The law of INTERNATIONAL *business* TRANSACTIONS

Larry A. DiMatteo
Associate Professor,
Warrington College of Business
University of Florida
J.D., The Cornell Law School
L.LM., The Harvard Law School

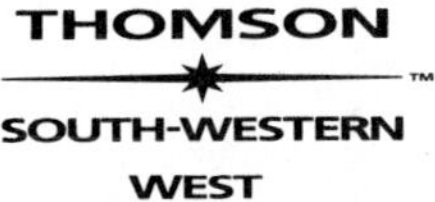

Australia · Canada · Mexico · Singapore · Spain · United Kingdom · United States

The Law of International Business Transactions by Larry A. DiMatteo

Editor-in-Chief: Jack W. Calhoun
Vice President/Team Director: Michael P. Roche
Sr. Acquisitions Editor: Rob Dewey
Developmental Editor: Jennifer E. Baker
Marketing Manager: Nicole C. Moore
Production Editor: Starratt E. Alexander
Manufacturing Coordinator: Rhonda Utley
Production House & Compositor: Pre-Press Company, Inc.
Printer: Phoenix Color/Book Technology Park
Internal Designer: Chris Miller
Cover Designer: Chris Miller
Cover Photograph: © Stone Images
Photo Manager: Deanna Ettinger
Photo Researcher: Sam Marshall

Printed in the United States of America
1 2 3 4 5 04 03 02

For more information contact West Legal Studies in Business, 5191 Natorp Boulevard, Mason, Ohio 45040. Or you can visit our Internet site at: http://www.westbuslaw.com

For permission to use material from this text or product, contact us by
- **telephone: 1-800-730-2214**
- **fax: 1-800-730-2215**
- **web: http://www.thomsonrights.com**

Library of Congress Cataloging-in-Publication Data

DiMatteo, Larry A.
The law of international business transactions / Larry A. DiMatteo.
p. cm.
ISBN: 0-324-04097-0
1. Export sales contracts—United States. 2. Foreign trade regulation—United States. 3. Export sales contracts. 4. Foreign trade regulation. 5. Risk I. Title.
KF915 .L386 2002
343.73'087—dc21 2002019406

To my heart and my soul: my wife Colleen for her love and support and my son, Ian, for his inspiration.

Brief Contents

Part 1: Legal and Ethical Environment of International Business

1 Introduction to International Business Transactions 1
2 The Ethics of International Business 38
3 Strategies for International Business 66
4 International Commercial Dispute Resolution 98

Part 2: Trade Regulation

5 International Trade Regulation 126
6 National Import and Export Regulation 150

Part 3: International Contracting

7 International Contract Law 177
8 International Sales Law 211

Part 4: Exporting and Importing: The Documentary Transaction and Trade Finance

9 The Documentary Transaction 243
10 Transport of Goods 271
11 International Trade Finance 309

Part 5: Sales of Services, Licensing of Intellectual Property, and Electronic Transactions

12 Sale of Services 336
13 Law of Intellectual Property Rights 366
14 Intellectual Property Licensing 402
15 Electronic Business Transactions 434

Appendix A: United Nations Convention on Contracts for the International Sale of Goods 465
Appendix B: Uniform Commercial Code (Selected Provisions) 484
Appendix C: Agreement Establishing the World Trade Organization (Selected Provisions) 493
Appendix D: Agreement on Trade-Related Aspects of Intellectual Property Rights (Selected Provisions) 499
Appendix E: Excerpts from International Convention for the Unification of Certain Rules of Law Relating to Bills of Lading ("Hague Rules") 508

Contents

PREFACE

Part 1: Legal and Ethical Environment of International Business

1: INTRODUCTION TO INTERNATIONAL BUSINESS TRANSACTIONS 1

The Global and Regional Marketplace 2

Laws of International Business Transactions 4
International Customary Law 6

Scope of International Business Transactions 8
Indirect and Direct Exporting 9

Evaluating Risks Through Market Research 10

Risks of International Business Transactions 13
Transaction Risks 13 Risks in Developing Countries 15 Language and Cultural Risk 16 Currency Risks 20 Legal Risk 23 Political Risk 26

Risk Management 28
Managing Risk Through Insurance 29 Managing Risk Through Intermediaries 30 Countertrade 30

Developing an Export Plan 34

Finding and Managing Foreign Lawyers 35

Chapter Problems 37

2: THE ETHICS OF INTERNATIONAL BUSINESS 38

International Business Ethics 39
Utilitarianism 39 Rights and Duties 41 Virtue Ethics 44 Ethics of Care 44

Integrative Approach to International Business Ethics 45

The Amoral International Businessperson 46

Organizational Ethics 47

Environmental Ethics 48

Host-Home Country Standards 49

Foreign Corrupt Practices Act 50
FCPA Accounting Provisions 56

International Standards 60

The Ethics of Advertising 61
Professional Standards of International Advertising 62

Chapter Problems 64

3: STRATEGIES FOR INTERNATIONAL BUSINESS 66

Strategies for Doing Business in the United States 67

Strategies for Entering a Foreign Market 68
Foreign Corporation Law 69

Establishing a Business in a Foreign Country 74
Foreign Competition Law 75 Foreign Trade Zones 77 International Taxation 78

Joint Ventures and Franchising 78
Joint Ventures 78 Franchising 85 International Franchising 92 Foreign Regulation of Franchising 95

Chapter Problems 97

4: INTERNATIONAL COMMERCIAL DISPUTE RESOLUTION 98

International Litigation 99
International Discovery 104 Enforceability of Judgments 104

Choice of Law 107
Judicial Abrogation of Choice of Law Clauses 107

Arbitration of Disputes in International Transactions 109
Arbitration and Mediation Clauses 113

Legality of Arbitration and Forum Selection Clauses 116

Force Majeure *Clause 120*

Liquidated Damages Clause 123

Chapter Problems 125

Part 2: Trade Regulation

5: INTERNATIONAL TRADE REGULATION 126

World Trading System 127

GATT Principles 128

The WTO Agreements 130
WTO Dispute Settlement System 132 Antidumping Procedures 135 Section 301 136 Section 337 of the Tariff Act 140

Future of Multilateral Trade Negotiations 141

Regional Expansion of Free Trade 141
North American Free Trade Agreement (NAFTA) 145 European Union Expansion 146

Chapter Problems 148

6: NATIONAL IMPORT AND EXPORT REGULATION 150

Import Requirements and Duties 151
Assessment of Duties 155 U.S. Foreign Trade Zones 161 Country of Origin 162 Marking Requirements 164 Foreign National Import Restrictions, Requirements, and Standards 165 Standards Requirements 166

Export Regulations 167

Chapter Problems 176

Part 3: International Contracting

7: INTERNATIONAL CONTRACT LAW 177

Negotiating an International Contract 178

Principles of International Contract Law 181
Contract Interpretation 184 Convergence and Divergence of National Laws 185 National Contract Codes 188 Precontractual Liability 200

Chapter Problems 209

8: INTERNATIONAL SALES LAW 211

International Sales Law 212
Choice of Law and Conflict of Laws 212 Commercial Sale of Goods 214

CISG and Uniform Commercial Code 219
Mechanics of Formation 219 Battle of Forms 221 Contract Interpretation 226 Duty to Inspect and Proper Notice 228 *Nachfrist* Notice 229 Seller's Right to Cure 231 Anticipatory Breach and Adequate Assurance 231 Damages 231 Warranty Provisions 232 Contractual Excuses 237 The *Force Majeure* Clause 238

Limitation Period 239

Chapter Problems 241

Part 4: Exporting and Importing: The Documentary Transaction and Trade Finance

9: THE DOCUMENTARY TRANSACTION 243

Methods of Payment 244
The Sales Contract and Documentary Transaction 245 *Pro Forma* Invoice 246

The Documentary Transaction 247

The Documentary Collections Transaction 250

Documentation 252
Bill of Lading 255 Trade Terms 257

Incoterms 2000 262

Chapter Problems 270

10: TRANSPORT OF GOODS 271

Air Waybill and The Warsaw Convention 272

International Ocean Carriage Conventions 273

COGSA 275
Carrier Liability 277 Carrier Duties 278 Per Package Limitation 280 COGSA Coverage 283 Material Deviation 286 Fair Opportunity 288 Misdelivery of Goods 288 COGSA Exemptions 291

Freight Forwarders and Multimodal Transport Operators 292

Marine Insurance 297
Marine Cargo Insurance 299

Chapter Problems 308

11: INTERNATIONAL TRADE FINANCE 309

Letters of Credit 310
The Letter of Credit Transaction 314

Uniform Customs and Practices for Documentary Credits 320

Standby Letters of Credit 325
Alternative Methods of Guaranteeing Performance 327

Sources of Trade Finance 328
Commercial Banks 329 Factoring and Forfaiting 330 Buyer and Supplier Financing 330 Government Assistance Programs 332

Chapter Problems 334

Part 5: Sales of Services, Licensing of Intellectual Property, and Electronic Transactions

12: SALE OF SERVICES 336

International Sale of Services 337
General Agreement on Trade in Services 339 Services and the Internet 340

Hiring Foreign Personnel 343
The Employment Relationship 344 The Independent Contractor Contract 349 The Foreign Sales Representative 349 The Commercial Agency Contract 350 Foreign Competition Law 356

Logistical Services 357
Law of Freight Forwarding 358

Advertising Services and Law 358

Cross-Border Security Offerings 361

Internationalization of Accounting and Taxation 362

Chapter Problems 364

13: LAW OF INTELLECTUAL PROPERTY RIGHTS 366

Intellectual Property Rights in the United States 367
Trademark Protection 368 Copyright Protection 371 Patent Protection 374 Trade Secrets 375

Extraterritorial Application of United States Law 376
The Gray Market 377

International Property Rights Protection 381
Paris Convention and Patent Cooperation Treaty 381 Berne Convention and Universal Copyright Convention 383

Agreement on Trade-Related Aspects of Intellectual Property 384
General Principles 386 Copyright and Related Rights 387 Trademark Protection 387 Patent Protection 388 Trade Secrets 388 Remedies and Penalties 388 Enforcement of Intellectual Property Rights 389

Foreign Intellectual Property Laws 391
Foreign Trademark Law 391 Foreign Patent Law 394 European Union 395

Protection in Transitional and Emerging Economies 396

Developing an Intellectual Property Protection Strategy 398

Chapter Problems 400

14: INTELLECTUAL PROPERTY LICENSING 402

Licensing and Intellectual Property Transfer 403

Protecting Intellectual Property Rights 404

Preventive Due Diligence 405

Intellectual Property License Registration 407

Intellectual Property Licensing Agreement 408
Common Licensing Clauses 409 License Grant and Limitations 410

Review of Typical License Agreement 415

Law of Licensing 425
Uniform Computer Information Transactions Act 425

Foreign Transfer Restrictions 427
European Union Regulations 427 Regulations of the People's Republic of China 430
Foreign Registration and Approval 431

Chapter Problems 432

15: ELECTRONIC BUSINESS TRANSACTIONS 434

Personal Jurisdiction 436

Trademark Infringement, Dilution, and Cybersquatting 442

Internet Privacy and Database Protection 445

E-Commerce and E-Contracting 449
Framework for Global Electronic Commerce 450 E-Contracting Law Issues 451
Uniform Computer Information Transactions Act 452 International E-Commerce Developments 456

Electronic Documentation 458

New Electronic Services Industry 459

Internet Securities Offerings 460

E-Commerce Ethics 460
Advertising and Marketing Ethics 461

Chapter Problems 463

APPENDIX A: UNITED NATIONS CONVENTION ON CONTRACTS FOR THE INTERNATIONAL SALE OF GOODS 465

APPENDIX B: UNIFORM COMMERCIAL CODE (SELECTED PROVISIONS) 484

APPENDIX C: AGREEMENT ESTABLISHING THE WORLD TRADE ORGANIZATION (SELECTED PROVISIONS) 493

APPENDIX D: AGREEMENT ON TRADE-RELATED ASPECTS OF INTELLECTUAL PROPERTY RIGHTS (SELECTED PROVISIONS) 499

APPENDIX E: EXCERPTS FROM INTERNATIONAL CONVENTION FOR THE UNIFICATION OF CERTAIN RULES OF LAW RELATING TO BILLS OF LADING ("HAGUE RULES") 508

Index 513

Table of Cases and Laws

Abbott Laboratories v. Diamedix Corp., 47 F.3d 1128 (Fed. Cir. 1995), **423**
Allied Chemical International v. Companhia De Navegacao Lloyd Brasileiro, 775 F.2d 476 (2d Cir. 1985), **290**
All Pacific Trading v. M/V Hanjin Yosu, 7 F.3d 1427 (9th Cir. 1993), **285–286**
Alpine View Co., Ltd. v. Atlas Copco AB, 205 F.3d 208 (5th Cir. 2000), **100–101**
Anheuser-Busch Brewing v. United States, 207 U.S. 556 (1908), **162–163**
Arizona Retail Systems, Inc. v. The Software Link, Inc., 831 F. Supp. 759 (D.C. Ariz. 1993), **454**
Avery Dennison Corp. v. Sumpton, 189 F.3d 868 (9th Cir. 1999), **443**
Banque Libanaise Pour le Commerce v. Khreich, 915 F.2d 1000 (5th Cir. 1990), **107**
Beijing Metals & Minerals Import/Export Corp. v. American Bus. Ctr., Inc., 993 F.2d 1178 (5th Cir. 1993), **218**
Bende & Sons, Inc. v. Crown Recreation, Inc., 548 F. Supp. 1018 (E.D. Louisiana 1982), **121**
Bensusan Restaurant Corp v. King, 126 F.3d 25 (2d Cir. 1997), **436–437, 438**
Bernina Distributors v. Bernina Sewing Machines, 646 F.2d 434 (1981), **22–23**
Best Cellars Inc., v. Grape Finds at Dupont, Inc., 90 F. Supp. 2d 431 (S.D.N.Y. 2000), **368, 369–370**
Bower v. Gateway, 676 N.Y.S.2d 569 (App. Div. 1999), **119**
Bremen v. Zapata Off-Shore Co., 407 U.S. 1 (1971), **118**
Brennan v. Carvel Corp., 929 F.2d 801 (S.D.Fla. 1992), **89**
Broussard v. Meineke Discount Muffler Shops, 155 F.3d 331 (4th Cir. 1998), **87–88**
Steele v. Bulova Watches, 344 U.S. 280 (1952), **377**
Capital Currency Exchange v. National Westminster Bank and Barclays Bank, 155 F.3d 603 (2d Cir. 1998), **101, 103**
Carell v. The Shubert Organization, Inc., 2000 U.S. Dist. LEXIS 8807 (S.D.N.Y. 2000), **389, 390**
C-Art, Ltd. v. Hong Kong Islands Line America, 940 F.2d 530 (9th Cir. 1991), **291**
Caterpillar Overseas v. Marine Transport, Inc., 900 F.2d 714 (4th Cir. 1990), **278**
Central Bank of the Philippines v. Ferdinand E. Marcos, 665 F. Supp. 793 (N.D. Cal. 1987), **99, 102–103**
Cohen v. Paramount Pictures Corp., 845 F.2d 851 (9th Cir. 1988), **414–415**
Columbia Broadcasting System, Inc. v. Scorpio Music Distributors, Inc., 569 F. Supp. 47 (E.D. Pa. 1983), **378, 380**
Compuserve, Inc. v. Patterson, 89 F.3d 1257 (6th Cir. 1996), **436–437**
Community for Creative Non-Violence v. Reid, 490 U.S. 730 (1989), **373, 374**

Constructores Tecnicos v. Sea-Land Service, Inc., 945 F.2d 841 (5th Cir. 1991), **293, 295**
Courtaulds NO. America, Inc. v. North Carolina National Bank, 528 F.2d 802 (4th Cir. 1975), **322, 323–324**
Cybersell, Inc. v. Cybersell, Inc., 130 F.3d 414 (9th Cir. 1997), **436**
Daedalus Enterprises, Inc., v. Baldrige, 563 F. Supp. 1345 (D.C. 1983), **172, 173**
Dart v. United States, 848 F.2d 217 (D.C. Cir. 1988), **176**
Delchi Carrier, S.P.A. v. Rotorex Corp., 71 F.3d 1024 (2d Cir. 1995), **232, 233**
Delverde USA, Inc., v. United States, 202 F.3d 1360 (F. Cir. 2000), **139–140**
Dupont de Nemours Int'l v. Mormacvega, 493 F.2d 97 (2d Cir. 1974), **287**
E-Data Corp. v. Micropatent Corp., 989 F. Supp. 173 (D.Conn 1997), **438, 463**
Enrique Bernat, S.A. v. Guadalajara, Inc., 210 F.3d 439 (5th Cir. 2000), **375**
Estee Lauder, Inc. v. L'Oreal, S.A., 129 F.3d 588 (Fed. Cir. 1997), **400**
Europcar Italia, S.P.A. v. Maiellano Tours, Inc., Docket No. 97-7224 (2d Cir. 1997), **120**
Falcoal, Inc. v. Kurumu, 660 F. Supp. 1536 (S.D. Tex. 1987), **16–18**
Farrel Corporation v. International Trade Commission, 949 F.2d 1147 (Fed Cir. 1991), **114, 115**
Fernandez v. Wynn Oil Co., 653 F.2d 1273 (9th Cir. 1981), **21**
Filanto, S.P.A. v. Chilewich International Corp., 789 F. Supp. 1229 (S.D.N.Y. 1992), **225–226**
Finnish Fur Sales Co., Ltd. v. Juliette Shulof Furs, Inc., George Shulof and Juliette Shulof, 770 F. Supp. 139 (S.D.N.Y. 1991), **72–73**
Folger Coffee Company v. Olivebank, 201 F.3d 632 (5th Cir. 2000), **306–307**
Frigaliment Importing v. B.N.S. International Sales Corp., F. Supp. 116 (S.D. N. Y. 1960), **226, 227, 228**
General Electric Co. v. Inter-Ocean Shipping, 862 F. Supp. 166, 169 (S.D. Tex. 1994), **277**
George E. Warren Corp., v. U.S. Environmental Protection Agency, 164 F.3d 676 (D.C. Cir. 1998), **128, 129**
GPL Treatment, Ltd. v. Louisiana-Pacific, 914 P.2d 682 (Or. Sup. Ct. 1996), **216, 217**
Green River Bottling Co. v. Green River Corp., 997 F.2d 359 (7th Cir. 1993), **432–433**
Habib Bank Ltd. v. Convermat Corp., 554 N.Y.S.2d 757 (1990), **324**
Harriscom Svenska, AB v. Harris Corp., 3 F.3d 576 (2d Cir. 1993), **120–121, 239**
Heritage Mutual Insurance v. Advanced Polymer Tech., 97 F. Supp. 2d 913 (S.D. Ind. 2000), **359–360**
Hewlett-Packard Co. v. Bausch & Lomb, Inc., 909 F.2d 1464 (Fed. Cir. 1990), **421**
Hilton v. Guyot, 159 U.S. 113 (1895), **104, 105**
In re Application of Mohamed Al Fayed, 92 F. Supp. 2d 137 (D.D.C. 2000), **125**
In re Union Carbide Corp. Gas Plant Disaster at Bhopall, 809 F.2d 195 (1987), **43–44**
Interpane Coatings, Inc. v. Australia and New Zealand Banking Group, 732 F. Supp. 909 (N.D. Ill. 1990), **319, 320**
Iran Aircraft Industries v. Avco Corporation, 980 F.2d 141 (2d Cir. 1992), **112, 113**
Itar-Tass Russian News Agency v. Russian Kurier, Inc., 153 F.3d 82 (2nd Cir., 1998), **400**
Itek Corp. v. First National Bank of Boston, 730 F.2d 19 (1st Cir. 1984), **326–327**
Kern v. Dynalectron Corp., 577 F. Supp. 1196 (N.D. Texas 1983), **20–21**
Komatsu, Ltd. v. States S.S. Co., 674 F.2d 806 (9th Cir. 1982), **288**
Kumar Corp. v. Nopal Lines Ltd., 462 So.2d 1178 (Fl. Ct. Appeals 1985), **260**
Lamb v. Phillip Morris, Inc., 915 F.2d 1024 (6th Cir. 1990), **53**
Made in the USA Foundation v. United States of America, 56 F. Supp. 2d 1226 (N.D. Ala. 1999), **144**
Mallinckrodt, Inc. v. Medipart, Inc., 976 F.2d 700 (Fed. Cir. 1992), **412, 413**
Mannesman Demag Corp. v. M/V Concert Express, 225 F.3d 587 (5th Cir. 2000), **296–297**
Marobie-FL, Inc. v. Natl. Assn. of Fire Equipment Distributors, F. Supp. (1997 Wl 709747, N.D. Ill.), **463**
Marchetto, v. Dekalb Genetics Corp., 711 F. Supp. 936 (N.D. Illinois 1989), **37**
Marcraft Clothes, Inc. v. M/V Kurobe Maru, 575 F. Supp. 239 (S.D.N.Y. 1983), **285**
Mattel, Inc. v. Internet Dimensions Inc., 2000 U.S. Dist. LEXIS 9747 (S.D.N.Y. 2000), **444–445**
McAlpine v. AAMCO Automatic Transmission, Inc., 461 F. Supp. 1232 (E.D. Mich. 1978), **92–93**
MCC-Marble Ceraminc Center v. Ceramica Nuova D'Agostino, S.P.A., 144 F. 3d (1384 11th Cir. 1998), **216, 218–219**
McCoy v. Mitsuboshi Cutlery, Inc., 67 F.3d 917 (Fed. Cir. 1995), **432**
Micro Data Systems, Inc. v. Dharma Systems, 148 F.3d 649 (7th Cir. 1998), **214–215**

Mori Seiki USA, Inc. v. M/V Alligator Triumph, in rem, Mitsui O.S.K. Lines, Ltd., and Marine Terminals Corp., 990 F.2d 444 (9th Cir. 1993), **283, 284**
National Foreign Trade Council, v. Baker, 26 F. Supp. 2d 287 (D.C. Mass. 1998), **154, 156**
NEC Electronics v. Cal Circuit Abco, 810 F.2d 1506 (9th Cir. 1987), **378, 379**
Nelson Bunker Hunt v. BP Exploration, Ltd., 492 F. Supp. 885 (N.D. Tex. 1980), **104, 105–106**
Nimrod Marketing v. Texas Energy Corp., 769 F.2d 1076 (5th Cir. 1985), **201**
Novecon Ltd. v. Bulgarian-American Enterprise Fund, F.3d (1999 Wl 683006, D.C. Cir.), **204**
Orbisphere Corp. v. United States, 765 F. Supp. 1087 (Ct. Int'l Trade 1991), **160**
Oregon Natural Resources Council, v. Animal and Plant Health Inspection Service, 1997 U.S. Dist. LEXIS 9521 (N.D. Cal. 1977), **131–132**
Paramount Pictures Corp. v. Metro Program Network, Inc., 962 F.2d 775 (8th Cir. 1992), **422, 424–425**
Phillips Puerto Rico, Inc. v. Tradax Petroleum, 782 F.2d 314 (1985), **121–122, 261**
Polo Ralph Lauren, L.P. v. Tropical Shipping & Construction Co., 215 F.3d 1217 (11th Cir. 2000), **282–283**
Prima U.S. Inc. v. M/V Addiriyah, 223 F.3d 126 (2d Cir. 2000), **275–276**
Quality King Distributors, Inc. v. L'anza Research Int'l, Inc., 118 S.Ct. 1125 (1998), **378**
Ravens Metal Products v. McGann, 699 N.Y.S.2d 503 (1999), **70–71, 73**
Raymond Dayan v. McDonald's Corp., 466 N.E.2d 958 (Ill. App. 1984), **93–94**
R.G. Group, Inc. v. Bojangles' of America, Inc., 751 F.2d 69 (2d Cir. 1984), **202–203, 204**
Rodriguez De Quijas v. Shearson/American Express, Inc., 490 U.S. 477 (Sup. Ct. 1989), **125**
Samsonite Corp. v. United States, 889 F.2d 1074 (Fed. Cir. 1989), **157, 158**
St. Johns N. F. Shipping Corp. v. S. A. Companhia Geral Commercial de Rio de Janeiro, 263 U.S. 119 (1923), **286, 287**
St. Paul INS. v. Sea Land Service, 745 F. Supp. 186, 188 (S.D. N.Y. 1990), **288**
Scotch Whiskey Assoc. v. Barton Distilling, 489 F.2d 809 (7th Cir. 1972), **376–377**
SEC v. Tesoro Petroleum Corp., 2 FCPA Rep. (1980), **55**
Secrest Machine Corp. v. S.S. Tiber, 450 F.2d 285 (5th Cir. 1971), **276**
Shaver Transportation Co. v. The Travelers Indemnity Co., 481 F. Supp. 892 (D.C. Oregon 1979), **301–305**
Smith v. Pillsbury Co., 914 F. Supp. 97 (E.D. Pa., 1996), **463**
Sony Magnetic Products Inc. v. Merivienti, 863 F.2d 1537 (11th Cir. 1989), **281, 293**
Sporty's Farm, L.L.C. v. Sportman's Market, Inc., 202 F.3d 489 (2nd Cir., 2000), **463**
Stromberg-Carlson Corp. v. Bank Melli Iran, 467 F. Supp. 530 (S.D.N.Y. 1979), **334**
Sztejn v. J. Henry Schroder Banking Corp., 31 N.Y.S.2d 631 (Sup. Ct. 1941), **327**
TACS Corp. v. Trans World Communications, 155 F. 3d 659 (3rd Cir. 1998), **209**
Tennessee Imports, Inc. v. Pier Paulo, 745 F. Supp. 1314 (Mid D. Tenn. 1990), **118–119**
Texaco v. Pennzoil, 729 S.W.2d 768 (Tex. Ct. App. 1987), **204–205**
T.J. Stevenson & Co. v. Bags of Flour, 629 F.2d 338 (5th Cir. 1980), **234, 235–236**
Toys "R" Us v. Feinberg, 1998 Dist. LEXIS 17217 (S.D.N.Y. 1998), **443–444**
Travelers Indemnity Company, v. Waterman Steamship Corp ("The Vessel Sam Houston"), 26 F.3d 895 (9th Cir. 1994), **288, 289**
United States v. Ali Moghadam, 175 F.3d 1269 (11th Cir. 1999), **379, 385**
United States v. Balsys, 118 S.Ct. 2218 (1998), **125**
United States v. Donald Shetterly, 971 F.2d 67 (7th Cir.), **170–171**
United States v. Haggar Apparel Company, 526 U.S. 380 (1999), **154–155**
United States v. Hsu, F.3d (1998 Wl 538221, 3rd Cir.), **376**
United States v. Liebo, 923 F.2d 1308 (8th Cir. 1991), **52–53, 54, 55**
Valente-Kritzer Video v. Callan Productions, 881 F.2d 772 (9th Cir. 1989), **408**
Vegas v. Compania Anonima Venzolana, 720 F.2d 629 (11th Cir. 1983), **281**
Vimar Seguros Y Reaseguros v. M/V Sky Reefer, 515 U.S. 526 (1995), **279**
Voest-Alpine International v. Chase Manhattan Bank, 707 F.2d 680 (2d Cir. 1983), **316, 317–318**
Warner Bros. & Co. v. Israel, 101 F.2d 59 (2d Cir. 1939), **261**
Warner-Jenkinson Co. v. Hilton Davis Chemical, 117 S. Ct. 1040 (1997), **375**
Wood v. Lady Duff-Gordon, 222 N.Y. 88 (1917), **209**

Yarway Corp. v. Eur-Control, Inc., 775 F.2d 268 (Fed. Cir. 1985), **420, 421**
Zippo Manufacturing Co. v. Zippo Dot Com, Inc., 952 F. Supp. 1119 (W.D.Pa. 1997), **439–440**

United States Statutory Law

Anticybersquatting Consumer Protection Act, **444, 445**
Carriage of Goods by Sea Act (COGSA), 46 U.S.C. §§ 1300-1315, **272, 275–277**
Convention on the Recognition and Enforcement of Foreign Arbitral Awards (New York Convention), 9 U.S.C. § 207, **111**
Copyright Act of 1976, 17 U.S.C. § 102, **372–373, 407–408**
Electronic Communications Privacy Act of 1986, 18 U.S.C. § 2510, **446**
Export Administration Act of 1979, 50 U.S.C. App. §§ 2401-2420, **170–171, 172**
Federal Bills of Lading Act, 49 U.S.C.A. §§ 80101–16, **283**
Federal Trademark Dilution Act, 15 U.S.C. § 1125(c), **371, 442–444**
Federal Trade Commission Act, 15 U.S.C. § 45(a)(1)(1982), **358**
Federal Rules of Civil Procedure, **25**
Foreign Corrupt Practices Act (FCPA), 15 USC § 78dd-1 (2000), **50–51**
Foreign Sovereign Immunities Act of 1976, 28 U.S.C. §§ 1332 (1982), **99**
Harter Act, 46 U.S.C. App. §§ 190-196 (1988), **273, 283**
Harmonized Tariff Schedule (HTS), 19 U.S.C.A. § 1202, **151–154, 157**
Lanham Act, 15 U.S.C. 1125(a) (1988), **358, 368, 371**
North American Free Trade Agreement (NAFTA), **145–146**
Overseas Private Investment Corp. (OPIC), 22 U.S.C. § 2194 (1988), **12, 14, 28, 29**
Patent Act, 35 U.S.C. §§ 100, 271 (a) (1994), **375**
Section 301 Antidumping Provisions, 19 U.SC. §§ 2411-19 (1994), **137–138**
SEC, Statement of the Commission Regarding the Use of Internet Web Sites to Offer Securities, Solicit Transactions, or Advertise Investment Services Offshore, **361–362**
SEC, Release 33-7233 (1995) (direct public offerings), **460**
Agreement on Trade-Related Aspects of Intellectual Property Rights (TRIPS), 35 U.S.C. § 271(a), **127**
Uniform Commercial Code, Section 2–718, **186**
United States Tariff Act of 1930, 19 U.S.C. § 1304(a) (1982), **140**
United States Sentencing Guidelines, **58–59**

English Case Law

Chemco Leasing Spa. v. Rediffusion Plc., Transcript Assoc. (Q.B.1985), **208**
Hadley v. Baxendale, 156 Eng. Rep. 145 (1854), **193, 232**
J.H. Rayner & Co. v. Hambros Bank Ltd., 112 K.B. 27 (1943), **322**
Lamb Head Shipping v. Jennings, 1 Lloyd's L. R. 624 (C.A. 1994), **294**
Manifest Shipping v. Uni-Polaris Insurance Co., 1 Lloyd's L. R. 651 (Q.B. 1995), **280**
Noten v. Harding, 2 Lloyd's Law Report 283 (C.A. 1990), **308**
Reardon SmithLine Ltd., [1976] 1 W.L.R. 989, **228**
Rose & Frank Co. v. Crompton, 1924 All E.R. 245, 255 (Ct. App. 1923), **208**

English Statutory Law

English Unfair Contract Terms Act of 1977, **185**
Frustrated Contracts Act (1943), **238**

European Union Law

Grifoni v. European Atomic Energy Community, [1992] 3 CMLR 463, **206**
Sa Pasquasy v. Cosmair, Inc., [1989] ECC 508, **207**
Commission Decision of 17/11/1999 (1999 OJ C 357) (Case No Iv/M.1652), **76**

Commission Regulation (EC) No 2868/95 (implementation of community trademark directive), **396**
Commission Regulation (EEC) No 4087/88 Of 30 November 1988 (Franchise Regulations), **91–92, 95–96**
Commission Regulations 556/89 (know-how licensing), **428**
Council Regulation 2913/92 (European Union Customs Code), **159, 161**
Directive on Unfair Terms in Consumer Contracts, 93/13/EEC: L 95/29 (1993), **189–190**
Directive 97/55/EC on Comparative Advertising (1997), **62**
Directive 97/7/EC on Protection of Consumers in Distance Contracts (1997), **342**
Directive 94/45/EC of 22 September 1994 (European Works Council Directive), **348**
Directive 96/9/EC on the Legal Protection of Databases, **446, 449**
Directive 95/46 on the Protection of Individuals with Regard to the Processing of Personal Data and the Free Movement of such Data, **446–448**
Directive 84/450/EEC (1984) (Misleading Advertising Directive), **62**
Directive 93/13/EEC of 5 April 1993 on Unfair Terms in Consumer Contracts, **189**
Directive 86/653/EEC of December 18, 1986 Regarding Commercial Agents, **354**
European Union Commission on Contract, *Principles of European Contract Law,* **188, 194–198**
EU Regulation 1983/83 (exclusive distribution agreements), **356–357**
EU Regulation No. 4087/88, "Application of the Treaty to Categories of Franchise Agreements" (Nov. 30, 1988), **92–93, 96**
Mutual Recognition of Professional Qualifications (December 13, 1993), **338**
Partnership and Cooperation Agreement Between the European Communities and Georgia (April 22, 1996), **147**
Technology Transfer Regulation 240/96 of January 31, 1996, **427–430**

Other European Laws

Organization for Economic Cooperation and Development (OECD) Convention on Combating Bribery of Foreign Public Officials in International Business Transaction, **57–58**
Council of Europe, Resolution (78) 3 on Penal Clauses in the Civil Law (1978), **186**

Brazilian Law

Brazilian Industrial Property Law of May 15, 1997, **391–392**

Canadian Law

Braintech, Inc. v. Kostiuk, 1999 D.L.R. LEXIS 134 (British Columbia Court of Appeal 1999), **441, 442**

Chinese Law

Chinese Company Law, **70**
Foreign Contract Law of the People's Republic of China, **192**
Foreign Contract Law of the People's Republic of China, **192–194**
Law on Joint Ventures Using Chinese and Foreign Investment (1990), **69**
Law on Chinese-Foreign Contractual Joint Ventures (1988), **68, 85**
Law on Enterprises Operated Exclusively with Foreign Capital, **69**
Measures for the Examination of Contracts for the Importation of Technology, **430–431**
People's Republic of China Patent Law, **394, 395**
People's Republic of China Trademark Law, **394**
Regulations Governing Contracts for the Importation of Technology, **430–431**
Regulations on Labor Management in Joint Ventures Using Chinese and Foreign Investment, **84–85**

Dutch Law

Plas v. Valburg, Hoge Road, 18-6 Nederlandse Jurisprudentie 723 (1983), **205, 206**

French Law

Article 1152 of the French Civil Code, **123**
Article 1590 of the French Civil Code, **124, 187**

German Law

General Court of Stuttgart, 3 KFh 97/89, The CLOUT Case No. 4 (Case Law on UNCITRAL Text (CLOUT is a reporting service accessible through the United Nations document services.), **229**
General Court of München, 17 HKO 3726/89, The CLOUT Case No. 3, UNCITRAL Abstract, A/CN.9/SER.C/Abstracts/1 (May 19, 1993), **229**
Municipal Court of Holstein, 5 C 73/89, The CLOUT Case No. 7, **230**

Hungarian Law

Hungarian Conflict of Law Rules, **108**
Pratt & Whitney Corp. v. Malev Hungarian Airlines, 13 Bp. P.O.B. 16 (Metropolitan Court of Budapest 1991), **222**

ICC Arbitration Cases

ICC Arbitration Case No. 7531 of 1994, **231**
ICC Arbitration Case No. 5713 of 1989, **214**
ICC Arbitration Case No. 6281 of 1989, **239**

Indonesian Law

Indonesian Civil Law, Article 1338, **85**

International Treaties and Conventions

Brussels Convention on Jurisdiction and Judgments in Civil and Commercial Matters, **106, 458**
Convention on Contracts for the International Sale of Goods (CISG), **213, 220, Appendix A**
Convention on the Limitation Period in the International Sale of Goods, **239–241**
Convention for the Unification of Certain Rules Relating to International Transportation by Air (Warsaw Convention), **272, 273**
Convention on the Service Abroad of Judicial and Extrajudical Documents in Civil or Commercial Matters (Hague Service Convention), **99**
Convention on the Taking of Evidence Abroad in Civil or Commercial Matters (Hague Evidence Convention), **104**
Hague Rules, **272, Appendix E**
Hague-Visby Rules, **272, 274**
Hamburg Rules, **272, 274**

Italian Law

Italian Civil Code, Article 2596, **416**

Korean Law

Basic Environmental Policy Act (BEPA) (1990), **48–49**

Mexican Law

Foreign Investment Act of 1993, **16**

New Zealand Law

Comite Interprofessional du Vin de Champagne v. Wineworths, Ltd., 2 NZLR 432 (1991), **392**

Russian Law

Law on Enterprises (1996), **75**
Russian Civil Code (1994), **190–191**
Patent Law of the Russian Federation, **394**
Russian Trademark Law, **391, 394**

Preface

The international marketplace offers great opportunity for a domestic enterprise seeking to expand. It is also a place where the risks of loss are somewhat unique in character. Accordingly, the American businessperson must become an astute manager of international business risk in order to minimize the chances of financial loss. This book will illuminate the risks of doing business internationally, while providing the student of international business with tools to help minimize those risks.

The legal issues relevant to international business transactions can be seen as a due diligence checklist.The sophisticated international entrepreneur directly addresses the legal issues discussed in this book before transacting international business.The tremendous expansion of international business is a testament to the fact that the legal issues in international business transactions are discernible. Furthermore, the real world often provides solutions to the risks associated with such issues.

The trend towards increased international trade is likely to continue. It began at the end of World War II with the establishment of the World Bank, International Monetary Fund, United Nations, and the evolution of the General Agreement on Tariffs and Trade (GATT). The trend continued to accelerate with the adoption of the North American Free Trade Agreement (NAFTA), the deepening of the European Union (EU), and the establishment of the World Trade Organization (WTO). It will continue to accelerate with the opening of new markets occasioned by the fall of communism, the culmination of the 2000 trade pact between the United States and the People's Republic of China, and the explosion of e-commerce.

In order to obtain profits in the international marketplace, small to large size companies will have to develop an "international business strategy" in order to stay competitive. This book provides an introduction to the legal issues that need to be addressed in formulating such a strategy.

ABOUT THE AUTHOR

Larry A. DiMatteo is a professor at the Warrington College of Business Administration at the University of Florida. He previously taught at the University of Miami Graduate School of Business. His primary teaching responsibilities have been teaching graduate courses in international business law, commercial law, and the legal environment of business. Professor DiMatteo graduated from with a B.A. in Economics and a B.A. in Political Science from the State University of New York at Buffalo where he was Phi Beta Kappa. He received his J.D., *magna cum laude*, from The Cornell Law School and a LL.M. from the Harvard Law School. Professor DiMatteo is the author of 3 books and more than a dozen law review articles with a primary focus on contract and international business law. His previous books include *The Equitable Law of Contract* (2001), *The Law of International Contracting* (2000), and *Contract Theory: The Evolution of Contractual Intent* (1998). His articles have appeared in the *Harvard International Law Journal, Yale Journal of International Law, American Business Law Journal, Hofstra Law Review*, and the *University of Pittsburgh Law Review*. His article in Volume 38 of the *American Business Law Journal* won the prestigious 2001 Ralph C. Hoeber Award as "best article." Professor DiMatteo is a past president of the International Law Section of the Academy of Legal Studies in Business.

TRANSACTIONAL APPROACH

The title of this book, *The Law of International Business Transactions*, was selected to distinguish it from the more generic texts on "International Business Law." As such, it focuses on transactional international business law. The text presents international business transactions with an emphasis on rules and practice. The topics of coverage have been selected to place predominant emphasis on matters that most directly impact private business transactions: export-import, licensing and technology transfer, and sales of services. It is the author's belief that it is these practical legal aspects of international business that are most relevant to today's business student. Therefore, extensive coverage of more "macro" issues like expropriation or nationalization, workings of the United Nations, and international monetary policy are abandoned due to the increasingly minor role they play in today's international business arena. This is not to say that these areas of coverage are not important but that in a relatively stable free trade environment they are unlikely to be of direct importance to the international entrepreneur. Given the time limitations in a standard college course, it is to the basics of transactional business law that this textbook's coverage is directed.

Managerial Perspective

Throughout the book capsules and materials will be provided to illustrate the law of international business transactions *as practiced*. A variety of methods will be utilized to provide the student with a real world perspective. These methods include case studies, checklists, forms, tables, and summaries.

Capsules and Exhibits

The Chapters contain numerous capsules and exhibits that emphasize the transactional and managerial emphasis of the text. The "Doing Business Internationally" and "Focus on Transactions" capsules provide checklists and practical information relevant ot the international entrepreneur. "Exhibits" expose the student to the forms used in carrying out international business transactions, along with charts and statistics.

Special Features

A number of *hot topics* are included to make the textbook more comprehensive and "cutting edge." These topics include in-depth coverage of international commercial arbitration; recent interpretations of the United Nations Convention for the International Sale of Goods (CISG); the legal issues of e-commerce and other types of electronic transactions; the expanding recognition of international franchising; the problems of international bribery, including the adoption of the OECD Anti-Corruption Code; the development of international standards such as the International Standards Organization's ISO 9000 and ISO 14000; and the unique issues pertaining to joint venturing.

Electronic Transactions

The growing importance of electronic means of communicating and contracting in the international business arena is reflected in the allotment of an entire chapter to the topic, along with coverage of electronic developments pertaining to the other substantive topics discussed throughout the book.

Ethics Coverage

Ethical questions in international business can arise in various contexts. These contexts include the ethics of negotiations, disclosure of information, dealing with foreign governments, and the divergence between home country and host country laws. The student will be encouraged to form a mind-set in which ethical behavior will become an inherent part of their approach to international business. An entire chapter is devoted to the topic, along with a number of ethics capsules placed throughout the book.

Sources and References

The text reflects an earnest attempt to expose the student to a sampling of foreign law. National laws from approximately a dozen and a half countries are referenced and used for purposes of illustration. There are a numerous references throughout the text to a number of primary sources. All references to the Uniform Commercial Code or UCC are references to the law of the United States. The book also makes ample use of a variety of European Economic Community (EEC), European Community (EC), and European Union (EU) directives and regulations. I often refer to this body of law, apologetically, simply as EU Regulations. The reader may refer to the footnotes for the proper citations. In order to emphasize the nature of national laws' impact upon international business transactions, the laws of the European Union, the People's Republic of China, and the Russian Federation have been singled out for extra attention. These three bodies of law were also selected because of the importance of these markets in world trade. The use of national law serves to illuminate the typical issues found in international business transactions.

Case Law

A concerted effort has been made to "update" the case law in order to provide a more contemporary flavor to the text. Over 70 of the cases are from 1990 to the present; of those, 37 cases were decided no later than 1997. Of course, some older cases remain because of their power as precedents or as clear illustrations of a given legal principle. Along with a presentation of American law, more than a dozen cases have been selected from the countries of Great Britain, Hungary, Germany, New Zealand, Holland, Canada, and the European Union, along with a number of International Chamber of Commerce Arbitration cases.

Style and Structure

A premium has been placed upon readability by the use of clear narrative, carefully edited case summaries and articles, and concise use of tangential materials. Also, in the spirit of the practical-managerial focus of the book, more in-depth insight is offered in certain areas so that the student is exposed not only to the *why* a given rule of law has evolved, but also *how* it is applied in practice. The chapter coverage allows for the use of the chapters as individual modules or as blocks of chapters. The first seven chapters can be viewed as foundational in that they provide the legal environment of international business, including: International Business Risks, International Business Ethics, Strategies for Doing Business Internationally, International Dispute Resolution, National and International Trade Regulation, and International Contract Law. Chapters 8-11 focus upon the legalities of exporting-importing, covering International Sales Law, the Documentary Transaction, Transport of Goods, and International Trade Finance. Chapter 12 provides coverage of the growing area of the international sale of services. Chapters 13 and 14 pertain to the important area of technology transfer and the international licensing of intellectual property rights. Finally, Chapter 15 provides coverage of the evolving area of electronic transactions that cuts across all of the ways of doing business internationally.

Internet Exercises

A number of Internet exercises have been placed in the end-of-chapters' problems section. These provide important web sites that students can use for reference or to answer a question or project posed. These projects can be used in individual or group assignments.

Key Terms

Learning the terminology of international business is an important part of any international business law course. The key terms used in the chapters are listed at the end of each chapter. Definitions of terms are provided in the text and in a special glossary found on the book's web site at http://dimatteo.westbuslaw.com.

Case Highlights

Following each case is a capsule listing principles of law, concepts, and business practices highlighted in the case. Some of the highlights summarize the reasons why the case was inserted into the textbook. Other highlights alert the student to the fact that most legal disputes involve multiple issues. Many of these "external" highlights are examined elsewhere in the textbook. The instructor may also use these points as a starting point for a more in-depth discussion of the multiple issues of the case.

Chapter Problems

Each chapter concludes with problems appropriate for classroom discussion. The Instructor's Manual provides the answers and relevant case citations to the problems, along with other ideas for class discussion. The Test Bank provides additional essay questions that provide an additional source for discussions.

Appendices

The Appendices selected are to be actively used by the student. Appendix A provides the text of the Convention for the International Sale of Goods (CISG) and should be referred to in conjunction with Chapter 8's law of sales. Selected provisions of the Uniform Commercial Code (UCC) appear in Appendix B. These are the provisions listed in the Comparative Law Capsule comparing the CISG with the UCC. Appendix C is the Agreement Establishing the World Trade Organization. This is supplemental to the material in Chapters 5 and 6 on trade regulation. Students' interested in the WTO should read this foundational document to better understand the scope, governance, and purpose of this international trade organization. Appendix D is selected provisions of the Agreement on Trade-Related Aspects of Intellectual Property Rights (TRIPS). The TRIPS Agreement is discussed in Chapter 13. A review of TRIPS will help the student better understand the reach of intellectual property law. Finally, the Hague Rules that are the central focus of Chapter 10 should be referred to when there is an issue of carrier liability.

Instructor's Manual and Test Bank

The Instructor's Manual provides additional source materials including a chapter-by-chapter bibliography, Chapter topics and objectives, lecture outlines, answers to end-of-chapter problems, and additional student in-class and take-home exercises. The Manual also provides supplemental material, such as statutes. These materials can be used in preparation for class or given as handouts. The Test Bank provides 750-short answer (true-false and multiple choice) questions, along with approximately 75 essay questions.

Acknowledgments

I would like to thank the editorial staff at West Legal Studies in Business, Thomson Learning, especially my editors Rob Dewey and Jennifer Baker. I am grateful for the help of a former student of mine, Brian O'Keefe, in preparing the Test Bank.

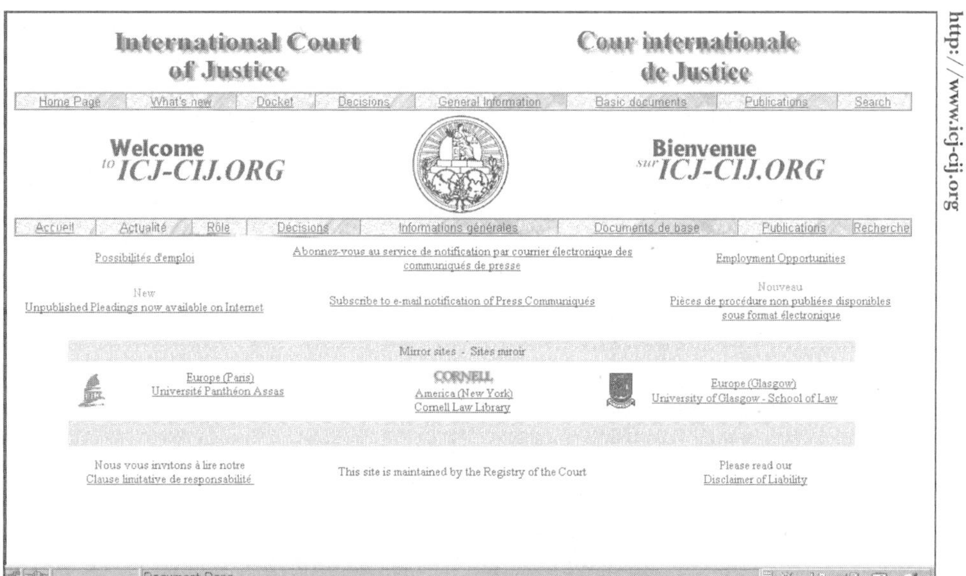

http://www.icj-cij.org

Chapter 1 Introduction to International Business Transactions

The purpose of this chapter is to review briefly some of the major topics and issues involved in international business transactions. The remaining chapters of the book will expand on the topics outlined in this chapter. The first part of Chapter 1 will highlight the tremendous growth in international business transactions and some of the causes behind this expansion. One factor that has aided the expansion of international trade is the development of a supranational trade law. Chapter 1 will therefore introduce the reader to the concept of international customary law.

We will examine the ways international business is transacted. The concepts of direct and indirect exporting, licensing, and direct foreign investment will be introduced. This discussion will provide a basic understanding of the perceived advantages and disadvantages of each method of transacting international business. These methods will be explored further in Chapter 3 along with hybrid ways of transacting business, such as franchising and joint venturing.

The second half of Chapter 1 will focus on the risks involved in international business transactions. The great opportunities presented by international business transactions do not come without risk. Some risks are the same as those in purely domestic transactions; others are more unique to the international business environment. First, we will analyze how companies evaluate such risks. Second, we will review the generic risks associated with international business transactions. These include risks associated with cultural and language differences, currency risks, legal risks, and political risks. Finally, we will explore briefly the tools that have been developed to minimize and manage such risks. We conclude by discussing strategies for managing international business risks, including the development of an export plan, use of intermediaries, and a form of international business known as countertrade.

Ultimately, the goal of teaching international business law is to sensitize future entrepreneurs to the risks of international business and the ways to manage such risks: A savvy entrepreneur is adept at analyzing risk and knowledgeable about the techniques to minimize risk. Chapter 1 will introduce the reader to the risks of international business transactions. The rest of the textbook will explore more fully how such risks are minimized in the areas of exporting, direct foreign investment, and intellectual property transfer.

THE GLOBAL AND REGIONAL MARKETPLACE

Increasing volumes of world trade in goods, services, and technology licenses have resulted from the relaxation of international trade barriers. A number of factors have played a role in the expansion of international trade. Some of the important events and forces that have paved the way to the growth of international trade include the following:

- General Agreement on Tariffs and Trade (GATT)
- The expansion of GATT with the adoption of the 1994 World Trade Organization (WTO) Agreements into other areas, such as trade in services, technology transfer, and foreign investment
- The deepening of regional trading blocks, such as the European Union (EU) and the North American Free Trade Area (NAFTA)
- The disintegration of the Soviet Union and Warsaw Pact and the advent of "emerging economies"
- Dramatic advances in telecommunications and information technology
- The development of vibrant international capital markets in Europe and North America

This list is far from exhaustive, but it illustrates the fact that we live in an age of dynamic global economic development and interdependence.

The forces listed above have resulted in significant increases in cross-border trade in manufacturing goods and in services, international joint ventures, mergers, acquisitions, strategic alliances and affiliations, infrastructure projects, privatization, and international direct investment. The liberalization of trade and investment rules has created a "world of opportunities" for the international entrepreneur.[1] The draw of profits from international business transactions has

1. See generally, Ward Bower, "The Future Structure of the Global Legal Marketplace," *The Metropolitan Corporate Counsel* (1999).

made purely domestic businesses rare. The mobility of goods and services has allowed domestic companies to search the world for new markets to sell their products or to procure component parts used in the manufacture of their products. The producer of goods and services, or the innovator of technology, can maximize profits with a global business strategy. This strategy encompasses not only developing foreign markets for a company's products but also outsourcing materials, labor, and component parts. Even a company that takes a more isolated domestic sales strategy is likely to be affected by international developments.

The best measure of globalization has been the tremendous growth in the international **trade in goods.** Exhibit 1.1 illustrates the trend in world trade over the past few decades and into the early part of the current decade.

A second measure of globalization is **foreign direct investment** (FDI). FDI represents the capital investments made by companies in other countries. This includes the purchase of real estate, manufacturing plants, service and distribution centers, or foreign businesses. Between 1981 and 1985 total world FDI averaged $98 billion per year. In 1997, FDI had reached $440 billion. The increase in world FDI has, much like trade, occurred mostly in the three major regional trade areas of Europe, the Americas, and East Asia. Globalization is likely to expand both at the regional level and at the truly global level. The causes of this expected growth include the advance of global telecommunications and the increased transferability of services and intellectual property (see Exhibit 1.2). The service and knowledge industries, such as entertainment, education, and health care, will benefit from the expansion of the **General Agreement on Tariffs and Trade (GATT)** into the non-sale of goods area. The trend in services and intellectual property trade will dominate

http://
U.S. Bureau of Economic Affairs: **http://www.state.gov/e/eb/tpp**. Information on U.S. trade programs with links to NAFTA and WTO web sites.

http://
U.S. Department of Commerce Bureau of Economic Analysis: **http://www.bea.doc.gov**. Provides statistics pertaining to economic activity.

http://
World Bank: **http://www.worldbank.org**. Provides statistics and information on international trade and finance.

EXHIBIT 1.1 *Trends in World Trade Integration (Trillion of dollars)*

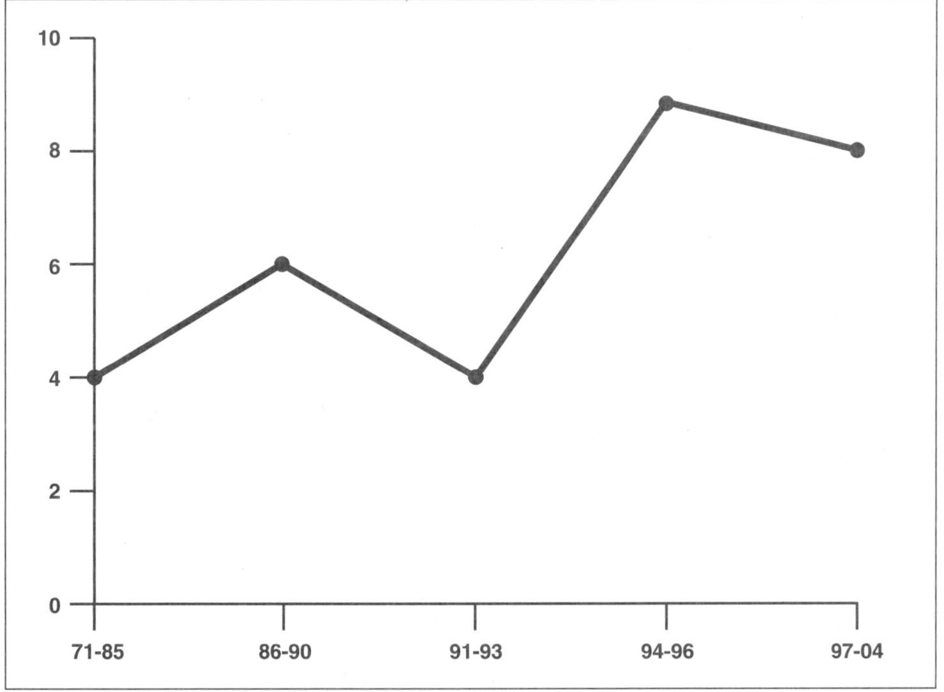

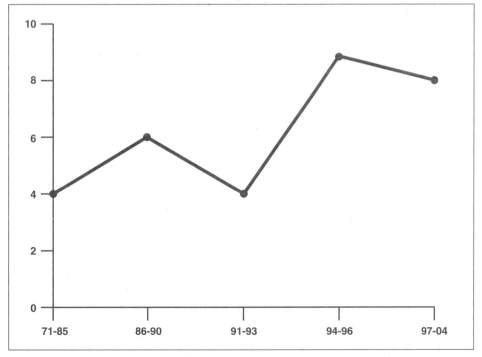

Source: The World Bank, *Global Economic Prospects* 15 (Wash. D.C. 1995)

EXHIBIT 1.2 *World Trade in Services (Billions of dollars)*

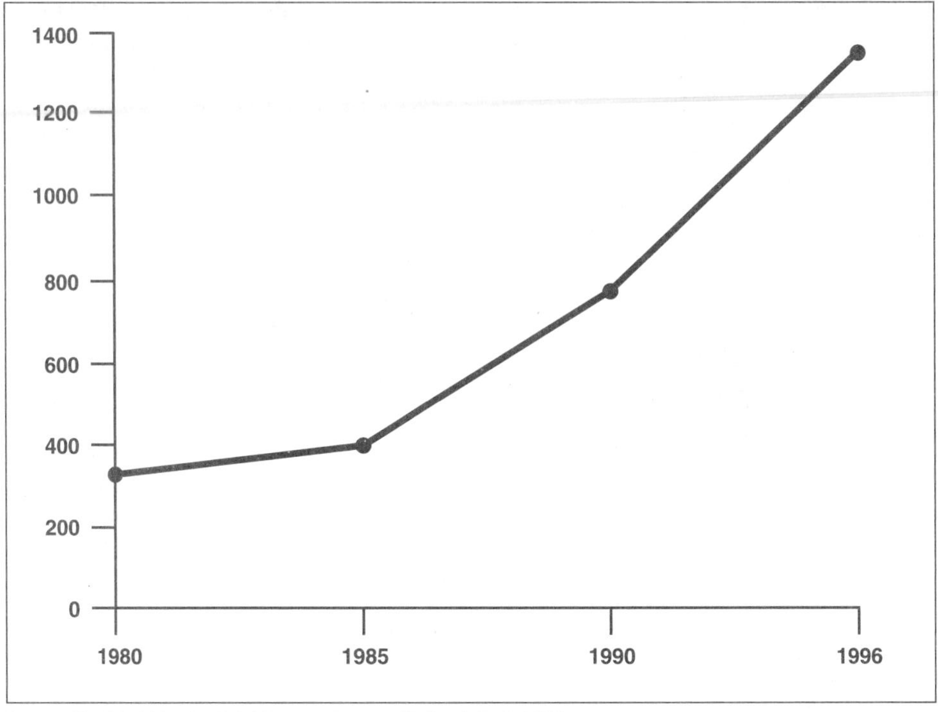

Source: The World Bank, *Global Economic Prospects* 47 (Wash. D.C. 1995)

the next decade and beyond (see Exhibit 1.3). The average annual growth rate for trade in commercial services between 1980 and 1993 was 7.7 percent, compared to 4.9 percent for trade in goods.

LAWS OF INTERNATIONAL BUSINESS TRANSACTIONS

International law generally refers to the historically developed transnational rules and norms that national courts use to regulate three primary relationships: (1) the relationship between two nations, (2) the relationship between a nation and an individual, and (3) the relationship between persons or entities from different countries. This book is primarily concerned with the person-to-person relationship between two parties transacting business across national borders. The first two types of relationships will be reviewed, at times, because of their effect upon private business relationships. Thus, the regulations promulgated by the World Trade Organization (WTO) will be studied because of their direct impact on the export and import of goods, services, and intellectual property rights.

There are numerous sources of international business law. **Article 38** of the Statute of the **International Court of Justice**[2] lists the sources of international law. In order of superiority they are: (1) international conventions[3] and

2. The International Court of Justice (ICJ) or World Court is located at The Hague in the Netherlands. Its Statute, a part of the United Nations Charter, dictates the jurisdiction and powers of the court.
3. The term *convention* is used in connection with multilateral agreements, as opposed to bilateral arrangements.

EXHIBIT 1.3 *Trade in Services as Percentage of World Trade*

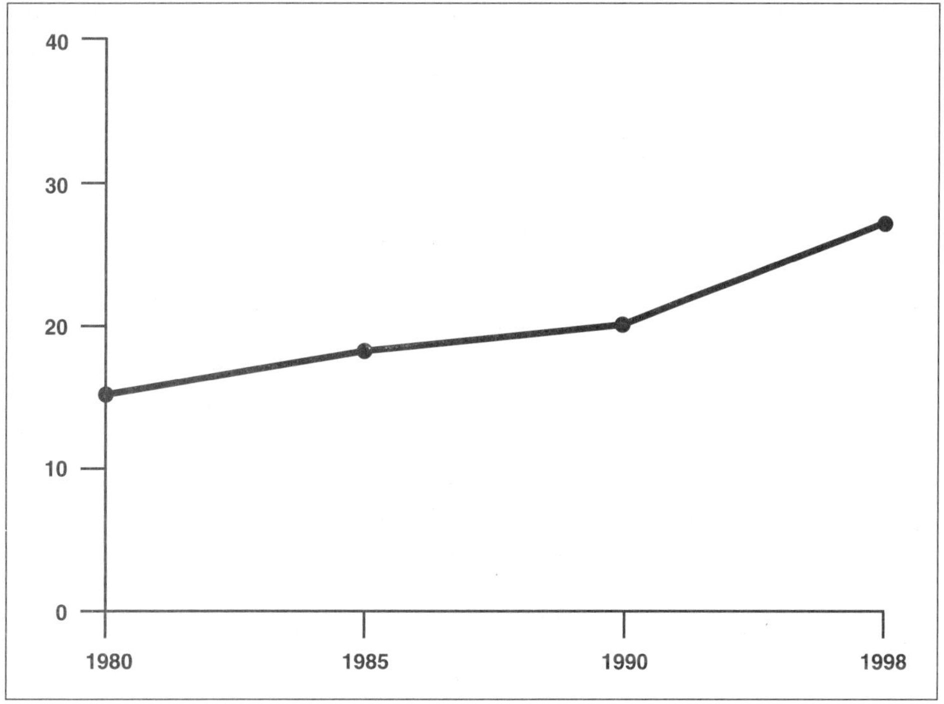

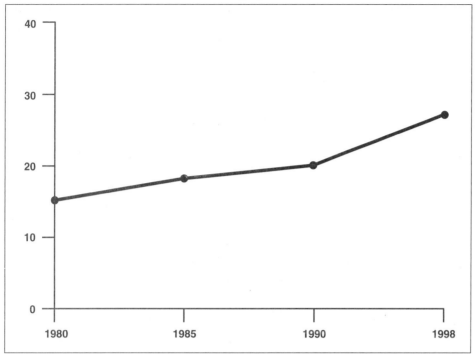

Source: The World Bank, *World Development Indicators* 1998 (Wash. D.C. 1998)

treaties,[4] (2) international custom or general practice, (3) general principles of law recognized by civilized nations, and (4) judicial decisions and scholarly writings. These are the same sources of law often used by private parties in international litigation or arbitration proceedings.

http://
International Court of Justice:
http://www.icj-cij.org.

The primary source of law in international business transactions is, however, the private contract entered into by the business parties. The contract will be the primary source of law in case of a dispute. At times, however, the contract may fail to provide a solution either because it does not deal with the issue in dispute or because the parties interpret the contract differently. It was once said that "no written contract is ever complete; even the most carefully drafted document rests on volumes of assumptions that cannot be explicitly expressed."[5] This quote illustrates that a substantial core of any international business transaction is non-legal in nature. Businesspersons prefer the language of business and are often unconcerned with the legal language of the formal contract document.

Despite this informal attitude, the language of business does have a tendency to be "codified" into legally recognizable custom and trade usage. This transformation is a well-worn tradition that dates back to the medieval ***lex mercatoria***.[6] The *lex mercatoria*, or law of merchants, provides the mechanism in which day-to-day uses

4. The Vienna Convention on the Law of Treaties defines a treaty as "an international agreement between States and governed by international law." Under U.S. law a treaty becomes federal law and is binding on federal, state, and local governments.
5. Arthur Rosett, "Critical Reflections on the CISG," 45 *Ohio State Law Journal* 265, 287 (1984).
6. See generally, R. Goode, "Usage and Its Reception in Transnational Commercial Law," 46 *I.C.L.Q.* 1 (1997); Lord Mustill, "The New Lex Mercatoria: The First Twenty-Five Years," 4 *Arbitration International* 86 (1988).

http://

Links to *lex mercatoria* developments: **http://lexmercatoria.net**. This web site describes itself as a monitor for developments in international customary law and Internet infrastructure.

and practices are recognized by businesspersons, as well as courts and arbitral tribunals, as international customary law. It has also been said that "the transformation of international business law signifies more than just an incremental normative change; it signifies a quite radical revision in the very prism through which we view transnational deals and disputes."[7] This statement indicates that the latter half of the twentieth century saw a broad transformation in international trade and business. This transformation has resulted in a radical expansion of international business law.

The reality of trade liberalization and the rapid expansion of exporting in services and licensing, combined with the technological enhancement of business relationships, have increased the number of international conventions and supranational responses to globalization. Business students should incorporate these conventions and standards in their perspective of international business transactions because they are often the vehicle for overcoming cultural, language, and legal differences in cross-border transactions.

The acceptance of generally recognized contract principles, the trend toward economic trade unions, the adoption of international conventions, and the growth of international customary law have all led to common approaches among national legal systems in the area of international contract law. In the long term, international unification and harmonization are likely to reduce transaction costs relating to international contract formation.

Most legal international business disputes stem from poorly written contracts or the parties' failure to recognize key substantive issues. Given the universal nature of business transactions and the globalization of the marketplace, contractual failures attributable to inherent linguistic and cultural differences have significantly diminished, but when they do occur, they can lead to high transaction costs. Another cause of legal disputes is the existence of fundamental differences in national rules about interpreting contractual terms. Thus, a primary way to understand the risk of international business transactions is to research cases and arbitral decisions dealing with key issues.

International Customary Law

Following standard practices, custom, and trade usage can minimize the risk of legal disputes stemming from contractual misunderstandings. These secondary sources of international business law can be divided into two general groups, the first of which includes international conventions or regional initiatives aimed at harmonizing rules about cross-border transactions. Examples include the Hague Rules[8] on the liability of international carriers of goods by sea and the Agreement on Trade-Related Aspects of Intellectual Property Rights (TRIPS) within the General Agreement on Tariffs and Trade (GATT).[9] Regional efforts generally revolve around major free trade areas such as NAFTA and the European Union, and also include broader-based institutions such as the Organization for Economic Cooperation and Development (OECD).

7. Kenneth C. Randall & John E. Norris, "A New Paradigm for International Business Transactions," 71 *Washington University Law Quarterly* 599, 624 (1993).
8. The Hague Rules were codified in the United States as the Carriage of Goods by Sea Act (COGSA) in 1936, which applies to an international export or import shipment involving a bill of lading for transport from or to a United States port.
9. Agreement on Trade-Related Aspects of Intellectual Property Rights (TRIPS), General Agreement on Tariffs and Trade (GATT), April 15, 1994.

The second group, the *lex mercatoria* or customary international law, has developed to bridge language, cultural, and legal differences between businesspersons throughout the world. The materials produced by the **International Chamber of Commerce (ICC)** in Paris illustrate the evolution of the *lex mercatoria.* The ICC was created in 1919 to promote free trade and private enterprise and to represent business interests at the international level. Members include national councils from more than sixty countries. Headquartered in Paris, France, the ICC is a nongovernmental organization whose current mission is to promote world trade, harmonize trade practices, and provide practical services to businesspersons. These services include the International Court of Arbitration in Paris, the Centre for Maritime Cooperation in London, the Counterfeiting Intelligence Bureau in London, and the Institute of International Business Law and Practice in Paris. The ICC's UCP 500 (Uniform Customs and Practices for Documentary Credits)[10] and its INCOTERMS 2000 manual (of trade terms) are examples of international trade customs that have risen to near-universal acceptance in the international banking and business communities.

http://

Department of State Private International Law Database: **http://www.state.gov/www/global/legal_affairs/private_intl_law.html**. Provides information on international transactional law compiled by the Office of Legal Adviser.

International business transactions require a firm understanding of the substantive laws of the country in which one is intending to transact business, and of any relevant international conventions. Clarity of writing will not overcome the immutable rules of a given country or even some international conventions. For example, a clearly written, principal-friendly termination clause in an agency agreement will not survive the **evergreen provisions** found in a number of European countries. An evergreen provision is a statutory preemption of the termination and commission clauses of an agency contract.

Under the **United Nations Convention on Contracts for the International Sale of Goods (CISG),**[11] a writing is not required and a contract may be proved by "any means including witness testimony."[12] In practice, many business transactions are characterized by a high degree of informality. As an English court noted: "One has to bear in mind that commercial men do not look at things from the lawyer's point of view."[13] Despite the informal nature of business contracting and the common use of standard forms, however, it is likely that sophisticated businesspersons are fully aware of their national rules of contract and the supportive legal sanctions. For that reason, it is recommended that even sale of goods transactions governed by the CISG should be based upon at least a semiformal writing. This seems especially necessary given the difficulty of procuring reputable business partners in foreign countries, and the obstacles of language and culture, including differences in negotiating styles. These factors, and the potential difficulty and expense of obtaining a legal remedy in a foreign country, justify the additional time spent researching legal issues and writing a contract. A carefully written contract will often highlight the latent differences of language and law while there is time to reconcile differences before the execution of the contract. Preventive contracting diminishes the likelihood of disputes about contract interpretation.

What are the generally recognized principles of international business law? What are some of the fundamental contract law differences among the major

10. The UCP was first published in 1933 and subsequently revised in 1951, 1962, 1974, 1983, and 1993. UCP 500 came into effect on January 1, 1994.
11. United Nations Convention on Contracts for the International Sale of Goods, April 11, 1980, U.N. Doc. A/CONF.97/18, Annex I, reprinted in 19 I.L.M. 668.
12. CISG at Article 11.
13. Hugh Beale & Tony Dugdale, "Contracts Between Businessmen: Planning and the Use of Contractual Remedies," 2 *British Journal of Law & Society* 45, 49 (1975).

national legal systems of which the U.S. entrepreneur should be aware? What are the typical characteristics of the export or import contract? These questions will be addressed in Chapter 7, International Contract Law and Chapter 8, International Sales Law.

Behind every business transaction is the fear of nonperformance and the threat of one party using the law to obtain a legal remedy. Understanding international contract dispute resolution is important in order to negotiate and draft an effective contract. Just as prenuptial agreements are written in anticipation of a possible divorce, contracts should be written in anticipation of possible contract disputes. What can international businesspersons write into their contracts to make dispute resolution less likely to be needed? What can they write into the contract that would make dispute resolution less painful or costly in the event it is necessary? What can be included in the contract to increase the chances for success in a dispute resolution? These questions will be addressed in Chapter 4, International Commercial Dispute Resolution.

SCOPE OF INTERNATIONAL BUSINESS TRANSACTIONS

All business transactions involve considerable risk. The essence of being a businessperson or entrepreneur is a willingness to confront loss, or risk, in the search for profits, and profit seeking or risk taking underscores the capitalistic, free-market system. The most consistently successful entrepreneurs are those who take steps to avoid or at least minimize risk, and risk-aversion techniques and strategies have been developed to provide stability and security to business transactions. Risk minimization is essential for both domestic transactions and those that cross national boundaries, but there are profound differences in approach between international and domestic business transactions.

The **basket of risks** associated with an international transaction is different in many ways from that of a U.S. domestic transaction. Businesses' efforts to minimize risk differ, too. Many international risk management devices, although longstanding, are likely to be unfamiliar to the U.S. businessperson on his or her initial foray into exporting, licensing, or direct foreign investment. International dealings are further complicated by the fact that the basket of risks to be confronted is constantly fluctuating, depending on the type of business entity, the type of good or service being sold, the country of the other party, the country of performance, and the means of transportation.

http://
International Trade Administration: **http://www.trade.gov**. Provides export assistance and information on doing business with foreign countries.

At the broadest level of analysis, the risk characteristics will depend largely on the type of transaction. Transactions are categorized under four general groupings: **exporting-importing** (sale of goods), **sale of services** (consulting, distribution, transportation, marketing, sales), **licensing** (technology or intellectual property transfer), and **direct foreign investment** (foreign operations). This classification is overly simplified because many transactions display characteristics of two or more categories. We will examine vehicles of doing business—like franchising, joint venturing, and countertrade—independently of classification, since these three vehicles are hybrids of one or more of the four broader categories. The **franchise** transaction generally involves the contractual transfer or licensing of a bundle of intellectual property rights, know-how, trade secrets, and possibly the sale of goods or services. The **joint venture** is most closely associated with direct foreign investment, but may also involve the transfer of goods, services, technology, and capital. **Countertrade** is a form of exporting used to overcome the risks of currency convertibility, local participation requirements, and restrictions against the repatriation of capital, profits, or hard currency. Countertrade can also be used within the framework of a joint venture or technology transfer. These forms of doing business internationally will be more fully explored in Chapter 3, Strategies for International Business.

Indirect and Direct Exporting

The most popular method of transacting business internationally remains the exporting of goods and services, which is generally divided into indirect and direct exporting. A number of different kinds of intermediary firms are utilized in the area of **indirect exporting.** The principal advantage of indirect exporting for a smaller company is that it provides a way to penetrate foreign markets without the complexities and risks of direct exporting. A company may contact **commission agents** or **buying agents** who find foreign firms that want to purchase U.S. products. Such agents seek to obtain the desired items at the lowest possible price and are paid a commission by their foreign clients. In some cases, the agents may be foreign government agencies or quasi-governmental firms empowered to locate and purchase desired goods.

An indirect exporter may also hire an **export management company** (EMC). An EMC, in essence, acts as the export department for one or several producers of goods or services. A private business, it solicits and transacts business in the names of the producers it represents or in its own name for a commission, salary, or retainer plus commission. Some EMCs offer immediate payment for products either by arranging financing or by directly purchasing products for resale. EMCs usually specialize by product line or by foreign market. The best EMCs know their products and markets very well and usually have well-established networks of foreign distributors already in place. This immediate access to foreign markets is one of the principal reasons for using an EMC. One disadvantage to using an EMC is that a manufacturer may lose control over foreign sales. Control is an important issue for a manufacturer concerned with maintaining their product and company image in foreign markets.

A manufacturer that wants to minimize its involvement may sell its goods to an **export trading company** (ETC). An ETC takes title to the product and exports for its own account, and for the manufacturer the transaction is essentially a domestic sale. Some special ETCs are organized and operated by producers. These types of ETCs can be organized along multiple- or single-industry lines and can represent producers of competing products. The U.S. Congress has encouraged the growth of ETCs through the enactment of the Export Trading Company Act of 1982, which allows banks to make equity investments in commercial ventures that qualify as ETCs. In addition, the Export-Import Bank (Eximbank) of the United States is allowed to make working capital guarantees to U.S. exporters. The Office of Export Trading Company Affairs (OETCA), within the U.S. Department of Commerce, promotes the formation and use of U.S. export intermediaries and issues export trade certificates that provide limited immunity from U.S. antitrust laws.

http://

U.S. government links: **http://firstgov.gov.** Provides links to all relevant government web sites.

An indirect exporting method similar to using an ETC is selling goods to an **export agent** or **remarketer.** Export agents or remarketers purchase products directly from the manufacturer, packing and marking the products according to their own specifications. They then sell overseas through their contacts in their own names and assume all account risks. The U.S. manufacturer relinquishes control over the marketing and promotion of its product, which could have an adverse effect on future sales efforts abroad.

DIRECT EXPORTING

A company new to direct exporting generally treats export sales no differently from domestic sales, using existing personnel and organizational structures, but the advantages of separating international from domestic business include centralizing the specialized international market skills and focusing marketing efforts. Regardless of how a company organizes for exporting, it should ensure that the structure facilitates the marketer's job. Experience shows that a company's success in foreign markets depends less on the attributes of its products than on its marketing methods.

Once a company has been organized to handle exporting, it must select the proper channel of distribution in each market. These channels include sales representatives, agents, distributors, retailers, and end users. A **foreign sales representative** is the equivalent of a manufacturer's representative in the United States. The representative uses the company's product literature and samples to present the product to potential buyers; a representative often handles many complementary lines from different manufacturers. The sales representative usually works on a commission basis, assumes no risk or responsibility, and is under contract for a definite period of time. The contract defines territory, terms of sale, method of compensation, reasons and procedures for terminating the agreement, and other details. In contrast, a **foreign agent** normally has authority to make commitments on behalf of the firm he or she represents. Any contract should state whether the representative or agent does or does not have legal authority to obligate the firm.

The **foreign distributor** is a merchant who purchases merchandise from a U.S. exporter, resells it at a profit, and generally provides after sales support and service. The distributor usually carries an inventory of products and spare parts and maintains adequate facilities and personnel for normal servicing operations. The U.S. exporter must screen carefully all potential representatives, agents, or distributors. The following information should be obtained and reviewed: (1) current status and history, including background on principal officers; (2) personnel and other resources (salespeople, warehouse and service facilities); (3) sales territory covered; (4) current sales volume; (5) typical customer profiles; (6) methods of introducing new products into the sales territory; (7) names and addresses of U.S. firms currently represented; (8) trade and bank references; (9) if a foreign company, the company's view of the in-country market potential for the exporter's products. This information is not only useful in gauging how much the representative knows about the exporter's industry, it is also valuable market research in its own right. Credit reports are available from commercial firms and from the Department of Commerce's World Traders Data Report program. To protect itself against possible conflicts of interest, a U.S. firm must also learn about other product lines that the foreign firm represents.[14]

EVALUATING RISKS THROUGH MARKET RESEARCH

To be successful, international entrepreneurs and exporters must assess foreign markets through market research. Exporters engage in market research primarily to identify their marketing opportunities and constraints and also to identify and

14. Most of the material in the section on Direct Exporting was taken from the National Trade Data Bank, a product of STAT-USA, U.S. Department of Commerce.

Focus on Transactions

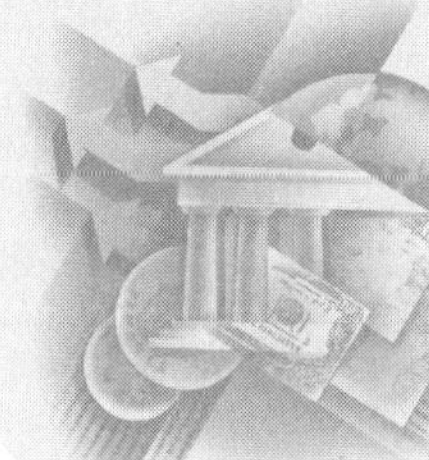

General Sources for Market Research

- **Business America.** This biweekly publication of the U.S. Department of Commerce contains country-by-country marketing reports, incisive economic analyses, worldwide trade leads, advance notice of planned exhibitions of U.S. products worldwide, and success stories of export marketing.
- **Commerce Business Daily (CBD).** Published daily, Monday through Friday, by the U.S. Department of Commerce, CBD lists government procurement invitations, contract awards, subcontracting leads, sales of surplus property, and foreign business opportunities as well as certain foreign government procurements.
- **Trade Information Center.** A comprehensive source for U.S. companies seeking information on federal programs and activities that support U.S. exports, including information on overseas markets and industry trends, the center maintains a computerized calendar of U.S. government-sponsored domestic and overseas trade events.
- **Economic Bulletin Board (EBB).** The PC-based EBB is an online source for trade leads as well as the latest statistical releases from the Bureau of the Census, the Bureau of Economic Analysis, the Bureau of Labor Statistics, the Federal Reserve Board, and other federal agencies.
- **National Trade Data Bank (NTDB).** The NTDB contains export promotion and international trade data collected by 15 U.S. government agencies. Updated each month and released on CD-ROM, the data bank enables access to more than 100,000 documents. The NTDB contains the latest census data on U.S. imports and exports by commodity and country; the complete Central Intelligence Agency (CIA) World Factbook; the complete Foreign Traders Index, which contains more than 50,000 names and addresses of individuals and firms abroad interested in importing U.S. products; and many other data sources.
- **Small Business Administration (SBA).** The SBA markets research-related general resources.

find prospective customers. A company's market research should determine the largest foreign markets for its products and identify trends, outlook, conditions, practices, and competitors in those markets.

In conducting primary market research, a company collects data directly from the foreign marketplace through interviews, surveys, and other direct contact with representatives and potential buyers. Primary market research has the advantage of being tailored to a company's needs and answering specific questions, but it is time-consuming and expensive. Because of the expense of primary market research, most firms rely on secondary data sources (see Focus on Transactions: General Sources for Market Research).

Secondary market research is conducted in three basic ways. The first is by keeping abreast of world events that influence the international marketplace, watching for announcements of specific projects, or simply visiting likely markets. The second is by analyzing trade and economic statistics. Trade statistics are generally compiled by product category and by country. These statistics provide the U.S. firm with information about shipments of products over specified periods of time.

Doing Business Internationally

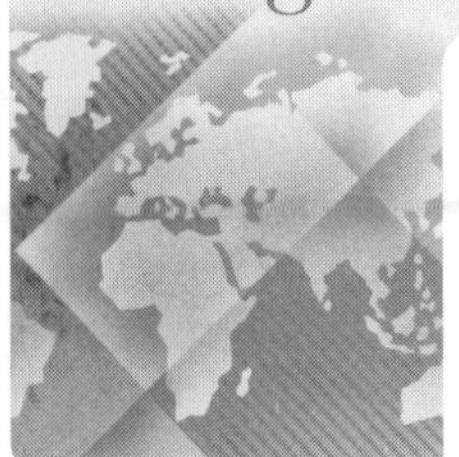

A Step-by-Step Approach to Market Research

1. **Screen potential markets**
   Step 1. Obtain export statistics that indicate product exports to various countries. Foreign Trade Report: Monthly Exports and Imports (SITC Commodity by Country) (Department of Commerce) provides statistics on all U.S. exports and imports. Firms should also consult the Export Information System (XIS) Data Reports (SBA), or U.S. Industrial Outlook (Department of Commerce).
   Step 2. Identify five to ten large and fast-growing markets for the firm's product. Examine them over the past three to five years. Has market growth been consistent year to year? Did import growth occur even during periods of economic recession? If not, did growth resume with economic recovery?
   Step 3. Identify some smaller but fast-emerging markets that may provide ground-floor opportunities. If a market is just beginning to open up, there may be fewer competitors. Growth rates should be substantially higher in these countries to qualify as up-and-coming markets, given the lower starting point.
   Step 4. Target three to five of the most statistically promising markets for further assessment. Consult with Department of Commerce district offices, business associates, freight forwarders, and others to help refine targeted markets.
2. **Assess targeted markets**
   Step 1. Examine trends for company products as well as related products that could influence demand. Calculate overall consumption of the product and the amount accounted for by imports. Industry Sector Analyses (ISAs), alert reports, and country marketing plans, all from the Department of Commerce, give economic backgrounds and market trends for each country. Demographic information (population, age, etc.) can be obtained from World Population (the Bureau of the Census) and Statistical Yearbook (United Nations).
   Step 2. Ascertain the sources of competition, including the extent of domestic industry production and the countries of origin of the major competitors in each targeted market, by using ISAs and competitive assessments (all from the Department of Commerce). Look at each competitor's U.S. market share.
   Step 3. Analyze factors affecting marketing and use of the product in each market, such as end user sectors, channels of distribution, cultural idiosyncrasies, and business practices. Again, ISAs are useful, as is the Comparison Shopping Service (CSS) offered by the Department of Commerce.
   Step 4. Identify any foreign barriers (tariff or nontariff) to the product being imported into the country. Identify any U.S. barriers (such as export controls) affecting exports to the country. Country information kits produced by the Overseas Private Investment Corporation (OPIC) can be helpful.
   Step 5. Identify any U.S. or foreign government incentives to promote exporting of the product or service.
3. **Draw conclusions**
   After analyzing the data, the company may conclude that its marketing resources would be applied more effectively to a few countries. In general, efforts should be directed to fewer than ten markets if the company is new to exporting; one or two countries may be enough to start with. The company's internal resources should help determine its level of effort.

Source: National Trade Data Bank, a product of STAT-USA, U.S. Department of Commerce.

Demographic and general economic statistics such as population size and makeup, per capita income, and production levels by industry can be important indicators of the market potential for a company's products. The third method of secondary market research is obtaining the advice of experts, including contacting experts at the U.S. Department of Commerce and other government agencies; attending seminars, workshops, and international trade shows; hiring an international trade and marketing consultant; talking with successful exporters of similar products; and contacting trade and industry association staff.

Working with secondary sources is less expensive and helps the company focus its marketing efforts. However, the most recent statistics for some countries may be more than two years old. Also, statistics on sale of services are often unavailable. Yet, even with these limitations, secondary research is a valuable and a relatively easy first step for a company to take (See, Doing Business Internationally: A Step-by-Step Approach to Market Research).

RISKS OF INTERNATIONAL BUSINESS TRANSACTIONS

The numerous risks associated with international business transactions vary depending on the method of transaction, such as trade, licensing, or direct investment. They will also vary depending on what countries the business parties are located in or what country the transaction is to be performed in. The country where a party is a citizen or national is its **home country.** If a party is transacting business in a foreign country, then that country is referred to as the **host country.** The varieties of risk that generally exist to some degree for all countries and all methods of transacting business can be grouped into categories. This section will analyze four categories of international business risks: cultural and language, currency, legal, and political.

The types of risks that an international businessperson faces, and the methods utilized to minimize such risks, will vary from transaction to transaction depending on a number of variables. Two of the most fundamental variables are the identity of the host country and the type of transaction. In general, the level of risk escalates in the three basic ways of conducting international business, from exporting-importing to licensing, and from licensing to direct foreign investment. We will investigate the different types of risks involved in these areas of international business transactions. The importance of assessing host country risk is highlighted by a review of three comparative scenarios (see pages 14–15). In each scenario, representatives of a U.S.-based company must weigh the risks of doing business in two countries using one of the three basic market entry strategies discussed in the previous section. The *italicized words* represent key concepts that will be defined and explored throughout the textbook.

Using these three scenarios we can begin to understand the complexity of the risks involved in international business transactions. A successful international businessperson is sophisticated and able to recognize risks and take the appropriate precautions.

Transaction Risks

One of the primary risks in all international business transactions is the application and enforcement of foreign laws. Host country laws may include restrictions on

Scenario 1: Sale of Goods to Nigeria and Canada

Nigeria has been rated at the top of the recent *Corruption Index* published by Transparency International, a Non-Governmental Organization (NGO). It may be difficult to undertake business dealings in Nigeria without being asked to give a bribe. To best understand the risks of doing business with such a country, it is prudent to order a *political risk report* from a professional risk assessment company. It is also advisable to contact the U.S. State Department for information. It is imperative to fully investigate the foreign party, including credit and reference checks. A strong *ethics compliance program* will need to be in place in order to prevent the giving of bribes in violation of the U.S. *Foreign Corrupt Practices Act*. Also, the Nigerian currency is not *convertible* to a hard currency like the U.S. dollar, European euro or English pound. Payment in one of these hard currencies is unlikely because of government restrictions against the *repatriation* of such currencies from the country. Thus, the risk of doing business, even in the relatively risk-free method of exporting, may be too great a problem in a place like Nigeria.

Any exporting to such a country needs to be supported by a *confirmed letter of credit* from a reputable international bank. The currency convertibility and repatriation problems could be overcome through a *countertrade* transaction in which goods are exchanged for each other or an export transaction is linked to an import transaction. Another device to eliminate the risk to a company is to find an *export trading company* willing to perform the transaction on its own account. Finally, the costs and feasibility of obtaining political and credit risk insurance should be investigated. The *Overseas Private Investment Corporation* (OPIC), *Eximbank*, and the *Multilateral Guarantee Agency* (MIGA) provide various types of insurance.

In contrast to exporting to Nigeria, exporting to Canada offers a low level of risk. *Country* and *currency risks* are minimal given that Canada is a stable, industrialized country and a member of the *North American Free Trade Agreement* (NAFTA). Although currency fluctuations are possible, the Canadian dollar is freely convertible into the U.S. dollar. Currency fluctuation risk may be a concern in a long-term transaction, and both parties may manage that risk through a variety of *hedging* techniques. In a one-shot export transaction, the risk of a dramatic currency rate change is unlikely. The U.S. exporter can eliminate all currency risk simply by requiring payment in U.S. dollars.

Scenario 2: Licensing Technology to the People's Republic of China and France

The licensing of technology and the transfer of *intellectual property rights* presents the next level of risk in international business transactions. Any time a company discloses confidential information and trade secrets to a third party there is always a risk that the information may be further disclosed to unauthorized parties. The problem is confounded when that disclosure is made in a foreign country that is not protective of intellectual property.

China has acceded to numerous intellectual property rights' conventions, such as the *Berne Convention*, but in the past the level of trademark, copyright, and patent infringement through piracy and counterfeiting has been relatively high. The cost and time of legal action to prevent the importation of illegal *gray market* goods has been the only effective countermeasure. It is hoped that Chinese membership in the *World Trade Organization* (WTO) will result in greater enforcement of intellectual property law. In the meantime, the *licensor* needs to negotiate a *transfer agreement* that includes contractual protections against the misuse of the licensed information. The problem remains whether such protections will be enforced. In order to reduce the cost of enforcement and increase the likelihood of success, the licensor should consider alternative dispute resolution methods such as *mediation* and *arbitration*. It is also important for the licensor to understand that, unlike in the United States, the licensing agreement may not be a totally private affair. Lesser-developed countries, former communist countries, and China often require government approval and registration of licensing agreements. The contract is likely to be reviewed and pro-licensor clauses modified. Clauses most susceptible to revision include the *royalty*, *confidentiality*, *termination*, and *grant back* clauses.

In contrast to China, France has an established record of intellectual property protection. It is important for the intellectual property owner to register its rights under the patent, copyright, and trademark laws of France before entering any transfer agreement. The license or transfer agreement is generally enforced as written under French law, but superseding *European Union Regulations* dealing with licensing of patents and intellectual property must be addressed and certain provisions that are legal under U.S. laws may be illegal under EU *competition* (antitrust) *law*.

Scenario 3: Purchasing a Company in the Russian Federation and Germany

The most risky of all international business transactions is direct foreign investment, which can range from opening a branch office to purchasing an existing company or building a manufacturing facility. Foreign direct investment is risky primarily because it makes a company susceptible to a wide range of *host country laws.* These laws cover the areas of employment and labor, environmental, health and safety, product liability, and taxation. In considering direct foreign investment, the first decision is what type of legal vehicle should be chosen to operate the foreign enterprise. The most popular way of doing business is to establish an independent subsidiary under the laws of the host country.

In purchasing an existing company in Russia, the greatest risk is the uncertainty in the meaning and enforcement of commercial laws. Most of the current Western-styled laws were enacted following the fall of communism in 1991. The supporting jurisprudence found in Western legal systems has yet to be developed by the Russian courts; in fact, the widespread ineffectiveness of the Russian legal system has been well chronicled. Russia is a country where the use of a *joint venture* with an established Russian partner might be advantageous. A joint partner can share the risks and provide a portion of the capital or offer necessary government contacts and distribution system. Joint ventures have to be approved or registered with government agencies and failure to register can lead to severe negative consequences such as the dissolution of the joint venture.

In contrast, purchasing a company in Germany is much the same as buying a company in the United States. There is little likelihood of a government *expropriation* or *nationalization* in Germany. Germany's pro-worker labor laws, however, prohibit an acquiring firm from ignoring existing collective bargaining agreements. The employment-at-will doctrine of the United States allows an acquiring firm to downsize the workforce with little legal restraint, but in Germany employment is viewed as a *property right* that must be respected. Any substantial changes in the workforce, such as layoffs or plant closings, must be submitted to a *works council* made up of employees. Finally, the corporation laws in both Russia and Germany should be researched. The limited liability provided by the corporate entity is sacrosanct in U.S. law, but in foreign legal systems an attempt to *pierce the corporate veil* to hold a parent company or a joint venture partner liable is more likely to be successful.

currency conversion and repatriation of profits. If a company is deemed to be doing business in a foreign country, then it may become amenable to the legal jurisdiction of a foreign court. Companies that establish a presence in a foreign country must also be concerned with local employment laws. Many countries impose severe restrictions on the termination of employees or agents, such as requiring lengthy notice requirements and substantial severance payments. Other host country laws that should be examined include labeling, marketing, and advertising laws; income and sales tax laws; environmental laws; product and consumer liability laws; health and safety laws; and antitrust or competition laws. In order to decrease the uncertainty due to the risks of foreign laws, the United States has entered into **bilateral investment treaties** with many foreign countries. These treaties provide the basic legal framework for a company investing in a foreign country. They generally address issues of convertibility of currency, repatriation of profits, compensation for expropriation, protection of intellectual property, and nondiscriminatory treatment of foreign investors.

Risks in Developing Countries

The level of risks in transacting business in many developing countries is considerably higher than in developed countries. Some countries are marked by arbitrary government actions, excessive taxation, ineffective legal and dispute resolution systems, and a high degree of corruption. These countries find it difficult to interest foreign investment. Therefore, the best and possibly the only way to conduct business in these countries is by exporting. Some countries have passed laws to assure foreign investors and businesspersons by legally attempting to reduce the risks of doing business. Mexico passed the Foreign Investment Act of 1993 in order to attract and protect foreign investment. It opened large portions of the Mexican market to foreign ownership. In certain strategic economic industries, approval of the National Commission of Foreign Investments is needed for foreign ownership of greater than 49%, while some industries, such as oil, electricity, and railroads, remain reserved for Mexican nationals. The Foreign Investment Act provides expedited procedures to gain governmental approvals.

Russia has enacted a Regulation on Hard Currency Control that attempts to placate foreign investors' fears about the repatriation of hard currencies. The law requires any purchase or sale of foreign currencies to be approved by the Central Bank of the Russian Federation. Currency control is also delegated to the State Customs Committee, the Ministry of Finance, and Inspector of Currency Control. However, Article 8 of the Hard Currency Law recognizes the right of nonresidents "to freely transfer, export, and transmit hard currency if that hard currency was previously transferred or imported to the Russian Federation." The law mandates strict bookkeeping requirements for all hard currency transactions. Residents and nonresidents must maintain records of their hard currency operations for a period of five years.

Language and Cultural Risk

In the past, a major obstacle to international business transactions involved the differences in language and the cultural backgrounds of the transacting parties. Language difficulties have diminished significantly due to the precipitous rise in foreign language proficiency. Nonetheless, even when dealing with a foreign counterpart who speaks English it is important to understand that misunderstandings can still occur. One device to overcome language differences is to have the contract drawn in the languages of both parties. But the *Falcoal, Inc. v. Kurumu* case that follows illustrates that even this precaution may fail to overcome inconsistencies that may result from translation. The language problem in this case revolves around the pivotal issues of where the parties may sue under the contract's forum selection clause and whether the U.S. court had personal jurisdiction over the foreign defendant.

Falcoal, Inc. v. Kurumu

660 F. Supp. 1536 (S.D. Tex. 1987)

David Hittner, District Judge. Plaintiff Falcoal, Inc. is an American corporation having its principal place of business in Houston, Texas. Defendant Kurumu (TKI) is a commercial entity, owned and controlled by the Turkish government. TKI decided to import a portion of Turkey's coal supply. In an attempt to solicit bids, TKI issued a notice announcing a "sartname" ("terms and conditions"). This announcement was made in local Turkish-language publications. The sartname distributed by TKI was issued in Turkish and provided by its terms that any conflicts as to its terms would be settled by reference to the original Turkish language version. Falcoal submitted the bid that was ultimately accepted by TKI. Falcoal's bid was signed and submitted by its authorized agent, Zihni, a Turkish company. The negotiation of the contract took place entirely in Ankara, Turkey.

After the parties had agreed to the terms, Zihni prepared two copies of the contract, an English version and a Turkish version. Although the parties assert that they believed the content of the two versions to be identical, the English contract and the Turkish contract contain forum selection clauses which directly contradict each other. The Turkish-language version provides that "the final jurisdiction for the settlement of any disputes, in the case of the PURCHASER [TKI] submitting a claim, lies within the jurisdiction of the Houston commercial courts and, in the case of the SUPPLIER [Falcoal] submitting a claim lies within the jurisdiction of the Ankara commercial courts." The English-language contract, by contrast, provides that any dispute "shall be finally settled in Houston and submitted to the jurisdiction of the Courts of the U.S.A. if the claim is put forward by Supplier [Falcoal] and in Ankara, Turkey, and submitted to the Turkish Courts if the claim is put forward by Buyer [TKI]."

Pursuant to the contract, Falcoal was to deliver 100,000 tons of coal to a shipper of TKI's choice. Falcoal agreed to post a performance bond in an amount equal to 10 percent of the contract price and, pursuant to this agreement, Citibank International-Ankara issued a performance bond in favor of TKI in the amount of $400,000. This bond was secured by a letter of credit opened by Falcoal at Citibank International-Dallas. The contract further provided that, to secure payment for the coal, TKI was to open a letter of credit in New York forty-five days before shipment. TKI failed to open this letter of credit. When the coal was not shipped, TKI, allegedly wrongfully and without authorization, drew on Falcoal's performance bond. Falcoal subsequently brought this suit against TKI alleging breach of contract for failing to open the New York letter of credit in Falcoal's favor, conversion and fraud for wrongfully drawing on Falcoal's performance bond, and injury to Falcoal's business reputation. TKI has moved to dismiss, alleging lack of subject matter jurisdiction and lack of personal jurisdiction.

Subject Matter Jurisdiction

TKI asserts that this Court lacks subject matter jurisdiction because TKI, as an entity of the Turkish government, has sovereign immunity under the Foreign Sovereign Immunities Act of 1976 (FSIA), 28 U.S.C. § 1602 *et seq.* However, Falcoal contends that TKI waived sovereign immunity by agreeing to a forum selection clause and falls within the commercial exception of the FSIA. The waiver provision and commercial exception are found in section 1605(a):

Section 1605 (a) A foreign state shall not be immune from the jurisdiction of courts of the United States or of the States in any case—

(1) in which the foreign state has waived its immunity either explicitly or by implication, notwithstanding any withdrawal of the waiver which the foreign state may purport to effect except in accordance with the terms of the waiver;

(2) in which the action is based upon a commercial activity carried on in the United States by the foreign State; or upon an act performed in the United States in connection with a commercial activity of the foreign state elsewhere; or upon an act outside the territory of the United States in connection with a commercial activity of the foreign state elsewhere and that act causes a direct effect in the United States;

This Court would find merit to Falcoal's "waiver" argument, were the English version forum clause the only clause at issue. However, the Court cannot ignore the existence of the Turkish contract, whose forum clause provides for suit in Houston when TKI is the plaintiff. That contract expressly provides for suit *against* TKI in Turkey. Clearly, under the facts of this case where, as here, there are two contradictory forum clauses and where the issue of which forum clause should control is vigorously contested, the English-language clause cannot be said to constitute a waiver of sovereign immunity.

The Court next reviews Falcoal's argument that TKI's actions place it within the exceptions to sovereign immunity set forth in section 1605(a)(2). Clearly this action is not one "based upon commercial activity carried on [by TKI] in the United States." The FSIA defines such commercial activity as activity "having substantial contact with the United States." The mere provision for payment in the United States, however, is not a "substantial contact" meeting the test for commercial activity under the FSIA. It remains for this Court to determine whether TKI's conduct falls within the third clause of section 1605(a)(2) as to whether the conduct alleged against TKI constitutes "an act outside the territory of the United States in connection with a commercial activity of the foreign state elsewhere" which "causes a direct effect in the United States." At issue is the definition of "direct effect."

TKI asserts, and Falcoal has not shown otherwise, that it has had no contacts with the Texas forum, nor in fact with the United States, other than its involvement in the contract which is the subject of this suit. That contract was solicited, negotiated, drafted, and executed in Turkey and in the Turkish language. The contract itself does not establish minimum contacts with the Texas forum. Nor does TKI's agreement to pay through a letter of credit in New York create personal jurisdiction. Thus, in the instant case the constitutional requirements for exercise of in personam jurisdiction are lacking.

In an effort to resolve the tension between 28 U.S.C. § 1605(a)(2) and 28 U.S.C. § 1330(b), courts have taken two approaches. Some have held that an effect cannot reach the level of "direct" effects described in the statute and thus sovereign immunity cannot be overcome, unless the effect fulfills the "minimum contacts" requirement.

Other courts have given "direct effect" its literal meaning and found such an effect when an American corporation has suffered a direct financial injury due to a foreign sovereign's conduct. This Court finds the latter approach to be most reasonable. The Court holds that the conduct of TKI in drawing on Falcoal's performance bond was an action which caused a direct effect in the United States, and thus TKI cannot claim sovereign immunity from this suit. Subject matter jurisdiction, therefore, exists.

Personal Jurisdiction

Constitutionally, this Court cannot exercise personal jurisdiction over TKI unless TKI has taken some action that may be construed as an expression of waiver or implied consent to the exercise of such jurisdiction. Falcoal contends that such an implied consent is found in the forum selection clause of the English version contract. This Court could find waiver, however, only if it were found that the Turkish-language clause is unenforceable and the English version valid. The Court thus faced with the existence of two contradictory clauses, must look to the law of the appropriate forum to determine which clause to enforce. Because the contract was solicited, negotiated and executed in Turkey, Turkish law must apply. Both parties agree that, were Texas law to apply, the existence of contradictory clauses would evidence a lack of meeting of the minds on the issue of forum for suit, and the clause should be dropped from both contracts. However, in the absence of a determination of similar Turkish law, the clauses cannot be eliminated from the contract. Although this Court finds that TKI has been divested of its sovereign immunity to this suit by its actions in Turkey having a direct effect in the United States and, thus, subject matter jurisdiction exists, the Court finds that it lacks personal jurisdiction over TKI. Motion to Dismiss is GRANTED.

Case Highlights

- Importance of the forum selection clause in international contracts
- Use of letters of credit and performance bonds to secure payments and performances
- Defense of sovereign immunity, along with the waiver and "commercial activity" exceptions
- Determining if a court has personal jurisdiction over the defendant through the "minimum contacts" or "direct effects" standards
- Importance of determining the appropriate law to be applied
- Importance of selecting the language that controls when more than one language contract is executed

RISKS OF CULTURAL DIFFERENCES

Business executives who hope to expand abroad should learn about the history, culture, and customs of the countries to be visited. Business manners and methods, religious customs, dietary practices, humor, and acceptable dress vary widely from country to country. For example, never touch the head of a Thai or pass an object over it—the head is considered sacred in Thailand. Avoid using triangular shapes in Hong Kong, Korea, and Taiwan—the triangle is considered a negative shape. The number 7 is considered bad luck in Kenya and good luck in Czechoslovakia, and it has magical connotations in Benin. The number 10 is bad luck in Korea, and 4 means death in Japan. Red is a positive color in Denmark, but it represents witchcraft and death in many African countries. A nod means no in Bulgaria, and shaking the head from side to side means yes. The OK sign commonly used in the United States (thumb and index finger forming a circle and the other fingers raised) means zero in France, is a symbol for money in Japan, and carries a vulgar connotation in Brazil. The use of a palm-up hand and moving index finger signals "come here" in the United States and some other countries, but it is considered vulgar in others. In Ethiopia, repeatedly opening and closing the palm-down hand means "come here."

Understanding and heeding cultural variables such as these is critical to success in international business and travel. Lack of familiarity with the business practices, social customs, and etiquette of a country can weaken a company's position in the market and prevent it from accomplishing its objectives and ultimately lead to failure. Some of the cultural distinctions that U.S. firms face most often include differences in business styles, attitudes toward development of business relationships, attitudes toward punctuality, negotiating styles, gift-giving customs, greetings, significance of gestures, meanings of colors and numbers, and customs regarding titles. U.S. firms must pay close attention to different styles of doing business and the degree of importance placed on developing business relationships. In some countries business people have a very direct style, while in others they have a more subtle style and value a personal relationship more than most U.S. businesspersons. For example, in the Middle East, engaging in small talk before engaging in business is standard practice.

The U.S. businessperson must also consider foreign customs. For example, attitudes toward punctuality vary greatly from one culture to another and, if misunderstood, can cause confusion and misunderstanding. Romanians, Japanese, and Germans are very punctual, whereas people in many of the Latin countries have a more relaxed attitude toward time. The Japanese consider it rude to be late for a business meeting, but acceptable, even fashionable, to be late for a social occasion. In Guatemala, on the other hand, one might arrive anytime from 10 minutes early to 45 minutes late for a luncheon appointment.

http://

Department of State: **http://www.state.gov**. The U.S. State Department publishes commercial guides for numerous foreign countries. This is a good place to start to learn about differences in culture and business customs.

Proper use of names and titles is often a source of confusion in international business relations. In many countries (including the United Kingdom, France, and Denmark) it is appropriate to use titles until use of first names is suggested. First names are seldom used when doing business in Germany. Visiting businesspeople should use the surname preceded by the title. Titles such as "Herr Direktor" are sometimes used to indicate prestige, status, and rank. In Thailand, people address one another by first names and reserve last names for very formal occasions and written communications. In Belgium it is important to address French-speaking business contacts as "Monsieur" or "Madame," while Dutch-speaking contacts should be addressed as "Mr." or "Mrs." To confuse the two is a great insult.

Customs concerning gift-giving are extremely important to understand. In some cultures gifts are expected, and failure to present them is considered an insult, whereas in other countries offering a gift is considered offensive. Business executives also need to know when to present gifts; where to present gifts; what type of gift to present; what color the gift should be; and how many to present. Gift-giving is an important part of doing business in Japan, where gifts are usually exchanged at the first meeting. In sharp contrast, gifts are rarely exchanged in Germany and are usually considered inappropriate. Gift-giving is not a normal custom in Belgium or the United Kingdom either, although in both countries flowers are a suitable gift when invited to someone's home.

Customs concerning the exchange of business cards vary, too. Although this point seems of minor importance, observing a country's card-giving customs is a key part of business protocol. In Japan, for example, the Western practice of accepting a business card and pocketing it immediately is considered rude. The proper approach is to carefully look at the card after accepting it, observe the title and organization, acknowledge with a nod that the information has been digested, and perhaps make a relevant comment or ask a polite question. In addition, it is essential to understand the importance of rank in the other country, to know who the decision-makers are, to be familiar with the business style of the foreign company, and to understand the negotiating etiquette and nature of agreements in the country.[15]

15. The material in this section was taken from the National Trade Data Bank, a product of STAT-USA, U.S. Department of Commerce.

Another facet of international business concerns selling practices. Because cultures vary, there is no single code by which to conduct business. Certain business practices, however, transcend culture barriers: (1) answer requests promptly and clearly; (2) keep promises—a first order is particularly important because it shapes a customer's image of a firm as a dependable or undependable supplier; (3) be polite, courteous, and friendly; and (4) personally sign all letters.

The importance of religious practices should not be underestimated; religious and cultural differences not only impact a foreign entrepreneur directly in the negotiation of a contract but also will subsequently impact employees and agents in the performance of the contract. The *Kern v. Dynalectron Corp.* case that follows illustrates the challenges faced by an organization in conducting its business in a foreign country.

Currency Risks

Currency risks are a concern in almost all business transactions that cross national borders. There are three separate risks that relate to currency and international business transactions: **convertibility, repatriation,** and **currency rate fluctuation.** A buyer and a seller in different countries rarely use the same currency. Payment is usually made in either the buyer's or the seller's currency or in a mutually agreed-on currency that is foreign to both parties. Convertibility is the issue of whether one currency is convertible into another currency. Other than the world's hard currencies, such as the U.S. dollar, English pound, European euro, and Swiss francs, and Japanese yen, most national currencies are

Kern v. Dynalectron Corp.

577 F. Supp. 1196 (N.D. Tex. 1983)

Belew, District Judge. Wade Kern filed this religious-discrimination suit pursuant to Title VII of the Civil Rights Act of 1964, 42 U.S.C. § 2000e-2000e-17 (1976) against Dynalectron Corporation. On August 17, 1978, Wade Kern entered into a written contract of employment with the Defendant, Dynalectron Corporation, to perform duties as a helicopter pilot. The work to be performed in Saudi Arabia consisted of flying helicopters over crowds of Moslems making their pilgrimage along Muhammad's path to Mecca. Those pilots who were stationed at Jeddah would be required to fly into the holy area, Mecca. Saudi Arabian law, based upon the tenets of the Islamic religion, prohibits the entry of non-Moslems into the holy area, Mecca, under penalty of death. Thus, Dynalectron, in accordance with its contract with Kawasaki, requires all pilots stationed at Jeddah to be (or become) Moslem. Had Wade Kern continued to work for Dynalectron, he would have been based in Jeddah and, therefore, his conversion from Baptist to Moslem would have been required. Defendant later offered Kern a job as a member of the air crew, a position not requiring his conversion. However, Kern declined to take that job. Kern filed a sworn complaint with the Equal Employment Opportunity Commission alleging that he was denied an employment opportunity with Defendant due to its discrimination against him because of his religious beliefs.

One of the several ways in which the defendant can carry his burden is by establishing that the discrimination was not unlawful since religion may be a bona fide occupational qualification (B.F.O.Q.). The B.F.O.Q. defense is set forth in § 703(a) of Title VII:

Notwithstanding any other provision of this title it shall not be an unlawful employment practice for an employer to hire and employ employees on the basis of religion, sex, or national origin in those certain instances where religion, sex, or national origin is a bona fide occupational qualification reasonably necessary to the normal operation of that particular business or enterprise.

The use of the word "necessary" in section 703(e) requires that we apply a business necessity test, not a business convenience test. There can be no question but that non-Moslem pilots stationed in Jeddah are not safe as compared to Moslem pilots. Therefore, Dynalectron's discrimination against non-Moslems in general, and Wade Kern specifically, is not unlawful since to hire Moslems exclusively for this job "is a bona fide occupational qualification reasonably necessary to the normal operation of that particular business," § 703(a) of Title VII. Notwithstanding the religious discrimination in this case, the Court holds and finds that the B.F.O.Q. exception is properly applicable.

In *Fernandez v. Wynn Oil Co.*, 653 F.2d 1273 (9th Cir. 1981), a female plaintiff sued her employer for discriminatorily not promoting her because she was female. The job to which she would have been promoted required her to deal with South American businessmen who preferred not to do business with females. There, the Court stated that the mere fact that it was an international case did not distinguish it from other cases wherein it was held that mere customer preference would not justify the use of the B.F.O.Q. exception. The requirement that an individual be a Moslem to perform the duties of a helicopter pilot in certain portions of Saudi Arabia is a bona fide occupational qualification within the meaning of 42 U.S.C. § 2000e-2(e). Thus, Kern voluntarily and unilaterally rescinded his agreement to work for Defendant and thus breached his obligation under the contract.

Case Highlights

- The use of a written employment contract to limit the employer's liabilities
- Extraterritorial application of U.S. employment discrimination laws
- The Bona Fide Occupational Qualification Defense (BFOQ) to an employment discrimination claim
- Religion as a BFOQ in some international business situations

not easily convertible. Hard currency is sometimes referred to as convertible currency.

Unlike countries with hard currency, countries with soft currency do not possess sizeable exchange reserves and surpluses in their balance of payments. Russian rubles cannot be converted to U.S. dollars. That leaves the U.S. businessperson with limited options—reinvest the rubles in the Russian economy or find an alternate means of payment, such as countertrade. An exporter or investor can overcome any convertibility problem by requiring payment in a hard currency.

The second currency risk, that of repatriation, may present itself when a foreign party attempts to remove hard currency from a host country. Some foreign countries have enacted currency laws that block the movement of hard currencies outside of the country. Less developed countries, for example, have limited hard currency reserves and do not allow them to be used for the purchase of private goods. Once again, countertrade may be the only option available to overcome the repatriation risk of doing business in such countries.

The third and broadest type of currency risk is the devaluation of the currency of payment. The relative value between the dollar and the buyer's currency may change between the time the deal is made and the time payment is received. If the exporter is not properly protected, a devaluation of the foreign currency could cause the exporter to lose money in the transaction. One of the simplest ways for a U.S. exporter to avoid this type of risk is to quote prices and require payment in U.S. dollars. Then the burden and risk are placed on the buyer to make the currency exchange. If the buyer asks to make payment in a foreign currency, the exporter should consult an international banker before negotiating the sales contract. International banks can help one hedge against such a risk if necessary, by agreeing to purchase the foreign currency at a fixed price in dollars regardless of the value of the currency when the customer pays. If this mechanism is used, the fees charged by the bank should be included in the price quotation.

The *Bernina Distributors v. Bernina Sewing Machines* case illustrates how a party did not anticipate the risk of a currency rate fluctuation. In this case, a poorly written *open price term* resulted in significant monetary losses due to an unanticipated currency fluctuation.

A foreign importer or exporter can minimize the risk of a negative currency rate change through techniques of hedging. This is accomplished by entering into forward, future, or option contracts. **Arbitrage** is the simultaneous buying and selling of the same foreign exchange in two or more markets in order to take advantage of price differentials. A **forward contract** requires two parties to exchange specified amounts of two currencies at some future time. The problem with a forward contract is that if the underlying deal falls through, the party is still required to purchase (exchange) the other currency. The **futures contract** is like a bond that can be sold prior to maturity. Either party can avoid their obligations under the contract by selling it in the secondary market.[16] A well-developed futures market provides a high level of liquidity but, just as in the bond market, the value of the futures contract will fluctuate depending on the underlying values of the currencies.

http://
International Finance Corporation: **http://www.ifc.org**. This is the finance arm of the World Bank.

In the *Bernina* case the importer could have hedged by entering a futures contract to purchase Swiss francs for a fixed amount of dollars. This would have protected it against the subsequent devaluation of the dollar. In fact, the value of the futures contract would have increased in value in the futures market since the con-

Bernina Distributors, Inc. v. Bernina Sewing Mach.

646 F.2d 434 (10th Cir. 1981)

Distributor of sewing machines brought action against importer of sewing machines for breach of contract. Defendant Bernina Sewing Machine Co. (Importer), a Utah corporation, imports and supplies Bernina sewing machines to plaintiff Bernina Distributors (Distributor). The problems that have arisen relate mostly to pricing and are caused by the fluctuations of exchange rates and decreases in the value of the U.S. dollar versus the Swiss franc. The case involves a long-term supply contract to run for seven years. Contract contained an open price term in which "prices are automatically subject to change when factory costs are increased." Importer is required to pay in Swiss francs. The open price term allowed Importer to increase price as follows: "(a) To the extent of any increase of factory invoice costs to Importer. (b) To the extent of any increase in duty charges. (c) To the extent of increases in insurance, freight, handling, broker and port fees, or other similar charges. Increases to duty or factory invoice costs shall be adjusted as they occur. Increases to all other charges shall be adjusted at the commencement of each calendar year." But with the precipitous decline of the dollar in relation to the Swiss franc, Importer's costs nearly doubled and thus halved its rate of return per dollar invested.

Logan, Circuit Judge. Importer maintains that the risk of currency fluctuations had not been considered or allocated in the contract and that under the Uniform Commercial Code, this "open price term" should be determined according to what the court finds to be reasonable. We believe that the contract provisions are quite comprehensive and hence, the statutory provision is inapplicable to this case. Thus, we believe the contract places the risk of a diminishing profit margin on the Importer and that the Importer bears the risk of currency fluctuations. The Importer also asserts that the court's interpretation makes the contract impracticable under § 2-615 of the Uniform Commercial Code. The U.C.C. excuses performance under a contract when performance "has been made impracticable by the occurrence of a contingency the nonoccurrence of which was a basic assumption on which the contract was made." In our view the instant contract is not one made impracticable by the contingency of the devalued dollar. Comment 8 to § 2-

16. The Chicago Mercantile Exchange established in 1972 the International Monetary Market for trading in currency futures contracts.

615 states that this excuse does "not apply when the contingency in question is sufficiently foreshadowed at the time of contracting." Also, cost increases alone do not render a contract impracticable. The loss would have to be especially severe and unreasonable. Importer was aware of the possibility of a reduction in profits due to exchange rate fluctuations and could have guarded against this contingency. For example, a cost-plus formula for determining the price could have been utilized. Furthermore, Importer was represented by counsel throughout and should have known that the contract provided for price increases only to the extent of actual cost increases.

To grant relief on this issue would be to disturb an agreed-upon allocation of risk between commercial equals. The district court did not err in prohibiting Importer from charging Distributor under the contract's "open price term" a margin of ten percent on increased cost due to exchange rate fluctuations. Furthermore, the contract was not rendered impracticable due to the increase in costs to the Importer related to the currency fluctuation.

Case Highlights

- Common practice of entering into long-term supply contracts
- Use of open price or price escalation clauses to adjust the contract price over the term of the contract
- A determination that a risk has been allocated to one of the parties defeats demand for a contract adjustment
- Contract law allows for an excuse from not fulfilling a contract. In the sale of goods the Uniform Commercial Code § 2-615 grants an excuse for commercial impracticability. The law also allows the parties to write an express excuse or *force majeure* clause.
- An excuse for commercial impracticability will not be granted if the risk was foreseeable or where the burden on a party is not unduly severe.
- Since currency fluctuations are foreseeable courts are likely to view them as allocated risks and not to grant an excuse.
- It is important to write clear and detailed clauses, especially in long-term contracts. The Court suggested the use of a "cost-plus" formula in the open price term.

tract gives a right to buy Swiss francs at a lower fixed price. Another device used to hedge currency risks is the option contract. A **currency option** gives a party a right, but not the obligation, to buy or sell a currency at a fixed rate in the future; a purchaser and a seller of foreign currencies agree on a specific rate of exchange at a future date. The purchaser may choose to exercise or pass on the option, thus limiting the effect of unfavorable exchange rate fluctuations. The seller is paid a fee for tendering the option. The right to sell a currency in the future is a *put option*, while the right to buy is a *call option*. The option is obtained by paying a substantial premium whether the option is exercised or not.

Legal Risk

Because of differences in language, culture, and legal systems, the intentions of parties in an international transaction may not be easily discernable from their contract. Therefore, it is imperative, more so than in a purely domestic undertaking, for the parties to express carefully intended rights and obligations in a written contract. At the time of execution, it is important that the parties, with the assistance of their lawyers, review each contract clause to make sure all parties understand them.

Of course, such a model approach to contract review is not often practical. For example, in the typical export transaction there is no single form that both parties read and sign. The parties simply exchange their own forms in order to effect an offer and acceptance. Nonetheless, each party should take the time to carefully review the terms and conditions found in the other party's form before entering into the contract. This is especially important if it is the first transaction between the contracting parties. It is also important, especially in large transactions with a corporation or partnership, to verify the other party's authority to bind his company to a contract.

Often the quality of a contract is evident not in what it says but in what it fails to say and an international contract may be the product of "studied ambiguity."[17] Vagueness or ambiguity in contractual language is employed in order to achieve the illusion of agreement. Parties make use of "a kind of Esperanto" in which "parties often leave a draft contract in ambiguous form in order to achieve agreement."[18] The roots of contract ambiguity come from two sources: (1) the parties negotiating the contract and (2) those charged with drafting the contract. A common scenario is that the principals negotiate the general framework for an agreement and then turn the task of writing the language of the agreement over to their attorneys. Such brief negotiations increase the risk of ambiguity inherent in interpersonal communication, especially within a cross-cultural context. A key issue for international businesspersons is to determine at what stage they should enlist the services of a lawyer.

http://

European Law Dictionary: **http://library.ukc.ac.uk/library/lawlinks/european.html**. Provides definitions of legal terms used in Europe.

Businesspersons often do not use lawyers in the negotiation stage of contracting, viewing them as obstacles to rather than facilitators of agreement. The businessperson-to-businessperson, face-to-face exchange is a paradigm of how business is done, while lawyers are relegated to the task of writing the formal documents. In international contracting, the businessperson, especially one new to international dealings, would be well advised to enlist an astute international transactional lawyer, along with foreign counsel. The issue of trust aside, international dealings should be evidenced by clearly written and highly negotiated agreements.

Legal systems can differ in substantive laws, procedures, remedies, and levels of enforcement. Although the fundamental legal concepts dealing with business transactions are similar in the civil, common, and socialist legal systems, idiosyncratic differences in the rules can result in unexpected legal liabilities. For example, in Germany the civil law system recognizes the notion of *nachfrist* notice[19] in the area of sale of goods. In U.S. law, a party has the right to strictly enforce the delivery date stated in the contract and can summarily reject a request for more time. In contrast, the civil law concept of *nachfrist* notice dictates that such dates should not be strictly enforced. A request for additional time should be granted unless the non-breaching party can give a commercially viable reason for not granting the requested extension.

Suppose that a U.S. businessperson enters a contract with a German supplier for delivery of goods on June 1. On May 25 the German supplier sends a letter re-

17. Johan Steyn, "A Kind of Esperanto?" *The Frontiers of Liability*, Vol. 2. P.B.H. Birks, Ed. New York: Oxford University Press 1994.
18. Ibid. p. 13.
19. *Nachfrist* notice is the requirement that a party grant an extension of time to perform the contract upon the request of the other party. *Nachfrist* notice will be examined in Chapter 8.

questing an extension for delivery to June 30. Under U.S. law, the buyer may simply reject the request and hold the German supplier in breach of contract if the goods are not delivered on June 1. In fact, the U.S. buyer in this instance responds by saying that the contract provides for delivery on June 1 and any delivery beyond that date will not be accepted. On June 1 the goods are not delivered and the U.S. buyer obtains substituted goods from another supplier. On June 30 goods are received from the German supplier. The U.S. buyer responds by rejecting the "late" delivery. Under *nachfrist* notice, it is the U.S. buyer and not the German supplier who has breached the contract. Because the U.S. buyer failed to give a commercially viable reason for not granting the additional time, the civil law automatically awards the time extension. Therefore, the delivery on June 30 was timely and the German can now sue for full contract damages under German law.

http://

American Society of International Law: **http://www.asil.org**. Provides information on current developments in international law, along with links to international documents and analysis.

In other instances, the rules of law may be similar but the procedures and remedies available may differ significantly. In some countries the cultural abhorrence to litigation results in difficulty finding adequate legal counsel and restricted discovery options.[20] The United States' Federal Rules of Civil Procedure provide a liberal set of rules that allow for full discovery of the other party. Such sweeping discovery techniques may not be available in other countries. Also, the remedies available to the plaintiff may be of a different order. The U.S. notions of treble (triple) and punitive damages are not found in most foreign legal systems, and the U.S. and common law views that prefer to give monetary damages are not found in civil law countries. In civil law the plaintiff is allowed the choice of suing for monetary damages or receiving an order of specific performance that forces the other party to honor the contract.

Finally, similarities in the substantive laws of a country may mask differences in the enforcement of those laws. This can be seen in the areas of intellectual property protection and corruption. A number of countries have ratified the primary international property rights conventions, such as the Paris and Berne Conventions, but have been lax in their enforcement. Lax enforcement has resulted in high levels of counterfeiting and piracy of trademarks, patents, and copyrights. All countries prohibit the bribing of government officials, but lack of enforcement in some countries has resulted in a culture where bribery has become common. Such an environment places limitations on U.S. businesspersons prohibited from making illegal payments to foreign officials under the Foreign Corrupt Practices Act.

A number of countries, especially in the developing world, have enacted laws specifically targeted to foreign investment and trade. Examples of such specialized host country laws include laws that protect host country agents and distributors of foreign products from termination without notice or payment. In some countries—notably within the European Union—a foreign exporter or manufacturer may not terminate its host country agent without paying statutorily determined indemnity compensation or damages in concordance with evergreen statutes. Evergreen statutes limit the ability of a principal or employer to discharge an employee or agent.

Some countries limit the amount of equity ownership that a foreign company may hold in a host country enterprise. These local participation requirements often result in the foreign company creating a partnership or joint venture with

20. Discovery is the pre-trial process whereby the litigants uncover evidence by questioning the other party either in writing (interrogatories) or in person (depositions) and by examining documents provided by the other party to the litigation.

nationals of the host country. Because of the limited amount of hard currency in some countries, other laws restrict a foreign investor or exporter from withdrawing or repatriating their profits or royalties from the country.

Another common area of host country intervention is in the area of technology transfers. In some countries private licensing agreements must be registered and approved by the government. Pro-licensor clauses involving royalty payments, termination, and training may be rewritten to be more favorable to the licensee. These types of specialized host country laws need to be analyzed to determine their impact on a potential foreign investment, export transaction, or intellectual property transfer.

Political Risk

Political or country risk broadly refers to the negative consequences that stem from a change in government policies. In the area of import-export, **trade barriers** represent the most common risk. The United States Trade Representative classifies trade barriers into seven general categories.

- Import policies including tariffs and other import charges, quantitative restrictions,[21] and import licensing
- Standards, labeling, testing, and certification
- Government procurement restrictions
- Export subsidies
- Lack of intellectual property protection
- Service barriers
- Investment barriers

A number of international agreements have been adopted that address trade barriers. The **Uruguay Round** of the General Agreement on Tariffs and Trade (GATT) addressed all of these trade barriers in some fashion. GATT negotiations traditionally targeted tariff barriers and quantitative restrictions. The original 1947 GATT contained provisions aimed at "reducing fees and formalities connected with importation and exportation" (Article VIII), "general elimination of quantitative restrictions" (Article XI), and the "publication of trade regulations" (Article X). The World Trade Organization (WTO) Agreements that followed the Uruguay Round of GATT committed the newly formed WTO to a reduction and elimination of all categories of trade barriers. **Non-tariff barriers** include import quotas and other quantitative restrictions, non-automatic import licensing, customs charges and fees, customs procedures, export subsidies, unreasonable standards, discriminatory labeling, and discriminatory government procurement policies.

http://
World Trade Organization: **http://www.wto.org**. Provides links to all WTO Agreements.

The 1994 WTO Agreements included a separate Agreement on Import Licensing. **Technical barriers** to trade are addressed by a number of the **WTO Agreements** including the Agreement on Technical Barriers, Agreement on the Application of Sanitary and Phytosanitary Measures, Agreement on Customs Valuation, and the Agreement on Preshipment Inspection. Restrictions on foreign government procurement are the subject of the Agreement on Government Procurement. Export subsidies were addressed in the 1947 Agreement in Article VI (Antidumping and Countervailing Duties) and Article XXIII (Nullification and Impairment). The 1994 Agreements also included an Antidumping Agreement.

21. A quota is an example of a quantitative restriction.

Intellectual property protection, barriers to trade in service, and barriers to investment are dealt with directly in separate agreements: the Agreement on Trade-Related Investment Measures (TRIMs), General Agreement on Trade in Services (GATS), and the Agreement on Trade-Related Aspects of Intellectual Property Rights (TRIPS). The Investment Agreement prohibits countries from requiring the purchase of domestically produced products, from conditioning the importation of products on a company's agreement to export products, and from restricting access to foreign exchange. The Agreement on Services prohibits the use of qualification and licensing requirements as barriers to the establishment of a business or the practicing of a profession by a foreign party. Any such requirements are to be based upon "objective and transparent criteria" and must include "adequate procedures to verify the competence of professionals" from foreign countries. The TRIPS Agreement is a comprehensive framework that covers all areas of intellectual property including copyright, trademark, country of origin indicators, patent, industrial designs, and trade secrets. This Agreement will be reviewed in Chapter 13.

http://
Political Risk Information: **http://www.political-risk.net**. Provides data and information on political risk.

A prevalent form of political risk involves changes in government regulation of foreign business activity, sometimes referred to as creeping expropriation. This includes changes in formal regulations, licensing procedures, and the enactment of price controls. Creeping expropriation can also be a less legitimate form of interference such as the extortion of bribes, arbitrary changes in standards and inspection requirements, and the nonenforcement of intellectual property laws. Another major form of political risk is tax calculation and enforcement. A change in the rates, a denial of a tax credit, or a change in accounting rules can be used to manipulate corporate income taxes. Other forms of taxes, such as revenue taxes, can also be manipulated. These taxes are associated with the importation and exportation of goods and include the value-added tax,[22] sales tax, excise tax, and tariffs.

EXPROPRIATION AND NATIONALIZATION

The most extreme form of political risk is **expropriation** and **nationalization.** Expropriation is a government seizure of foreign businesses and assets. Nationalization refers to the seizure of all businesses, foreign and domestic, in a particular industry. Both include some form of compensation, but in the past the compensation has not equalled the value of the lost investments. Fortunately, the threats of a foreign government nationalizing an industry or expropriating a foreign company's assets have severely diminished. The free trade era has made it clear that countries need to attract foreign investment and trade in order to continue to develop. In fact, the opposite of nationalization and expropriation, the **privatization** of government-owned industries, has been the dominant trend over the past few decades.

http://
Readings on privatization issues: **http://www.privatization.md/**.

In order to encourage foreign investments, many developing countries and former communist countries have passed laws protecting them. In May 1993, for example, Russia enacted Foreign Economic Activity legislation that states that foreign investments on its territory "shall enjoy full and unconditional legal protection." More specifically, it states that foreign investments "shall not be subject to nationalization or confiscation except when such measures are adopted in the social interests." In

22. Value-added tax or VAT is a popular method of taxation in Europe. It imposes a tax on goods and services at each stage of the production process equal to the value added to the product at each stage. It is similar, but not identical, to a sales tax.

case of nationalization or confiscation, Russia states it will give prompt, adequate, and effective compensation to the foreign investor.

In the past, the key area of dispute was not whether a country had the legal right to nationalize or expropriate, but the amount of compensation to be paid. Often, the foreign government was willing to pay only the cost paid by the foreign investor. Russia's foreign investment protection law commits it to pay "the real value of the investments being nationalized." It further requires the government to pay in hard currency and to pay interest in the event of any delay in the making of the payment.

Bilateral Investment Treaties (BIT) are another avenue by which countries safeguard foreign investment from expropriation and other investment risks. BITs provide that a host country must not discriminate against foreign investors and agree to pay prompt, adequate, and effective compensation in case of expropriation. They also provide for alternative dispute resolution by way of arbitration with the **International Center for Settlement of Investment Disputes** (ICSID).

http://
Overseas Private Investment Corporation: **http://www.opic.gov**.

Finally, an investor may obtain insurance to protect its investments in foreign countries. To encourage U.S. companies to invest in developing countries, the U.S. government established the **Overseas Private Investment Corporation (OPIC).** The OPIC is a government corporation that assists U.S. private investments in developing countries by providing loans, loan guarantees, investment services, and insurance against political risks. The OPIC provides low-cost expropriation insurance to U.S. companies. The Export-Import Bank of the United States (**Eximbank**) provides financing assistance to U.S. exporters and through the **Foreign Credit Insurance Association** (FCIA) provides different types of insurance coverage. The FCIA works with the Eximbank to provide political and commercial risk insurance to U.S. exporters. Political risk insurance protects against the expropriation of goods, the nonconvertibility of currency, and the inability of a foreign purchaser to obtain an import license.

RISK MANAGEMENT

Before entering a foreign market, a business should measure the degree and likelihood of political risk by performing a formal risk assessment. This may be done internally through research using materials obtained through the U.S. State Department and the Overseas Private Investment Corporation (OPIC). Some businesses enlist private companies that specialize in risk assessment. If a project is very large, however, then management should meet with government officials of the foreign country to discuss the company's goals. If possible, a formal **concession agreement** should be negotiated outlining the duties of the foreign government and the rights of the company. It should specify the level of tariffs to be charged, the right of the company to repatriate profits, the host country's commitment to intellectual property protection, the applicable level of taxation, and the government's **transfer pricing** policy.[23] It is also prudent to require the use of mediation and arbitration in case of a dispute.

23. Transfer pricing is the price that an affiliated company, such as a subsidiary, charges another affiliated company. Manipulation of transfer prices can be used to move profits and costs from a high tax to a low tax country.

Managing Risk Through Insurance

Once the potential risk is assessed, a business can insure against a loss by obtaining political risk insurance. OPIC offers four types of insurance coverage.[24] First, it insures against restrictions on the repatriation of profits. Second, it insures against expropriation and nationalization. Third, it insures against damage to assets due to war or civil strife. Fourth, it provides business interruption insurance for losses of income resulting from political disturbances. The OPIC will also insure banks willing to finance export transactions, enabling a bank to confirm a letter of credit from a risky importer and its bank. OPIC insurance is available only to American investors or exporters undertaking business in a foreign country with which the United States has entered into a bilateral investment treaty (BIT). In addition, OPIC is allowed to sue a foreign country because BITs require the foreign country to waive sovereign immunity protection.

An internationally based investment insurance company is the Multilateral Investment Guarantee Agency (**MIGA**). Established in 1988 as part of the World Bank, MIGA encourages investment in developing countries through the mitigation of noncommercial investment barriers. It provides insurance against expropriation, war, and other noncommercial risks and offers investment guarantees for direct foreign investments, as well as licensing, franchising, and transfers of technology.

The determination of whether political or commercial risk insurance will be needed should be made when negotiating the underlying contract and the cost and type of insurance to be procured should be stated in the contract. Insurance procurement may be subject to foreign government regulation. In China, for example, insurance in conjunction with a joint venture must be obtained through a Chinese insurance company. The decision to obtain commercial insurance may be dictated by the commercial lender. Provisions in the underlying contract should also be reviewed for their potential impact on subsequent insurance claims. For example, choice of law clauses should be reviewed to determine if there are laws that preclude the insured from making a claim under its insurance policy.

The application for insurance, like the application for a letter of credit, is contractual in nature. The applicant should read the form carefully and answer it as honestly and comprehensively as possible. The general rule is that the applicant must disclose any information that would "materially" influence the insurance company's decision to grant the requested insurance.[25] In the related area of marine insurance, a court stated that "an applicant for a marine insurance policy is bound to reveal every fact within his knowledge that is material to the risk."[26] In that case, an owner of a company failed to disclose that he had previously filed claims for more than two dozen losses at sea. The court found that there was sufficient evidence for fraud in intentionally concealing material facts and allowed rescission of the insurance policy.

Typical provisions found in most insurance contracts include a description of the insured property, a definition of expropriatory act, waiting period, notice, warranties, recoveries, duty to minimize loss,[27] and definition and computation of

24. 22 U.S.C. § 2194 (1988).
25. See New York Insurance Law § 3105 (McKinney's).
26. Cigna Property & Casualty Insurance Co. v. Polaris Pictures Co., 1998 WL 734391 (9th Cir. 1998).
27. See Slay Warehousing Company Inc. v. Reliance Insurance Co., 471 F.2d 1364 (8th Cir. 1973).

loss.[28] The definition of what expropriatory acts are covered by expropriation insurance policy should be closely scrutinized. Does the policy cover both partial and total loss or expropriation? A "waiting period" is often required between the expropriatory loss and collecting on the insurance policy. In large projects the waiting period can be as long a year. The duties of the insured regarding the preservation of the investment and any claims pertaining to the loss should be clearly defined. A warranty provision often requires the insured to take steps in order to preserve its coverage. For example, the insured may have to certify that it will comply with relevant host country laws and that the uninsured portion of the investment will remain uninsured. Also, rights to recoveries made after payment on the claim should be defined.

Managing Risk Through Intermediaries

Exporting, licensing, and direct foreign investment risks can be reduced by using professional consultants and agents. International specialists such as freight forwarders, customs brokers, political risk analysts, international lawyers, and commercial insurance companies all offer expertise and services.

Customs brokers assist importers with the entry and admissibility of goods, its classification and valuation, and the payment of duties. In the United States, customhouses are licensed under Part III of Title 19 of the Code of Federal Regulations in order to transact business with the Customs Service. They can be hired to provide the necessary import and customs documents. Generally, the seller or exporter hires the freight forwarder, while the customs broker is the agent for an importer or purchaser. An "export" freight forwarder must be certified by the Federal Maritime Commission to handle ocean freight.

The **freight forwarder** often arranges all documentation needed to move a shipment from origin to destination and assembles documents for presentation to the bank in the exporter's name. The forwarder arranges for cargo insurance, notifies the buyer of the shipment, and advises the shipper of marking and labeling requirements. In exchange, the forwarder is paid a fee by the exporter and may receive a percentage of the freight charge from the common carrier. The international banker offers financing assistance, provides guarantees of payment, and facilitates the movement of documents between the parties.

Countertrade

Countertrade is used to overcome currency convertibility and repatriation problems or the capital shortcomings of a foreign party.[29] This section will discuss some of the common forms of countertrade including barter, buy-back, and counterpurchase. A **barter transaction** involves an exchange of goods or services, but barter agreements are not always simple, cashless, single document arrangements. They sometimes involve two separate documentary sales, often with separate letters of credit. A form of countertrade known as **counterpurchase** is an economic transaction in which one party sells goods to the second party and, in return, the first party agrees to purchase goods from the second party so as to achieve an agreed ratio

28. S. Linn Williams, "Political and Other Risk Insurance: OPIC, MIGA, EXIMBANK, and Other Providers," 5 *Pace International Law Review* 59, 106–112 (1993).

29. See generally Grabow, "Negotiating and Drafting Contracts in International Barter and Countertrade Transactions," 9 *North Carolina Journal of International Law & Commercial Regulation* 255 (1984).

between the reciprocal performances.[30] A variant is the **offset agreement.** "Offsets constitute an agreement by the foreign seller to include as part of the sale in the foreign nation the use of parts or services from local suppliers."[31] An offset satisfies local content requirements where the host country mandates that a certain percentage of a good be a product of local materials and labor. In **buy-back** or compensation transactions, exporters of heavy equipment, technology, or entire manufacturing facilities agree to purchase a certain percentage of the output of the facility. The following section describes the variations found in the area of countertrade.

Doing Business Internationally

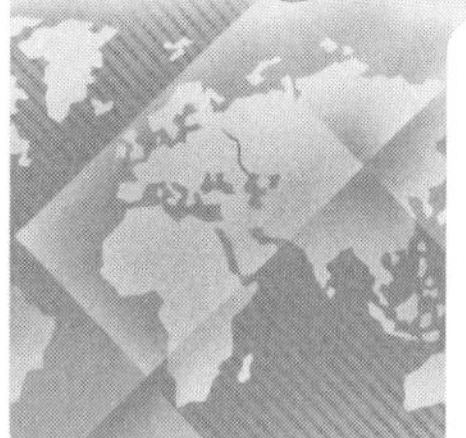

McVey, "Countertrade: Commercial Practices, Legal Issues, and Policy Dilemmas"

16 *Law & Policy Int'l Bus.* 1 (1984)

Countertrade frequently is confused with the concept of barter. Barter is an exchange of goods effectuated without the use of currency. Countertrade is most frequently used to refer to two reciprocal sales transactions in which each party is paid in currency. Despite this technical distinction most observers view barter transactions as a subcategory of countertrade. The two most common types of countertrade are known as counterpurchase and compensation (buy-back) trade.

Counterpurchase

In a counterpurchase arrangement, a private firm agrees to sell products to a sovereign nation and to purchase from the nation goods which are unrelated to the items which it is selling. For example, in a series of transactions between a major U.S. manufacturer of commercial aircraft and the government of Yugoslavia, the U.S. firm sold jet aircraft to Yugoslavia and agreed to purchase substantial quantities of Yugoslav crystal glassware, cutting tools, leather coats, and canned hams.

In a counterpurchase transaction, each party is paid in currency upon the delivery of its products to the other party. It is common in such transactions for a private firm to be allowed a period of time following the delivery of the goods that it is selling in which to fulfill its purchase obligation. Periods of from three to five years, for example, are not uncommon in counterpurchase obligations imposed by the Soviet Union and Eastern European nations. Often, the parties agree upon a list of goods from which the private firm later will be able to select items to purchase.

Private firms resort to a variety of methods to dispose of goods which they are forced to purchase, but most frequently resell these goods to trading companies or directly to end users, often at a discount or "disagio." Sometimes the private firm will resell the countertraded goods at a price below that which it paid for them, seeking to offset this loss by larger profits generated by the sale of its own product to the nation.

Compensation

The most common form of countertrade is referred to as "compensation" or "buy-back." In a compensation transaction, a private firm will sell equipment, technology, or even an entire plant to a sovereign nation and agree to purchase a portion of the output produced from the use of the equipment or technology. For example, in the celebrated

(continued)

30. See UNCITRAL, "Preliminary Study of Legal Issues in International Countertrade" (1988).
31. Folsom & Gordon, *International Business Transactions* 35 (1995).

Doing Business Internationally *(continued)*

$20 billion Occidental Petroleum ammonia countertrade transaction with the Soviet Union, Occidental assisted the Soviets in constructing and financing ammonia plants and agreed to purchase quantities of ammonia produced in these plants over a twenty-year period.

Compensation transactions frequently involve significantly longer periods of time during which the private firm will be permitted to fulfill its purchase obligation than in counterpurchase. In addition, compensation transactions are generally of larger dollar value than counterpurchase transactions. Unlike counterpurchase transactions, the products which the private firm purchases in compensation are frequently of marketable quality and in demand in the international marketplace. Further, Western firms frequently are able to negotiate a purchase price for the output that is below the world market price so that the firm can earn a profit in reselling the product which it is forced to buy.

Barter

Barter, swap, and other types of noncurrency transactions are frequently viewed as forms of countertrade. In many cases, the sovereign nation will impose a barter requirement in a coercive fashion for purposes of disposing of surplus or low quality goods which it otherwise cannot sell. Barter transactions are frequently utilized in crude oil transfers as a means of conveying crude below official OPEC prices. Similarly, barter is occasionally used as a means of "liberating" blocked currencies or otherwise circumventing foreign exchange controls.

Clearing Agreements

Although countertrade is conducted most frequently between a sovereign nation and a private firm, countertrade arrangements also occur between and among sovereign nations. Nations have historically entered into bilateral or multilateral "clearing agreements" under which they agree to purchase equal values of each other's products over a specified period of time. This is a form of reciprocal trading not unlike the private firm-sovereign nation relationships discussed above. When an imbalance develops in an account that a nation cannot rectify, private firms known as "switch trading" firms offer to assist the recalcitrant nation in disposing of the goods which it is required to purchase, usually for a fee.

Framework Agreements

In a countertrade "framework agreement" a private firm establishes a formal, long-term "crediting" mechanism with the host nation under which exports generated by the private firm are routinely credited to the countertrade commitments of numerous third-party firms on an ongoing basis. The key to a framework agreement is that the "crediting" of the offsetting purchases or the escrowing and payment of funds is undertaken on a routine and ongoing basis under

http://
United Nations:
http://www.un.org/law.
Provides links to United Nations initiatives in the area of private international business.

The Department of Commerce can advise and assist U.S. exporters faced with countertrade requirements. The Finance and Countertrade Division of the Office of Finance, Industry, and Trade Information monitors countertrade trends, disseminates information, and provides general assistance to enterprises seeking barter and countertrade opportunities. Another source for information and contract clauses dealing with countertrade is the United Nations Commission on International Trade Law (**UNCITRAL**). It publishes a *Legal Guide on International Countertrade Transactions* that provides information on how best to structure a countertrade transaction. It also discusses the types of clauses generally found in a prearranged agreement rather than on the more common case-by-case basis.

"Positive" or "Reverse" Countertrade

In certain instances, private firms prefer countertrade arrangements over conventional transactions. In so-called "positive" or "reverse" countertrade, the private firm views the goods that it will be required to purchase as more valuable than hard currency. This is most often the case when a firm seeks to establish a guaranteed supply of a valuable commodity or production component when it anticipates future shortages of these items. For example, in one of the proposed East-West "gas-for-pipes" transactions, a group of private firms was negotiating with the Soviet Union to transfer equipment and technology for the transportation and production of natural gas to the Soviets in return for guarantees of quantities of natural gas produced through the use of this equipment and technology.

Performance Requirements

A performance requirement is a condition imposed by a sovereign government that requires foreign parties who wish to undertake an investment in that nation to agree to take certain steps to increase exports from the nation. Such steps include the agreement by the foreign investors to export a certain percentage of the output from the investment project, to employ a certain level of local inhabitants in the project, to use a predetermined level of locally produced components in the manufactured product, and to transfer certain technology to the host nation. Performance requirements are distinguishable from other types of countertrade requirements in that the former involve a private firm's investment in the imposing nation rather than its sale of goods to the nation. Both practices involve intervention by the host nation in the free market process, however, and in view of their similarity are frequently treated as the same phenomenon.

Collection-through-Export Transactions

A major problem for U.S. firms doing business abroad is the collection of overseas funds which have been restricted from repatriation due to foreign exchange controls. In such instances, a private firm might be owed funds by a foreign party as a result of a trade debt or have profits denominated in local currency which are earned by a foreign subsidiary. The private firm will have possession of the local currency in the host country, but due to foreign exchange shortages will be unable to convert this currency into dollars. In a collection-through-export transaction, the firm will use the local currency to purchase locally produced goods, export the goods from the host nation, and sell the goods overseas for dollars or another convertible currency.

countertrade contracts. The clauses discussed in the *Guide* include: type, quality, and quantity of goods; pricing of goods; participation of third parties; payment; restrictions on resale; liquidated damages; security for performance; failure to perform; choice of law; and settlement of disputes.

Because of the difficulty in finding marketable goods in a foreign country to fulfill a countertrade commitment, certain clauses take on added importance. First, an extended period of time should be allotted to the exporter to obtain host country goods to satisfy its countertrade obligations. Second, a broad list of countertrade goods should be negotiated to enhance the exporter's chances of finding marketable goods. Third, because of the poor quality of some foreign goods, the exporter should negotiate broad inspection rights. Also, the costs and uncertainty of the countertrade arrangement may warrant the granting of a ***disagio*** (discount) of the amount of goods needed to be purchased to fulfill the countertrade commitment.

Another provision included in countertrade contracts is a penalty clause for nonperformance of the countertrade commitment. In some cases, paying a penalty instead of purchasing unmarketable goods may make better economic sense for the exporter. Of course, the penalty clause should make clear that payment of the penalty releases the exporter from any further liability.[32]

DEVELOPING AN EXPORT PLAN

Before attempting to export, a firm should develop an export plan that answers the following ten questions: (1) What countries are targeted for sales development? (2) What products are selected for export? What modifications, if any, must be made to adapt them for overseas markets? (3) In each country, what is the basic customer profile? What marketing and distribution channels should be used to reach customers? (4) What special challenges pertain to each market (competition, cultural differences, import controls, etc.), and what strategy will be used to address them? (5) How will the product's export sales price be determined? (6) What specific operational steps must be taken and when? (7) What will be the time frame for implementing each element of the plan? (8) What personnel and company resources will be dedicated to exporting? (9) What will be the cost in time and money for each element? (10) How will results be evaluated and used to modify the plan? The next Focus on Transactions feature provides an outline for a generic export plan.

The way a company chooses to export its products can have a significant effect on its export plan. One goal of the export plan will be to determine whether the firm should export directly or indirectly. The basic distinction between these approaches to exporting relates to a company's level of involvement in the export process. Firms that are new to exporting or are unable to commit staff and funds to more complex export activities may find indirect exporting appropriate. Exporting indirectly through intermediaries leaves it to the intermediary firm to find foreign markets and buyers for its products. Export management companies (EMCs), export trading companies (ETCs), international trade consultants, and other intermediaries can give the exporter access to well-established expertise and trade contacts. A firm contemplating a greater involvement in a foreign market will need to seek the expertise of a foreign lawyer.

The direct exporting approach is the more ambitious and difficult, since the exporter personally handles every aspect of the exporting process from market research and planning to foreign distribution and collections. Consequently, a significant commitment of management time and attention is required to achieve good results. However, this approach may also be the best way to achieve maximum profits and long-term growth. With appropriate help and guidance from third-party experts including freight forwarders and international banks, even small or medium-sized firms can export directly if they are able to commit enough staff time to the

32. William G. Frenkel, "Legal Protection against Risks Involved in Doing Business in the Republics of the Former U.S.S.R.," 10 *International Quarterly* 395, 431 (1998).

Focus on Transactions

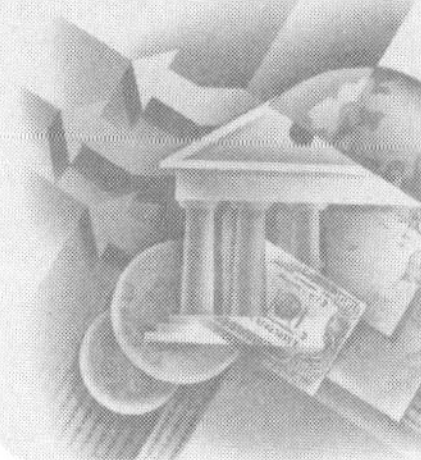

Sample Outline for an Export Plan[33]

Introduction: Why this Company Should Export
Part I. Export Policy Commitment Statement
Part II. Situation/Background Analysis

- Product or Service
- Operations
- Personnel and Export Organization
- Resources of the Firm
- Industry Structure, Competition, and Demand

Part III. Marketing Component

- Identifying, Evaluating, and Selecting Target Markets
- Product Selection and Pricing
- Distribution Methods
- Terms and Conditions
- Sales Goals: Profit and Loss Forecasts

Part IV. Tactics: Action Steps

- Primary Target Countries
- Secondary Target Countries
- Indirect Marketing Efforts

Part V. Export Budget

- Pro Forma Financial Statements

Part VI. Implementation Schedule

- Follow-up
- Periodic Operational and Management Review (Measuring Results Against Plan)

effort. For those who cannot make that commitment, the services of an EMC, ETC, trade consultant, or other qualified intermediary is indispensable.

A company may take a multifaceted approach to exporting. For example, it may elect to export directly to nearby markets such as Canada or Mexico, while letting an EMC handle more ambitious sales to Saudi Arabia or China. An exporter may also choose to gradually increase its level of direct exporting, after it has gained experience and sales volume appears to justify added investment.

FINDING AND MANAGING FOREIGN LAWYERS

One of the best ways to find foreign legal counsel is to follow the recommendations of U.S. lawyers or businesspersons with experience in a given country. Other sources for foreign lawyers are national or local bar associations or chambers of

33. Source: National Trade Data Bank, a product of STAT-USA, U.S. Department of Commerce.

commerce. Some foreign bar association rules are more restrictive in the area of advertising. German lawyers, for example, are prohibited from advertising or actively seeking clients. Also, there are a number of international bar associations and societies that publish membership lists. Examples of international law societies include the German-American Lawyers' Association and the German-British Jurists' Association.

http://
Legal Directory: **http://www.westbuslaw.com.** Includes links to West's Legal Directory for a listing of lawyers in the United States.

When selecting a foreign legal representative, a number of criteria should be considered. Language skills are vital to an effective dialogue; international law directories will often list the language capabilities of foreign lawyers. Also, it is important to understand the type of assistance that will be required. In complicated international business transactions numerous national laws are likely to be applicable. In addition, the timing of commercial transactions is of great importance to the businessperson. It is therefore imperative that the U.S. businessperson communicates clearly the time frame of the transaction to his foreign counsel.

Key Terms

arbitrage, 22
Article 38, 4
barter transaction, 30
basket of risks, 8
bilateral investment treaty (BIT), 15
buy-back, 31
buying agent, 9
commission agent, 9
concession agreement, 28
convertibility, 20
counterpurchase, 30
countertrade, 8
currency option, 23
curency rate fluctuation, 20
customs broker, 30
direct foreign investment, 8
disagio, 34
evergreen provision, 7
Eximbank, 28
export agent, 9
export management company (EMC), 9
export trading company (ETC), 9
exporting-importing, 8
expropriation, 27
foreign agent, 10
Foreign Credit Insurance Association (FCIA), 28
foreign direct investment, 3
foreign distributor, 10
foreign sales representative, 10
forward contract, 22
franchise, 8
freight forwarder, 30
futures contract, 22
General Agreement on Tariffs and Trade (GATT), 3
home country, 13
host country, 13
indirect exporting, 9
International Center for Settlement of Investment Disputes, 28
International Chamber of Commerce (ICC), 7
International Court of Justice, 4
joint venture, 8
lex mercatoria, 5
licensing, 8
Multilateral Investment Guarantee Agency (MIGA), 29
nationalization, 27
non-tariff barriers, 26
offset agreement, 31
Overseas Private Investment Corporation (OPIC), 28
privatization, 27
remarketer, 9
repatriation, 20
sale of services, 8
technical barriers, 26
trade barriers, 26
trade in goods, 3
transfer pricing, 28
UNCITRAL, 32
United Nations Convention on Contracts for the International Sale of Goods (CISG), 7
Uruguay round, 26
WTO Agreements, 26

Chapter Problems

1. You are a manager at a U.S. company that manufactures moderately priced personal computers. The company is contemplating expanding overseas with an initial emphasis on exporting to Latin America. You have been assigned the task of preparing a preliminary market analysis for the country of Brazil. Using the sources found in the Focus on Transactions feature on page 11, conduct market research. Prepare a report that focuses on the opportunities and pitfalls of exporting to Brazil and offer recommendations.

2. As Vice President for Foreign Operations of a U.S. multinational corporation you have been asked to prepare a report for the Board of Directors regarding "doing business" in Germany and Nigeria. Please discuss the following in your report: (1) The different ways of "doing business" in foreign countries, (2) The way you would recommend for each of the two countries mentioned, (3) The risks of doing business in these countries, and (4) Ways of minimizing those risks.

3. A U.S. businessperson enters into a joint venture with an Italian company in the business of manufacturing and selling agricultural and vegetable products. The joint venture agreement gives the U.S. businessperson a 50% equity ownership in the joint venture. The parties also enter into a shareholder agreement that restricts the shareholders' ability to transfer shares without offering the other shareholders the opportunity to purchase the shares and that provides for arbitration of any shareholder disputes in Rome, Italy. The Italian defendant attempted to purchase ownership interest in the joint venture of the Italian company. The U.S. businessperson sues in the United States on the ground of tortious interference with the shareholder agreement. The plaintiff asserts that the tort claim is not subject to the arbitration clause and argues that a tort claim is outside the scope of the arbitration clause since it is restricted to contract claims directly related to the shareholder agreement. Is the plaintiff correct on the issue of arbitrability or will the plaintiff be forced to arbitrate in Rome, Italy? *Marchetto v. DeKalb Genetics Corp.*, 711 F. Supp. 936 (N.D. Ill. 1989).

4. Your company is contemplating exporting goods to the following countries: France, Hungary, and Nigeria. Research the following: (1) The currency of each country and the current conversion rate into U.S. dollars. (2) Restrictions in each country pertaining to the conversion of the national currency into U.S. dollars and any repatriation limitations. Check the U.S. Department of State Country Commercial Guides for each of these countries for relevant information. If the currency risks are severe for any of these countries, what alternatives should you explore in order to do business in these countries?

Internet Exercises

1. Review the web site of the International Finance Corporation, the private investment arm of the World Bank, for information on the political risks of doing business in a country from the developing world: **http://www.ifc.org**.

2. Review the online catalog of materials published by International Chamber of Commerce Publishing, SA, at **http://www.iccbooks.com**.

3. Review the web site of the World Intellectual Property Organization at **http://www.wipo.org** for materials that would be of assistance to someone contemplating the international licensing of intellectual property rights.

4. Review the international trade law database at **http://lexmercatoria.net/**.

5. Search the web for sites of international law firms that provide assistance to companies undertaking international business transactions. Some of these sites provide interesting articles and links to current developments in the law of international business transactions.

6. Your company manufactures a popular brand of clothing with a world-recognized trademark. You are asked to prepare a political risk report on exporting to two countries in Europe of your choosing. One country is to be a member of the European Union and the other is in Eastern Europe. Compare the different types of risk for the two countries. Recommend a market entry strategy (exporting, licensing, direct investment) for each country. A good place to start is the U.S. Department of State Country Commercial Guides for each country at **http://www.state.gov**.

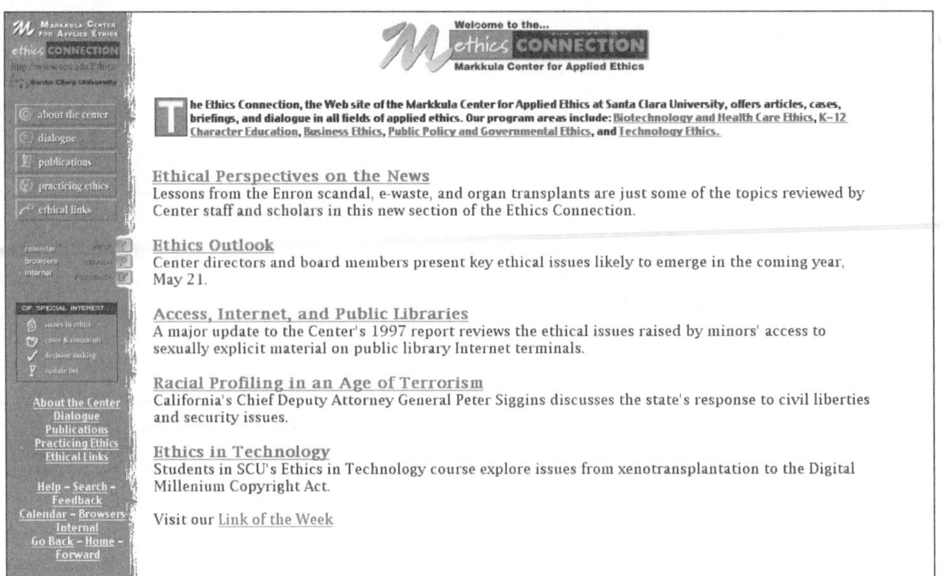

http://www.scu.edu/SCU/Centers/Ethics

Chapter 2
The Ethics of International Business

This textbook's primary focus is on the *legal* implications of doing business internationally. This chapter will emphasize some of the important *ethical* implications of international business dealings and will explore how a multinational business confronts the issues of transnational ethics. It will also discuss various **standards.**

Standards refer to government regulations pertaining to labor, health, safety, and environmental concerns. A variety of "voluntary standards" also exist, advanced by either trade associations or non-governmental organizations. The **International Labor Organization** is an example of a non-governmental agency that publishes standards for the workplace.

http://
International Labor Organization:
http://www.ilo.org.

Most international business decisions have both legal and ethical implications—how to address differences between host country and home country standards, for example. Generally the legal answer to this dilemma is quite clear—since the business activity transpires within the jurisdiction of the host country, then the businessperson need only comply with the standards of the host country assuming no extraterritorial application of home country law. The ethical answer is much more complicated. If the host country's standards are lower than those of the home country, is complying with the lesser standards ethical? Most U.S. companies face this question when starting business operations in lesser-developed countries. Answering becomes more difficult if the lesser standards are likely to result in harm to people or the environment. Ultimately a multinational company may be *ethically* required to apply standards higher than those of the host country.

Demarcating the line between law and ethics and accounting for ethical factors in business decisions is crucial to international business transactions. The ethical assessment is complicated by differing cultural and national outlooks on what is ethically appropriate and will be influenced by the nuances of culture, religion, and economics. **Ethical or cultural relativism,** which holds that because different countries or cultures have different ethical belief systems there is no supranational way of determining whether an action is right or wrong, is often used to argue that ethical decisions are confined within the boundaries of a given country or culture. Ethical relativism asserts that the correctness of an action is to be measured by whatever a majority within a society believes is morally correct.

http://

Business Ethics—Wharton Ethics Program: **http//ethics.wharton.upenn.edu/**.

The problem of cultural relativism that confronts all multinational enterprises will be examined in the context of four common areas of concern: environment, standards, bribery, and advertising. Before exploring these issues in detail, an exploration of general ethical schools and approaches will provide insight.

INTERNATIONAL BUSINESS ETHICS

Business managers often do not recognize the ethical implications of their decisions. From the perspective of corporate profits and credibility, a good reputation in the global marketplace has become paramount for most multinational enterprises, partly because bad ethical practices are readily apparent in an increasingly transparent global economy. Multinational companies are often the target of surveillance by the media, government agencies, competitors, private watch groups, and even their own employees. Public relations disasters resulting from unethical practices can be catastrophic.

http://

For materials on ethical relativism see Ethics Update: **http://ethics.acusd.edu**.

To better sensitize employees to ethical issues, there must be some agreement on what is right or wrong. Some basic assumptions regarding the rightness of certain practices and activities must be made. These basic assumptions are descriptive, not normative, in nature. For example, the issue will not be whether bribery is wrong, but whether Americans or citizens of most civilized nations believe that bribery is wrong. A review of the traditional schools of ethics provides a starting point for the U.S. businessperson's approach to ethical decision-making, and will enable the businessperson to better apply moral reasoning to ethical problems in the international setting. The ethical schools to be reviewed include utilitarianism, rights and duties, virtue, and ethics of care.

Utilitarianism

The **utilitarian** approach is a teleological approach to ethics. Teleology or consequentalism looks to the consequences of a decision or an action to determine if it was ethically appropriate. There are many different formulations of this approach.

Egoism simply determines the rightness of an action, whether it produces more good than bad, for the individual decision-maker. In the area of business, egoism is often associated with the economics of Adam Smith, an eighteenth-century Scottish philosopher generally regarded as the father of modern economics. His masterwork, *The Wealth of Nations,* was published in 1776. In it Smith provided the rationalization for free market economics: Individuals should be allowed to make decisions based upon their own narrow self-interests. If not interfered with, such rational self-interest will produce an efficient economy that benefits society as a whole. Smith's view of self-interest and the free market has largely been misunderstood, however. Smith's moral philosophy as described in his other masterwork, *A Theory of Moral Sentiments,* saw *rational* self-interest as incorporating many altruistic factors not normally associated with the economic man of free market theory.

http://
For a review of utilitarianism see Ethics Update: **http://ethics.acusd.edu.**

Another, simplified version of utilitarianism is the economic concept of benefit-cost. **Benefit-cost analysis** attempts to monetize the ethical determination by placing a dollar value on the benefits and costs of an action from the narrow perspective of the decision-maker. The danger of this narrow interpretation of utilitarianism was demonstrated in the infamous Pinto automobile case. The decision not to install a relatively inexpensive device to prevent rear-end explosions was based upon a narrow dollar calculation, which concluded the cost to defend and settle personal injury and wrongful death lawsuits was less than the costs of incorporating the safety feature. This analysis raises the questions: Is an examination of benefits and cost performed solely from the perspective of the automobile company ethically sufficient? How does one place a value on human life or well-being? Are certain concerns, such as human life, **dominant considerations** that outweigh the other factors in the benefit-cost equation?

A true utilitarian analysis attempts to weigh all direct and indirect effects from the perspectives of all parties or stakeholders affected and not just from the perspective of the decision-maker. It is imperative for the decision-maker to continuously expand the utilitarian analysis to take into account as many effects and stakeholders as possible. It is also important to seek out alternatives that would minimize costs (harm) and increase the net benefit. Benefit-cost utilitarianism may fail to take into account how the net benefit of an action is distributed. Thus, a multinational company decision that creates a net benefit is unlikely to be ethical if the company retains the entire net benefit and the host country and its people receive none. In some developing countries a few leaders and their associates might hoard the host country's benefits.

Dominant considerations relate to **incommensurability.** How does one value life, equality, health, and so on? One can argue that we make those valuations every day in determining what is a reasonable level of safety or what is a reasonable level of pollution. A utilitarian would argue that the market establishes society's preference level of safety or pollution. Did the market establish reasonable levels in the Pinto decision, where safety concerns were ignored? Did the individual consumers? Would the actions of the manufacturer have been more ethical if they had disclosed the dangers of rear-end explosions? Would they have been absolved of moral responsibility if they had offered the consumer the option of purchasing the safety device?

Critics argue that the utilitarian calculation should be, the first stage in a two-stage process. A second stage would analyze how the net benefits are distributed. This process is associated with the notion of **distributive justice.** The second stage may also weigh the effects of an action from the perspective of individual rights and entitlements. For example, if a net benefit results in the diminishment of basic human rights, then the action would be considered unethical. In essence, certain concerns, such as human rights, would take priority over the results of a purely utilitarian analysis. This idea that certain things are sacrosanct is part of the concept of dominant considerations. Certain negative consequences can preempt the determination that an action creates the "greatest good for the greatest number."

If an action produces the greatest good at the expense of the rights of a minority, then utilitarianism fails in its sanctioning of such an action as ethical. In sum, an international businessperson using a utilitarian approach to decision-making should list all those affected by the decision. The businessperson then must value the good and bad consequences of the decision from the perspective of all those found on the list. Next, the analysis should be expanded to include any indirect effects not previously considered. In determining the net benefit or cost of a decision, the decision-maker should seek out alternatives that would produce greater amounts of net benefits. If alternatives are found, then the decision-maker should ask some fundamental questions in comparing the alternatives: Which alternative best promotes the common good? Which alternative best respects the rights of the individual? Which alternative best maintains the valuable traits of character espoused in the company's code of conduct? Finally, the decision-maker must attempt to uncover any dominant considerations that would preclude the action despite the net benefits.

Rights and Duties

While the utilitarian approach focuses upon the net benefits to society, a rights and duties approach views morality from the perspective of the individual. A **moral right** of someone creates a correlative **moral duty** of others not to interfere in the exercise of that right. John Locke championed the notion of inalienable rights that antecede the social contract that binds people together in a society and binds a government to the people. These inalienable rights, as enunciated in the United States' foundational documents (Declaration of Independence, Constitution, Bill of Rights) and the French *Rights of Man*, recognize the sanctity of individual autonomy and equality in the pursuit of personal interests. This sanctity of individual freedom is embodied in the U.S. right to vote, right of association, freedom of religion, and right to a free press. In the area of international documents, the **United Nations Declaration of Human Rights** adopts a basic rights approach to international human rights concerns. More recently, the United Nations passed a resolution titled the **Declaration on the Right to Development,**[1] which asserts that every person has a basic human right to development. The Declaration places responsibility on individual nations and the international community to ensure that everyone shares in the benefits of development. Article 3 of the Declaration states that countries have "the duty to cooperate in ensuring development and eliminating obstacles to development," including the formulation of international development policies that promote the "more rapid development of developing countries." International cooperation is required to provide these countries with "appropriate means to foster their comprehensive development."

The rights approach views morality from the perspective of the individual while utilitarianism measures morality from a societal perspective. Thus, rights can be seen as dominant considerations that trump a strictly utilitarian calculation of net

1. United Nations General Assembly Resolution 41/128 (December 16, 1986).

Comparative Law

Universal Declaration of Human Rights

(Adopted by the United Nations General Assembly on December 10, 1948)

Article 2 states that "everyone is entitled to certain rights and freedoms, without distinction of any kind, such as race, color, sex, language, religion, political or other opinion, national or social origin, property, birth, or other status." This nondiscrimination principle applies to the enumerated rights listed in the declaration. Article 3 provides the general recognition that "everyone has the right to life, liberty, and security of person." Other articles provide specific rights, including the right against torture or degrading treatment (Article 5), right to recognition everywhere as a person under the law (Article 6), right to an effective remedy for acts violating fundamental rights (Article 8), right to a fair and public hearing by an impartial tribunal (Article 10), freedom of movement (Article 13), right to own property (Article 17), freedom of religion (Article 19), right to take part in government (Article 21), and the right to social security, including "the economic, social, and cultural rights indispensable for his dignity" (Article 22). In the area of nondiscrimination, Article 7 states that "all are entitled to equal protection against discrimination." Article 23 provides that "everyone, without any discrimination, has the right to equal pay for equal work." Quality of life and a living wage are considered fundamental human rights. Article 23 states that everyone has a right to work, to just and favorable working conditions, to a just remuneration ensuring for himself and his family "an existence worthy of human dignity." Article 25 further defines just remuneration as one that provides a "standard of living adequate for health and well-being, including food, clothing, housing and medical care and necessary social services, and the right to security in the event of unemployment, sickness, disability, or old age."

benefits. Because of the firm belief in individual rights in U.S. political culture, a U.S. corporation will always have difficulty doing business in a culture that openly discriminates against women or minority groups. The developmental benefits of a foreign investment must be weighed against the need to honor and protect the rights of the individual. Ethical issues like this often surface because of the **conflict of relative development,**[2] which questions the appropriateness of considering whether a certain standard is acceptable in the home country of the multinational company. Instead, it suggests considering whether the practice or standard would have been acceptable at the time the home country was at a similar stage of development. Past sins, however, may not be sufficient to justify contemporary practices. Sometimes a host country's standards can be considered inadequate for any level of development. This is the issue in the ethics of wage determination. Do foreign workers have a moral right to a subsistence wage that is likely to be above the market rate in most developing countries? Is it right for a foreign company to pay a wage far below those paid in their home country and one that fails to improve the standard of life in the impoverished host country?

Another conflict that produces ethical concerns is the **conflict of cultural tradition**[3] in which an unethical practice in a home country is considered ethically

2. Thomas Donaldson, "Values in Tension: Ethics Away from Home," *Harvard Business Review* (Sept.-Oct. 1996).
3. Ibid.

proper in the host country. How does a company contend with the low "glass ceiling" against women that is an overt part of Saudi Arabian culture and religious beliefs? How did the open discrimination against blacks under South African apartheid law influence U.S. investment in that country? The initial response to the subjugation of blacks in South African society was not to boycott foreign investment. Instead, multinational corporations (MNCs) agreed as a group to do business in South Africa but to openly defy the apartheid laws. The hope was that the MNCs could do more good in overturning the apartheid law by working within the system than by outside pressure. Although this approach was eventually abandoned in favor of boycott-embargo, it is an example of moral imagination that overcame the bipolar all-or-nothing approach. It also demonstrates the power of concerted acts of moral behavior. Because the Western companies agreed to defy the laws as a group, the government of South Africa elected not to enforce the laws and punish them.

A form of a rights approach to ethics is **Kantian ethics.** Like the rights approach, this school is deontological in nature. It is premised on the belief that there are absolute duties (or rights) that cannot be changed despite the consequences created by such a duty. Immanuel Kant constructed an ethical system that recognized the existence of absolute moral duties or laws that he referred to as **categorical imperatives.** These duties were nonnegotiable and were *a priori* to any utilitarian calculation. One common formulation of the categorical imperative is that human beings can never be used as a "means to an end." All individuals are to be recognized as equal, rational persons. It is thereby wrong to subject anyone to a risk without their informed consent. Thus, a MNC that constructs a hazardous chemical plant in a developing country has a moral duty to fully disclose the health risks to its host country, the local community, and its foreign workers. The problem with disclosure is that the low level of economic development and per capita income may render the information meaningless. Does the foreign company have to do more than disclose and obey whatever host country regulations may apply? Kantian ethics would hold that we have a universal duty not to intentionally harm one another.

http://

For materials on Kantian ethics see Ethics Update: **http://ethics.acusd.edu**.

The categorical imperative requires that a MNC do more than merely disclose or comply with host country regulations. Thus, Union Carbide of America's arguments that it was not morally responsible for the Bhopal disaster[4] is difficult to support under the duty not to harm. Union Carbide argued that it lacked control over the safety and operations of the Indian plant. It argued that its independent subsidiary, which was 49% owned by the Indian government and citizens, was responsible for the plant. Furthermore, it argued that it had no responsibility for the safety of the plant because all management and safety personnel were Indian and the Indian government controlled safety inspections and standards. In fact, the blueprints for the Bhopal plant provided by Union Carbide were rejected in favor of an Indian designed alternative. Does the forced abdication of all control by Union Carbide to the Indian government absolve it of moral responsibility for the accident or is it simply an excuse used by the parent company to avoid liability? Critics would argue that such companies have a moral responsibility not to locate hazardous plants in a foreign country unless they retain sufficient control. Should the fact that the pesticides produced by the Bhopal plant helped feed millions of Indians be entered into this ethical equation?

4. In re Union Carbide Corp. Gas Plant Disaster at Bhopal, 809 F.2d 195 (1987).

Focus on Transactions

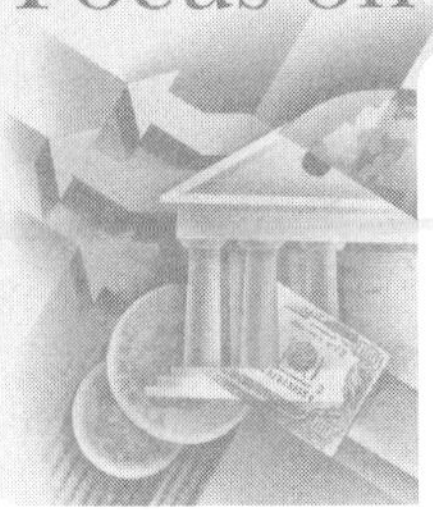

Ethical Issues Raised by Bhopal Disaster

- To what extent should multinational companies maintain identical standards at home and abroad, regardless how lax laws are in the host country?
- How wise are laws that require plants to be staffed entirely by local employees?
- What is the responsibility of corporations and governments in allowing the use of otherwise safe products that become dangerous because of local conditions (e.g., proximity of residences in Bhopal)?
- Should certain kinds of plants not be located in developing nations?
- Was the true moral responsibility for Bhopal that of the Indian government because of its local participation and management requirements (which reduce parent company control and the flow of technical expertise)?
- Did the parent company have an ethical responsibility to protect workers and the public? Does this responsibility have priority over the duty to earn a profit?
- Does the absence of sufficient government regulations excuse the parent company from any legal responsibility?
- Did the parent company have a social responsibility not to locate a plant in a foreign country where it did not have sufficient control? Should a parent company be held liable as parents are held liable for the damage done by their children?

Virtue Ethics

http://

For a fuller analysis of virtue ethics see Ethics Update: **http://ethics.acusd.edu**.

Virtue ethics[5] focuses not upon the morality of an action but on the moral character or motivation of the actor. It separates motives into virtues and vices. Vices are seen as destructive to human relationships and include selfishness, deceptiveness, and unfairness. In contrast, Aristotle saw virtues as acquired moral traits that allow a person to act according to right and practical reason. This approach is useful in understanding the importance of corporate culture. Clearly, a corporate culture that emphasizes profit at any cost is not conducive to encouraging moral business virtues among the company's employees.

Ethics of Care

The **ethics of care**[6] approach focuses on the importance of preserving a web of relationships. A company's weighting of the benefits and costs of a decision should take into account certain concrete relationships. It is ethically appropriate, for example, for a company to place greater weight on the benefits and costs of a decision to its workers and community. Utilitarianism, deontological, and justice approaches to ethics emphasize the impartiality and equality of all parties. The ethics of care allows for the recognition that we owe an obligation to some more than to others.

5. See generally Alasdair MacIntyre, *After Virtue: A Study in Moral Theory* (1984). See also Aristotle, *Nicomachean Ethics*.
6. See generally Carol Gilligan, *In a Different Voice: Psychology Theory and Women's Development* (1982).

The potential influence of this approach can be illustrated by the typical case of plant relocation. The board of directors must decide whether to relocate a long-established and aging plant in its country to a more economically friendly location in a developing country. A utilitarian approach would justify the move purely on efficiency grounds. The rights perspective would recognize the right of an owner to move its business in order to maintain the financial viability of his company. Furthermore, under the employment at will doctrine, prevalent in the United States, an employer owes no duty of continued employment to his workers. Finally, since business and corporations are organized under the fairly enacted laws of a country, they are entitled to respect as artificial beings and their fairly arrived-at decisions should not be subject to interference. In contrast, the ethics of care would recognize the special obligation a company has to its workers and community. Thus, the cost of the relocation to the company's workers and community may override the determinations made under the other approaches.

INTEGRATIVE APPROACH TO INTERNATIONAL BUSINESS ETHICS

The different ethical approaches to business decision-making all offer insight into how to decide or act. An **integrative approach,** incorporating the best of each, is especially prudent in international business dealings given the problem of ethical and cultural relativism. Such an approach would weigh the benefits and harms of a decision and compare them to alternatives (utilitarian). It would take into account whether a given action would disrespect the basic rights of persons (rights). It would also judge the distributive effects of the decision and see how the benefits and burdens are ultimately distributed (justice). Finally, it would weigh the impact of the decision upon those who have a concrete relationship with the company (care). The integrative approach would help ensure a fuller stakeholder analysis of international business decisions. The concerns of individuals (rights) and society (utilitarian) are considered both impartially (justice) and preferentially (care). Such an approach can be found in many **corporate codes of conduct.** An examination of Motorola's approach to ethical conduct illustrates the uses of the various approaches to ethics. The reader can see in its mandates the influences of utilitarian, rights, justice, and virtue-based approaches to ethical decision-making.

Motorola's corporate code (see Doing Business Internationally) states that "employees of Motorola will respect the laws, customs, and traditions of each country in which they operate, but will, at the same time, engage in no course of conduct which, even if legal, customary, and accepted in any such country, could be deemed to be in violation of the accepted business ethics of Motorola or the laws of the United States relating to business ethics." However, cross-cultural misunderstandings still limit the ability of multinational companies to fashion a code of ethics that can be internationally understood and applied.[7] The problem is that abstract terms, such as human rights or bribery, have various connotations that depend upon cultural values and local customs. In fact, corporate codes of ethics are not as prevalent in many countries of the world.

http://

Code of Ethics Online Project, Center for Study of Ethics in the Professions, Illinois Institute of Technology: **http://csep.iit.edu/codes**. Database with over 850 corporate, professional, and government codes of ethics.

7. See generally Warren A. French & John Granrose, *Practical Business Ethics* 165–169 (1995).

Doing Business Internationally

Motorola's Approach to Ethical Decision-Making[8]

Motorola's Language	Ethical Approach
"Look carefully at the consequences of the action"	Utility Calculation
"*All* parties are to be considered—not just an individual or company and includes both monetary and *nonmonetary* variables"	Expanded Utilitarian
"The action produces more overall good to *compensate* for harm done"	Utilitarian & Justice (compensatory)
"Give each person his due"	Justice & Fairness
"Respect human and civil rights"	Rights
"Duties are found in law, contracts, policies, and religions, but they are always subject to interpretation"	Duties/Relativism (Respect for Local Culture)
"It is important to recognize the influence of admirable behavior in decision-making such as honesty and courage."	Virtues

Even when a code of ethics is implemented, cross-cultural misunderstandings can occur between managers in a host country and those in the home office. Motorola attempts to strike a balance between respecting the customs and laws of a host country while remaining true to its own code of ethics and that of its home country. Ultimately, this statement directly addresses the notion of ethical relativism in the interpretation of the code. Nonetheless, it firmly obligates its employees to be guided by home country and not host country beliefs. The issue of cross-cultural morality as represented in the divergence between host and home country standards will be more fully addressed later in this chapter.

THE AMORAL INTERNATIONAL BUSINESSPERSON

Nobel laureate Milton Friedman wrote in 1970 that the only social responsibility of business is to increase profits.[9] Under Friedman's analysis, corporations have no social conscience and should not be concerned with being good "corporate citizens." In his view it is wrong for a corporation to spend corporate profits on social or charitable concerns since the practice of social responsibility applies only to individuals and not to corporations. It is the prerogative of the individual stockholder to voluntarily spend his share of the corporate profits on behalf of social ends. From an ethical perspective, corporations need conform only to the **moral minimum.**

8. See R. S. Moorthy, Richard T. DeGeorge, Thomas Donaldson, William Ellos, Robert Solomon & Robert Textor, *Uncompromising Integrity: Motorola's Global Challenge* (1998).
9. Milton Friedman, "The Social Responsibility of Business Is to Increase Profits," *New York Times Magazine* (1970).

The moral minimum, according to Friedman, is simply obeying the "basic rules" or laws of society in the pursuit of greater profits. What are the "basic rules" of society? Should the definition of basic rules be restricted to the mandatory laws of the country? Do you agree with Friedman that a corporation has no social conscience and should not promote desirable "social ends"?

One approach to reconciling these questions is the **myth of the amoral businessperson.** It asserts that good ethics is consistent with the pursuit of profits. Moreover, this school of business argues that good ethical business practices are necessary for long-run profitability. Francis Fukayama in his study of why some societies were more prosperous than others isolated the notion of trust as the crucial factor.[10] Under his notion of trust, business is essentially a cooperative venture whose very existence requires ethical behavior. The rational self-interest depicted in Adam Smith's economic man results in uncooperative behavior. In fact, the nature of business shows that even people motivated solely by self-interest still have good reason to be ethical in their business dealings.

http://

Web sites discussing corporate social responsibility: Web Watch—Resources for Corporate Social Responsibility at **http://business-ethics.com** or Business for Social Responsibility at **http://www.bsr.org** or Corporate Social Responsibility in Europe at **http://www.ebnsc.org**.

Merck, an international pharmaceutical company, sees its reputation for ethical behavior as a competitive advantage. Merck's code of ethics is a clear rejection of the amoral businessperson perspective. Instead, it views one of its functions as a corporation is to be a good corporate citizen. In short, profits are important, but not necessarily the determinant factor in corporate decision-making. The Merck company's motto as espoused by its founder states: "We try never to forget that medicine is for people. It is not for profits. The profits follow, and if we remember that, they have never failed to appear. The better we have remembered that, the larger they have been." The next section focuses on the special problems of accountability in the organizational setting.

ORGANIZATIONAL ETHICS

Organizational ethics can be a crucial problem for the multinational enterprise. How do moral standards, developed in conjunction with personal will or responsibility, apply to corporations? Assuming that organizations are morally responsible, what individuals within the organization should be held accountable for violations of the corporation's moral duties? The traditional view is that those who *knowingly* partake in unethical actions should be held accountable. In the case of insider trading, for example, all those who knowingly give and use inside information are morally responsible. The problem is the fragmentation of responsibility in large organizations. An unethical action may be performed by many loosely connected actors. Some may simply be following organizational rules and may be unaware of the outcome of their contribution to the process; their ignorance may absolve them of moral responsibility.

http://

Organizational Ethics: Ethics Resource Center at **http://www.ethics.org**. For an interesting avenue for exploring the ethics of a company's corporate culture scroll to "Ethical Effectiveness Quick Test."

The problem of **subordinate responsibility** was documented by Hannah Arendt in her 1963 work *Eichmann in Jerusalem: A Report on the Banality of Evil.* Adolph Eichmann was a typical middle-level bureaucrat in charge of delivering the trains carrying Jews to the death camps. His response to the morally reprehensible nature of his behavior was that he was "just following orders." Eichmann seemed to possess no ill will for the Jews, but was incapable of thinking from the perspective of another person. His "inability to think [ethically]" was as dangerous as someone

http://

Database of 921 links on ethics including business and environmental ethics, see Markkula Center for Applied Ethics: **http://www.scu.edu/SCU/Centers/Ethics**. Click on "Ethical Links," then on "Browse Ethical Links."

10. Francis Fukayama, *Trust: The Social Virtues and the Creation of Prosperity* (1995).

acting with evil intent. Viewing an action from the perspectives of different stakeholders inside and outside of the organization will sensitize corporate decision-makers to ethically relevant issues.

http://
The Caux Round Table: **http://www.cauxroundtable.org**.

In 1994, a group of business leaders introduced the **Caux Round Table Principles for International Business,** which blend the Western concept of the dignity of all human beings with the Japanese concept of *kyosei*—that a primary value of society is working together for common good. The Caux Principles list the factors companies should take into account when making business decisions. Principle 1 makes it the responsibility of business to go *beyond shareholders toward stakeholders.* Businesses should take into consideration not only the well-being of their shareholders but also that of their customers, employees, suppliers, competitors, and communities.

Principle 2 deals specifically with companies transacting business in a foreign country. It requires that the social and economic impact of business be directed at advancing *innovation, justice, and world community.* Businesses in foreign countries should create productive employment and raise the standard of living of its citizens.

Principle 3, *Business Behavior: Beyond the Letter of Law Toward a Spirit of Trust,* admonishes that it may not be appropriate for a company to enforce its rights strictly under the law. In the area of intellectual property rights, disclosure of some information demonstrates a concern for the long-term development of an impoverished country.

Principle 6 makes *respect for the environment* a moral minimum for all international businesses. Environmental protection includes improving the environment, promoting sustainable development, and avoiding the wasteful use of natural resources.

Principle 7, *Avoidance of Illicit Operations,* targets bribery and corruption and their damaging effect on a country's development. The assumption that corporations have social and environmental responsibilities is further recognized in the United Nations Global Impact Program. The Global Impact initiative is a voluntary program that invites companies to commit themselves to protecting the environment, abolishing child labor, and supporting free-trade unions.

ENVIRONMENTAL ETHICS

http://
For additional materials on environmental ethics, see Environmental Ethics at **http://www.cep.unt.edu/enethics.html** or International Society for Environmental Ethics at **http://www.cep.unt.edu/ISEE.html**.

As illustrated previously by the Bhopal tragedy, rapid economic development and industrialization may come at a price: harm to the local and world environments. It is important to balance the goals of industrialization with environmental protection. For the least developed nations, assistance from the developed world is imperative. Those countries that have successfully evolved from a poor country to a developed country or one considered an emerging economy must themselves ensure a healthy environment for their citizens. Korea, now the twelfth largest trading nation in the world, is one such country. It has achieved tremendous economic growth with an annual growth rate of about 8% through rapid industrialization at the expense of the environment. In one of its largest industrial centers there is a monument to the country's drive toward industrialization that bears the inscription: "Dark smoke arising from factories are symbols of our nation's growth and prosperity."[11]

11. See Hong Sik Cho, "An Overview of Korean Environmental Law," 29 *Environmental Law* 501 (1999). (This article was drawn upon in the current section's discussion of Korean environmental laws.)

Because of environmental neglect, environmental protection became an important political issue beginning in the 1980s. By 1997, more than three hundred non-governmental organizations (NGOs) had been established, including the Korean Environmental Preservation Association and the Korea Action Federation for the Environment. Eventually, the government began to respond to the people's increased sensitivity to environmental concerns. The country had never had a separate agency assigned to the enforcement of environmental laws. In 1979, the government established the Environmental Administration (EA) to monitor environmental enforcement and duties. This was followed by an amendment to the Korean Constitution giving all citizens a right to a clean and healthy environment. Beginning in the 1990s, Korea began to model its environmental laws after those in the United States. This began with the enactment of the Basic Environmental Policy Act (BEPA) in 1990. At the same time, the EA was elevated to cabinet level as the Ministry of Environment.

http://

Envirolink: **http://envirolink.org/envirohome.html** provides environmental news and links.

The Korean experience shows the importance of public awareness of environmental problems and the instrumental role of NGOs in pressuring the government to act. It is important to realize that economic development and the emergence of strong democratic principles allowed public awareness to flourish. However, major shortcomings remain in Korea's environmental laws. Economic development has been successful in raising the Korean standard of living and in supporting the creation of democratic principles but at a cost to the environment. The current issue is whether a sufficient amount of the monies produced by its economic expansion will be used to modernize more fully its environmental laws.

HOST-HOME COUNTRY STANDARDS

A multinational enterprise is confronted with different standards in the various countries that it does business and it must resolve whether to apply host or home country standards to a foreign operation. It can choose among three approaches. First, it may decide that a company is ethically and legally obligated to apply only host country standards to its activities within that country. One exception is made for home country laws that apply extraterritorially, such as the **Foreign Corrupt Practices Act**[12] and U.S. antitrust laws. This approach is closely associated with the moral minimum school of business ethics where complying with applicable law is a company's only moral imperative.

Second, the company may determine that an ethical company should apply the higher standards of its home country's laws and regulations, critical in areas where harm is a foreseeable consequence of the activity. This approach requires that the more stringent environmental, health, and safety regulations found in U.S. law should be used in foreign operations.

The third approach is a variation of the second. This approach asserts that although higher standards are preferred they may not be ethically required in all instances. This approach allows a U.S. company to take into account the stage of development of the host country. Using this approach, an ethical company must answer the following question: Will the application of the more stringent requirements of the home (developed) country be harmful to the host (developing)

http://

"Ethical Considerations in International Start-up Companies" at Babson College—Business Ethics Program: **http://roger.babson.edu/ethics/entrepre.htm**.

12. The Foreign Corrupt Practices Act prohibits U.S. individuals, companies, and direct foreign subsidiaries of U.S. companies from offering, promising, or paying anything of value to any foreign government official in order to obtain or retain business.

country or its development? An alternative formulation of this question is whether good consequences from a corporate presence in a country override the unethical national standards? For example, can the economic benefits of a corporate operation in an impoverished country justify operation in a country that openly discriminates against groups within the population?

There are a number of ways to answer the questions above. One utilizes ethical relativism. It holds that ethics is culture bound and thus the ethical determination of the host country should be honored. However, it is problematic for a U.S. company to do something considered ethically repugnant by Americans. A second way has been labeled the "Righteous American" perspective, dictating the use of U.S. rules and standards in foreign business operations. The danger of such an approach is that it may diminish the importance of respecting local culture and lifestyles. A third and more radical perspective is that international companies need not follow any ethical rules. Since their competitors may not do so, following high ethical standards would place them at a competitive disadvantage. This perspective was advanced by those critical of the Foreign Corrupt Practices Act.

FOREIGN CORRUPT PRACTICES ACT

The Foreign Corrupt Practices Act (FCPA) was intended to have and has had a major impact on the way U.S. companies do business overseas. Since the passage of the FCPA, several firms convicted of bribing foreign officials have been subject to criminal and civil enforcement actions, resulting in large fines, exclusion from federal government contracts, and jail terms for employees and officers. The antibribery provisions of the FCPA make it illegal for a U.S. person or company to make corrupt payments to a foreign official for the purpose of obtaining business (See Comparative Law: FCPA Bribery Provisions and Focus on Transactions: Five Elements of a FCPA Offense). The FCPA also requires companies whose securities are traded in the United States to meet strict accounting provisions. These provisions require corporations to make and keep books and records that accurately reflect the transactions of the corporation and to devise an adequate system of internal accounting controls.

http://

Legislative history of FCPA at Justice Department web site: **http://www.usdoj.gov/criminal/fraud/fcpa.html**.

The international entrepreneur should always be cautioned against activities that involve the corruption of a foreign official. Most national laws outlaw the payment of bribes in order to obtain a service, contract, license, approval, or other regulatory consideration from a government official. Unfortunately, anti-corruption laws in some countries are not enforced and bribes are openly solicited. **Transparency International,** a non-governmental group of business leaders and former government officials, is dedicated to promoting international business ethics and the elimination of corruption. Its primary concern is the damage that bribery causes to the economic and democratic development of developing countries.

http://

Transparency International: **http://www.transparency.org**.

Transparency International has used statistics to link corruption with lost development opportunities such as foreign direct investment. It is important to understand, however, that the definition and practice of bribery varies significantly across different cultures. For example, in the Indonesian concept of *sharism,* a bribe is shared and loses the character of a bribe in the Latin American sense. The Indonesian bribe is best understood as an "express fee" to move requests to a higher level in order to get them processed more expeditiously. It is important to note that the amount is usually reasonable and somewhat standardized and the money doesn't remain with the official that received it—it is shared with others in the office. It has been argued that in Latin America low ethical standards in politics have had a strong impact on individuals, companies, and the economic systems. "Deception, bribery, fraud, and dishonest negotiations have been means to succeed in private and public organizations in Latin American countries."[13] There is an implication that in order to level the competitive playing field, the foreign businessperson will need to make facilitation payments or bribes.

The pressure to give bribes is especially troublesome for the U.S. businessperson because of the severe civil and criminal penalties available through the Foreign Corrupt Practices Act.[14] The act applies extraterritorially to foreign activities of U.S. citizens, companies, and foreign entities controlled by them. Furthermore, U.S. companies are liable for bribes made by its foreign agents. Actual knowledge of the bribery is not required. Prosecutors need only prove that the firm should have been aware of a high probability that bribing would occur. Incorporated within the Act are stringent accounting provisions that require companies doing business abroad to maintain records and auditing controls that provide reasonable assurances that bribing is not occurring. A company will be liable for violating the accounting provisions even if no illegal bribing has occurred. Violations of the statute can result in large fines and imprisonment for up to five years for an individual.

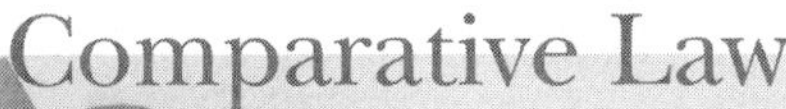

Comparative Law

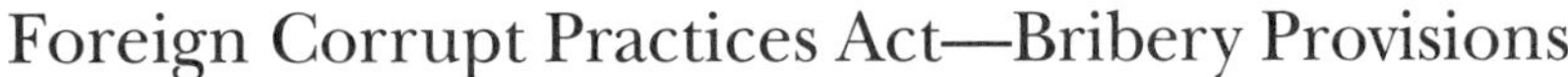

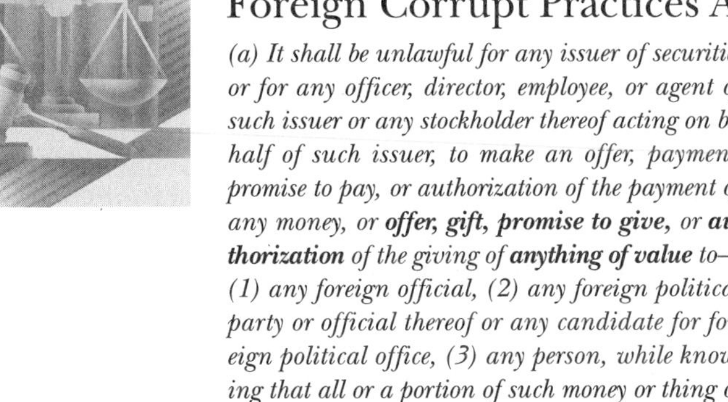

Foreign Corrupt Practices Act—Bribery Provisions

(a) It shall be unlawful for any issuer of securities or for any officer, director, employee, or agent of such issuer or any stockholder thereof acting on behalf of such issuer, to make an offer, payment, promise to pay, or authorization of the payment of any money, or ***offer, gift, promise to give,*** *or* ***authorization*** *of the giving of* ***anything of value*** *to—(1) any foreign official, (2) any foreign political party or official thereof or any candidate for foreign political office, (3) any person, while knowing that all or a portion of such money or thing of value will be offered, given, or promised, directly or indirectly, to any foreign official for purposes of—*

(A) influencing any act or decision of such foreign official in his official capacity

(B) inducing such foreign official to use his influence with a foreign government or instrumentality thereof,

in order to assist such issuer in ***obtaining or retaining business*** *for or with, or directing business to, any person;*

(b) Exception for ***routine governmental action.*** *Subsection (a) shall not apply to any facilitating or expediting payment to a foreign official, political party, or party official the purpose of which is to expedite or to secure the performance of a routine governmental action by a foreign official, political party, or party official.*

(c) ***Affirmative defenses.*** *It shall be an affirmative defense to actions under subsection (a) that—*

(1) the payment, gift, offer, or promise of anything of value that was made, was ***lawful under the written laws*** *and regulations of the foreign official's, political party's, party official's, or candidate's country; or*

(2) the payment, gift, offer, or promise of anything of value that was made, was a reasonable and ***bona fide expenditure,*** *such as travel and lodging expenses, incurred by or on behalf of a foreign official, party, party official, or candidate and was directly related to—*

(A) the promotion, demonstration, or explanation of products or services; or

(B) the execution or performance of a contract with a foreign government or agency thereof.

13. M. Cecilia Arruda, "Business Ethics in Latin America," 16: *Journal of Business Ethics* 1597 (1997).

14. Amended in 1988 in 15 U.S.C. § 78.

Because of the vagaries of the FCPA, Congress sought to clarify some of its provisions and meanings in order to provide additional guidance, and the **Amendments of 1988** provided more detailed definitions of some of the crucial terms of the FCPA. Of foremost importance, it gave examples of expenditures that would be considered "routine government expenditures." Fees paid to an official for an action "ordinarily" done in the performance of his official duties are exempted. These include obtaining permits, licenses, or other official documents to qualify a person to do business in a foreign country; processing governmental papers, such as visas and work orders; providing police protection, mail pickup and delivery, or scheduling inspections associated with contract performance or inspections related to transit of goods across the country; providing phone service, power and water supply, loading and unloading cargo, or protecting perishable products or commodities from deterioration; or actions of a similar nature.

The question remains what other payments will be allowed for "actions of a similar nature"? The Amendments provide a possible solution to such uncertainty by allowing a private party to obtain an **Attorney General Opinion.** The Attorney General, after consultation with appropriate departments and agencies of the United States and after obtaining the views of all interested persons through public notice and comment procedures, shall establish a procedure to provide responses to inquiries concerning conformance of an action with the Department of Justice's enforcement policy regarding the FCPA. The Attorney General is required to issue an opinion within 30 days after receiving a request. The crucial distinction for the determination of whether a payment is "routine" is that between a discretionary act and a clerical one. Therefore, the term "routine governmental action" does not include any decision by a foreign official whether, or on what terms, to award new business. These types of decisions are discretionary in nature and the payment would be considered a bribe.

The 1988 Amendments state that a minor payment made to "any employee of a foreign government or any department, agency, or instrumentality thereof whose duties are essentially ministerial or clerical" would not be considered a bribe under the FCPA. What is considered a minor payment remains to be determined on a case-by-case basis. As we're about to see, it is important to note that a Federal Appeals Court in *Lamb v. Philip Morris, Inc.*[15] ruled that the FCPA does not provide a private right of action. Thus, a businessperson cannot bring a lawsuit against a competitor for obtaining a contract in violation of the FCPA. He is limited to bringing the alleged violation to the attention of the Justice Department.

Two other important definitional changes were made by the 1988 Amendments. First, the definition of "foreign official" was broadened to include "any officer or employee of a public international organization." Second, the "knowing" requirement for criminal liability under the FCPA was substantially modified. Actual knowledge of a bribe is not required. Instead, the government needs to prove only that a party had reason to know that some of its money would be used to bribe a foreign official. A party can be found guilty of bribery if such person is aware that another person is "engaging in such conduct, that such circumstance exists, or that such result is substantially certain to occur." When knowledge of the existence of a particular circumstance is required for an offense, such knowledge is established if a person is "aware of a high probability of the existence of such circumstance."

The issue remains what is evidence of "substantial certainty" or "high probability." The court in *United States v. Liebo* found that evidence of knowledge of bribery

15. 915 F.2d 1024 (6th Cir. 1990).

Lamb v. Philip Morris, Inc.

915 F.2d 1024 (6th Cir. 1990)

Guy, Circuit Judge. Since we find that no private right of action is available under the Foreign Corrupt Practices Act of 1977 (FCPA), we affirm the dismissal of the plaintiffs' FCPA claim. On May 14, 1982, a Philip Morris subsidiary known as C.A. Tabacalera National and a B.A.T. subsidiary known as C.A. Cigarrera Bigott, SUCS, entered into a contract with La Fundacion Del Nino (the Children's Foundation) of Caracas, Venezuela. The agreement was signed on behalf of the Children's Foundation by the organization's president, the wife of the then President of Venezuela. Under the terms of the agreement, the two subsidiaries were to make periodic donations to the Children's Foundation totaling approximately $12.5 million dollars. In exchange, the subsidiaries were to obtain price controls on Venezuelan tobacco, elimination of controls on retail cigarette prices in Venezuela, tax deductions for the donations, and assurances that existing tax rates applicable to tobacco companies would not be increased. In the plaintiffs' view, the donations promised by the defendants' subsidiaries amount to unlawful inducements designed and intended to restrain trade. The plaintiffs further assert that the district court erred in prohibiting them from pursuing a private cause of action under the FCPA.

Although the Foreign Corrupt Practices Act was enacted more than a decade ago, the question of whether an implied private right of action exists under the FCPA apparently is one of first impression at the federal appellate level. The Supreme Court recently explained that: In determining whether to infer a private cause of action from a federal statute, our focal point is Congress' intent in enacting the statute. Our central focus is on congressional intent, "with an eye toward" four factors: (1) whether the plaintiffs are among "the class for whose especial benefit" the statute was enacted; (2) whether the legislative history suggests congressional intent to prescribe or proscribe a private cause of action; (3) whether implying such a remedy for the plaintiff would be consistent with the underlying purposes of the legislative scheme; and (4) whether the cause of action is one traditionally relegated to state law.

First, the defendants contend, and we agree, that the FCPA was designed with the assistance of the Securities and Exchange Commission (SEC) to aid federal law enforcement agencies in curbing bribes of foreign officials. The authorization of stringent criminal penalties amplifies the foreign policy and law enforcement considerations underlying the FCPA. As such, individual private citizens are not part of a class for whose "especial benefit" the statute was enacted. Second, the availability of a private right of action apparently was never resolved (or perhaps even raised) at the conference that ultimately produced the compromise bill passed by both houses and signed into law. Third, recognition of the plaintiffs' proposed private right of action, in our view, would directly contravene the carefully tailored FCPA scheme presently in place. Congress recently expanded the Attorney General's responsibilities to include facilitating compliance with the FCPA. Because this legislative action clearly evinces a preference for compliance in lieu of prosecution, the introduction of private plaintiffs interested solely in post-violation enforcement, rather than pre-violation compliance, most assuredly would hinder congressional efforts to protect companies and their employees concerned about FCPA liability.

Finally, because the potential for recovery under federal antitrust laws in this case belies the plaintiffs' contention that an implied private right of action under the FCPA is imperative, we attach no significance to the absence of state laws proscribing bribery of foreign officials. We AFFIRM the district court's dismissal of the FCPA claim.

Case Highlights

- The main statutory purpose of the FCPA is pre-violation compliance and not post-violation persecution.
- There is no implied private cause of action permitted under the FCPA.
- The Justice Department and the SEC are solely responsible for the enforcement of the FCPA.

can be proven circumstantially. It held that giving airline tickets as a "gift" to a cousin of a foreign official was sufficient to sustain conviction of a business executive where approval of the foreign official was necessary to obtain contracts. This case illustrates a number of provisions of the FCPA. First, third-party bribery is just as illegal as "direct" bribery. Second, the minor payment or expenditure exception is to be narrowly construed.

United States v. Liebo

923 F.2d 1308 (8th Cir. 1991)

Gibson, Circuit Judge. Richard H. Liebo appeals from his convictions for violating the bribery provisions of the Foreign Corrupt Practices Act and making a false statement to a government agency. The background leading to Liebo's conviction has all the earmarks of a modern fable. Between January 1983 and June 1987, Liebo was vice-president in charge of the Aerospace Division of NAPCO International, Inc., located in Hopkins, Minnesota. NAPCO's primary business consisted of selling military equipment and supplies throughout the world. Liebo flew to Niger to get the President of Niger's approval of a supply contract. He flew to Niger and met with Captain Ali Tiemogo. Tiemogo was the chief of maintenance for the Niger Air Force. Tiemogo testified that during the trip, Liebo told him that his company would make "some gestures" to him if he helped get the contract approved. When asked whether this promise played a role in deciding to recommend approval of the contract, Tiemogo stated, "I can't say 'no', I cannot say 'yes', at that time," but "it encouraged me." Following Tiemogo's recommendation that the contract be approved, the President signed the contract.

Tahirou Barke, Tiemogo's cousin and close friend, testified that in August 1985 he returned to Niger to be married. After the wedding, he and his wife honeymooned in Paris, Stockholm, and London. He testified that before leaving for Niger, he informed Liebo of his honeymoon plans, and Liebo offered to pay for his airline tickets as a gift. Liebo paid for the tickets, which cost $2,028. Barke testified that he considered the tickets a "gift" from Liebo personally.

Over a two-and-a-half-year period beginning in May 1984, NAPCO made payments totaling $130,000 to three "commission agents." The practice of using agents and paying them commissions on international contracts was acknowledged as proper, legal, and an accepted business practice in third-world countries. NAPCO issued commission checks to "agents," identified as Amadou Mailele, Tiemogo's brother-in-law, and Fatouma Boube, Tiemogo's sister-in-law. At Tiemogo's request, both Mailele and Boube set up bank accounts in Paris. Evidence at trial established that NAPCO's corporate president, Henri Jacob, or another superior of Liebo's, approved these "commission payments." To obtain foreign military sales financing, NAPCO was required to submit a Contractor's Certification and Agreement with the Defense Security Assistance Agency. In the Contractor's certification submitted in connection with the third Niger contract, Liebo certified that "no rebates, gifts or gratuities have been given contrary to United States law to officers, officials, or employees" of the Niger government. Following a three-week trial, the jury acquitted Liebo on all charges except the count concerning NAPCO's purchase of Barke's honeymoon airline tickets and the related false statement count.

Liebo first argues that his conviction for violating the bribery provisions of the Foreign Corrupt Practices Act by giving Barke airline tickets for his honeymoon should be reversed. First, Liebo contends that there was insufficient evidence to show that the airline tickets were "given to obtain or retain business." Second, he argues that there was no evidence to show that his gift of honeymoon tickets was done "corruptly." We believe that there is sufficient evidence that the airplane tickets were given to obtain or retain business. The relationship between Barke and Tiemogo could have allowed a reasonable jury to *infer* that Liebo made the gift to Barke intending to buy Tiemogo's help in getting the contracts approved. Accordingly, a reasonable jury could conclude that the gift was given "to obtain or retain business."

Next, Liebo contends that his conviction should be reversed because the court erred in the giving of jury structions distinguishing a "gift or gratuity" from a bribe. Here, the court instructed the jury that the term "corruptly" meant that "the offer, promise to pay, payment or authorization of payment, must be intended to induce the recipient to misuse his official position or to influence someone else to do so," and that "an act is 'corruptly' done if done voluntarily and intentionally, and with a bad purpose of accomplishing either an unlawful end or result, or a lawful end or result by some unlawful method or means." We agree. A jury may infer a corrupt intent if a payment is given voluntarily or intentionally. AFFIRMED

Case Highlights

- Third-party bribery under the FCPA includes the use of agents to make payments to government officials and indirect payments to persons associated with a government official.
- Merely classifying something as a gift (as in *United States v. Liebo*) or a donation (as in *Lamb v. Philip Morris*) is not conclusive in assessing whether it constitutes a bribe.
- Direct evidence of actual intent to give a bribe is not required under the FCPA. (Intent may be inferred from circumstantial evidence.)
- Despite the multimillion-dollar size of the government contracts, two airline tickets satisfies the "anything of value" requirement and is not considered a "minor expense."

The FCPA provisions dealing with "substantial certainty" or "high probability" of **third-party bribery** was illustrated in the *Liebo* case. In that case should Liebo have been concerned by the fact that the "commission agents" were related to the government official or that monies were being deposited into foreign bank accounts? Third-party bribery exists when a company hires another and has "reason to know" that a portion of money would be used to bribe. A third party may be a joint venture partner or an agent. How can one determine if one has "reason to know" of a bribe made by a third party?

The type of circumstantial evidence that can be used to satisfy the "reason to know" requirement was illustrated in *SEC v. Tesoro Petroleum Corp.*[16] In that case a company was prosecuted even though it did not directly pay or authorize any bribes. It hired a foreign agent to obtain contracts from a foreign government. It was alleged to have been guilty of third-party bribery. The evidence included the payment of a commission considerably larger than the market rate, a disproportionately small contract price compared to the commission paid, and a large degree of secrecy including the use of Swiss bank accounts. No written contract was entered into with the foreign agent. U.S. companies are expected to exercise *due diligence* and take steps to ensure they have formed a business relationship with a reputable partner or representative. These parties should be investigated to determine if they are qualified, whether they have ties to the government, the number and reputation of their clients, and their reputation with the U.S. Embassy, local bankers, and other business associates.

The *Tesoro* and *Liebo* cases show that a number of red flags need to be addressed in any company's FCPA compliance program. These red flags are especially important where express and direct bribery is not present. Red flags include paying a commission substantially higher than the going rate, the existence of family or business ties between an agent and government officials, and commission payments made in a third country. Are there any other red flags that may indicate the potential for third-party bribery? A company's compliance program should require any potential agent to disclose past or current ties to government officials, a report on the agent's character by way of reference checks, and a carefully worded written agreement with the agent. The written agreement should expressly state that the agent is working as an independent agent and is not authorized to make any illicit payments on behalf of the principal. The agreement should contain FCPA-oriented clauses, including a clause that requires the agent to comply with all laws and regulations of both the home and host countries.

http://
Lay-Person's Guide to the FCPA:
http://www.usdoj.gov/criminal/fraud/fcpa.html.

Whether a U.S. parent company is liable for the acts of a foreign subsidiary depends on the degree of ownership and control exerted by the parent over its foreign subsidiary. The benchmark for degree of ownership is whether the U.S. company is a majority or minority owner. If it is a majority owner, then it is vicariously liable for the violations of its subsidiary. If it owns less than 50%, then it need only make a good-faith effort to have its subsidiary comply with the FCPA. Finally, the FCPA does not distinguish between violations involving direct bribery, third-party bribery, and bribery committed by a controlled subsidiary. In fact, the 1988 Amendments stiffened the fines for violations of any of the bribery provisions. Currently, the FCPA provides for individual criminal fines of $100,000 and imprisonment of up to five years. A company may be fined up to $2 million per violation. The Amendments also implemented a new individual civil fine of $10,000 which cannot be reimbursed by the company.

16. 2 FCPA Rep. (1980).

Focus on Transactions

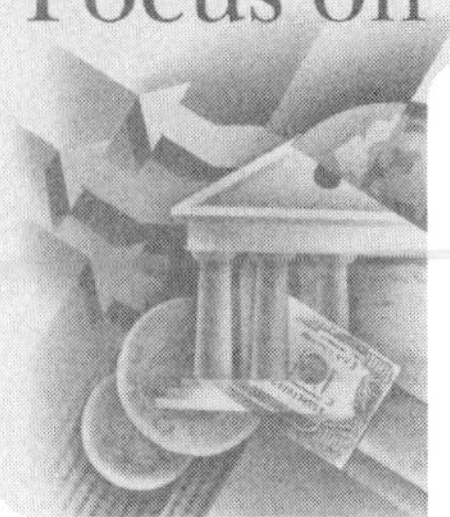

Five Elements of a FCPA Offense

Who

The FCPA potentially applies to any individual, company, officer, director, employee, or agent of a company and any stockholder acting on behalf of a U.S. controlled company. U.S. parent companies may be held liable for the acts of foreign subsidiaries where they authorized, directed, or controlled the activity in question, as can U.S. citizens or residents who were employed or acting on behalf of such foreign-incorporated subsidiaries.

Corrupt Intent

The person making or authorizing the payment must have corrupt intent and must have intended to induce the recipient to misuse his official position.

Corrupt Act

The FCPA prohibits paying, offering, promising to pay, or authorizing to pay or offer money or anything of value.

Recipient

The prohibition extends to corrupt payments to a foreign official, a foreign political party or party official, or any candidate for foreign political office.

Business Purpose

The FCPA prohibits only payments to assist the firm in obtaining or retaining business or directing business to any person.

FCPA Accounting Provisions

Section 102 of the FCPA requires anyone covered by the Act to "make and keep records in reasonable detail, that accurately and fairly reflect the transactions and dispositions of assets." Failure to do so subjects that person or company to the same types of fines as imposed under the bribery provisions. Thus, a company can violate the FCPA without committing any acts of bribery. The problem with the accounting requirements is that the original Act did not define what is meant by "reasonable." It does not provide a materiality standard to assist in the determination of what needs to be reported.

The 1988 Amendments defined reasonableness as that exhibited by the "prudent person." Therefore, a company is not expected to show an unrealistic degree of exactitude. Implied in the notion of the prudent person is the use of a benefit-cost approach. Therefore, the accounting requirements are satisfied if the system of internal accounting controls is sufficient to provide reasonable assurance that (1) transactions are executed in accordance with management's specific authorizations, (2) transactions are recorded to permit preparation of financial statements in conformity with generally accepted accounting principles, (3) access to assets is permitted only with specific management authorization, and (4) accountability for assets is reviewed at reasonable intervals. Under the original act a company could technically be held criminally liable for inadvertent errors. The 1988 Amendments limited criminal liability under the accounting provisions to those who *knowingly* falsify records.

OECD CONVENTION ON COMBATING BRIBERY

The magnitude of foreign bribery has resulted in some recent movement at the international and regional levels. In 1988, the U.S. Congress directed the President to commence negotiations in the **Organization for Economic Cooperation and Development (OECD)** to obtain agreement among its members on anti-bribery provisions. The OECD, a Paris-based organization with 29 member countries,[17] was formed after World War II to help build a new economic system based on free international trade. On February 15, 1999, the OECD Convention on Combating Bribery of Foreign Public Officials in International Business Transactions went into effect. The OECD Convention sets forth the following goals:

- To achieve the highest sustainable economic growth and employment and a rising standard of living in member countries, while maintaining financial stability, and to contribute to the development of the world economy
- To contribute to sound economic expansion in member countries as well as nonmember countries in the process of economic development
- To contribute to the expansion of world trade on a multilateral and nondiscriminatory basis in accordance with international obligations

The OECD provides a venue for countries to develop economic and social policies. Even though all countries have laws that make the bribery of officials a crime, only the FCPA is applied extraterritorially to the bribery of foreign officials. The relative success of the FCPA, the growth of the global marketplace, and the recognition of the economic costs to the bribe-giver and to foreign economics provided the impetus for the OECD Convention.

Before the adoption of the OECD Convention on Bribery, a number of predecessor acts were adopted. In 1996, for example, the OECD passed a resolution on the *Tax Deductibility of Bribes to Foreign Public Officials.* Incredibly, a number of countries, such as France, Germany, Norway, and Denmark, had previously allowed for the deductibility of bribes paid as a cost of doing business. In order to study issues of corruption the OECD has established the Development Centre on Corruption. The major focus of the Centre is to assist developing countries in the fight against corruption.

http://

For the text of the OECD Convention on Combating Bribery of Foreign Public Officials: **http://www.oecd.org/daf/cmis/bribery/20nov1e.htm**.

The Convention provides a framework and guidance to signatories regarding the steps to be taken to combat bribery of their public officials. It defines public officials broadly to include public agencies, public enterprises, and public international organizations. Like the FCPA, it adopts the extraterritorial approach to the international bribery of foreign government officials. It mandates that countries prosecute their nationals for offenses committed abroad. In the accounting area, it requires that each signatory enact "dissuasive civil, administrative, or criminal penalties for such omissions and falsifications in respect of the books, records, accounts, and financial statements." Companies will be required to disclose, on their financial statements, any potential liabilities under the act that rise to the level of a material contingent liability.

The United States is a member of the OECD and is bound by its new Bribery Convention. The 1998 Amendments to the FCPA recognize the newly enacted

17. The 29 members of the OECD are Australia, Austria, Belgium, Canada, the Czech Republic, Denmark, Finland, France, Germany, Greece, Hungary, Iceland, Ireland, Italy, Japan, Korea, Luxembourg, Mexico, Netherlands, New Zealand, Norway, Poland, Portugal, Spain, Sweden, Switzerland, Turkey, United Kingdom, and the United States. It should be noted that along with the OECD members, a number of nonmember countries have also signed, including Argentina, Brazil, Slovakia, Bulgaria, and Chile.

OECD Convention on Combating Bribery. The Amendments require the Secretary of Commerce to submit a report to Congress of the following information: (1) A list of the countries that have ratified the Convention, the dates of ratification by such countries, and the entry into force for each country; (2) A description of domestic laws enacted by each party to the Convention that implement commitments under the Convention; (3) An assessment of the measures taken by each party to the Convention during the previous year to fulfill its obligations under the Convention; and (4) An explanation of the domestic laws enacted by each party to the Convention that would prohibit the deduction of bribes in the computation of domestic taxes. Under item (3), foreign countries are to be evaluated by the degree that they enforce their domestic anti-bribery laws, their efforts to promote public awareness of the evils of corruption, and their effectiveness in monitoring and enforcement.

UNITED STATES FEDERAL SENTENCING GUIDELINES

The United States' **Federal Sentencing Guidelines,** which became effective on November 1, 1991, fundamentally altered the approach to organizational accountability. Previously, enforcement actions relating to crimes committed in the corporate context were directed only against the employees responsible for the act. Under the guidelines, the corporate or organizational entity can be held vicariously liable for the criminal acts of its employees. The guidelines also allow for the mitigation of fines for those companies that demonstrate **due diligence** in attempting to prevent misconduct. They provide for more lenient treatment of corporate executives who had implemented an ethics program.

The importance of these guidelines has increased with a recent Delaware court decision that held that corporate directors could be personally liable for subordinates' wrongdoing if they had failed to establish an ethics program. In short, the guidelines "reward organizations for establishing a legal and ethical compliance program."[18] By law, a company's penalties for violating the law are adjusted based upon the degree of cooperation exhibited by the company during the government investigation. The penalties can also be reduced if the company had an existing compliance program (See Focus on Transactions: Designing an Effective Compliance Program), along with exhibiting due diligence in policing the program. It is in a company's best interest to develop a compliance program in such areas as the Foreign Corrupt Practices Act, export regulations, environmental compliance, and health and safety laws.

http://

For an excellent overview of the Organizational Guidelines go to the web site of the U.S. Sentencing Commission: **http://www.ussc.gov/orgguide.htm**. See "Overview" in the section on Organizational Guidelines and Compliance.

The base or minimum fines to be assessed under the guidelines range from $5,000 to $72.5 million. The levels of base fines are based upon two calculations: the seriousness of the offense and the culpability of the organization. Some of the offenses targeted by the guidelines include customs violations, bid rigging, fraud, antitrust violations, transportation of hazardous materials, environmental crimes, commercial bribery, and copyright infringement. Culpability factors include history of past infractions and the rank of the employees within the company. The higher the rank of the employee the higher the culpability of the organization. The guidelines also expressly recognize mitigating factors that can result in the lessening of the punishment. These include the implementation of an effective compliance program, self-reporting of infractions, and cooperating with the government investigation.

18. O.C. Ferrell, Debbie Thorne LeClair & Linda Ferrell, "The Federal Sentencing Guidelines for Organizations: A Framework for Ethical Compliance," 17 *Journal of Business Ethics* 353, 354 (1998).

Focus on Transactions

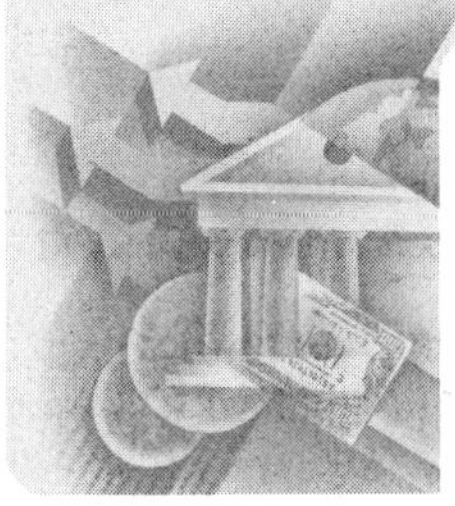

Fines Under the Federal Sentencing Guidelines[19]

A company convicted of mail fraud for systematically overcharging customers for the costs of repair for damages to its rental automobiles is subject to fines ranging from $685,000 to $54.8 million. The exact amount of the fine is dependent on the existence of mitigating factors recognized under the Federal Sentencing Guidelines:

	Maximum	**Minimum**
Existence of compliance program, self-reporting crime, cooperation with government investigation	$2.74 million	$685,000
Compliance program only	10.96 million	5.48 million
No program, reporting, or cooperation	27.4 million	13.7 million
No program, reporting, or cooperation, and involvement by high-ranking personnel	54.8 million	27.4 million

An example of the use of an effective compliance system would be the improvement of a company's global working conditions. The compliance program would specifically state the criteria to be addressed such as the nonuse of forced labor, controlled use of child labor, the implementation of minimum health and

Focus on Transactions

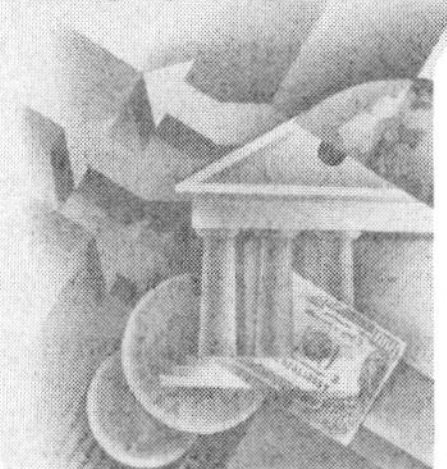

Designing an Effective Compliance Program

Features

- Implementation of codes of conduct
- Custom-designed standards and procedures
- Compliance supervised by high-level managers or by an ethics officer
- Employee education—publications and training
- Effective reporting procedure
- Development of monitoring and auditing procedures
- Infractions appropriately disciplined
- Annual reviews and amendments to program
- Reporting violations to appropriate authorities
- Compensation adjusted for effective compliance

Other Techniques

- Compliance programs required for suppliers and business associates
- Third-party verification: Compliance audit performed by independent third party

19. United States Sentencing Commission, Case No. 88-266, as discussed in Lynn Sharpe Paine, "Managing for Organizational Integrity," *Harvard Business Review* 110 (March-April 1994).

safety standards, maximum working hours, payment of a "living wage," and antidiscrimination policies. The implementation of customized standards and third-party verification are essential to a compliance program with these types of objectives.

INTERNATIONAL STANDARDS

Standards to ensure adequate levels of quality, labor, and environmental sensitivity in the production and marketing of goods and services are important and evolving. The wide variety of national standards in these areas produces a number of problems. First, it promotes the lowest common denominator in the production of goods. Companies that are motivated only by short-term profits will attempt to cut costs by searching for countries with the most lax environmental and labor laws. Second, a company seeking to market its products internationally has to contend with differing standards that may act as barriers to importing a company's goods into various countries. One solution to both problems has been the development of international standards, which can both reduce barriers to trade and ensure minimum levels of quality, labor, and environmental compliance.

A non-governmental organization established in 1947, the **International Organization for Standardization (ISO)** is a worldwide federation of national standards bodies from some 130 countries, one from each country. The mission of ISO[20] is to promote the development of standardization and related activities in the world in order to facilitate the international exchange of goods and services and to develop cooperation in the spheres of intellectual, scientific, technological, and economic activity. International standardization is well-established for many technologies in such diverse fields as information processing and communications, textiles, packaging, distribution of goods, energy production and utilization, shipbuilding, banking, and financial services. It will continue to grow in importance for all sectors of industrial activity for the foreseeable future.

The ISO has developed international codes for country names, currencies, and languages that have helped to eliminate duplication and incompatibilities in the collection, processing, and dissemination of information. As resource-saving tools, universally understandable codes play an important role in both automated and manual documentation. The ISO and many of its members are actively involved in consulting and training services which include seminars on the application of standards in quality assurance systems, technical assistance to exporters concerning standards requirements in other countries, workshops on consumer involvement in standardization, and conferences and symposia covering recent developments in testing and certification.

The most recognized international standard is the **ISO 9000.** The purpose of the ISO 9000 Standard is to facilitate international commerce by providing a single set of quality standards that people everywhere recognize and respect. The ISO 9000 Standards apply to all types of organizations in all kinds of areas. The ISO provides guidelines for developing a quality management system. If ISO auditors like what they see, they will certify that a company's quality system has met ISO's requirements. They will then issue an official certificate and record the company's name in their registry. The company can then promote the quality of its products and services as ISO 9000 certified.

20. *ISO* is derived from the Greek *isos,* meaning "equal," which is the root of the prefix "iso-" that occurs in *isometric* (of equal measure or dimensions) and *isonomy* (equality of laws, or of people before the law), among others.

The ISO's most recent effort, **ISO 14000,** is a series of international, voluntary environmental management standards. The ISO 14000 series of standards effectively address the needs of organizations worldwide by providing a common framework for managing environmental issues. ISO 14000 standards require a company to establish an environmental management system (EMS). An EMS enables an organization of any size or type to control the impact of its activities, products, or services on the natural environment. The benefits of installing an EMS include: (1) assuring customers of a commitment to demonstrable environmental management, (2) maintaining good public/community relations, (3) obtaining insurance at reasonable cost, (4) reducing incidents that result in liability, and (5) facilitating the attainment of permits and authorizations. The standards in the ISO 14000 series fall into two major groups: organization-oriented standards and product-oriented standards. Organization-oriented standards provide comprehensive guidance for establishing, maintaining and evaluating an EMS. Product-oriented standards are concerned with determining the environmental impacts of products and services over their life cycles and with environmental labels and declarations. Product-oriented standards will help an organization communicate specific environmental information to consumers and other interested parties.

http://
International Standards Organization: **http://www.iso.ch/iso/en/ISOOnline.frontpage**.

The activities of the European Union (EU) deserve special attention. EU requirements include the placement of a **CE mark** by the manufacturer on all regulated products. Importers who obtain the CE mark will be guaranteed access to the markets of all EU members. The CE mark asserts that the product meets mandatory health, safety, and environmental requirements of the EU. A newer development is the establishment of a voluntary mark known as the **EU Ecolabel.** Products without the Ecolabel may still enter the EU, but the label, if used, replaces the existing national equivalents. In order to obtain an Ecolabel, the manufacturer must show that its products are less harmful to the environment than other similar products.

The ISO has been successful in raising the level of awareness in areas of product quality and the environment. Its certifications under ISO 9000 and ISO 14000 provide both practical and ethical benefits to companies. From a practical perspective, products with these certifications are likely to find fewer obstacles in the area of importation. Most countries recognize the significance of the ISO certifications. From an ethical perspective, these certifications can be used by companies as evidence of their commitment to producing quality products and to being an environmentally conscious company.

The Council on Economic Priorities Accreditation Agency has used the ISO model to develop a **Social Accountability Standard.** The SA 8000 standard insures that a company and its suppliers provide an equitable and safe workplace for their employees. The SA 8000 certification requires a company to restrict the use of child or forced labor, to respect the right of workers to unionize, to limit the work week to 48 hours, to provide a safe working environment, and to pay a living wage that meets the basic needs of the workers. The SA 8000 allows companies to demonstrate a commitment to international human rights standards. Firms that wish to avoid bad publicity should adopt the SA 8000 standards as a preventive measure.

THE ETHICS OF ADVERTISING

How a company markets its products internationally will play a major role in whether it is successful. Failure to take into account the differences in national cultural and legal approaches to advertising is a recipe for failure. Internationally, the development of supranational rules of advertising has been sporadic. The best example of a multinational effort is the Marketing Supervision Network. The United States and about 20 other countries have agreed to cooperate in resolving advertising disputes that cross national boundaries.[21] At the regional level, the European Union has enacted two directives aimed at harmonizing European law on misleading and **comparative advertising.**[22] Before the 1997 Directive 97/55/EC on Comparative Advertising was enacted, such advertising was banned in Italy, Belgium, and Luxembourg, and was highly restricted in such countries as Germany and France. In contrast, in the United States more than 25 percent of all advertising is comparative.[23]

The 1997 Directive legalizes the use of comparative advertising that is defined as "any advertising which explicitly or by implication identifies a competitor or goods or services offered by a competitor." However, comparative advertising is permitted only if: (1) it does not mislead, (2) it compares goods or services meeting the same needs or serving the same purpose, (3) it objectively compares one or more material, relevant, verifiable, and representative features of the goods and services, (4) it does not create confusion in the marketplace between the advertiser and a competitor or with the competitor's trademarks or trade names, (5) it does not discredit or denigrate the trademarks, trade names, goods, or services of a competitor, (6) for products with designation of origin, it relates in each case to products with the same designation, and (7) it does not present goods or services as imitations or replicas of trademarked goods or services.

The EU Directive also requires that the advertiser demonstrate promptly the accuracy of its comparative claim. In contrast, the U.S. Federal Trade Commission only requires the proof of a *reasonable basis.* The use of subjective features such as taste or feel is permitted in the United States. Under the EU Directive's requirement of objective proof, such comparative advertising is prohibited. "Comparison on the basis of subjective factors, and opinion-based puffery are therefore prohibited under the Directive. Furthermore, it seems that the adopted formula bans the use of objectively administered consumer preference tests." Thus, the U.S. exporter should not assume that its comparative advertisements are automatically legal under the new Directive. This is especially true in countries that have traditionally prohibited such advertisements.

Professional Standards of International Advertising

http://

For a menu of ICC advertising codes: **http://www.iccwbo.org/home/menu_advert_marketing.asp**.

The International Chamber of Commerce has sponsored a number of ethical codes relating to international advertising and marketing, including the International Code of Advertising Practice, International Code of Sales Promotion, International Code of Practice on Direct Marketing, Code on Environmental Advertising, Code on Sponsorship, and the ICC/ESOMAR International Code of Marketing and Social Research Practice. The ICC International Code of Advertising Practice was first issued in 1937 and was revised in 1997. The main principles contained in the ICC code on advertising are summarized in the Comparative Law feature that follows. The ICC code applies to advertising in *any* medium for the sale of goods *or* services.

21. Allyson L. Stewart, "International Marketing Police Resolve Trading Disputes," *Marketing News* 15 (June 7, 1993).
22. Directive 84/450/EEC (1984) ("Misleading Advertising Directive") and Directive 97/55/EC (1997) ("Comparative Advertising Directive").
23. Paul Spink & Ross Petty, "Comparative Advertising in the European Union," 47 *International & Comparative Law Quarterly* 855 (1998). See also Ross D. Petty, "Advertising Law in the United States and European Union," 16 *Public Policy & Marketing* 2 (1997).

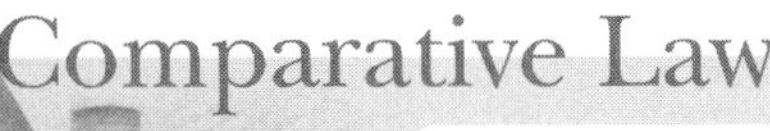

Comparative Law

ICC International Code of Advertising Practice

Article 2: Decency
Should not offend prevailing standards of decency.

Article 3: Honesty
Should not exploit consumers' lack of experience or knowledge.

Article 4: Social Responsibility
Should not condone any form of discrimination, play on fear, or play on superstition.

Article 5: Truthful Presentation
Should not mislead with regard to characteristics, value, terms of guarantee, intellectual property rights, or official recognition or approval and should not misuse research results.

Article 6: Comparisons
Comparison to other products should be based on facts that can be substantiated and should not be unfairly selected.

Article 7: Denigration
Should not denigrate any firm, organization, profession, or product.

Article 8: Testimonials
No use of personal testimonials or endorsements unless genuine, verifiable, relevant, and based upon personal experience or knowledge. Testimonials that have become obsolete should not be used.

Article 11: Imitation
Should not imitate other advertisements or unduly imitate others' advertising campaigns in other countries.

Article 12: Identification
Should not be made to appear as an editorial or news item. Should be presented so that it is readily recognized as an advertisement.

Article 14: Children
Applies to children as defined as minors under applicable national laws. Should not exploit their inexperience or give unreal perception of the true value of the product. For example, the use of the word *only* should be avoided. Should not directly appeal to children to persuade their parents to buy the advertised products.

Article 15: Guarantees
Should not contain any reference to a guarantee that does not provide the consumer with rights additional to those provided by law.

Article 10: Exploitation of Goodwill
Should not infringe upon intellectual property or goodwill.

The introduction to the Code describes it as a voluntary, self-regulating ethical code, but noted its use in a legal proceeding: "The Code is designed primarily as an instrument of self-discipline but it is also intended for the use of the courts as a reference document within the framework of applicable law."[24] The underlying principle of the Code is that "all advertising should be legal, decent, and truthful." Articles 3 through 17 provide some details regarding the meaning of "decent and truthful." Article 18 allots responsibilities to any professional advertising agency and any firm or company that advertises. Furthermore, anyone employed within these companies or agencies shall be liable to "a degree of responsibility commensurate with their positions." This liability is levied against both the selling company and its advertising agency, along with responsible officers and employees.

24. ICC, *International Code of Advertising Practice,* Introduction (1997 edition).

Key Terms

Amendments of 1988, 52
Attorney General Opinion, 52
benefit-cost analysis, 40
categorical imperatives, 43
Caux round Table Principles for International Business, 48
CE mark, 61
comparative advertising, 62
conflict of cultural tradition, 42
conflict of relative development, 42
corporate code of conduct, 45
cultural relativism, 39
Declaration on the Right to Development, 41
distributive justice, 40
dominant considerations, 40
due diligence, 58
ethical relativism, 39
ethics of care, 44
EU Ecolabel, 61
Federal Sentencing Guidelines, 58
Foreign Corrupt Practices Act (FCPA), 49
incommensurability, 40
integrative approach, 45
International Labor Organization, 38
International Organization for Standardization (ISO), 60
ISO 9000, 60
ISO 14000, 61
Kantian ethics, 43
moral duty, 41
moral minimum, 46
moral right, 41
myth of the amoral businessperson, 47
Organization for Economic Cooperation and Development (OECD), 57
organizational ethics, 47
Social Accountability Standard, 61
standards, 38
subordinate responsibility, 47
third-party bribery, 55
Transparency International, 50
United Nations Declaration of Human Rights, 41
utilitarian ethics, 39
virtue ethics, 44

Chapter Problems

1. How can a parent company insulate itself from liability under the Foreign Corrupt Practices Act for acts of its foreign subsidiaries, affiliates, and partners? See Brown, "Parent-Subsidiary Liability Under the Foreign Corrupt Practices Act," 50 *Baylor Law Review* 1 (1998).

2. Devise a program for your company to ensure compliance with the Foreign Corrupt Practices Act. What is the importance of *corporate culture* to any such compliance program? See Goelzer, "Designing an FCPA Compliance Program: Minimizing the Risks of Improper Foreign Payments," 18 *Northwestern Journal of International Law & Business* 282 (1998). See also Head, "The Development of Compliance Programs: One Company's Experience," 18 *Northwestern Journal of International Law & Business* 535 (1998).

3. What is the difference between a bribe and a facilitation fee? Does it make a difference if payments or bribes are a crime in a foreign country, but such crimes are not enforced? If such payments are not considered illegal in a foreign country, is it proper to make such payments? From an ethical point of view should the FCPA be read broadly or narrowly? Is giving a bribe a victimless crime? Does bribe-giving affect the free-market system? How? Do you believe that the FCPA places U.S. companies at a competitive disadvantage?

4. Your company has been trying for more than a year to obtain the assets of a formally government-owned petroleum business. However, the approval process and review of the contract documents have been held up for months in the government bureaucracy. An official approaches your Vice President of Acquisitions and suggests that if your company pays the expenses for a ten-day "negotiating" trip for himself and his family to Disney World and Miami the approval process could be completed within one week. Should your company authorize the expenditure? Would your answer be different if it were a $200 "fee" to expedite the importation of your company's products into the country?

5. You have obtained a United States government grant to help train physicians in a developing country on new techniques for fighting AIDS. While working within the developing country's Ministry of Disease Control you have uncovered evidence that certain monies received through the International Red Cross had been misappropriated by certain officials in the Ministry. The money was to be used to test and ensure the safety of the country's blood supply. Instead, it seems that the money was used to buy new ambulances for some of the country's hospitals. Should you report this transgression? Do you have any legal duty to report? Do you have an ethical duty to report? If so, to whom? Does the fact that such reporting may jeopardize your relationship with members of the Ministry and the U.S. agency that hired you enter into to your decision? Does the FCPA apply to this case? How can materials on "whistleblowing" be applied to this hypothetical? Do you have an obligation to obtain a sufficient amount of evidence before reporting?

6. Your company transfers you to a foreign subsidiary as an assistant manager of operations. The purpose of the assignment is to be trained by one of the company's "top managers." Soon after arriving you discover that the manager had instituted an unusual accounting system. You have no real evidence, but the talk around the office is that the manager's success is due to his payments to his government connections. It is also rumored that some of the hidden transactions have profited the manager personally. The subsidiary remains one of the most profitable of your company's foreign operations. What do you do?

7. Lord Coke had this to say about bribery: "Though the bribe be small, yet the fault is great." Do you agree that the size of the bribe is unimportant in determining legal or ethical wrongdoing?

8. What are the elements of an effective ethics or environmental compliance program? How would you develop an ethics or environmental compliance program that would satisfy the dictates of the Federal Organizational Sentencing Guidelines? See Paul Fiorelli, *Fine Reduction through Effective Ethics Program*, 56 *Alb. L. Rev.* 403 (1992); Paul Fiorelli, *The Environmental Sentencing Guidelines for Business Organizations*, 22 *B.C. Envtl. Aff. L. Rev.* 481 (1995).

9. It is currently estimated that only 13% of middle managers posted overseas by U.S. companies are women, even though women make up nearly half of the middle managers at these companies. What do you think are the reasons for such an imbalance? At the same time, a poll of human resources executives show that 80% of them believed that global work experience was essential for advancement. Can this be seen as the potential for creating a global glass ceiling? What can companies due to overcome such bias?

10. In 1971, John Rawls published his masterwork, A *Theory of Justice*. Simply stated, he equated justice with notions of procedural fairness. Rawlsian justice judges a decision or rule on whether it was arrived at through a process of procedural fairness. Thus, a decision is just or ethical if it was fairly made. A decision or rule is fairly made if each person affected by it is given the most extensive basic liberties compatible with the similar rights of others. Furthermore, social and economic inequalities are arranged to the greatest benefit of the least advantaged persons and such inequalities are attached to positions open to all under conditions of fair equality of opportunity. Although Rawls' approach is targeted at political and not moral theory, its use in dealing with the least advantaged countries of the world may be productive. These rules are to be applied behind a *veil of ignorance* where the parties are unaware of their status or positions. How can this approach be used to ethically judge dealings between developed and developing countries? If these rules were applied behind such a veil, then would such dealings likely result in more equitable transactions?

11. One of the negative by-products of the corporate ethics movement is a decrease in employee privacy. In order to ensure ethical compliance in the workplace employers will feel pressure to monitor employee activities. To discourage employee misbehavior, employers have begun to monitor employee use of the company's e-mail system to discourage its use for personal purposes and as a vehicle of sexual harassment. Some companies have installed video cameras to monitor employee movements. How should companies balance their ethics monitoring with employee privacy concerns? Need they fully disclose to their employees the extent of their monitoring practices?

Internet Exercises

1. Review the Corruption Perception Index published by Transparency International at **http://www.transparency.org/**.

2. Review the web site of *Sweatshop Watch* for recent developments involving the problem of low labor standards in the international production of goods: **http://www.sweatshopwatch.org**.

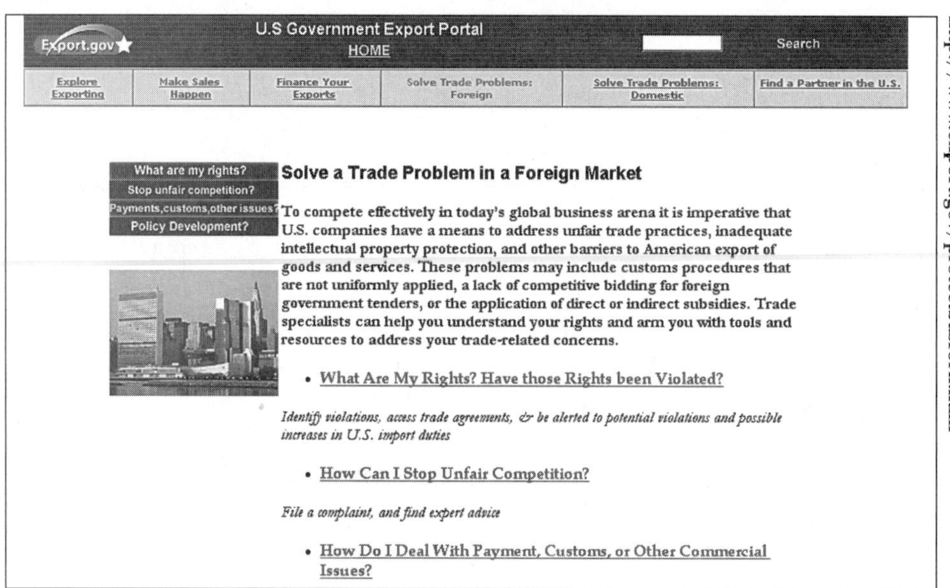

http://www.export.gov/protectbusforn.html

Chapter 3 Strategies for International Business

A U.S. company must develop a strategy or business plan when deciding to establish a foreign business operation. A foreign business strategy encompasses activities like hiring foreign employees, establishing a foreign office, and acquiring foreign business assets, including the acquisition of companies or the incorporation of a subsidiary. The factors that affect planning foreign operations, like the risks of international business transactions, vary depending on the country, type of industry, size of operation, and legal issues such as foreign regulations and taxation.

As discussed in Chapter 1, the first major decision is whether entry into a foreign country should be through a direct or indirect presence. The most indirect form of foreign entry is through exportation of goods or the licensing of technology. These transactions can involve little direct contact or the use of surrogates or agents within the country. A company that wants to do more than just sell to a foreign importer but that does not want a direct presence within a country will often hire agents or independent contractors to help market, sell, and distribute its products. These agents are generally hired as independent contractors and not as direct employees. The next two sections will review the ways a foreign company can conduct business in the United States and the ways a U.S. company can operate internationally.

STRATEGIES FOR DOING BUSINESS IN THE UNITED STATES

The various forms of doing business in the United States are organized and controlled under state laws. Although there are technical variations among state laws, the common forms of doing business are similar in all the states. A foreign company planning to do business in the United States may do so through a **branch office.** Generally, the only formal procedure required of a branch is to register to do business with the appropriate state regulatory agency. The branch is considered simply an extension of the foreign corporation, and the corporation is liable for the debts of the branch under U.S. common law.

Alternatively, the foreign corporation may elect to operate one of a number of independent entities recognized under state laws, including the joint venture, general partnership, limited partnership, corporation, and limited liability companies. The **joint venture** is a hybrid that forms either a partnership or a corporation. A joint venture can be loosely defined as an association between two or more parties with an agreement to share the profits and often the management of a particular project. In the United States, the joint venture is commonly treated as a partnership, especially for tax purposes. The joint venture is a common method for international business investment, in which a foreign company seeks out a domestic company in order to penetrate the host country's market. The advantages of joint venturing will be discussed in greater detail later in the chapter.

In a **general partnership,** all the partners are jointly and severally liable for partnership debts. Unlike in a joint venture, a partnership mandate is more flexible and ongoing. Where a joint venture is established to accomplish a narrow business objective, a general partnership generally envisions a long-term evolution of the business, including the development of goals not contemplated by the partners at the time of inception. In a partnership, as in the partnership-style joint venture, the losses and profits of the business *pass through* directly to the partners for purposes of taxation. This avoids the problem of double taxation most closely associated with the corporation.

http://

For general information on U.S. business law, including the laws of partnership and corporations, see **http://www.westbuslaw.com**.

The **limited partnership** couples the pass-through feature of a general partnership with the concept of limited liability found in a corporation. Limited liability is achieved through the division of the partners into two classes: general and limited partners. The general partner has unlimited liability, while the limited partners are liable only up to the amount of their capital contributions. A limited partnership, however, is a statutorily created mode of doing business. Unlike the general partnership, which originates in common law, the limited partnership must fulfill a state's limited partnership statute requirements. In contrast, the general partnership is formed simply through the agreement, express or implied, of the partners. The benefit of limited liability comes at a price; state law requires that a limited partner be a silent or passive investor. A limited partner who becomes involved in the day-to-day management of the business by law acquires the status of a general partner and, as a general partner, will possess unlimited liability for the debts of the partnership.

http://
Materials on corporate law: FindLaw Corporate Law at **http://www.findlaw.com/01topics/08corp** or Hieros Gamos Corporate Law at **http://www.hg.org/corp.html** or Cornell at **http://www.law.cornell.edu/topics/corporations.html**.

A more recent development is the **limited liability company (LLC).** Established under specific state statutes, these entities take various forms. The greatest advantage of LLCs is that they provide limited liability without the formalism of the corporation. In some instances, an LLC may be an alternative to a joint venture or limited partnership, offering both the flexibility of a partnership and the limited liability of the corporation. Types of limited liability companies vary by state law.

The most common form of doing business for the foreign investor is the **corporation,** whereby an investor purchases shares in an existing or newly formed corporation. As a shareholder, the investor's liability is generally limited to the amount paid for the shares of stock. The corporation is created when the shareholders file a *certificate of incorporation* with one of the fifty Secretaries of State. In the past, Delaware was the most popular state of incorporation because of its liberal corporate laws. Today, most states have simplified their laws to make it easier for corporations to conduct business. Once incorporated, a business is required to file annual reports or pay state franchise taxes. Most states do not differentiate between corporations owned by residents or by foreign nationals. Once a corporation receives its charter from the state, other parties are prohibited from using its corporate name when doing business in that state.

STRATEGIES FOR ENTERING A FOREIGN MARKET

A U.S. company that wants a direct foreign presence has a number of options, including establishing a representative office, a joint venture with an established company, setting up a branch office, or forming a full-scale foreign subsidiary. Forming a foreign subsidiary requires deeper business and legal involvement than establishing a representative office. A **representative office** is established for limited purposes, such as undertaking market analysis and product promotion. Host country laws dictate what types of activities a representative office may pursue. For example, a representative office may obtain leads of potential customers, but cannot negotiate or enter into contracts, tasks reserved to the parent company in the home country. The advantage of operating a representative office is that the company is not considered to be *doing business* in the foreign country, so it will avoid host country regulations and will not be subject to foreign taxation. Such offices are relatively inexpensive and the easiest to establish.

In order to have a full-time presence and to transact business, a company will need to establish an operation to do business within a foreign country. The joint venture vehicle allows a company to share expertise and risks with a **local partner,** who often brings benefits such as customer and distribution networks, existing contacts with important government officers, and knowledge of the host country's legal and regulatory system. A joint venture may also be the only option in a country that prohibits wholly owned foreign subsidiaries. A joint venture is usually a partnership, but can also be undertaken by establishing a corporation or limited liability company with each party owning a portion of the equity. These types of enterprises are referred to as **equity joint ventures.**

http://
Chinese Foreign Equity Joint Venture Law: **http://www.qis.net/chinalaw/prclaw11.htm**.

A third option, where the parties agree to perform certain tasks without forming a new entity, is a **contractual joint venture.** In 1988, China enacted the Law on Chinese-Foreign Contractual Joint Ventures. That law allows the parties to operate as separate companies and does not require a minimum capital contribution from the foreign investor. Factors like taxation, liability, and host country commercial and corporate laws, however, will influence the form of the joint venture. China has enacted separate laws to regulate different types of joint ventures. Equity joint ventures are governed by the Law on Joint Ventures Using Chinese and Foreign Investment, most recently amended in 1990. This law requires the establishment of a Chinese corporation for which the foreign participant must provide a minimum of 25 percent of the capital. In addition, the ownership rights of the foreign investor are nontransferable. The parties to a joint venture will need to research whether the joint venture can be formed under U.S. law, the law of the host country, or the laws of a third country, and which will be the most favorable.

http://

http://www.state.gov: For brief descriptions of the different strategies or methods of doing business in a particular country see the "Country Commercial Guide" for the country in the "Business Center" section.

Another means of entering a foreign market is the **foreign subsidiary** or **affiliate.** A company may elect to establish an independent foreign subsidiary or an affiliate. An affiliate is a business enterprise located in one country that is directly or indirectly owned or controlled by a company located in another country. Ownership of 10 percent of its voting securities is generally considered "control." The subsidiary is generally established under the laws of the foreign country and pays taxes on the profits it earns in the foreign country, but the parent company's income will not be subject to host country taxation. Companies with foreign subsidiaries often attempt to reduce the enterprise's overall tax liability through **transfer pricing,** where one subsidiary of an enterprise charges another for goods or services. Companies manipulate these transfer prices in order to move profits to countries with lower tax rates. Foreign subsidiaries may be heavily regulated in some countries; some host countries require that a portion of the subsidiary be locally owned and that the board of directors include nationals of the host country. In some countries the establishment of a wholly owned foreign subsidiary may not be possible.[1] Also, foreign corporation laws may not be as friendly as U.S. law in limiting the liability of the parent company. In certain countries, a creditor is allowed to pierce the corporate veil more easily to sue the parent company. The crucial advantages of a foreign subsidiary over the branch office are that the parent company has limited liability and is able to carry on a broad range of business activities.

http://

Information and links about market access and foreign government regulations: **http://www.ita.doc.gov/ita_home/itamac.html**.

No matter what type of enterprise is selected, joint venture or foreign subsidiary, a company must submit to a vigorous approval process in countries like China. China has a dual approval process whereby the enterprise or venture must first be approved by the Minister of Foreign Economic Relations and Trade and then registered with the Administration of Industry and Commerce, which reviews financing and debt-equity guidelines. Upon approval, the foreign enterprise is issued a business license to conduct business in China. The use of a Chinese consultant familiar with the approval process and having *quanxi* (connections) with central and local government authorities is essential.

Foreign Corporation Law

The roles and duties played by different constituent groups, such as the shareholders and board of directors, vary under foreign corporate laws (see Comparative Law: Corporate Governance in the U.S., Germany, and Japan). Japanese corporate law is strikingly similar to U.S. corporate law: A single board of directors is elected by the shareholders and the directors owe the traditional duties of loyalty and care to the corporation and its shareholders. Securities laws in Japan, however, do not play the

1. For example, Chinese *Law on Enterprises Operated Exclusively with Foreign Capital* permits such an enterprise only if it uses advanced technologies or markets its products outside of China.

central role that they play in the United States. Bank financing, not security offerings, remain the fundamental vehicle for financing corporate expansion in Japan. Because corporate capital is largely privately funded, the need for disclosure, as mandated under U.S. securities laws, is not as important in Japan as it is in the United States.

In contrast, the corporate laws of Germany,[2] China, and France reflect fundamentally different views of the objectives of the board of directors and the role of the corporation in society. Germany mandates a two-tiered board of directors: the supervisory board and the management board. The employees and the shareholders each elect one-half of the **supervisory board,** which then appoints the management board members. The supervisory board oversees the **management board** and approves the financial statements and major corporate decisions. The management board carries out the strategic objectives established by the supervisory board and makes the day-to-day decisions in managing the company. The German corporate structure places a primary emphasis on the interests of the employees and a secondary emphasis on shareholder interests.

In China, shareholders' interests are the dominant vehicle for corporate decision making. Unlike in the United States, shareholder power pervades the day-to-day operation of the company. The Chinese Company Law requires large companies to establish a **supervisory committee** of shareholders which has the power to investigate and supervise the financial affairs of the company. Furthermore, shareholders are authorized to pass their own resolutions that must be implemented by the board of directors. Business plans and investment decisions are formulated by the board of directors, but must be submitted to the shareholders for approval.

French corporate law is unique because it provides alternate governance structures for the public corporation, or *S.A.*[3] The articles of incorporation may select a management structure that is headed by a U.S.-style board of directors or one that consists of a management committee or executive board and a **shareholders' council.** The latter form acts in many ways like the two-tiered system found in Germany. The shareholders' council possesses most of the powers that are delegated to the board of directors under U.S. corporate law.

PIERCING THE CORPORATE VEIL

U.S. corporate law and practice is considered to be corporation friendly. The limitation on personal liability offered by the corporate form is highly guarded by U.S. courts. The formation of a corporation with minimal capitalization is sufficient to shield the corporate shareholders from personal liability for the debts and obligations of the corporation. This protection is given whether the shareholder is an individual or a parent corporation. Thus, a corporation may use an independent incorporated subsidiary to shield itself from liability. However, U.S. law does allow a court to disregard the corporate form through the doctrine of **piercing the corporate veil.** If the corporate form is considered a sham, U.S. courts may allow the shareholders to be sued personally for the debts of the disregarded corporation.

The case of *Raven Metal Products v. McGann*[4] illustrates some of the factors a court assesses when deciding if a corporate entity should be disregarded and the entity's owners exposed to personal liability. Raven Metal brought suit for breach of contract for nonpayment for materials delivered to Northeast Trailer, Inc.

2. It is important to note that there are no European Union directives that require any particular corporate form. Corporate law is found solely in the individual national laws of the members of the EU.
3. S.A. stands for *Sociedad Anonyme.*
4. 699 N.Y.S.2d 503 (1999).

Comparative Law

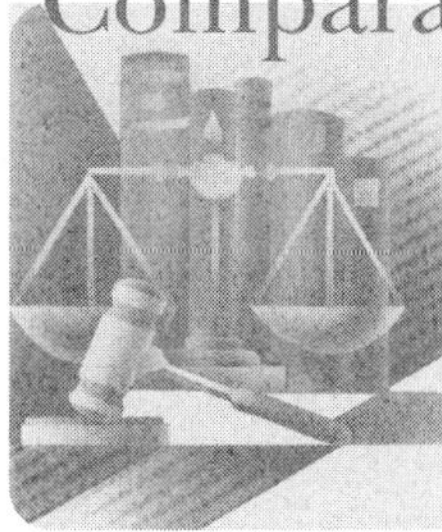

Corporate Governance in the United States, Germany, and Japan[5]

Corporate Goals and Objectives

What differentiates the governance structures of the U.S., Japan, and Germany are the roles the various stakeholders play in monitoring and controlling the firm. For example, in the United States, the primary stakeholder has been the shareholder, whereas in Japan and Germany, labor historically also has had a relatively strong voice. The American Law Institute asserts that a corporation's primary objective should be "corporate profit and shareholder gain." Traditionally, Japanese corporations have operated to benefit a small group of owners, rather than to maximize shareholder value. Its corporate governance system emphasizes the protection of employees and creditor interests as much or more than shareholder interests. Management has had few direct incentives to enhance shareholder value. German law clearly defines the goals of German corporations. Its business corporation statute states that "the managing board, on its own responsibility, is to manage the corporation for the good of the enterprise and its employees, the common weal of society, and the State." German law dictates that managers operate the firm for the benefit of multiple stakeholders, not just shareholders.

Management Structure

In the United States, shareholders typically elect directors at annual shareholder meetings. Labor is rarely involved in the corporate governance system. Japan, like the U.S., uses a single-tier board structure. Traditionally, Japanese boards have been large, with some of the largest firms having more than 50 directors. Most typically, board members will be current or former senior and middle management. The mixing of management and director roles in Japanese corporate governance is in stark contrast to the separate, independent roles encouraged in U.S. corporate governance law. The system used in Germany is significantly different from those in either the United States or Japan. In large German firms, employees select half the board of directors. This practice is known as *codetermination.* Modern German corporations with over 500 employees have a two-tiered board structure. A supervisory board performs the strategic oversight role, while a management board performs the operational and day-to-day management role. In firms with over 2,000 employees, employees must comprise half of the supervisory board; shareholder representatives make up the other half. Supervisory boards also may include representatives of firms with whom the corporation has vertical relationships, such as suppliers and customers. The supervisory board appoints and oversees the management board. The German board structure thus functions to explicitly represent the interests of non-shareholder constituents and ensures that major strategic decisions are not made without the consent of employees and their representatives.

Brenda McGann was the sole director, officer, and shareholder of Northeast Trailer. Northeast held no corporate meetings and no corporate records existed. McGann used corporate funds to pay personal expenses. The court stated that there are two general elements that must be met in order to pierce the corporate veil. First, the owners must exercise complete domination of the corporation in

5. Excerpted from Timothy L. Fort & Cindy A. Schipani, "Corporate Governance in a Global Environment: The Search for the Best of All Worlds," 33 *Vanderbilt Journal of Transnational Law* 829 (2000).

Finnish Fur Sales Co., Ltd. v. Juliette Shulof Furs, Inc., George Shulof and Juliette Shulof

770 F. Supp. 139 (S.D.N.Y. 1991)

Leisure, District Judge. This is an action to collect sums allegedly owed in connection with furs purchased at two auctions in Vantaa, Finland. Plaintiff Finnish Fur Sales Co., Ltd. ("FFS"), asserts its claim of failure to pay for and clear 2,469 fox pelts against defendants Juliette Shulof Furs, Inc. ("JSF"), and George Shulof. Plaintiff Okobank Osuuspankkien Keskuspankki Oy ("Okobank") asserts its claim of failure to honor a bill of exchange against defendants JSF and Juliette Shulof. FFS is a limited company organized under Finnish law, which sells fur pelts raised by Finnish breeders at public auctions held several times each year. The auctions are conducted under certain Conditions of Sale ("Conditions"), which are listed in the auction catalogue, a copy of which is given to each prospective bidder in advance of the auction. A one-page English translation of the Conditions appears on the inside cover of the catalogue.

JSF is a New York corporation that has conducted a fur business for approximately 15 years. George Shulof, an officer of JSF, has been in the fur business since 1935. Mr. Shulof attended the FFS auctions held in Vantaa, Finland, in January and May 1987. He purchased over $500,000 worth of skins at the January auction, and some $700,000 worth of skins at the May auction. FFS claims that, in addition to the liability of JSF, Mr. Shulof is personally liable for this debt, based on Finnish law, the custom and practice of the fur trade, and the provisions of section 4 of the Conditions. Section 4 provides: "Any person bidding at the auction shall stand surety as for his own debt until full payment is made for purchased merchandise." George Shulof denies any personal liability on the grounds, *inter alia*, that the provision is unenforceable under both New York and Finnish law. JSF made a cash down payment and accepted a bill of exchange (the "Bill of Exchange") for $30,328.39. According to plaintiffs, in January 1989, Okobank became holder in due course of the Bill of Exchange, which was presented for collection on or about February 7, 1989, at Bank Leumi in New York, but was dishonored. The Bill of Exchange was signed "Juliette A. Shulof" above the printed name "Juliette Shulof Furs Inc."

Liability of George Shulof

In this case, application of New York choice of law analysis is required. Section 15 of the Conditions provides that "these conditions are governed by Finnish law." Choice of law clauses are routinely enforced by the courts of this Circuit "if there is a reasonable basis for the choice. Finland's contacts with the transactions at issue are substantial, rendering the choice of law clause enforceable unless a strong public policy of New York is impaired by the application of Finnish law. Mr. Shulof also argues that, under New York law, Section 4 of the Conditions would be invalid as contravening New York's policy against imposing personal liability on corporate officers.

It is also well-established under New York law, as under Finnish law, that "the owner of property offered for sale at auction has the right to prescribe the manner, conditions and terms of sale. The conditions of a public sale, announced by the auctioneer at the time and place of the sale, are binding on the purchaser, whether or not he knew or heard them." In the case at bar, George Shulof contends that the provisions of Section 4 are unconscionable and would not be enforced by a New York court. Nevertheless, a perusal of the Conditions reveals that their entire text is only a single page long, and that all of the Conditions, including Section 4, are printed in the same size print, which, although small, is legible. Under these circumstances, it seems unlikely that a New York court would refuse to enforce Section 4 in an arm's-length commercial transaction involving a sophisticated defendant accustomed to bidding at fur auctions.

Given the lack of a clear conflict with either New York law or policy, this Court concludes that a New York court would apply Finnish law to the issue before the Court. The Court also notes that a similar result has often been reached under New York conflicts rules even in the absence of a contractual choice of law clause. Thus, Mr. Shulof must be held jointly and severally liable with JSF for any damages owed to FFS for the furs purchased at its 1987 auctions.

Liability of Juliette Shulof

The parties agree that New York law governs the issue of the liability of Juliette Shulof on the Bill of Exchange, which was executed and payable in New York. The parties do not dispute that the Bill of Exchange is a negotiable instrument, and therefore subject to the provisions of Article 3 of the Uniform Commercial Code, as adopted by the state of New York. The relevant section of the Code is § 3-403, which governs signatures by authorized representatives. Under subsection (2), An authorized representative who signs his own name to an instrument:

(a) is personally obligated if the instrument neither names the person represented nor shows that the representative signed in a representative capacity;
(b) except as otherwise established between the immediate parties, is personally obligated if the instrument names the person represented but does not show that the representative signed in a representative capacity, or if the instrument does not name the person represented but does show that the representative signed in a representative capacity.

An Official Comment to this section offers examples of signatures and the legal implication of each type of signature. An authorized representative will not be personally bound by the following: a signature in the name of the represented party; "Peter Pringle by Arthur Adams, Agent"; or "Arthur Adams, Agent" (assuming that the principal is named in the instrument). In the case of a signature such as "Arthur Adams, Agent," or "Peter Pringle Arthur Adams," parol evidence may be offered in litigation between the immediate parties to prove representative capacity.

In the case at bar, Mrs. Shulof signed as "Juliette A. Shulof" above a typed name of "Juliette Shulof Furs Inc.," which had been typed in by the preparer of the instrument, FFS. The cases interpreting signatures of this type demonstrate the special treatment of negotiable instruments under New York law. As reflected in the discussion in an earlier section of this opinion, New York has, as a general rule, a policy against imposing personal liability on corporate officers if the circumstances are ambiguous. However, this policy gives way before the policy considerations underlying N.Y.U.C.C. § 3-403, which "aims to foster certainty and definiteness in the law of commercial paper, requirements deriving from the 'necessity for takers of negotiable instruments to tell at a glance whose obligation they hold.'"

It is undisputed that Okobank never dealt with either of the Shulofs or JSF. Mrs. Shulof offers no evidence sufficient to raise a triable issue of fact as to either Okobank's status as a *holder in due course* or her allegations of fraud in the inducement on the part of FFS. Accordingly, the Court finds that Mrs. Shulof's signature on the Bill of Exchange did not give notice that she signed in a representative capacity only, and therefore she is personally liable for the amount of the bill. SO ORDERED.

Case Highlights

- There is a strong public policy in U.S. corporate law against imposing personal liability on corporate officers for actions performed on behalf of the corporation.
- It is customary under Finnish law for an agent to be held personally liable as a surety for goods purchased at an auction.
- A corporate officer who signs a bill of exchange or draft must state she signs *only* in a representative capacity in order to avoid personal liability.
- The public policy underlying negotiable instrument law is that a *holder in due course* may collect against the signer of the instrument.
- A choice of law clause in a contract will be enforced if there is a reasonable connection between the choice and the transaction, unless a strong public policy of the forum court is threatened.
- Owners at an auction have the right to prescribe the manner, conditions, and terms of sale.

respect to the transaction being attacked. Second, such domination is used to commit a fraud or wrong against the plaintiff. The court refused to pierce the corporate veil because there was no wrongful act, and despite the domination of McGann over Northeast, there was no evidence of actual fraud. Furthermore, the court noted that the corporate money used to pay personal expenses was not in excess of what McGann's services were worth to the corporation. This case illustrates the U.S. view in favor of upholding the limited liability of the corporate form.

The *Finish Fur Sales v. Shulof* case above shows that the U.S. presumption against piercing the corporate veil is not held as strongly in other countries. The case also introduces the bill of exchange instrument and the law of negotiable instruments as separate vehicles of liability. This area of law will be more fully explored in Chapter 11, International Trade Finance.

Another method used to pierce the corporate veil is **enterprise liability.** Although this theory has been widely rejected by U.S. courts, some foreign courts recognize it. Enterprise liability looks at affiliated companies as an enterprise to be held liable individually or as a whole. Thus, a parent company may be held liable for the acts of its subsidiaries, or a franchisor may be held liable for the acts of its franchisees. Taken to an extreme, each individual subsidiary or franchisee can be held liable for the acts of other subsidiaries or franchisees. This was the path taken by the Grand Court of the Cayman Islands in *Touche-Ross & Co. v. Bank Intercontinental, Ltd.* In that case, Touche-Ross of the Cayman Islands performed audit work in the Cayman Islands for Bank Intercontinental. Bank Intercontinental then attempted to sue Touche-Ross International and all its affiliated companies. Touche-Ross of New York brought suit in the Cayman Islands to obtain an injunction against being sued by Bank Intercontinental. The Cayman Court held that Touche-Ross of New York, Touche-Ross of the Cayman Islands, and Touche-Ross International, headquartered in Switzerland, formed a common enterprise. As a common enterprise, the affiliated company was held to be jointly liable for the acts of an associated member.

ESTABLISHING A BUSINESS IN A FOREIGN COUNTRY

http://

http://www.export.gov/tcc/ provides links to topics pertaining to foreign employment and labor laws.

The requirements to establish a business or an office in a foreign country vary dramatically from one country to the next. The least level of involvement in entering a foreign market is hiring a foreign sales representative or agent. Some countries, however, limit foreign companies to hiring nationals as sales representatives or agents. The foreign exporter, however, can exert substantial control over its agents through **management agreements.** Such agreements do not *establish* the foreign exporter for purposes of tax liability; the tax liability of the foreign company is generally restricted to the income of any expatriates assigned to the representative office.

The next level of entry into a foreign market is the establishment of a representative or branch office. With a branch office, the parent company establishes any type of operation—sales office, manufacturing plant, or distribution facility—without setting up an independent legal entity. The branch office generally operates under the trade name of the parent company. Advantages of such an operation include ease in establishment, central management, and fewer required disclosures of confidential information to third parties. The major disadvantages are the risk of host country taxation and unlimited liability for the activities of the branch office, such as product liability. A business permit is required in most countries, and in some countries registering to establish a foreign office entails multiple filings with multiple agencies. In Indonesia, the activities of a representative office are limited to signing sales contracts, collecting payments, and other general business activities. In other countries other activities may also be limited.

An important issue in entering a foreign market is the protection of the company's trade name. In the United States, corporate and trade names are protected under the individual states' incorporation statutes. Once a business name is reserved, all other persons or companies are precluded from using that or a similar name. In many foreign countries the only avenue of protection for a business name is for a company to register it as a foreign trademark.

Companies planning a permanent presence in a foreign country may choose to establish an independent subsidiary or purchase an existing company. The corporate entity is recognized in almost all countries in the world, but names and abbreviations for corporations vary in different legal systems. In the United States, a corporation is signified by the use of "Inc." after the company's name to indicate that it is an "incorporated" entity. The term "Limited" or "Ltd." is used in Canada and Great Britain. "SA" for *Sociedad Anonyme* is the corporate designation in France and Spain. "SpA" or *Societa per Azioni* is the Italian symbol for corporation, and "Y.K." or *Yugen-Kaisha* is the Japanese designation for a corporation. The number of options for establishing a business in a given country can be staggering. In Russia, for example, the 1990 Law on Enterprises recognizes no fewer than ten forms of business enterprises.[6]

The number of recognized enterprises in Russia was subsequently reduced by the 1994 Civil Code.[7] Even though the nomenclature is similar to that found in the United States, there are key differences in the Russian forms of enterprise. The Russian partnership is considered a separate entity for purposes of taxation, and does not benefit from the pass-through feature of U.S. partnerships. Double taxation, at the partnership and individual levels, is the result.

Another variation not found in U.S. law is the limited liability company *with additional liability*. The standard Russian limited liability company, like those in the United States, limits the owners' liability for the debts of the company to the value of their contributions. The limited liability company with additional liability makes the owners liable for a *pro rata* share of the company's debts in bankruptcy. This form is intended to provide additional security to creditors.

The **joint stock company** is the Russian form of corporation and is regulated under the 1996 Law on Enterprises. Under this law, a joint stock company may be open or closed. The closed version is limited to no more than fifty shareholders who can maintain their ownership interests through a preemptive right to purchase a *pro rata* share of any subsequent issuance of stock. Unlike U.S. laws, this Russian law grants subsidiaries express rights that can be used against the parent company. The parent company is jointly and severally liable for any orders it gives to its subsidiaries. It is also liable for the insolvency of a subsidiary because of the parent's fault. Finally, shareholders of the subsidiary have the right to sue the parent company for losses caused by the fault of the parent company.[8]

Foreign Competition Law

If the market entry strategy decided upon is the purchase of an existing foreign company, then the legalities of acquiring a company under host country laws must be thoroughly researched, particularly whether the acquisition conforms to the host country's **competition law.**[9] The European Union provides one example of an advanced competition law system. In order to purchase a company situated in a European Union country a purchaser must obtain clearance from Directorate IV of the European Commission. The following *Commission Decision of 17/11/1999* provides insight into the nuances of European competition law.

6. These include the state enterprise, municipal enterprise, individual or family private enterprise, full partnership, mixed partnership, closed joint stock company or limited liability partnership, open joint stock company, association of enterprises, branch of an enterprise, and labor collective enterprise.
7. The Civil Code recognizes the individual partnership (general and limited), limited liability company (ordinary or additional liability), joint stock company (open and closed), and the industrial or unitarian enterprise (state or municipal).
8. This material was taken from Edward C. Vandenberg, "The Evolution of Russian Forms of Business Enterprise," 28 *Ottawa Law Review* 343 (1996–1997).
9. Competition law in the United States is referred to as antitrust law.

Commission Decision of 17/11/1999

(1999 OJ C 357) (Case No IV/M.1652)

On October 14, 1999, the Commission received a notification of proposed concentration pursuant to Article 4 of Council Regulation (EEC) No 4064/89 of the acquisition by the Belgian company, s.a. D'Ieteren n.v. ("D'Ieteren"), of sole control over the South African company, Plate Glass & Shatterprufe Industries Limited ("PGSI"). Following examination of the notification, the Commission has concluded that the notified operation falls within the scope of Council Regulation (EEC) No 4064/89 and does not raise serious doubts as to its compatibility with the common market and with the EEA Agreement.

D'Ieteren is involved in a range of business activities in the automotive sector, comprising broadly: i) wholesale and retail motor vehicle distribution, ii) servicing and repair and the supply of spare parts for motor vehicles, iii) short term car rental, and iv) long term car rental and financing. D'Ieteren has practically no activities outside the EU, and within the EU some 70% of its turnover is achieved in Belgium. PGSI is a group involved in the manufacture, distribution, repair, and replacement of glass and board products. It has activities in South Africa, Central Africa, the United States, Australia, New Zealand, and Brazil, as well as in the EU.

The transaction consists of a number of steps through which D'Ieteren will acquire sole control of PGSI. D'Ieteren will carry out these steps through a joint venture company, S.A. Dicobel ("Dicobel"), in which it will hold 70% of the shares. The remaining 30% are held by S.A. Copeba Novo ("Copeba"), a Belgian listed holding company. In the Shareholders' Agreement of Dicobel, Copeba's role is stated to be that of "financial partner" and provision is made for a majority representation by D'Ieteren on the Board, whose majority will make the strategic decisions of the company. Dicobel will, in turn, acquire the majority shareholding of each of three companies, namely, Old Belron Rest of the World, HoldCo Southern Africa, and Glass SA, which between them comprise the PGSI group of companies. Through its majority presence on the Boards of these companies and the arrangements for strategic decision-making, Dicobel will enjoy sole control over PGSI. Thus D'Ieteren, through its sole control of Dicobel, will have sole control of PGSI.

Concentration of a Community Dimension

The operation constitutes an acquisition by D'Ieteren of sole control of PGSI, and is, therefore, a concentration within the meaning of Article 3.1.b. of the Merger Regulation. D'Ieteren and PGSI have a combined aggregate worldwide turnover in excess of EUR 2,500 million. In each of three member states their combined aggregate turnover is more than EUR 100 million. The operations have, therefore, a Community dimension.

Relevant Product Markets

The activities of D'Ieteren and PGSI, through its subsidiary, Belron International n.v., overlap in two areas, in themselves vertically related, i.e., i) the supply of automotive glass to the independent aftermarket, consisting of independent car dealerships, garages, and bodyshops ("IAM"), which the Commission has already considered to constitute a product market in itself, and ii) the repair and replacement of automotive glass, which would constitute another product market.

Relevant Geographic Markets

The IAM market has already been considered of a Community-wide geographic scope by the Commission and this definition is retained in the present case. With regard to the repair and replacement of automotive glass, D'Ieteren submitted that the existence of national distribution networks with national pricing and single (free call) telephone numbers indicated a national geographic scope for this market. Other characteristics, such as different suppliers in different member states and appreciable price differences from one member state to another, can be considered further indicators of a national scope for the market for these services. However, given that the operation does not raise any serious concerns, either at a national or wider level (D'Ieteren does not have these activities outside of Belgium), the Commission does not need to define the geographic scope of the market for the repair and replacement of automotive glass more precisely in the present case.

Assessment—The Repair and Replacement of Automotive Glass

The repair and replacement of automotive glass would constitute an affected market in Belgium, due to the addition of PGSI/Belron's share of some 39% to D'Ieteren's own share of some 1%. D'Ieteren's activities have been limited to services provided in its own car dealerships situated in the Brussels area, whereas PGSI/Belron operates from a network of 40 branches throughout Belgium, replacing the glass at the branches or at the location chosen by the customers. Although the operation strengthens considerably D'Ieteren's market share, the actual change brought about in the overall structure of supply in the market is very small indeed, given D'Ieteren's very limited share. Furthermore, D'Ieteren has indicated that it will be confronted with competition from a variety of competitors, including: (i) independent service providers who market as a single source and supply a network assistance of the type provided by PGSI/Belron, which between them enjoy some 5%–15% of the market, (ii) independent car dealerships who as a block account for some 25%–35%, and (iii) bodyshops and garages who make up the remaining 15%–25% or so of the market. The Commission's market investigation did not result in the expression of any significant concerns by the other players with regard to the competitive impact of the operation. In the circumstances and in the light of the factors mentioned above, i.e., the marginal change in market structure and the range of competitors, the Commission considers that the operation will not lead to the creation or strengthening of a dominant position in the repair and replacement of automotive glass in Belgium.

For the above reasons, the Commission has decided not to oppose the notified operation and to declare it compatible with the common market and the EEA Agreement.

Case Highlights

- Directorate IV of the European Commission is responsible for the enforcement of EU Competition Law.
- Before acquiring a European company, a foreign investor should *notify* (consult) with Directorate IV.
- Factors used to determine whether an acquisition or merger will create a *dominant position* (monopoly) subject to abuse include whether the acquisition has a community dimension, the relevant product markets, the geographic scope of the market, and the market shares of the companies.

Foreign Trade Zones

A foreign or free trade zone can minimize legal exposure in a foreign country. Foreign and domestic merchandise may enter the designated foreign trade zones without a formal customs entry. Therefore, importation and subsequent reexportation are not subject to customs duties or excise taxes. While in the trade zone, the merchandise may be:

http://
Directorate IV of the European Commission regarding EU competition law: **http://europa.eu.int/comm/competition.**

- Stored
- Sampled
- Relabeled
- Repaired
- Assembled
- Processed
- Tested
- Displayed
- Repackaged
- Cleaned
- Manufactured
- Mixed

If the final product is exported, no customs duty or excise tax is levied. If the final product is imported into the country, then customs duties and excise taxes are due at the *time of transfer* from the foreign trade zone and formal entry into the country. The fact that duties are due only at the time merchandise is transferred out of the trade zone can be used by foreign exporters to improve their cash flow by shortening the time between paying customs duties and receiving income from the sale of goods. A foreign exporter may ship unsold goods into a trade zone for storage purposes without incurring the costs of duties or formal entry. The goods may be transshipped without penalty or prospective buyers can inspect goods and rejected goods can be transferred out or destroyed duty-free. Foreign free trade zones are found in many countries in the world and conform to the free trade principles of GATT.

International Taxation

No matter what vehicle is chosen to transact foreign business operations, the foreign investor is subject to the tax ramifications of doing business across national borders. International taxation is one of the most complicated issues of doing business internationally, because taxation is dealt with differently among the countries of the world. In the United States, for example, citizens or resident aliens must pay federal income tax on their worldwide income. International tax treaties and federal statutes grant certain exemptions, deductions, and credits in order to protect against being double-taxed by two countries.

In the United States, nonresident aliens are taxed only on their U.S. source business income—a nonresident alien providing services within the United States for either a foreign or U.S. employer must pay U.S. income tax on wages or compensation received for services. However, nonresident aliens are exempt from paying income tax in the United States if their: (1) stay in the United States does not exceed 90 days in any one taxable year, (2) compensation does not exceed $3,000 (or $10,000 for Canadian residents), and (3) the services are performed for a foreign employer not currently engaged in business in the United States. In contrast, resident aliens in the United States are taxed the same as U.S. citizens on their worldwide income.

JOINT VENTURES AND FRANCHISING

An international joint venture or franchising arrangement is attractive for a number of reasons.[10] First, it allows a party to utilize the partner's or franchisee's local expertise, marketing skills, and established lines of distribution. Joint ventures and franchises are well suited for entry into a foreign market through the use of a host country national familiar with the local language, law, and culture. Second, a joint venture or franchise may provide a means to avoid host country protectionist trade requirements. Joint ventures, for example, are used to provide technology to a foreign partner who has production facilities and access to the local market.

Joint Ventures

International joint ventures are used in a wide variety of manufacturing, mining, and service industries and are frequently undertaken in conjunction with technology licensing by the U.S. firm to the joint venture. The host country may require that a certain percentage, often 51 percent, of manufacturing or mining operations be owned by nationals of that country, thereby obligating U.S. firms to operate through joint ventures. In addition, U.S. firms may find it desirable to enter into a joint venture with a foreign firm in order to spread the high costs and risks frequently associated with foreign operations. Moreover, the local partner may bring to the joint venture its knowledge of the customs and tastes of the people, an established distribution network, and valuable business and political contacts. Having local partners also decreases the foreign status of the firm and may provide some protection against discrimination or expropriation, should conditions change.

10. See generally Karen J. Hladik, *International Joint Ventures* (1985); Robert Radway, "Overview of Foreign Joint Ventures," 38 *Business Lawyer* 1040 (1983); Susan Goldenberg, *Hands Across the Ocean: Managing Joint Ventures with a Spotlight on China & Japan* (1988).

There are, of course, possible disadvantages to international joint ventures. A major potential drawback to joint ventures, especially in countries that limit foreign companies to 49 percent or less participation, is the loss of effective managerial control. A loss of effective managerial control can result in reduced profits, increased operating costs, inferior product quality, and exposure to product liability and environmental litigation and fines. U.S. firms that wish to retain effective managerial control will incorporate this issue in negotiations with the prospective joint venture partner and frequently the host government.

Like technology licensing agreements, joint ventures can raise U.S. or foreign antitrust issues in certain circumstances, particularly when the prospective joint venture partners are major existing or potential competitors in the affected national markets. Firms may wish to consider applying for an **export trade certificate of review** from the Department of Commerce or a **business review letter** from the Department of Justice when significant federal antitrust issues are raised by the proposed international joint venture.

U.S. firms contemplating international joint ventures should also consider retaining experienced legal counsel in the host country. It may be disadvantageous for a U.S. firm to rely upon its potential joint venture partner to negotiate approvals and advise on legal issues, since its prospective partner's interests may not always coincide with its own. Qualified foreign counsel can be very helpful in obtaining government approvals and providing ongoing advice regarding the host country's patent, trademark, copyright, tax, labor, corporate, commercial, antitrust, and exchange control laws.[11]

THE JOINT VENTURE AGREEMENT

A simple definition of joint venture[12] is "a contract that creates a partnership for the purpose of performing some kind of business operation."[13] It is a business collaboration in which the joint venture participants share resources, risks, and profits. Joint ventures often involve joint management and are established for a specific objective and sometimes for a fixed duration. In order for a joint venture to succeed, it must be carefully thought out and researched by all the prospective partners. "Feasibility studies are undertaken, confidential information is exchanged, and huge amounts of money are committed,"[14] before parties enter a joint venture contract. The parties must move cautiously in order to gain the trust of other participants; the parties' capacities, motives, prior relationships, and project objectives should be fully discussed during the preliminary stage of the negotiations.

A joint venture is an elastic vehicle for doing business and can take numerous forms. For example, the parties can enter into an agreement to work together in order to achieve certain business goals as joint venturers or they can agree to create an entirely separate entity, such as a corporation, in order to transact business. Two of the common uses of the joint venture in conducting international business

11. See generally National Trade Data Bank, a product of STAT-USA, U.S. Department of Commerce.
12. The term *joint venture* is not legally defined in many foreign legal systems (one important exception is the European Union, which has adopted rules for joint ventures). Therefore, there is often no foreign joint venture law. It is important to research foreign law to familiarize oneself with the forms of doing business recognized under the national law that can be utilized to approximate the joint venture concept.
13. William F. Fox, Jr., *International Commercial Agreements: A Primer on Drafting, Negotiating and Resolving Disputes* 79 (1992).
14. Denis Philippe, "Drawing Up a Joint Venture Contract," 20 *The Comparative Law Yearbook of International Business* 25, 27 (1998).

are the single project and business alliance joint ventures.[15] The single project venture exists when a number of parties or companies agree to enter into a partnership in order to develop specific business opportunities with a single, identifiable goal. These single project joint ventures generally have a relatively short life span. An example would be a joint venture for a single construction project. The business alliance venture envisions a more fluid, long-term business relationship.

Under U.S. law, a joint venture is generally considered a general partnership. The core issues in the partnership agreement include the scope of the business enterprise, the capitalization of the venture, the organization and management of the venture, and the termination of the business. A major concern in most joint venture agreements is providing the mechanisms for decision-making. The joint venturers may disagree on how best to deal with post-formation events. It is important, especially in the long-term joint venture agreement, to provide a mechanism to prevent decisional deadlock.

In negotiating and structuring joint ventures, proper attention should be given to the issues of share allocation, financing the enterprise, protecting minority interests, confidentiality, and the transfer and continuation of the business.[16] Shares may be allocated based upon each party's contribution, or joint venturers may authorize different classes or types of shares in order to attract other investors such as venture capitalists. Funding decisions have a direct impact on the location of profits for tax purposes.[17] Investors may structure their contributions as either equity contributions or loans and should give full consideration to all accounting and tax ramifications. For example, one would like to avoid the European Union's 1 percent duty on company capital.

The **purpose clause,** which maps the scope and goals of the business enterprise, is crucial for maintaining the long-term viability of the joint venture arrangement.[18] Scope should be defined along three parameters: geography, products and services, and duration. A careful balance must be struck between a clause that is precise but restricts future expansion and one that allows the venture to develop in different directions, since an overly specific statement of the venture's purpose can lead to an undesirable termination. This can be accomplished by a specific purpose clause coupled with an **exceptions clause** that allows for adjustments to the purpose clause along prescribed parameters. An alternative provision would allow for a periodic review of the purpose clause with a renegotiation requirement.

Joint venturers must also establish the initial level of capitalization, including the amount and form of currency to be invested by each partner and a method for adjusting foreign currency differences. If noncurrency contributions are contemplated, the agreement should specify a valuation method. Also, the parties should expressly agree to the adoption of accounting standards such as United States or European Union accounting standards and practices. The agreement should also specify the level and type of indebtedness the venture is authorized to undertake. Establishing an acceptable debt-to-equity ratio for the venture is prudent.

A successful joint venture agreement will provide the means to make future funding decisions. The most likely cause of joint venture failure is the parties' disagreement regarding future capital infusions. If external funding is likely to be

15. See Mark Pery-Knox-Gore, *Joint Ventures* in *Structuring International Contracts* 87 (ed. Dennis Campbell 1997).
16. See generally Hooton, "Structuring and Negotiating Joint Ventures," 27 *Creighton Law Review* 1013 (1994).
17. See Dolan, "Special Issues in Structuring International Joint Ventures," 22 *Tax Management Int'l Journal* 51 (1993).
18. A number of valuable suggestions for those considering a joint venture contract may be found in Steven R. Salbu & Richard A. Brahm, "Strategic Considerations in Designing Joint Venture Contracts," *Columbia Business Law Review* 253 (1992).

sought in the future, an agreement is needed as to whether the joint venture partners will provide guarantees in order to procure external financing. The joint venture agreement should also have a **counter-indemnity clause** in which the joint venture partners agree to be responsible on multiple-party guarantees only to the proportion of their shareholdings.

If the joint venture is between numerous parties, then provisions to protect minority interests may be necessary. One way to protect minority interests is to categorize decisions as "ordinary" or "extraordinary." Extraordinary decisions would require a supermajority vote for approval; for example, a two-thirds or 75 percent vote would be required to approve extraordinary decisions. Extraordinary decisions could include:

- capital expenditures in excess of a certain amount
- borrowings in excess of a certain amount
- increasing of share capital
- issuance of new stock or admittance of a new joint venture partner
- giving guarantees; appointment or removal of directors
- setting employee remuneration above a certain level
- material changes in the business operation or nature of the business
- sale or transfer of assets
- making contracts with principals of the joint venture
- approval of budgets

In case of a deadlock regarding an important decision, a party may be offered the right to leave the joint venture; a provision should address the transfer or sale of ownership to the other partners. Share price should be fair, to be determined by an independent accounting firm. The shares being sold should be offered to all remaining partners in proportion to their existing ownership interests. The agreement should also provide whether, in the event of termination, the joint venture partners have the right to continue in the same business after the termination.

Strict confidentiality and noncompetition provisions are also necessary. The partners may be prohibited from competing with the joint venture by stipulations that include being unable to hire employees of the joint venture for a period of time, maintaining the secrecy of all confidential information, and not soliciting customers of the joint venture. Of course, these restrictions must be reasonable or may be subject to challenge as illegal restraints of trade under U.S. common law or the European Union's Competition Law pertaining to ancillary restrictions.

Another crucial set of provisions to ensure the ongoing viability of the venture is the management provisions. *Double parenting* is a pervasive problem in which both joint venturers attempt to assert independent control over the joint venture. The degree of managerial control to be placed with the different joint venturers should be carefully delineated in the agreement. Will the owner of the greater share have greater managerial control? Will a local minority partner be allowed a degree of control greatly exceeding its proportional ownership? Other issues that will need to be dealt with by management clauses include: (1) Should veto power be given to the partners, including minority partners, for particular classes of important decisions? (2) How will the selection of the top manager and management team be decided? (3) What reporting and information systems will be used to communicate between the joint venture and its owners?[19] Ultimately, these provisions

19. Salbu & Brahm, 292–294.

will reflect the essential nature of the joint venture as one controlled by a dominant parent or as one with a shared management structure.

Finally, the joint venture should have a detailed termination provision stating the events that allow the parties to terminate their involvement. The following list suggests the types of considerations that should be discussed in drafting a termination clause:[20]

(1) Failure of a participant to make required capital contributions
(2) Failure of a participant to obtain necessary government approvals
(3) Failure of the venture to reach a pre-agreed level of profitability
(4) Management deadlock
(5) Failure of one partner to purchase the shares of another (buy-sell agreement)
(6) An adverse and debilitating change in the law
(7) Bankruptcy or insolvency of one of the participants

The termination clause should also describe how unforeseeable or *force majeure* events will affect a termination of the joint venture.

ANCILLARY AGREEMENTS

The joint venture agreement is likely only one of a number of documents to be prepared for a well-planned joint venture undertaking. Other documentation commonly used includes a formal business plan, distribution agreement, intellectual property transfer or licensing agreement, management agreement, service contracts, and secondment agreements. A carefully written **business plan** is vital to maintaining cordial relationships among the joint venture partners. It should be sufficiently long-term in nature, set realistic revenue and profit goals, and provide for a "cushion" in capital and time in meeting the plan's objectives. The business plan should include other necessary studies such as a long-term strategic plan and a marketing plan.

Secondment agreements are used to require the "lending" of employees of the joint venture partners to the joint venture. It is important to determine whether these employees are to be treated as independent contractors or employees of the joint venture. From the point of view of the joint venture, treatment as independent contractors is preferred. The joint venture partner would then remain primarily obligated to the employees being lent. Service contracts between the partners and their joint venture could also be utilized in the management of the joint venture enterprise.

Sometimes, one of the joint venture partners is given the formal responsibility to manage the joint venture. In that case, the managing partner should enter into a formal management agreement with the joint venture. The management agreement, among other things, should outline the allocation of costs between the partner's core business and the joint venture business. Often one of the contributions of a joint venture partner is its expertise in its home country regarding the distribution of goods or services. An express **distribution agreement** should be entered into between that partner and the joint venture. The distribution agreement's termination provisions should be tied to those in the joint venture agreement. This may be important if the distributor is removed as a joint venture partner.

International joint ventures may include the use of the know-how or intellectual property rights of one of the joint venture partners. In such a situation, an

20. Taken from William G. Frenkel, "Legal Protection against Risks Involved in Doing Business in the Republics of the Former U.S.S.R.," 10 *International Quarterly* 395, 467 (1998).

Doing Business Internationally

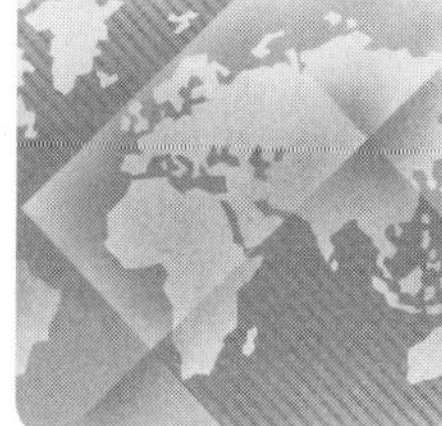

Joint Ventures and Licensing in Indonesia[21]

Since 1994 the government has removed most requirements for domestic equity and joint ventures. Foreign investors who opt for 100 percent initial ownership are obligated to divest to Indonesians some share—as little as 1 percent—after 15 years. This can be accomplished through the stock market. As a practical matter a local joint venture partner is often essential for success in this market, for the same reason that an Indonesian agent or distributor has advantages over a foreign trade representative office. The choice of an Indonesian joint venture partner is critical for many reasons, especially for knowledge of the local scene and contacts, which are important for successful operations. A partnership in Indonesia is difficult to dissolve, however, so the first choice has to be the correct choice. Business sense is crucial to any commercial endeavor and contacts in Indonesia, while important, cannot substitute for business skills in a local partner. Because Indonesians place great importance on personal relationships and mutual understanding, partnerships tend to be based primarily on genuine accord, with the written contract playing a less significant role. It is therefore important that any agreement be well understood by both sides. A contract over which there are conflicting interpretations is certain to cause future problems.

independently negotiated **intellectual property transfer** or licensing agreement is necessary and should deal with the withdrawal of the licensor-partner. A name change of the joint venture may be required if the existing name is associated with the intellectual property of the withdrawing partner. The licensor-partner may demand a provision that makes the licensing of intellectual property rights "coterminous with the licensor's involvement in the joint venture."[22]

FOREIGN GOVERNMENT REGULATION

Foreign governments commonly regulate joint venture transactions. The most common restrictions are foreign participation requirements in which control of the enterprise must vest in a local company. The trend, however, has been toward a liberalization of such participation requirements. The above Doing Business Internationally feature summarizes the practice and law of joint venturing in Indonesia. Note that it is now possible for a foreign investor to obtain almost total ownership of a Indonesian joint venture.

More unique types of government regulations can be found on a country-by-country basis. For example, the People's Republic of China enacted Regulations on Labor Management in Joint Ventures Using Chinese and Foreign Investment. It requires that a labor contract, approved by the Chinese government, be entered into between the joint venture and a trade union. It further provides that all workers of the joint venture "shall be selected for employment through examinations conducted by the joint venture." The joint venture's ability to discharge employees is also restricted. "Punishment by discharge must be reported to the department in charge of enterprises and the labor management department for approval."

http://

World Trade Organization links to foreign investment laws: **http://www.wto.org**.

21. U.S. State Department's Country Commercial Guide for Indonesia.
22. Pery-Knox-Gore at 99.

Doing Business Internationally

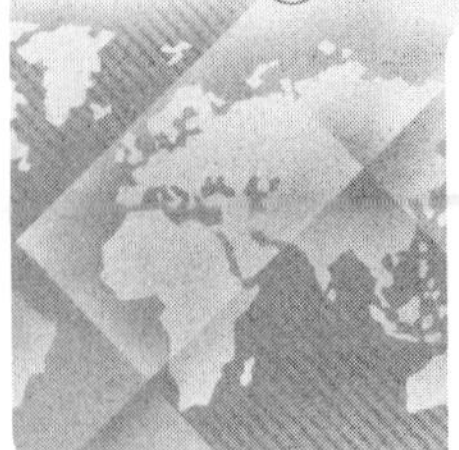

Approval and Establishment of a Joint Venture in China

Step 1
Signing of Cooperative Joint Venture Contract

Step 2
Submission of Joint Venture Contract and Articles of Association to the "Examination and Approval Authority" (as designated by the State Council) [Approval Authority must render a decision within 45 days]

Step 3
Application for Registration (to appropriate industry and commerce agency) [Within 30 days of receipt of approval certificate from Approval Authority]

Step 4
Receipt of Business License (date of establishment)

Step 5
Register Venture with appropriate tax authority

Step 6
Post-Establishment Concerns
Any changes in the joint venture contract must be submitted to the Approval Authority. Any transfers of rights and obligations under the cooperative joint venture contract must be approved by the Approval Authority.

Any changes in the management and operation of the joint venture (to a party not an original partner) must be by unanimous vote of the board of directors and with the approval of the Approval Authority.

Record-keeping and certifications must be verified by an accountant registered in China. The joint venture must establish and support a labor union to represent its employees.

Open a foreign exchange account.

http://

PRC Cooperative Joint Venture Law, amended in 2000: **http://www.chinalegalchange.com**.

http://

http://www.jus.uio.no/lm/china.laws/index.html gives texts of the commercial laws of the People's Republic of China including trade law, labor law, company law, and "foreign contract law."

China's more generic law on joint ventures, the Law of the People's Republic of China on Chinese-Foreign Cooperative Joint Ventures, was promulgated on April 13, 1988. It should be carefully reviewed before beginning any negotiations. It provides that the parties should agree in a *cooperative venture contract* on the terms and conditions of cooperation, the distributions of earnings or products, the sharing of risks and losses, the form of operation and management, and the ownership of property. All such contracts need to be approved by the relevant "Examination and Approval Authority."

The list in Doing Business Internationally above demonstrates that governmental regulation is pervasive in the establishment and operation of a joint venture in China. The cooperative joint venture law is merely a framework or enabling statute; detailed regulations must be consulted before establishing a joint venture. Also, ancillary laws must be reviewed in conjunction with the operation of the joint venture. Article 13 of the Chinese law states that "matters such as employment, discharge, remuneration, welfare, labor protection, and labor insurance should be stipulated through the making of contracts in accordance with the law." In fact, a foreign investor is required to enter into a labor contract as a condition for joint venture approval. The labor contract must be submitted to the municipal or provincial government for approval. Furthermore, the labor-management relationship is regulated throughout the term of employment. Most workers are hired from a pool of workers provided by the local government labor department. They are to be selected for employment through an approved examination. Finally, any discharge of an employee must be reported to the labor management department for approval. When contemplating a joint venture in China it is good practice to obtain copies of form contracts (available in English) used by Chinese enterprises and to consult with the Chinese Ministry of Foreign and Economic Relations and Trade (MOFERT) created in 1982 to expedite foreign trade contracts.

Franchising

Though franchising is an attractive arrangement, it does pose some problems. Franchising is a uniquely U.S. form of doing business. Franchising is allowed in most countries of the world, but many foreign laws do not expressly recognize the franchise form of business. For example, even though franchises have been registered in Germany, franchising itself has not been explicitly codified in German law, so other more general bodies of law, such as licensing or partnership law, are used by analogy to regulate the franchise relationship. In Germany, franchises are regulated through application of German commercial, trademark, competition, and consumer credit law.

Since the franchise is not expressly recognized in some countries, imposing exclusive franchise territories is susceptible to attack under foreign competition or antitrust laws. In Europe, an EU **block exemption** that provides a general exemption from the ban on cartels for franchise arrangements has alleviated the problem. The EU block exemption has resulted in the franchise industry in Europe being primarily self-regulated. The European Franchise Federation acts as an umbrella organization for the different national franchise associations, guiding those promoting franchise operations. The European Franchise Federation has issued a code of ethics that should be reviewed by a foreign party intending to franchise in Europe. National franchise associations have also issued guidelines, such as the German Franchise Association's Pre-Contract Disclosure Requirements.

Before entering into a franchising contract with a foreign entity, it is important to thoroughly research the investment climate in the host country. For example, in Indonesia, franchising became a popular vehicle for foreign entry until the devaluation of the rupiah. "The depreciation of the rupiah has made virtually impossible the payment of franchise royalties in foreign exchange."[23] Aside from the convertibility issue, Indonesia places no major restrictions on the repatriation of profits and maintains no capital controls, and foreign exchange may flow freely in and out of the country. Foreign investors have the right to repatriate capital and profits at the prevailing rate of exchange.

The U.S. State Department's *Commercial Guide for Indonesia* summarizes the law pertaining to franchising as follows:

> *Although there is no specific law regulating franchising, the legal underpinnings for franchising are specified in article 1338 of the Indonesian Civil law (KUH Perdata—Kitab Undang Undang Hukum Perdata) which states that business persons are free to conclude contracts. Further legal grounding for franchising can be found in the 1992 law on trademarks No. 19, article 44-50.*

23. U.S. State Department Country Commercial Guide for Indonesia.

> *There are no widely accepted models for business contracts covering franchise agreements. However, the foreign principal usually provides the franchisee with his own standard contract format which is used as a basis for developing franchise agreements with the local business enterprise. The franchise agreement should be reviewed and notarized by a public notary in Indonesia in order to make it legally binding.*
>
> *Franchise agreements should be accompanied by other contractually binding arrangements such as loan agreements, site leases, building agreements, graphics, employee selection, standard description and promotion. Franchise agreements should also include a provision regarding the settlement of disputes through arbitration which may arise out of breach of contract or disagreements between the contracting parties.*

Because Indonesian law does not prescribe any specific form or registration requirements for franchise agreements, the foreign franchisor is free to use its own standard forms. The agreement must be reviewed and notarized in Indonesia to become legally binding.

The State Department Guide notes that joint venturing with an established Indonesian company is the preferred method of market entry. This means of market entry has been enhanced by recent developments. First, in 1994 the Indonesian government removed most local participation requirements. Second, a number of firms will provide background and credit checks on Indonesian firms. Third, an Indonesian company can provide the necessary knowledge and contacts with the local market. One drawback to establishing an Indonesian franchise relationship is the difficulty of dissolving a joint venture or franchise partnership under Indonesian law. Therefore, careful background research, prior dealings, and a clear, comprehensive agreement are necessary.

Other areas of interest for those contemplating franchising, licensing, or joint venturing in a foreign country include the protection of intellectual property rights, the use of a local attorney, transferability of ownership interests, and expropriation and dispute settlement polices. Intellectual property protection, for example, is wanting in Indonesia. "Because of this one U.S. company's strategy is to identify counterfeiters and then proceed to sign them as legal licensees of its products."[24] Nonetheless, it is important to register intellectual property as soon as possible and to challenge any unauthorized registrations. The Commercial Guide suggests acquiring a local partner as the best way to defend against the infringement of intellectual property rights.

As with the record for intellectual property protection, the Indonesian record for the enforcement of foreign arbitration awards is dismal. In the area of dispute resolution, Indonesia is a party to the New York Convention on the enforcement of foreign arbitration awards, but because an Indonesian court is more likely to enforce an award issued by an Indonesian arbitration panel, the Guide suggests an arbitration clause that designates Indonesia as the place of arbitration.[25] The transfer

24. U.S. State Department Country Commercial Guide for Indonesia.

25. "Because Indonesia's legal system is currently being overhauled and modernized, firms are strongly advised to locate and retain a local attorney early in the investment process. In the event of a commercial dispute, one should first attempt to reach consensus through negotiation, using a mediator acceptable to both parties if necessary. If deliberation fails to achieve consensus, then companies may enter into arbitration. To prepare for this eventuality, an arbitration clause should be included in any commercial contract with Indonesia chosen as the site of arbitration. This is recommended because foreign arbitral awards have proven difficult to enforce locally. Badan Arbitrase Nasional Indonesia (BANI) is the local arbitration board and companies may employ BANI or select their own arbitration vehicle and procedures (i.e., ICC or UNCITRAL)." U.S. Department of State, Country Commercial Guide for Indonesia (1999).

and expropriation polices of the Indonesian government are conducive to foreign entry. Foreign investors have the right to repatriate capital and profits and no permits are required to transfer foreign exchange.

FRANCHISE LAW

The advantage of franchising is aptly stated as its method for facilitating "the transfer of know-how and managerial expertise to the franchisee companies while simultaneously allowing the franchisor to quickly establish a presence in the country. Under a typical franchising agreement, the franchisor receives royalties and fees as stipulated in the contract. In exchange, the franchisee has the right to use (and manufacture) copyrighted, patented, or service-marked materials identifying the enterprise. The franchisor typically provides training and organizational guidance in return for a guarantee that the franchisee will follow these operational directions."[26]

The expertise of the franchisor is reflected in areas of the franchise contract including the opening and financing of the franchise, along with the means and content of advertisement. Contractual clauses pertaining to the franchisor's assistance in obtaining financing and opening the franchise should state specific obligations. In the area of advertisement, the clause should state the franchisor's control over the content and placement of advertisements. Also, it may mandate a minimum level of franchisee expenditures on advertisements.

http://

Franchise and distribution law—recent legal developments: **http://www.franchisedistriblaw.net.**

Some franchise agreements provide for a pool of funds contributed by franchisees that the franchisor then uses to place advertisements. The franchise agreement should detail how advertising monies are to be spent by the franchisor. The franchisees may request a clause allocating advertising monies between a national or international campaign and local advertisement. The *Broussard v. Meineke Muffler Shops* case involves a dispute over such an advertisement provision. It illustrates some of the nuances of U.S. franchise law and how courts are reluctant to pierce the limited liability protection that franchising offers to the franchisor.

The franchise relationship is a uniquely American creation. "Over half a million franchises operate in the United States, and they account for more than a third of the nation's total retail sales."[27] The United States has developed an extensive body of law regulating the franchise relationship: A large number of states

Broussard v. Meineke Discount Muffler Shops

155 F.3d 331 (4th Cir. 1998)

Wilkinson, Chief Judge. This case is a study in the tensions that can beset the franchisor-franchisee relationship. Ten owners of Meineke Discount Muffler franchises sued franchisor Meineke Discount Muffler Shops, Inc. ("Meineke"), Meineke's in-house advertising agency New Horizons Advertising, Inc. ("New Horizons"), three officers of Meineke, and Meineke's corporate parents GKN and GKN Parts Industries Corporation ("PIC"). Plaintiffs claimed that Meineke's handling of franchise advertising breached the Franchise and Trademark Agreements ("FTAs") that Meineke had entered into with every franchisee. Plaintiffs also advanced a raft of tort and statutory unfair trade practices claims arising out of the same conduct. Plaintiffs won a $390 million judgment against Meineke and its affiliated parties.

26. U.S. Department of State, Country Commercial Guide for Indonesia (1999)
27. Robert W. Emerson, "Franchise Contract Clauses and the Franchisor's Duty of Care Toward its Franchisees," 72 *North Carolina Law Review* 905, 909 (1994) (hereinafter "Franchise Contract Clauses").

Under all versions of the FTA, each franchisee was to pay Meineke an initial franchise fee and thereafter some percentage of its weekly gross revenue (generally 7%–8%) as a royalty. Franchisees also paid Meineke 10 percent of weekly revenues to fund national and local advertising. Initially, franchisees made these advertising contributions directly to a third-party advertising agency, M&N Advertising ("M&N"), which placed ads on a commission basis. In 1982, franchisees paid their 10 percent contributions to a central account maintained by Meineke, the Weekly Advertising Contribution ("WAC") account.

Franchise advertising is addressed in two sections of the FTAs. All versions of the FTA oblige Meineke "to purchase and place from time to time advertising promoting the products and services sold by FRANCHISEE." The FTAs provide that "all decisions regarding whether to utilize national, regional, or local advertising, or some combination thereof, and regarding selection of the particular media and advertising content, shall be within the sole discretion of MEINEKE and such agencies or others as it may appoint." Three categories of disbursements from the WAC account, totaling approximately $32.2 million, are at the heart of this lawsuit. At a dealers' meeting in April 1993, a Meineke official read from a December 1992 Uniform Franchise Offering Circular ("UFOC") that disclosed New Horizons' 5%–15% commission rates. Plaintiffs knew before the meeting that New Horizons took commissions from WAC funds but claim they were unaware that its rates were so high.

The jury returned a verdict against Meineke for breach of contract and against Meineke and New Horizons for breach of fiduciary duty, negligence, and unjust enrichment. The jury found that GKN and PIC had utilized Meineke and New Horizons as mere instrumentalities, and that PIC was merely an instrumentality of GKN, which justified piercing the corporate veil and imposing vicarious liability on GKN. Along with Meineke and New Horizons, GKN, PIC, and three officers of Meineke were found to have committed fraud, and of making negligent misrepresentations. The jury awarded plaintiffs $196 million in compensatory damages, which, over Meineke's objection, was not allocated among the various theories of liability or among defendants. The jury awarded a total of $150 million in punitive damages: $70 million against Meineke; $7 million against New Horizons; $1.8 million against PIC; $70 million against GKN; and $1.2 million total against the three Meineke officers.

The district court erred by allowing plaintiffs to advance their claims for breach of fiduciary duty when there is no indication that North Carolina law would recognize the existence of a fiduciary relationship between franchisee and franchisor. "Rather," in North Carolina "parties to a contract do not thereby become each others' fiduciaries; they generally owe no special duty to one another beyond the terms of the contract and the duties set forth in the U.C.C." Though plaintiffs would portray franchisees as helpless Davids to the franchisor's Goliath, size, as that story teaches, is not a reliable indicator of strength or influence. Our hesitation is strengthened by the refusal of courts in many other jurisdictions to superimpose fiduciary duties on a franchisor-franchisee relationship.

Furthermore, shareholders who take an active interest in the affairs of the corporation are "non-outsiders" and thus protected from tortious interference claims by the same qualified privilege that protects directors and officers of the corporation. And if those shareholders do not completely dominate the affairs of the corporation, the corporate veil will not be pierced and they will be shielded from vicarious liability. Setting up such a safe harbor preserves the advantages of limited liability while encouraging shareholders to actively monitor corporate affairs.

REVERSED AND REMANDED

Case Highlights

- The franchise arrangement is contractual in nature, however, U.S. regulations require certain disclosures through a Uniform Franchise Offering Circular (UFOC)
- Because of the contractual nature of the franchise arrangement, the franchisor does not owe a fiduciary duty to its franchisees
- Note the size of the punitive damages component of the jury award. Punitive damages are unique to American law and are not found in foreign legal systems.
- Note also that the corporate veil will only be pierced to hold shareholders or a parent corporation vicariously liable when the shareholders or parent exercises complete *domination* over the corporation or its subsidiary, or if they fail to observe corporate formalities

regulate the offer and sale of franchises; Many state laws require franchisors to register a detailed offering before being able to solicit franchisees; Some statutes provide the franchisee with a right to cure any of its defaults under the franchise agreement and grant a minimum notice period prior to termination by the franchisor. The popularity of franchising in the United States, along with this increased governmental regulation, has produced a number of franchise clauses that are commonly used and recognized in the franchise industry. The next section will review some of the clauses commonly found in the franchise agreement.

THE FRANCHISE AGREEMENT

The following commonly used clauses place various obligations upon the franchisor and the franchisee. These clauses should be completely understood when negotiating a franchise agreement. A **site selection clause** delineates the franchisor's responsibilities in the site selection process. Such clauses range from placing an affirmative duty on the franchisor to find an appropriate site to simply requiring the franchisor's approval. An approval clause should state the criteria for the franchisor's disapproval of a site. In *Brennan v. Carvel Corp.*[28] the court went outside the boundaries of the franchise site selection clause in finding that the franchisor had failed to meet its obligations in the site selection process. The court found the franchisor's Deposit Agreement stated that the franchisor would expend a "substantial amount of time and effort in seeking, surveying, and showing locations available for a store." This case illustrates the importance in reviewing all franchise documentation for consistency. A merger clause in the final franchise agreement is unlikely to prevent courts from reviewing preliminary agreements, ancillary agreements, promotional materials, and governmental filings for purposes of clarification or to substantiate a claim of misrepresentation.

Physical layout and signage, along with operational standards, are important areas of control for the franchisor. Clauses relating to these matters are essential to maintain system-wide integrity and uniformity of standards. Most retail franchises utilize layouts that maintain the uniformity of appearance at all franchise locations. "The design or display *package* may be in conjunction with the trademarks and service marks provided by the franchisor or as part of the advertising controls."[29] Failure of the franchisee to adhere to these and other operational standards generally provides the franchisor with good cause for termination of the franchise operation. Most layout clauses give the franchisor the absolute right of approval.

An **operational standards clause** provides a detailed description of quality standards and operational goals. It generally refers to an operating manual provided by the franchisor. In order to defend a decision to terminate, the franchisor should ensure that the franchise agreement has a clear notice provision and provides for a reasonable period of time to cure deficiencies. An associated concern is the training of the franchisee and its employees, since training and consultation provided by the franchisor are the heart of many franchise arrangements. Key employees of the franchisee are trained in all facets of the business. Consultation involves dealing with problems that occur from time to time. A franchisor's failure to provide adequate training and consultation under these clauses would be grounds for a lawsuit by the franchisee.

28. 929 F.2d 801 (S.D.Fla. 1992).
29. Emerson, "Franchise Contract Clauses," at 938, n. 143.

Most franchise systems are premised on uniform treatment between the franchisor and all its franchisees. However, franchisors sometimes incorporate a clause in their franchise agreements that allow them to vary contractual terms among their different franchisees. Such clauses have been grounds for claims of discriminatory treatment. Other common clauses include those on territorial exclusivity and protection, noncompetition, transfers and assignments, terminations and nonrenewals, and those pertaining to pricing, purchase of supplies, hours of operation, franchisor's rights of inspection, and audits. **Territorial clauses** grant the franchisee an exclusive territory within which the franchisor is barred from competing. The problem with such clauses is that the franchisor and franchisee may disagree regarding the scope of expansion of franchise operations within the territory. An alternative is to give the franchisee a period of time to fully develop the franchise territory. After the expiration of that time, the franchisor is then allowed to further develop the territorial market. The franchisee is protected somewhat by being granted a right of first refusal for any new locations within the territory.

The termination of the franchise by the franchisor, either for cause or nonrenewal, is the action most likely to lead to litigation. Most franchise agreements contain a clause that allows the franchisor to terminate for any violation, but termination for a minor breach will not be viewed favorably by most courts. Likewise, the **renewal clause** often provides an absolute right of the franchisor not to renew. Instead of absolute rights to terminate or not to renew, termination or nonrenewal clauses should specify the violations that are considered material for termination and grounds for nonrenewal. Appropriate grounds for termination or nonrenewal include the loss of a lease, failure to operate the business, franchisee insolvency, denial of franchisor access to inspect, and repeated violations of quality standards.[30] Internationally, termination without good cause or without a reasonable period to correct deficiencies will be vulnerable to legal challenge. In the United States, a number of state statutes require good cause for the termination of franchises.[31]

Other provisions deal with the mechanics of the franchise relationship. Foremost is the franchise fee or **royalties clause.** The franchise agreement commonly requires that an initial fee be paid for the right to obtain a franchise and then payment of royalties based upon a percentage of gross or net sales. The agreement should provide a commencement and expiration date. One common means of fixing the dates is to provide for expiration a certain number of years from commencement, the date the franchise opens for business. Since most franchise arrangements include the transfer of intellectual property rights, the agreement should expressly retain the title to those rights to the franchisor. The following Comparative Law feature illustrates a franchise clause dealing with the transfer of trade secrets and intellectual property. The clause makes clear that that the franchisor owns the intellectual property being licensed and that on the franchise's termination all of the property rights return to the franchisor.

The final two clauses to be discussed are the insurance and the franchisee review clauses. It is prudent for the franchisor, especially in the international setting, to require the franchisee to maintain certain types and amounts of insurance. The franchisee can be required to carry specific amounts of comprehensive general liability and products liability insurance. The contract should provide that the fran-

30. See Dayan v. McDonald's Corp., 466 N.E.2d 958 (Ill. 1984).

31. See Robert W. Emerson, "Franchising and the Collective Rights of Franchisees," 43 Vanderbilt Law Review 1503, 1511, n. 27 (1990).

Comparative Law

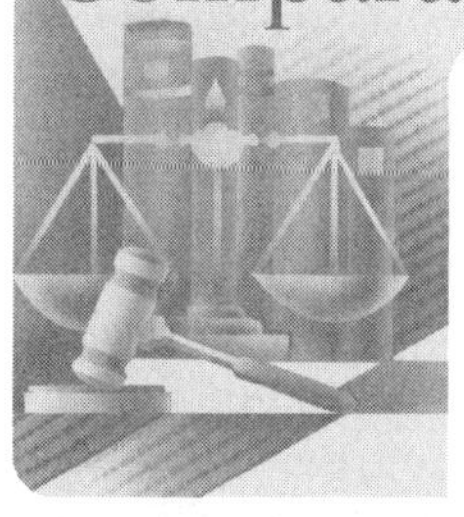

Intellectual Property Transfer Clause

FRANCHISEE acknowledges that ownership of all right, title, and interest to the ABC franchise system and its marks are and shall remain vested solely in the franchisor, and the FRANCHISEE disclaims any right or interest therein or the goodwill derived therefrom. FRANCHISEE agrees that all materials loaned or otherwise made available to him by the franchisor at any time before or during the term of this Agreement relating to the franchise system, including, without limitation, the Manual in its entirety, financial information, marketing strategy, and programs are to be considered trade secrets of the franchisor and shall be kept confidential and used by FRANCHISEE only in connection with the franchise operation. FRANCHISEE agrees not to divulge any of the trade secrets to any person other than its employees and then only to the extent necessary for the operation of the franchise and, specifically, that FRANCHISEE will not, nor permit anyone to, reproduce, copy, or exhibit any portion of the Manual or any other trade secrets of the franchisor. FRANCHISEE shall immediately notify franchisor of all infringements or limitations of franchisor's marks which come to its attention.[32]

chisor should be an "additional endorsee" on all such policies. The **insurance clause** should be coupled with a hold harmless clause that requires the franchisee to defend the franchisor against any liability claims arising from or related to its operation of the franchise.

The **franchisee review clause** is used to combat future claims of misrepresentation or overbearing by the franchisor. They generally incorporate a number of provisos including "a statement that the franchisee has received no guarantees, representations, warranties or the like as to the profitability of the franchise being purchased and that the franchise has conducted its own independent investigation of the merits of the investment."[33] Another clause vital to the franchisor's defense against misrepresentation is the merger clause. The merger clause attempts to prevent the entry of any parol evidence in a subsequent adversarial proceeding. The role of parol evidence in contract disputes will be discussed in Chapter 7, International Contract Law, and Chapter 8, International Sales Law.

UNIDROIT GUIDE TO INTERNATIONAL MASTER FRANCHISING

One way to avoid entering multiple franchise agreements with individual franchisees in a foreign country is the **master franchise** arrangement. In the master franchise arrangement, the franchisor enters into an agreement with a subfranchisor or master franchisee in order to develop an entire franchise territory. The subfranchisor is entitled to establish individual franchise locations or to find subfranchisees to operate within its territory. The contractual relationship may run between the subfranchisee and the subfranchisor or, most commonly, between the subfranchisee and the franchisor. In fact, master franchise agreements are defined in the EU Franchise Regulations as those in which "the relationship between

32. Emerson, "Franchise Contract Clauses" at 958.
33. Ibid.

franchisor and franchisees is made through a third undertaking, the master franchisee." In this way the franchisor can directly exercise control over the individual franchise operations.

http://
UNIDROIT:
http://www.unidroit.org.

The International Institute for the Unification of Private Law (UNIDROIT) has published an elaborate document titled *UNIDROIT Guide to International Master Franchise Arrangements.* It provides an array of information, along with standard clauses to be used in the drafting of a master franchise contract. The approach of the publication is to provide clauses that are fair to all parties concerned and are based on best practices. Some of the issues addressed include the types of franchising arrangements available, the relationship between the franchising agreement and other types of agreements (commercial agency, license, technology transfer, distribution), and the differences in the franchisor-franchisee and subfranchisor-subfranchisee relationships. The contract issues discussed include the nature and extent of the rights granted (e.g., exclusivity of rights granted to subfranchisor); duration of agreement and provisions for renewal; alternative fee structures; calculation of payments (timing, accounting, currency, tax issues); costs and control of advertising; supply of equipment, products, and services; the transfer and protection of intellectual property (confidentiality clauses, noncompetition clauses, grant-back clauses, post-termination clauses); assignment and transfer; indemnification and insurance (franchisor liability to third parties); remedies for breach; and termination.

International Franchising

European Union regulations define franchising as "a gathering of industrial or intellectual property rights relative to trademark, commercial denominations, insignia, utility models, designs, copyrights, know-how, or patents to be utilized for the resale of goods or services to a final user."[34] Under this definition, the franchisor sells to the franchisee the right to exploit a franchise and to commercialize specific goods or services. The franchise agreement generally requires a common and uniform presentation of franchise operations, the transfer of expertise and know-how from the franchisor to the franchisee, and the supplying of technical assistance by the franchisor. Principles recognized under U.S. franchise law do not always translate well into other legal systems, however.[35] For example, the U.S. State Department's Country Commercial Guide for Russia downplays the use of franchising as a viable option in entering the Russian market: "Franchising is little understood in Russia. Several early attempts to establish franchise distribution have foundered, due to confusion regarding ownership and the responsibilities of the parties to a franchise agreement." However, the Guide qualifies the previous statement by noting that "some have been quite successful, and the potential remains quite high." The court in *McAlpine v. AAMCO Automatic Transmission, Inc.* described the synergy of franchising and the inherent seeds for its own destruction:

http://
International Franchise Federation:
http://www.franchise.org.

> *The franchise arrangement starts as a mutually advantageous business relationship. Both the franchisor and the franchisee contribute to this arrangement in order to obtain benefits they could not obtain independently. The franchisor's contribution is a combination of factors: trademark, recognized product or service, experience, advertising, and management support. The franchisee's contribution is capital, day-to-day management and the payment of franchise fees. The franchisor benefits from the use*

34. Regulation EEC 4087/88.
35. See generally Avner, "Franchising in Eastern Europe and the Soviet Union," 3 *DePaul Business Law Journal* 307 (1991).

of franchisee capital, fees, and lower-level management, for it allows the franchise organization to expand more rapidly. As the franchise becomes successful, the partnership arrangement which seemed reasonable at its inception begins to appear burdensome to the franchisee who comes to regard the payment of franchise fees as restricting its profitability.[36]

To further illustrate the point, the *Dayan v. McDonald's Corp.* case exemplifies the two major risks of international franchising, namely, loss of control over franchise operations and the inability to terminate the franchise relationship.

Raymond Dayan v. McDonald's Corp.

466 N.E.2d 958 (Ill. App.1984)

This appeal arises out of a suit brought to enjoin McDonald's Corporation from terminating Raymond Dayan's restaurant franchise in Paris, France. Other issues relating to this controversy have been considered twice before by this court. After a 65-day trial, the circuit court of Cook County denied plaintiff's request for a permanent injunction. The trial court issued a 114-page memorandum and an order terminating plaintiff's franchise to operate McDonald's restaurants in and around Paris.

This case has a lengthy legal and historical background involving prior litigation. Dayan originally filed an action against McDonald's in 1970 alleging the defendant corporation had breached a prior agreement giving Dayan the right to purchase certain franchises and to develop and operate certain restaurants in Paris. The unique character of the 1971 license agreement was a key factor at trial. The record reveals that the terms of this agreement were the subject of extensive negotiations between McDonald's and Dayan and differed substantially from McDonald's standard licensing agreement. McDonald's submitted three alternate proposals to Dayan. Proposal 1 was McDonald's standard license agreement with a 3% royalty fee on gross receipts, real estate to be bought and developed by McDonald's with rental rates comparable to U.S.A. leases. Proposal 2 was a joint venture with McDonald's and Dayan each owning 50% equity. Proposal 3 was a developmental license similar to the original Canadian franchises and provided for a 1% royalty fee, Dayan to develop his own real estate, and no McDonald's service except as ordered and paid for by Dayan. Under the standard McDonald's license embodied in proposal 1, McDonald's would be obligated to provide extensive services to Dayan in all areas of restaurant operations and Dayan would pay a correspondingly higher royalty fee. Dayan insisted upon the 1% developmental license.

The necessity of maintaining the Quality, Safety, and Cleanliness (QSC) standards is explicitly recognized in the Master License Agreement (MLA). It recites the rationale for maintaining QSC standards—"departure of Restaurants anywhere in the world from these standards impedes the successful operation of Restaurants throughout the world, and injures the value of its [McDonald's] Patents, Trademarks, Trade name, and Property." In addition, the individual operating license agreements (OLA) included the following termination provision:

Licensee acknowledges that uniform quality and taste of food, excellence of service, cleanliness, appearance, and general performance are of the utmost importance to the successful operation of the business venture of the Licensee and of all other Licensees using said System. The Licensee agrees that any violation of this paragraph shall be deemed to be a substantial breach of this Agreement and shall give the Licensor the right to terminate this Agreement.

Witnesses called by McDonald's testified as to the deplorable condition of Dayan's restaurants. In particular, their testimony revealed that Dayan was not using approved products; he used no pickles; he charged extra for catsup or mustard; he hid straws and napkins under the counter; he refused to take a refresher course at McDonald's "Hamburger University;" the stores were filthy and without many items of necessary equipment; the store crews were poorly trained and frequently out of uniform, and customer complaints were numerous. Barnes, the president of McDonald's international division, testified that in June 1976 he informed Dayan that he would be given six months to bring his restaurants up to standard and at the end of this period McDonald's would exercise its right to formal inspection. The inspectors found gross violations of McDonald's QSC standards

36. 461 F. Supp. 1232, 1238-39 (E.D. Mich. 1978).

at all the stores they visited. In July 1977, a stern warning letter was sent to Dayan advising him that the number, variety, and severity of QSC deficiencies justified a default declaration but that such declaration would be held in abeyance for six months to "give you an opportunity to take immediate corrective action." Ultimately, McDonald's brought suit in Paris to terminate the MLA, which resulted in Dayan filing the present suit in Illinois to enjoin termination.

In Illinois, as in the majority of American jurisdictions, a *covenant of good faith* and *fair dealing* is implied in every contract absent express disavowal. Problems relating to good faith performance typically arise where one party to the contract is given broad discretion in performance. The dependent party must then rely on the party in control to exercise that discretion fairly. It remains to be seen, however, what limitation the implied covenant of good faith imposes on franchisor discretion in terminating a franchise agreement. A Utah Supreme Court held that the implied covenant of good faith limited the power of the franchisor to terminate a franchise agreement without good cause. The court stated that "when parties enter into a contract of this character, and there is no express provision that it may be cancelled without cause, it seems fair and reasonable to assume that both parties entered into the arrangement in good faith, intending that if the service is performed in a satisfactory manner it will not be cancelled arbitrarily." These cases reflect judicial concern over longstanding abuses in franchise relationships, particularly contract provisions giving the franchisor broad unilateral powers of termination at will. Taken collectively, they stand for the proposition that the implied covenant of good faith restricts franchisor discretion in terminating a franchise agreement to those cases where good cause exists. However, plaintiff would have us go further and argues that even if McDonald's had good cause for termination, if it also had an improper motive the termination would be a breach of the implied covenant of good faith. Dayan would attribute to McDonald's a desire to recapture the lucrative Paris market as an impermissible motive. We cannot agree. As a general proposition of law, it is widely held that where good cause exists, motive is immaterial to a determination of good faith performance.

Our review of the evidence admits of no doubt; the trial court properly resolved this issue in favor of McDonald's. To characterize the condition of Dayan's restaurants as being in substantial noncompliance with McDonald's QSC standards is a profound understatement. Throughout trial the various witnesses struggled to find the appropriate words to describe the ineffably unsanitary conditions observed in these restaurants, as did the trial court in its memorandum opinion. Terms describing the uncleanliness—such as "indescribable," "extremely defective sanitary conditions," "filthy, grimy, cruddy," "deplorable," "significantly unsanitary," "contaminated," "unsanitary," "very dirty," "very, very dirty," "disgusting," "abundance of filth," "pig pens"—tell only part of the story. The accuracy of these epithets is supported by voluminous, detailed testimonial evidence which consumed many weeks of trial and thousands of pages of transcript and is also corroborated by over 1,000 photographs admitted in evidence at trial. Dayan also argues that McDonald's was obligated to provide him with the operational assistance necessary to enable him to meet the QSC standards. As the trial court correctly realized: "It does not take a McDonald's trained French speaking operational man to know that grease dripping from the vents must be stopped and not merely collected in a cup hung from the ceiling, that dogs are not permitted to defecate where food is stored, that insecticide is not blended with chicken breading, that past-dated products should be discarded, that a potato peeler should be somewhat cleaner than a tire-vulcanizer and that shortening should not look like crank case oil."

Contrary to plaintiff's contention, the MLA negotiated by him explicitly stated what he had to do if he wished such assistance; he had to request it in writing and pay for it. Accordingly, we reject Dayan's argument that he was entitled to the same operational assistance prior to termination as the standard licensee. The judgment of the trial court denying plaintiff's request for a permanent injunction and finding that McDonald's properly terminated the franchise agreement is AFFIRMED.

Case Highlights

- Note the length and complexity, and ultimately the costs, of the litigation pertaining to this termination of a franchise agreement.
- A master license agreement (MLA) is often used to develop an entire territory, while each franchise location is also governed by individual operating license agreements (OLA).
- Under U.S. law, the franchisor's right to terminate a franchise is limited by the duty of good faith and fair dealing, along with individual state statutes.
- Standards relating to quality, safety, and cleanliness (QSC) are vital to maintaining the integrity and reputation of the franchise system as a whole.

Another issue especially important when franchising in a foreign country is to provide the appropriate means of termination and the protection of **trade secrets.** There is no generally accepted definition of trade secrets. It is a much broader concept than statutorily protected intellectual property rights (patent, copyright, trademark). The Uniform Trade Secrets Act offers this definition:

> *"Trade Secret" means information, including a formula, pattern, compilation, program, device, method, technique, or process, that: (i) derives independent economic value, actual or potential, from not being generally known to, and not being readily ascertainable by proper means by other persons who can obtain economic value from its disclosure or use, and (ii) is the subject of efforts that are reasonable under the circumstances to maintain its secrecy.*[37]

The franchisor should determine if the information being given is a trade secret. If so, it should expressly list in the franchise agreement the information that it intends to treat as trade secrets. The agreement may list information not generally considered trade secrets and expressly state that the information is to be deemed "secret and confidential." For example, customer lists provided by the franchisor have been held to be legally protected trade secrets. A trade secret designation in the agreement is enhanced if: (1) the information is not readily obtainable through alternative sources and (2) the franchisor treats the lists as "secret and confidential." The agreement can further protect the franchisor with a separate confidentiality clause and a noncompetition clause. The noncompetition clause should balance the goal of protecting the franchisor with the need to devise reasonable restrictions regarding scope, duration, and territory. Overly restrictive noncompetition clauses are likely to be reviewed and modified by most courts.

A franchise agreement that provides for a large amount of franchisor control may create problems under host country regulation. "Excessive control or the public appearance of such control may give rise to an agency relationship between the franchisor and the franchise"[38] under foreign law. If viewed as a dependent agency relationship, as discussed in Chapter 12, the franchisor may become susceptible to the tax and labor laws of the host country, as well as vulnerable to lawsuits such as products liability claims. The next section briefly reviews foreign regulation of franchising.

Foreign Regulation of Franchising

A number of restrictions on franchising can be found in U.S. and foreign laws. For example, in the United States a number of state franchise statutes limit the ability of the franchisor to terminate the franchise at will. Internationally, some countries offer a less friendly environment for franchising than is found in the United States. Host country laws vary significantly—from laws that do not even recognize the franchise form of business to laws that limit the types of contract provisions that will be enforced. The effectiveness of using model forms is limited by the fact that vast differences in contractual issues occur from industry to industry and under host country laws. The next subsection will review EU Franchise Regulations for purposes of negotiating legally enforceable franchise agreements. The Regulations offer insight about what types of clauses can be incorporated into an international franchise agreement.

http://

Franchise law in Canada:
http://www.trytel.com/~pbkerr/franchise.html.

37. Uniform Trade Secrets Act § 1(4), 14 U.L.A. 541 (1980).
38. Ralph H. Folsom & Michael W. Gordon, *International Business Transactions* 428 (1995).

EU FRANCHISE REGULATIONS

The European Union (EU) places limits on franchises in order for them to conform to its competition law.[39] The **EU Regulations on Franchise Agreements**[40] provides an exemption from the application of EU competition law found in Article 85 of the Treaty of Rome.[41] However, it is also an indispensable source to be used in the drafting of a franchise agreement. Commission Regulation 4087/88 pertains to franchise agreements involving the distribution of goods or services, along with master franchise agreements. The Regulation expressly exempts from its coverage industrial franchises that generally include the manufacture of products through the transfer of intellectual property rights. It notes that those types of franchises may make use of the block exemptions pertaining to patent and know-how licensing. EU Regulations in those areas will be discussed in Chapter 13, Law of Intellectual Property Rights, and Chapter 14, Intellectual Property Licensing.

The EU Regulations recognize that some restrictions on the rights of the franchisee are needed in order to maintain the "homogeneity of the network and the constant cooperation between franchisor and franchisees [in order to] ensure a constant quality of the products and services" being provided. Article 2 provides a list of clauses that, although restrictive of competition, have a strong nexus to the above philosophical goals. They allow for the development of exclusive franchise territories and prohibit actively seeking customers outside the franchise territory.

Along those lines, a master franchisee can be prohibited from entering a subfranchise agreement with an entity outside the territory of the master franchise. The agreement may also prohibit the franchisee from selling the goods or services of a competitor. The franchisor may insert clauses mandating that the franchisee sells only goods or services "matching minimum objective quality specifications." Generally, the franchisee cannot be restricted in determining its sources of supply. However, an exemption from this prohibition is given if requirements to purchase supplies from the franchisor or other designated third-party suppliers are necessary in order to meet "objective quality specifications."

Other clauses that are expressly permitted include best efforts, minimum sales quotas, customer service and warranty requirements, advertising requirements, confidentiality (including post-termination confidentiality), training requirements, rights to improvements, location restrictions, nonassignment without prior consent, notice of infringement and sales restricted to end users, other franchisees and resellers.

Prohibited clauses include those that restrict a franchisee from purchasing from another franchisee, from filling orders from parties outside its territory that were not actively sought, unduly limiting the franchisee's choice of suppliers or customers, and restrictions on pricing. These prohibited restrictions relate to a stated purpose of the Regulation that ensures that "parallel imports and cross deliveries between franchisees remain possible." In the event that a contract clause restriction does not come within one of the "approved restrictions enumerated in the Regulation, then the parties will have to *notify* the European Commission for an approval or negative clearance."

39. See Schmitz & Van Hamme, "Franchising in Europe—The First Practical EEC Guidelines," 22 *The International Lawyer* 717 (1988).

40. Commission Regulation (EEC) No 4087/88 of 30 November 1988 on the Application of Article 85(3) of the Treaty to Categories of Franchise Agreements.

41. For a fuller explanation on how European Union competition law relates to franchising, see Paul Ridgeway, "Franchising in the Common Market: A Survey of the Application of Competition Law of the European Community to Retail Franchising," 13 *North Carolina Journal of International Law & Commercial Regulation* 74 (1988).

Key Terms

affiliate, 69
block exemption, 85
branch office, 67
business plan, 82
business review letter, 79
competition law, 75
contractual joint venture, 68
corporation, 68
counter-indemnity clause, 81
distribution agreement, 82
enterprise liability, 73
equity joint venture, 68
EU Regulations of Franchise Agreements, 96
exceptions clause, 80
export trade certificate of review, 79
foreign subsidiary, 69
franchisee review clause, 91
general partnership, 67
insurance clause, 91
intellectual property transfer, 83
joint stock company, 75
joint venture, 67
limited liability company (LLC), 68
limited partnership, 67
local partner, 68
management agreements, 74
management board, 70
master franchise, 91
operational standards clause, 89
piercing the corporate veil, 70
purpose clause, 80
renewal clause, 90
representative office, 68
royalties clause, 90
secondment agreement, 82
shareholders' council, 70
site selection clause, 89
supervisory board, 70
supervisory committee, 70
territorial clause, 90
trade secrets, 95
transfer pricing, 69

Chapter Problems

1. Read the following articles and do a comparative analysis: Ronald J. Gilson & Mark J. Roe, "Lifetime Employment: Labor Peace and the Evolution of Japanese Corporate Governance," 99 *Columbia Law Review* 508 (1999); Mark J. Roe, "German Codetermination and German Securities Markets," 1998 *Columbia Business Law Review* 167 (1998); Mark J. Roe, "Some Differences in Corporate Structure in Germany, Japan, and the United States," 102 *Yale Law Journal* 1927 (1993).

2. Select two of the following countries: China, United States, Japan, Germany. Compare and contrast corporate law in the two countries you have selected. Discuss how corporate law reflects society's fundamental view of the role of the corporation.

3. What does the phrase "piercing the corporate veil" mean? When might the corporate veil be pierced? How does this philosophy compare with that of many of the United States' trading partners?

4. What are some of the issues that potential joint venture partners need to discuss in detail before entering into an agreement? Discuss some of the contractual clauses that can be incorporated into an agreement in order to minimize potential conflict.

Internet Exercises

1. Research a foreign country or countries for opportunities and restrictions on the different ways of transacting business discussed in this chapter using the U.S. Department of State's Country Commercial Guides. Individual Country Commercial Guides can be obtained at **http://www.state.gov**.

2. Research the status of franchising in a foreign country. A good place to start is the web site for the International Franchising Federation at **http://www.franchise.org**. A growing number of national franchise associations, along with the European Franchise Federation, can also be assessed.

3. Compare the Contractual Joint Venture Law of the People's Republic of Korea at **http://www.korea-np.co.jp** with the Chinese Foreign Equity Joint Venture Law at **http://www.qis.net/chinalaw/prclaw11.htm**.

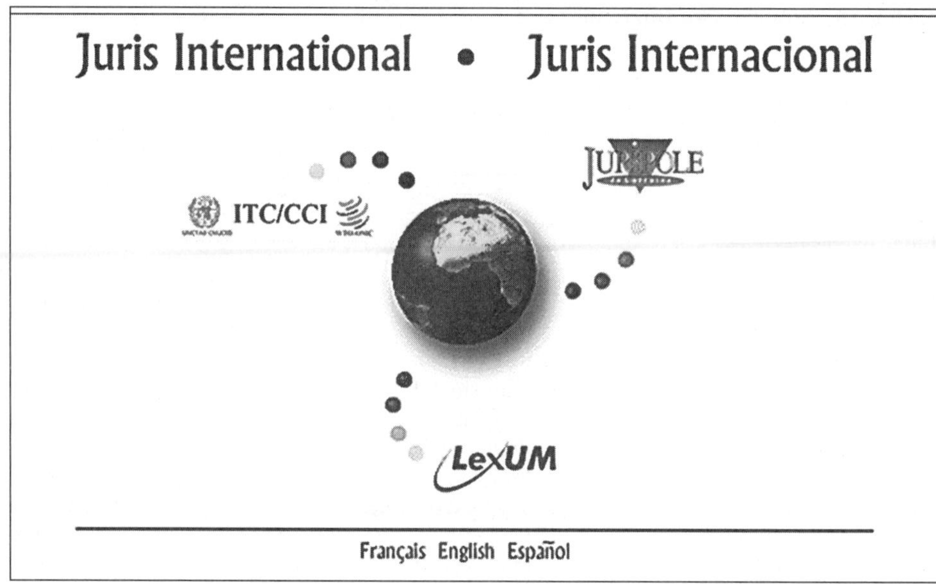

Chapter 4 International Commercial Dispute Resolution

The cost and uncertainty of potential litigation with a foreign citizen or company can act as a deterrent to entering an international business transaction. The prospect of having to pursue a claim or to defend a claim in a foreign court using foreign law may prove too risky for some businesspersons. At the least, anyone contemplating a business transaction with a foreign entity should ask the following questions: (1) What are the alternatives to transnational litigation? (2) Where will a future dispute be argued or settled? (3) What country's law would be applied to such a dispute? (4) Will a settlement or decision be enforceable in a foreign country? These questions should be discussed during the earlier stages of contract negotiation, and an international contract should expressly answer these questions through the use of forum selection, choice of law, and alternative dispute resolution clauses. The answer to question (1) is that international commercial arbitration is a popular alternative to international litigation. The contractual devices represented by choice of law and forum selection clauses provide the avenue for dealing with questions (2) and (3). Finally, a review of national laws and international conventions will help answer question (4).

INTERNATIONAL LITIGATION

Anyone seeking to undertake international litigation faces three areas of concern. First, how does one properly begin a lawsuit against a foreign company? Second, once the litigation begins, how do the parties gather evidence in foreign countries? Third, if successful in the litigation, how does one enforce a judgment in a foreign country?

To bring a lawsuit against a foreign company, one must properly serve process. **Service of process** is the formal notification of a defendant to defend himself in court. Proper service of process is necessary in order for a court to obtain **personal jurisdiction** over the defendant. Failure to obtain legally sufficient service of process is likely to result in the nonenforceability of any *default judgment* obtained in the event that the defendant fails to appear. In order to require a foreign party to defend itself in a suit brought in the United States, the service of process should meet the requirements of both the United States and the country of the party being served. This is especially crucial if the judgment will need to be enforced in a foreign country. Service of process requirements, however, vary widely throughout the world. The United States Federal Rules of Civil Procedure state that service in a foreign country may be made "by any form of mail, requiring a signed receipt, to be addressed and dispatched by the clerk of the court to the party to be served." In contrast, service by mail is generally not recognized by foreign court systems.

http://

International Bar Association—Sections on business law and legal practice: **http://www.ibanet.org**.

Adoption of the Convention on the Service Abroad of Judicial and Extrajudical Documents in Civil or Commercial Matters, or **Hague Service Convention,** is one response to the problem of international service of process. The Hague Service Convention provides a government means to ensure effective and recognizable service of process. The signatory countries to the Convention are required to establish a Central Authority for processing foreign plaintiffs' service of process requests. The Central Authority serves the defendant directly or arranges to have it served by the appropriate government agency. Although many countries have not adopted the Hague Service Convention, a number of important trading countries have adopted it, including the United States, Japan, China, France, Germany, Great Britain, Italy, Spain, and Canada. In countries not party to the Convention, **dual service** of process is recommended. Dual service aims to satisfy the service requirements of the country of the forum court and the country of the defendant in order to enhance the enforceability of any future judgment. The issues of personal jurisdiction over a foreign defendant are discussed in *Alpine View Co., Ltd. v. Atlas Copco AB.*

http://

Text of Hague Service Convention: **http://www.hcch.net/e/conventions/text14e.html**.

There are a number of defenses to a foreign court's exercise of jurisdiction even when such an exercise would be proper under the requirements of due process. The *Central Bank of the Philippines v. Ferdinand E. Marcos* case introduces the nondiscretionary defenses of foreign sovereign immunity, head-of-state immunity, and diplomatic immunity.[1] These defenses to jurisdiction are limited to lawsuits

http://

Text of the Foreign Sovereign Immunities Act (FSIA), Title 28, Chapter 97 of the United States Code: **http://www4.law.cornell.edu/uscode/28/pIVch97.html**.

1. The United States' doctrine of sovereign immunity has been codified as the *Foreign Sovereign Immunities Act of 1976*, Public Law 94-583, 90 Stat. 289, 28 U.S.C. §§ 1332 (a)(2), (3), (4), 1391(f), 1441(d), 1602-1611 (1982). For the English law counterpart (State Immunity Act of 1978) see Chapter 33, 17 I.L.M. 1123 (1978).

Alpine View Co., Ltd. v. Atlas Copco AB

205 F.3d 208 (5th Cir. 2000)

King, Chief Judge. This case arises out of an alleged breach of a 1992 Intentional Agreement ("1992 Agreement") between Alpine View Company, Limited ("Alpine View"), and Uniroc AB ("Uniroc"), a wholly-owned subsidiary of the Swedish holding company, Atlas Copco AB ("ACAB"). In 1989, Bjorn Hansen, the president of Alpine View, was granted exclusive worldwide rights to the distribution and sale of offshore drill bits manufactured by Shanghai Machinery & Equipment Import/Export Corporation ("SMEC"), a Chinese company.

To facilitate the sale of these products, Hansen sought an established distributor, and eventually executed the 1992 Agreement with Uniroc. Under the 1992 Agreement, Uniroc was to purchase drill bits from Bjorn Hansen A/S, and eventually become the exclusive distributor of those products in certain specified sectors of the world market. Uniroc was to pay Alpine View a commission based on net sales to users and distributors outside the Atlas Copco Group, which comprises ACAB and its 71 subsidiaries. To enhance its ability to deal directly with SMEC, Uniroc was also to enter into a separate distributorship agreement with that company. The existence of the separate distributorship agreement was a precondition for the effectiveness of the 1992 Agreement. Alpine View is incorporated under the laws of the British Virgin Islands and Hansen is a resident of Norway. Compressors and Comptec are each Delaware corporations, with Compressors having its principal place of business in Massachusetts and Comptec having its in New York. Robbins is a Washington corporation and has its principal place of business in that state. Compressors, Comptec, and Robbins are all subsidiaries of ACAB.

Dismissal for Lack of Personal Jurisdiction

We review *de novo* a district court's dismissal for want of personal jurisdiction. The Due Process Clause permits the exercise of personal jurisdiction over a nonresident defendant when (1) that defendant has purposefully availed himself of the benefits and protections of the forum state by establishing *minimum contacts* with the forum state; and (2) the exercise of jurisdiction over that defendant does not offend traditional notions of fair play and substantial justice. Minimum contacts can be established either through contacts sufficient to assert specific jurisdiction, or contacts sufficient to assert general jurisdiction. *Specific jurisdiction* over a nonresident corporation is appropriate when that corporation has purposefully directed its activities at the forum state and the "litigation results from alleged injuries that arise out of or relate to those activities." *General jurisdiction*, on the other hand, will attach where the nonresident defendant's contacts with the forum state, although not related to the plaintiff's cause of action, are "continuous and systematic."

1. Specific Jurisdiction and the Stream-of-Commerce Theory

The Supreme Court stated that the "foreseeability that is critical to due process analysis is that the defendant's conduct and connection with the forum State are such that he should reasonably anticipate being haled into court there." Appellants rely heavily on the stream-of-commerce theory. In support of their argument that the *stream-of-commerce theory* is applicable to cases other than those involving products liability, Appellants point to courts applying the theory to cases raising antitrust or intellectual property related claims. When a nonresident's contact with the forum state stems from a product, sold or manufactured by the foreign defendant, which has caused harm in the forum state, the court has specific jurisdiction if it finds that the defendant delivered the product into the stream of commerce with the expectation that it would be purchased by or used by consumers in the forum state. However, delivery of products into the stream of commerce does not support assertion of specific jurisdiction over ACAB and Robbins. Appellants argue that putting products into the stream of commerce with the expectation that Texans will purchase or use those products suffices to establish jurisdiction with respect to "any claims." This is more akin to a general jurisdiction argument than to a specific jurisdiction argument. Appellants make no attempt to link Appellees' contacts with Texas and the instant litigation. This is a link that specific jurisdiction requires. Appellants have not asserted that the alleged misdeeds occurred in Texas, or that the 1992 Agreement was negotiated or executed in Texas. Neither Alpine View nor Hansen is considered a Texas resident.

2. General Jurisdiction and the Alter-Ego Doctrine

Appellants also challenge the district court's conclusion that they had not shown that assertion of general jurisdiction was proper in this case. To make a *prima facie* showing of general jurisdiction, Appellants must produce evidence that affirmatively shows that ACAB's and Robbins' contacts with Texas that are unrelated to the litigation are sufficient to satisfy due process requirements. Those unrelated contacts must be substantial, continuous, and systematic. Examining the submitted evidence, it is clear that Appellants have not demonstrated that Robbins' direct contacts with Texas during the relevant period were sufficient to establish general jurisdiction. The evidence shows, at best, that Robbins sold, on isolated occasions, products to entities located in Texas and that Robbins' personnel made field service visits to Texas. These contacts are neither substantial, continuous, nor systematic.

The same conclusion is compelled with regard to ACAB. Appellants rely on evidence that indicates that the products of ACAB's subsidiaries are sold in Texas. However, "a foreign parent corporation is not subject to the jurisdiction of a forum state merely because its subsidiary is present or doing business there; the mere existence of a parent-subsidiary relationship is not sufficient to warrant the assertion of jurisdiction over the foreign parent." Appellants must make a *prima facie* showing that ACAB so controls other organizations that the activities of those organizations may be fairly attributed to ACAB for purposes of asserting jurisdiction over it. Under Texas law, the *alter-ego doctrine* applies when there is such unity between the parent corporation and its subsidiary that the separateness of the two corporations has ceased and holding only the subsidiary corporation liable would result in injustice. We have said, however, that "100% stock ownership and commonality of officers and directors are not alone sufficient to establish an *alter-ego* relationship between two corporations." Instead, "the degree of control exercised by the parent must be greater than that normally associated with common ownership and directorship." Such control has not been indicated here. The existence of intercorporate loans does not establish the requisite dominance, and in fact, interest-bearing loans suggest separation of corporate entities. We conclude that the district court did not err in dismissing Appellants' claims against Robbins and ACAB for lack of personal jurisdiction.

Case Highlights

- International litigation is often complex due to the diversity of the parties. In this case, the parties were from China, Sweden, Norway, the British Virgin Islands, and the states of New York, Massachusetts, Washington, and Delaware.
- Under the due process clause of the U.S. Constitution, personal jurisdiction over a defendant must be based on either "minimum contacts" for purposes of gaining specific jurisdiction or "substantial, continuous, and systematic" contacts for purposes of gaining general jurisdiction.
- Specific jurisdiction requires a nexus between the minimum contacts and the injuries claimed, while general jurisdiction allows for lawsuits on even unrelated claims.
- The "stream-of-commerce" theory is only applicable if the defendant delivers a product into the stream of commerce with the expectation that it would be purchased in the forum state.
- A foreign parent company does not become subject to the jurisdiction of a foreign court simply because its subsidiary is amenable to that state's jurisdiction.
- The "alter ego-theory" allows for jurisdiction over a parent company if the parent company "dominates" the activities of a subsidiary that has sufficient contacts with the forum court.

involving a foreign country and its officers. The courts have also developed a general discretionary principle known as the ***forum non conveniens* doctrine.** The *forum non conveniens* doctrine can be applied to any case if the court determines that there is another more convenient forum to hear the case. The *Capital Currency Exchange* case examines some of the nuances of this judge-made doctrine.

The doctrine of sovereign immunity protects foreign governments only from essentially governmental activities and not from *commercial* activities. The problem with this type of categorization of activities is that government procurement has become increasingly commercialized, making the distinction between sovereign and commercial activities difficult to define. The gravity of this problem becomes apparent in developing countries where almost by necessity a governmental entity is

http://

State Department's questions and answers on Foreign Sovereign Immunities Act: **http://travel.state.gov/fsia.html**.

involved with international transactions. For example, a government partner is common in joint venture undertakings in developing countries. It is important in such dealings to negotiate a contract clause in which the governmental entity *waives* its potential sovereign immunities and **Act of State**[2] defenses.

Central Bank of the Philippines v. Ferdinand E. Marcos

665 F. Supp. 793 (N.D. Cal. 1987)

Orrick, District Judge. Ferdinand Marcos, former President of the Republic of the Philippines, is presently involved in a lawsuit in the United States District Court of Hawaii. In the course of discovery, Marcos served a subpoena on Philippine Solicitor General Sedfrey Ordonez, during a recent visit of his to San Francisco to appear for a deposition. The United States filed the present motion to quash the subpoena on the grounds that Ordonez was entitled to immunity pursuant to a "Suggestion of Immunity" issued by the United States Department of State.

The Central Bank of the Philippines brought suit in the United States District Court of Hawaii against former President Marcos seeking the return of certain gold and currency. The Embassy of the Philippines sent a letter to the United States Department of State invoking "diplomatic immunity" on behalf of Ordonez. The government relies primarily upon the doctrine of foreign sovereign immunity, and the "derivative" of that immunity now treated separately as "head-of-state" immunity. Although head-of-state immunity has its origins in sovereign immunity, arising in a period when the head of state and the state itself were considered one, the doctrine is now independent of sovereign immunity and guided by separate principles.

Foreign Sovereign Immunity

In arguing that the subpoena should be quashed, the government relies on cases holding that an executive "Suggestion of Immunity" under the foreign sovereign immunity doctrine is binding on the courts. First, the executive "Suggestion" of foreign sovereign immunity doctrine has been abrogated by the Foreign Sovereign Immunities Act (FSIA). Congress enacted the FSIA to "transfer the determination of sovereign immunity from the executive branch to the judicial branch." The FSIA sets forth comprehensive standards for determining when a foreign state is entitled to immunity, and vests sole responsibility for the application of those standards in the judiciary. Second, the sovereign immunity doctrine may not serve as a basis for Ordonez' immunity in this instance because it is not applicable to individual government officials. The FSIA provides that a "foreign state shall be immune from the jurisdiction of the courts of the United States" with certain exceptions. A "foreign state" is defined as "a political subdivision of a foreign state or an agency or instrumentality of a foreign state."

Head-of-State Immunity

The government also argues that Ordonez is entitled to head-of-state immunity, despite the fact that he is neither a sovereign nor a foreign minister, the two traditional bases for a recognition or grant of head-of-state immunity. In fact, the government in this instance seeks to expand the head-of-state doctrine to encompass all government officials of a foreign state to whom the State Department chooses to extend immunity. There is no precedent for such a radical departure from past custom.

Diplomatic Immunity

The final potential ground for recognition of the immunity of Ordonez is found in the doctrine of "diplomatic immunity." There is a rich jurisprudential and statutory history surrounding the international practice of diplomatic immunity. The Diplomatic Relations Act of 1978 established the Vienna Convention on Diplomatic Immunity ("Vienna Convention") as the sole United States law on the subject. Article 31 of the Vienna Convention provides that, with certain exceptions, a diplomatic agent shall be immune from the civil jurisdiction of the "receiving" state's courts, and shall "not be obliged to give evidence as a witness." Article 32 states that this immunity may be waived by the "sending" state, but that the waiver must always be *express*.

Marcos has argued that any immunity in the Philippines' diplomatic agents has been waived by the institution of this lawsuit by the Central Bank of the Philip-

2. See Banc Nacional de Cuba v. Sabbatino, 376 U.S. 398 (1964).

pines. A sending state does not waive any and all diplomatic immunity for its agents merely through the institution of a suit in the receiving state. Unlike sovereign immunity, whether a diplomatic agent is entitled to diplomatic immunity is a matter for the State Department to decide. Although some have asserted that the State Department's decisions are reviewable by the courts, "the courts have generally accepted as conclusive the views of the State Department as to the fact of diplomatic status." This Court finds that the State Department has provided the Court with a letter certifying Ordonez as a diplomatic agent and requesting diplomatic immunity on his behalf. Out of respect for the foreign policy decisions of the Executive Branch, this Court finds that Ordonez is entitled to diplomatic immunity.

Case Highlights

- A grant of diplomatic immunity is considered a discretionary decision of the executive branch through certification by the Department of State.
- Foreign sovereign immunity, as provided for under the Foreign Sovereign Immunity Act, is reserved for foreign states and the agencies or instrumentalities of a foreign state.
- Head-of-state immunity is limited to top level officials and does not apply to all foreign government officials or employees.

Capital Currency Exchange v. National Westminster Bank and Barclays Bank

155 F.3d 603 (2d Cir. 1998)

McLaughlin, Circuit Judge. Capital Currency Exchange, N.V. ("CCE"), is a financial company organized under the laws of the Netherlands Antilles. CCE and its affiliates are engaged principally in two kinds of international financial transactions: (1) retail currency exchange and (2) money transfers from the United States to England. CCE and its affiliates had a longstanding banking relationship with Barclays UK. In 1991, CCE, on behalf of Worldcash, sought a New York State money transmission license. To qualify for this license, Worldcash had to post a $500,000 bond in favor of the New York State banking authorities. CCE arranged with Barclays UK's New York office to issue an irrevocable letter of credit as security for the bond. In May 1995, for reasons that the parties dispute, Barclays UK told CCE to find another banker. In August 1995, NatWest UK declined to provide CCE with banking services. CCE maintains that NatWest UK and Barclays UK conspired to drive CCE out of the money transfer business by depriving it of banking services in violation of the antitrust laws, specifically Sections 1 and 2 of the Sherman Act. On November 6, 1996, defendants moved to dismiss the complaint under the *forum non conveniens* doctrine.

In a *forum non conveniens* analysis, a court must determine that an adequate alternative forum exists. An alternative forum is adequate if: (1) the defendants are subject to service of process there; and (2) the forum permits "litigation of the subject matter of the dispute." We believe there is an adequate, alternative forum. Plaintiffs may challenge defendants' allegedly anticompetitive actions under Articles 85 and 86 of the Treaty of Rome, which English courts are bound to enforce. Although English courts have not yet awarded damages in an antitrust case, it appears that English courts have the power to do so. It is well established, however, that the unavailability of treble damages does not render a forum inadequate. Thus, suits brought under the Sherman Act are subject to dismissal under the *forum non conveniens* doctrine.

AFFIRMED.

Case Highlights

- In order for a court to dismiss a case under the *forum non conveniens* doctrine, it must determine that an adequate alternative forum exists.
- The unavailability of certain remedies under the laws of the alternative forum does not render that forum inadequate.

International Discovery

http://

Text of Hague Evidence Convention: **http://www.hcch.net/e/conventions/index.html**.

Once the defendant is properly served and personal jurisdiction is obtained, the next issue is the ability to pursue **discovery** against him. Discovery is the process of gathering evidence from one's adversary and other third parties. Discovery is often the most difficult and costly part of international litigation. The United States Federal Rules of Civil Procedure allow for numerous and broad methods of discovery; other countries with less liberal discovery methods are less receptive to requests for the discovery of their nationals. The purpose of the Convention on the Taking of Evidence Abroad in Civil or Commercial Matters (**Hague Evidence Convention**) is to facilitate the discovery of foreign parties. This Convention provides for the use of Letters of Request that require foreign courts to perform the discovery process. It also provides for the "taking of evidence by diplomatic officers, consular agents and commissioners."

A number of factors limit the effectiveness of the Convention. First, few countries outside of the United States and Western Europe have adopted the Convention. Second, a foreign court may reject a letter of request if the court deems it to be in violation of its national laws. Nonetheless, a U.S. plaintiff having problems with foreign discovery should seek the help of the U.S. State Department in gathering evidence through the Hague Evidence Convention.

Enforceability of Judgments

After obtaining a judgment in an international litigation, the winning party will often need to enforce the judgment in a foreign country. This is likely when the foreign defendant does not possess enough assets in the forum court to satisfy the judgment. International litigation judgments are more difficult to enforce than arbitral awards. The court in *Hunt v. BP Exploration Ltd.*[3] reviewed U.S. law on the enforcement of foreign judgments. The case involved the enforcement of an English judgment against a U.S. defendant. The court recognized that *Hilton v. Guyot*[4] was still good law. In *Hilton*, the Supreme Court held that a foreign judgment is entitled to enforcement if the defendant had an opportunity for a fair trial. A fair trial is predicated on the foreign court possessing personal and subject matter jurisdiction, conducting trials using *regular* procedures, and acting "under a system of jurisprudence likely to secure an impartial administration of justice." Despite this embrace of international comity, however, the court in *Hilton* failed to enforce the French judgment under a **rule of reciprocity.** The rule of reciprocity holds that a country will not enforce judgments rendered in a foreign country that does not likewise enforce its judgments. Because of the convergence of national legal systems and the United States' recognition of other legal systems, the rule of reciprocity has rarely been used in recent years as a defense to the enforcement of a foreign judgment.

The most effective grounds for attacking a foreign judgment are procedural ones centered on due process and public policy concerns. In *Hunt*, the court held that given the historical deference received by English judgments, the *Hilton* due process standards were met given the similarities of the legal systems. However, a

3. 492 F. Supp. 885 (N.D. Tex. 1980).
4. 159 U.S. 113 (1895).

Nelson Bunker Hunt v. BP Exploration Company (Libya) Ltd.

492 F. Supp. 885 (N.D. Tex 1980)

Higginbotham, District Judge. This parallel London/Dallas litigation stems from a relationship between BP and Hunt with respect to an oil field located in Libya. In 1957, Libya granted Hunt Concession No. 65 in the province of Cyrenaica. In June 1960, Hunt entered into a letter agreement as to Concession No. 65 with BP accompanied by an Operating Agreement. The 1960 Agreement provided that Hunt would convey to BP an undivided one-half interest in Concession No. 65. On May 2, 1975, BP instituted suit in England, relying primarily on Section 1(3) of the Frustrated Contracts Act, 1943 ("Act"). BP's claim under the Act was that its contract with Hunt was frustrated when BP's interest in the concession was expropriated, and that, because of BP's contractual performance before expropriation, Hunt obtained a valuable benefit. Hunt declined to accept service of the writ issued on May 2, 1975, through agents and solicitors in the U.K. and attempts to serve him personally during a short visit also proved unsuccessful.

On June 19, 1975, the High Court of Justice, Queen's Bench Division, Commercial Court, granted BP's request for service by mail. On June 30, 1978, Mr. Justice Goff entered judgment against Hunt, and held that the counterclaim under the Act failed. On March 26, 1979, an English court awarded BP $15,575,823 and $8,922,060. Both Hunt and BP appealed but the Court of Appeals in England has not yet decided the appeals.

The Law of Recognition

Hilton v. Guyot is the leading American decision on the recognition and enforcement of foreign country judgments. The Supreme Court held that:

Where there has been opportunity for a full and fair trial abroad before a court of competent jurisdiction, conducting the trial upon regular proceedings, after due citation or voluntary appearance of the defendant, and under a system of jurisprudence likely to secure an impartial administration of justice between the citizens of its own country and those of other countries, and there is nothing to show either prejudice in the court, or in the system of laws under which it is sitting, or fraud in the procuring of the judgment, or any other special reason why the comity of this nation should not allow it full effect, the merits of the case should not, in an action brought in this country upon the judgment, be tried afresh, as on new trial or an appeal, upon the mere assertion of the party that the judgment was erroneous in law or in fact.

Applying the *Hilton v. Guyot* principles of comity in order to determine whether a foreign country judgment should be recognized presents difficult social and public policy judgments. Comity is a recognition which one nation extends to the legislative, executive, or judicial acts of another. It is not a rule of law, but one of practice, convenience, and expediency. It is a nation's expression of understanding that demonstrates due regard both to international duty and convenience and the rights of persons protected by its own laws. Comity should be withheld only when its acceptance would be contrary or prejudicial to the interest of the nation called upon to give it effect.

In this case, Hunt cannot seriously assert that there was not timely notice and opportunity to defend, that fraud was involved, or that the proceedings were not rendered according to a civilized jurisprudence. Hunt asserts, correctly, that if the English court had no personal jurisdiction over him, the judgment should not be recognized. The record reflects, however, that the English court did have jurisdiction over Hunt. This court turns to a minimum contacts analysis in order to determine if the English court's exercise of jurisdiction comports with our own notions expressed in due process terms. Hunt's contacts with England are of such an extent and of such nature that the maintenance of this suit does not offend fair play and substantial justice. Hunt has engaged in much purposeful activity in England. The contract was executed in England, Hunt has personally traveled to England to participate in meetings with BP, he had agents resident in England to represent his interests, and BP's principal place of business was in London.

Public Policy

Hunt's argument that an American judgment would not be recognized in England and so should not, on public policy grounds, be recognized here is in essence an assertion that reciprocity is an essential element of recognition. The court disagrees. Though the *Hilton* case required reciprocity as a condition of recognition, American decisions since *Hilton* have moved "decisively away from the requirement of reciprocity as a condition of recognition." Indeed, the draftsmen of the Uniform Foreign Money-Judgment Recognition Act consciously rejected reciprocity as a factor to consider in recognizing foreign money judgments.

Effect of the Appeal

Hunt next argues that the English judgment is not entitled to recognition because it is now on appeal; and the decision of the Court of Appeal will be subject to review by the House of Lords. Existing precedent on comity, the principle under which foreign country judgments are recognized, lends support to this assumption. The Uniform Foreign Money-Judgments Recognition Act provides that "if the defendant satisfies the court either that an appeal is pending or that he is entitled and intends to appeal from the foreign judgment, the court may stay the proceedings until the appeal has been determined or until the expiration of a period of time sufficient to enable the defendant to prosecute the appeal." Therefore, it is necessary for this court to stay the proceedings until a final determination of the proceedings in England.

Case Highlights

- Comity is a recognition that one nation extends to the legislative, executive, or judicial acts of another.
- Reciprocity is no longer a factor considered in the recognition of a foreign judgment.
- A foreign judgment is not due recognition while it is in the process of being appealed.

major substantive difference in the laws of the court rendering judgment and the enforcing court will be scrutinized during the enforcement stage. For example, U.S. courts will generally not enforce foreign country penal and tax judgments.[5] The court in *Hunt v. BP Exploration* did not enforce the English judgment pending its appeal in the English court system. It cited the Uniform Foreign Money-Judgments Recognition Act which states that "if the defendant satisfies the court either that an appeal is pending or that he is entitled and intends to appeal from the foreign judgment, the court may stay the proceedings until the appeal has been determined or until the expiration of a period of time sufficient to enable the defendant to prosecute the appeal."[6]

A number of international conventions have been promulgated to help enforce judgments internationally. Three are regional in nature: Members of the European Union can use the **Brussels Convention on Jurisdiction and Judgments in Civil and Commercial Matters.** The **Lugano Convention** applies to all countries in the European Free Trade Area. Finally, the **Inter-American Convention on the Extraterritorial Validity of Foreign Judgments** applies to members of the Organization of American States. The only truly "international" convention, the **Hague Convention on International Jurisdiction and Foreign Judgments in Civil and Commercial Matters,** has not been widely accepted and has failed to be effective in facilitating the enforcement of foreign judgments.

http://

The Hague Conference on Private International Law has begun work on a new judgment convention—Hague Convention on International Jurisdiction and Foreign Judgments in Civil and Commercial Matters: **http://www.cptech.org/ecom/jurisdiction/hague.html** or **http://www.hcch.net/e/workprog/jdgm.html**. The proposed Convention would likely also deal with issues of Internet jurisdiction.

In contrast, the United Nations Convention on the Recognition and Enforcement of Foreign Arbitral Awards or **New York Convention** has been widely accepted and enforced. Thus, the enforcement of a judgment in a foreign country is dependent upon the nuances of enforcement in that particular country. For example, France and Switzerland refuse to enforce a foreign judgment against their nationals unless there is a clear indication that the national voluntarily intended to submit to the jurisdiction of the foreign court. Many countries will not enforce U.S. judgments that are contrary to their public policy. Foreign courts, for example, are unlikely to enforce punitive and treble damage awards because there are no such counterparts under their laws. Faced with such obstacles, a plaintiff may choose to file suit directly in the country of the defendant or to arbitrate the claim.

5. See von Mehren & Patterson, "Recognition and Enforcement of Foreign-Country Judgments in the United States," 6 *Law & Policy in International Business* 37, 61 (1974).
6. The Uniform Foreign Money-Judgments Recognition Act, 13 Uniform Laws Annotated (U.L.A.) 263 (1962). The shortcoming of the act is that it has not received a significant degree of international adoption.

CHOICE OF LAW

How do courts determine which national laws apply in a given case? Generally, absent a **choice of law clause** in which the parties to a contract expressly state the law that will govern any disputes, the law of the country most *closely connected* to the agreement will govern. Sometimes the courts may apply the principle of *depecage* to apply different governing laws to different parts of the contract. In short, different parts of the contract may have closer connections to different countries. The country of closest connection will often be the country of the residence of the performing party. Courts have fashioned **conflict of law rules** to assist them in making choice of law decisions. These rules are essentially a list of factors used to determine the country with the closest connection to the case.

Under the Restatement (Second) of Conflicts of Laws,[7] the law of the jurisdiction with the "most significant contacts" governs both tort and contract claims. In evaluating tort claims, the following four factors are relevant: (1) the domicile, place of incorporation, and place of business of the parties; (2) the place where a tort occurred; (3) the place where the relationship of the parties is centered; and (4) the place where the injury occurred. With respect to contract claims, the factors are: (1) the place of contracting; (2) the place of negotiation; (3) the place of performance; (4) location of the subject matter of the contract; and (5) the domicile, place of incorporation, and place of business of the parties. The Restatement also states that if the place of negotiating the contract and the place of performance are in the same country, the law of that country will usually be applied. If a specific contract clause or issue is invalid in a country with a close connection to the contract, then that country's laws may be deferred to because of its strong interest in enforcing its laws and public policies. The **doctrine of *renvoi*** is when a court uses another country's conflict of law rules that direct the court to apply its own country's law. Other factors considered include the place the contract was negotiated, the place the contract was signed, the place of performance, and the place the breach occurred.

Before a contract and a choice of law clause are drafted, the conflict of law rules in the national law of the other party should be researched. This will help determine whether an express choice of law clause is needed and, if so, the factors the foreign country will use in assessing the enforceability of the choice of law selection. The conflict of law rules found in Hungarian law are shown in the Comparative Law capsule on the following page.

One principle used in determining the law to be applied by the forum court is that absent sufficient proof to establish with reasonable certainty the substance of the foreign principles of law, the court should apply the law of the forum. A court is not expected to decide a case based on incomplete and frequently confusing explanations of foreign law. In *Banque Libanaise Pour Le Commerce v. Khreich*,[8] the Federal Circuit Court stated that it was the plaintiff's "burden to provide the legal pigment and then paint the district court a clear portrait of the relevant foreign (Abu Dhabi) law." It affirmed the right of the lower court to apply Texas law to what was primarily a foreign transaction.

Judicial Abrogation of Choice of Law Clauses

Internationally, courts and arbitration tribunals have generally enforced contractual choice of law clauses. Courts, however, will usually require that the choice of

7. §187: Law of the State Chosen by the Parties
8. 915 F.2d 1000 (5th Cir. 1990).

Comparative Law

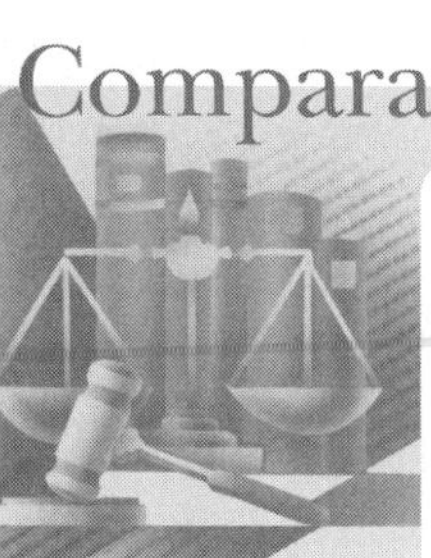

Hungarian Conflict of Law Rules

Specific Rules

Sale/purchase contracts	law of the country of the seller
Lease contract	law of the country of the lessor
Banking/credit contract	law of country of the financial institution
Employment contract	law of the country in which the services are performed when services are to be performed in more than one country, then law of the country of the employer

General Default Rule

If specific rules are not applicable	law of the country of the party performing the principle obligation

law have some connection to the parties or the contract. Arbitration tribunals, on the other hand, are more likely to enforce a reasonable choice of law selection even if the choice is not connected to the contract or the transaction. Arbitrators may see an unconnected choice of law selection as a fair compromise given the international nature of the transaction. This is especially true if the parties' choice is the laws of one of the more popular neutral countries, such as Great Britain, the United States, Switzerland, and Germany.

At times, statutory mandates may preempt this reasonableness inquiry. For example, the English Unfair Contract Terms Act of 1977 adopts a presumption of unreasonableness for indemnity clauses through which "by reference to any contract term a party is made to indemnify another party in respect of liability for negligence or breach of contract."[9] For international sales contracts, the Act voids any choice of law clause whose purpose is the avoidance of the Unfair Terms Act.

Courts have used a number of factors in scrutinizing choice of law clauses. The following excerpts from the Restatement (Second) of the Law of Conflicts provide the rationale for the need for such rules and the factors that courts review in deciding whether to honor a choice of law selection.

Section 1: Reason for the Rules of Conflict of Laws

The world is composed of territorial states having separate and differing systems of law. Events and transactions occur, and issues arise, that may have significant relationships to more than one state, making necessary a special body of rules and methods for their ordering and resolution.

Section 6: Choice of Law Principles

The factors relevant to the choice of law include:

(a) the needs of the international system,

(b) the relevant policies of the forum,

9. Unfair Contract Terms Act § 4(1) (1977).

(c) the relevant policies of other interested states and the relative interests of those states in the determination of the particular issue,
(d) the protection of justified expectations,
(e) the basic policies underlying the particular field of law,
(f) certainty, predictability, and uniformity of result, and
(g) ease in the determination and application of the law to be applied.

In weighing these factors, the modern judicial trend is to give great deference to the choice made by the parties in their contractual choice of law clause. "In the area of contracts, where choice-of-law rules are uncertain, some measure of predictability and certainty is achieved by allowing the parties, within broad limits, to select the law to govern the validity and effect of their contract."[10] This deference also advances the policy goal of protecting "the justified expectations" of the contracting parties.

The *Restatement* also provides two grounds for abrogating the parties' choice of law clause. First, the chosen law has no substantial relationship to the parties or the transaction and there is no reasonable basis for the parties' choice. Second, application of the law of the chosen state would be contrary to a fundamental policy of a country which has a materially greater interest than the chosen state in the determination of the particular issue. A forum court is unlikely to enforce a choice of law that would be contrary to its county's law and policy.

ARBITRATION OF DISPUTES IN INTERNATIONAL TRANSACTIONS

The simplest solution to a payment problem is to contact and negotiate with the customer. With patience, understanding, and flexibility, one can often resolve conflicts to the satisfaction of both sides. If, however, negotiations fail and the sum involved is large enough to warrant the effort, a company should obtain the assistance and advice of its bank, legal counsel, and other qualified experts. If both parties can agree to take their dispute to an arbitration agency, this step is preferable to legal action, since arbitration is often faster and less costly. The **International Chamber of Commerce (ICC)** handles the majority of international arbitrations and is usually acceptable to foreign companies because it is not affiliated with any single country.

http://
ICC International Court of Arbitration—International Dispute Resolution Center: **http://www.iccwbo.org/index_court.asp.** Provides links to ICC rules and model clauses.

Litigation is the less-preferred method of dispute resolution in many countries. It is seen in some countries, most notably in Japan, as a failure of the businessperson *qua* businessperson. (See Doing Business Internationally: The Role of Alternative Dispute Resolution in Japan.) In "some cultures arbitration may prove a 'face-saving' approach to dispute resolution."[11] From a more practical perspective, litigation is an expensive process likely to permanently damage the business relationship and is inherently unpredictable as to result. International litigation is often unduly delayed because of a lack of uniformity in procedural rules. For example, the liberalized nature of U.S. discovery rules often meets with hostility in foreign courts.

The uncertainty of dispute resolution in a foreign country is generally more manageable through arbitration than through the national court system. This is especially true in former Soviet-bloc countries and developing countries where the

10. Willis Reese, "Conflict of Laws and the Restatement Second," 28 *Law & Contemporary Problems* 679 (1963).
11. Steven C. Nelson, "Alternatives to Litigation of International Disputes," 23 *International Lawyer* 187, 199 (1989).

Doing Business Internationally

The Role of Alternative Dispute Resolution in Japan[12]

The Japanese have characteristically been reluctant to litigate disputes. The Japanese litigation system promises up to a ten-year wait before a controversy is resolved. There is a cultural aversion to conflict based on ingrained notions of *wa* or peace and harmony. Informal resolution usually preserves the relationship between the parties. It removes the stigma of blame or fault associated with one who is found guilty or liable. The Japanese attitude toward compromise, conciliation, and arbitration is discussed below.

Compromise. Compromise or *wakai* differs from out-of-court settlement negotiations in that it involves a judge. In *benron-ken wakai* the parties present their cases orally before the judge and, with the judge, explore areas of compromise. In *soshjno wakai* or "compromise before the court," after thorough discussions with both parties, the judge generates compromise proposals. Compromise offers obvious benefits not found in traditional litigation. A compromise may preserve peace and the status quo and come at the expense of the legitimate expectations of one of the parties; unlike in a court of law, the judge in compromise proceedings is free to disregard the legal merits and standing of the parties in order to settle the dispute equitably and restore a sense of harmony between the parties. As a ruler under Confucian principles, the judge is bound to act with compassion and benevolence. The compromise proceedings are confidential. The compromise agreement represents a voluntary contract; parties are always free to refuse a judicially sponsored settlement, but the same judge presiding over the compromise proceedings would also hear the case at trial.

Conciliation. Conciliation or *chtei* may be initiated by application of the parties or by the court, and may occur while a lawsuit is pending. Unlike with court-sponsored compromise, a court appoints a conciliation committee. A conciliation commissioner must be a lawyer, must have expert knowledge and experience useful in settling disputes, and must possess "rich knowledge and experience in public life." There is, however, no guarantee that the outcome will reflect the legal merits of the case. Indeed, it has been described as "OK, OK (*maamaa*)" or "fifty/fifty (*seppan*)" conciliation because of the overriding emphasis placed on settling the dispute and restoring harmony.

Arbitration. Japanese arbitration or *chsai* can be divided into two categories: arbitration conducted between two Japanese parties and arbitration conducted between a Japanese party and a foreign party. Arbitration has not been favored as a method of dispute resolution among the Japanese because, like litigation, arbitration involves the "imposition" of a settlement by a third party and therefore cannot restore the harmony disrupted by the dispute. Arbitration has, however, gained widespread acceptance as a means of resolving disputes in international business transactions between Japanese and foreign parties. Arbitration allows Japanese concerns to negotiate "equitable positions as opposed to purely legal technicalities," and to avoid extensive pretrial discovery battles that serve only to "exacerbate the conflict."

enforcement of new substantive laws is uncertain and uneven. Furthermore, even when enforced, the remedies granted may be insufficient to fully protect the contract and property rights of the foreign party. In general, arbitral awards rendered in countries party to the New York Convention are readily enforceable in all other signatory countries.[13]

12. Andrew M. Pardieck, "Virtuous Ways and Beautiful Customs: The Role of Alternative Dispute Resolution in Japan," 11 *Temple International & Comparative Law Journal* 31, 33, 37–42, 44–45, 55 (1997).
13. Ibid. at 538.

The parties to a commercial transaction may provide in their contract that any disputes over interpretation or performance of the agreement will be resolved through arbitration. Arbitration is appealing for a variety of reasons. Frequently cited advantages over conventional litigation include potential savings in time and expense, confidentiality, and expertise of the arbitrators. For export transactions, in which the parties to the agreement are from different countries, additional advantages are neutrality, the avoidance of either party's domestic courts, and ease of enforcement. In an agreement to arbitrate, usually consisting of a clause inserted in the contract, the parties also have broad powers to specify many significant aspects of the arbitration. The arbitration clause may appoint an arbitration institute and may name the arbitration location, the law and rules that will govern, qualifications of the arbitrators, and the language in which the arbitral proceedings will be conducted.

For an international arbitration to work effectively, the national courts in the countries of both parties to the dispute must recognize and support arbitration. Should one party attempt to avoid arbitration after a dispute has arisen, the other party must be able to rely on the judicial system in either country to enforce the

Comparative Law

Convention on the Recognition and Enforcement of Foreign Arbitral Awards (June 10, 1958)[14]

Article I

When signing, ratifying or acceding to this Convention any State may on the basis of reciprocity declare that it will apply the Convention to the recognition and enforcement of awards made only in the territory of another Contracting State. It may also declare that it will apply the Convention only to differences arising out of legal relationships, whether contractual or not, which are considered as commercial under the national law of the State making such declaration.

Article II

Each Contracting State shall recognize an agreement in writing under which the parties undertake to submit to arbitration all or any differences which have arisen or which may arise between them in respect of a defined legal relationship, whether contractual or not, concerning a subject matter capable of settlement by arbitration.

The term "agreement in writing" shall include an arbitral clause in a contract or an arbitration agreement, signed by the parties or contained in exchange of letters or telegrams.

Article III

Each Contracting State shall recognize arbitral awards as binding and enforce them in accordance with the rules of procedure of the territory where the award is relied upon, under conditions laid down in the following articles.

Article IV

To obtain the recognition and enforcement mentioned in the preceding article, the party applying for recognition and enforcement shall, at the time of the application, supply a duly authenticated original award or certified copy.

14. Title 9 U.S.C. Sections 1–14 codify the United States Arbitration Act, the Convention on the Recognition and Enforcement of Foreign Arbitral Awards, and the Inter-American Convention on International Commercial Arbitration.

agreement to arbitrate. In addition, the party that wins in the arbitration proceeding must be confident that the national courts will enforce the decision of the arbitrators. The federal policy of the United States is to approve and support resolution of disputes by arbitration. Through the UN Convention on the Recognition and Enforcement of Foreign Arbitral Awards (New York Convention), which the United States ratified in 1970, more than 80 countries have undertaken international legal obligations to recognize and enforce arbitral awards, of which the People's Republic of China is the most recent. (See Comparative Law: Convention on the Recognition and Enforcement of Foreign Arbitral Awards.) The New York Convention is by far the most important international agreement on commercial arbitration and may be credited for much of the explosive growth of arbitration in international business disputes.[15]

Iran Aircraft Industries v. Avco Corporation

980 F.2d 141 (2d Cir. 1992)

Lumbard, Circuit Judge. The district court declined to enforce an award of the Iran-United States Claims Tribunal which resulted in an award of $3,513,086 due from Avco to the Iranian parties. The Iranian parties contend that the Award is enforceable under the United Nations Convention on the Recognition and Enforcement of Foreign Arbitral Awards (the "New York Convention").

The New York Convention

Avco argues that the district court properly denied enforcement of the Award pursuant to Article V(1)(b) of the New York Convention because it was unable to present its case to the Tribunal. Article V(1)(b) of the New York Convention "essentially sanctions the application of the forum country's standards of due process." The New York Convention, however, provides for nonenforcement where: "The party against whom the award is invoked was not given proper notice of the appointment of the arbitrator or of the arbitration proceedings or was otherwise unable to present his case." In this case, Avco was not made aware that the Tribunal required actual invoices to substantiate its claim. Having thus led Avco to believe it had used a proper method to substantiate its claim, the Tribunal then rejected Avco's claim for lack of proof. We believe that by so misleading Avco the Tribunal denied Avco the opportunity to present its claim in a meaningful manner. Accordingly, Avco was "unable to present its case" within the meaning of Article V(1)(b), and enforcement of the Award was properly denied.
AFFIRMED.

Cardamone, Circuit Judge, dissenting. The New York Convention obligates U.S. courts to enforce foreign arbitral awards unless certain defenses provided in article V(1) of the Convention are established. The specific defense with which we deal in the case at hand appears in article V(1)(b). That section states that enforcement of an arbitral award may be denied if the court is satisfied that the party against whom the award is sought to be enforced was unable to present its case before the arbitration panel. The standard, as the majority points out, essentially involves a due process inquiry to see whether the party against whom enforcement is sought has been put on notice and has had an opportunity to respond.

Avco was not denied due process before the Iran-U.S. Claims Tribunal. The ruling by the Hague Tribunal in the instant matter was not high-handed or arbitrary. A reading of prior cases reveals that they involved arbitration hearings actually cut short and not completed before an award was rendered. The present picture is vastly different. Avco had a full opportunity to present its claims, and was on notice that there might be a problem with its proof. Accordingly, I dissent and vote to enforce the award.

Case Highlights

- The New York Convention requires U.S. courts to enforce foreign arbitration awards.
- Enforcement of an arbitration award may be withheld if the losing party was denied due process.
- Due process requires the defendant be given proper notice and an opportunity to be heard.

15. Material taken from Trade Database, U.S. Dept. of Commerce.

The Convention provides for the full recognition of contract arbitration clauses and outlines a narrow set of grounds for the nonenforcement or vacating of an arbitration award. These include: (1) where an award was procured by corruption, fraud, or undue means; (2) where there was evident partiality or corruption in the arbitrators; (3) where the arbitrators were guilty of misconduct in refusing to postpone the hearing or in refusing to hear evidence pertinent and material to the controversy; (4) where the arbitrators exceed their powers; (5) where there was evident miscalculation of figures; and (6) where the arbitrators have awarded upon a matter not submitted to them. The *Iran Aircraft Industries* case above examined the issue of the enforceability of a foreign arbitration award.

It should be noted that an arbitration clause does not and should not completely separate the arbitration from the court system. At least in two instances the court system is crucial to the vitality of the arbitration process. The first is the most obvious—the arbitration award must be enforced through the court system. An unenforceable award renders the arbitration process an empty exercise. Fortunately, the New York Convention has provided security of enforcement in many national jurisdictions. Nonetheless, the arbitration clause should expressly state that the parties consent to the jurisdiction of any competent court for purposes of the enforcement and satisfaction of any award. Establishing an escrow account before arbitration commences will make enforcement less problematic and court-dependent. The parties can be required to deposit money, letters of credit, or insurance bonds. The arbitration clause should then provide that the arbitrator is empowered to release the funds held in escrow to satisfy any award.

A second role for the court system is in granting injunctive relief pending the outcome of the arbitration. The arbitration clause may provide that the parties can apply to the arbitrators for injunctive relief, but the arbitrator's ability to restrain the parties may be legally ineffective. Thus, the clause should also allow the parties to resort to the court system. This provision is especially important in the area of intellectual property, where the critical need to restrain the release of confidential information and trade secrets makes injunctive relief a necessity. It is important for the aggrieved party to maintain the *status quo* pending the outcome of the arbitration process.

The sensitivity of the information may also dictate a clause that restrains the release of information within the arbitration process. First, the clause should reiterate that all information provided in the arbitration is to remain private and confidential. Release of such information by one of the parties would be a ground for a separate claim. Second, the clause should provide that information is to be provided to the arbitrators during the resolution process and not during the selection process. The next section discusses the parameters for negotiating a proper arbitration clause

Arbitration and Mediation Clauses

Arbitration is the most common vehicle for dispute resolution in international commercial transactions.[16] It can be institutionalized through the use of standard rules provided by such organizations as the American Arbitration Association

16. "When businesses enter into transnational relationships such as contracts for the sale of goods, joint ventures, construction projects, or distributorships, the contract typically calls for arbitration in the event of any dispute." Yves Dezalay & Bryant Garth, "Merchants of Law as Moral Entrepreneurs: Constructing International Justice from the Competition for Transnational Business Disputes," 29 *Law & Society Review* 27, 30 (1995). Compare Christina S. Romano, "1996 Brazilian Commercial Arbitration Law," 5 *Annual Survey of International & Comparative Law* 27 (1999) (Brazil was slow in accepting the desirability of international commercial arbitration).

http://

American Society of International Law's Guide to Electronic Resources for International Law (section on Commercial Arbitration): **http://www.asil.org/**. Includes a database with 61 national arbitration statutes. Click on "Dispute Resolution."

(AAA) or the International Chamber of Commerce (ICC), or it can be done on an *ad hoc* basis.[17] Arbitration offers the potential for a shortened, cost-effective, confidential, and hopefully more amicable means to resolve a dispute. It allows the parties to select arbitrators with the necessary expertise to understand the technicalities of the issues in dispute. Also, an unusual choice of law is more likely to be sustained by a panel of arbitrators than by national courts of law. Unlike courts, arbitrators' primary mandate comes from the contractual arbitration clause and not national public policy concerns.

Confidentiality, especially in areas involving sensitive information, and the finality of arbitration awards (compared to the multiple appeals common in litigation) make alternative dispute resolution the preferred means for solving contractual disputes. Most courts will honor the dictates of an arbitration clause. The *Farrel Corporation* case demonstrates that there are some instances when a court will ignore such a clause.

THE CUSTOM ARBITRATION CLAUSE

A vague, simple arbitration clause is often not worth the paper it's printed on, since issues it does not deal with will likely need to be resolved in court. An arbitration clause should state the specific rules to be applied, such as the rules of the International Chamber of Commerce[18] or the **American Arbitration Association (AAA)**. The American Arbitration Association's standard clause states: "Any controversy or claim arising out of or relating to this contract shall be settled by arbitration administered by the American Arbitration Association in accordance with its applicable rules and judgment may be entered in any court having jurisdiction thereof." This clause makes clear that *all* issues pertaining to the contract are to be arbitrated and it provides a complete set of rules and procedures in referencing the AAA rules of arbitration. The *entry of judgment* language ("may be entered in any court") is essential to show intent that any arbitration award is to be final and binding. In short, in international contracting it is important "to make absolutely clear in the contract that both parties desire arbitration, are willing to accept judgment of an award, and are willing to accept judgment in any jurisdiction."[19]

http://

American Arbitration Association: **http://www.adr.org**.

The AAA standard clause does not provide for mediation or conciliation[20] as a means to resolve a dispute before a formal arbitration. It is highly recommended that a **med-arb clause** be utilized in most contracts. Conciliation or mediation as a required precursor to any arbitration is generally advantageous to both parties. First, mediation has been shown to be highly successful in resolving disputes promptly and preserving the long-term solidarity of the contractual relationship. Second, if mediation is unsuccessful, the parties will have a better understanding of the issues in dispute, which is likely to lead to a more efficient arbitration. Mediation may be more appealing if the clause states that the arbitrators may include mediation costs in their arbitration award. The downside of mediation is minimal,

17. Dezalay & Garth note that the arbitration rules of the United Nations Commission on International Trade Law are often used for *ad hoc* arbitration. Ibid. at 31. To find the UNCITRAL arbitration rules see 31 U.N. GAOR, Supp. No. 17, Doc. A/31/17 at 33 (1976), reprinted in 15 I.L.M. 701 (1976).
18. *International Chamber of Commerce*, Public Law No. 291, ICC 9-21, *Rules for the ICC Court of Arbitration* (1980).
19. James H. Davis, Kenneth E. Payne & John R. Thomas, "Drafting the Technology License Agreement," 13 *ALI-ABA Course Materials Journal* 27 (1996).
20. Some commentators distinguish between mediation and conciliation. Since there is no generally accepted definition to base any such differences, the two words will be used interchangeably. Mediation or conciliation refers to the use of a third party to negotiate a settlement of a dispute. The mediation is a nonbinding proceeding. The mediator has no power to issue a binding ruling.

Farrel Corporation v. International Trade Commission

949 F.2d 1147 (Fed. Cir. 1991)

Farrel manufactures and distributes worldwide heavy machinery used in mixing rubber and plastics. Pomini, an Italian company, also sells imported rubber and plastics processing machinery in competition with Farrel. From 1957 until 1986, Farrel and Pomini entered into a series of licensing agreements allowing Pomini to manufacture, using Farrel's technology, and sell a line of rubber and plastics mixing machines worldwide, with the exceptions of the United States, the United Kingdom and Japan.

The agreements included provisions requiring that Pomini return all designs, specifications, and other materials on the expiration of the contractual relationship. Each of the licensing agreements contained an arbitration clause requiring that "all disputes" be resolved by arbitration under the International Chamber of Commerce ("ICC"): "All disputes arising in connection with the present Agreement shall be finally settled by arbitration. Arbitration shall be conducted in Geneva, Switzerland, in accordance with the rules of Arbitration of the International Chamber of Commerce. Judgment upon the award rendered may be entered in any Court having jurisdiction, or application may be made to such Court for a judicial acceptance of the award and an order of enforcement, as the case may be."

On January 1, 1986, in accordance with the license provisions, Farrel terminated Pomini's rights to use or to retain Farrel technology. Approximately seven months later, Pomini announced that it planned to enter the U.S. market and supply American customers with internal mixing devices and components it manufactured in Italy. Farrel later alleged that Pomini was only able to do this by using trade secrets that Pomini had misappropriated from Farrel. Farrel filed a complaint against Pomini in the Tribunal of Busto Arsizio, an Italian civil court, alleging the misappropriation of trade secrets and infringement of various patents and trademarks registered in Italy. A similar suit was filed in the Scottish Court of Sessions, in which Farrel alleged that Pomini infringed certain of its patents and trademarks registered in the United Kingdom. In both suits, Pomini asserted, as an affirmative defense, the "existence of binding arbitration agreements between the parties requiring that all disputes be resolved by an arbitration panel of the ICC."

Meanwhile, on July 24, 1990, Farrel filed a complaint against Pomini with the Commission. It alleged that Pomini violated 19 U.S.C. § 1337(a) in the importation and sale of internal mixing machines and their components by misappropriating trade secrets, committing trademark infringement, and falsely representing the manufactures' source. Farrel petitioned for an immediate cease and desist order under 19 U.S.C. § 1337(f) and a limited permanent exclusion order forbidding entry into the United States of Pomini's internal mixing devices. On October 3, 1990, the administrative law judge ("ALJ") assigned to the case issued an initial determination terminating the investigation based on the existence of the arbitration clauses in the technology licensing agreements.

We have jurisdiction over appeals from the International Trade Commission. The Commission has exclusive authority to investigate, either on the basis of a complaint or on its own initiative, allegations that foreign importers are engaging in unfair methods of competition and unfair acts in the importation of articles. The ITC, through its staff, conducts the investigations. Farrel contends that the Commission, by relying on a private contractual arbitration agreement to terminate its investigation, acted contrary to its authority. We conclude that the Commission acted contrary to law by terminating its investigation on the basis of an arbitration agreement without first determining whether a violation existed as required under Section 1337. The Commission's decision terminating the instant investigation is REVERSED AND REMANDED.

Case Highlights

- The existence of an arbitration clause in a contract provides an affirmative defense against a party's commencement of litigation.
- The U.S. International Trade Commission (ITC) has exclusive jurisdiction over the issuance of cease and desist orders preventing infringing foreign goods from being imported into the United States.
- The ITC must research the merits of any claims of violations of the Tariff Act or intellectual property laws despite the existence of an arbitration agreement

since either party retains the power to end the mediation at any time in order to proceed to arbitration.

The standard arbitration clause above can be transformed easily into a med-arb clause by inserting the following language: "The parties agree first to attempt to settle the dispute through mediation administered by the AAA and its Commercial Mediation Rules or ICC Rules of Optional Conciliation before resorting to arbitration." Conciliation makes especial sense in an international business dispute because of the increased chance that misunderstandings are due to cultural and language differences.[21] Unfortunately, international mediation or conciliation is an underutilized dispute resolution device. Therefore, it is recommended that the arbitration clause state expressly that the parties have agreed to submit voluntarily to conciliation before they proceed with a formal arbitration.

http://
Mediation Information and Resource Center: **http://www.mediate.com** or ADR and Mediation Resources: **http://adrr.com**.

In order to stimulate interest in conciliation, the ICC updated its Conciliation Rules on January 1, 1988. The ICC Rules of Optional Conciliation, discussed in the next section, are made up of 11 concise articles intended to encourage simplicity, flexibility, timeliness, cost-savings, and confidentiality in the conciliation process. In practice, it is best for the parties to negotiate a custom clause. The additional time spent negotiating and drafting the clause will be well spent given the costs of international dispute resolution. Focus on Transactions: Issues in Drafting a Custom Arbitration Clause lists a number of issues that should be addressed in negotiating a custom arbitration clause.

ICC RULES OF OPTIONAL CONCILIATION

The ICC Rules of Optional Conciliation simplify the process of beginning conciliation. The parties simply submit an application for conciliation, along with a $500 application fee. The Secretary General of the ICC appoints a single conciliator. The conciliator then sets a time period for the parties to present their arguments. Flexibility is enhanced by the fact that the Rules place few restraints upon the conciliator. For example, the conciliator may or may not make settlement recommendations and, unlike in arbitration, may meet individually with either party. The ICC's position regarding costs is that they should be considerably less than the costs of arbitration. The ICC Schedule of Conciliation and Arbitration Costs fixes administrative expenses for conciliation at one-quarter of the amount of arbitration.

Concerns for confidentiality are emphasized in the rules' general mandate that the "confidential nature of the conciliation process shall be respected by every person." Use of the following conciliation-generated information in a subsequent arbitration or court proceeding is specifically prohibited: (1) any views expressed or suggested by any party with regard to a possible settlement; (2) any proposals enunciated by the conciliator; and (3) the fact that one of the parties was agreeable to the conciliator's recommendations.

LEGALITY OF ARBITRATION AND FORUM SELECTION CLAUSES

A well-written arbitration clause will answer not only the question of how a contract dispute is to be resolved, but also where the dispute is to be resolved. In the latter sense, an arbitration clause acts as a forum selection clause. In the past, U.S. courts

21. Eric A. Schwartz, "International Conciliation and the ICC," 5 *The ICC International Court of Arbitration Bulletin* 5, 6 (Nov. 1994).

Focus on Transactions

Issues in Drafting a Custom Arbitration Clause[22]

- **Governing Law:** Given the diversity of national legal systems, all international contracts should have a clearly written choice of law clause. The choice of law clause can direct the arbitrator away from any specific national law and require a decision based upon international law or the *lex mercatoria.* Also, the arbitrator may be empowered to grant any remedy that fairness or equity dictates.
- **Provisional Remedies:** The arbitration clause should clearly state whether or not provisional remedies, such as injunctions, might be obtained through application to the arbitrator. Failure to do so would require a party to incur the costs of obtaining a court order.
- **Escrow Provision:** Given the cost of enforcing judgments and arbitral awards in the international setting, the parties may want to ensure payment by requiring the establishment of an escrow fund. The fund may be established with the arbitration association (AAA, ICC), a law firm, or an independent escrow agent such as a commercial bank.
- **Venue of Arbitration:** A specific city should be named as the place of arbitration. The selection of the city of arbitration rests upon a number of factors, including convenience for parties, availability of qualified arbitrators, location within a country that is a signatory to the New York Convention, and the language of the proceeding.
- **Selection of Arbitrators:** The two types of selection are party-appointed and association appointed. The parties, especially when only one arbitrator is being used, may delegate their selection to the arbitration association. For a three-person arbitration panel, each party commonly selects one arbitrator from a list provided by the association. The party-selected arbitrators select the third arbitrator jointly.
- **Qualifications of Arbitrators:** The parties may list within their arbitration clause the requirements of the arbitrators to be appointed. In a complicated transaction, such as an intellectual property transfer, the parties may list different qualifications for each arbitrator. [23]
- **Discovery:** Most arbitration rules minimize the amount of discovery allowed. Depending on the complexity of the claims and sensitivity of the information, the parties may want to provide for discovery. It is suggested, however, that the contract language be specific as to what type of discovery is permitted. Furthermore, the clause should limit the time available for discovery in order to avoid the dangers of creating a litigation-type of arbitration. The clause may, for example, provide for discovery under the United States Federal Rules of Civil Procedure, but limit the discovery period to 120 days.
- **Remedies:** The parties may elect to restrict the type and amount of damages to be awarded through arbitration. For example, they may prohibit punitive damage awards or limit the amount of consequential damages.
- **Reasoned Awards:** Most arbitration rules do not require the arbitrators to itemize awards or to give reasons for their decision, but a reasoned award may offer future guidance for the parties. Therefore, the arbitration clause should require an itemized or reasoned award; it should state that the "award shall be in writing and shall specify all findings of fact and conclusions of law."

22. Source: American Arbitration Association at **http://www.adr.org**.
23. For example, the parties could require that one arbitrator be a certified public accountant familiar with the determination of gross and net revenues and the calculation of royalties, the second be an intellectual property attorney who specializes in a specific area of intellectual property law, and the third be a former administrative law judge or governmental regulatory official with expertise in the regulatory side of intellectual property protection or someone in the computer or technology transfer business.

often voided forum selection clauses as usurping the court's jurisdiction. One of the public policy concerns was to preserve the U.S. plaintiff's right to bring a lawsuit in a U.S. court. The United States Supreme Court in the *Bremen v. Zapata Off-Shore Co.*[24] case held that a forum selection clause should be voided only in unusual cases. The court determined that forum selection clauses are to be enforced fully unless the attacking party meets "the heavy burden of showing that its enforcement would be unreasonable, unfair, or unjust." The court explained that the challenging party needed to show that the "contractual forum will be so gravely difficult and inconvenient" that the plaintiff will, for all practical purposes, be deprived of her right to proceed with her claim. The court's stated rationale was that the expansion of U.S. business would be retarded if "we insist on a parochial concept that all disputes must be resolved under our law and in our courts." Furthermore, it reasoned that the security and predictability of international contracts and contract dispute resolution must be ensured. "The elimination of uncertainties by agreeing in advance on a forum acceptable to both parties is an indispensable element in international trade and contracting." The *Tennessee Imports, Inc.*, case explores the issues of the arbitrability of specific issues and the enforceability of arbitration clauses.

Tennessee Imports, Inc. v. Pier Paulo

745 F. Supp. 1314 (Mid D. Tenn. 1990)

Nixon, District Judge. Plaintiff, Tennessee Imports, Inc., brought this action for breach of contract and tortious interference with contract against defendant Prix Italiais an Italian corporation with its principal place of business in Venice, Italy. The contract provided that "should any dispute arise between the contractual parties or in connection with the relations stipulated by this contract and no settlement can be achieved, then both parties agree to the competence of the Arbitration Court of the Chamber of Commerce in Venice, Italy." Tennessee Imports argued that enforcement of this provision would result in substantial inconvenience and would deny it effective relief. Furthermore, that the tortious interference claim is not within the scope of the forum selection clause. The defendants have responded to the plaintiff's arguments as follows: (1) That the Arbitration Court referred to in Article 8 is the Arbitration Court of the International Chamber of Commerce, a well-recognized and competent arbitral body which may conduct proceedings in Venice, (2) That the contract between Prix and Tennessee Imports was the result of "arms length negotiations by experienced and sophisticated business entities," and (3) That, because of the expansion of American trade and commerce in world markets, public policy now supports upholding forum selection clauses.

A. The Federal Arbitration Act

Because the forum selection clause at issue is also an arbitration clause found in the contract involving international commerce, its validity, interpretation, and enforcement are governed by the Federal Arbitration Act, 9 U.S.C. § 1 et seq. Congress enacted the Arbitration Act in 1924 "to ensure judicial enforcement of privately made agreements to arbitrate." The Act sets up "a presumption in favor of arbitration," and requires that courts "rigorously enforce agreements to arbitrate." In the field of international commerce, this presumption in favor of arbitration was strengthened by adoption of the United Nations Convention on the Recognition and Enforcement of Foreign Arbitral Awards ("New York Convention"). The United States ratified the Convention on September 30, 1970, with certain reservations as allowed by Article I (3) of the Convention. These reservations include the following: "The United States of America will apply the Convention, on the basis of reciprocity, to the recognition and enforcement of only those awards made in the territory of another Contracting State." Italy ratified the Convention on January 31, 1969, without reservations.

The language of the Convention contemplates a very limited inquiry by the courts in determining the enforceability of arbitration clauses found in international com-

24. 407 U.S. 1 (1971).

mercial agreements. In making this determination, the Court must first address three questions: (1) Is there an agreement in writing to arbitrate the subject of the dispute?, (2) Does the agreement provide for arbitration in the territory of a signatory country?, and (3) Does the agreement arise out of a legal relationship, whether contractual or not, which is considered as commercial? In the case of narrow arbitration clauses, the court will determine if issues fall within the scope of an arbitration clause before referring them to arbitration.

In the case of broad arbitration clauses, arbitrability of issues arguably falls within the scope of the clause and it will be left to the arbitrators to determine whether an issue falls within the scope of a clause. Nevertheless, in certain cases, a stay or preliminary injunction may be a more appropriate solution. A court may issue a preliminary injunction if it deems preliminary injunctive relief necessary to ensure that the arbitration process remains a meaningful one.

B. The Enforceability of the Arbitration Clause

Each of the two parties is incorporated and has their principal place of business in different countries that are signatories to the New York Convention. The sales contract contains an express agreement to arbitrate and provides for arbitration in Italy. Thus, if the disputes between these parties fall within the scope of their arbitration agreement, this Court must enforce that agreement unless the Court finds that it falls within the Tennessee Imports' claim of inducing and procuring breach. A party cannot tortiously induce a breach of its own contract. Tennessee Imports cannot escape arbitration merely by characterizing these claims as sounding in tort. Courts have consistently held that broad arbitration clauses encompass contract-based tort claims.

Tennessee Imports argues that Prix used its superior economic power to obtain Tennessee Imports' assent to the arbitration clause without negotiation and, as such, it is adhesive and unconscionable. The Uniform Commercial Code addresses the subject of unconscionability in §2-302. It states that "the basic test is whether, in the light of the general commercial background and the commercial needs of the particular trade or case, the clauses involved are so one-sided as to be unconscionable under the circumstances existing at the time of the making of the contract and not of disturbance of allocation of risks because of superior bargaining power." The clause is not hidden in the small print boilerplate of a standard form contract. It is not the product of a battle of forms. It is not buried among the provisions of a lengthy and complex sales agreement. On its face, the contract appears to be one specifically drawn to define the relationship between these two parties. Tennessee Imports appears to have had ample opportunity to examine the contract before executing it. Having made its choice, Tennessee Imports must now abide by it.

The parties are hereby REFERRED to arbitration.

Case Highlights

- Arbitration clauses that state the place for arbitration also serve as forum selection clauses.
- In a case involving a "narrow" arbitration clause, the court will determine if issues fall within the scope of an arbitration clause before referring them to arbitration.
- In case of "broad" arbitration clauses, the arbitrators will generally determine the arbitrability of an issue.
- A court may issue a preliminary injunction if it deems preliminary injunctive relief necessary to ensure that the arbitration process remains a meaningful one.
- Courts are not receptive to attacks on the enforceability of an arbitration clause on ground of unconscionability, especially when both parties are merchants.

In the area of consumer purchases, some courts continue to void arbitration clauses. In a 1999 case, a New York court voided an arbitration clause as unconscionable under Section 2-302 of the Uniform Commercial Code. *Bower v. Gateway*[25] involved the sale of a Gateway computer. After receiving an order either by mail, phone, or internet, Gateway mails its "Standard Terms and Conditions of Agreement." The Standard Terms state that any dispute will be resolved under the arbitration rules of the International Chamber of Commerce. The court in *Bower* held that the high cost of arbitration would unconscionably deter the purchaser from invoking a claim.

25. 676 N.Y.S.2d 569 (App. Div. 1999).

In contrast, arbitration is accepted without question in most international business settings. The court in *Europcar Italia, S.P.A. v. Maiellano Tours, Inc.*[26] held that any party to a foreign arbitration award may seek confirmation in a U.S. court within three years after the award was made.[27] The case involved the enforcement of an award made through an informal procedure in Italy. The United States Circuit Court held that "in light of the differences in arbitration among the signatory countries, the New York Convention should be read broadly to cover both formal and informal arbitration. A stay of confirmation should not be lightly granted lest it encourage abusive tactics by the party that lost in arbitration."[28]

The next two sections examine two clauses, *force majeure* and liquidated damages, that should also be analyzed in conjunction with the dispute resolution clause. The *force majeure* clause provides excuses against breach of contract claims. The occurrence of a *force majeure* event precludes the nonbreaching party from pursuing litigation or arbitration against the breaching party. The liquidated damages clause, where the parties agree in advance to damages in the event of breach, may make litigation or arbitration unnecessary.

FORCE MAJEURE *CLAUSE*

A ***force majeure*** (superior force) clause allows a party to terminate its obligations under a contract due to the occurrence of something described in the clause. *Force majeure* events may include wars, blockades, strikes, governmental interference or approval, fire, transportation problems, and others. Any event expressly designated by the parties will be given *force majeure* effect. Often overlooked, a *force majeure* clause should be custom drafted to take into account the type of industry, the countries, and type of carriage involved.

In *Harriscom Svenska*[29] the *force majeure* clause enabled a seller to avoid liability for not performing on a contract. An Iranian distributor filed a breach of contract claim against a manufacturer of radio communications products. The manufacturer claimed an excuse under the agreement's *force majeure* clause. It claimed that the U.S. government prohibition on all sales to Iran of goods it categorized as military equipment was a *force majeure* event. The U.S. State Department began a commodity jurisdiction proceeding, authorized by the Arms Export Control Act, to decide whether the radio was a military product that should be on the government's Munitions List. Placement on the list would require the manufacturer to obtain export licenses for all its sales of the radio, not just those to Iran. The manufacturer negotiated a compromise in which it agreed to "voluntarily withdraw from further sales to the Iranian market." In exchange, the government agreed that the radio was not subject to the stringent export controls of Munitions List products.

One of the issues before the court was whether the manufacturer's failure to ship spare radio parts was a voluntary act or a *force majeure.* Other issues included whether the defendant was released under the *force majeure* clause that excused performance under circumstances of governmental interference, whether the voluntary nature of defendant's compliance negated the excuse, and whether the defendant was required to give substituted performance through its Indian licensee.

26. Docket No. 97-7224 (2d Cir. 1997).
27. 9 U.S.C. § 207.
28. See also Fertilizer Corp. of India v. IDI Management, Inc., 517 F.Supp. 948 (S.D. Ohio 1981).
29. 3 F.3d 576 (1993).

Despite the voluntary nature of the defendant's actions, the court held that the government had undoubted power to compel compliance. Like commercial impracticability, a *force majeure* clause excuses nonperformance when circumstances beyond the control of the parties prevent performance. The court held that the governmental interference in this case was such a circumstance.

The *force majeure* clause that excuses a breaching party from liability for nonperformance is common under most national legal systems. *Force majeure* refers to "extraordinary events independent of the parties' will that cannot be foreseen or averted by them with due diligence, being beyond their control and preventing the contracting party from fulfilling the obligation undertaken in the contract."[30] Most *force majeure* events require four criteria in order to satisfy the requirements of most national laws: (1) the event must be external to the transaction and the parties, (2) it must render the performance radically different from that originally contemplated, (3) it must have been unforeseeable (objectively), and its (4) occurrence must be beyond the control of the party concerned.[31]

The importance of a well-drafted *force majeure* clause is illustrated by the case of *Bende & Sons, Inc. v. Crown Recreation, Inc.*[32] In that case a U.S. seller of combat boots sought an excuse for nonperformance due to the derailment of the train transporting the boots. He sought the excuse of commercial impracticability under Section 2-615 of the Uniform Commercial Code. Section 2-615 provides for an excuse for nonperformance when performance is "made impracticable by the occurrence of a contingency the nonoccurrence of which was a basic assumption on which the contract was made." Surprisingly, the court rejected the defense, holding that the derailment was an allocated risk because "common sense dictates that they could easily have foreseen such an occurrence[!]"[33]

In *Phillips Puerto Rico Core, Inc. v. Tradax Petroleum*[34] liability rested upon the interpretation of a standard *force majeure* clause in relationship to the trade term. The clause in question read as follows:

> FORCE MAJEURE: *In the event of any strike, fire or other event falling within the term* Force Majeure *preventing or delaying shipment or delivery of the goods by the seller . . . then the contract period of shipment or delivery shall be extended by 30 days on telex request made within seven days of its occurrence. Should shipment or delivery of the goods continue to be prevented beyond 30 days, the unaffected party may cancel the unfulfilled balance of the contract. Should the contract thus be cancelled and/or performance be prevented during any extension to the shipment or delivery period neither party shall have any claim against the other.*[35]

In *Phillips Puerto Rico Core, Inc.*, the Cost and Freight (C & F) contract was entered for the purchase of a product to be shipped from Algeria to Puerto Rico. The U.S. Coast Guard unexpectedly detained the ship while in transit. The purchaser

30. Theo Rauh, "Legal Consequences of *Force Majeure* Under German, Swiss, English, and United States' Law," 25 *Denver Journal of International Law & Policy* 151 (1996).
31. Ibid. at 152.
32. 548 F. Supp. 1018 (E.D. Louisiana 1982).
33. Ibid. at 1022.
34. 782 F.2d 314 (1985).
35. This clause does possess a number of good features even though it does not adequately define the term *force majeure.* It does define the responsibilities of the party attempting to declare *force majeure.* It also provides an automatic 30-day performance extension before allowing the purchaser to cancel the contract. A graduated response to a *force majeure* event should be considered when drafting a *force majeure* clause. The drafter should attempt to define not only the events to be considered as *force majeure*, but also the relative duties and rights of each party stemming from such an event.

brought suit against the seller for breach of contract, and the seller claimed an excuse by invoking the *force majeure* clause. The court held that the defense was not necessary because under the C & F term the risk of loss had already passed to the purchaser at the port of shipment.

The *force majeure* clause should be a highly negotiated, customized provision dealing with the particulars of the specific parties and specific type of contract. Unfortunately, most contracts, domestic and international, utilize vaguely worded standard excuse or exemption clauses. The International Chamber of Commerce has developed a more elaborate *force majeure* clause.[36] The following is an edited version of the ICC clause:

> *A party is not liable for a failure to perform if he can prove that: (1) the failure was due to an impediment beyond his control, (2) he could not have reasonably foreseen the impediment at the time of contract formation, and (3) he could not have reasonably avoided or overcome its effects.*
>
> *An impediment includes but is not limited to:*
> *(a) war, hostilities, and acts of piracy,*
> *(b) natural disasters,*
> *(c) explosions, fires, and destruction of machinery,*
> *(d) boycotts, strikes, lock-outs, and work stoppages which occur in the enterprise of the party seeking relief,*
> *(e) acts of authority.*
>
> *A party seeking relief pursuant to this clause shall give notice as soon as practicable. Failure to give timely notice makes the party liable in damages for losses that could otherwise have been avoided. Notice shall also be given when the impediment ceases.*
>
> *The relief granted under this clause is a postponement of the time for performance for such period as may be reasonable. The nonbreaching party may also suspend his own performance. Either party may terminate the contract in the event that the impediment persists for a period of ____days. Upon the termination of the contract, each party may retain whatever he has received, but must account to the other party for any unjust enrichment.*

The concept of *force majeure* or excuse has been incorporated in Article 79 of the Convention for the International Sale of Goods (see Chapter 8). Article 79 refers to a *force majeure* event as an **impediment.** *Impediment* does not mean inconvenient, or more costly, or difficult to perform. The nonforeseeable requirement is generally interpreted as reasonably nonforeseeable since technically everything is foreseeable. "The clause refers to what a party could reasonably be expected to take into account and to make contingency plans for when entering into the contract." Regarding the impediments enumerated above: work stoppages or strikes at a supplier or subcontractor are generally not sufficient causes. This presumption may be overcome if, for example, the contract specifies the use of the particular supplier or subcontractor.

Since the *force majeure* clause generally does not recognize changes in circumstances that result in mere hardship, the parties may expand the clause to include events that make performance not impossible but unduly costly. Such a clause is referred to as a **hardship clause.** The ICC has published a manual titled "*Force Majeure* and Hardship," which asserts that an occurrence that "fundamentally alters the contractual equilibrium by placing an excessive burden on one of the parties"

36. ICC Publication No. 421, "*Force Majeure* and Hardship" (1985).

allows that party to request a revision of the contract. The requesting party must make the request within a reasonable time. The parties are to consult in good faith in the hope of amicably revising the contract. If no agreement is reached within a specified period of time then "the parties are to submit the case to the ICC Standing Committee for the Regulation of Contractual Relations for a nonbinding decision or either party may submit the issue for binding arbitration pursuant to the contract's arbitration clause." The hardship provision is especially warranted for long-term or multiple installment contracts.

Another *force majeure*-type of clause that can be considered is the **government approval clause.** If some government permit, license, or approval is required in order to perform under the contract, then the parties may elect to have the approval be a *condition precedent* to the contract. This type of provision is especially appropriate in an intellectual property transfer transaction in a country where government approval is required. A simple government approval clause in an export contract would read: "Seller shall obtain all necessary permits, licenses, or approvals to export the goods. Buyer shall obtain all necessary permits, licenses, or approvals to import the goods. This contract is not fully executed and enforceable until such approvals have been received."[37]

LIQUIDATED DAMAGES CLAUSE

Liquidated damages clauses state in advance the damages that the parties agree to voluntarily pay upon breaching the contract, technically eliminating the need for a court action or arbitral proceeding. These clauses, however, also known as penalty clauses, are not uniformly enforced under all national legal systems. This section will compare substantive differences in liquidated damages law among different legal systems. The common law system requires courts to void liquidated damages clauses that act as penalties. A penalty is an inflated amount aimed at punishing the breaching party. This voiding of penalties is a minority approach under most national laws.[38] The French Civil Code deals directly with the issue of liquidated damages or penalty clauses: Article 1152 allows the courts to provide alternative relief if the stipulated amount is "manifestly excessive." It expressly grants courts the authority to reduce or increase the penalty if it is deemed to be manifestly excessive or low. In Japan, there is a strong presumption that penalty clauses are enforceable,[39] but Article 420(1) of the Japanese Civil Code precludes a court from reforming the contract amount.

The laws of Denmark, Sweden, Finland, and Norway allow either the voiding or reformation of a penalty clause deemed unreasonable. The Russian Civil Code provides that "the debtor must pay the penalty established for the breach regardless of whether or not the creditor has suffered damages as a result of the breach" and, in Article 190, allows a court to reduce the amount of the penalty or liquidated damages if it is "extraordinarily large in comparison with the creditor's actual losses." In contrast, Anglo-American common law simply allows for the voiding of a penalty clause when the stipulated amount is considered unreasonably large.

37. William F. Fox, Jr., *International Commercial Agreements: A Primer on Drafting, Negotiating and Resolving Disputes* 145 (2d ed. 1992).
38. Courts are required simply to set aside a clause which is found to impose a true penalty.
39. Article 420(3) of the Japanese Civil Code states that "a penalty clause is presumed to be a determination in advance of the amount of compensation due for damages." *International Chamber of Commerce, Guide to Penalty and Liquidated Damages Clauses* 37 (1990).

In order to provide some uniformity between common law and civil law, the Council of Europe adopted *Resolution (78) 3 on Penal Clauses in the Civil Law.*[40] It adopts the civil law approach that the "sum stipulated may be reduced by the court when it is manifestly excessive." In its Explanatory Memorandum, the Committee on Legal Cooperation explained that some penal clauses are "*stricto sensu* whose main purpose is to act as a threat to induce the promisor to perform" while others are "a genuine preassessment of damages or liquidated damages." However, unlike in the common law, the clauses that are *stricto sensu* are not invalid *per se* under the civil law. In short, it is acceptable under the civil law for a liquidated damages clause to serve as not only a means for just compensation, but also an incentive to induce performance.

A further review of foreign national laws demonstrates that the common law approach to liquidated damages is not the only viable alternative. For example, the Foreign Contract Law of the People's Republic of China[41] does not deal directly with the issue of liquidated damages, but allows for the use of deposits as a way of fixing damages unrelated to actual damages. Article 14 of the law allows a party to retain the deposit if the other party fails to perform. Alternatively, if the party holding the deposit fails to perform, then it must return twice the amount of the deposit. This concept of deposit forfeiture mimics the doctrine of *arrhes* found in Section 1590 of the French Civil Code. Under the doctrine of *arrhes* a deposit is forfeited when the deposit giver cancels a contract. If the deposit holder cancels the contract, then that party must refund twice the amount of the deposit. The rules embodied in the doctrine of *arrhes* can be understood as the use of deposits as liquidated damages. Furthermore, the potentially penal nature of retaining the entire deposit or doubling the amount refunded is disregarded under this doctrine.

Key Terms

Act of State, 102
American Arbitration Association (AAA), 114
Brussels Convention on Jurisdictional Judgments in Civil and Commercial Matters, 106
choice of law clause, 107
conflict of law rules, 107
discovery, 104
doctrine of *renvoi*, 107
dual service, 99
force majeure, 120
forum non conveniens doctrine, 101
government approval clause, 123
Hague Convention on International Jurisdiction and Foreign Judgemwnts in Civil and Commercial Matters, 106
Hague Evidence Convention, 104
Hague Service Convention, 99
hardship clause, 122
impediment, 122
Inter-American Convention on the Extraterritorial Validity of Foreign Judgments, 104
International Chamber of Commerce (ICC), 109
Lugano Convention, 104
med-arb clause, 114
New York Convention, 106
personal jurisdiction, 99
rule of reciprocity, 104
service of process, 99

40. Adopted by the Committee of Ministers on January 20, 1978, at the 281st meeting of the Ministers' Deputies.
41. See generally Zhang Yuqing & James S. McLean, "China's Foreign Economic Contract Law: Its Significance and Analysis," 8 *Northwestern Journal of International Law & Business* 120 (1987).

Chapter Problems

1. Abraham Lincoln once gave this advice relating to litigation: "Persuade your neighbors to compromise whenever they can. Point out to them how the nominal winner is often the real loser—in fees, expenses, and waste of time. As a peacemaker the lawyer has a superior opportunity of being a good man." The Roman philosopher Cicero once admonished that "the litigious spirit is more often found with ignorance than with knowledge of law." Do you agree with this view of litigation? Do you believe that alternative dispute resolution is adequately used by U.S. business enterprises? What would you recommend for improving the U.S. dispute resolution system?

2. Several securities investors who were customers of a broker signed a standard agreement that included a clause requiring the arbitration of any controversies relating to their accounts. When the investments turned sour, the investors sued the broker and the broker's principal in the United States District Court for the Southern District of Texas under the 1933 Securities Act. The defendant moved that the claims be submitted to arbitration, under the agreement. Should the plaintiffs be forced to arbitrate their federal securities law claims? Does the public policy of full enforcement of the securities laws prevail over the public policy favoring arbitration? *Rodriguez de Quijas v. Shearson/American Express, Inc.*, 490 U.S. 477 (Supreme Court 1989).

3. Your son has been killed in a car accident in a foreign country. You believe a U.S. agency is holding information that may provide insight into the cause of the accident. You file a motion to compel the agency to comply with your subpoena requesting certain documents. Will the court compel the agency to comply with the subpoena? Does the notion of sovereign immunity enter into the court's determination? *In re Application of Mohamed al Fayed*, 92 F.Supp.2d 137 (D.D.C., 2000).

4. Pursuant to a request by a foreign court, a legal alien resident of the United States is asked to testify about his activities during World War II and his immigration to the United States. Can he be compelled to testify against himself? Does the Fifth Amendment's privilege against self-incrimination extend to the fear of being prosecuted by a foreign nation? *United States v. Balsys*, 118 S.Ct. 2218 (1998).

5. A U.S. seller and an English purchaser of services enter into a contract for servicing of heavy machinery at the purchaser's factory. The service contract included an exculpatory clause that relieved the seller of all liability relating to his work. U.S. law generally enforces such clauses while English law often voids such clauses. The choice of law clause in the contract provided that U.S. law would apply to the contract. Soon after the U.S. seller serviced the machinery it malfunctioned, injuring two workers and causing substantial property damage to the English company's factory. The English party brought suit in an English court. The U.S. company seeks a dismissal citing the exculpatory clause. What factors will the English court look at in determining the validity of the choice of law clause as it relates to the issues of this case?

Internet Activities

1. Review the model arbitration and mediation clauses published by the International Chamber of Commerce at **http://www.iccwbo.org/index_court.asp**.

2. Review the index of the 35 international conventions sponsored by the Hague Conference on Private International Law at **http://www.hcch.net/e/conventions/index.html**.

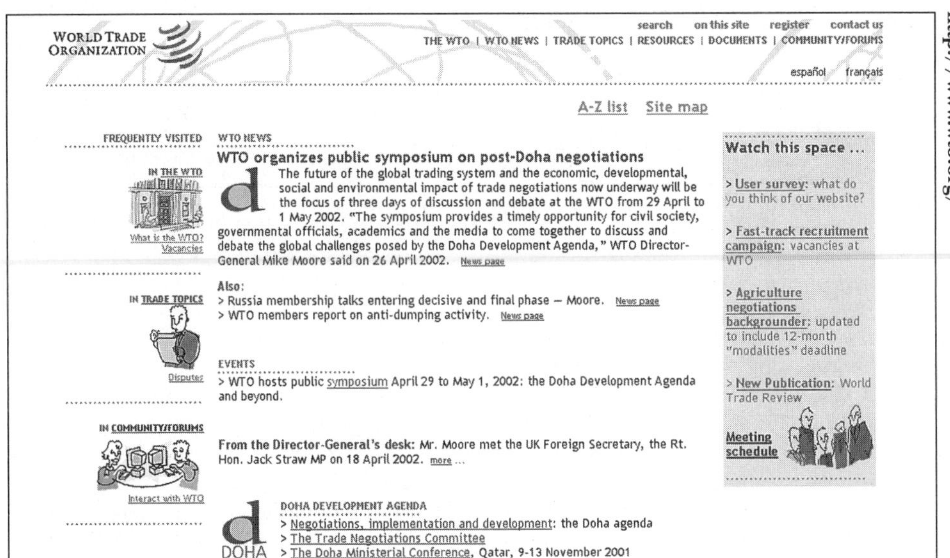

http://www.wto.org/

Chapter 5 International Trade Regulation

This chapter is the first of two covering international and governmental regulation of international trade. We will first look at the world trading system as it has evolved under the General Agreement on Tariffs and Trade (GATT). The postwar success of GATT has led to the establishment of a permanent international institution known as the World Trade Organization (WTO). The primary purpose of the WTO is to remove barriers to international free trade. Chapter 5 will review the WTO and the agreements it has been empowered to enforce. International trade has also been affected by the development of strong regional trading blocs. Two of the more successful attempts at regional trade integration, the European Union and the North American Free Trade Agreement (NAFTA), will be examined.

Extending the coverage of trade regulation to the national level, Chapter 6 will examine the relationship between national trade regulation and the world trading system, particularly export and import regulations. Topics include import requirements, the assessment of tariff duties, country of origin rules, marking requirements, and national standards regulations. Chapter 6 concludes with an examination of the U.S. export regulation system. The student should read Chapter 6 after becoming familiar with the requirements of the WTO system presented in this chapter.

WORLD TRADING SYSTEM

The multilateral trading system known as the **General Agreement on Tariffs and Trade (GATT)** has been guided by a number of foundational principles. The initial aim of GATT was to expand free trade through the reduction of tariffs worldwide. Since GATT's creation in 1947, there have been eight rounds of GATT negotiations. As a result of these negotiations, by 1990 tariff rates among the industrial countries have fallen to an average rate of 6.3%. This can be compared to the tariff rates enacted by the United States in the Smoot-Hawley Act of 1930. Under that act tariffs ranged from 50 percent to 100 percent.

http://
Kluwer Law International, *Journal of World Trade*: **http://www.kluwerlaw.com**.

Promising not to raise a trade barrier is as important as lowering one. Under GATT, when countries agree to open their markets they are required to bind their commitments. In the area of tariffs, bindings amount to placing ceilings upon customs tariff rates. Countries may reduce their tariff rates below the bound rates but may not exceed the bound rates. One of the achievements of the final rounds of GATT was to increase the amount of trade covered by **binding commitments:**

Increased Bindings Due to Uruguay Round

Percentages of tariffs bound	Before 1986	After 1994
Developed Countries	78	99
Developing Countries	21	73
Transition Economies	73	98

For example, 100% of agricultural products are now subject to bound tariffs. Expansion of binding commitments has resulted in a tremendous increase in market stability and security.

Because of the great success of reducing tariffs, the eighth round of GATT, the **Uruguay Round,**[1] expanded for the first time into nontariff areas such as services and intellectual property. The U.S. Department of Commerce now defines trade barriers to include not only tariffs, but also quantitative restrictions, import licensing, and customs barriers; standards, testing, labeling, and certification; government procurement, export subsidies, service barriers, lack of intellectual property protection, and investment barriers. Most important, the Uruguay Round culminated with the establishment of a permanent body to oversee the implementation of GATT principles and agreements—the **World Trade Organization (WTO).** Other WTO agreements produced by the Uruguay Round include the **General Agreement on Trade in Services (GATS)** and the **Agreement on Trade-Related Aspects of Intellectual Property Rights (TRIPS).**

http://
World Trade Organization: **http://www.wto.org**.

1. The United States Congress ratified and implemented the Uruguay Round agreements in December 1994 under the Uruguay Round Agreements Act. See Public Law No. 103-465, 108 Stat. 4809.

GATT PRINCIPLES

The three founding principles of GATT are the most-favored-nation principle, national treatment principle, and the principle of transparency. All three are aimed at advancing the notion of nondiscrimination by which countries are mandated not to discriminate among different foreign trading partners or between domestic goods and imported goods. The **most-favored-nation principle** requires that members of the WTO offer all other members their most favorable tariff rates. If a country grants benefits to a trading partner through a bilateral agreement, then it must also grant those benefits to all other members of the WTO. Thus, when a country lowers a trade barrier or opens up a domestic market it has to do so for all its trading partners.

There are two major exceptions to the most-favored-nation principle. First, a country can raise barriers to the importation of goods from specific countries that have violated the principles of GATT. These punitive barriers are generally enacted in response to the giving of illegal **subsidies** by a foreign government or when a foreign exporter is accused of **dumping** goods on a foreign market. A subsidy is when a government grants a domestic industry some benefit not granted a foreign industry. Dumping is when a foreign company exports and sells goods at below-market prices. Dumping can be proven by showing that the goods are sold below cost or at a price that is lower than the price the goods are sold at in the exporter's home country. Before enacting any countervailing measures, the country that has been victimized must seek WTO permission through the WTO dispute resolution process. The respective cases of both countries are presented to an *ad hoc* WTO panel, which then renders a decision. If the complainant wins the panel will sanction a specific remedy, generally a tariff increase for an illegal subsidy or a **countervailing duty** in dumping cases.

The second major exception to the most-favored-nation principle is the formation by countries of regional free trade areas whose agreements do not apply to goods from outside the regional group. The countries within the group may lower barriers among themselves without having to grant the reduced barriers to other WTO countries. Thus, the trade agreements embodied in the **European Union (EU)**[2] and the **North American Free Trade Agreement (NAFTA)**[3] do not violate the WTO Agreements.

The **national treatment principle** applies only once goods enter a foreign market. Once a product, intellectual property right, or service enters a foreign market it must receive the same treatment given to domestically produced goods, services, and intellectual property rights even though it can be treated differently at the time of importation. Therefore, charging customs duties on imported goods is not a violation of the national treatment principle. Import requirements that are disguised trade barriers would be subject to attack as a violation of national treatment. For example, requiring foreign goods to satisfy higher standards or to pass more rigorous testing or inspections than domestic goods would be illegal. The *Warren Corp. v. EPA* case that follows illustrates the fact that international obligations as required under GATT may conflict with domestic requirements.

The **transparency principle** is the third founding principle of GATT. The transparency principle prohibits a country from making its import standards and

2. Members of the European Union include Austria, Belgium, Denmark, Finland, France, Germany, Greece, Ireland, Italy, Luxembourg, Netherlands, Portugal, Spain, Sweden, and the United Kingdom.

3. The NAFTA members are United States, Canada, and Mexico.

George E. Warren Corp. v. U.S. Environmental Protection Agency

164 F.3d 676 (D.C. Cir. 1998)

A rule promulgated by the Environmental Protection Agency regulates emissions from conventional gasoline for motor vehicles, and changes the way importers and foreign refiners of conventional gasoline sold in the United States had been treated under the prior rule. In 1994 the EPA announced standards for setting individual baselines under which domestic refiners, foreign refiners, and importers were all treated differently. Domestic refiners were each required to establish an individual baseline because the EPA determined they have adequate and reliable data with which to do so. Each importer was permitted to establish an individual baseline, but because they generally lacked the data to do so, importers were in practice assigned the statutory baseline.

In 1995 the World Trade Organization held the 1994 rule violated the antidiscrimination norm of the General Agreement on Tariffs and Trade because domestic refiners were allowed to set individual baselines while foreign refiners were not. The United States Trade Representative in June 1996 advised the WTO that the United States intended to comply with that decision. The EPA accordingly solicited public comment to identify its choices and later proposed to adopt the optional baseline approach it had rejected in the 1994 rule, allowing each foreign refiner either to accept the statutory baseline or to petition the EPA for permission to establish an individual baseline. The petitioners challenge the legality of this 1997 rule.

Again proceeding from the mistaken premise that the maintenance or improvement of air quality is the sole focus of the antidumping provision, the petitioners argue that the EPA may not consider factors other than air quality. Thus do they challenge the EPA's consideration of the WTO's decision interpreting the GATT. The EPA responds that nothing in the statute precludes consideration of such factors, and that its approach is congruent with that employed by the Congress when it enacted the antidumping provision. We think the agency's interpretation is permissible. "Since the days of Chief Justice Marshall, the Supreme Court has consistently held that congressional statutes must be construed wherever possible in a manner that will not require the United States to violate the law of nations." If the United States is to be able to gain the benefits of international accords and have a role as a trusted partner in multilateral endeavors, its courts should be most cautious before interpreting its domestic legislation in such manner as to violate international agreements. There is a fundamental distinction between EPA's ability to monitor and enforce regulatory requirements that would apply against domestic as opposed to foreign refiners. Simply put, domestic refiners are subject to the full panoply of EPA's regulatory jurisdiction and compliance monitoring, while not all foreign refiners desiring to produce reformulated and/or conventional gasoline may be subject to EPA's regulatory jurisdiction with equivalent certainty. Accordingly, the petitions for review are DENIED.

Case Highlights

- GATT's national treatment principle requires that individuals and firms of foreign countries are given the same competitive opportunities, including market access, as are available to domestic parties.
- International agreements prevail over conflicting national statutory mandates.
- Federal regulatory agencies may weigh different factors (such as international commitments) when rendering a decision or applying a regulation to a situation with international ramifications and a purely domestic one.

requirements secretive. It also precludes a country from constantly changing import requirements without reason. Most WTO agreements require governments to fully disclose import polices and practices publicly including formally notifying the WTO of any changes. Disguised barriers often violate both the national treatment and transparency principles.

THE WTO AGREEMENTS

http://
Harvard Law School—WTO documents and press releases: **http://www.law.harvard.edu/library/ref/ils_ref/world_trade.htm**.

The 1980s and 1990s witnessed a tremendous liberalization of international trade law. The breadth of trade liberalization was evident in the successful conclusion of the Uruguay Round of GATT. The expansion beyond GATT's traditional mandate of tariff reduction shows how pervasive the free trade movement has become. Its side agreements on investment, services, technology protection, and government procurement, along with the creation of the World Trade Organization (WTO), indicate that the internationalization of business transactions will continue to flourish. Tariffs in the range of 5 percent or less have become common. A number of provisions, mostly of a technical nature, of immediate importance to international exporters and importers include Agreement on the Application of Sanitary and Phytosanitary Measures, Agreement on Technical Barriers to Trade, Customs Valuation Code, Agreement on Preshipment Inspection, Agreement on Rules of Origin, and Agreement on Import Licensing Procedures.

The **Agreement on the Application of Sanitary and Phytosanitary Measures (SPS)** is aimed at promoting international standards for import restrictions aimed at protecting human, animal, and plant life and health. As defined in GATT's Agreement on Technical Barriers to Trade (Standards Code), a standard is a technical specification contained in a document that specifies the characteristics of a product such as levels of quality, performance, safety, or dimensions. Standards may include terminology, symbols, testing, packaging, marking, or labeling requirements.

SPS mandates that countries not use such measures or restrictions "as disguised devices" to restrict the importation of goods. "Countries are required to accept one another's measures as equivalent; but the exporting country may need to demonstrate that its measures achieve the importing country's SPS protection level and for this purpose to give the importing country access for inspection, testing, and similar procedures."[4] The parallel Agreement on Technical Barriers to Trade requires that the importing country allow importers access to its testing and certification standards and procedures. Countries party to this agreement are to "use international standards wherever possible; maintain transparency through publication and notification of all relevant information . . . through 'enquiry points' established in each country."[5] The problems of conflicting national standards and conformity to GATT principles was addressed in *Oregon Natural Resources v. Animal and Plant Health Inspection Service.*

Other agreements are also directly related to national import requirements. The **Customs Valuation Code** attempts to standardize country challenges to the valuations placed on goods being imported. It places the burden of proof on the importer to provide additional evidence of valuation. However, a country must give the importer adequate opportunity to respond to the country's challenge. An associated accord, **Agreement on Preshipment Inspection** pertains to an importing country's right to preshipment inspection. This right to preinspect goods for quality, quantity, and value is afforded only to developing countries. Because of the limited resources of developing countries, GATT recognizes their right to hire private companies to inspect the goods in the country of export. The **Agreement on Import Licensing Procedures** is based upon the principle that application procedures

4. John Kraus, *The GATT Negotiations: A Business Guide to the Results of the Uruguay Round,* ICC Pub. No. 533 (E) 18 (1994).
5. Ibid. at 22.

Oregon Natural Resources Council v. Animal and Plant Health Inspection Service, an agency of the United States Department of Agriculture

1997 U.S. Dist. LEXIS 9521 (N.D.C. Cal. 1997)

Claudia Wilken, District Judge. Plaintiff Oregon Natural Resources Council ("ONRC") move for a preliminary injunction. In its February 27, 1997, Order, the Court found that the Environmental Impact Statement ("EIS") prepared for the Animal and Plant Health Inspection Service (APHIS) regulations governing the importation of unmanufactured wood products ("Regulations"), did not comply with the National Environmental Policy Act ("NEPA"), or with Council on Environmental Quality ("CEQ") regulations, 40 C.F.R. pt. 1500 et seq. The Court, however, rejected Plaintiffs' argument that APHIS had applied an incorrect legal standard when framing the Regulations. The Court ordered the parties to submit briefs on the appropriate form of relief. Plaintiff ONRC filed a motion for a preliminary injunction, requesting that the Court enjoin APHIS from issuing any new import permits under the Regulations until the agency complied with its obligations under NEPA. ONRC's proposed injunction would not prevent the import of wood products pursuant to the general permits granted in Title 7 C.F.R. § 319.40-3 nor would it rescind permits that have already been granted under the Regulations. At oral argument, ONRC expressed particular concern about the anticipated commencement of large-scale imports of unfinished wood products from Mexico.

An injunction returning regulation of the importation of unfinished wood products to the status *quo ante,* i.e., reliance on visual inspection as the principal means of preventing the entry of infested wood into the United States, would clearly be inappropriate and is not requested by any of the parties. The Court is required to shape equitable relief in light of the substantive policies of the underlying statutes. One of the purposes of NEPA is "to promote efforts which will prevent or eliminate damage to the environment." This includes preventing the introduction and spread of exotic pests. The parties agree that the current regulations are an improvement over the status *quo ante;* they simply disagree about whether they are an adequate improvement. It would therefore be an abuse of discretion for the Court to issue an injunction which would result in less protection to the environment and less protection against the entry of exotic pests into the United States than exist under the current Regulations.

The record indicates a significant threat of infestation from forests comparable to those in the United States, but does not indicate a significant threat from tropical hardwoods. APHIS does not deny that if exotic pests did establish themselves in American forests, the consequences could be devastating and difficult to mitigate.

Compliance with GATT

APHIS contends that enjoining the issuance of new permits is contrary to the General Agreement on Tariffs and Trade ("GATT"). Article 2.2 of the agreement on sanitary and phytosanitary measures provides that "members shall ensure that any sanitary or phytosanitary measure is applied only to the extent necessary to protect human, animal, or plant life or health, is based on scientific principles, and is not maintained without sufficient scientific evidence." When relevant scientific evidence is insufficient, "a Member may provisionally adopt sanitary or phytosanitary measures on the basis of available pertinent information. Members shall seek to obtain the additional information necessary for a more objective assessment of risk within a reasonable period of time."

Article 5.7 states that phytosanitary measures may not arbitrarily or unjustifiably discriminate between member nations where similar conditions prevail and may not constitute disguised restrictions on international trade. By enjoining only the issuance of new permits for imports that pose a threat of infestation to North American forests, the injunction is not broader than necessary to protect plant life. The injunction will last only until APHIS conducts a new EIS and promulgates regulations that comply with NEPA. By permitting imports to continue under existing permits, the impact on international trade is minimized. The injunction proposed by ONRC, as modified to allow the importation of wood products that do not pose a threat to the health of North American forests, is therefore consistent with the United States' obligations under GATT.

The Court finds that ONRC has established a substantial likelihood of irreparable harm resulting from the introduction of exotic pests into United States forests by means of imports of non-tropical unfinished wood products. The balance of harm tips in favor of enjoining APHIS from issuing new permits for such products but allowing imports to continue under permits that have already been issued. For the foregoing reasons, Plaintiff ONRC's motion for a preliminary injunction is GRANTED in part. The Court therefore ENJOINS APHIS from issuing any new permits for the importation of unfinished non-tropical wood products.

Case Highlights

- A country's product, health, and safety standards should not be used as disguised trade barriers.
- National regulatory agencies need to balance potential health, safety, and environmental concerns with the nation's obligations under GATT.
- GATT requires that health, environmental, and safety standards are based on scientific evidence, that they are made transparent to foreign importers, and that they not be any broader than necessary.

should be made as simple as possible. Finally, the work on developing uniform **Country of Origin Rules** is ongoing and should be monitored in the future.

WTO Dispute Settlement System

The member countries of the WTO have agreed that if they believe that another member country has violated trade rules, they will use the WTO system of resolving disputes instead of taking unilateral action. The **WTO Dispute Settlement Understanding (DSU),** enacted in 1994, provides for the prompt handling of international trade disputes. Its procedures for settling disputes provide fixed time periods for prompt resolution; in urgent cases, the rules provide for a final decision within three months. In cases that use the maximum time periods and that are appealed, the dispute resolution process should not take more than 15 months. The settlement system provides the following maximum time periods: 60 days for consultation and mediation, 45 days for the appointment of the Dispute Panel; 6 months for the Panel to issue its decision and report; 3 weeks for the submission of the report to WTO members; 60 days for the Dispute Settlement Body to adopt the report. In case of an appeal the appeals court has 90 days to issue its report and the Dispute Settlement Body has 30 days to adopt the appeals report.

The **Dispute Settlement Body** is the sole authority for appointing the panel of experts to decide cases. Before taking any formal action the disputing countries must consult with each other in an attempt to settle the dispute. They can also ask the WTO director-general to mediate the dispute. Upon the failure of consultation, the complaining country can request that a panel be established to hear the dispute. **WTO Panels** are like tribunals, usually consisting of three, sometimes five, experts. The two countries usually agree on the panel members. If they cannot agree, then the director-general will appoint the panelists. The activities of the panel are confidential. Before the hearing each side prepares its case in writing. At the first hearing, both parties present, along with any other country that voices an interest in the case. At a second hearing, both parties submit written rebuttals and present oral arguments. The panel may also consult experts or appoint an advisory group of experts to prepare a report.

The panel prepares a first draft report and submits it to both parties for comments. It then submits an interim report consisting of its findings and conclusions,

Comparative Law

WTO's Understanding Governing the Settlement of Disputes

The dispute settlement system of the GATT is generally considered to be one of the cornerstones of the multilateral trade order. The system has already been strengthened and streamlined as a result of reforms agreed following the Mid-Term Review Ministerial Meeting held in Montreal in December 1988. Disputes currently being dealt with by the Council are subject to these new rules, which include the new rule that decisions on the establishment and composition of panels are no longer dependent upon the consent of the parties to a dispute.

The DSU emphasizes the importance of consultations in securing dispute resolution, requiring a Member to enter into consultations within 30 days of a request for consultations from another Member. If after 60 days from the request for consultations there is no settlement, the complaining party may request the establishment of a panel. Where consultations are denied, the complaining party may move directly to request a panel. The parties may voluntarily agree to follow alternative means of dispute settlement, including good offices, conciliation, mediation, and arbitration.

Where a dispute is not settled through consultations, the DSU requires the establishment of a panel. Panels normally consist of three persons of appropriate background and experience from countries not party to the dispute. The Secretariat will maintain a list of experts satisfying the criteria. Panel procedures are set out in detail in the DSU. It is envisaged that a panel will normally complete its work within six months or, in cases of urgency, within three months. Panel reports may be considered by the DSB for adoption 20 days after they are issued to Members. Within 60 days of their issuance, they will be adopted, unless the DSB decides by consensus not to adopt the report or one of the parties notifies the DSB of its intention to appeal.

The concept of appellate review is an important new feature of the DSU. An Appellate Body will be established, composed of seven members, three of whom will serve on any one case. An appeal will be limited to issues of law covered in the panel report and legal interpretations developed by the panel.

Once the panel report or the Appellate Body report is adopted, the party concerned will have to notify its intentions with respect to implementation of adopted recommendations. Further provisions set out rules for compensation or the suspension of concessions in the event of nonimplementation. Disagreements over the proposed level of suspension may be referred to arbitration.

The DSU contains a number of provisions taking into account the specific interests of the developing and the least-developed countries. It also provides some special rules for the resolution of disputes which do not involve a violation of obligations under a covered agreement but where a Member believes nevertheless that benefits are being nullified or impaired.

Source: World Trade Organization

allowing either party one week in order to request a review. If a review is requested the panel has two weeks to hold additional meetings with the parties. The panel then submits a *final report,* which becomes the ruling of the Dispute Settlement Body unless it is rejected. However, the final report can only be rejected by a unanimous vote of the DSB. The losing party then must prepare and submit a proposal to implement the ruling within a reasonable period of time. In cases where the losing party fails to implement the ruling within a reasonable period of time the parties must negotiate

Comparative Law

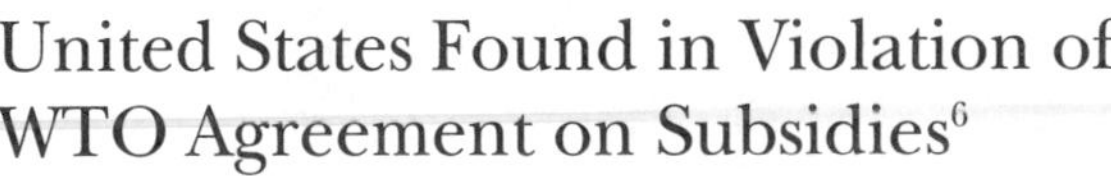

United States Found in Violation of WTO Agreement on Subsidies[6]

In October 1999, a panel created by the Dispute Settlement Body of the World Trade Organization issued its final report concluding that the U.S. Foreign Sales Corporation tax regime creates illegal export subsidies. A Foreign Sales Corporation (FSC) is a corporation given special tax treatment under the U.S. tax laws, and the purpose of the FSC provisions is to promote U.S. exports in a manner compatible with the agreements negotiated between the United States and its trading partners. The European Union, which has opposed the FSC regime since its enactment in the mid-1980s, filed a complaint against the United States in 1997. Specifically, the EU complaint alleged that the FSC regime violates certain export subsidy prohibitions of the WTO Agreement on Subsidies and Countervailing Measures by granting tax subsidies contingent upon export performance and tax subsidies contingent upon the use of domestic over imported goods.

The U.S. position has consistently been that the FSC regime is not an illegal export subsidy. The FSC represents a partial adoption of the territorial approach to taxation, common in Europe, and intended to equalize the position of U.S. manufacturers in markets outside the United States such as the EU, where the availability of VAT rebates along with territorial taxing schemes make non-U.S. goods cheaper than those manufactured in the United States In July 1998, after consultations between the EU and the United States failed to resolve differences, the EU requested that the WTO's Dispute Settlement Body form a panel to rule on the issue. In October 1999, the WTO's panel released its findings in a 298-page report. The panel concluded that the U.S. FSC regime creates illegal export subsidies and should be abolished by October 1, 2000. In reaching that conclusion, the WTO panel found that the FSC regime "clearly confers a benefit, in as much as both FSC's and their parents need not pay certain taxes that would otherwise be due" and that the subsidies are "contingent upon export performance" because they are available only with respect to "foreign trade income."

compensation pending a full implementation. If the parties do not agree on compensation, then the Dispute Settlement Body will authorize measures of retaliation for the winning country. These sanctions usually entail withholding or suspending tariff concessions previously mandated under GATT. The next section illustrates the WTO Dispute Settlement System at work in the famous U.S.–EU Bananas Dispute.

THE UNITED STATES–EU "BANANAS DISPUTE"

On January 14, 1999, the United States requested the Dispute Settlement Body as required by the Dispute Settlement Understanding of the World Trade Organization to authorize the suspension of existing tariff concessions to the European Union (EU) in the amount of $520 million. This was requested pursuant to a decision of a WTO Dispute Resolution Panel that the EU had illegally placed restrictions on the importation of bananas into EU countries. The EU objected to the

6. Julie E. McGuire, "WTO Rules U. S. in Violation of EU Trade Agreements," *The Legal Intelligencer* (2000).

amount of the **suspension** as not being "equivalent to the level of **nullification** or **impairment** of benefits suffered by the United States.

The level of the suspension was submitted for arbitration. Pursuant to the DSU the level of suspension is to be determined following the following principles: (1) the complaining party should first seek suspension of benefits in the *same sector* as that in which the impairment or nullification was found, (2) if this is not practical, then it should seek suspension or concessions "in other sectors under the same agreement," and (3) if that is not practical, then it should seek a suspension under another covered agreement.[7] The basic rationale of these principles is to ensure that suspensions or concessions across different sectors remain the exception and not the rule. It would seem that sector-specific concessions or suspensions are preferred in order to prevent an escalation of animosities and a broader trade war.

The panel decision held that the EU import regime pertaining to bananas violated both the goods sector (GATT) and the services sector (GATS). It should be noted that the United States requested the suspension only after it had won the dispute before the WTO panel and the EU had failed to abide by the panel's decision. The revised import regime instituted by the EU in response to the decision continued to place tariff quotas on bananas imported from the Caribbean and South America. This violated the national treatment principle of GATT and GATS in which like products are to be treated equally, irrespective of their origin. In order to be in violation of this nondiscrimination principle two elements must be proved. First, the services or goods at issue must be sufficiently alike. Second, the imported goods or services are treated less favorably than those of domestic origin. The arbitration panel held that the revised bananas import regime of the EU continued to violate the national treatment principle. It was a "continuation of nullification or impairment of United States benefits" found under the previous EU regime.

The arbitration panel then turned to the remaining issue of whether the concessions requested by the United States were appropriate. In determining the level of concessions, the WTO panel may consider both direct and indirect benefits. Consideration of *indirect benefits* was especially important in this case because the United States is not an exporter of bananas. Instead, the United States argued that the restrictions on Latin American banana exports indirectly impaired U.S. exports. For example, the U.S. exports farm products, such as fertilizers, used in the production of bananas that would have been exported to the EU. The arbitration panel ultimately decided that the concessions requested were excessive even with the consideration of indirect benefits. It reduced the concession amount from the approximately $500 million requested by the United States to $191.4 million.

Antidumping Procedures

The GATT system of enforcement does allow for retaliation at the national level for violations of the GATT agreements. The most common trade violation is the dumping of goods on foreign markets. **Dumping** or price discrimination is when a foreign exporter sells goods below what it sells them in its home country or below the cost of production. The lower pricing may be the result of an illegal subsidy given to the exporter by its home country. Under the U.S. **Tariff Act of 1930** a subsidy occurs when a foreign government authority "provides a financial contribution, any form of income or price support, makes a payment to a funding mechanism to

7. In the area of services, the WTO has developed a "Services Sectoral Classification List" that identifies service sectors.

http://
Text of WTO codes and agreements: **http://www.wto.org/english/docs_e/docs_e.htm**.

provide a financial contribution, or entrusts or directs a private entity to make a financial contribution." U.S. manufacturers can petition the Department of Commerce (DOC) to place antidumping duties on such imports. The DOC is required to conduct an administrative review to determine the amount of any antidumping duty that should be assessed. Such duties are popularly referred to as countervailing duties. They are extra duties or charges countries place on imported goods to offset the subsidies granted to the exporters by their home governments. GATT's **Code on Subsidies and Countervailing Duties** allows such duties when the importing country can prove that the subsidy would cause injury to a domestic industry. Antidumping duties, however, are considered the last resort in protecting domestic industries from unfair foreign competition.

The antidumping duty is assessed on an entry-by-entry basis in an amount equal to the difference between the U.S. price of the good and the foreign market value of similar goods. Antidumping duties can be as high as 400 percent of the value of the goods being imported and can be assessed for periods of up to 20 years. To be successful in its position a company or industry must provide evidence to the DOC that foreign exporters are dumping their goods on the U.S. market. It must also persuade the U.S. International Trade Commission (ITC) that the dumping threatens to cause material injury to U.S. industry.

Injury due to goods being imported at "less than fair value" can be proven showing one of the following: (1) sales lost to imports sold at "less than fair value," (2) suppression of export prices through underselling, (3) lost profits, (4) reduced employment or capacity utilization, (5) declining sales, (6) growth of imports, (7) reduced product development abilities, or (8) magnitude of the dumping margin.[8] If the DOC finds a case of dumping and the ITC finds material injury, then the DOC issues an *antidumping order* fixing the duties to be levied against the foreign exporters. The next two sections discuss in more detail the unilateral statutory devices, found in Section 301 and Section 337 of the Tariff Act, a U.S. party can use to combat unfair trade practices of foreign competitors.

Section 301

The Office of the **U.S. Trade Representative (USTR)** is authorized by statute to retaliate against activities of other countries that are deemed to violate U.S. rights under international trade agreements. The USTR coordinates the development of U.S. trade policy, leads activity on U.S. international trade regulations, and seeks to expand U.S. exports by promoting the removal of foreign trade barriers and the procurement of rights to foreign markets. USTR retaliation is popularly referred to as Section 301 sanctions.[9] (See Doing Business Internationally: Applying Section 301.) A business that is being unfairly treated in a foreign market may petition the USTR to intervene in the matter under Section 301 of the Trade Act of 1974.

http://
U.S. International Trade Administration: **http://www.ita.doc.gov/**.

Section 301 provides a means to counter a broad range of unfair foreign practices, including discriminatory rules of origin, discriminatory government procurement, licensing systems, quotas, exchange controls, restrictive business practices, discriminatory bilateral agreements, taxes that discriminate against U.S. products, and discriminatory product standards. "Since the conclusion of the multiple, wide-ranging Uruguay Round trade agreements in 1994, Section 301 has assumed

8. 19 U.S.C. § 1677.
9. Section 301 retaliation is found in 19 U.SC. §§ 2411-19 (1994). For a table of Section 301 cases see http://www.ustr.gov/reports/301report/act301.htm.

Doing Business Internationally

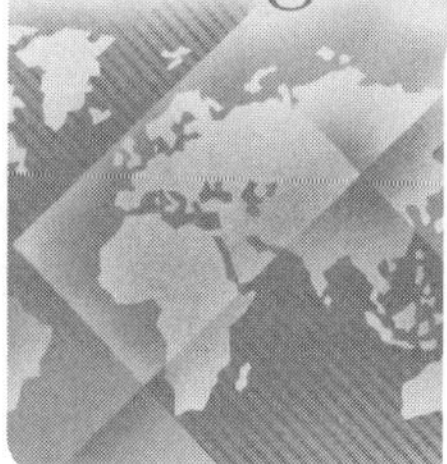

Applying Section 301[10]

Actionable practices under Section 301 are acts or policies engaged in by U.S. trading partners that violate a trade agreement, or are found to be unjustifiable, unreasonable, or discriminatory, and burden or restrict U.S. commerce:

(a) **Trade Agreement Violations:** Where a country violates the terms of a bilateral or multilateral agreement with the United States, or acts in a manner that effectively denies the benefit of the agreement to the United States, Section 301 can be invoked to impose sanctions against imports of that country.

(b) **Unjustifiable, Unreasonable, and Discriminatory Practices:** An act, policy, or practice is regarded as "unjustifiable" if it denies most-favored-nation treatment to U.S. exports or national treatment to U.S. business interests, if it fails to protect U.S. intellectual property rights, if it denies U.S. businesses the right of establishment in the foreign country concerned, or if it is otherwise inconsistent with the international rights of the United States. The term "unreasonable" refers to acts, policies, or practices that are "unfair and inequitable," even though they may fall short of violating the international legal rights of the United States. If any country treats U.S. products, services, or investments less favorably than those supplied by domestic or third-country sources, that country could become the subject of a "discriminatory practices" determination. A determination that a foreign practice is unjustifiable, unreasonable, or discriminatory is not *per se* sufficient to trigger retaliatory authority under Section 301. The USTR must also determine that the practice burdens or restricts U.S. commerce.

(c) **Burdens or Restricts U.S. Commerce:** The term "U.S. commerce" refers to the transnational flow of U.S. goods, as well as trade-related services and investments. It includes U.S. exports to countries other than the one whose practice is being questioned. As a general proposition, it can be said that a foreign practice "burdens or restricts" U.S. commerce if it causes immediate harm to U.S. interests in some significant and measurable way, or forecloses future market opportunities that would otherwise be available.

Retaliation and Settlement. Section 301 provides that, before any trade sanctions may be imposed, the USTR must consult with the government of the country charged with an offending practice. Where a trade agreement that is the subject of a Section 301 action contains provisions governing the resolution of disputes, such dispute resolution mechanisms must be utilized within 150 days if consultations have not produced an accord. These requirements apply even when retaliation is mandatory. Thus, in every Section 301 action the USTR's first step is to discuss the problem with the country involved, with a view toward a negotiated settlement of the dispute. This process often results in elimination or satisfactory codification of the practice in question or in an agreed compensation package. It is only when this process fails that retaliatory steps are taken.

Since the enactment of Section 301, 90 cases have been initiated by the USTR. While most of the cases were settled without resort to sanctions, the threat that U.S. market access could be reduced or eliminated was often instrumental in achieving an agreement under Section 301. Moreover, since 1995, Section 301 has gained increased importance as a means of enforcing the re-

10. Peter B. Feller & Vincent M. Routhier, "Invoking Section 301 to Overcome Foreign Trade Barriers," *The Metropolitan Corporate Counsel* (1999) p138.

Doing Business Internationally *(continued)*

sults of binding dispute settlement before the WTO: countries that fail to implement the recommendations of WTO panels can face trade retaliation. In the United States such retaliation is implemented through Section 301. Written in broad terms, Section 301 gives the USTR considerable discretion to investigate virtually any type of foreign trade practice. The types of unfair trade practices found actionable include:

Discriminatory Government Procurement Practices: USTR initiated several investigations concerning discrimination by the Japanese government involving outright prohibitions on the procurement of foreign satellites or certain Japanese exclusionary practices such as technical standards favoring Japanese producers.

Quotas, Tariffs and Licensing Schemes: Section 301 was also invoked in the celebrated bananas case. In April 1999, retaliatory tariffs were imposed as a result of the EU's failure to modify its banana quotas and import licensing schemes. The dispute originated with a section 301 petition filed by Chiquita Brands International, Inc., alleging discriminatory treatment against U.S. commercial interests in certain banana-producing countries.

http://

International Trade Law Monitor: **http://www.jus.uio.no/lm/international.economic.law/itl.html**.

greater importance as a compliance tool for USTR to assure that U.S. commercial interests can realize the benefits promised by our trading partners."[11]

Section 301 investigations are initiated by the USTR in response to an interested party's petition. The USTR allows U.S. businesses to approach it on an informal and confidential basis with pertinent information and a justification. This confidential alternative diminishes the risk that a foreign country will seek retribution against the party for instigating a Section 301 proceeding. Whether by formal or informal means, the interested party seeking to invoke section 301 must provide detailed information on both the foreign trade practice complained of and its impact on U.S. commerce.

The deadline for completing Section 301 investigations involving rights under a trade agreement is 18 months, while investigations of alleged unreasonable, discriminatory, or unjustified practices must be completed within 12 months. An expedited investigation not exceeding 6 months is undertaken when there are allegations that a foreign country has failed to provide adequate and effective intellectual property rights protection. "The range of actions that may be taken under section 301 is broad and may include: suspension of trade agreement concessions, the imposition of duties or other import restrictions, the imposition of fees or restrictions on services, the restriction of service sector authorizations or to provide compensatory benefits for the United States."[12] Before such sanctions can be administered, the Tariff Act requires that the Commerce Department determine that a government is providing, directly or indirectly, a **countervailing subsidy** with respect to the manufacture, production, or export of that merchandise. If the USTR determines that such an illegal subsidy has been given, then it will pursue bilateral negotiations

11. Ibid.
12. Ibid.

with the offending country and, if necessary, will institute a formal dispute resolution proceeding. If the dispute remains unresolved, the USTR is authorized to impose *unilateral* trade restrictions equal to the amount of burden placed on U.S. commerce. The *Delverde USA v. United States* case that follows explores the meaning of an illegal foreign subsidy and the assessment of a countervailing duty by the Department of Commerce.

Delverde USA, Inc. v. United States

202 F.3d 1360 (Fed. Cir. 2000)

Lourie, Circuit Judge. Delverde, SrL ("Delverde") and Delverde USA, Inc., appeal from the September 25, 1998, decision of the United States Court of International Trade affirming the Department of Commerce's ("Commerce's") countervailing duty determination. Because Commerce's methodology for determining whether Delverde indirectly received countervailable subsidies from the Italian government is inconsistent with § 771(5) of the Tariff Act of 1930 ("Tariff Act"), as amended by the Uruguay Round Agreements we vacate and remand. In 1995, Commerce launched a countervailing duty investigation of certain non-egg dry pasta in packages of five pounds or less imported in 1994 from Italy. Upon investigation of 17 Italian manufacturer-importers, Commerce discovered that, in 1991, Delverde purchased certain corporate assets, namely, a pasta factory and related production assets, name, and trademark, from a private company that had previously received several nonrecurring countervailable subsidies from the Italian government from 1983 to 1991.

First, when Commerce determines that a company has received a *nonrecurring subsidy*, Commerce divides the amount of that subsidy by the number of years equal to "the average useful life of renewable physical assets in the industry concerned" and allocates an amount to each year accordingly. Second, Commerce assumes that when a company sells "productive assets" during "the average useful life," a *pro rata* portion of that subsidy "passes through" to the purchaser at the time of the sale. Commerce then quantifies the assumed "pass through" amount, makes adjustments based on the purchase price, allocates an amount to the year of investigation, and calculates the *ad valorum* subsidy rate. In Delverde's case, Commerce determined that the average useful life of renewable physical assets in the food processing industry was 12 years. Commerce thus held Delverde responsible for a *pro rata* portion of the nonrecurring subsidies that were granted to the former owner between 1983 and 1991 because they fell within that 12-year period.

The Tariff Act of 1930 defines a subsidy as including "financial contributions" and "benefits" conferred and defines them as follows:

A "financial contribution" includes:
Section 337

(i) the direct transfer of funds, such as grants, loans, and equity infusion, or the potential direct transfer of funds or liabilities, such as loan guarantees,

(ii) foregoing or not collecting revenue that is otherwise due, such as granting tax credits or deductions from taxable income,

(iii) providing goods or services, other than general infrastructure, or

(iv) purchasing goods.

A "benefit" shall normally be treated as conferred where there is a benefit to the recipient, including—

(i) in the case of equity infusion, if the investment decision is inconsistent with the usual investment practice of private investors, including the practice regarding the provision of risk capital, in the country in which the equity infusion is made,

(ii) in the case of a loan, if there is a difference between the amount the recipient of the loan pays on the loan and the amount the recipient would pay on a comparable commercial loan that the recipient could actually obtain on a market,

(iii) in the case of a loan guarantee, if there is a difference, after adjusting for any difference in guarantee fees, between the amount the recipient of the guarantee pays on the guaranteed loan and the amount the recipient would pay for a comparable commercial loan if there were no guarantee by the authority, and

(iv) in the case where goods or services are provided, if such goods or services are provided for less than adequate remuneration, and in the case where goods are purchased, if such goods are purchased for more than adequate remuneration.

A change in ownership of all or part of a foreign enterprise or the productive assets of a foreign enterprise does not by itself require a determination by an administering authority that a past countervailable subsidy received by the enterprise no longer continues to be countervailable, even if the change of ownership is accomplished through an arm's length transaction.

We conclude that the statute does not contemplate any exception to the requirement that Commerce determine that a government provided both a financial contribution and benefit to a person, either directly or indirectly, by one of the acts enumerated, before charging it with receipt of a subsidy, even when that person bought corporate assets from another person who was previously subsidized. In other words, the Change of Ownership provision does not change the meaning of "subsidy." A subsidy can only be determined by finding that a person received a "financial contribution" and a "benefit" by one of the acts enumerated in §§ 1677(5)(D) and (E).

Having determined that the meaning of the statute is clear, we need only determine whether Commerce's methodology is in accordance with the statute. We have concluded that it is not. Nowhere following its methodology did Commerce determine whether Delverde directly or indirectly received a financial contribution and benefit from one of the acts enumerated. Rather, Commerce's methodology conclusively presumed that Delverde received a subsidy from the Italian government—i.e., a financial contribution and a benefit—simply because it bought assets from another person who earlier received subsidies.

Lastly, an "effect" of a subsidy may be a competitive advantage that the subsidy recipient obtained from the subsidies. A subsidy may enable a recipient to manufacture and sell products at lower price due to the subsidies it received. The issue here, however, is not whether Delverde was able to produce and sell pasta products at lower price, but whether it received a subsidy in the first place. It is undisputed that Delverde was not the direct recipient of any subsidy. The question is whether Delverde was an indirect recipient by having purchased assets from a company that did directly receive one. As we stated earlier, the statute does not permit Commerce simply to assume that Delverde received a *pro rata* portion of those subsidies.

Commerce's methodology for determining whether Delverde received a countervailing subsidy is invalid as being inconsistent with 19 U.S.C. § 1677(5). For the reasons stated above, the decision of the Court of International Trade is VACATED and REMANDED.

Case Highlights

- An illegal subsidy given by a foreign government can be attributed to the purchaser of the company that had received the subsidy.
- The Department of Commerce cannot assume that when a company sells "productive assets" during "the average useful life," a *pro rata* portion of the subsidy used to purchase those assets "passes through" to the purchaser at the time of the sale.
- The Department of Commerce must show that an illegal subsidy was given and that the purchaser of the company at least indirectly benefited from the earlier subsidy before assessing a countervailing duty.

In 1999, the European Union challenged the unilateral nature of Section 301 as a violation of the World Trade Organization Agreements. It alleged that the speed of retaliation under Section 301 violated the WTO Dispute Settlement Understanding. On January 27, 2000, the WTO Dispute Settlement Body upheld a WTO panel's report that held that the rights of the United States under Section 301 did not violate the WTO Dispute Settlement Understanding. The practice of the USTR to consult with the foreign government in order to resolve the dispute before authorizing sanctions satisfied the requirements of the WTO.

Section 337 of the Tariff Act

Section 337 of the Tariff Act of 1930 provides for relief to be given by the International Trade Commission for "unfair methods of competition" in the importation or sale of imported goods. Proof of infringement of intellectual property rights relating to the imported goods is usually sufficient to prove injury. Section 337 is most commonly used to prevent the import of illegal pirated or counterfeited *gray market* goods. Standing to seek relief from the ITC requires showing some use of an intellectual property right in the United States. Ownership of a U.S. trademark or patent, without use in the United States, is not sufficient. Section 337 does not define "unfair competition," but patent, copyright, and trademark infringement are all considered unfair competition.

The sole remedy under Section 337 is the exclusion of the goods from the United States. No damages can be granted. A permanent exclusion order prohibits entry of any of the specified goods produced by the named foreign producer or importer into the United States. A party may also obtain a **cease and desist order** prohibiting future imports by the accused importer or distributor. The minimum daily penalty for violating an exclusion or a cease and desist order is $100,000 or twice the domestic value of the imported goods. An investigation may be opened upon petition from a domestic producer. Any decision of the ITC may be appealed to the Court of Appeals for the Federal Circuit.

FUTURE OF MULTILATERAL TRADE NEGOTIATIONS

Attempts to commence the new **Millennium Round** of WTO talks collapsed in December 1999 in Seattle. The collapse was preceded by weeks of protests and riots in Seattle against the WTO. The protestors included public interest, environmental, consumer, and labor groups. Labor groups protested the alleged dumping of foreign products, a lack of international labor standards, and the movement of production to countries with lower standards. Environmental groups have accused the WTO of not considering the environmental impacts of its decisions. Consumer and public interests groups protested the WTO's failure to give food safety priority over trade. These groups also protested the secretiveness of WTO decision-making and the undemocratic nature of WTO decisions that override local and national rules. Comparative Law: Criticism of the WTO on the next page develops the parameters of the prevailing controversies surrounding the WTO.

http://

Check results of Fourth Ministerial Conference in Doha, Qatar, November 9–13, 2001: **http://www.wto.org**.

REGIONAL EXPANSION OF FREE TRADE

The regionalization of trade, as evidenced by the European Union (EU) and the North American Free Trade Agreement (NAFTA), have removed trade barriers and created larger markets for foreign goods. Exporters and importers should constantly monitor the impact on the broader developments of international trade policy represented by the creation of the EU and NAFTA. Regional trading blocs can help overcome the obstacles of nontransparent national standards and the need to evaluate different national standards. The European Union has made significant strides under its Common Community Customs Code to lessen the paperwork problems of different national standards. "Technical regulations cannot now be used to keep imports out if the other country's technical requirements are *equivalent.* Where standards do not involve risks to health, safety, or the environment, the *rule of mutual recognition* holds. A country cannot prevent the importation of a product from another country simply because that product meets a different but qualified standard. Instead of harmonizing standards in these other areas, the Community relies on labeling and consumer choice."[13]

13. Ibid. at 102.

Comparative Law

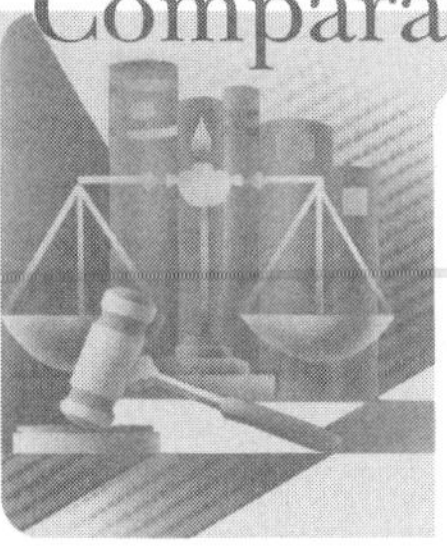

Criticism of the WTO[14]

Last fall's protests in Seattle, targeted at the WTO, and subsequent demonstrations against the World Bank in Washington reflected intense, if often contradictory, frustration with both organizations, and with the broader process of "globalization," by those who believe that powerful transnational corporations and the multilateral financial institutions have altered the global marketplace to the detriment of the world's consumers, workers, and ordinary people, as well as the natural environment. The world's economy is undergoing some of the same changes that the United States experienced at the beginning of the last century and with some of the same demands for reform by those left out of the decision-making process.

This is a summary of the principal complaints underlying the Seattle and Washington protests, and an offering of suggestions, both substantive and procedural, for reconciling the competing interests involved. Our goal is to suggest a path toward barrier-free world trade that is compatible with the sustainable development, environmental protection, and respect for human rights to which the international community is nominally committed but which it casts aside—or appears to—whenever they conflict with expanded commerce.

WTO Environmental Conflicts

The Seattle protesters directed their anger at the WTO's alleged failure to respect environmental standards and its indifference to "human rights" in promoting global trade. Their raucous demonstrations were widely credited with disrupting a WTO meeting at which the world's major trading nations seemed poised to advance still further toward unrestricted global trade. Yet the WTO Seattle meeting was almost certainly doomed to failure even before the protests. Many members believed the conference should have been postponed because of the sharp differences among the United States, the European Union (EU), and many developing countries over trade in agricultural commodities, continuing resentment by WTO members at U.S. insistence on preserving its "antidumping" legislation as a unilateral trade sanction, U.S. concerns at the pace of EU (and other nations') compliance with decisions by the WTO Dispute Settlement Panels, and the slow pace at which many states were implementing WTO agreements on trade in services (GATS) and intellectual property rights (TRIPS).

For most WTO members, environmental issues were at best ancillary to these core trade disputes. But they were by no means incidental to the Seattle protesters, many of whom wore sea turtle or dolphin insignias in reference to international trade decisions holding portions of U.S. environmental laws inconsistent with GATT's Article XX, which exempts certain kinds of domestic legislation from GATT's overall ban on discriminatory trade restrictions. The potential sacrifice of U.S. environmental standards on the altar of free trade had been a rallying cry for many environmentalists and labor activists who opposed both NAFTA and the WTO. The WTO's "Shrimp/Turtle" decision in particular seemed to validate the protesters' fears by its finding that Section 609 of the Endangered Species Act (requiring the United States to ban the importation of shrimp from nations that did not require their commercial fishing vessels to employ U.S.-specified turtle excluder devices) was inconsistent with Article XX because it unjustifiably restricted international trade. Other protesters pointed to an earlier WTO decision finding EPA's "Reformulated Gasoline Rule" under the Clean Air Act similarly invalid or to the WTO's refusal to permit

14. The content of this feature is based upon materials presented in Stephen L. Kass & Jean M. McCarroll, "Having it All: Trade, Development, Environmental, and Human Rights," *New York Law Journal* (May 5, 2000).

non-governmental organizations (NGOs) to participate in trade disputes over the legitimacy of environmental measures adopted by member states.

The World Bank

Beyond specific WTO disputes lies the deeper question of the impact of global trade on the environment generally, and on the environment of developing countries in particular. NGOs are the engine that drive environmental enforcement in the context of trade, where most governments and most competitors have little independent incentive to do so. One lesson familiar to U.S. environmentalists and human rights advocates is the power of public disclosure. This has been most evident in the case of Mexico, which is eager to avoid lending credence to U.S. labor and NGO claims that it habitually fails to enforce its environmental laws.

The World Bank's experience with environmental issues is also instructive for the WTO. During its formative years, the Bank largely ignored environmental considerations in financing infrastructure and other development projects in poorer countries. As the adverse environmental impacts of many of those projects became evident both within and without those countries, intense NGO criticism forced the Bank to adopt, and later to strengthen, internal guidelines aimed at incorporating environmental assessments, public comments, and ongoing mitigation commitments into its loan approval process. In formal terms, the Bank's Environmental Impact Assessment process represents a significant advance over environmental impact assessment practices in most developed countries, including U.S. practice under the National Environmental Policy Act (NEPA). The Bank established a special inspection panel to evaluate complaints of noncompliance with such environmental commitments.

Reforming WTO

Unlike the Bank, the WTO has no affirmative charge to alleviate poverty or stimulate development; its task is essentially negative—to remove barriers to increased international trade in goods and services. Ironically, it was only through the Seattle protests that the developing country NGOs were able to focus world attention on their complaint that the WTO offered no forum at all to consider, much less correct, the devastating short-term impacts produced by unrestrained global trade.

Drawing from the lessons of NAFTA, the World Bank, and the human rights movement some initial steps can be undertaken. First, the WTO can adopt formal rules for the participation of NGOs as *amici* in its environmental disputes. The WTO should also move rapidly to establish and fund its technical assistance center for developing countries and their NGOs in order to permit more effective participation in both formal dispute settlement proceedings and the underlying trade debates that shape the rules of global trade. Second, the environmental impact assessments required by the Bank, particularly for its national development programs, could provide a model for periodic assessments of the environmental impacts of global trade on individual countries, regions, or industries. Such assessments could be prepared on a regular basis either by the WTO or independent agencies and should include significant opportunities for public comment by both affected states and NGOs. While such WTO environmental assessments would not carry any specific sanctions or penalties, they would almost certainly help inform future WTO negotiations and dispute settlement proceedings. Few industries like being classified as environmentally irresponsible.

Made in the USA Foundation v. United States of America

56 F. Supp. 2d 1226 (N.D.C. Alabama 1999)

Propst, District Judge. In 1990 the United States, Mexico, and Canada initiated negotiations with the intention of creating a "free trade zone" through the elimination or reduction of tariffs and other barriers to trade. After two years of negotiations, the leaders of the three countries signed the North American Free Trade Agreement ("NAFTA" or the "Agreement") on December 17, 1992. Congress approved and implemented NAFTA on December 8, 1993, with the passage of the NAFTA Implementation Act ("Implementation Act").

The President purportedly negotiated and concluded NAFTA pursuant to his constitutional responsibility for conducting the foreign affairs of the United States and in accordance with the Omnibus Trade and Competitiveness Act of 1988 under the so-called "fast-track" procedure. Congress then approved and implemented NAFTA by enacting the Implementation Act, pursuant to its power to legislate in the areas of tariffs and domestic and foreign commerce. The plaintiffs contend that this failure to go through the Treaty Clause in Article II, Section 2, of the U.S. Constitution renders the Agreement and, apparently, the Implementation Act, unconstitutional.

The issues are the following:

(1) Do NAFTA and the Implementation Act constitute a "treaty" as contemplated by Article II, Section 2, of the Constitution?
(2) Even if NAFTA and the Implementation Act constitute a "treaty" as contemplated by Article II, Section 2, of the Constitution, was the making and implementation of NAFTA authorized under other provisions of the Constitution?

Remarkably, in the over two hundred years of this nation, the Supreme Court of the United States has not specifically and definitively decided the principles applicable to these issues.

The Constitutionality of NAFTA

The Treaty Clause states that the President "shall have the Power, by and with the Advice and Consent of the Senate, to make Treaties, provided two-thirds of the Senators present concur." The plaintiffs' ultimate argument in this case is that the Treaty Clause should be read as an exclusive grant of power with respect to those international agreements that may be called "treaties," and that NAFTA falls within the bounds of the proper definition of the term. The plaintiffs acknowledge that the text of the Constitution fails to establish a test for determining when an international agreement is a "treaty" as opposed to some other type of agreement.

It is also clear that under international law the Agreement would be considered to be a treaty and there is no clear distinction between what constitutes a treaty under international law as opposed to a treaty "in the constitutional sense." While NAFTA is likely a treaty, it may not be a "treaty," as contemplated by the Treaty Clause. Nevertheless, I will assume that it is such. The most significant issue before the court is whether the Treaty Clause is an exclusive means of making an international agreement under the circumstances of this case.

The fact that the President has the power to make treaties by and with the advice and consent of the Senate is not saying that agreements with foreign nations cannot otherwise be made and implemented. However, it should be noted that the Supreme Court has upheld the power of Congress to delegate to the President the ability to negotiate and conclude agreements with foreign nations or to implicitly approve the President's actions with respect to such agreements. Under such circumstances, the President is said to "exercise not only his powers but also those delegated by Congress," and has been allowed to conclude international agreements settling claims of United States citizens. I hold that the President had the authority to negotiate and conclude NAFTA pursuant to his executive authority and pursuant to the authority granted to him by Congress in accordance with the terms of the Omnibus Trade and Competitiveness Act of 1988.

Case Highlights

- The Treaty Clause of the U.S. Constitution grants the President the power to make treaties by and with the advice and consent of the Senate.
- NAFTA is considered a treaty according to international law.
- Congress may also delegate additional powers to negotiate international agreements to the President, as it did under its "fast-track" legislation.

Both regional trading blocs are the result of years of contention in negotiation, approval, and implementation. The *Made in the USA Foundation* case, involving a constitutional challenge to the NAFTA agreement, serves to illustrate the comparative powers of the U.S. President and Congress in the area of international trade agreements.

North American Free Trade Agreement (NAFTA)[15]

NAFTA aims to reduce tariff and nontariff barriers among the United States, Canada, and Mexico. On the tariff side, NAFTA has had an immediate impact on reducing barriers, especially on manufactured goods. Its long-term goal is the elimination of all tariffs over a 15-year period. The complete elimination of tariffs is likely to harm some domestic industries in the short term, so NAFTA contains **snapback provisions** that allow for the reinstitution of previous tariff levels at times in order to alleviate short-term negative impacts on industry and business.

http://

NAFTA Secretariat—rules, decisions, status reports, text of all 22 chapters of NAFTA, links: **http://www.nafta-sec-alena.org**. University of Texas—NAFTA resources, Mexico: **http://lanic.utexas.edu/la/mexico/nafta**.

NAFTA enacted a series of complicated rules of origin that the North American businessperson must master in order to earn the lower NAFTA tariff rates. Goods must be certified as **regional goods** in order to cross NAFTA borders freely. The traditional test of **substantial transformation**[16] (where a good or material is further processed), which usually results in a tariff classification change for the goods, is not sufficient when certain goods are imported from outside of NAFTA and then moved within NAFTA. For example, textile products must go through a *triple transformation* in order to obtain regional goods status. Other products, like automobiles, electronics, and machinery, have to pass stringent *cost tests*. Depending on the good, somewhere between 50 percent and 62.5 percent of the good's costs must be regional in origin.

NAFTA's ultimate long-term impact on trade is more likely to come in its nontariff provisions, which include an agreement to reduce barriers to direct foreign investment, to eliminate performance standards, to ensure the free flow of capital, to offer expropriation assurances, and to institute a dispute resolution mechanism. The breadth of NAFTA and its potential impact on regional trade can be seen in the following chart which lists some of the committees and groups authorized by NAFTA articles[17] (reference to NAFTA articles are in brackets).

Working Groups:	Working Group on Rules of Origin [513]
	Working Group on Customs [513(6)]
	Working Group on Agricultural Subsidies [705(6)]
	Working Group on Trade and Competition [1504]
Committees:	Trade in Goods [316]
	Sanitary and Phytosanitary Measures [722]
	Financial Services [1412]
	Private Commercial Disputes [2022(4)]

continued

15. The enumerated goals of NAFTA are to: (1) eliminate trade barriers; (2) promote conditions of fair competition; (3) increase investment opportunities; (4) provide adequate protection for intellectual property rights; (5) establish effective procedures for its implementation and application; and (6) provide for the resolution of disputes among the parties to the agreement. See generally Bernard D. Reams, Jr. & Jon S. Schultz, eds. *The North American Free Trade Agreement* (1994).
16. Substantial transformation will be discussed more fully in Chapter 6.
17. See Leonard Waverman, "Post-NAFTA: Can the United States, Canada, and Mexico Deepen their Economic Relationships?" in *Integrating the Americas: Shaping Future Trade Policy,* Sidney Weintraub, ed. 1994.

Land Transportation Standards [913(5)]
Telecommunications Standards [913(5)]
Automotive Standards [913(5)]
Small Business [1021]

Only time will tell whether the standing committees and working groups will produce harmonization or mutual recognition of national rules and standards. Such efforts should be closely monitored by the businessperson operating within the NAFTA countries.

European Union Expansion

http://

Europa—The European Union Online: **http://europa.eu.int** or European Union Internet Resources—University of California, Berkeley: **http://www.lib.berkeley.edu/GSSI/eu.html**.

With the success of the European Union and the fall of Soviet-dominated Eastern Europe, the expansion of the EU has become a defining issue on the European continent. Ten countries have indicated a strong interest in joining the EU: the Baltic countries of Latvia, Estonia, and Lithuania, along with Poland, the Czech Republic, Slovakia, Hungary, Slovenia, Romania, and Bulgaria. There are two types of relationship between the European Union and the countries of Central and Eastern Europe. The first is a relationship that will lead to full membership in the EU. These relationships are characterized by the existence of a **"Europe Agreement."** The stated purposes of such an agreement are the establishment of a political dialogue and a free trade area between the EU and the contracting country.

In 1995, the European Commission of the EU published a White Paper titled "The Preparation of the Associated Countries of Central and Eastern Europe for Integration into the Internal Market of the Union," which details the steps needed in order for a country to be considered for accession into the EU. The requirements of accession include the ability of the prospective new member to meet the economic, political, and monetary obligations of membership, through the existence of a functioning market economy and stable political institutions that guarantee democracy, the rule of law, and human rights protection. The white paper contains wide-ranging provisions on the free movement of goods, safety of industrial products, free movement of capital, competition law (antitrust and unfair competition), social policy, agriculture, transport, telecommunications, and environmental requirements.

The second relationship is a looser legal framework characterized by entering a **Partnership and Cooperation Agreement.** The feature Comparative Law: Partnership and Cooperation Agreement Between the European Communities and Georgia illustrates the concerns that these agreements address. Compare the provisions of the agreement discussed with the provisions addressed by the WTO agreements covered earlier in this chapter. It should be apparent that these Partnership and Cooperation Agreements are simply more qualified trade agreements.

Comparative Law

Partnership and Cooperation Agreement between the EU and Georgia

[Selected provisions]

DESIROUS of encouraging the process of regional cooperation in the areas covered by this Agreement with neighboring countries in order to promote the prosperity and stability of the region,

BEARING IN MIND the utility of a wider area of cooperation in Europe and neighboring regions and its progressive integration into the open international system,

CONSIDERING the commitment of the Parties to liberalize trade, in conformity with World Trade Organization (WTO) rules, [THE PARTIES] HAVE AGREED AS FOLLOWS:

Article 2: Respect for democracy, principles of international law, and human rights as defined in particular in the United Nations Charter, the Helsinki Final Act, and the Charter of Paris for a New Europe, as well as the principles of market economy.

Article 9: The Parties shall accord to one another most-favored-nation treatment in all areas in respect of customs duties and charges applied to imports and exports, including the method of collecting such duties and charges; provisions relating to customs clearance, transit, warehouses and transshipment; taxes and other internal charges of any kind applied directly or indirectly to imported goods; methods of payment and the transfer of such payments; and the rules relating to the sale, purchase, transport, distribution and use of goods on the domestic market.

Article 42: Pursuant to the provisions of this Article, Georgia shall continue to improve the protection of intellectual, industrial, and commercial property rights in order to provide for a level of protection similar to that existing in the Community, including effective means of enforcing such rights.

Article 57: Cooperation shall aim at combating the deterioration of the environment and in particular the effective monitoring of pollution levels and assessment of the environment; system of information on the state of the environment; combating local, regional, and transboundary air and water pollution; safety of industrial plants; classification and safe handling of chemicals; and global climate change,

Article 66: The Parties will enter into close cooperation aimed at achieving compatibility between their systems of consumer protection. This cooperation may include the improvement of information provided to consumers especially on prices, and characteristics of products and services offered and increasing the compatibility of consumer protection policies.

Article 89: Within the limits of their respective powers and competencies, the Parties shall encourage the adoption of arbitration for the settlement of disputes arising out of commercial and cooperation transactions and to arbitration by any center of a State signatory to the Convention on Recognition and Enforcement of Foreign Arbitral Awards (New York Convention).

Key Terms

Agreement on Import Licensing Procedures, 130
Agreement on Preshipment Inspection, 130
Agreement on the Application of Sanitary and Phytosanitary Measures (SPS), 130
Agreement on Trade-Related Aspects of Intellectual Property Rights (TRIPS), 127
binding commitments, 127
cease and desist order, 141
Code on Subsidies and Countervailing Duties, 136
countervailing subsidy, 138
countervailing duties, 128
Country of Origin Rules, 132
Customs Valuation Code, 130
Dispute Settlement Body, 132
dumping, 128, 135
Europe Agreement, 146
European Union (EU), 128
General Agreement on Tariffs and Trade (GATT), 127
General Agreement on Trade in Services (GATS), 127
impairment, 135
Millennium Round, 141
most-favored-nation principle, 128
national treatment principle, 128
North American Free Trade Agreement (NAFTA), 128
nullification, 135
Partnership and Cooperation Agreement, 146
regional goods, 145
snapback provisions, 145
subsidies, 128
substantial transformation, 145
suspension, 135
Tariff Act of 1930, 135
transparency principle, 128
U.S. Trade Representative (USTR), 136
Uruguay Round, 127
World Trade Organization (WTO), 127
WTO Dispute Settlement Understanding (DSU), 132
WTO panels, 132

Chapter Problems

1. How can the free trade mandate of the World Trade Organization be reconciled with the concerns of labor, environmental, and consumer groups? What is meant by the word *free* in the term *free trade?* Does free mean no restrictions on the flow of labor, capital, goods, services, and technology? Should free trade be limited by other concerns such as local disruption? Should local cultural concerns be a limitation on the nonregulation of trade? How can the WTO dispute resolution and enforcement process be reconciled with a country's assertion of national sovereignty over its national laws and regulations?

2. The United Nations Conference on Trade and Development (UNCTAD) asserts that the 48 poorest nations of the world, including 33 in Africa, are failing to benefit from globalization and freer trade. In fact, there is evidence that poverty is worsening in many of these countries. What can be done to improve the effect of free trade on these impoverished countries? Should the WTO take a greater role in obtaining preferential tariff treatment for goods exported from these countries? How can developed countries continue to justify protection of domestic industries such as agriculture and textiles through the granting of subsidies?

3. How can one reconcile restrictive immigration policies with the notion of free trade? Why should goods, services, and capital be allowed to move freely and not persons? How do the restrictive immigration laws sanctioned under NAFTA compare with the EU's "Four Freedoms" of goods, services, capital, and persons and the EU's movement toward EU passports and citizenship? How does one reconcile U.S. interests in "border control" with its own liberal democratic principles? How does one reconcile the call to "regain control of our borders" with the government's policy not to harass employers of illegal aliens in industries where their labor is needed? What are the ethical arguments against proposals to prohibit undocumented immigrants from receiving emergency medical care or public schooling? One argument can be found in the United States Constitution, where no distinction is made between legal and illegal immigrants in the admonition that "all [persons] are endowed by their Creator with inalienable rights."

4. The United States had requested that a WTO Dispute Settlement Panel review an alleged Canadian violation of the intellectual property provisions of TRIPS. The United States argued in its complaint that the TRIPS Agreement requires WTO members to grant a minimum term of protection to all patents existing as of the date of application of the Agreement, and that Canada must apply the Agreement as of January 1, 1996. Canada's Patent Act provides that patent applications filed before October 1, 1989, would receive patent protection for only 17 years from the date the patent is issued. Article 33 of the TRIPS Agreement requires WTO members to provide a patent protection term of at least 20 years from filing for all patents existing on January 1, 1996. Canada relied on Article 28 of the Vienna Convention, arguing that there is a presumption against retroactivity for treaties. Which country do you think won? Why?

5. One can argue that regional trade areas like the European Union work like "mini-GATTS." In such systems it is inevitable that national concerns and sovereignty will conflict with the free trade dictates of the union. National subsidies traditionally given to domestic agricultural industries are one instance. France has a long-standing policy of granting aid to olive growers. Can France continue to give such aid under the auspices of the European Union? If so, does it need the permission of the EU?

6. Ralph Nader and Lori Wallach had this to say about the World Trade Organization: "The binding provisions that define the WTO's functions and scope do not incorporate any environmental, health, labor, or human rights considerations. There is nothing in the institutional principles of the WTO to inject any procedural safeguards of openness, participation, or accountability. The WTO 'dispute resolution system' is the mechanism that enforces WTO control over democratic governance. WTO panel members are selected from qualifications that produce panelists with a uniformly protrade perspective. The new rules favor the largest, most developed nations. Unlike the old GATT rules, the new WTO requires all members to agree to be bound by all Uruguay Round accords. The rule forces many countries, usually small ones, to accept trade in areas that might be undesirable in the long run. WTO rules are now enforceable as regards all existing federal, state, and local laws. In effect, countries have voluntarily sacrificed their own sovereignty. The WTO's rules and powerful enforcement mechanism promote downward harmonization of wages, environmental, worker, and health standards. Some international trade is useful, while other global trading favors corporate advantages over those of workers, consumers, and the environment. Concentrating power in international organizations, as trade pacts do, tends to remove critical decisions from citizen control."[18] Do you agree with Nader and Wallach's assessment of the dangers of the WTO? Do you think the dangers outweigh the benefits? What role should governments play in balancing the promotion of free trade through organizations like the WTO and the concerns addressed in the quote above?

Internet Excercises

1. Review recent developments in the area of trade law by reviewing the following web sites: **http://www.jus.uio.no/lm/international.economic.law/itl.html** (In-ternational Trade Law) and **http://www.ita.doc.gov/** (U.S. International Trade Administration).

2. Read the overview of the WTO and GATT at **http://www.wto.org/**.

3. Review recent WTO decisions that highlight the intersection between free trade and environmental issues. See, for example, **http://www.lib.uchicago.edu/~llou/wto/** and **http://www.worldtradelaw.net**.

18. Ralph Nader & Lori Wallach, "GATT, NAFTA, and the Subversion of the Democratic Process" in *The Case Against the Global Economy,* Jerry Mander & Edward Goldsmith, eds.

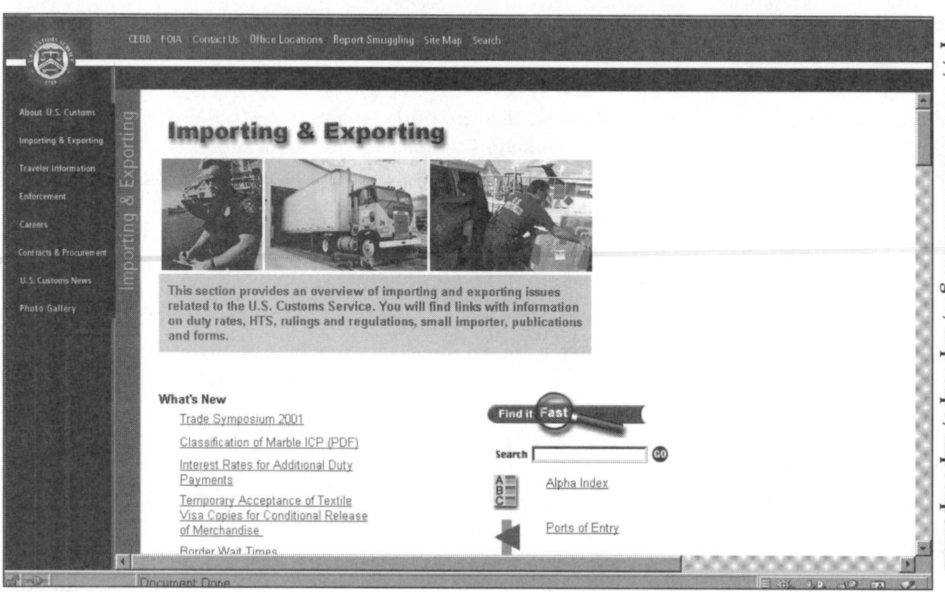

http://www.customs.ustreas.gov/impoexpo/impoexpo.htm

Chapter 6 National Import and Export Regulation

Countries' export and import regulations directly impact an exporter or importer's ability to undertake profitable international trade transactions. National regulation may bar an exporter's ability to honor a contract if he is precluded from exporting his goods. Also, the cost of importing can be dramatically changed in the event that the duties assigned to a transaction through customs regulations is different from what was expected by the importer. This chapter addresses the relationship between U.S. customs regulations and private business transactions. Does the typical U.S. exporter need to be concerned with violating U.S. export regulations? What do U.S. export regulations demand of the exporter? What are the consequences for violating the regulations?

In importing the assessment of duties and marking requirements are crucial. A miscalculation of duty owed to the government of import could convert an otherwise profitable import transaction into a loss. In addition to duties, penalties for violating the customs laws can be substantial. Failure to conform to a country's marking or country of origin requirements can result in the goods being barred from importation. We will discuss import regulations first, then review the export regulations of the United States.

IMPORT REQUIREMENTS AND DUTIES

In order to import goods into a foreign country, the importer must satisfy a number of requirements. The three basic types of laws that regulate the importation of goods are the assessment of duties, marking requirements, and standards requirements. Unlike in export regulation, which tends to be more country specific, there is general agreement among most countries on how to classify goods and assess import duties. The fundamental factors used to determine the customs duties are classification, valuation, and country of origin. Duties vary with the type of goods, their value, and where they originated.

Most countries have enacted a uniform classification system known as the **harmonized tariff schedule (HTS).** The U.S. version is published by the U.S. International Trade Commission. In 1989, the new HTS replaced older schedules in more than 50 countries, including the United States. Classification involves selecting the HTS product classification that best describes the goods being imported. This classification determines the duty rate to be applied. The goods must then be valued in order to determine the amount of duty owed. The duty owed is the product of multiplying the value of the goods by the duty rate provided by the classification. The **country of origin** determination is made to determine if the goods are subject to a most-favored-nation rate, NAFTA rate, or a rate provided by the **generalized system of preferences (GSP).** The GSP is a framework under which developed countries give preferential tariff treatment to manufactured goods imported from developing countries.

http://

Harmonized Tariff Schedule: **http://www.customs.gov/download/htsusa/htsusa.pdf**.

http://

USTR—General System of Preferences: **http://www.ustr.gov/gsp/general.shtml**. Click on "GSP Guidebook."

In some circumstances no duties may be owed or the duties payable may be deferred to some future time. For instance, goods placed in a government **bonded warehouse** or entered into a **free trade zone** are not subject to duties until officially entered into the country. A bonded warehouse is more limited in scope than the free trade zone: Duty is deferred until the goods are formally entered into United States commerce, but manufacturing is not permitted unless the goods are subsequently exported. To encourage and facilitate international trade, more than 300 free ports, free trade zones, and similar customs-privileged facilities are now in operation in some 75 foreign countries, usually in or near seaports or airports. Federal regulations define a free trade zone as a "restricted-access area, in or adjacent to a Customs port of entry." Customs duty is not due when goods enter into the free trade zone, only when they enter the commerce of the United States. The importer pays customs on the lower of the finished goods after assembly or manufacture in the zone or of the imported parts and components. Many U.S. manufacturers and their distributors use free ports or free trade zones for receiving shipments of goods that are reshipped in smaller lots to customers throughout the surrounding areas.

Bonded warehouses are also found in many locations. Here, goods can be warehoused without duties being assessed. Once goods are released, they are subject to duties. An importer may use a free trade zone to assemble or manufacture a product from imported components in order to take advantage of duty preferences. An importer may store finished products in a bonded warehouse for a period of time if the importer expects duty rates to decrease.

When importing into the United States, an importer must classify the goods, subject to review by the U.S. Customs Service, by selecting a category from the HTS. The HTS used in the United States is taken from an international classification scheme administered by the **World Customs Organization (WCO).** HTS classification consists of a series of numbers that identify categories of goods beginning with broad categories. As numbers are added the description becomes increasingly more specific. The HTS uses the following groupings: section, chapter, heading, and subheading. Twenty-two sections broadly cover products from different industries; 99 chapters group products by industry ranging from agricultural and component products to finished products. Each grouping is represented by a series of numbers. The first six digits of a tariff classification, uniform for all countries using the WCO system, represent the chapter and heading levels. The first two digits refer to the chapter and the next four to the heading and subheadings. Countries may add more detail by using an additional four digits. In the United States, digits seven and eight denote tariff items and digits nine and ten are used for statistical purposes.

http://
World Customs Organization: **http://www.wcoomd.org**.

Exhibit 6.1 is from the HTS and gives the tariff rates for a number of leather products. The "General Rate of Duty" is that provided to WTO members under the most-favored-nation principle. The success of GATT in reducing the overall level of world tariff rates is apparent. The WTO rates in this excerpt range from 0 to 14 percent. Note column "2" in Rates of Duty. These are the rates that would be applicable under the Tariff Act of 1930—the rate that would be applied if the United States removed most-favored-nation status from the imports of a certain country. Most of the rates in this column are between 35 percent and 40 percent. Elsewhere in the HTS the non–most-favored-nation rates reach as high as 100 percent. These types of exorbitant rates are meant to punish an exporting country and effectively prevent the importation of goods from that country.

GENERAL RULES OF INTERPRETATION

Despite the fact that there are more than 5,000 tariff classifications in the HTS, there is often no exact fit between the good being imported and a HTS tariff classification. When the importer makes a selection of a tariff classification he should consult the **General Rules of Interpretation** found at the beginning of the HTS.[1] When more than one tariff selection is possible, the Rules are the means by which the importer and Customs Service make the final selection. When a good is subject to more than one section or chapter heading number, then the General Rules of Interpretation are applied to determine the appropriate classification number.

http://
Bureau of Export Administration (BXA): **http://www.bxa.doc.gov**.

The primary rule of interpretation is the **rule of specificity.** It requires the use of a heading that provides a more specific description of the good over one that gives a more general description. If neither description is considered more specific, then the heading for the material, component, or function that provides the **essential character** of the good is to be used. In the event that neither the rule of specificity nor the essential character rule determine a classification, then the heading that occurs last in numerical order shall apply. The **Customs Electronic Bulletin Board** provides information on classification rulings, quotas, currency conversion rates, customs valuation provisions, and directives.

Over time, as more headings are added to the HTS, the rule of specificity and the essential character rule may result in a change of classification for a specific product.

1. See also "United States Customs Service, Guidance for Interpretation of Harmonized System," 54 *Federal Register* 35127 (1989).

EXHIBIT 6.1 *Excerpt from Harmonized Tariff Schedule*

Harmonized Tariff Schedule of the United States (2002)

Annotated for Statistical Reporting Purposes

VIII
42-12

Heading/ Subheading	Stat. Suf- fix	Article Description	Unit of Quantity	Rates of Duty		
				1		2
				General	Special	
4203 (con.)		Articles of apparel and clothing accessories, of leather or of composition leather (con.):				
		Gloves, mittens and mitts (con.):				
4203.29 (con.)		Other (con.):				
		Other:				
4203.29.20	00	Not seamed	doz. prs. .	12.6%	Free (CA,D,E,IL,J) 1.4% (MX) 7.5% (JO)	25%
		Other:				
4203.29.30		Men's	. . . .	14%	Free (CA,D,E,IL,J) 1.4% (MX) 8.4% (JO)	25%
	10	Not lined	doz. prs.			
	20	Lined	doz. prs.			
		For other persons:				
4203.29.40	00	Not lined	doz. prs. .	12.6%	Free (CA,D,E,IL,J) 1.4% (MX) 7.5% (JO)	25%
4203.29.50	00	Lined	doz. prs. .	12.6%	Free (CA,D,E,IL,J) 1.4% (MX) 7.5% (JO)	25%
4203.30.00	00	Belts and bandoliers with or without buckles	X	2.7%	Free (A,CA,E,IL,J, JO,MX)	35%
4203.40		Other clothing accessories:				
4203.40.30	00	Of reptile leather	X	4.9%	Free (A,CA,E,IL,J, JO,MX)	35%
4203.40.60	00	Other	X	Free		35%
4204.00		Articles of leather or of composition leather of a kind used in machinery or mechanical appliances or for other technical uses:				
4204.00.30	00	Belting leather cut or wholly or partly manufactured into forms or shapes suitable for conversion into belting . . .	kg	2.9%	Free (A,CA,E,IL,J, JO,MX)	12.5%
4204.00.60	00	Other	X	Free		35%
4205.00		Other articles of leather or of composition leather:				
4205.00.20	00	Shoelaces	X	Free		15%
4205.00.40	00	Straps and strops	X	1.8%	Free (A,CA,E,IL,J, JO,MX)	35%
		Other:				
4205.00.60	00	Of reptile leather	X	4.9%	Free (A*,B,CA,E, IL, J,JO,MX)	35%
4205.00.80	00	Other	X	Free		35%
4206		Articles of gut (other than silkworm gut), of goldbeater's skin, of bladders or of tendons:				
4206.10		Of catgut:				
4206.10.30	00	If imported for use in the manufacture of sterile surgical sutures	X	3.5%	Free (A,CA,E,IL,J, JO,MX)	40%
4206.10.90		Other	. . . .	3.9%	Free (A,CA,E,IL,J, JO,MX)	40%
	10	Racquet strings	m			
	30	Other	X			
4206.90.00	00	Other	X	Free		40%

A change of classification may result in a different duty rate being applied, so it is important for importers to keep up to date on changes or additions made to the HTS. The need for additions to tariff classifications is especially apparent in the area of technology products. On December 13, 1996, the first Ministerial Meeting of the World Trade Organization issued a Declaration on Trade in Information Technology Products (ITA), which established a framework for expanding world trade in information technology products and enhancing market access opportunities for such products. To implement that declaration, 42 WTO members and governments agreed on the common objective of achieving, where appropriate, a common classification of such goods for tariff purposes within the existing nomenclature of the Harmonized Commodity Description and Coding System (HS). It further called for a future joint session with the World Customs Organization to update existing HS nomenclature.

The general rule-making authority in customs classification and assessment of duties in the United States is vested in the Customs Service. U.S. courts will generally defer to Customs Service rule-making authority when the Tariff Law is unclear.

The Supreme Court in the *United States v. Haggar Apparel Co.* case that follows held that the courts will grant deference to the Customs Service when it writes regulations that clarify parts of the tariff statutes that are unclear as to particular goods or services. So long as Customs Service is reasonable in its interpretation, its rules should stand. The *Haggar* case also exposes the reader to Section 9802 of the HTS, which provides a special exemption from tariff duties for items temporarily exported for assembly and then returned to the United States.

The *United States v. Haggar* case dealt with the relationship between an executive branch agency (Customs Service) and the courts. Another issue is the ability of individual states to enact laws that may impact international trade. The *National Foreign Trade Council v. Baker* case on page 156 deals with a state statute limiting the procurement of goods from the country of Myanmar.

United States v. Haggar Apparel Company

526 U.S. 380 (1999)

Justice Kennedy. This case concerns regulations relating to the customs classification of certain imported goods issued by the United States Customs Service. The question is whether these regulations are entitled to judicial deference in a refund suit brought in the Court of International Trade. Contrary to the position of that Court and the Court of Appeals for the Federal Circuit, we hold the regulation in question is subject to the analysis required by *Chevron U.S.A. Inc.* v. *Natural Resources Defense Council, Inc.*, and that if it is a reasonable interpretation and implementation of an ambiguous statutory provision, it must be given judicial deference.

Respondent Haggar Apparel Co. designs, manufactures, and markets apparel for men. This matter arises from a refund proceeding for duties imposed on men's trousers shipped by respondent to this country from an assembly plant it controlled in Mexico. The fabric had been cut in the United States and then shipped to Mexico, along with the thread, buttons, and zippers necessary to complete the garments. There the trousers were sewn and reshipped to the United States. If that had been the full extent of it, there would be no dispute, for if there were mere assembly without other steps, all agree the imported garments would have been eligible for the duty exemption which respondent claims.

Respondent, however, in the Government's view, added one other step at the Mexican plant: permapressing. Permapressing is designed to maintain a garment's crease in the desired place and to avoid other creases or wrinkles that detract from its proper appearance. The Customs Service claimed the baking was an added process in addition to assembly, and denied a duty exemption; respondent claimed the baking was simply part of the assembly process, or, in the words of the controlling statute, an "operation incidental to the assembly process." After being denied the exemption it sought for the permapressed articles, respondent brought suit for refund in the Court of International Trade. The court declined to treat the regulation as controlling. The court ruled in favor of respondent. On review, the Court of Appeals for the Federal Circuit declined to analyze the regulation under *Chevron*, and affirmed.

The statute on which respondent relies, Section 9802, provides importers a partial exemption from duties otherwise imposed. The relevant regulation interpreting the statute with respect to permapressed articles provides as follows:

Any significant process, operation, or treatment other than assembly whose primary purpose is the fabrication, completion, physical or chemical improvement of a component, or which is not related to the assembly process, whether or not it effects a substantial transformation of the article, shall not be regarded as incidental to the assembly and shall preclude the application of the exemption to such article. The following are examples of operations not considered incidental to the assembly:

(4) Chemical treatment of components or assembled articles to impart new characteristics, such as showerproofing, permapressing, sanforizing, dying or bleaching of textiles.[2]

The Customs Service (which is within the Treasury Department) is charged with the classification of imported goods under the proper provision of the tariff schedules in the first instance. In addition, the Secretary is directed by statute to "establish and promulgate such rules and regulations not inconsistent with the law . . . as may be necessary to secure a just, impartial and uniform appraisement of imported merchandise and the classification and assessment of duties thereon at the various ports of entry."

2. 19 CFR § 10.16(c) (1998).

For the reasons we have given, the statutes authorizing customs classification regulations are consistent with the usual rule that regulations of an administering agency warrant judicial deference. We turn to respondent's second major contention, that the statutes governing the reviewing authority of the Court of International Trade in classification cases displace this customary framework. The Court of Appeals held in this case, and in previous cases presenting the issue, that these regulations were not entitled to deference because the Court of International Trade is charged to "reach the correct decision" in determining the proper classification of goods. The whole point of regulations such as these, however, is to ensure that the statute is applied in a consistent and proper manner. Deference to an agency's expertise in construing a statutory command is not inconsistent with reaching a correct decision. If the agency's statutory interpretation fills a gap or defines a term in a way that is reasonable in light of the legislature's revealed design, we give that judgment controlling weight.

The customs regulations may not be disregarded. Application of the *Chevron* framework is the beginning of the legal analysis. Like other courts, the Court of International Trade must, when appropriate, give customs regulations *Chevron* deference. The judgment is VACATED and the case is remanded for further proceedings consistent with this opinion.

Case Highlights

- The Court of International Trade is the U.S. court that has jurisdiction over any civil matters against the United States arising out of federal laws governing import transactions. The court hears cases dealing with antidumping, product classification, valuation, and countervailing duty matters.
- Permapressing clothes is not assembly under Section 9802 or an "operation incidental to the assembly process."
- Merely because a process, operation, or treatment fails to produce a *substantial transformation* does not automatically result in it being able to obtain a duty exemption under Section 9802.
- The Customs Service has been delegated the authority to promulgate rules associated with the classification of imported goods and assessment of duties.
- Courts must give deference to the regulations published by the Customs Service.

Assessment of Duties

The assessment of import tariffs or duties is a product of three variables: (1) classification of the goods being imported, (2) valuation of the goods, and (3) the country of origin. Focus on Transactions: The Dutiable Status of Goods outlines the factors involved in applying the above three variables in U.S. import or customs law.

The viability of export contracts, especially long-term supply contracts, revolves around the parties' abilities to quantify and predict costs. The amount of customs duties to be paid is an important factor that must be analyzed before any long-term contract is signed. An import duty is a tax imposed on imports by a customs authority. Duties are generally based on the value of the goods **(*ad valorem* duties);** some other factors include weight or quantity **(specific duties),** or a combination (compound duties). *Ad valorem* literally means according to value and refers to any charge, duty, or tax that is applied as a percentage of value. The classification of goods will determine the specific *ad valorem* tariff rate. The value of the goods is influenced by many factors. It would be prudent for an exporter to obtain an official ruling on the customs classification of, tariff rate for, and other import fees applying to a specific product before entering into a contract.

SECTION 9802

The *United States v. Haggar* case introduced **Section 9802,** which allows importers to deduct the value of assembly from duty assessment. This exemption is given for "articles assembled abroad in whole or in part of fabricated components that are

National Foreign Trade Council v. Baker

26 F. Supp. 2d 287 D.C. Mass. (1998)

Tauro, District Judge. Plaintiff National Foreign Trade Council ("NFTC") brings this action against two officials of the Commonwealth seeking a declaratory judgment that the so-called "Massachusetts Burma Law" is unconstitutional. The Massachusetts Burma Law is a procurement statute that prohibits the Commonwealth and its agents from purchasing goods or services from anyone doing business with the Union of Myanmar (formerly known as the Nation of Burma). The statute authorizes the establishment of a "restricted purchase list" of companies "doing business with Burma." Plaintiff claims that the Burma Law is invalid because it: (1) intrudes on the federal government's exclusive power to regulate foreign affairs; (2) discriminates against and burdens international trade in violation of the Foreign Commerce Clause; and (3) is preempted by a federal statute and an executive order imposing sanctions on Myanmar.

Under our constitutional framework, the federal government has exclusive authority to conduct foreign affairs. The Supreme Court has consistently recognized the exclusive role assigned to the federal government in the area of foreign affairs. The Court has admonished, "power over external affairs is not shared by the States; it is vested in the national government exclusively." The Massachusetts Burma Law has more than an "indirect or incidental effect in foreign countries," and a "great potential for disruption or embarrassment." It, therefore, unconstitutionally impinges on the federal government's exclusive authority to regulate foreign affairs. The Commonwealth concedes that the statute was enacted solely to sanction Myanmar for human rights violations and to change Myanmar's domestic policies. The European Union (EU), as an *amicus*, observes that the Massachusetts Burma Law: (1) interferes with the normal conduct of EU-U.S. relations; (2) raises questions about the ability of the U.S. to honor international commitments it has entered in the framework of the World Trade Organization (WTO). Japan and the Association of the South East Asian Nations (ASEAN) also filed complaints against the statute with the U.S. government.

"Buy American" statutes can be distinguished because their whole purpose and effect were to create jobs and promote economic development at home. Although these statutes benefited Americans economically, they did not single out a particular foreign country for particular treatment, as does the Massachusetts Burma Law. For example, a Pennsylvania statute applied to "steel from any foreign source, regardless of whether the source country might be considered friend or foe," and therefore did not involve the state in the conduct of foreign affairs. However, at least one court has held that even Buy American statutes may violate the foreign affairs doctrine. The court in *Bethlehem Steel Corp. v. Board of Comm'n,* 80 Cal. Rptr. 800 (1969) held unconstitutional a California "Buy American Law" that awarded state construction contracts only to companies that agreed to use American-made products. Massachusetts' concern for the welfare of the people of Myanmar as manifested by this legislative enactment, may well be regarded as admirable. But, under the exclusive foreign affairs doctrine, the proper forum to raise such concerns is the United States Congress. For the foregoing reasons, Plaintiff's Motion for Summary Judgment is ALLOWED.

Case Highlights

- The foreign affair doctrine states that it is the exclusive domain of the federal government to enact laws regulating international trade.
- A state law that prohibits the procurement of goods from the country of Myanmar is an unconstitutional intrusion of federal government powers.

http://

New Mexico Economic Development Department—The Maquiladora Industry: **http://www.edd.state.nm.us/TRADE/ISSUES/maq.htm**.

products of the United States." It also extends the exemption to any advancement in value or improvement in condition that is a result of "operations incidental to the assembly process such as cleaning, lubricating, and painting." This exemption has resulted in the creation of a corridor of assembly plants, popularly known as *maquiladoras,* along the United States-Mexican border. ***Maquiladora*** or "in-bond" industry allows foreign importers to ship components into Mexico duty-free for assembly and reexport. The key issue of contention between the Customs Service and importers is the definition of "fabrication."

Focus on Transactions

The Dutiable Status of Goods

CLASSIFICATION +	VALUATION +	COUNTRY-OF-ORIGIN
The Harmonized Tariff Schedule Rules of Interpretation:	**Transaction Value**	**"Rules-of-Origin"**
Common/Commercial Meaning	Price paid	grown, mined, produced, manufactured
Rule of Relative Specificity	Packing Costs	"Substantial Transformation Test"
Essential Character Principle	Commissions (by buyer)	• new article • value added • process v. assembly
Principle Use Rule	Value of "Assists"	• producer to consumer good
Latest Entry Rule	Royalties/Fees (by buyer)	
Doctrine of the Entireties	Proceeds of Resale (accruing to seller)	
Chief Weight Rule (Textiles)		

Dutiable Status is the Customs Service determination of the amount of money or duty owed by the importer. The above three columns summarize the factors used in calculating the duty owed. Column 1 (Classification) and Column 3 (Country-of-Origin) determine the rate (%). Column 2 (Valuation) determines the value of the imported goods. The value of the goods is then multiplied by the rate to determine the amount of duty (tax) owed.

In *Samsonite Corp. v. United States*[3] on page 158 the Customs Service successfully challenged an importer's deduction for the value of assembling luggage in Mexico. Steel strips were produced in the United States and then sent to the company's assembly plant in Mexico. The case involved the deductibility of the costs of the steel strips upon importation into the United States. The Court agreed with the Customs Service that shaping the steel strips before placing them within the luggage constituted a further fabrication and not mere assembly.

http://

Legal Information Institute—Tariff Act of 1930: **http://www4.law.cornell.edu/uscode/unframed/19/ch4.html**. See also, International Trade Data System—Major Trade Laws Since 1930: **http://www.itds.treas.gov/tradelaws.html**.

TRANSACTION VALUE

Section 402 of the Tariff Act of 1930 provides the basic method for determining the value of goods for customs purposes. United States Customs law has subsequently enacted the GATT Valuations Code. The Valuations Code uses the concept of **transaction value**[4] as the basis of customs valuation. Transaction value requires that the value of imported goods be determined on a *commercially realistic basis*. This

3. 889 F.2d 1074 (Fed. Cir. 1989).
4. See 19 U.S.C.A. § 1401a (a)(1)(A).

Samsonite Corp. v. United States

889 F.2d 1074 (Fed. Cir. 1989)

Friedman, Senior Circuit Judge. This is an appeal from a judgment of the United States Court of International Trade upholding the denial by the Customs Service of a deduction from assessed duties of the cost of an item that had been manufactured in the United States and, after undergoing certain changes in Mexico, was incorporated into the finished product shipped from Mexico to the United States. The Court of International Trade described the metal strips and Samsonite's use of them in assembling the luggage, as follows: "When they left Tuscon [sic], the strips were straight, approximately 1-7/8 inches wide and 55 inches long. After arrival at plaintiff's assembly facility in Nogales, the strips were bent by machine into a squared-sided form and riveted on the open outsides to sheets of plastic, which thereby became the bottom plates of completed frame assemblies."

The Customs Service classified the imported merchandise as luggage under Item 706.62 of the Tariff Schedules of the United States and assessed the 20 percent *ad valorem* duty that that item provides, less the cost or value of certain components of the luggage that had been manufactured in the United States. The latter deduction was made pursuant to Item 807.00 of those schedules. The Customs Service denied a deduction from the value of the luggage for the cost of the steel strips. The Court of International Trade upheld Customs' denial of the deduction.

The court held that the steel strips "were not exported in condition ready for assembly." It found that the "bending process" to which the strips were subjected "did more than 'adjust' the article. The process created the component to be assembled, the essence of which is its configuration. Without the resultant shape, the plastic plate could not be attached so as to constitute the bottom, and the completed frames could not be inserted into plaintiff's bags, thereby imparting the intended overall form and structural stability of the finished luggage."

To obtain a deduction for American-fabricated articles assembled abroad, the components (a) must have been exported from the United States "in condition ready for assembly without further fabrication," (b) not have lost their physical identity in the articles by change in form, shape, or otherwise, and (c) not have been advanced in value or improved in condition "except by being assembled" and except "by operations incidental to the assembly process such as cleaning, lubricating, and painting." The critical inquiry is whether the bending and shaping that the strips underwent constituted "fabrication" or mere assembly and operations incidental to the assembly process. We hold that what was done to the strips in Mexico was fabrication and not mere assembly. The judgment of the Court of International Trade dismissing the action is AFFIRMED.

Case Highlights

- In order to obtain the duty exemption for offshore assembly found in Section 9802 the exported items must be ready for assembly without further fabrication.
- The "bending process" to which the strips were subjected to in *Samsonite* "did more than 'adjust' the article" and thereby constituted further fabrication.

means goods must be priced at a value that would be the result of a sale between two unrelated parties in the ordinary course of business. The valuation of goods is based upon the calculation of transaction value—namely the costs of the goods to the importer. It is in the interest of the importer to keep the transaction value as low as possible and so conflict may arise over what items of costs should be included in the transaction values. Those items most contested include commissions paid by the buyer,[5] royalties or fees paid by the buyer after importation,[6] the value of *assists*[7]

5. See 19 U.S.C.A. § 1401a (b)(1)(B). See also Monarch Luggage Co. v. U.S., 715 F.Supp. 1115 (1989); Rosenthal-Netter, Inc. v. U.S., 861 F.2d 261 (Fed. Cir. 1988).
6. See 19 U.S.C.A. § 1401a (b)(1)(D).
7. See 19 U.S.C.A. §§ 1401a (b)(1)(C0 7 1401a (h)(1). See also Texas Apparel Co. v. U.S., 698 F.Supp 932 (Ct. of Int'l Trade 1988).

(material, equipment, or services provided to seller by the buyer), and proceeds of resales paid to the original seller.

Transaction value in a transaction occurring partly in a free trade zone may be difficult to determine because the import transaction is not the product of an arm's length sale, as would be the case, for example, for a transfer of raw materials or inventory between affiliated companies. The Tariff Act provides four alternative valuation methods when an arm's length transaction is not present. These alternative methods are to be followed in order of preference. The most preferred method is to use the transaction value of identical goods. This is the price charged by the same manufacturer or importer to an unrelated customer. If there is no such information available, then the transaction value of similar goods is to be used. This would be the price charged for nearly identical goods sold by the same manufacturer.

The third preferred alternative value is the use of the **deductive value** of the goods. The deductive value is the price that the goods being imported are ultimately sold at in the United States. The importer is allowed to *deduct* a number of costs from that price, including international freight, duties, and certain commissions. For example, foreign inland freight costs can be deducted but only if they are separately invoiced. Purchasing goods using the "ex-factory" trade term will remove the costs of inland shipment.[8] Although selling commissions are included in determining dutiable value, commissions paid by the buyer are not dutiable. Therefore, by proving that any middleman is acting as the buyer's purchasing agent, the buyer's commission can be excluded from the valuation.

In order to reduce the transaction value and hence the amount of tariff duties a sophisticated importer will attempt to *unbundle* the import transaction into dutiable and non-dutiable parts. If goods are purchased on credit that requires the payment of interest, the importer should separate the credit part of the sale from the sale of goods. If the price of goods reflects the interest charged by the seller, then the interest becomes part of dutiable value. In contrast, interest alone is not dutiable. Another example of unbundling is when an import contract provides for an inspection of goods at the port of shipment. If the seller obtains and pays for an inspection certificate as part of the documentary transaction, those costs are included in the transaction value, but inspection services paid for by the buyer are not part of the transaction value.

The final, least-preferred alternative valuation method is the **computed value** of the goods. This value is fabricated by adding the manufacturer's actual labor and material costs, along with an estimate of its general expenses and profits. The *Orbisphere Corp. v. United States* case that follows explores the concept of deductive value and the types of expenses that may be deducted before duties are assessed.

CUSTOMS VALUATION IN THE EUROPEAN UNION

The European approach to customs valuation is similar to that in the United States. EU Council Regulation 2913/92 established the **European Union's Customs Code,** which bases the valuation of imported goods on the notion of transaction value or the "price actually paid" (Article 28). Article 29 provides that transaction value must be adjusted for any proceeds of subsequent sales that are remitted by the buyer to the exporter, directly or indirectly. Article 32 provides a list of the types of charges that must be included in transaction value. Customs

http://
EU Taxation and Customs Union—Taric: **http://europa.eu.int/comm/taxation_customs/databases/taric_en.htm**.

8. Trade terms are explained in Chapter 9.

Orbisphere Corp. v. United States

765 F. Supp. 1087 (Ct. Int'l Trade 1991)

Musgrave, Judge. Plaintiff contests certain aspects of the Customs Service's valuation of plaintiff's products. Plaintiff alleges that in revaluing its merchandise on the basis of the "deductive value" of that merchandise, as ordered by the Court and as opposed to the earlier valuation on the basis of "transaction value," Customs improperly failed to subtract from the deductive value amounts of certain commissions, profits, and expenses involved in the sales as required by statute. Defendant argues that its failure to subtract those amounts was justified because the three items at issue—commissions, profits, and expenses—did not qualify as deductible under the applicable statute.

A. Controlling Statutes

Section 1401a(d)(2)(A)(i), under which the merchandise was appraised pursuant to the earlier opinion, defines "deductive value" as "the unit price at which the merchandise concerned is sold in the greatest aggregate quantity at or about the date of importation." Paragraph (3)(A) of that section prescribes a number of downward adjustments to the unit price stated above, including the following at issue in this case: "The price determined under paragraph (2) shall be reduced by an amount equal to any commission actually paid or agreed to be paid, or the addition usually made for profit and general expenses, in connection with sales in the United States of imported merchandise that is of the same class or kind, regardless of the country of exportation." Paragraph 3 also provides that "the deduction made for profit and general expenses shall be based upon the importer's profit and general expenses, unless such profits and general expenses are inconsistent with those reflected in sales in the United States of imported merchandise of the same class or kind, in which case the deduction shall be based on the usual profit and general expenses reflected in such sales, as determined from sufficient information." The principal question concerning this section in the present case is what kind of connection must be shown between the items of expenses or profits to be deducted and the U.S. sales of the imported merchandise.

The rule emanating from these decisions concerning the requisite connection between the expenses to be deducted from the import sales price and the underlying sales transactions appears to be that an importer may not prove that connection by merely multiplying the amount of its total expenses by the percentage that its sales of the subject merchandise make up of its total sales. It requires a specific listing of expenses involved in, and added in the price of, sales of the particular products or line at issue. Subparagraph (B) of paragraph (3) further provides, for purposes of applying the above adjustment that "the deduction made for profit and general expenses shall be based upon the importer's profits and general expenses, unless such profits and general expenses are inconsistent with those reflected in sales in the United States of imported merchandise of the same class or kind, in which case the deduction shall be based on the usual profit and general expenses reflected in such sales, as determined from sufficient information."

The disputed expenses in the present case are:

1. salary and expenses for travel;
2. costs for "U.S. accounting services";
3. costs for "U.S. legal services";
4. director's fees and expenses for travel to Geneva.

Accordingly, the Court orders that the deductive value computed by Customs for this merchandise be reduced by the amount of those expenses. The deduction for profits is provided not based on where the profits end up but in order to provide a value of the goods sold in the United States that approximates the cost of the goods before shipment, resale, and expenses associated therewith. Accordingly, it is clear that in this case plaintiff's profits on the sales in question should have been deducted from the deductive value of the merchandise. Therefore, Customs is hereby ordered to amend its previous calculation of the deductive value of the subject merchandise by subtracting therefrom amounts equal to plaintiff's expenses and profits discussed herein.

Case Highlights

- Items such as profits and expenses occurring within the United States relating to imported goods should be subtracted when using the deductive method of calculating value for purposes of duty assessment.
- Other items that may be deducted from the value of imported goods include the cost of legal services, travel expenses, and accounting costs.
- The importer of goods must show the connection between the items being deducted and the U.S. sale of the imported goods.

value includes the costs of packing, commission and brokerage, and royalty and license fees. Items that are not included in the customs valuation include freight charges, charges incurred subsequent to import, and finance charges (Article 33). One advantage of the EU tariff is that it is fully harmonized in the area of import licensing. The single tariff structure known as ***Taric*** provides rules for determining whether an import license is required for a particular good. It should be noted that most EU members also maintain their own country lists of goods requiring an import license.[9]

DRAWBACK OF CUSTOMS DUTIES

Drawback is a form of tax relief in which a lawfully collected customs duty is refunded or remitted wholly or in part because of the particular use made of the commodity on which the duty was collected. U.S. firms that import materials or components that they process or assemble for reexport may obtain drawback refunds of all duties paid on the imported merchandise, less 1 percent to cover customs costs. This practice encourages U.S. exports by permitting exporters to compete in foreign markets without the handicap of including in their sales prices the duties paid on imported components.

The U.S. **Trade and Tariff Act of 1984** revised and expanded drawbacks. Under existing regulations several types of drawback have been authorized, but only three are of interest to most manufacturers. First, if articles manufactured in the United States using imported merchandise are exported, then the duties paid on the imported merchandise used may be refunded as a drawback. Second, if both imported merchandise and domestic merchandise of the same kind and quality are used to manufacture articles, some of which are exported, then duties paid on the imported merchandise are refundable as a drawback, regardless of whether that merchandise was used in the exported articles.

Finally, if articles of foreign origin imported for consumption are exported from the United States or are destroyed under the supervision of U.S. Customs within three years of the date of importation, in the same condition as when imported and without being "used" in the United States, then duties paid on the imported merchandise are refundable as a drawback. Incidental operations on the merchandise, such as testing, cleaning, repacking, or inspection, are not considered "uses" of the article. To obtain drawback, the U.S. firm must file a proposal with a regional commissioner of customs or with the Entry Rulings Branch of the Customs Service.

U.S. Foreign-Trade Zones

Exporters should also consider the customs privileges of U.S. **foreign (free) trade zones.** These zones are domestic U.S. sites that are considered outside U.S. customs territory and are available for activities that might otherwise be carried on overseas for customs reasons. For export operations, the zones offer accelerated export status for purposes of excise tax rebates and customs drawback. For import and reexport activities, no customs duties, federal excise taxes, or state or local *ad valorem* taxes are charged on foreign goods moved into foreign-trade zones unless and until the goods, or products made from them, are officially moved into the United States. This means that the use of zones can be profitable for operations involving

http://

List of world's free trade zones with links to government agencies: **http://www.escapeartist.com/ftz/ftz_index.html**.

9. Information on import forms for the EU is contained in Title VII of EU Council Regulation 2454/93 and Title III of EU Council Regulation 2913/92.

foreign dutiable materials and components being assembled or produced here for reexport. In addition, quota restrictions do not ordinarily apply.

There are now 180 approved foreign-trade zones in port communities throughout the United States. Associated with these projects are some 200 subzones. These facilities are available for operations involving storage, repacking, inspection, exhibition, assembly, manufacturing, and other processing. Information about the zones is available from the Foreign-Trade Zones Board of the International Trade Administration.

Country of Origin

The modern trend is to use resources in a number of locations in the manufacture of goods. The global marketplace includes the global manufacture of goods. Globalization presents problems in determining the country of origin for a good that is a product of processes that take place in different countries. Recognizing that there is a lack of international uniformity for country of origin criteria, the Uruguay Round of GATT adopted the **Agreement on Customs Valuation.** Although it is currently only a framework agreement, it establishes fair valuation as an internationally recognizable principle. It further makes transaction value as the internationally preferred means of calculating dutiable value.

The country of origin of a good is used to determine the applicable tariff rate and whether any quantitative restrictions are relevant. For example, a product of a less developed country is often given a reduced tariff rate under the General Systems of Preferences. Also, lower tariffs and restrictions are available for goods produced within a free trade area. Thus, the NAFTA provides a unique set of "country of origin" rules to determine if a good is to be considered a regional or NAFTA product.

http://
NAFTA Secretariat: **http://nafta-sec-alena.org**. See also NAFTA Customs Web site: **http://www.nafta-customs.org**. Click on "United States" link for information on rules of origin and valuation matters.

Country-specific or industry-specific restrictions like anti-dumping duties, quotas, and voluntary restraint agreements are dependent upon the determination of the country of origin. Unfortunately, country of origin determinations can be complicated and uncertain for a number of reasons. First, country of origin rules have generally come from national import laws; individual countries have used different criteria and have varied in their interpretations. Second, the rise of the global marketplace for goods, services, and raw materials, along with the development of global corporations, has resulted in products being manufactured in different stages in different countries with component parts coming from all over the world. Thus, the true country of origin is often difficult to determine.

Country of origin rules are also used to conform to import laws pertaining to the labeling of products manufactured, produced, assembled, or made from materials from different countries. A number of methods have been developed to make this determination. **Substantial transformation** is considered the primary test in country of origin determinations and is the one adopted under U.S. law. Under this approach, the country of origin is the last country in which a good or product was substantially transformed. A substantial transformation occurs when a product is changed into a new or different product. For example, if a good has changed from a producer good to a consumer good, a substantial transformation has occurred.

The Supreme Court in *Anheuser-Busch Ass'n v. United States*[10] defined a substantial transformation as one where a good is "manufactured into a new and different article, having a distinctive name, character, or use from that of the original article." Factors often utilized in applying this test include whether the good went through a

10. 207 U.S. 556 (1908).

tariff classification change, the amount of value added because of the transformation, and the complexity of the processing operation. For example, the greater the value added the more likely that a substantial transformation has occurred.

An alternative method to determine country of origin is to perform a value-added analysis. The **value-added test** is based upon the use of percentages, either of the value added or percentage of component parts coming from imported materials, to determine the country of origin. Used in the European Union, this method was adopted under NAFTA for goods transported from one NAFTA country to another. NAFTA's country of origin rules use the value-added test as part of a multistep approach depending on the type of product being imported. In general, nonregional (non-NAFTA) materials or components need to be sufficiently transformed in order to result in a tariff classification change.

In some areas, not only do nonregional goods have to be substantially transformed, but the final end product needs to contain a specified percentage of regional (NAFTA) content (value-added). The value-added percentage applied under NAFTA varies according to the type of good. Automobiles, for example, are required to have a regional content equal to 62.5 percent or more of NAFTA-originating materials and labor.

A number of problems are associated with the value-added method. First, it penalizes lesser-developed countries because of their low costs of labor and raw materials. Second, multinational enterprises may manipulate transfer pricing among its affiliated companies to reduce the value of imported materials in order to avoid tariff duties or to ensure a certain country of origin designation.[11]

Some countries use value-added percentage to determine the country of origin of a component part that is then applied in whole or excluded in whole in determining the country of origin of the final product. The **Canada-United States Free Trade Agreement**[12] uses a 50 percent value-added rule in determining the country of origin of a component part. A component part is considered to be a wholly domestic part if the regional value of its content is 50 percent or more. The part then earns a roll-up in which it is considered 100 percent domestically produced for determining the country of origin for the final product. If the regional content value is less than 50 percent, then the entire component will be considered as wholly imported, known as a roll-back.

http://
National Bureau of Economic Research—"Lessons from the Canada-U.S. Free Trade Agreement": **http://www.nber.org/digest/sep01/w8293.html**.

The **specified processes test** expressly lists the types of processes or operations that are considered to confer country of origin status. However, this test has not been used comprehensively. Instead, it has been used in a piecemeal fashion to target certain products. For example, EU Commission Regulation 288/99 grants origin status to an integrated circuit wherever it undergoes diffusion. An example of a negative version of the test is EU Regulation 2071/89, which holds that the location of the assembly of the optical system does not provide a presumption that that location is the country of origin for imported photocopiers.

The final method of origin determination is the **change in tariff classification** approach. This test bases country of origin status upon any change in a product that results in a change in its tariff classification. Tariff classifications are almost universally affixed using the Harmonized Commodity Description and Coding System. This classification system has been enacted in the United States in the Harmonized Tariff Schedule. The most recent attempt at harmonizing country

11. Joseph A. LaNasa, III, "Rules of Origin and the Uruguay Round's Effectiveness in Harmonizing and Regulating Them," 90 *American Journal of International Law* 625 (1996). This article provides an excellent review of country of origin methods and the WTO Origin Agreement. The material in this section was taken from the above article.
12. Note that the Canada-U.S. Free Trade Agreement has been formally folded into NAFTA.

of origin rules is the **Origin Agreement** of GATT. The Origin Agreement adopts the change in tariff classification as the primary method to determine origin.

In conjunction with the Origin Agreement, the **Technical Committee on Rules of Origin** and the **Committee on Rules of Origin** have been established to interpret the rules. The Origin Agreement also emphasizes the importance of transparency. It requires all WTO countries to publish their nation's origin rules and applications of their rules. It also requires members to give a **binding assessment** to anyone who requests an advanced determination of origin. The binding assessment must then be honored for a period of three years for all comparable goods or imports.

The United States Customs Service administers a number of laws that revolve around the country of origin of imported goods. These laws include those relating to marking requirements, qualification for trade preferences under a free trade agreement, application of antidumping duties and quota restrictions, and granting of a special duty status for tariff reductions. The country of origin determinations may vary under the different statutes. Therefore, it is possible for the same good to be considered from Country A for purposes of marking and from Country B for purposes of assessing a duty. The next section explores the application of country of origin rules to national marking requirements.

Marking Requirements

United States law requires that the country of origin must be marked on all imported goods. This **marking requirement** is found in Section 304(a) of the Tariff Act of 1930. It states that "every article of foreign origin imported into the United States shall be marked in a conspicuous place in such manner as to indicate to an ultimate purchaser the English name of the country of origin."[13] Civil actions pertaining to marking requirements are set in the Court of International Trade. There are a number of exceptions to the marking requirements: Goods that are incapable of being marked such as crude substances, personal goods, and goods not native to the United States need not be marked.

A key issue in determining the type of marking necessary to comply with the Act is defining the **ultimate purchaser.** Customs regulations define the ultimate purchaser as "the last person in the United States who will receive the article in the form in which it is imported."[14] Therefore, if the imported item is used in a manufacturing process, then the manufacturer is the ultimate purchaser. The manufacturing process must result in a substantial transformation of the article for this to be the case. If the identity of the article remains essentially the same after the manufacturing process, then the user or consumer who uses the article after the process is regarded as the ultimate purchaser. The Tariff Act provides severe punishment including fines and imprisonment for anyone destroying, removing, or altering any mark required under the Act. In addition, anyone importing unmarked items is subject to civil penalties including an additional 10 percent *ad valorem* duty.

Marking requirements vary widely from country to country. NAFTA, for example, includes a number of marking provisions. Formulas are provided in order to determine whether a good was produced in a NAFTA country in order to take advantage of the lower tariff rates between the United States, Canada, and Mexico. The labeling of a product regarding its country of origin may mean different things depending upon the law or test being applied. The use of the label "Made

13. 19 U.S.C. § 1304(a).
14. 10 C.F.R. § 134.1(d) (1986).

in the USA" may vary depending on the appropriate regulations. NAFTA defines something made in a NAFTA country, whether in the United States, Canada, or Mexico, as something in which at least 55 percent of the labor and component parts were supplied by a NAFTA country. In contrast, the U.S. Department of Transportation requires that a motor vehicle must be 75 percent the product of the United States before it may be considered "Made in the USA." The Federal Trade Commission states that the "Made in the USA" label should be used in advertising only when "all, or virtually all, of the components and labor are of U.S. origin."

CUSTOMS MODERNIZATION ACT

The **Customs Modernization Act** has implemented a number of changes to U.S. customs law. Prior to the act's enactment the Customs Service was primarily responsible for classifying and valuing imported products. Legal responsibility in these areas is now entirely upon the importer of the goods. The importer is under a duty of *reasonable care* to correctly classify and value the goods being imported. This duty cannot legally be delegated to a customs broker. The importer remains liable for any misclassification or undervaluation.

The importer's secondary responsibility under the Modernization Act is to implement a proper record-keeping system. Failure to maintain adequate records that substantiate the importer's customs declarations can result in substantial penalties. Because of this shifting of responsibility to the importer, goods now enter the United States more quickly without the need for Customs inspections. Instead, the Customs Service will rely on the examination of documents and post-entry audits.

http://

United States Automated Export System at U.S. Customs web site: **http://www.customs.treas.gov**.

Another innovation mandated by the Customs Modernization Act is the implementation of a new **Automated Export System (AES).** Use of the AES by exporters and their freight forwarders has exceeded Customs' forecasts, representing 38.9 percent of total export trade in January 2000. AES was jointly developed by Customs, the Commerce Department's Census Bureau and Bureau of Export Administration, the State Department's Office of Defense Trade Controls, and other government agencies involved in exports.

Foreign National Import Restrictions, Requirements, and Standards

A good source for general information on import restrictions and requirements of foreign countries is the Country Commercial Guides provided by United States government agencies. The Country Guide for Indonesia, for example, provides information on trade regulations, standards, and import requirements. It notes that beginning in 1996, the Indonesian government began to drastically reduce tariffs, along with quantitative restrictions. "In May 1995, the Indonesian government unveiled a comprehensive tariff reduction package covering roughly two-thirds of all traded goods, designed to reduce most tariffs to under 5 percent by 2003." However, technical barriers remain in the area of services. "Foreign law firms, accounting firms, and consulting engineers must operate through technical assistance or joint venture with local firms."

http://

U.S. State Department—Country Commercial Guides: **http://www.state.gov**.

In the area of import control, the Indonesian government has drastically reduced the types of good subject to import restrictions and special licensing requirements. However, goods such as alcoholic beverages, motor vehicles, hand tools, sweeteners, engines and pumps, tractors, rice, lube oil, and explosives continue to be regulated. Customs valuation has been transformed from an inspection system to one that relies on verification and auditing. Beginning in 1997, the Customs Directorate in the Ministry of Finance has operated an entry audit system. An **electronic data interchange (EDI)** system links importers, banks, and the

Directorate. Import documentation generally includes the *pro forma* invoice, commercial invoice, certificate of origin, bill of lading, and insurance certificate. The government requires advance notification in which these documents are presented in diskette form. Like Indonesia's import tariff regime, export controls are in a state of rapid flux as the government works to implement reforms to reduce the restrictions and taxes placed on exports that affect agricultural products, including crops like rubber, palm oil, coffee, and copra.

The import regime of countries of the former Soviet bloc is still evolving. New customs codes have been adopted, but enforcement may still be unpredictable.[15] For example, Russia has adopted customs valuation procedures as approved by GATT. The tariff rate to be applied will be taken from a list of rates that became effective on May 15, 1996. If a preferential rate is being requested, for example for products originating from a less developed country, a certificate of origin will be required.

In addition, a number of exemptions can be obtained for goods imported to Russia for processing and sale or for processing and export, or for goods exported for processing. The first exemption is often difficult to obtain. The second type (processing and export) does not allow an exemption for customs duties or value-added taxation (VAT), but does give a right to reclaim those taxes and duties if the processed goods are exported within two years. This exemption applies only to the processing value. Other than the certificate of origin, an importer must complete a customs declaration in the Russian language and may have to obtain bank approval pertinent to any hard currency transactions. Because of the evolving nature of the new customs laws, it is wise to contact the Russian Ministry of Foreign Economic Relations for updates and to enlist the services of a Russian customs agent to handle the import documentation.

Standards Requirements

The existence of non-harmonized standards for similar products or technologies in different countries or regions can contribute to so-called "technical barriers to trade." Standards are technical specifications or other precise criteria to be used as rules, guidelines, or definitions of characteristics, to ensure that materials, products, processes, and services are fit for their intended purposes. All countries have enacted requirements that certain goods or services meet their country's standards before being allowed entry. These country-specific standards are not always transparent and in the past may have acted as barriers to trade.

In more recent times, there have been regional efforts to harmonize product standards. In the European Union standards harmonization has allowed for the free movement of goods within the Union. Most recently, voluntary standards have been developed that allow a company to affix an **eco-label** to its products. An eco-label is a voluntary mark awarded by the European Union to producers who can show that their products are significantly less harmful to the environment than similar products. A more recent development is the EU's **CE Mark.** This "umbrella" label warrants that the good bearing the mark meets all relevant EU Directives relating to that type of product.

http://
EU eco-label homepage: **http://europa.eu.int/comm/environment/ecolabel.**

http://
CE Mark: **http://www.cemarking.net**

Internationally, the 1994 WTO Agreements include a framework for the harmonization of some health and safety standards. The two framework agreements are the WTO Agreement on Technical Barriers to Trade (TBT) and under the WTO Agreement on Sanitary and PhytoSanitary Measures (SPS). The further de-

15. See Price Waterhouse, *Doing Business in the Russian Federation* 64–70 (1997).

velopment of international standards will contribute to making life simpler, and to increasing the reliability and effectiveness of the goods and services we use.

In the area of service standards, the General Agreement on Trade in Services (GATS) requires that all countries review their laws so that "qualification requirements and procedures, technical standards, and licensing requirements do not constitute unnecessary barriers to trade in services." Any such requirements should be "based on objective and transparent criteria." In the area of professional services, each country "shall provide for adequate procedures to verify the competence of professionals" of any other country.

http://
European Commission—Standards: **http://www.europa.eu.int/comm/dgs/health_consumer/library/surveys/sur16_en.html**.

Historically, the International Labor Organization (ILO) has been active in developing international labor standards. The ILO was established in 1919 and became a specialized agency of the United Nations in 1946. It seeks to promote social justice in areas such as employment, pay, health, working conditions, and freedom of association among workers. Its headquarters is in Geneva, Switzerland.

EXPORT REGULATIONS

The **Export Administration Regulations (EAR)** provide a general overview of United States export restrictions as published by the **Bureau of Export Administration (BXA).** The BXA is organized into two branches: Export Administration and Export Enforcement. Export Administration implements and administers the export controls as detailed in the EAR. It consists of five offices: Office of Nuclear and Missile Technology Controls, Office of Chemical and Biological Controls and Treaty Compliance, Office of Strategic Trade and Foreign Policy Controls, Office of Strategic Industries and Economic Security, and Office of Export Services. The last office provides assistance to exporters and reexporters, conducts educational seminars, and maintains the EAR. The Export Enforcement branch has three offices: Office of Export Enforcement, Office of Environmental Support, and Office of Antiboycott Compliance. The last office enforces the Restrictive Trade Practices and Boycotts restrictions enacted under U.S. law.

http://
Bureau of Export Administration (BXA): **http://www.bxa.doc.gov**.

The United States controls the exportation of goods by issuing two types of export licenses. The **general license** is a grant of authority to all exporters for certain types of goods. In some instances, exporters must obtain a **validated license** for certain products and for export to certain countries. A validated license grants authority to a specific exporter to export specific products. Whether a validated license is required will be determined through a review of a number of regulations: First, whether the country of import is on the **country groups list.** Second, whether the product being exported is on the **commodity control list.** Third, whether any "special restrictions" apply to the export. The Country Group List consists of countries that are being boycotted by the U.S. government. The Commodity Control List is a list of sensitive products whose export is restricted or regulated.

If a validated license is not required, then the goods may be exported under a general license without any specific application. However, the exporter will have to provide a **Shipper's Export Declaration (SED)** (Exhibit 6.2) and may have to provide a **Destination Control Statement.** Exporters are required to place this statement on commercial invoices and bills of lading for most export sales. These statements alert foreign buyers of goods and documents that diversion contrary to U.S. law is prohibited. The Destination Control Statement requires that the following language be placed upon all export documents including the bill of lading and commercial invoice: "These commodities, technology, or software were exported

EXHIBIT 6.2 *Shipper's Export Declaration*

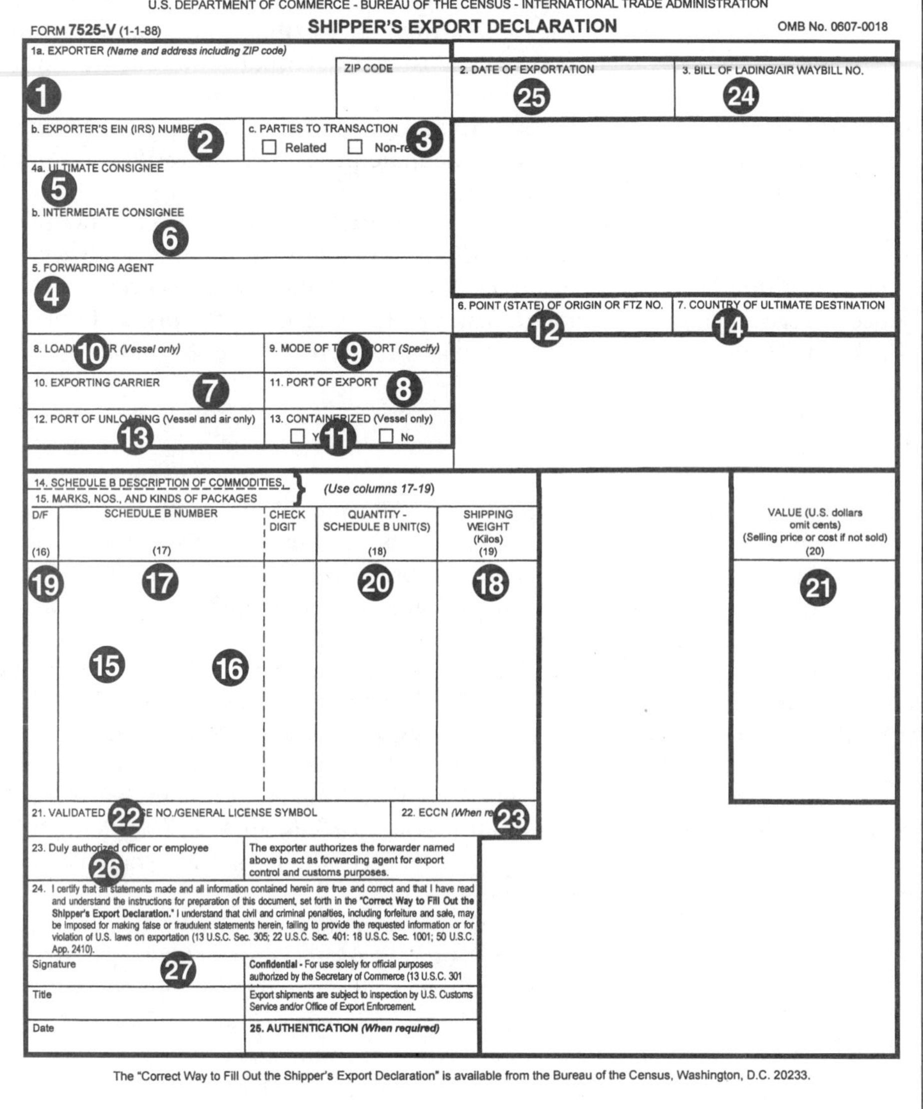

U.S. DEPARTMENT OF COMMERCE - BUREAU OF THE CENSUS - INTERNATIONAL TRADE ADMINISTRATION

FORM **7525-V** (1-1-88) **SHIPPER'S EXPORT DECLARATION** OMB No. 0607-0018

1a. EXPORTER *(Name and address including ZIP code)* 1 | ZIP CODE

2. DATE OF EXPORTATION 25

3. BILL OF LADING/AIR WAYBILL NO. 24

b. EXPORTER'S EIN (IRS) NUMB[ER] 2

c. PARTIES TO TRANSACTION 3 ☐ Related ☐ Non-re[lated]

4a. ULTIMATE CONSIGNEE 5

b. INTERMEDIATE CONSIGNEE 6

5. FORWARDING AGENT 4

6. POINT (STATE) OF ORIGIN OR FTZ NO. 12

7. COUNTRY OF ULTIMATE DESTINATION 14

8. LOAD[ING PIE]R *(Vessel only)* 10

9. MODE OF T[RANSP]ORT *(Specify)* 9

10. EXPORTING CARRIER 7

11. PORT OF EXPORT 8

12. PORT OF UNLOADING (Vessel and air only) 13

13. CONTAINERIZED (Vessel only) 11 ☐ Y[es] ☐ No

14. SCHEDULE B DESCRIPTION OF COMMODITIES,
15. MARKS, NOS., AND KINDS OF PACKAGES } *(Use columns 17-19)*

D/F (16)	SCHEDULE B NUMBER (17)	CHECK DIGIT	QUANTITY - SCHEDULE B UNIT(S) (18)	SHIPPING WEIGHT (Kilos) (19)	VALUE (U.S. dollars omit cents) (Selling price or cost if not sold) (20)
19	17 15 16		20	18	21

21. VALIDATED [LICEN]SE NO./GENERAL LICENSE SYMBOL 22

22. ECCN *(When re[quired])* 23

23. Duly authorized officer or employee 26 | The exporter authorizes the forwarder named above to act as forwarding agent for export control and customs purposes.

24. I certify that all statements made and all information contained herein are true and correct and that I have read and understand the instructions for preparation of this document, set forth in the **"Correct Way to Fill Out the Shipper's Export Declaration."** I understand that civil and criminal penalties, including forfeiture and sale, may be imposed for making false or fraudulent statements herein, failing to provide the requested information or for violation of U.S. laws on exportation (13 U.S.C. Sec. 305; 22 U.S.C. Sec. 401: 18 U.S.C. Sec. 1001; 50 U.S.C. App. 2410).

Signature 27 | **Confidential** - For use solely for official purposes authorized by the Secretary of Commerce (13 U.S.C. 301

Title | Export shipments are subject to inspection by U.S. Customs Service and/or Office of Export Enforcement.

Date | **25. AUTHENTICATION** *(When required)*

The "Correct Way to Fill Out the Shipper's Export Declaration" is available from the Bureau of the Census, Washington, D.C. 20233.

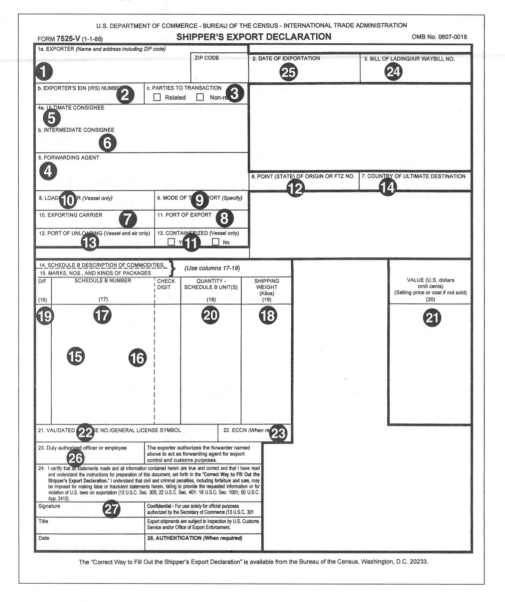

from the United States in accordance with the Export Administration Regulations. Diversion contrary to U.S. law is prohibited."[16]

Section 2403 of the EAR explains the types of licenses available for exporting goods. The general license requires only the submission of the Shipper's Export Declaration. Validated licenses, including those for specific exports along with those for multiple exports, require written approval from the Department of Commerce. The following excerpt from the EAR lists the varieties of export licenses.

16. For a good overview of United States export documentation, see Braumiller & Rodriquez, "Export Process and Documentation: Focus on the New Export Administration Regulations," 9 *International Quarterly* 697. They distill all of the Export Administration Regulations to five questions: What is the item (Commerce Control List)? Where is it going? Who will receive it? What will be the item's end-use? What else does my end-user do?

EXHIBIT 6.2 *(continued)*

1. **Exporter**—The name and address of the principal party responsible for effecting export from the United States. The exporter as named on the Export License. Report only the first five digits of the ZIP code.
2. **Exporter Identification Number**—The exporter's Internal Revenue Service Employer Identification Number (EIN) or Social Security Number (SSN) if no EIN has been assigned.
3. **Related Party Transaction**—One between the U.S. exporter and the foreign consignee, that is, an export from a U.S. person or business enterprise to a foreign business enterprise or from a U.S. business enterprise to a foreign person or business enterprise, when the person owns (directly or indirectly) at any time during the fiscal year, 10 percent or more of the voting securities of the incorporated business enterprise, or an equivalent interest if an unincorporated business enterprise, including a branch. Otherwise, check UNRELATED.
4. **Agent of Exporter**—The name and address of the duly authorized forwarding agent.
5. **Ultimate Consignee**—The name and address of the party actually receiving the merchandise for the designated end use or the party so designated on the validated export license.
6. **Intermediate Consignee**—The name and address of the party in a foreign country who effects delivery of the merchandise to the ultimate consignee or the party so named on the export license.
7. **Exporting Carrier**—The name of the carrier transporting the merchandise out of the United States. For vessel shipments, give the vessel's flag also.
8. **U.S. Port of Export**
   - **Overland**—the U.S. Customs port at which the surface carrier crosses the border.
   - **Vessel and air**—the U.S. Customs port where the merchandise is loaded on the carrier which is taking the merchandise out of the United States.
   - **Postal**—the U.S. Post Office where the merchandise is mailed.
9. **Method of Transportation**—The mode of transport by which the merchandise is exported. Specify by name, i.e., vessel, air, rail, truck, etc. Specify "own power" is applicable.
10. **Loading Pier**—(For vessel shipments only) The number or name of the pier at which the merchandise is laden aboard the exporting vessel.
11. **Containerized**—(For vessel shipments only) Cargo originally booked as containerized cargo and that is placed in containers at the operator's option.
12. **Point (State) of Origin or Foreign Trade Zone (FTZ) Number**
    - The two digit U.S. Postal Service abbreviation of the state in which the merchandise actually starts its journey to the port of export, or
    - The state of origin of the commodity of the greatest value, or
    - The state of consolidation, or
    - The Foreign Trade Zone Number for exports leaving a FTZ.
13. **Foreign Port of Unloading**—(For vessel and air shipments only) The foreign port and country at which the merchandise will be laden from the exporting carrier.
14. **Country of Ultimate Destination**—The country in which the merchandise is to be consumed, further processed, or manufactured; the final country of destination as known to the exporter at the time of shipment; or the country of ultimate destination as shown on the validated export license.
15. **Marks, Numbers, and Kinds of Packages**—Marks, numbers, or other identification shown on the packages and the numbers and kinds of packages (boxes, barrels, baskets, etc.).
16. **Commodity Description**—A sufficient description of the commodity to permit verification of the Schedule B Commodity Number or the description on the validated export license.
17. **Schedule B Commodity Number**—the commodity number and "check digit" as provided in Schedule B—Statistical Classification of Domestic and Foreign Commodities Exported from the United States. When form 7513 is used, report only the first six digits of the Schedule B commodity number.
18. **Gross Shipping Weight**—(For vessel and air shipments only) The gross shipping weight in kilograms, including the weight of containers but excluding carrier equipment (Multiply lbs. by 0.4536 to get kilos; round off to whole numbers.).
19. **"D" (Domestic) or "F" (Foreign)**
    - Domestic exports—Merchandise grown, produced, or manufactured (including imported merchandise which has been enhanced in value) in the United States.
    - Foreign exports—merchandise that has entered the United States and is being reexported in the same condition as when imported.
20. **Net Quantity**—The amount in terms of the unit(s) specified in Schedule B with the unit indicated or the unit as specified on the validated export license. (Report whole units.)
21. **Value**—Selling price or cost if not sold, including inland freight, insurance, and other charges to U.S. port of export, but excluding unconditional discounts and commissions (nearest whole dollar, omit cents).
22. **Export License Number or Symbol**—Validated export license number and expiration date or general license symbol.
23. **Export Commodity Control Number (ECCN)**—(When required) ECCN number of commodities listed on the Commodity Control List (commodities subject to U.S. Department of commerce export controls) in the Export Administration Regulations.
24. **Bill of Lading or Air Waybill Number**—The exporting carrier's bill of lading or air waybill number.
25. **Date of Exportation**—(Not required for vessel and postal shipments) The date of departure or date of clearance, if date of departure is not known.
26. **Designation of Agent**—Signature of exporter authorizing the named agent to effect the export when such agent does not have power of attorney.
27. **Signature**—Signature of exporter or authorized agent certifying the truth and accuracy of the information on the SED.

Under such conditions as may be imposed by the Secretary which are consistent with the provisions of this Act, the Secretary may require any of the following types of export licenses:

(1) A validated license, *authorizing a specific export, issued pursuant to an application by the exporter.*

(2) Validated licenses authorizing multiple exports, *issued pursuant to an application by the exporter, in lieu of an individual validated license for each such export, including, but not limited to, the following:*

(A) A distribution license, *authorizing exports of goods to approved distributors or users of the goods in countries other than controlled countries, except that the Secretary may establish a type of distribution license appropriate for consignees in the People's Republic of China. The Secretary shall grant the distribution license primarily on the basis of the reliability of the applicant and foreign consignees with respect to the prevention of diversion of goods to controlled countries.*

(B) A comprehensive operations license, *authorizing exports and reexports of technology and related goods, including items from the list of militarily critical technologies which are included on the control list in accordance with that section, from a domestic concern to and among its foreign subsidiaries, affiliates, joint venturers, and licensees that have long-term, contractually defined relations with the exporter, are located in countries other than controlled countries (except the People's Republic of China), and are approved by the Secretary. The Secretary shall grant the license to manufacturing, laboratory, or related operations on the basis of approval of the exporter's systems of control, including internal proprietary controls, applicable to the technology and related goods to be exported rather than approval of individual export transactions.*

(C) A project license, *authorizing exports of goods or technology for a specified activity.*

(D) A service supply license, *authorizing exports of spare or replacement parts for goods previously exported.*

(3) A general license, *authorizing exports, without application by the exporter.*

United States v. Donald Shetterly

971 F.2d 67 (7th Cir.)

Kanne, Circuit Judge. After a jury trial, Donald Shetterly was convicted of attempting to export a controlled microwave amplifier to (then) West Germany without an export license in violation of § 2410(a) of the Export Administration Act of 1979, and was sentenced to 41 months imprisonment. He now appeals his conviction and sentence.

Mr. Shetterly was introduced to Karl Mann, a West German businessman. From 1987 through 1989, Mr. Shetterly sent electronic equipment, including microwave amplifiers and computer software, to Mr. Mann in West Germany. In October 1988, Mr. Mann sent a letter to Mr. Shetterly requesting him to purchase an amplifier from Berkshire Technologies, Inc., of Oakland, California. Mr. Shetterly called Berkshire to inquire about the amplifier and spoke with William Lum, the president of Berkshire. The amplifier was on the Department of Commerce's commodity control list and therefore a validated license was required for its exportation out of the United States. Export licenses are required for exporting certain commodities under the Export Administration Act. A general license merely requires that the commodity meets certain standards—no license application is necessary and no license document is issued.

A validated license requires the exporter to file a license application before exporting commodities that cannot be exported under a general license or with other authorization by the Office of Export Licensing. Such commodities are included in the Department of Commerce's commodity control list. See 15 C.F.R. § 799.1 Supp. 1. At the time of the offense, a validated license was required for exportation of the Berkshire amplifier because its value exceeded $5,000.00.

This case arose prior to the breakup of the former Soviet Union. In line with cold war attitudes, Mr. Lum testified that he was suspicious that the destination of the amplifier was overseas because he "had become aware of significant attempts by the Soviets to obtain the amplifier." Mr. Shetterly argues that the statement was improper because it implied that his goal was to supply technology to the Soviet Union. However, there was evidence that the technology involved was already known to the Soviets; therefore, any error was harmless.

50 U.S.C. § 2410(a) states that one who "knowingly violates or conspires to or attempts to violate any provision of the Export Administration Act, or any regulation, order or license issued thereunder" commits a crime. Mr. Shetterly contends that an exportation or attempted

exportation of a controlled commodity without a license becomes a crime under § 2410(a) only when the exporter knows that a license is required. We agree with the government's assertions that specific intent is not required for a violation of § 2410(a). In order to establish that Mr. Shetterly violated § 2410(a), the government was required to prove beyond a reasonable doubt that Mr. Shetterly knowingly exported or attempted to export a controlled commodity, without obtaining the appropriate export license, in violation of 15 C.F.R. § 799.1 Supp.1 (the commodities control list).

Finally, Mr. Shetterly argues that the district court misapplied the Sentencing Guidelines by refusing to depart below the Guidelines. Mr. Shetterly was sentenced pursuant to Guideline § 2M5.1, which provides for a base offense level of 22 "if national security or nuclear proliferation controls were invaded." One of the bases of the Export Administration Act is to protect national security. See 50 U.S.C. § 2402. Accordingly, the district judge sentenced Mr. Shetterly to 41 months of imprisonment, the minimum sentence in the applicable Guideline range. Mr. Shetterly alleges that trial counsel's petition to depart downward from the Guidelines was inadequate, and that the district court erred in failing to consider the implication of Application Note 2 of Guideline § 2M5.1, whereby a court can consider the degree to which the violation threatened a security interest of the United States, the volume of commerce involved, the extent of planning or sophistication, and whether there were multiple occurrences in determining a sentence within the Guidelines. Therefore, we must review the record to determine whether the district judge exercised his discretion in refusing to depart from the Guidelines or whether he felt that he lacked authority to depart.

The district judge's statements indicate he considered that it would no longer be illegal to export the Berkshire amplifier out of the country without a license. It is clear that the judge used his discretion in refusing to depart. Therefore, we have no jurisdiction to review his refusal to depart. AFFIRMED.

Case Highlights

- Export licenses are required for exporting certain commodities under the Export Administration Act.
- A general license requires merely that the commodity meets certain standards—no license application is necessary and no license document is issued.
- A good that is on the Department of Commerce's Commodity Control List requires a validated license.
- Knowingly exporting or attempting to export a controlled commodity without a license is a crime.

Subsections (1) and (2) describe the various types of *validated licenses* that are provided for under the regulations. The validated license described in subsection (1) covers only a single shipment of goods. Subsection (2) provides licenses for "multiple exports" including the distribution license, project license, service supply license, and the comprehensive operations license. Subsection (3) authorizes the generic *general license*. The term general license is a misnomer because it does not result in a license being issued by the government. Subsection (3) authorizes exports "without application by the exporter."[17]

EAR covers more than exports: It also covers reexports of some foreign products such as those products produced abroad under U.S. licenses, activities of U.S. citizens anywhere in the world involving technical assistance with respect to encryption commodities or software, and certain transactions within the United States. The last category includes the release of technology to a foreign national in the United States. It also includes the return of foreign equipment to its country of

17. When mailing goods through the U.S. Postal Service, Postal Service Form 2976-A needs to be completed. It is a two-part document incorporating a "Customs Declaration" and "Dispatch Note." It requests the seller's address, addressee's address, list of contents, quantity, value, and net weight. It allows the sender to classify the materials as a commercial sample, documents, gift, or merchandise. The sender must certify the accuracy of the list of contents and that the item "does not contain any dangerous article prohibited by postal regulations." Therefore, the sender must be familiar with both U.S. export regulations and postal regulations. The "Dispatch Note" portion requires the declaration of customs duty and a customs stamp. The form must be filled out in English but instructs the sender that she "may add a translation of the contents to facilitate Customs treatment in the destination country." It also states that one's signature is a "guarantee that the particulars given are correct."

http://
Code of Federal Regulations:
http://www.access.gpo.gov/nara/cfr/index.html.

origin after repair in the United States, shipments from United States foreign trade zones, and the electronic transmission of nonpublic data. The severity of punishment for failing to obtain the appropriate export license is demonstrated in *United States v. Shetterly,* on page 170.

Title 15 of the **Code of Federal Regulations (CFR)** provides information and guidance on the issuance of general and validated licenses.[18] Section 730.8 of the EAR provides a simple schematic for the exporter to follow. First, Part 732 of the EAR

Daedalus Enterprises, Inc. v. Baldridge

563 F. Supp. 1345 (D.C. 1983)

Parker, District Judge. Export license applicant brought suit to enjoin the Department of Commerce's noncompliance with the Export Administration Act's timetable for processing applications for export licenses. Section 10 of the Export Administration Act of 1979 provides for a timetable that governs the Department of Commerce's processing of applications for certain export licenses. Plaintiff, Daedalus Enterprises, Inc. ("Daedalus"), brings this suit to enjoin the Department of Commerce's noncompliance with the Export Administration Act's timetable. Under the authority of the Export Administration Act of 1979 ("the Act"), the Department of Commerce ("the Department") administers export controls in consultation with other United States agencies and departments. Under Section 10(h), whenever the export license being sought implicates national security, the application for the export license—after being referred to the other agencies and departments—is referred by the Secretary for multilateral review to the Coordinating Committee ("COCOM"), which includes representatives of the NATO countries plus Japan, less Iceland.

Daedalus engages in research, development, manufacture, and service in the field of remote sensing of the environment. Within this field, Daedalus specializes in airborne infrared and visual line-scanning devices and associated data analysis equipment. Daedalus manufactures infrared equipment, conducts surveys using such equipment, and analyzes data derived therefrom for governmental and commercial clients. An integral component of the Daedalus system is a magnetic instrumentation tape recorder. Daedalus entered into an agreement with Romania whereby Romania agreed to purchase a Daedalus multispectral airborne scanner. Soon after entering into the agreement, Daedalus filed an application with the Department for a license to export the scanner. Some 29 months after the filing of the first license application, and some 21 months after the filing of the second application, the Secretary has not reached a final decision to grant or deny the licenses.

The Secretary's strongest argument is that plaintiff has not exhausted the statutorily prescribed administrative remedies. Under the Act, an applicant may file a petition with the Secretary requesting compliance with the time periods established by the Act. Nonetheless, the fact that Daedalus failed to submit a written petition does not bar its claim here. The doctrine of exhaustion is intended, in part, to afford the administrative agency the first opportunity to correct any error. When the agency has already made it abundantly obvious that it would not correct the error and would not conform its actions with the strictures of the Act, it would be meaningless to compel the hapless plaintiff to pursue further administrative remedies simply for form's sake. Here, plaintiff sought repeatedly to ascertain the status of the application. The Court will not force plaintiff to submit to the futile formality of petitioning the same officials yet again.

Case Highlights

- The Export Administration Act vests authority and discretion in the Secretary of Commerce in the processing of export license applications. However, this discretion is limited.
- The doctrine of exhaustion of remedies found in administrative law requires an applicant to follow all administrative appeals processes before seeking judicial relief.
- The Secretary of Commerce cannot unduly delay a decision on an export license application and then receive a dismissal based on the exhaustion of remedies doctrine.

18. See Information to Exporters, 15 C.F.R. § 770.11; The Commerce Control List, 15 C.F.R. § 799.1; and Export Administration Forms, 15 C.F.R. § 770.12.

provides the steps to follow to determine the exporter's obligations under the EAR. Second, Part 734 defines the items and activities that are subject to the EAR. Third, Part 736 lists all the prohibitions that are contained in the EAR. Fourth, the Commodities Control List is found in Supplement No. 1 to § 774.1 of the EAR. A validated license is required for items on the Commodities Control List or if export is to a country found on the Country Chart in Part 738. Also of concern for exporters of hazardous materials is the **Basel Convention.** Adopted in 1989 by a United Nations-sponsored conference of 116 nations in Basel, Switzerland, this Convention restricts trade in hazardous waste. Licensing requirements for exports to embargoed destinations are found in Part 746. Once the exporter determines that a license will be required, the mechanics of filing an application for a license are found in Parts 748 and 750. If the exporter is denied a license, Part 756 provides the rules for appealing the denial. Once a license is procured, Part 758 should be reviewed to determine the requirements for export clearance through the United States Customs Service. Finally, Part 762 sets out the exporter's record-keeping requirements.

http://

Secretariat of the Basel Convention: **http://www.unep.ch/basel/about.html**.

The BXA provides assistance on understanding the EAR, obtaining forms, training programs, and electronic services. This assistance can be obtained through the Office of Exporter Services in the Department of Commerce. The *Daedalus Enterprises v. Baldridge* case on page 172 illustrates that the process for obtaining a validated license may be costly and time-consuming.

If a validated license is required, the exporter must submit an "Application for a Validated Export License." In order to expedite the application process the exporter may have to obtain an "International Import Certificate" and/or a **Statement of Ultimate Consignee and Purchaser** (Exhibit 6.3). The former is issued by the government of importation and certifies that the goods will be disposed of in the designated country. The Statement of Ultimate Purchaser is an assurance from the purchaser that the goods will not be resold or disposed of contrary to the requirements of the export license.

http://

Tradeport is a comprehensive site on international shipping and trade: **http://www.tradeport.org**.

A freight forwarder or customs broker may assist the exporter in preparing documentation, including the Statement of Ultimate Purchaser form. However, it is important to know that the exporter is ultimately responsible for the accuracy of all the export documents. In order to protect itself from violations of government reexport restrictions, the exporter should reensure that an export prohibition clause is written into the export contract. The clause should state the country of importation and prohibit the purchaser/importer from selling, delivering, or reexporting the goods to another country or any country prohibited under U.S. law.

Most exporters will have to deal with either the Bureau of Export Administration or the Office of Export Licenses. The Office of Export Enforcement in the Department of Commerce has published the following "Helpful Hints" to help exporters comply with the Export Administration Act and Regulations:

- Determine if a validated export license is required. When in doubt contact the Exporters Service Staff Office of Export Administration.
- Fully describe commodities or technical data on export shipping documents.
- Use the applicable destination control statement on commercial invoices, airway bills, and bills of lading.
- Avoid shipments after the expiration date on the validated export license.
- Enter the applicable validated export license number or general license symbol on the Shipper's Export Declaration.
- Make certain the export documents clearly identify the exporter, intermediate consignee, and ultimate consignee.

EXHIBIT 6.3 *Statement of Ultimate Purchaser (Form ITA-629P)*

OMB NO. 0625-0136

FORM ITA-629P
(REV. 6-84)

U.S. DEPARTMENT OF COMMERCE
INTERNATIONAL TRADE ADMINISTRATION

STATEMENT BY ULTIMATE CONSIGNEE AND PURCHASER

GENERAL INSTRUCTIONS – This form must be submitted by the importer (ultimate consignee shown in Item 1) and by the overseas buyer or purchaser, to the U.S. exporter or seller with whom the order for the commodities described in Item 3 is placed. This completed statement will be submitted in support of one or more export license applications to the U.S. Department of Commerce. **All items on this form must be completed.** Where the information required is unknown or the item does not apply, write in the appropriate words "UNKNOWN" or "NOT APPLICABLE." If more space is needed, attach an additional copy of this form or sheet of paper signed as in Item 8. Submit form within 180 days from latest date in Item 8. Information furnished herewith is subject to the provisions of Section 12(c) of the Export Administration Act of 1979, 50 USC app. 2411(c), and its unauthorized disclosure is prohibited by law.

1. Ultimate consignee name and address

Name

Street and number

City and Country

Reference *(if desired)*

2. Request *(Check one)*

a. ☐ We request that this statement be considered a part of the application for export license filed by

____
U.S. exporter or U.S. person with whom we have placed our order (order party)

for export to us of the commodities described in item 3.

b. ☐ We request that this statement be considered a part of every application for export license filed by

____
U.S. exporter or U.S. person with whom we have placed or may place our order (order party)

for export to us of the type of commodities described in this statement, during the period ending June 30 of the second year after the signing of this form, or on ______________

3. Commodities

We have placed or may place orders with the person or firm named in Item 2 for the commodities indicated below:

COMMODITY DESCRIPTION	*(Fill in only if 2a is checked)* QUANTITY	VALUE

4. Disposition or use of commodities by ultimate consignee named in Item 1 *(Check and complete the appropriate box(es))*

We certify that the commodity(ies) listed in Item 3:

a. ☐ Will be used by us (as capital equipment) in the form in which received in a manufacturing process in the country named in Item 1 and will not be reexported or incorporated into an end product.

b. ☐ Will be processed or incorporated by us into the following product(s) ______________ *(Specify)*

to be manufactured in the country named in Item 1 for distribution in ______________ *(Name of country or countries)*

c. ☐ Will be resold by us in the form in which received in the country named in Item 1 for use or consumption therein.

The specific end-use by my customer will be ______________ *(Specify, if known)*

d. ☐ Will be reexported by us in the form in which received to ______________ *(Name of country(ies))*

e. ☐ Other *(Describe fully)* ______________

NOTE: If Item (d) is checked, acceptance of this form by the Office of Export Administration as a supporting document for license applications shall not be construed as an authorization to reexport the commodities to which the form applies unless specific approval has been obtained from the Office of Export Administration for such reexport.

(Reproduction of this form is permissible, providing that content, format, size and color of paper are the same)

Please continue form and sign certification on reverse side.

USCOMM-DC 84-21766

- Stay current with export control requirements by subscribing annually to the Export Administration Regulations.
- Avoid inadvertent sales to persons or firms denied U.S. export privileges by obtaining a copy of the Table of Denial Orders Currently in Effect, available from the Office of Export Administration.

- Designate an appropriate person to monitor export transactions to ensure compliance with the Regulations.
- Enroll appropriate personnel in the Office of Export Administration's export licensing training program.

Exportation of certain specific goods may also require approval from a number of other government agencies. The following Focus on Transactions lists some of these other relevant government agencies.

Focus on Transactions

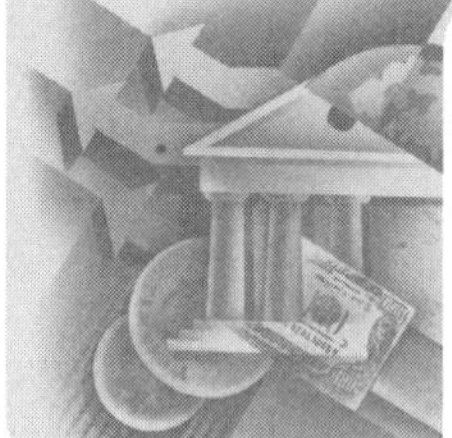

Government Agencies Relevant to Exporting

Types of Goods	Agency
Nuclear Technology Natural Gas	Department of Energy
Drugs	Department of Justice
Munitions	Department of State
Chemicals and Pesticides	Environmental Protection Agency
Nuclear Equipment and Materials	Nuclear Regulatory Commission
Technology in conjunction with foreign patent application	Patent & Trademark Office

Key Terms

ad valorem duties, 155
Agreement on Customs Valuation, 162
Automated Export System (AES), 165
Basel Convention, 173
binding assessment, 164
bonded warehouse, 151
Bureau of Export Administration (BXA), 167
Canada-United States Free Trade Agreement, 163
CE Mark, 166
change in tariff classification test, 163
Code of Federal Regulations (CFR), 172
Committee on Rules of Origin, 164
commodity control list, 167
computed value, 159
country groups list, 167
country of origin, 151
Customs Electronic Bulletin Board, 152
Customs Modernization Act, 165
deductive value, 159
Destination Control Statement, 167
drawback, 161
eco-label, 166
electronic data interchange (EDI), 165
essential character, 152
European Union Customs Code, 159
Export Administration Regulations (EAR), 167
foreign (free) trade zones, 161
free trade zone, 151
general license, 167
General Rules for Interpretation, 152
generalized system of preferences (GSP), 151
harmonized tariff schedule (HTS), 151
maquiladora, 156
marking requirement, 164
Origin Agreement, 164
rule of specificity, 152
Section 9802, 155
Shipper's Export Declaration (SED), 167
specific duties, 155
specified processes test, 163
Statement of Ultimate Consignee and Purchaser, 173
substantial transformation test, 162
Taric, 161

Technical Committee on Rules of Origin, 164
Trade and Tariff Act of 1984, 161
transaction value, 157
ultimate purchaser, 164
validated license, 167
value-added test, 163
World Customs Organization (WCO), 152

Chapter Problems

1. The Customs Service classified aluminum ingots that were shipped to the United States from Canada as not of Canadian origin. The ingots contained less than 1 percent materials from countries other than Canada. The U.S. Customs Service imposed a tariff of 0.19 percent on aluminum ingots imported from Canada. The Court of International Trade ruled in favor of the Customs Service, finding that the aluminum underwent "substantial transformation" because a foreign-origin substance (grain refiner) was mixed with the aluminum to make the ingots less likely to crack and therefore, worked a substantial transformation. Alcan protested that the tariff should be the 0.038 percent that would apply under NAFTA if the ingots had not undergone "substantial transformation" with goods that originated from outside of Canada. Do you think that the Court's decision was correct? *Alcan Aluminum Corp. v. U.S.,* 165 F.3d 898 (Fed. Cir., 1999)

2. William C. Dart sought to overturn a decision by the Secretary of Commerce imposing civil sanctions for violations of the Export Administration Act. The Export Act precludes judicial review of such fines under its so-called "finality clause." What are the competing concerns of the person fined and the limited appeal procedure provided in the Export Act? Has the world changed in a way that has changed the balance between these concerns? *Dart v. United States,* 848 F.2d 217 (D.C. Cir. 1988)

3. Import documentation requirements and other regulations imposed by foreign governments vary from country to country. It is vital that exporters be aware of the regulations that apply to their own operations and transactions. Many governments, for instance, require consular invoices, certificates of inspection, health certification, and various other documents. Select a country and research its basic documentary requirements for the importation of goods.

Internet Exercises

1. Visit the web site at **http://www.tradecompass.com** (Trade Compass). Review the materials on the procedure for the electronic filing of customs forms with United States Customs.

2. You are an importer of synthetic sails used for recreational sailboats. You import the sails from the People's Republic of China. Look at the Harmonized Tariff Schedule to determine the rate of duty that will be charged for the sails. The HTS can be accessed at **http://dataweb.usitc.gov/SCRIPTS/tariff/toc.html** and **http://www.itds.treas.gov/HTSindex.html**.

3. Research the customs law of Japan and compare them to those of the United States. To compare the customs law of another country see the web site for Japanese Customs at **http://www.mof.go.ip/~customs/iport-e.htm**.

4. You have completed an export contract and need to ship goods from Miami, Florida, to Buenos Aires, Argentina. Determine which shipping lines are available for such a shipment and research the documentation need for such a shipment. See the following web sites: **http://www.mglobal.com** ("Maritime Global Net") and **http://www.tradeport.org**. ("Tradeport" is a comprehensive site on international shipping and trade).

5. How does the new United States Automated Export System work? See U.S. Customs web site at **http://www.customs.treas.gov**.

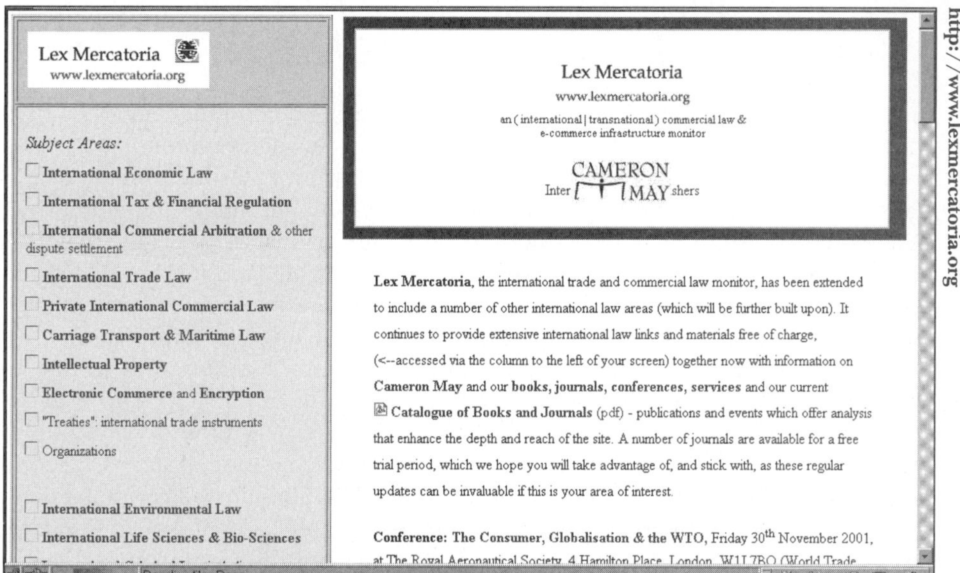

http://www.lexmercatoria.org

Chapter 7
International Contract Law

A thorough knowledge of substantive law rules and principles is imperative in drafting a good contract. At the domestic level a working knowledge of the **Uniform Commercial Code** provides a solid foundation for drafting a sales contract. At the international level, however, the general principles of contract law are less specific and are applied sporadically by national courts. Thus, it may be necessary to know the law of the country of your foreign contracting party in order to avoid misunderstandings. Cultural and language differences, however, may prevent a contract from ever being formed. Knowledge of the other party's culture and negotiating style is important if an initial inquiry is to develop into a long-term contractual relationship.

Business behavior differs among cultures. Some cultures focus on the importance of developing a contractual and social relationship and not on the importance of the deal as is prevalent in the United States. Many cultures view a formal, detailed contract as unnecessary and hindering a good faith, evolving contractual relationship where the parties mutually work through problems. "For many Asian cultures the contract may not represent finality but a starting point of a relationship. It is assumed that the contract will be reexamined, reinterpreted, or renegotiated if conditions change. In these more traditional cultures, negotiators seek mainly broad-based agreements that are general, flexible, and implicit."[1] In contrast, U.S. businesspersons view a contract as the operative tool for ensuring full and complete performance—something that should be honored at any cost.

Many foreign cultures view the negotiation phase of contracting as one in which a relaxed development of the relationship should be pursued. This is in opposition to the U.S. "time is money" approach. Without a firm understanding of the cross-cultural differences in negotiating styles, the likelihood of successful completion of the negotiations is greatly diminished. This chapter will review some of the cultural nuances in negotiating a contract in an international setting with a focus on Japan. It will then shift focus to the nuances of substantive contract law at the national and international levels with a particular emphasis on the area of precontractual liability.

NEGOTIATING AN INTERNATIONAL CONTRACT

The substantive laws and commercial means of doing business are amazingly similar among the world's different legal systems, but the differences in negotiating styles and contract customs are profound. For example, even though the importance of a written contract is universally recognized in principle, executing a long, detailed contract may be frowned upon in some countries. "In many cultures, if one is required to write down the agreement, it will destroy the trust and render the agreement invalid."[2]

International contract negotiation is a very difficult and complicated affair; the nuances of language and culture make it risky for the unsophisticated importer or exporter. The negotiation of the export or sales contract is generally more time-consuming than in a domestic transaction because foreign contractors need to develop a trust in their U.S. counterpart before entering into a contract. It is important for the U.S. businessperson to understand these cultural differences.

The added time invested to negotiate an international contract carefully will provide significant dividends in the long term. First, an agreement that successfully overcomes language, cultural, and legal differences will better reflect basic understandings and minimize misunderstandings. For example, it is difficult for U.S. businesspersons "to realize that in some countries, especially in Asia, it is characteristic for a businessperson to speak in vague terms with nuances that only experience can help decipher."[3] Second, the trust developed early in a contractual relationship will help ensure a long-term international business contact.

The following excerpt discusses some of the nuances associated with Japanese negotiators and business practices:

> *The story about Japanese contracting that emerges is that law is largely irrelevant. Instead, the business relationship is paramount, and the Japanese favor unwritten,*

1. Claude Cellich, Review of *Cross-Cultural Business Negotiations* by Donald W. Hendon, Rebecca A. Hendon & Paula Herbig, 10 *Journal of International Consumer Marketing* 120 (1998).
2. Magoroh Maruyama, "Contracts in Cultures," 10 *Human Systems Management* 33 (1991).
3. WARREN A. FRENCH & JOHN GRANROSE, PRACTICAL BUSINESS ETHICS 166 (1995).

> *or very brief agreements; do not regard themselves bound by the letter of such agreements but rely on the notion of* changed circumstances *to seek renegotiation; and, in the case of a dispute, will seldom, if ever, allow the matter to proceed to court. . . . The relationship, rather than the formalities or potential legal sanctions, traditionally gave the contract its binding force in Japan. . . . Commercial custom in contemporary Japan often revolves around transaction types identified as* traditional contracting practices. *My personal favorite is the* cry-yourself-to-sleep *transaction, in which the seller is faced with a sudden cancellation of an order and simply absorbs the consequent loss, in the hope that it will be made up in the future. Not all of these practices are supported by classical contract law, but all represent commercial expectations, and to that extent, they can be viewed as a kind of* unwritten law. . . . *In Japan, a continuing contract will invite some relational analysis. Specifically, it is not improbable that a court would seriously consider the effect of removing a retailer's* ikigai *(reason for living) as well as the legal merits and economic rationality of a termination.*[4]

Such cultural differences have crucial practical importance in the negotiation and formation of a contract. The Confucian influence of harmony permeates contracting in Japan. Thus, the U.S. style of hard bargaining and pressure tactics is likely to meet with failure. It is important to state a position firmly and at the same time not disturb the *wa* or harmony of the negotiation. The Japanese aversion to litigation stems from the belief that it is their societal "duty to avoid discord."[5] Interestingly, the Japanese also dislike arbitration. They believe that parties should negotiate directly in resolving disputes. In case of failure in negotiating a solution, the Japanese prefer the use of conciliation or *chotei*.[6]

http://

International Trade Administration—Information on foreign culture and customs: **http://www.ita.doc.gov/td/tic**.

The ***wa*** concept is reflected in the Japanese approach to negotiation as the process of developing a trusting business relationship and not the simple formation of a contract. (See Doing Business Internationally: Contract Characteristics in Japan.) From a practical perspective, this results in Japanese contracts being simple, short, and vague. All problems are to be dealt with through acts of conciliation. All questions are to be answered through a process of *reconcilement.* "Reconcilement is the process by which parties in the dispute confer with each other and reach a point at which they come to terms and restore *harmonious* relationships."[7] The contract provides a basic framework that allows for modification and flexibility. Performance standards are not defined restrictively. Thus, the U.S. businessperson may have to modify his proclivity for long, detailed agreements.

Cultural differences can have a profound impact on new business relationships. The U.S. exporter should be careful in how he approaches a prospective contact in Japan. The Japanese place a high premium on personal contact; a Japanese importer may not respond to written inquiries. Therefore, any initial inquiry should be followed by a personal contact. The best approach is to ask to be introduced by an intermediary known to the other party.[8]

4. Veronica L. Taylor, "Continuing Transactions and Persistent Myths: Contracts in Contemporary Japan," 19 *Melbourne University Law Review* 352, 353, 356, 364, 393 & 395 (1993).
5. Comment, "'Working it Out': A Japanese Alternative to Fighting it Out," 37 *Cleveland St. Law Review*. 149, 157 (1989).
6. Ibid. at 164. See generally KAWASHIMA, "DISPUTE RESOLUTION IN CONTEMPORARY JAPAN," LAW IN JAPAN 42 (1963); D. HENDERSON, CONCILIATION AND JAPANESE LAW (1965).
7. Ibid. at 163.
8. See Elliot Hahn, "Negotiating Contracts with the Japanese," 14 *Case Western Reserve Journal International Law* 377 (1982).

Another possible conflict resulting from cultural differences comes from the U.S. businessperson's propensity to send a written agreement when negotiations have entered into their final stages. A U.S. businessperson may ask his attorney to confirm the terms discussed and agreed upon before the negotiations are complete. The lawyer may respond by sending a letter or a proposed agreement to the other party. "But the letter may get no response because the unexpected arrival of a contract probably appears abrupt and possibly coercive to a foreign recipient."[9] In order to avoid cultural *faux pas* one attorney gives this advice:

> *Do some reading on the country—at least you'll know where it is. Know something of the history. Talk to someone who's done business there, an American businessman or someone from the Department of Commerce—find out who the trade specialist is in that country and talk to that person. And once you get there, don't hop off the plane and set up meetings . . . Don't do the trilogy of hotels, restaurants, and office buildings. Instead of staying in your hotel room answering e-mail, get up in the morning and walk around.*[10]

It is important to understand the authority of the other negotiating party and her place in the chain of command. A longer negotiation period may be due not to the other party's reluctance or gamesmanship but to her lack of authority to complete a deal on her own. For example, the Japanese often make business decisions based upon a consensus or *ring-sho,* which takes time to formulate.

A number of criteria must be satisfied in order for cross-cultural contract negotiations to conclude successfully. First, the negotiations should lead to a written contract that is enforceable in the countries of both parties. Second, conflicts that result from cross-cultural misunderstandings are avoided through a carefully nego-

Doing Business Internationally

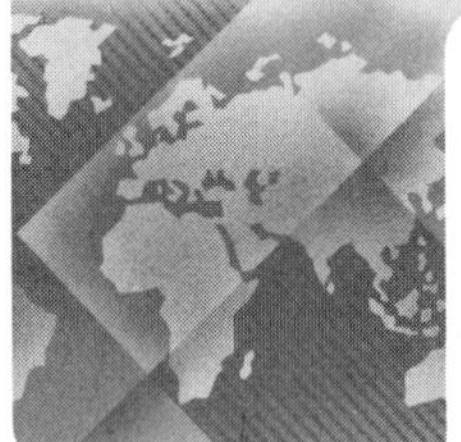

Contract Characteristics in Japan

- "Contract" assumes not opposition of parties, but cooperation.
- Parties attach more importance to establishing a collaborative human relationship than preparing a highly formal, legalistic written contract.
- Contract provisions are written not to be rigid, but to be flexible and changeable.
- Parties prefer clauses that in case of changed circumstances require the parties to act in good faith to renegotiate the term, rather than including detailed clauses to cover anticipated disputes.
- Contracts generally are simple, consisting of a few short clauses.
- There is an implied understanding that clauses are to be applied leniently in the area of performance and nonperformance.
- In case of dispute, the preferred means of resolution is the giving of mutual concessions and not litigation.
- To conclude a negotiation often means not to sign a written contract, but to establish a personal and cordial relationship.

Source: Shoji Kawami, "Japan" in *Precontractual Liability* 215 (ed. Ewoud H. Hondius) 1991.

9. See Henderson, "The Role of Lawyers in U.S.-Japanese Business Transactions," 38 *Washington Law Review* 1 (1963).
10. Laurel-Ann Dooley, "Culture Clashes Hinder Deals," *National Law Journal* B1, B4 (September 13, 1999).

tiated and written contract that informs both parties of their rights and duties. A full understanding of rights and duties provides the basis for the development of a strong business relationship. Third, dispute resolution should be completely and fairly addressed in the contract. Because of the cost, inconvenience, and uncertainty of transnational litigation, the contract should outline cost-effective and relationship-preserving means of dispute resolution. Some countries, such as China and Japan, have long emphasized conciliation without resort to litigation as the preferred manner of dispute resolution.

The risks of international business dealings addressed in Chapter 1 should be minimized by appropriate contract provisions. Special attention should be devoted to the issue of "changed circumstances," since various legal and business cultures deal with this issue differently. U.S. culture places a premium on the strict enforcement of contractual rights and duties regardless of circumstance. In contrast, some other cultures will not strictly enforce a contract if there has been a change in circumstances. Therefore, the contract should deal carefully with issues of renegotiation and modification of the contract in the event of such changes.

PRINCIPLES OF INTERNATIONAL CONTRACT LAW

Despite the differences in how foreign laws and culture deal with the negotiation, interpretation, and enforcement of contracts, there are tremendous similarities among the different legal systems in how the law supports commercial transactions. For example, the civil law and common law legal systems provide similar mechanisms for facilitating business transactions. Most differences are a matter of style and not substance.

Along with the similarities among legal systems in commercial law, a trend has been evidenced toward developing a unified body of international business law. This trend can be seen at work on a number of different levels. First, the growth of **customary international business law** is seen with the almost universal adoption of the International Chamber of Commerce's standards in the area of trade terms (Incoterms) and letters of credit (Uniform Customs and Practices for Documentary Credits). Second, the increased publication and citation of international commercial arbitration decisions are evidence of the development of an international commercial jurisprudence not tied directly to national laws. Finally, there have been important developments in the enactment of international treaties and conventions unifying international business law. The clearest example of this trend was the ratification of the United Nations Convention on Contracts for the International Sale of Goods on January 1, 1988. This pioneering effort to unify international sales law will be the subject of Chapter 8, International Sales Law.

It is impossible to adequately draft a contract without knowledge of substantive contract law. The need is compounded when drafting an international contract where there are at least three possible sources of law, including the national laws of each of the parties and international contract law or the ***lex mercatoria***. The *lex mercatoria* or "law of merchants" refers to business customs or trade usage developed by businesspersons throughout the world in order to facilitate business transactions. Some degree of *harmonization* has been achieved through the adoption of international conventions. These conventions often become enacted into national law or become a part of the *lex mercatoria*. The ideal situation is to have a working knowledge of trade usage, law of the seller, and law of the buyer, including any relevant international conventions.

http://

For links to "modern" *lex mercatoria:* **http://www.lexmercatoria.org**.

Even if the contract writer attempts to reduce his need to know a foreign law by using a choice of law clause, he still must be knowledgeable about the mandatory or immutable rules and regulations found in the foreign law. Also, arbitrators often resort to a supranational law or *lex mercatoria* in place of a full application of a national law designated by a choice of law clause. Danish professor Ole Lando listed the following seven sources[11] of the *lex mercatoria* that can be used in the interpretation of contracts:

- *Public International Law:* There are provisions in the Vienna Convention on Treaties that can be applied to private international contracts.
- *Uniform Laws:* The Hague Rules (codified as COGSA) and the Convention on Contracts for the International Sale of Goods (CISG) are examples of successful attempts at uniform international laws.
- *General Principles of Contract Law:* The best example of a general principle of contract law found in most national legal systems is *pacta sunt servanda* or what is referred to in the common law as *sanctity of contract.*
- *Rules of International Organizations:* Courts may look to nonbinding rules published by such international organizations as the United Nations, Organization for European Cooperation and Development (OECD), and the International Institute for the Unification of Private Law (UNIDROIT).
- *Custom and Usage:* The clearest examples of custom and usage or *customary international law* that has reached a level of almost universal acceptance are the standards and rules published by the International Chamber of Commerce in the area of trade terms (INCOTERMS) and letters of credit (Uniform Customs and Practices for Documentary Credits, or UCP).
- *Standard Form Contracts:* Once again, the ICC is a good source for standard form contracts and standard clauses. For example, the ICC publishes standard or model forms of Distribution and Agency Agreements. They also publish a manual to be used in the drafting of *force majeure* and hardship clauses.
- *Arbitral Decisions:* Although not widely reported, arbitral decisions provide an outstanding resource for principles.

Generally recognized international contract principles have a direct bearing on how one approaches the drafting of an international contract. These principles are brought to bear by courts and arbitration panels in the interpretation of contracts. They are also used to determine the parties' rights and duties regarding performance and subsequent requests for adjustments in the contract. The general principle is that contracts should *prima facie* be enforced according to their terms under the doctrine of ***pacta sunt servanda.*** However, *pacta sunt servanda* is also qualified by the concept of ***abus de droit***—the rule that unfair or unconscionable contracts and clauses should not be enforced.

The general duty of good faith in international contracting is a more expanded version of the good faith requirement found in the United States. The civil law concept *culpa in contrahendo* requires that the parties negotiate in good faith.[12] This civil law concept will be fully explored later in the chapter. The U.S. concept of good faith is applied only to the area of performance and enforcement of contrac-

11. Ole Lando, "The *Lex Mercatoria* in International Commercial Arbitration," 34 *International & Comparative Law Quarterly* 747 (1985).
12. See seminal but outdated work, Friedrich Kessler & Edith Fine, "*Culpa in Contrahendo,* Bargaining in Good Faith, and Freedom of Contract: A Comparative Study," 77 *Harvard Law Review* 401 (1964). For an analysis of the ethics of negotiation, see Gerald B. Wetlaufer, "The Ethics of Lying in Negotiations," 75 *Iowa Law Rev.* 1219 (1990).

Comparative Law

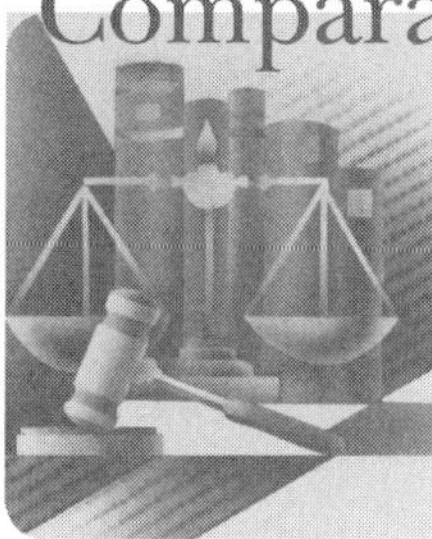

International Commercial Law Conventions

- United Nations Convention on Contracts for the International Sale of Goods, ratified January 1, 1988
- United Nations Convention on the Limitation Period of the International Sale of Goods, ratified January 1, 1988
- UNCITRAL (United Nations Commission on International Private Law) Independent Guarantees and Stand-by Letters of Credit
- United Nations Convention on Carriage of Goods by Sea (Hamburg Rules, ratified 1992)
- United Nations Convention on Multimodal Transport
- UNIDROIT (International Institute for the Unification of Private Law, or Rome Institute) Convention on International Financial Leasing
- UNIDROIT Convention on International Factoring
- UNIDROIT Principles of International Commercial Contracts
- United Nations Convention on the Recognition and Enforcement of Foreign Arbitral Awards (New York Convention)
- UNCITRAL Model Law on International Commercial Arbitration

tual obligations. Thus, in international contracting there is a possibility of liability before the conclusion of a contract. The principle of good faith is further extended to a duty to adjust the contract in the event of unforeseen circumstances.

The notion of good faith should guide the U.S. businessperson's response to all communications from a foreign party. Failure to respond to a letter or request is often regarded as evidence of assent to its terms. This concept can be seen at work in the **Convention on Contracts for the International Sale of Goods (CISG)** adoption of ***nachfrist* notice,** in which a party makes a request for additional time to perform. In the event that the receiving party fails to respond or fails to give a commercially viable reason for a denial of the request, then the extension is automatically granted.[13] There is no counterpart to this notion in the common law. It is important for the international lawyer to understand these principles when drafting and performing a contract.

Some contract codes, like the CISG, can be used to create a checklist of issues or clauses that should be dealt with in an international contract. Focus on Transactions: Checklist of Important International Contract Clauses, provides an example of a checklist prepared by the **International Chamber of Commerce (ICC),** illustrating how a substantive body of law or principles may be utilized as a checklist in the drafting of a contract.[14] This checklist lists issues covered in the **UNIDROIT Principles of International Commercial Contracts.**[15] The material in parentheses refers to the relevant articles of the *UNIDROIT Principles*.

http://

UNIDROIT—menu of sponsored conventions: **http://www.unidroit.org**.

13. See CISG Articles 47-48, 63. See Chapter 8.
14. International Chamber of Commerce, *The UNIDROIT Principles for International Commercial Contracts: A New Lex Mercatoria?* (1995).
15. See material on the UNIDROIT Principles later in this Chapter.

Focus on Transactions

Checklist of Important International Contract Clauses

- Exclusion of trade usage (Articles 1.8, 4.3(f))
- Four corners clause (integration or merger clause) (Articles 2.17 and 2.18)
- Time of performance, early performance, late performance (Articles 6.1.1, 6.1.5, and 7.1.5)
- Order of performance (Article 6.1.4)
- Place of performance, place of payment (Article 6.1.6)
- Form of payment (Articles 6.1.7 and 6.1.8)
- Currency of payment (Article 6.1.9)
- Transportation costs, other expenses (Article 6.1.11)
- Government approvals (Articles 6.1.13–6.1.17)
- Hardship clause (Articles 6.2.1–6.2.3)
- *Force majeure* clause (Article 7.1.7)
- Termination clause, notice provisions (Articles 7.3.1 and 7.3.2)
- Forum selection and arbitration clauses (Article 7.3.5(3))
- Limitation of liability clause (Article 7.1.6)
- Interest on delinquent payments (Article 7.4.9)
- Damages, liquidated damages clause (Articles 7.4.1–7.4.4 and 7.4.13)

Principles of international contracting are important for reasons other than drafting and performing contracts. Foreign courts and arbitration panels will use these principles of international contracting when interpreting an ambiguity in a contract. The next section examines the process of contract interpretation that is pivotal to the resolution of contract disputes.

Contract Interpretation

An important part of contract law pertains to the rules or standards used by courts in the interpretation of contracts. In U.S. contract law, the standard of review is embedded in the reasonable person approach. In the United States, the *imprimatur* of the reasonable person approach can be seen throughout the **Second Restatement of Contracts** and the Uniform Commercial Code. It can be seen whenever reference is made to the fact that a party had reason to know or should have known something. There is *reason to know* if a person "has information from which a person of similar intelligence would infer that the fact in question does or will exist." The line between *reason to know* and actual knowledge is often nonexistent. *Reason to know* is a factual determination based upon the circumstances and information available to the parties. In contrast, *should know* is generally associated with a legal duty to know. "Should know imports a duty to ascertain the facts."[16] Thus, *should know* is relatively unconcerned with actual knowledge.

16. Restatement (Second) of Contracts at § 19, Comment *b.*

The determination of whether a party had *reason to know* is accomplished through the **totality of the circumstances analysis.**[17] This analysis takes into account all the circumstances of the contract including the contract itself, prior dealings between the parties, how the parties performed the contract, subsequent modification to the contract, and relevant business customs and trade usage. *Should know* is more a judicial reflection regarding what is reasonable given the parties and the circumstances. The difference is that *reason to know* is more a party-specific analysis. In contrast, *should know* is community focused, that is, it determines what is a reasonable interpretation or result based on business or community standards.[18]

Modern contract law has witnessed an increasing preemption by statutory law of interpretation analysis. The **English Unfair Contract Terms Act of 1977** adopts a presumption of unreasonableness for indemnity or exculpatory clauses that "by reference to any contract term a party is made to indemnify another party in respect of liability for negligence or breach of contract."[19] For international sales contracts it voids any choice of law clause whose purpose is the avoidance of the Unfair Contract Terms Act. This statute is an example of how mandatory rules preempt a court's search for the contractual intent of the parties. The intent of the parties regarding such a clause becomes irrelevant because the statute invalidates it.

http://
United Kingdom Department of Trade and Industry—English unfair terms in consumer contracts regulations: **http://www.dti.gov.uk/access/unfair/part4.htm**.

Customary law, by way of examining current custom and trade usage, has often been the vehicle by which the common law has fabricated the reasonable person in interpreting contracts. Justice Turley in the 1842 case *Jacob v. State* convincingly states this grassroots metamorphosis. "Common law sources are to be found in the usage, habits, manners, and customs of a people. The common law of a country will be modified, and extended by analogy, *construction, and custom,* so as to embrace new relations, springing up from time to time, from an amelioration or change of society."[20] The courts use the reasonable person standard to discourage unconscionable practices and encourage the development of judicially approved standards of reasonableness.

Convergence and Divergence of National Laws

The interrelationship between national and international legal systems is critical to the entrepreneur and the legal practitioner in assessing the legal risks of a transaction. One commentator states that "with the world so interrelated, economic relations and their international aspects are influenced by the interests of and relations between subjects of commercial law from various countries."[21] Even without the development of uniform international laws like the CISG, there has been a significant convergence of contract law between different legal systems.

The differences in contract law, however, between the common law and civil law systems is more one of style than substance. The next Comparative Law feature is taken from a resolution of the **Council of Europe** pertaining to the enforceability

http://
Council of Europe: **http://www.coe.int**.

17. See generally Larry A. DiMatteo, "The Counterpoise of Contracts: The Reasonable Person Standard and the Subjectivity of Judgment," 48 *South Carolina Law Review* 293, 318 (1997).
18. For example, "what is reasonable depends on the circumstances; it may be reasonable to hold a non-merchant to mercantile standards if he is represented by a mercantile agent." Restatement (Second) on Contracts at § 221, Comment *b.*
19. Unfair Contract Terms Act § 4(1) (1977).
20. 22 Tenn. 493, 514–515 (1842) (emphasis added).
21. Tsvetana Kamenova, "Civil Law in Bulgaria: The Relationship Between International and Domestic Law and the Impact on Civil Law," in GEORGE GINSBURGS, DONALD D. BARRY, & WILLIAM B. SIMONS, THE REVIVAL OF PRIVATE LAW IN CENTRAL AND EASTERN EUROPE. 541 (The Hague: Martinus Nijhoff Publishers, 1996).

Comparative Law

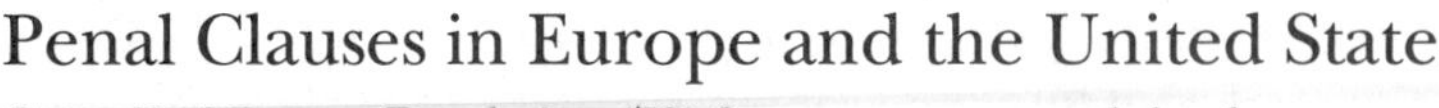

Penal Clauses in Europe and the United States

Council of Europe Resolution (78) 3
On Penal Clauses in Civil Law

Considering that the aim of the Council of Europe is to achieve greater unity between its members, in particular the adoption of common rules in the field of law and considering that it is necessary to provide judicial control over penal clauses in civil law in appropriate cases where the penalty is manifestly excessive.

Article 2

The promisee may not obtain concurrently performance of the principal obligation, as specified in the contract, and payment of the sum stipulated in the penal clause unless the sum was stipulated for delayed performance.

Article 7

The sum stipulated may be reduced by the court when it is manifestly excessive.

Explanatory Memorandum

The legal systems of member states have devised various means to enable courts to exercise a certain control over penal clauses, although the circumstances under which this control can be exercised differ considerably from one state to another. It is one of the essential aims of the present resolution to contribute towards a *harmonisation* of the laws of the member states.

It is left to each legal system to determine under what precise circumstances the sum concerned is manifestly excessive. It is suggested that in a given case the courts may have regard to a number of factors such as:

i. comparing the damage preestimated by the parties at the time of contracting and the damage actually suffered by the promisee.
ii. The legitimate interests of the parties including the promisee's nonpecuniary interests.
iii. the category of contract and the circumstances under which it was concluded, in particular the relative social and economic position of the parties, or the fact that the contract was a standard form contract.
iv. the reason for the failure to perform, in particular the good or bad faith of the promisor.

United States
Uniform Commercial Code, Section 2-718: Liquidation or Limitation of Damages

Damages for breach may be liquidated in the agreement but only at an amount which is reasonable in the light of the anticipated or actual harm caused by the breach, the difficulties of proof of loss, and the inconvenience of obtaining an adequate remedy. A term fixing unreasonably large liquidated damages is void as a penalty.

Restatement (Second) of Contracts, Section 356, Comment b.

Factor 1: The amount fixed is reasonable to the extent that it approximates the actual loss caused by the breach. Furthermore, the amount affixed is reasonable to the extent that it approximates the loss anticipated at the time of the making of the contract.

Factor 2: If the difficulty of proof is great, considerable latitude is allowed in the approximation of anticipated or actual harm.

of **penal clauses** or what U.S. legal practitioners call **liquidated damage clauses.** First, take note that the Council of Europe's membership includes both common law and civil law countries. Therefore, the resolution is itself an example of contract law convergence in Europe. Second, the similarities between the resolution and U.S. law, as described in the excerpts from the Uniform Commercial Code and the Restatement (Second) of Contracts, are further evidence of convergence.

Despite the growing similarities among the different legal systems, significant divergence remains. There are concepts within the civil law systems simply not found in common law. A review of the provisions below taken from the **French Civil Code** demonstrates that there are foreign contract law principles that have no American law counterpart.

> ***French Civil Code Section 1590***
>
> *If the promise to sell was made with payment of a deposit* (arrhes), *each of the contracting parties is at liberty to withdraw. The one who paid the deposit, on forfeiting it, and the one who received it, on returning double the amount.*
>
> ***Section 1587***
>
> *With regard to wine, oil, and other things which it is customary to taste before buying, there is no sale so long as the buyer has not tasted and approved them.*
>
> ***Sections 1674, 1681, and 1706***
>
> *If the price of an immovable is adequate by more than* seven-twelfths, *the seller has the right to demand rescission of the sale, even though he has expressly renounced in the contract the option to demand rescission.*
>
> *In case the action for rescission is upheld, the purchaser has the option either to return the thing upon recovering the price which he has paid, or to keep the property upon paying the balance of the* just price, *after deducting one-tenth of the total price. No rescission for inadequacy may take place in a barter contract.*

Note the differences between the **doctrine of *arrhes,*** as described in Section 1590 of the French Civil Code, and the normal deposit given in U.S. business transactions. Does the doctrine of *arrhes* invite either party to breach the contract if they change their minds? Can the doctrine of *arrhes* be used as an implicit liquidated damages or penalty clause? Why are the inspection rights for wine and other similar products so different than what is found in most sales of goods transactions? Why do you think the just price provision allows the buyer to retain 10 percent of the value of the goods?

It is important to realize that national differences in the requirements of and restrictions on contracting are often found throughout a country's regulatory network. These noncontract law regulations impact directly on contract issues. For example, Article 433 of the **German Civil Code** indicates that a producer or supplier of goods in an ongoing relationship, such as a distribution agreement, has a "collateral obligation to have replacement parts ready for delivery even if there is no special agreement." In contrast, in the United States, issues of after-sales service and replacement parts supply are left to the private agreement of the contracting parties.

Another area of concern for the international entrepreneur is the difference between "law in books" and "law in action." A number of countries have enacted modern, Westernized commercial codes, but uniformity in their interpretation and application is somewhat lacking. An example is the law of many Islamic countries where there is a direct interrelationship between religious and secular codes. The main body of law, the ***Shari'a*** comprises religious, social, and legal mandates. The main body of this source of law was completed by the early tenth century, at least as practiced by the majority Sunni sect. Beginning with the Ottoman Empire in the nineteenth century, however, "the *Shari'a* lost its exclusivity as the governing law of contracts to a combination of sacred and secular laws."[22]

The secular laws have included a modern codification of contract and commercial law with which a Western businessperson would be quite comfortable. For example, Saudi Arabia has enacted a set of regulations including ones governing commercial law, negotiable instruments, and corporate law. The problem for an outside businessperson is that the principles of the *Shari'a* still take precedence over these secular statutes. Most of the judges in the secular court system have religious training and their decisions are reviewed by a Commercial Board that ensures conformity with the dictates of the *Shari'a*.[23] The application and intrusion of religious principles into commercial law disputes is sporadic, but it is important to note that a party may seek to overcome a decision based on the commercial codes by resorting to *Shari'a* principles. "Often it becomes a means of perverting the course of justice by allowing the strongest party in a dispute to select among the components of the law of contract those legal provisions which will settle that dispute on the most favorable terms."[24]

National Contract Codes

A person attempting to do business in a foreign country should make a good faith effort to acquaint herself with that country's contract and sales laws. A thorough examination is not possible here, but the existence of statutory or commercial codes will allow a cursory review. Even a cursory review will highlight some of the similarities and differences between home and host country laws. I have selected the **Russian Civil Code,** the **Foreign Economic Contract Law of the People's Republic of China,** and the **Principles of European Contract Law** for review. The first two are examples of transitional economies enacting Western-style codes compatible with an emerging market economy. The latter example more closely resembles a "restatement" of general principles taken from the underlying national contract law systems.

RUSSIAN CIVIL CODE

A special concern in international contracting is the problem of assessing the laws in the countries of the former Soviet bloc and those countries that remain under a centrally planned economy or socialistic legal regime, such as the People's Republic of China. The enormous change in the legal systems of the Soviet-bloc countries often means that the substantive and procedural laws are still in flux[25] and that their enforcement is uncertain. A brief look at selected provisions of the Russian Civil Code will illustrate some of the similarities and differences between this first generation commercial statute and U.S. contract law. Chapter 13's coverage of intellectual property law will illustrate not only some of the substantive differences but also the problems with the legal enforcement of these new laws.

The most obvious observation in reviewing the contract provisions of the Russian Civil Code is how similar the rules are to our common law. The Code displays

22. Nabil Saleh, "The Law Governing Contracts in Arabia," 38 *Int'l & Comparative Law Quarterly* 761, 763 (1989).
23. Ibid. at 765–766.
24. Ibid. at 786–787.
25. It was noted that in the first half-decade of transition "the Hungarian Parliament passed over 350 laws" aimed at effecting the transition to a market-oriented system. Ilonka Jankovich, "Recent Developments in Privatization Laws, Banking Laws, and Dispute Resolution in Hungary," in *supra* note 21.

many of the principles and concepts found in U.S. contract law. Article 158 allows silence as a means of acceptance only if there was a prior agreement of the parties. Article 160 defines the requirements of the written form, or what is under U.S. law known as the **statute of frauds,** more broadly and is more modern than the definition currently found in Article 2 of the UCC. For example, Paragraph 2 of Article 160 states: "the use when concluding a transaction of a facsimile reproduction of a signature with the assistance of mechanical or other means of copying, electronic-cypher signature, or other analogue of a signature in one's own hand shall be permitted in the instances and procedure provided by a law, other legal acts, or by agreement of the parties." Section 162 expressly notes that foreign economic transactions are invalid unless in writing. Although oral contracts are recognized in some instances, the Russian Civil Code places strong emphasis on formalities including the written form, notarial certifications, and in some cases, governmental registration. As a general rule, a foreign party should not contemplate moving forward on a business transaction without a formal written contract. It is also good practice, even if not technically required in a given transaction, for the parties' signatures to be notarized.

Section 428 recognizes the U.S. notion of the **contract of adhesion** where a party signs the contract form provided by the other party on a take-it-or-leave-it basis. It grants to the contract form receiving party a right to demand dissolution. Thus, a term that is not contrary to the law may be voided if it deprives the adhering party of the rights "usually granted under contracts of that type, or excludes or limits the responsibility of the other party." The importance of disclosure as a means to preclude the right to demand dissolution is also recognized. The adhering party cannot demand dissolution if he "knew or should have known on what conditions the contract is concluded." The general mandate against the enforcement of unfair terms in an adhesion contract can be contrasted with the **European Union Directive on Unfair Terms** in consumer contracts. That directive is much

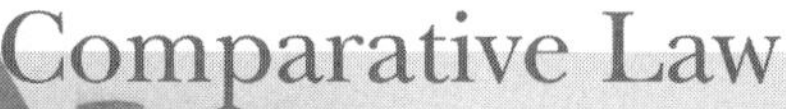

Comparative Law

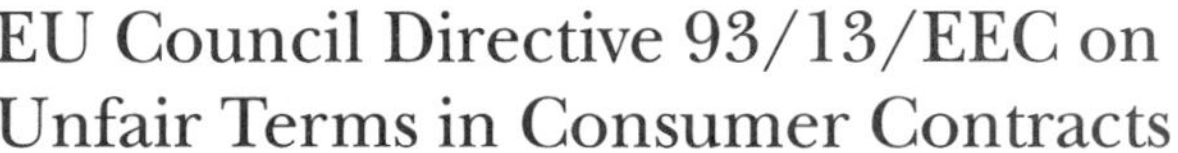

EU Council Directive 93/13/EEC on Unfair Terms in Consumer Contracts

- A nonnegotiated term is unfair when it establishes a significant imbalance, to the consumer's detriment, between the rights and obligations of the contracting parties.
- Assessing the unfair nature of a contractual term takes into account:
  (i) the nature of the goods or services covered by the contract;
  (ii) the circumstances surrounding the drawing up of the contract;
  (iii) the other terms in the contract or in another contract to which it relates.
- Neither the definition of the main aim of the contract nor the relationship between the price and the service or goods to be provided may be taken into account in assessing the unfair nature of clearly worded contractual terms.
- Where there is doubt as to the meaning of a term, the interpretation most favorable to the consumer will prevail.
- Consumers are not bound by unfair terms in a contract signed with a professional.

narrower in scope in that it invalidates only certain types of exculpatory clauses. An exculpatory clause generally insulates one of the parties from liability due to its own negligent acts.

Despite the overall similarities between the Russian Civil Code and U.S. contract law there are some unique provisions in the Russian Code foreign businesspersons should become familiar with. An example can be found in the types of contracts that need to be in written form. Contracts of a certain amount need to be in writing. The threshold when the contracting parties are individuals is when the amount exceeds "not less than ten times the minimum amount of payment of labor." Article 162 expressly states that in an international business transaction "the

Doing Business Internationally

Selected Contract Provisions of the Russian Civil Code

Article 429. Preliminary Contract

Under a preliminary contract the parties shall be obliged to conclude in future a contract concerning the transfer of property, fulfillment of work, or rendering of services (principal contract) on the conditions provided for by the preliminary contract.

The preliminary contract shall be concluded in the form established for the principal contract, and if the form of the principal contract has not been established, then in written form. The failure to comply with the rules concerning the form of the preliminary contract shall entail its being void.

A preliminary contract must contain conditions enabling the establishment of the subject, and also the other material conditions, of the principal contract.

A preliminary contract shall specify the period in which the parties are obliged to conclude the principal contract. If such period has not been determined in the preliminary contract, the principal contract shall be subject to conclusion within a year from the moment of concluding the preliminary contract.

Article 451. Change and Dissolution of Contract in Connection with Material Change of Circumstances

A material change of circumstances from which the parties proceeded when concluding a contract shall be a ground for the change or dissolution thereof unless provided otherwise by the contract or it arises from the essence thereof. A change of circumstances shall be deemed to be material when they have changed such that if the parties could reasonably foresee this, the contract would not have been concluded at all by them or it would have been concluded on significantly differing conditions.

If the parties have not reached agreement concerning bringing the contract into conformity with the materially changed circumstances or the dissolution thereof, the contract may be dissolved, and on the grounds provided for by point 4 of the present Article, changed by a court at the request of the interested party when the following conditions are present:

(1) at the moment of concluding the contract the parties proceeded from the fact that such a change of circumstances would not occur;
(2) the change of circumstances has been caused by reasons which the interested party could not overcome after they arose with that degree of concern and care which are required of him by the character of the contract and the conditions of turnover;
(3) the performance of the contract without a change of its conditions would so violate the correlation of property interests of the parties which correspond to the contract and entail for the interested party such damage it would be deprived

failure to comply with the simple written form of a foreign economic transaction shall entail the invalidity of the transaction." Furthermore, some types of contracts require a notary's certification and some international contracts need to be registered with government agencies. Failure to do so also results in the contract being invalidated. If the contract is executory or yet to be performed, then failure to register renders it null in void. However, in a partially performed or concluded contract the court has the option of enforcing the contract by ordering the parties to register the contract.

Of critical importance to the foreign contracting party are the provisions dealing with preliminary contract, changes of circumstances, and quality of goods. See Doing Business Internationally: Selected Contract Provisions of the Russian Civil Code.

to a significant degree of that which it had the right to count on when concluding the contract;

(4) it does not arise from the customs of business turnover or the essence of the contract that the risk of the change of circumstances is borne by the interested party.

In the event of the dissolution of a contract as a consequence of a material change of circumstances the court at the demand of any of the parties shall determine the consequences of the dissolution of the contract by proceeding from the need for a just distribution between the parties of the expenses incurred by them in connection with the performance of this contract.

The change of a contract in connection with a material change of circumstances shall be permitted by decision of a court in exceptional instances when dissolution of the contract is contrary to social interests or entails damage for the parties which significantly exceeds the expenditures needed to perform the contract on the conditions changed by the court.

Articles 469 and 475. Quality of Good

The seller shall be obliged to transfer a good to the purchaser when quality corresponds to the contract of purchase-sale.

In the absence in a contract of purchase-sale of conditions concerning the quality of a good the seller shall be obliged to transfer to the purchaser a good fit for the purposes for which a good of such nature is usually used. If the seller when concluding the contract was given notice by the purchaser of the specific purposes for the acquisition of the good, the seller shall be obliged to transfer to the purchaser a good fit for use in accordance with these purposes.

In the event of the sale of a good according to a sample and/or description, the seller shall be obliged to transfer to the purchaser of a good which corresponds to the sample and/or description.

If obligatory requirements for the quality of a good being sold have been provided in the procedure established by a law, then the seller effectuating entrepreneurial activity shall be obliged to transfer a good to the purchaser which corresponds to these obligatory requirements. By agreement between the seller and the purchaser a good may be transferred which corresponds to higher quality requirements in comparison with the obligatory requirements established in the procedure provided for by a law.

If the defects of a good were not stipulated by the seller, the purchaser to whom the good of improper quality was transferred shall have the right at his choice to require from the seller: commensurate reduction of the purchase price; elimination without compensation of the defects of the good within a reasonable period; compensation of his expenses to eliminate the defects of the good.

Article 451 recognizes an excuse for a "material change of circumstances." Paragraph 2 lists four conditions similar to those found in U.S. excuse doctrines: (1) the contract was premised on the change of circumstances not occurring, (2) the party could not avoid the occurrence even when using reasonable care, (3) the occurrence materially alters the contract, and (4) it was not an allocated risk under the contract or through industry custom. The subject of excuse will be studied more fully in Chapter 8.

http://
Overview of the Russian Civil Code: **http://www.russianembassy.org/RUSSIA/civil_code.htm.**

Article 429 recognizes the preliminary contract, which is not recognized under U.S. law. The parties have an affirmative obligation to conclude the contract under the Russian notion of preliminary contract. If the parties fail to state a time for concluding the contract, then the law provides that it should be concluded within one year from the conclusion of the preliminary contract. Thus, the potential for precontractual liability seems to be much greater under the Russian Civil Code than under U.S. law. Of course, "preliminary contract" can be a misnomer if the preliminary is considered as a contract unto itself.

The final topic to be examined is the recognition of implied warranties. Paragraph 2 of Section 469 adopts the language but not the nomenclature of the UCC's warranty of merchantability and warranty for a particular purpose. The Code, however, offers a broader selection of remedial options to the receiving party. As under the CISG,[26] the buyer is granted a price reduction option. Under the UCC the buyer must pay in full and then make a claim for damages under a breach of warranty claim. In contrast, the price reduction remedy allows the buyer to unilaterally reduce the price based on the diminishment of value caused by the defect. Also, the Russian Civil Code allows the buyer the option to demand specific performance by requiring "the replacement of the good of improper quality by a good corresponding to the contract."

CHINA'S FOREIGN ECONOMIC CONTRACTS LAW

http://
Foreign Economic Contract Law of PRC: **http://www.qis.net/chinalaw/prclaw20.htm.**

Another interesting codification of contract law, aimed at facilitating international trade, is the Law of the People's Republic of China on Economic Contracts Involving Foreign Parties (Foreign Economic Contracts Law). The law is divided into seven chapters: Chapter 1 deals with general provisions; Chapter 2 with contract formation; Chapter 3 with performance and remedies including the issues of breach, nonperformance, and liquidated damages; Chapter 4 with the transfer and assignments of rights; Chapter 5 with the modification and termination of contracts; Chapter 6 with dispute resolution; and Chapter 7 with miscellaneous provisions including a statute of limitations. An important consideration for the foreign contract negotiator is the authority of the Chinese party to the negotiations. The law applies to Chinese "enterprises or other economic organizations." It is important to determine that the other party is a member of such an entity and has authority to negotiate a foreign contract.[27]

A reading of the law reveals a great many similarities with the U.S. common law of contracts. Article 17 is a version of the U.S. concepts of anticipatory repudiation and adequate assurance. Upon providing "definite evidence" of breach and giving "immediate notice," a party "may temporarily suspend performance." However, such suspension must cease if the other party "has provided a complete guarantee." Article 17, however, does not seem to allow for the anticipation of breach, only the

26. See Chapter 8.
27. See generally Zhang Yuqing & James S. McLean, "China's Foreign Economic Contract Law: Its Significance and Analysis," 8 *Northwestern Journal of Int'l Law & Business* 120 (1987).

suspension of performance on the occurrence of a breach. It also fails to define "complete guarantee" or "definite evidence."

Article 19 adopts the Anglo-American *Hadley v. Baxendale* limitation on damages. Under the rules of *Hadley*, damages are not to exceed those that could have been foreseen at the time of contract formation by the party breaching the contract. Article 20 is a general adoption of the U.S. law of liquidated damages. Contracting parties "may agree on a certain amount of damages to be paid for breach." However, such stipulated damages may be reduced or increased by an arbitration panel or a court of law if they are "excessively higher or lower than the losses actually resulting." Such excessive damages would be considered as an unenforceable penalty under U.S. law.[28] Article 22 adopts the common law principle of mitigation. The nonbreaching party "should take appropriate measures in a timely manner to prevent the increase of losses."

Articles 24 and 25 recognize the excuse of ***force majeure***, ("superior force"). A *force majeure* event is some unforeseeable event that prevents one party from performing on the contract. The law will generally excuse the nonperforming party from the contract without liability. The requirements for a *force majeure* event are outlined in Article 24. Such events "shall mean events that are *unforeseeable*" at the time of contracting and whose "occurrence is *unavoidable* and cannot be overcome by the parties." The breaching party is required by Article 25 to notify the other party in a timely manner.

The foreign party should be aware of the high degree of formality required under the Foreign Economic Contracts Law. The law requires that all contracts be formalized in writing. It should be noted that the law does recognize the applicability of the CISG, which does not require a writing in order to form a contract. However, China opted out of that provision, and therefore an export or sale of goods contract must be in writing under Chinese law. In fact, Article 32 requires that any alteration or rescission of the contract must also be in written form. Article 7 does recognize that in international transactions there may be an exchange of instruments and not a single contractual document. It recognizes that an agreement may be reached through the exchange of letters, cables, or telexes, but it mandates that a contract is only formed when a "written confirmation is signed."

The Foreign Economic Contracts Law also indicates that the written contract should display a high degree of certainty of terms. Article 12 states that contracts should contain the following provisions:

- title, name, nationality, and place of business of the parties
- the date and place of its signing
- the contract type, along with the category and scope of contractual objectives
- objectives regarding technology terms, quality, standard, specifications, and quantity
- the time limit on, place of, and method of performance
- conditions on price, amount, and method of payment
- terms and conditions for assignment
- compensation and liabilities for breach
- methods of settlement
- language of the contract

Article 37, although not mandating alternative dispute resolution, encourages the mediation and then arbitration of any disputes. Finally, the law provides a statute

28. See U.C.C. § 2-718.

of limitations period of four years for bringing a lawsuit. The period begins from the "date the party knew or should have known that his rights were infringed."

PRINCIPLES OF EUROPEAN CONTRACT LAW

http://

The Principles of European Contract Law may be accessed at: **http://www.jus.uio.no/lm/eu.contract.principles.1998/** or **http://www.ufsia.ac.be/~estorme/PECL2en.html**.

In 1998, the European Union's Commission on Contract published its revised Principles of European Contract Law (European Principles). The stated purpose of the European Principles was to respond to a need for a Community-wide infrastructure of contract law to consolidate the rapidly expanding volume of Community law regulating specific types of contracts. Article 1.101 states that the European Principles will apply to a contract dispute in two main scenarios: when the parties select them as their choice of law and when the contract is to be governed by general principles of law or the *lex mercatoria*. The former scenario is likely to occur when the contracting parties are in disagreement over the application of a given national law. The European Principles, like the CISG, serve as a broad, fairly written compromise choice of law. The CISG is a better choice in a sale of goods transaction, while the European Principles apply to all types of contracts. The second scenario is likely to occur in the setting of international arbitration. Arbitrators, at times, want to avoid the application of an idiosyncratic rule of national law in favor of a "fairer" general principle found in international customary law. In time, arbitrators may recognize the European Principles as evidence of customary international law.

A review of the European Principles demonstrates a large amount of similarity with the U.S. common law of contracts and the UCC. It also shows significant differences that could potentially lead to unexpected liabilities for one who is familiar only with U.S. law. The following review outlines some of the differences and notes comparable provisions in the CISG. One caveat should be noted: The U.S. businessperson will find a great deal more of common ground than differences when comparing the European Principles with U.S. contract law. It is important, however, to understand the differences in order to avoid certain liabilities. For example, the European Principles adopt the CISG's approach to formalities. Article 2.101 is almost identical to Article 11 of the CISG: "A contract need not be concluded or evidenced in writing nor is it subject to any other requirement as to form. The contract may be proved by any means, including witnesses."

The European Principles go farther than even the CISG[29] in rejecting provisions that reduce the admissibility of evidence in a contract dispute. The enforceability of common contract clauses, such as written modification and merger clauses, is jeopardized under Articles 2.105 and 2.106. Under these articles, a **written modification clause** that requires a writing to make any changes to the contract provides only a presumption. The other party may still introduce evidence in order to rebut the presumption. The articles further state that "a party may by its statements or conduct be precluded from asserting such a clause."

In addition, a **merger clause** found in a standard form or in the general conditions[30] section of a contract does not fare very well under the European Principles. The standard merger clause states that the document into which it is incorporated is a final integration of the parties' agreement and supercedes all other statements, writings, or correspondences. A merger clause that is *individually negotiated* will be enforced, otherwise the clause establishes only a presumption. However, even

29. See CISG at Article 29(2).

30. The following definition of general conditions is provided in Article 2.209(3) (Conflicting General Conditions): "General conditions of contract are terms which have been formulated in advance for an indefinite number of contracts of a certain nature, and which have not been individually negotiated between the parties."

when fully negotiated a merger clause can be voided in the case of ambiguity in the contract or on grounds of waiver. Article 2.105 states that "the parties' prior statements may be used to interpret the contract." Regarding subsequent statements and conduct, it provides that such statements and conduct may preclude a party "from asserting a merger clause to the extent that the other party has reasonably relied upon the subsequent statements or conduct."

In the area of **notice,** the European Principles state that notice becomes effective "when it reaches the addressee." It qualifies this rule by stating that a properly dispatched notice of nonperformance, which is subsequently lost or delayed in transmission, "shall have effect from the time at which it would have arrived under normal circumstances."[31] Notice plays a much larger role in the actual negotiation of contract terms under the European Principles than it does under the common law system. Article 2.104 states that "contract terms which have not been individually negotiated may be invoked against a party who did not know of them only if the party invoking them took reasonable steps to bring them to the other party's attention before or when the contract is concluded." Note that the individual negotiation rule is not confined to standard form contracting or merchant-to-consumer transactions. Article 4.110 allows a party to void an unfair term that was not individually negotiated. It defines "unfair" as a term that "causes a significant imbalance in the parties' rights and obligations."[32]

A number of rules in the area of **offer** should be noted. First, the exporter should be aware that a circular, advertisement, or proposal, considered by him as an invitation to offer, may be construed as a standing offer under the European Principles. Article 2.201 states that "a proposal to supply goods or services at stated prices made by a professional supplier in a public advertisement or a catalogue, or by a display of goods, is *presumed* to be an offer to sell or supply at that price until the stock of goods, or the supplier's capacity to supply the service, is exhausted."

Second, the **firm offer rule** is expanded to further restrict the maker of an offer's ability to revoke the offer. Unlike Section 2-205 of the Uniform Commercial Code, the offer need not be from a merchant, be in writing, be signed, or be for a period less than three months. An offer may not be revoked if it indicates that it is irrevocable or fixes a time for acceptance. Thus, a statement that the offeree must accept within ninety-five days will be interpreted as a firm offer for ninety-five days. Under U.S. law, the offer would self-terminate after ninety days and nothing prevents the offeror from revoking the offer prematurely; to be considered a firm offer, the offer must expressly assure the receiving party that the offer will remain open for a fixed period of time. More important, under the *European Principles* any offer may be recognized as a firm offer if it is "reasonable for the offeree to rely on the offer being irrevocable and the offeree has acted in reliance on the offer." Thus, the offer need not give any assurance that it is to remain open.[33]

In the area of **acceptance,** not surprisingly, the common law's dispatch or **mailbox rule** is rejected for the civil law's receipt rule. Under the Principles, a contract is concluded when the acceptance reaches the offeror.[34] It would seem that the receipt rule for acceptance would provide the offeror with an additional period to

31. See Article 1.303 (Notice).

32. Article 4.110 makes an exception for terms that provide the "main subject matter of the contract" and are provided in "plain and intelligible language." Also, the adequacy of value exchanged between the parties is not a ground for voiding a term. See Article 4.110(2)(b) (Unfair Terms Not Individually Negotiated).

33. See also CISG Article 16.

34. European Principles at Article 2.205 (Time of Conclusion of the Contract).

revoke the offer. But like under Article 18 of the CISG, the right to revoke an offer is frozen when the acceptance is dispatched[35] even though the acceptance is not effective until receipt. However, in the event that the acceptance does not reach the offeror within a reasonable time, then it would seem that the revocation would be unfrozen and preclude the formation of a contract. In the case where a revocation has not already been sent, a late acceptance due to problems of transmission gives the offeror the option to reject the acceptance if he informs the offeree, "without delay," that the offer has lapsed.[36]

The **battle of forms** scenario[37] commonly found in international sale of goods transactions is dealt with in Article 2.208 titled "Modified Acceptance" and Article 2.209 titled "Conflicting General Conditions." The offeree's form that gives a definite assent to the offer creates a contract unless it possesses additional or different terms that materially alter the offer. Article 2.208 recognizes that the parties can include contract language to control the battle of the forms scenario. The offeror may incorporate a clause in its offer to the effect that it "expressly limits acceptance to the terms of the offer."

The offeree may condition its acceptance upon the offeror's assent to its additional terms. Article 2.208 requires that the offeror must expressly agree to the additional terms in order for the conditional acceptance to effectuate a contract. An agreement to the additional terms can be obtained by the offeree when he requires the offeror to sign and return the conditional acceptance. A conditional acceptance will be treated as a rejection if the offeror's assent to the additional or different terms "does not reach the offeree within a reasonable time." Article 2.209 provides that the fine print terms in offer and acceptance forms will generally be considered as "general conditions" and only the general conditions that are "common in substance" become a part of the contract. Thus, conflicting general conditions would not become a part of the contract.

The European Principles also recognize a general area of **precontractual liability** and the duty of good faith negotiation not recognized under U.S. contract law. The very real possibility of unexpected liability will be discussed later in this chapter in the section on Precontractual Instruments. It is sufficient for our current purposes to note that parties have a general duty to negotiate in good faith. Failure to do so, such as never intending to enter into a contract, is grounds for contractual liability. Thus, terminating a negotiation without giving a viable reason is not an appropriate approach. A party can be held liable for losses caused to the other party.[38] Furthermore, either party to a negotiation may be held liable for a breach of confidentiality.

Article 2.302, titled **Breach of Confidentiality,** recognizes an affirmative duty not to disclose confidential information obtained in the course of negotiations. Statements made during the negotiations may also provide separate grounds for an action. Article 6.101 (Statements Giving Rise to Contractual Obligation) states that if a professional supplier gives information about the quality or uses of services or goods when marketing or advertising or otherwise before a contract is concluded then the "statement is to be treated as giving rise to a contractual obligation." This precontractual line of obligation is further extended to agents of the supplier. The supplier is contractually liable for statements made "by a person in *earlier links* of the business chain." It is imperative that the exporter-supplier review his advertise-

35. European Principles at Article 2.202 (Revocation of an Offer). See also Chapter 8.
36. European Principles at Article 2.207(2) (Late Acceptance).
37. Compare U.C.C. §2-207 and CISG Article 19.
38. Article 3.101 (Negotiations Contrary to Good Faith).

ments, promotional brochures, and practices of foreign sales representatives in order to avoid such liability.

A unique feature of the European Principles is its coverage of the **agency** relationship. Since the agency relationship is common in international transactions, as in the hiring of a foreign sales representative or distributor, the section on agency law is appropriate. Its coverage of the agency contract is limited to the relationship between third parties and the principal or agent. It does not govern the relationship between the principal and agent. The rules on agency are divided into those governing **direct representation** and those governing **indirect representation.** Direct representation is when the agent acts in the name of the principal. In contrast, indirect representation is when a third party is unaware that the agent is acting as an agent.

The agency rules in the European Principles are consistent with most of the agency rules found in common law. A number of its specific rules are of note, however. First, in the case where the agent indicates it is acting as agent, it must identify the principal within a reasonable time of entering into the contract upon the request of the third party. If the agent unduly delays disclosing the principal, then the agent becomes bound by the contract.[39] Second, if the third party is in doubt regarding the authority of the agent, "it may send a written confirmation to the principal or request ratification" from the principal.[40] If the principal fails to respond in a timely fashion, the agent's act is considered authorized.

In the area of **genuineness of assent,** European Principles recognize many of the same contract voiding events found in the common law. The terminology in parentheses is the common law equivalent to the invalidating rule found in the European Principles. A party has the right to void a contract due to: Mistake as to Facts or Law (unilateral mistake),[41] Mutual Mistake,[42] Fraud,[43] Threats (duress),[44] Unfair Advantage (undue influence),[45] and Unfair Terms (unconscionability).[46] In the area of mutual mistake, the court is charged directly not with rescinding the contract but rather with adapting (reforming) the contract. It states that where both parties made the same mistake, the court may at the request of either party bring the contract into accordance with what might reasonably have been agreed had the mistake not occurred.

The notion of **economic duress** is placed not under the threats (duress) umbrella but within the notion of unfair advantage (undue influence). A party may avoid a contract if at the time of contracting "it was dependent on or had a relationship of trust with the other party, was in *economic distress* or had urgent needs, was improvident, ignorant, inexperienced, or lacking bargaining skills." In contrast, the notion that the party had "no reasonable alternative" is found in the article on threats. The article on fraud recognizes a substantial duty to disclose information. The general duty of good faith and fair dealing is also applied to require a duty to disclose under certain circumstances. Factors to be considered in determining the need for disclosure include whether one of the parties had "special expertise," the cost of obtaining the information, whether the other party could reasonably have acquired the information on his own, and whether the information would have been material to the decision-maker.[47]

39. European Principles at Article 3.203 (Unidentified Principal).
40. European Principles at Article 3.208 (Third Party's Right with Respect to Confirmation of Authority).
41. European Principles at Article 4.103 (Mistake as to Facts or Law).
42. European Principles at Article 4.105(3) (Adaptation of Contract).
43. European Principles at Article 4.107 (Fraud).
44. European Principles at Article 4.108 (Threats).
45. European Principles at Article 4.109 (Excessive Benefit or Unfair Advantage).
46. European Principles at Article 4.110 (Unfair Terms which have not been Individually Negotiated).
47. European Principles at Article 4.109(3) (Fraud).

The European Principles adopt the civil law notion of *nachfrist* notice.[48] The nonperforming party may obtain an extension of the time of performance by giving notice to the other party. Generally, the extension must be given unless the nonbreaching party gives a commercially viable reason for not granting the extension. After the expiration of the extension, the nonbreaching party may terminate the contract even for minor breaches. There is no such provision for requesting or granting additional time in U.S. law.

In the area of contractual excuse for breach, the European Principles adopt civil law rules consistent with common law contracts. Article 8.108 recognizes the notion of **impediment** as a ground to excuse a breaching party for his nonperformance. The test of impediment is similar to that found in the common law excuse doctrines. The impediment must not have been "reasonably expected" and must be beyond the control of the nonperforming party.[49] The nonperforming party must give prompt notice of the impediment or be liable for damages resulting from the nonreceipt of the notice. In the event that the impediment is perceived to be temporary in nature, the nonperforming party is not excused from the contract but is granted a temporary suspension of performance.

There are two fundamental differences between the European Principles and U.S. law in the area of remedies. First, a unique remedy of **price reduction** is given to the buyer of nonconforming goods. Under the UCC, the buyer may reject nonconforming goods under the **perfect tender rule,**[50] or may accept the goods, pay in full, and make a breach of warranty claim. The price reduction remedy in the European Principles, also found in the CISG,[51] allows the buyer to reduce unilaterally the price paid for the goods based on the diminution of value due to the nonconformity. Second, the right to **specific performance** is not considered an extraordinary remedy. Article 9.102 of the Principles states simply that "the aggrieved party is entitled to specific performance, including the remedying of a defective performance." In contrast, the UCC adopts the common law rule that specific performance is warranted only when the goods are *unique.*[52]

UNIDROIT PRINCIPLES OF INTERNATIONAL COMMERCIAL CONTRACTS

UNIDROIT is a specialized agency of the United Nations that promotes the unification of law. In May 1994 it published the Principles of International Commercial Contracts (Principles). The Principles primary differences from the CISG are threefold. First, it is not for adoption as a domestic law of international contracts. It is intended merely to provide neutral principles acceptable for guidance for lawyers and businesspersons from different legal systems. Second, it provides a set of general principles applicable to all types of contracts. In contrast, the CISG applies only to the commercial sale of goods and supplies a number of specific rules for that type of transaction. Third, the Principles cover contract negotiations, while the CISG deals merely with the mechanics of offer and acceptance.

Those drafting an international contract of any type may want to review the UNIDROIT Principles of International Commercial Contracts. Although they are non-binding general principles, some courts may utilize them in the interpretation of an international contract. "With the assistance of the Principles, judges or arbitrators called upon to decide questions of interpretation or to supplement interna-

48. See CISG Article 47 & 63.
49. European Principles at Article 8.108 (Excuse Due to an Impediment). Compare U.C.C. § 2-615 (impracticability) and CISG Article 74.
50. U.C.C. §2-601 (Perfect Tender Rule).
51. See CISG Article 50.
52. U.C.C. § 2-716 (Buyer's Right to Specific Performance).

tional legislative texts will find it easier to adopt an autonomous and internationally uniform solution."[53] A number of features of the Principles should be noted. The first group of features involves the formation of contracts.

- There is no writing requirement. The Principles simply state that a contract "may be proved by any means, including witnesses."[54] Representations made during the negotiation stage may be entered into evidence even if they conflict with the written contract.
- International trade usage is recognized. The parties are "bound by a usage that is widely known to and regularly observed in international trade."[55]
- Article 2.16 recognizes a duty of confidentiality for information obtained during the course of negotiations.
- Article 2.20, titled "Surprising Terms," provides a means for a party to void fine print terms in a standard form contract. It provides that such terms that a party "could not reasonably have expected" will not be enforced. A conspicuously and clearly written but unusual term is, however, enforceable.

The Principles expressly cover precontractual liability for conduct during the negotiation phase. Along with the potential of liability for bad faith negotiation, the Principles acknowledge the fine line between negotiation and contract in three ways: First, a contract does not require an agreement on all details of the transaction. The fact that no agreement needs to be reached on all details of a transaction implies that parties may not know exactly when they enter a transaction. Article 2.13 suggests that if a party wants to avoid being "dragged" into a contract by surprise, it must specify in advance that agreement on an issue it considers important has to be reached; if no agreement on that specific item is reached, there will be no contract.

Second, sometimes negotiations are not actually finished when one of the parties starts to perform. For instance, the legal departments of the two companies may still be discussing the contract terms when the sales department of the seller already delivers. In such a situation, the shipment of the goods can be considered as acceptance of the offer. Thus negotiations can be overtaken by contract performance. Third, sometimes parties to a contract intentionally leave **open terms**—terms to be agreed on in future negotiations.

U.S. law does not require that negotiations be conducted in good faith. In contrast, German, French, Italian, and Belgian law have elaborate rules on precontractual liability for conducting or terminating negotiations. One of the great innovations of the Principles is that they provide standards for conducting negotiations. Article 2.15 states that "a party who negotiates or breaks off negotiations in bad faith is liable for the losses caused to the other party." Also, Article 2.16 makes a party liable "when it discloses or improperly uses confidential information obtained in the course of negotiations." Breach of confidentiality entitles the other party to compensation for either the loss suffered by the breach of good faith or the benefit the party in breach received by disclosing the information."[56]

The UNIDROIT Principles are indicative of how most civil law legal systems are likely to affix liability in the negotiation stage. Parties are generally required to act in good faith during the negotiation phase. For example, a termination of lengthy

53. Michael J. Bonell, "Non-Legislative Means of Harmonization" in United Nations, *Uniform Commercial Law in the Twenty-First Century* 38 (1992).
54. Article 1.2. Compare U.C.C. §§ 2-201 & 2-202.
55. Article 1.8. Compare U.C.C. § 1-205.
56. Hans van Houtte, "The UNIDROIT Principles of International Commercial Contracts," 11 *Arbitration International* 373, 374-378 (1995).

negotiations without a justified reason will be considered bad faith and subject the party to a suit for damages or expenses. Such precontractual liability may include claims for expenses directly related to the negotiations including travel, research, and consulting expenses. It may also support a claim for indirect damages such as lost profits from other potential deals that the innocent party gave up to pursue negotiations with the terminating party.[57]

In the area of performance, the Principles include a section on **hardship.** Hardship is defined as "where the occurrence of events fundamentally alters the equilibrium of the contract."[58] In order for a party to claim a hardship he must show that the event causing the hardship could not reasonably have been taken into account at the time of contracting, that the event was beyond his control, and that the risks were not assumed by the party in the contract. Hardship allows the party to "request negotiations." In the event that the parties do not agree to an adjustment or settlement, the court is instructed to either terminate the contract or adjust the contract to restore its equilibrium.[59] The Focus on Transactions feature provides a number of practical tips for international contracting.

Precontractual Liability

Under U.S. common law, a negotiating party owes no duty of good faith to the other party.[60] One may terminate negotiations in bad faith and not be liable for the

Focus on Transactions

Practical Tips for International Contracting

Tip 1: Even if not legally required to, put the contract in writing!
Tip 2: Negotiate a choice of law clause.
Tip 3: Custom design a forum selection or arbitration clause.
Tip 4: Negotiate a specific *force majeure* clause.
Tip 5: Expressly allocate the risk of currency exchange rate fluctuations.
Tip 6: For a long-term or multiple installments contract, negotiate a detailed price escalation clause.
Tip 7: Assure payment and performance through third-party devices such as confirmed letters of credit, standby letters of credit, performance bonds, and bank guarantees.
Tip 8: Seek the expert advice of international lawyers, foreign legal counsel, international bankers, freight forwarders, customs brokers, insurance brokers, and governmental agencies.

57. The Civil Code countries make a distinction between mere negotiations and preliminary agreement. The line between the two is a very subtle one. In addition, the Civil Code countries provide for extended periods of time for the bringing of lawsuits. Under the Italian Civil Code, the statute of limitations to bring a breach of the duty of good faith negotiations is five years, extended to ten years for a breach of contract. In contrast, there is no cause of action in the United States for bad faith negotiation, while the statute of limitations under Section 2-725 of the Uniform Commercial Code is four years and the contracting parties are authorized to reduce the period to as little as one year.
58. Article 6.2.2. Compare U.C.C. § 2-615.
59. Article 6.2.3.
60. For an analysis of precontractual liability in conjunction with the Convention on Contracts for the International Sale of Goods, see Michael Joachim Bonnell, "Formation of Contracts and Precontractual Liability Under the Vienna Convention on International Sale of Goods," in FORMATION OF CONTRACTS AND PRECONTRACTUAL LIABILITY (175 Paris: ICC Publishing, S.A. 1990).

other party's expenses, with one major exception: *Reliance theory* may be used to extend contractual liability to protect someone who reasonably relied upon the belief that the parties would conclude a final agreement. Section 90 of the *Restatement (Second) of Contracts,* often referred to as **promissory estoppel,** allows a court to give a remedy if a person's promise, such as a promise to conclude negotiations, is reasonably relied upon and injustice can be prevented only by the enforcement of the promise.

The court in *Nimrod Marketing v. Texas Energy Corp.*[61] held that a purchasing agent who expended money in reliance of obtaining a contract from one of its clients could sue for damages when the client hired another subcontractor. The client had sent a letter to the agent that stated: "Acting pursuant to your responsibilities as our purchasing agent, it is our hope to begin construction of the housing shortly upon obtaining a contract with the foreign government." The court ruled that based upon the doctrine of promissory estoppel, the agent had reasonably relied upon the assurance in the letter. See Focus on Transactions: Reliance Factors (Liability for Oral Statements and Informal Business Letters).

Examining the legal system of the Federal Republic of Germany allows us to compare how other legal systems deal with the potential liability of precontractual correspondences and instruments. German law is less dependent than U.S. law upon the literal designation of writings or instruments as legal or nonlegal. This informalism provides parties greater flexibility in structuring transactions. The German courts look to the purpose of a letter or a writing to determine if it creates an enforceable contractual obligation. One might argue that even informal business

Focus on Transactions

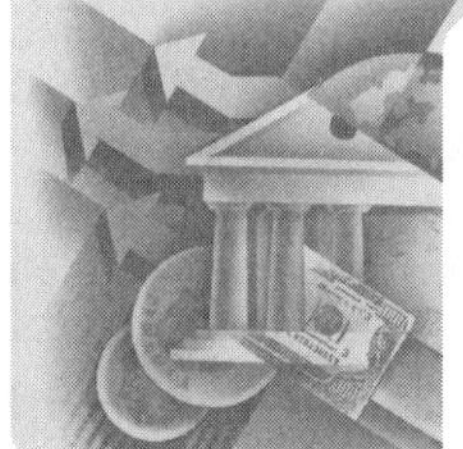

Reliance Factors (Liability for Oral Statements and Informal Business Letters)[62]

1. Does the language in the statement or letter border on a promise or a guarantee?
2. Is there a disclaimer of liability in the statement or letter?
3. Does the statement or letter invite one of the parties to take steps to ensure performance of an underlying obligation?
4. What was the intent of the party giving the statement or letter?
5. Did either party receive legal advice as to the legality of the statement or letter?
6. What was the relative sophistication of the parties regarding the purpose or legality of the statement or letter?
7. What were the prior dealings between the parties regarding such letters or statements?
8. What is the custom or practice in that particular business or industry regarding the purpose and legality of such statements or letters?
9. What was the length of negotiations pertaining to the statement or letter?
10. Was there actual reliance upon the statement or letter?

61. 769 F.2d 1076 (5th Cir. 1985).
62. See Larry A. DiMatteo & Rene Sacasas, "Credit and Value Comfort Instruments: Crossing the Line from Assurance to Legally Significant Reliance and Toward a Theory of Enforceability," 47 *Baylor Law Rev.* 357 (1995).

letters, seemingly not binding on the surface, are more likely to have legal consequences under this purpose-oriented approach to enforceability. The presumption is that most businesspersons would not spend time negotiating and drafting letters and documents unless they believed them to be legally binding. German and French courts often ask the following question when reviewing an instrument for enforceability purposes: Would two sophisticated commercial entities spend time to create a meaningless, unenforceable instrument?

The *R.G. Group v. Bojangles'* case provides an example of when negotiations and preliminary writings do not lead to contractual liability. It also introduces the

R.G. Group, Inc. v. Bojangles' of America, Inc.

751 F.2d 69 (2d Cir. 1984)

Pratt, Circuit Judge. Plaintiff R.G. Group, Inc., claim to have made an oral agreement with the defendants, Bojangles' of America, Inc., and its parent corporation, The Horn & Hardart Company, in which plaintiff gained the exclusive right to develop and operate some twenty "Bojangles' Famous Chicken 'N Biscuits" fast-service restaurants. Sometimes an oral promise or handshake is all that is needed, but when substantial sums of money are at stake it is neither unreasonable nor unusual for parties to require that their contract be entirely in writing and signed before binding obligations will attach. This case does not even present much of a cautionary tale. Its lesson is simply that when experienced businessmen and lawyers are told explicitly and clearly that a major and complex agreement will be binding only when put in writing, then they should be rather cautious about assuming anything different.

Bojangles' gave Gillman of R.G. Group a copy of its standard form development franchise agreement. Its general provisions include requirements that the entire agreement, and any modifications, be in writing and signed by the parties: "This Development Franchise Agreement together with all the Appendices and Exhibits annexed hereto contain the entire agreement and understanding between the parties hereto with respect to the subject matter hereof and supersedes all prior negotiations and oral understandings between the parties hereto, if any. There are no agreements, representations, or warranties other than those set forth, provided for or referred to herein." Gillman testified that he had asked Bojangles' representative Schupak over the telephone, "Do we have a handshake deal?" Schupak's answer, according to Gillman, was "Yes, we have a handshake deal today and right now." The agreement, however, was never signed. On December 14, 1982, Schupak called Gillman and told him that Bojangles' franchise committee had refused to approve the application put together by Gillman.

A. Was There a Contract?

Under New York law, if parties do not intend to be bound by an agreement until it is in writing and signed, then there is no contract until that event occurs. This rule holds even if the parties have orally agreed upon all the terms of the proposed contract. On the other hand, where there is no understanding that an agreement should not be binding until reduced to writing and formally executed, and "where all the substantial terms of a contract have been agreed on, and there is nothing left for future settlement," then an informal agreement can be binding even though the parties contemplate memorializing their contract in a formal document. The point of these rules is to give parties the power to contract as they please, so that they may, if they like, bind themselves orally or by informal letters, or that they may maintain "complete immunity from all obligation" until a written agreement is executed. Hard and fast requirements of form are out of place.

Freedom to avoid oral agreements is especially important when business entrepreneurs and corporations engage in substantial and complex dealings. In these circumstances there are often forceful reasons for refusing to make a binding contract unless it is put in writing. The actual drafting of a written instrument will frequently reveal points of disagreement, ambiguity, or omission which must be worked out prior to execution. Details that are unnoticed or passed by in oral discussion will be pinned down when the understanding is reduced to writing. These considerations are not minor; indeed, above a certain level of investment and complexity, requiring written contracts may be the norm in the business world, rather than the exception.

To begin with, it is not surprising that considerable weight is put on a party's explicit statement that it reserves the right to be bound only when a written agreement is signed. A second factor of major significance is whether one party has partially performed, and that performance has been accepted by the party disclaiming the contract. A third factor is whether there was literally nothing left to negotiate or settle, so that all that remained to be done was to sign what had already been fully agreed to. A fourth factor is whether the agreement concerns those complex and substantial business matters where requirements that contracts be in writing are the norm rather than the exception. In the present case the evidence on each of these factors unequivocally supports Bojangles' position. There was, first of all, the explicit wording of the development franchise agreement itself, which declared on its face that "when duly executed" it would set forth the parties' rights and obligations.

Here there was no performance, partial or otherwise, by either party. The third factor—whether there was literally nothing left to agree to—supports defendants' position as well. Winarick, RG Associates' chief operating officer, admitted in a deposition that the territory issue was an important one. The fourth factor concerns the extent to which, as a practical business matter, the agreement involved a scale of investment and complexity such that a writing requirement would be expected. Certainly this is the kind of agreement where it would be unusual to rely on an oral understanding. Bojangles' franchise contracts run for twenty years and cover detailed matters of capital structure for franchisees, purchase and development of real estate, construction of stores, trade secrets, transfers of interest, and rights on termination or default.

B. The Statute of Frauds.

The district court also decided that even if there had been an oral agreement, it would be rendered void by the New York statute of frauds. That statute provides in relevant part: "Every agreement, promise, or undertaking is void, unless it or some note or memorandum thereof be in writing, if such agreement, promise, or undertaking by its terms is not to be performed within one year from the making thereof." The required memorandum may consist of several documents, only some of which are signed, provided that they clearly refer to the same transaction.

Plaintiff argues that four documents, taken together, contain all the terms of the alleged contract. The writings put forward by plaintiffs, however, contradict the alleged oral agreement. Although plaintiffs rely in part on the standard form development franchise agreement to satisfy the statute, that agreement states that it is effective only when signed, that any modification or amendment to it must be in writing, and that any agreement concerning its subject matter must be in writing and signed. Our conclusion, therefore, is that the district court was correct in holding that there is no triable issue concerning plaintiffs' failure to satisfy the statute of frauds.

C. Promissory Estoppel.

Plaintiff also argues for recovery on the basis of promissory estoppel. In New York a claim for promissory estoppel requires "a clear and unambiguous promise; a reasonable and foreseeable reliance by the party to whom the promise is made; and an injury sustained by the party asserting the estoppel by reason of his reliance." However, there never was "a clear and unambiguous promise" to plaintiff that the development franchise was theirs. Plaintiff's counsel admitted in hearings before the district court that "the vast bulk" of plaintiffs' expenditures were made prior to December 3, the date of the alleged promise. Hence the district court was correct in rejecting the promissory estoppel claim both for lack of a clear promise and for lack of reliance. AFFIRMED.

Case Highlights

- If parties do not intend to be bound by an agreement until it is in writing and signed, then there is no contract until that event occurs.
- An informal agreement can be binding even though the parties contemplate memorializing their contract in a formal document.
- It is good business practice to place an agreement in writing because writing will frequently reveal points of disagreement, ambiguity, or omission that should be worked out before entering a contract.
- A court will weigh a number of factors to determine whether the parties intended to be bound before entering into a formal written contract, including whether one party reserved the right to be bound prior to a formal agreement, whether there has been a partial performance, whether there were still outstanding issues, and the complexity of the agreement.
- The statute of frauds requires any contract that cannot be performed within one year to be in a signed writing.
- Promissory estoppel is not available to recover expenses incurred before the making of a promise.

reader to the concepts of the statute of frauds and promissory estoppel. The former is an obstacle to contract formation and the latter is an alternative avenue of liability.

As the *R.G. Group, Inc.*, case demonstrates contractual liability under U.S. law becomes vested only when the parties move beyond mere negotiations. The importance of the line between negotiations and contract was more recently explored in *Novecon Ltd. v. Bulgarian-American Enterprise Fund.*[63] A Federal Appeals court held that no contract was formed when one party responded to a letter from a second party by stating that it agreed to the terms of the second party's proposal. The case involved Novecon, a company that develops business projects in Bulgaria. Novecon proposed a joint venture for a construction project in Sofia on land owned by Batsov, which was to get a share of the project for contributing land. A construction loan was to come from Bulgarian-American Enterprise Fund (BAEF). There were four letters between Novecon and BAEF concerning who would have what responsibility for the project. BAEF's last letter said that there were unresolved issues with Batsov that had to be settled before the matter could be finalized. Novecon replied that it accepted the terms of the offer, and that it understood that BAEF would resolve matters with Batsov.

Negotiations between BAEF and Batsov did not go well and BAEF withdrew from the project. Novecon sued for breach of contract. The court granted BAEF summary judgment. It stated that "for an enforceable contract to exist there must be both (1) agreement as to all material terms and (2) intention of the parties to be bound." The court held that there was no contract by reasoning that BAEF merely extended an offer to negotiate when it said that matters with Batsov needed to be resolved as a necessary part of any agreement. Parties "will not be bound to a preliminary agreement unless the evidence presented clearly indicates that they intended to be bound at that point." The exchange of communications did not constitute an agreement but were merely a part of the preliminary negotiations.

CULPA IN CONTRAHENDO

The famous case of *Texaco v. Pennzoil*[64] illustrates that simply knowing the black-letter rules of contract may not be enough to avoid liability. In that case Getty and Pennzoil reached an "agreement in principle" and held a news conference announcing the tentative agreement. Before the parties entered a formal agreement Getty entered into a formal contract to sell to Texaco. Despite the fact that the sale of Getty Oil to Pennzoil was never finalized, Texaco was held liable for tortious interference of contract for its attempt to buy Getty. A jury awarded Pennzoil $7.53 billion in compensatory damages and an additional $3 billion in punitive damages. Texaco subsequently filed for bankruptcy protection before settling out of court. Pennzoil and Getty had entered into a "memorandum of agreement" but a final, formal agreement was never signed. Furthermore, industry custom indicated that the term "agreement" is different than the term "contract." Thus, such memorandums were generally considered preliminary and conditional on the signing of a formal contract. Nonetheless, the jury found there was a contractual "meeting of the minds" and that but for the interference by Texaco the parties would have signed a formal contract.

63. 1999 WL 683006 (D.C. Cir.).
64. 729 S.W.2d 768 (Tex. Ct. App. 1987).

The *Texaco* case also serves to illustrate the importance of contract negotiations and the dangers of acting in bad faith during those negotiations. Unlike in the United States, the idea of precontractual liability is accepted in most of the world's national legal systems. In the civil law, one form of precontractual liability, ***culpa in contrahendo,*** has been a firm part of contract and tort laws. This liability is generally premised on the implied duty of the parties to act in good faith during the negotiations of a contract. In contrast, the American Uniform Commercial Code mandates good faith only during the performance and enforcement of contracts. Good faith under the civil law system means more than not breaking off negotiations in bad faith. Numerous duties are assigned to the negotiating parties. Under Dutch law there are duties to disclose essential information, to investigate in order to obtain necessary information, and to refrain from negotiating with third parties. A Dutch court in *Plas v. Valburg, Hoge Road*[65] divided precontract negotiations into three different stages.

Plas v. Valburg, Hoge Road

18-6 Nederlandse Jurisprudentie 723 (1983)

A construction firm, Plas, submitted a tender or bid to build a municipal swimming pool in the Town of Valburg. Its proposal was considered to be the best one by the Mayor and his municipal councilors agreed to the plan. The proposal was within the budget made available for the project. However, the City Council rejected the recommended bid in favor of an alternative tender by another company at a lower price. Plas sued for expenses and damages.

The court held that there are three steps in most contract negotiations that result in the creation of numerous rights and duties. During the initial stage of negotiations either party is free to break off negotiations without any liability to the other party. The next stage or "continuing stage" of negotiations allows either party to break off negotiations, but the breaking off party remains obligated to compensate the other party for at least some of its expenses. These types of damages are grounded upon Dutch tort law. In short, the breaking off of negotiations is deemed to be a tortious act.

During the third and final stage of negotiations the parties are not free to break off negotiations. To do so would be considered within the doctrine of *culpa in contrahendo* or an infringement of the rules of good faith. This stage is entered into when the parties mutually and reasonably expect that in any case a contract of some kind would result from the negotiations. The breaking off party is obligated to pay for the expectancy damages of the other party. These damages include any expenses incurred and, if deemed appropriate, the profits that would have been made by that party.

Decision. The parties had not entered into the third or final stage of negotiations. Therefore, it is inappropriate to award Plas damages for lost profits. The negotiations had entered into the second or continuing stage and therefore, Plas is awarded damages to cover the expenses incurred in preparing its bid proposal.

Case Highlights

- Dutch law divides contract negotiations into three stages.
- The preliminary or initial stage of negotiations result in no legal liability.
- Bad faith termination during the second or continuing stage of negotiations results in a claim for out-of-pocket expenses or what in U.S. contract law are referred to as reliance damages.
- The parties are prohibited from terminating negotiations during the third or final stage of negotiations without being liable for full contract damages, known under U.S. law as expectancy damages.

65. This case was extracted from Michael Tegethoff, "*Culpa in Contrahendo* in German and Dutch Law—A Comparison of Precontractual Liability," 5 *Maastricht Journal of European & Comparative Law* 341, 347 (1998).

What are the types of expenses that the terminating party is liable for under *Plas v. Valburg*'s second stage? These expenses include costs that can be connected directly to the negotiations, including travel and estimating expenses and possibly damages that result from the fact that the prejudiced party was not able to conclude a contract with a third party during the negotiations. Under German law, to find a party liable for breaking off negotiations it would have to be shown that the party breaking off negotiations: (1) indicated to the other party that the negotiations would lead to a conclusion of a contract and (2) failed to give a commercially reasonable explanation for the termination. German law also allows for liability for bad faith negotiation even when a contract is concluded; in short, when one of the parties' reasonable expectations are not satisfied. This type of liability includes cases involving the nondisclosure of essential information. Under U.S. law, the ordinary means of redress would be the tort of intentional misrepresentation or fraud.

Article 1337 of the Italian Civil Code states that "the parties, in the conduct of negotiations and the formation of the contract, shall conduct themselves according to good faith." The *Grifoni v. Euratom* case examines the Italian version of *culpa in contrahendo* as stated in Article 1337.

It is important for U.S. businesspersons to understand the potential for precontractual liability in international business dealings. First, there is no true counterpart to such liability in the common law system. Thus, what are considered *mere*

Grifoni v. European Atomic Energy Community (Euratom)

[1992] 3 CMLR 463

In the context of a tendering procedure for the performance of certain tin-plating and iron work to be carried out at the Euratom Research Center, the applicant, following Euratom's invitation to tender, submitted an offer, which was accepted by Euratom. A precontractual agreement was concluded governing the future relations between the parties including the following clause: "the successful tenderer has the sole responsibility to ensure that safety rules are obeyed and that order is maintained on the work site." Soon thereafter, the applicant climbed on to the roof of the Research Center in order to take measurements. The applicant fell from a height of 4.5 meters and suffered serious injuries

Opinion of Sig Giuseppe Tesauro. The accident occurred when the contract was not yet in force. It follows that contractual liability is precluded. However, it remains to be considered whether it is possible to find in Italian law, which is applicable by virtue of the precontractual agreement, and in particular in Section 1337 of the Italian Civil Code, a precontractual liability or *culpa in contrahendo*. Section 1337 provides that "in the negotiations and in the drawing up of the contract the parties shall act in good faith." As a matter of general legal theory, for precontractual liability to exist there must be some practical relationship with the subject-matter of the future contract, a relationship against which the traditional obligation of good faith is measured. A textbook example is the seller who significantly reduces the value of the object while negotiations are still in progress, or the party who unreasonably breaks off the negotiations. In the present case, the relationship between the event in question and the contract is merely chronological inasmuch as the event occurred prior to the entry into force of the contract. Consequently, it appears that in the present case neither contractual liability nor precontractual liability can be said to have been established.

Case Highlights

- The incurring of damages in relationship to negotiating a contract does not automatically lead to precontractual liability.
- The precontractual agreement shielded the owner from any liability relating to accidents and was enforceable against a claim for personal injuries.

negotiations in U.S. law can lead to unexpected legal liability in an international business negotiation. Second, the effect of damages granted for a bad faith termination of negotiations can be catastrophic. Under the doctrine of *culpa in contrahendo,* a court has the authority to grant full contract damages including lost profits.

One of the most common and important contracts that an exporter or manufacturer enters is with a foreign distributor for its products. This contract and relationship is vital to the successful marketing, sales, and distribution of products into a foreign market. The *SA Pasquasy v. Cosmair* case that follows deals with the negotiation of an exclusive distribution agreement.

SA Pasquasy v. Cosmair, Inc.

[1989] ECC 508

Where one party to negotiations with a view to entering an exclusive distributorship agreement, without valid reason breaks off negotiations just as they are about to be completed, he is at fault and incurs liability in damages. This is especially the case where the party knowingly allows the other party to incur considerable expense in order to be ready to perform his side of the contract and where both parties had clearly expressed their intention to enter into a permanent relationship. The facts of the case showed that the final version of the distribution agreement was at the point of being signed and that the correspondence between the parties showed that there was consensus on the essential elements of the agreement.

We find for the plaintiff on the tort claim of *culpa in contrahendo.* Furthermore we hold L'Oreal to be jointly liable with its subsidiary, despite the fact that it took no part in the negotiations itself, because the facts show that it induced its subsidiary to break off the talks. The plaintiff claims the following damages: (1) advertising expenses incurred in the promotion of defendant's products, (2) investments related to carrying out the expected contract, and (3) loss of opportunity. We find that the advertising expenses were reasonable and necessary because the products in question were unknown in Belgium and Luxembourg.

The plaintiff claims that it purchased a building, along with office equipment and a new computer system, in order to service the new distributorship agreement. It seeks to recover three years of the depreciation value (term of the distributorship) of these investments. Claims for damages are restricted by two principles. First, the damages must be assessed *in concreto* (certain, not speculative). Second, the victim is obligated to do everything to keep his damages to a minimum (duty to mitigate). The facts indicate that the plaintiff had acquired other distributorships that are also serviced by the new investments. We hold that the expenses in question do not appear to constitute injury having a necessary causal connection with the defendants' fault. Also, by acquiring new distributorships the plaintiff has been able to make a profit on its investment and therefore there is no damage.

Finally, plaintiff claims the loss of the opportunity of obtaining the profit anticipated by the grant of the distributorship for three years. In conformity with the prospective agreement and during the negotiations sales had already commenced over a period of ten months. The plaintiff estimates that its minimum loss profit amounts to 15 percent of the planned sales quota for the three years. We believe that 8 percent is more realistic because the plaintiff agreed to bear a number of expense items. Also, the profit would have accrued over the three-year period of the agreement. Therefore, the total amount of the calculated profits should be reduced by two-fifths. Judgment for the plaintiff for 8,864,788 Belgian francs.

Case Highlights

- Elements that favor an award in *culpa in contrahendo* include the suddenness of the termination, the finality of the negotiations, and knowingly allowing the other party to incur expenses.
- The nonterminating party is entitled to expenses and investments incurred in preparing to perform the contract, along with damages related to lost opportunity or profits.
- The nonterminating party's claims for damages are limited to losses that are provable with certainty and by its duty to mitigate.

PRECONTRACTUAL INSTRUMENTS

This section reviews the legal significance of preliminary writings, correspondences, and precontractual instruments. Precontractual instruments are found in most areas of trade and finance; examples include letters of intent, letters of support, and letters of assurance. For want of a better term, they will be referred to as **comfort instruments.**[66] Comfort instruments are generally given to encourage another party to enter into a contractual obligation. They may be made in conjunction with the direct negotiations between the parties or by a third party to the negotiations. For example, a parent company may send a letter of assurance or support "encouraging" a bank to lend money to its subsidiary. The issue becomes whether such informal letters can lead to contractual liability.

The potential for contractual liability lies in the internal inconsistency of many of these instruments. The typical comfort instrument tries to offer a guaranty-type of assurance without the resultant guaranty-type of liability. The 1923 English case of *Rose & Frank Co. v. Crompton*[67] is one of the earliest instances of a court coming to terms with a comfort instrument's internal contradiction. The Court expressly recognized the doctrinal inconsistencies in the language of the letter. It weighed the assurance language with the disclaimer language, ultimately deciding that the disclaimer language was the more dominant. It determined that the operative phrase in the letter was that it was a *contract of honor* and mere loss of honor is not a basis for contractual liability. The line between contract and noncontract remains ambiguous. The question of enforceability provides a framework for analyzing the twin pillars of contract: promissorial intent and promisee reliance.

Judge Vaisey in *Chemco Leasing Spa. v. Rediffusion Plc.* sarcastically frames the issue of comfort instrument enforceability. It is a *"gentlemen's agreement* which is not an agreement, made between two persons neither of whom is a gentlemen, whereby each expects the other to be strictly bound without himself being bound at all."[68] If this is true, then there is little ground for enforcement under either express intent or reliance. On its face, the instrument's ambiguous nature would make it difficult to find the requisite intent subjectively or objectively. The recipient of the comfort instrument would be hard pressed to prove justifiable reliance.

Internationally, courts have been more likely to enforce such instruments. The civil law system, for instance, seems to place less weight on the semantic labeling of instruments when determining the existence of a legally enforceable obligation. The lack of dependency upon legal literalism, both in the labeling of instruments and in the words of art used within the instruments, allows for greater flexibility in affixing contractual liability than is found in the common law system. For example, in the Federal Republic of Germany there are no specific provisions in the Civil or Commercial Codes concerning contractual guarantees. U.S. contract law would hold that comfort instruments are unenforceable because they lack clear contractual intent. French jurisprudence renders a contrary presumption, finding that such comfort instruments possess an implied intent to be binding ***obligations de faire*** (contracts). The presumption is grounded in the belief that parties generally do not intend to create meaningless contractual-type documentation.[69]

66. See generally Larry A. DiMatteo & Rene Sacasas, "Credit and Value Comfort Instruments," 47 *Baylor Law Review* 357 (1995).
67. 1924 All E.R. 245, 255 (Ct. App. 1923).
68. LEXIS Enggen library, Cases file (Q.B. July 19, 1985).
69. "There is a normal assumption that a business transaction is not meaningless and that the words have a purpose." Chelsea Industries, Inc. v. Accuray Leasing Corp., 699 F.2d 58, 60 (1st Cir. 1983). See also Cincinnati Enquirer, Inc. v. American Security & Trust Co., 160 N.E.2d 392, 398 (Ohio 1958).

Key Terms

abus de droit, 182
acceptance, 195
agency, 197
battle of forms, 196
breach of confidentiality, 196
comfort instruments, 208
contract of adhesion, 189
Convention on Contracts for the International Sale of Goods (CISG), 183
Council of Europe, 185
culpa in contrahendo, 205
customary international business law, 181
direct representation, 197
doctrine of *arrhes*, 187
economic duress, 197
English Unfair Contract Terms Act of 1977, 185
European Union Directive on Unfair Terms, 189
firm offer rule, 195
force majeure, 193
Foreign Economic Contract Law of the People's Republic of China, 188
French Civil Code, 187
genuineness of assent, 197
German Civil Code, 187
hardship, 200
impediment, 198
indirect representation, 197
International Chamber of Commerce (ICC), 183
lex mercatoria, 181
liquidated damage clause, 186
mailbox rule, 195
merger clause, 194
nachfrist notice, 183
notice, 195
obligations de faire, 208
open terms, 195
offer, 195
pacta sunt servanda, 182
penal clause, 186
perfect tender rule, 198
precontractual liability, 196
price reduction, 198
Principles of European Contract Law, 188
promissory estoppel, 201
Russian Civil Code, 188
Second Restatement of Contracts, 184
Shari'a, 187
specific performance, 198
statute of frauds, 189
totality of the circumstances analysis, 185
UNIDROIT Principles of International Commercial Contracts, 183
UNIDROIT, 198
Uniform Commercial Code, 177
wa, 179
written modification clause, 194

Chapter Problems

1. Justice Cardozo noted a profound change in the law of contracts and the reduced role of formality as a requirement for contractual liability in the following quote: "The law has outgrown its primitive stage of formalism when the precise word was the talisman, and every slip was fatal. It takes a broader view today. A promise may be lacking, and yet the whole writing may be *instinct with an obligation*, imperfectly expressed." Wood v. Duff-Gordon, 222 N.Y. 88 (1917). If this is true what are the consequences for precontractual liability? Do contracts have to be very detailed in order to be enforceable?

2. Two firms work together to prepare a complex bid for a buyer. One firm (Company A) drops the other (Company B) before getting the bid. After working for some time on specifications, negotiating with the buyer, and being chosen as a final candidate for the job, Company A told Company B that it was disappointed with Company B's behavior and obtained the contract on its own, with minor modifications from the joint proposal submitted previously. Company B sued Company A for breach after Company A subcontracted the work to another firm. Since there was no formal subcontract, what theory of recovery can Company B allege? What types of damages, if any, may Company B claim? *TACS Corp. v. Trans World Communications, Inc.*, 155 F. 3d 659 (3rd Cir.1998).

3. Review the *Bojangles, Plas, Grifoni,* and *SA Pasquasy* cases on preliminary agreements and *culpa in contrahendo* and answer the following questions. What could the party being sued have done differently to avoid liability? Would your answer be different under U.S. as compared to civil law?

Internet Exercises

1. Review and compare the English Unfair Contract Terms regulation at **http://www.dti.gov.uk/access/unfair/part4.htm** with the European Union Directive on Unfair Contract Terms at **http://europa.eu.int/comm/consumers/policy/ developments/unfa_cont_term/uct01_en.pdf**. In addition, the European Union Directive on Unfair Terms in Consumer Contracts (93/13/EEC) defines an unfair term as "any term which contrary to the requirement of good faith causes a significant imbalance in the parties' rights and obligations under the contract to the detriment of the consumer." *Exculpatory clauses* (clauses that excuse a party from his own negligent acts) and clauses limiting the liability of the seller are considered to create such imbalances. However, unfair terms are not voidable if the term was "individually negotiated." What is the importance of the notion of individual negotiation? Would your answer be different if the contract containing the exculpatory clause also had a choice of law clause directing the court to a non-EU country?

2. Review the European Commission's home page for Consumer Affairs at **http://europa.eu.int/comm/consumers/index_en.html**. What types of consumer protection initiatives has the EU undertaken? What areas in the subject index would be a concern for an international businessperson?

3. For a good review and explanation of Chinese commercial law see **http://www.qis.net/chinalaw/explan1.htm**.

4. Read the "overview" of the Council of Europe, along with the different subject areas within the organization, and associated links: **http://www.coe.int**.

5. For a more extensive review of the Russian Civil Code see: **http://www.cnr.it/CRDCS/frames21.htm**.

6. Review the site of the Commission on European Contracts for recent developments on the Principles of European Contract Law at **http://www.ufsia.ac.be/~estorme/CECL.html**.

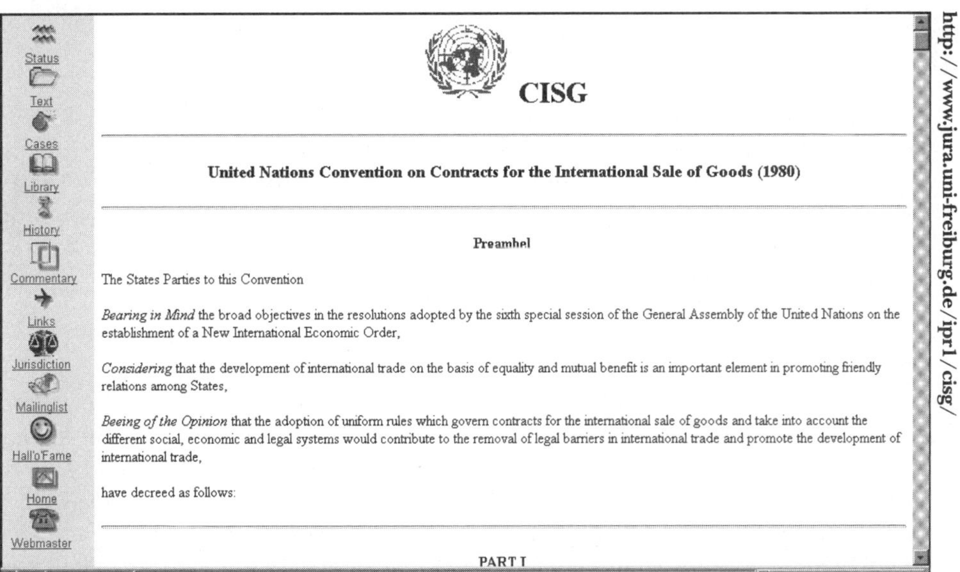

CISG

United Nations Convention on Contracts for the International Sale of Goods (1980)

Preambel

The States Parties to this Convention

Bearing in Mind the broad objectives in the resolutions adopted by the sixth special session of the General Assembly of the United Nations on the establishment of a New International Economic Order,

Considering that the development of international trade on the basis of equality and mutual benefit is an important element in promoting friendly relations among States,

Beeing of the Opinion that the adoption of uniform rules which govern contracts for the international sale of goods and take into account the different social, economic and legal systems would contribute to the removal of legal barriers in international trade and promote the development of international trade,

have decreed as follows:

PART I

http://www.jura.uni-freiburg.de/ipr1/cisg/

Chapter 8 International Sales Law

The success of international customary law or trade usage provided a strong foundation for an international convention on sales law. Examples of the expansion of international customary law in the area of commercial transactions are the universal acceptance of the International Chamber of Commerce's INCOTERM (glossary of trade terms) and its regulations relating to international letters of credit (Uniform Customs and Practices for Documentary Credits or UCP). The major area lacking uniformity was the law covering the underlying transaction—the sales contract. The **United Nations Convention on Contracts for the International Sale of Goods (CISG)** is the most successful attempt to fill in this gap; it promises to become the foundation for a uniform international law of sales for the twenty-first century.

This chapter will review the CISG in detail in order to expose the reader to this important international document and to review the major issues of international sales law. The CISG will be compared to the U.S. **Uniform Commercial Code (UCC)** and differences highlighted. These differences are most likely to result in unexpected legal liability for the U.S. businessperson. An in-depth review serves two major purposes: it familiarizes the reader with major sales law issues common to all legal systems and allows for a closer analysis of how these issues are treated differently among nations.

INTERNATIONAL SALES LAW

http://
General coverage of the *lex mercatoria:* **http://www.lexmercatoria.com**.

Most legal issues in international trade are settled by application of domestic national laws. At the beginning of the twenty-first century, however, we can begin to discuss the evolution of a truly international law of sales or a new ***lex mercatoria.*** *Lex mercatoria* or law of merchants refers to a system of rules of law created by international merchants, independent of any national legal system, for the purpose of governing international business transactions. The adoption in 1980 of the United Nations Convention on Contracts for the International Sale of Goods[1] marked a milestone in the development of the new *lex mercatoria.* Professor Farnsworth, the Reporter of the Second Restatement of Contracts, has predicted that the CISG will become the governing law of most export and import of goods transactions.

The CISG went into effect in the United States on January 1, 1988. Thus, the United States has two laws of contracts for the sale of goods: the UCC and the CISG. In a case where two contracting parties are residents of the United States and another CISG country, a U.S. court will apply the CISG rather than the UCC. The CISG, however, is an optional law and the parties may *opt out* of it through a choice of law clause in their contract. As of early 2002 the United Nations Treaty Section reported that 59 countries have adopted the CISG. (See Comparative Law: Contracting Parties to the CISG.) The list of the contracting states includes most of the United States major trading partners including Canada, Mexico, Germany, France, Russia, China, Italy, and Australia. Countries that have not adopted the CISG include Japan, South Korea, Britain, and Brazil.

http://
For an update on recent signatories and international case and arbitral law on the CISG refer to the following web site: **http://www.cisg.law.pace.edu**.

The coverage of the CISG can be grouped into three broad areas: substantive coverage, jurisdiction, and types of transactions. The CISG covers most substantive issues of contract law. There are, however, areas of law not covered under the CISG, including products liability, the legality of a contract, the capacity of the parties to contract, and whether the nonbreaching party is entitled to specific performance. These substantive areas would be decided under a national law of contract. The national law to be applied would be determined by applying the courts' conflict of law rules. The next section will review the area of conflict of laws and how it impacts on the applicability of the CISG.

Choice of Law and Conflict of Laws

A **choice of law clause** used to avoid application of the CISG must be carefully drafted. For example, the parties may intend the UCC to be the law of the transaction. To that end the parties negotiate the following choice of law clause: "the law of the State of New York shall apply to any disputes." Under Article 1(1)(a) of the

1. See generally ALBERT H. KRITZER, GUIDE TO PRACTICAL APPLICATIONS OF THE UNITED NATIONS CONVENTION ON CONTRACTS FOR THE INTERNATIONAL SALE OF GOODS (Kluwer 1989); Symposium, "Convention on the International Sale of Goods," 21 *Cornell Int'l Law Journal* 419–589(1988).

Comparative Law

Contracting Parties to the CISG

Argentina	Australia	Austria	Belarus
Belgium	Bosnia-Herzegovina	Bulgaria	Burundi
Canada	Chile	China	Croatia
Cuba	Czech Republic	Denmark	Ecuador
Egypt	Estonia	Finland	France
Georgia	Germany	Greece	Guinea
Hungary	Iraq	Italy	Latvia
Lesotho	Lithuania	Luxembourg	Mexico
Moldova	Mongolia	Netherlands	New Zealand
Norway	Peru	Poland	Romania
Russian Federation	Singapore	Slovakia	Slovenia
Spain	Sweden	Switzerland	Syria
Uganda	Ukraine	United States	Uruguay
Uzbekistan	Yugoslavia	Zambia	Kyrgystan
Mauritania	St. Vincent & Grenadines	Israel	

Source: United Nations Treaties at **http://www.un.org/Depts/Treaty/.**

CISG, however, the law of New York is the CISG if the two parties are from different CISG countries. In order to avoid such a quagmire, clear choice of law clauses should be drafted. For example, the above choice of law clause should specify that the "Uniform Commercial Code of the State of New York" is the applicable law.

The CISG has three areas of **jurisdiction.** Article 1 of the CISG states that unless there is an express choice of law clause in the contract, the CISG will be the law of dispute in two situations. First, CISG will apply if the two parties have their places of business in countries that have ratified the CISG. Article 10 of CISG offers guidance about how to determine **place of business** for multinational enterprises. "If a party has more than one place of business, the place of business is that which has the closest relationship to the contract and its performance." Therefore, if a foreign subsidiary of a corporation enters into a contract, the place of business for determining the jurisdiction of the CISG is the location of the subsidiary and not of the parent company.

The second ground for CISG jurisdiction is when only one of the parties is from a CISG country. In that event, the court or arbitral tribunal is instructed to use its **conflict of law rules** to determine the law of the dispute. If the conflict of law rules directs the court or tribunal to the party whose country has ratified the CISG, then the CISG becomes the law of the dispute. It should be noted, however, that the United States opted out of the second ground for jurisdiction. A U.S. court or arbitral tribunal will apply the CISG only when both parties are from different CISG countries.

http://

Legal Information Institute—U.S. conflict of law rules: **http://www.law.cornell.edu/topics/conflicts.html.**

http://

Department of State, Office of Legal Adviser—Private international law database: **www.state.gov/www/global/legal_affairs/private_intl_law.html.** Click on "Transactions Law."

A third ground for the use of the CISG in a dispute is based in customary international law. An arbitral panel or a court may use the CISG as evidence of trade usage instead of applying the law of an individual country. This is exactly what happened in *International Chamber of Commerce Arbitration Case No. 5713 of 1989.* In that case, the contract contained no provisions regarding the substantive law (no choice of law clause). Therefore, the arbitrators will apply the law designated as the proper law by applying conflict of law rules that they deem appropriate. The law of the country of the Seller appeared to be the proper law governing the contract. Instead, the Tribunal found that there is no better source to determine the prevailing trade usage than the terms of the CISG. This was so even though neither the country of the Buyer nor the country of the Seller are parties to that Convention. The issue in the case was the length of time a purchaser had to give notice of defect. The arbitration tribunal disregarded the domestic law's shorter statute of limitations period in favor of the two-year period provided in the CISG. In short, the arbitral tribunal used the CISG as evidence of international trade usage to avoid what it deemed to be an unfair domestic law. The arbitrator's decision stated that "as the applicable provisions of the law of the country where the seller had his place of business appeared to deviate from the generally accepted trade usage as reflected in the CISG in that it imposed extremely short and specific requirements in respect of the buyer giving notice to the seller in case of defects, the tribunal elects to apply the CISG."

This voluntary application of the CISG as evidence of customary international law in the above ICC case should not come as a surprise. The CISG is the product of compromise between the world's major legal systems—common law, civil law, and socialist law. Thus, it possesses a universal appeal that many arbitrators will find appealing in their search for a *lex mercatoria*-type of justification for their awards. The terse, clear, and nonlegal language of the CISG provides arbitrators a good source of supranational rules of commerce.[2]

Commercial Sale of Goods

The CISG covers only transactions for the sale of goods. Thus, sales of services and transfers of intellectual property rights would not come under the jurisdiction of the CISG. In addition, Article 2 excludes certain types of goods from coverage, including goods purchased at auction, electricity, securities, ships, vessels, and aircraft. There are many transactions, however, that include more than one subject matter. For example, the sale of computer software is often a **mixed sale** involving the sale of a tangible item, like a disk or a CD-ROM, along with a service or technical assistance agreement, and a license pertaining to intellectual property rights. Is this type of transaction covered by the CISG? Article 3 provides a two-part test to distinguish a service contract from a sale of goods. First, a contract is not for the sale of goods if the buyer provides a substantial part of the materials used in the production of the goods. This would be considered a contract for labor or assembly services. Second, a preponderant part of the contract is not for the supply of labor or services.

In *Micro Data Systems, Inc. v. Dharma Systems,*[3] the court held that labor can be considered as a component part of a good when determining the applicability of

2. See generally Larry A. DiMatteo, "The CISG as Source of International Customary Law," American Arbitration Association, *Dispute Resolution Journal* (1998).
3. 148 F.3d 649 (7th Cir. 1998).

the UCC to a mixed sale transaction. In that case, the buyer agreed to pay $125,000 for software and $125,000 for services necessary to adapt the system to the buyer's needs. The court ruled that the "services" were not services to be rendered directly to the buyer, but merely the labor to be extended in producing the modified software.

A **computer software sale** normally mixes the characteristics of a sale of goods, a sale of services, and a lease or license of technology, since software possesses both tangible and intangible elements. According to Article 3's second test a software sale will be considered within the scope of the CISG only if a preponderant part of the transaction is for tangible goods. If, for example, a company contracts for software to computerize its inventory the court may look to the allocation of the price within the contract among the different components. Thus, if the contract provided for $20,000 worth of database software and $15,000 worth of support service and labor for data entry, the contract would be considered predominantly one for the sale of goods and covered by the CISG.

One suggested resolution for the intangibility of technology and software is to treat such items as **virtual goods,**[4] the approach taken in applying the UCC to software products. Virtual goods are treated just like conventional goods for purposes of UCC and possibly CISG applications. Article 2 of the UCC covers "transactions in goods." Thus, its coverage is limited not to sales but by the word *transactions.* In contrast, the CISG expressly uses the term "sales" when defining its coverage. Its definition of goods is based primarily upon the concept of *movability.* Software clearly satisfies the requirement of movability.

The crucial determination of CISG applicability is if the sale of a copy of software, along with a license for its use, is considered a transaction in "goods." Generally, items sold by way of license are considered not to be sale of goods. Software licensing agreements, however, often have the characteristics of sale of goods transactions. If the copy being licensed is one for perpetual use for which the licensee pays a one-time licensing fee, then the software is essentially being sold even though the "license" retains title in the name of the licensor. In short, even though ownership over the technology is retained by the licensor, the licensee becomes the owner of the copy. Thus, the CISG is likely to cover sales of "off the shelf" software.

PAROL EVIDENCE RULE AND CISG

The UCC requires that "some writing sufficient to indicate that a contract of sale has been made" must evidence any sale of goods for a price of $500 or more. Also, the party against whom enforcement is sought must have signed the writing. In contrast, the CISG applies the view of many civil law countries that a writing is not required in order to enforce an agreement. By its adoption of the common law's **parol evidence rule,** the UCC writing requirement or **statute of frauds** also prevents the admission of evidence that contradicts the writing. The parol evidence rule protects the sanctity of a written contract intended to be the final agreement or integration of agreements of the parties. The rule prevents admitting into evidence any prior or contemporaneous oral statements or writings that contradict the form contract.

Along with stating the requirements for a legally sufficient writing, UCC Section 2-201 lists a number of exceptions, including the **written confirmation rule,** an order for **specially manufactured goods,** and where the parties' conduct has

4. See Marcus Larson, "Applying Uniform Sales Law to International Software Transactions," 5 *Tulane Journal of International & Comparative Law* 445 (1997).

overtaken the lack of a sufficient writing such as when payment or receipt of goods occurs. The written confirmation rule is available only in commercial transactions since it requires that both parties be merchants. It states that a writing sent by one of the parties confirming the conclusion of a contract is sufficient to satisfy the writing requirement. The other party need not sign or acknowledge receipt of the confirmation in order to be bound by it. Section 2-201 does allow the receiving party to object to the confirmation and thus prevent the formation of a contract. The notice of objection must be given within ten days of the receipt of the written confirmation. The court in *GPL Treatment Ltd. v. Louisiana-Pacific*[5] analyzed the intricacies of the written confirmation rule.

The parol evidence rule seeks to preserve the integrity of written contracts by refusing to allow the admission of oral statements or previous correspondence to contradict the written agreement. Under this rule, when parties place their agreement in writing, all previous oral and written documents merge into the final written agreement. However, such final written agreements may be explained or supplemented by prior dealings, trade usage, or course of performance information. **Prior dealings** include prior contracts and performances under prior contracts between the parties that establish a common basis of understanding and for interpreting subsequent contracts. **Trade usage** refers to the customs and practices regularly observed in a given trade or business. "Usages of trade furnish the background and give meaning to the language used by merchants in that trade."[6] **Course of performance** is premised on the fact that the parties' conduct in performing under the contract is a good indication of what they believe to be its meaning. Section 2-208 of the UCC states that "any course of performance accepted or acquiesced in without objection shall be relevant to determine the meaning of the agreement."

Unlike the UCC, the CISG in its Article 11 states that a "contract need not be evidenced by writing." Also, a contract and its terms may be proven "by *any* means," including witness testimony. Therefore, the potential for liability for representations made during the negotiation stage is greater under the CISG. The UCC's parol evidence rule allows a party to avoid liability for statements made during the negotiations if those statements are not placed within the final written contract. Under the CISG, prior oral statements regarding anything, including quality and performance, are potentially enforceable. An unknowing businessperson could be charged with unexpected liability for oral statements or representations made in informal correspondence. The CISG's lack of a writing requirement and of a parol evidence rule gives the recipient of a letter or documents a strategic advantage in proving enforceability. Also, oral assurances given to persuade another party to enter into a contract may be used to prove intent.

The CISG's lack of a writing requirement is further complicated by Articles 12 and 96, which allow contracting states to *opt out* of Article 11's no writing requirement. Some countries, mostly the former countries of the Soviet Union and socialist law countries, have opted out in favor of domestic laws that require a writing. These countries include Russia, Ukraine, Belarus, Estonia, Hungary, Argentina, Chile, and China.

The importance of the parol evidence rule to contract disputes is discussed in the *MCC-Marble Center* case on page 218. This is the most recent U.S. case involving the interaction of the CISG with other U.S. law. The court is asked to determine if the U.S. parol evidence rule is to be applied to cases involving the CISG.

5. 914 P.2d 682 (Or. Sup. Ct. 1996).
6. UCC Section 1-205, Comment 4.

GPL Treatment, Ltd. v. Louisiana-Pacific

914 P.2d 682 (Or. Sup. Ct. 1996)

This case involves the so-called merchant's exception to the statue of frauds in the Uniform Commercial Code. Plaintiff (GPL) sued defendant (Louisiana-Pacific) for breach of an oral contract to buy 88 truckloads of cedar shakes. Louisiana-Pacific denied the alleged contract and asserted the UCC statute of frauds as an affirmative defense. The relevant text of GPL's form that was entitled "ORDER CONFIRMATION" reads as follows:

"Conditions of Sale:"

All orders accepted subject to strikes, labor troubles, car shortages, or other contingencies beyond our power. Any freight rate increases, sales, or use taxes is for buyers account.

GPL LTD.

*BY:*____________________

"SIGN CONFIRMATION COPY & RETURN"

*BY:*______________________________

Thereafter, the price of cedar shakes dropped and defendant's needs changed. The defendant refused to place orders for more than 13 truckloads. Plaintiff brought a breach of contract action for lost profits.

Van Hoomissen, Justice. Under the written confirmation exception to the statute of frauds, the writing in confirmation of the [oral] contract must be signed by the sender, state a quantity, and evidence a contract for a sale of goods. A written confirmation sent pursuant to the merchant's exception need not contain all material terms of the contract; it must simply confirm a contract and include a quantity term. A merchant who receives a confirmatory writing may escape being bound only by giving a written objection within 10 days. A determination that a writing satisfies the merchant's exception does not prove the existence of a contract, however. It merely prevents the party against whom enforcement is sought from raising the UCC statute of frauds as an affirmative defense.

The defendant raises the issue that the "Sign Confirmation Copy and Return" language on the confirmation required the defendant to sign before a binding contract was to be formed. There is no single correct answer to the question of the effect of a "sign and return" clause. Each writing must be examined independently and in light of its own contents and context. Considering GPL's writing in its entirety, we conclude that notwithstanding the "sign and return" clause, GPL's order confirmation forms are sufficient to satisfy the merchant's exception.

The order confirmation forms that the sellers sent to buyer constituted a writing in confirmation of an alleged oral contract and sufficient against the sender and, thus, the forms satisfied the merchant's exception to the Uniform Commercial Code's statute of frauds, despite the fact that the forms contained a "sign and return" clause.

Graber, Justice, dissenting. The majority holds that the document does not require the recipient to sign the confirmation copy and return it. It reads the "sign and return" language to be nothing more than a request to acknowledge receipt of the form. The majority's reasoning is flawed. A true confirmation requires no response. Here, the document required the prospective buyer to sign and return a copy, thus reducing the document to the status of an offer that would take effect if and when it was "Accepted By" the buyer. In summary, because the document at issue required a response, it did not constitute a "writing in confirmation" of a prior oral agreement as required by the merchant's exception in the Uniform Commercial Code.

Case Highlights

- The Statute of Frauds is an affirmative defense that must be raised and proved by the defendant.
- The written confirmation exception to the Statute of Frauds provides that a writing sent by one merchant to another merchant satisfies the writing requirement unless the other merchant objects within 10 days.
- A sign and return clause may or may not convert a written confirmation into a mere offer.

MCC-Marble Ceramic Center v. Ceramica Nuova D'Agostino, S.P.A.

144 F. 3d 1384 (11th Cir. 1998)

"MCC" is a Florida corporation engaged in the retail sales of imported tiles. "D'Agostino" is an Italian manufacturer of tiles. At a trade show they orally agreed on a sale of tiles. The agreed terms were placed on one of D'Agostino's standard preprinted order forms. The executed forms were printed in Italian. MCC brought suit claiming a breach of the requirements contract when D'Agostino failed to satisfy a number of orders. D'Agostino responded that it was under no legal obligation to fill the orders because MCC had defaulted on payment for previous shipments. MCC responded that the earlier tiles they received were of a lower quality than contracted for and that it was entitled to reduce payment in proportion to the defects. D'Agostino replied that Clause 4 on the reverse side of the purchase order form required that all complaints for defects must be made in writing not later than 10 days after receipt of merchandise and this had not been done by MCC. MCC argued that the parties never intended the terms and conditions printed on the reverse of the order form to apply to their agreement.

Birch, Circuit Judge. Article 8 of the CISG provides: "For purposes of this Convention statements made by and other conduct of a party are to be interpreted according to his intent where the other party knew or should have been aware what that intent was. Due consideration is to be given to *all* relevant circumstances of the case including negotiations." The plain language of the Convention, therefore, requires an inquiry into a party's subjective intent as long as the other party to the contract was aware of that intent. MCC argues that it did not intend to be bound by the terms on the manufacturer's form since it was entirely in Italian. We find it nothing short of astounding that an individual, purportedly experienced in commercial matters, would sign a contract in a foreign language and expect not to be bound simply because he could not comprehend its terms. The general proposition is that they will bind parties who sign contracts regardless of whether they have read them or understand them. Nonetheless, Article 8(1) of the CISG requires a court to consider evidence of the parties' subjective intent. Affidavits of agents of MCC acknowledged that D'Agostino's representatives were aware of MCC's subjective intent not to be bound by the fine print terms.

The issue of whether the parol evidence rule applies to the CISG is a question of first impression in this circuit. It is important to whether the testimony of MCC's subjective intent and D'Agostino's awareness of it will be admitted to contradict or vary the terms of the written contract. We begin by observing that the parol evidence rule, contrary to its title, is a substantive rule of law, not a rule of evidence. The Uniform Commercial Code includes a version of the parol evidence rule that states that "a writing intended by the parties as a final expression of their agreement may not be contradicted by evidence of any prior agreement or contemporaneous oral agreement." The CISG contains no express statement on the role of parol evidence. Moreover, Article 8(3) [of the CISG] expressly directs the courts to give "due consideration to all relevant circumstances of the case including the negotiations." It is a clear instruction to admit and consider parol evidence regarding the negotiations to the extent they reveal the parties' subjective intents.

Another court, however, appears to have arrived at a contrary conclusion. In *Beijing Metals & Minerals Import/Export Corp. v. American Bus. Ctr., Inc.*,[7] a defendant sought to avoid summary judgment on a contract claim by relying on evidence of negotiated oral terms that the parties did not include in their written agreement. The court held that the parol evidence rule would apply regardless of whether Texas law or the CISG governed the dispute. We find the Beijing opinion is not particularly persuasive on this point. Moreover, the parties in the present case have not cited to us any persuasive authority from the courts of other States party to the CISG.

Our reading of Article 8(3) as a rejection of the parol evidence rule, however, is in accordance with the great weight of academic authority. Furthermore, a wide number of the other States that are parties to the CISG have rejected the rule in their domestic jurisdictions. One of the primary factors motivating the negotiation and adoption of the CISG was to provide parties to international contracts for the sale of goods with some degree of certainty as to the principles of law that would govern potential disputes. Courts applying the CISG cannot, therefore, upset the parties reliance on the Convention by substituting familiar principles of domestic law [such as the parol evidence rule] when the Convention requires a different result. Moreover, to the extent parties wish to avoid parol evidence problems they can do so by including a merger clause in their agreement that extin-

7. 993 F.2d 1178 (5th Cir. 1993).

guishes any and all prior agreements and understandings not expressed in the writing.

What a judge or jury does with the parol evidence once it is entered into evidence is within their discretion as the weighers of the evidence. A reasonable finder of fact is free to disregard the parol evidence that conflicts with the written contract. Thus, it may disregard testimony that sophisticated international merchants signed a contract without intending to be bound as simply too incredible to believe and hold MCC to the conditions printed on the reverse side of the contract. However, this is for the trier of fact to determine. Moreover, because Article 8 requires a court to consider any "practices which the parties have established between themselves, usage, and any subsequent conduct of the parties" in interpreting contracts, whether the parties intended to adhere to the ten day limit for complaints of defects, as stated on the reverse of the contract, will have an impact on whether MCC was bound to adhere to the limit in order to preserve its warranty claims.

The CISG precludes the application of the parol evidence rule, which would otherwise bar the consideration of evidence concerning a prior or contemporaneously negotiated oral agreement. Since material issues of fact remain, we cannot affirm the district court's summary judgment in D'Agostino's favor.

Case Highlights

- The court suggests that the use of a merger clause would be an effective means to prevent parol evidence from being admitted. A merger clause is a statement that the final written contract is evidence of the parties' agreement.
- Since the CISG has been adopted in numerous countries, any previous foreign decisions on a particular issue should be reviewed in order to obtain uniform interpretations of the CISG.
- The CISG provides a price reduction in its Article 50 as a remedy for the delivery of nonconforming goods.
- The two-year period found in Article 39 of the CISG is the outside limit for giving a notice of defect. A party must give notice within a reasonable time which will normally mean within days of finding the defect. In addition, the parties can agree to a shorter notice period.

CISG AND UNIFORM COMMERCIAL CODE

This section will focus on the substantive provisions of the CISG in order to instruct as to the potential for unintended legal liability in international contracting. These substantive provisions will be compared to relevant provisions in the UCC (see Comparative Law: Selective Comparison of CISG and UCC).[8] Although the UCC acted as a blueprint for the drafting of the CISG, the U.S. exporter must be cognizant of the fundamental differences between the two laws. Ten years after its adoption by Congress, the CISG remains a complete unknown to many businesspersons and lawyers. It is important that the CISG be understood and applied effectively by U.S. exporters and importers. It not only places some unique responsibilities on sellers and buyers of goods, it also provides a number of rights and remedies not found in U.S. law.

http://

Uniform Commercial Code: **http://www.law.cornell.edu/ucc/ucc.table.html**

Mechanics of Formation

The CISG can be divided into four groups: General Provisions (Articles 1–13), **Contract Formation** (Articles 14–24), **Rights and Obligations** (Articles 25–88), and **Ratification** (Articles 89–101). This section will examine the group dealing with Contract Formation, along with articles in the Ratification group that bear on formation. All legal systems recognize the formation of a contract when an **offer** and

8. See generally HENRY GABRIEL, PRACTITIONER'S GUIDE TO THE CISG AND UCC (1994); WILLIAM HANCOCK, ed., GUIDE TO THE INTERNATIONAL SALE OF GOODS (1986). See also B. Blair Crawford, "Drafting Considerations Under the 1980 United Nations Convention on Contracts for the International Sale of Goods," 8 *Journal of Law & Commerce* 187 (1988).

Comparative Law

Selective Comparison of CISG and UCC

CISG Description	CISG Articles	UCC Description	UCC Sections
Writing Requirement	11, 13, 14	Statute of Frauds	2-201
Parol Evidence Rule	8, 9	Parol Evidence Rule	2-202
Formation	14, 19, 20–21, 23	Formation	2-204
Obligation of Good Faith	None	Obligation of Good Faith	1-202
Revocability of Offer	16	Firm Offer Rule	2-205
Acceptance Upon Receipt	18	Mailbox Rule	2-206
Battle of the Forms	14, 19	Additional Terms	2-207
Fixing Price Term	14, 55, 56	Open Price Term	2-305
Fixing Place of Delivery	57	Place for Delivery	2-308
Time for Delivery; *Nachfrist*	33, 63	Time for Delivery, Performance	2-309
Place of Payment	57	Time for Payment	2-310
Avoidance; Rejection	81, 86	Manner of Rejection	2-602
Limited Right to Reject Goods	49	Perfect Tender Rule	2-601
Warranty Against Third Party	41, 42	Warranty of Title	2-312
Warranties	35	Warranties	2-313, 314, 315, 316
Inspection	38	Right to Inspection	2-513
Nonconformity; Nondelivery	36, 49, 51	Rights on Improper Delivery	2-601
Notice of Avoidance	49	Waiver of Failure to Particularize	2-605
Failure to Notify	49	Acceptance of Goods	2-606
Notice of Nonconformity (particularized notice)	39	Notice of Defect (generalized notice)	2-607(3)(a)
Fundamental Breach; Notice	25, 49, 73, 81–82	Revocation of Acceptance	2-608
Anticipatory Breach	71, 72, 73	Anticipatory Repudiation	2-609, 610
Price Reduction Remedy	50	Not Available	
Nachfrist Notice	47, 48, 63	Not Available	
Impediment Exemption	79	Commercial Impracticability	2-615
General Notice	27	Notice of Excuse	2-616

acceptance are exchanged. The key issue is determining the exact time of formation. This determination is important in order to decide the effectiveness of attempted **revocations** by the **offeror** and attempted **rejections** (subsequent to the sending of an acceptance) by the **offeree.** The offeror is the party making an offer to contract. The offeree is the party that receives an offer and is empowered to create a binding contract through an acceptance of the offer. Sometimes a contract is considered formed when the offer invites the offeree to accept by the commencing of performance and performance begins. Commencement of performance may not be sufficient, however. Most legal systems require the offeree to notify the offeror within a reasonable time that performance has commenced. Section 2-206(2) of the UCC states that "where the beginning of a requested performance is a reasonable mode of acceptance an offeror who is not notified of acceptance within a reasonable time may treat the offer as having lapsed before acceptance."

http://
Pace University Institute of International Commercial Law—recent cases and developments interpreting the CISG: **http://www.cisg.law.pace.edu**.

The common law rule known as the dispatch or **mailbox rule** holds that a contract is formed upon the sending of the acceptance by placing it into a reasonable means of transmission. All other legal systems of the world, and the CISG, find a contract only when and if the acceptance or notice of the acceptance is received by the original offeror. Article 1326 of the Italian Civil Code states that an acceptance must be communicated to the offeror within the term that is deemed reasonable according to the nature of the business or trade customs.

Most international commercial transactions involve long-term negotiations, along with numerous exchanges of correspondences and documents. It is often the difficult task of a court or arbitral tribunal to analyze the numerous exchanges to determine if and when a contract was formed. Articles 14–24 of the CISG, similar to those found in U.S. law, outline a number of offer-acceptance rules to be used to resolve formation issues. The following Hungarian court decision, *Pratt & Whitney v. Maler,* was one of the first to apply these rules.

Battle of Forms

Most international export transactions make use of standard forms to expedite the negotiation and conclusion of contracts. Exhibits 8.1 and 8.2 show a standard purchase order and the fine print or **boilerplate** found on the reverse of a *pro forma* invoice. Either one of such forms, along with others such as price quotes or written confirmations, may act as the offers and acceptances in the contract formation process. The chronological order of communication will determine, for example, if a purchase order acts as an offer or as an acceptance.

Most exporters and importers will review the front page of the other party's form (see Exhibit 8.1: Purchase Order). Few will take the time to read and understand the "Terms and Conditions" on the reverse. Not reading the boilerplate is dangerous because the terms on the reverse side of each party's respective forms are often in conflict or contain terms that the other party would not have agreed to if it was aware of them at the time of formation. For example, the "Terms and Conditions" in Exhibit 8.2 *Pro Forma* Invoice absolve the seller of any responsibility for the goods when they are delivered to any third party such as a freight forwarder or common carrier (paragraphs 1, 2, 3). This term may conflict with the trade terms on the face of the form.

Paragraph 4 in Exhibit 8.2 makes the seller's quotations as to freight and insurance *nonbinding*. Paragraph 5 limits seller's liability for its own negligent acts to $50 per shipment. Paragraph 6 requires the buyer to notify seller of any defects in the goods within 60 days of the date of exportation or lose its right to sue for breach of warranty. Paragraph 7 allows the seller to retain a lien on the goods for "all charges or expenses incurred by the Seller in connection with the shipment to the Purchaser." Paragraph 8 absolves seller from any governmental requirements pertaining to the shipment of the goods including marking and health regulations. Paragraph 9 mandates that any dispute must be settled in a court near the seller (City of Miami) and using the law of the Seller's place of business (State of Florida).

Pratt & Whitney Corp. v. Malev Hungarian Airlines

Metropolitan Court of Budapest, 13 Bp. P.O.B. 16 (1991)

Malev Airlines (defendant) entered into negotiations with Pratt & Whitney (plaintiff) to supply it with jet engines to be installed on jumbo jets that defendant was purchasing from Boeing Aircraft or Airbus of France. After carrying on thorough negotiations, Pratt & Whitney sent a meticulously written proposal of 15 pages to defendant on December 14, 1990, with a deadline for the proposal of December 21, 1990. Defendant accepted the proposal on December 21, 1990. After numerous other discussions and correspondences, defendant informed plaintiff in a March 25, 1991 letter that it no longer planned on buying plaintiff's engine. The issues for the court included whether the proposal without a fixed price or quantity was an offer, whether the defendant's response was an acceptance, and whether aircraft parts were covered under the CISG.

Hungarian Court. The applicable law of this case is the Vienna Sales Convention (CISG). Article 2 of the CISG excludes from coverage the sale of "ships, vessels, hovercraft, or aircraft." Does this exclusion include aircraft engines and parts? We believe that such component parts are covered as contracts relating to the production of goods as defined in Article 3 of the Convention. The defendant argues that Plaintiff's proposal of December 14, 1990, was of a general informative character, not an offer, but only a letter of intent. Furthermore, there were further discussions regarding the equipment after the December 14, 1990, proposal and the merchandise was not properly defined in that proposal.

According to Article 14 of the CISG, a proposal to be an offer need only be addressed to one or more definite persons, be adequately specified, and indicate the offerer's intention to bind itself in case of its acceptance. A proposal is adequately defined if it indicates the goods and fixes the quantity and price expressly or contains provisions for their definition. We hold that the proposal leaves no doubt about its subject, that it indicates unambiguously the goods subject of the sale. Because it leaves to the buyer the exact engine to be purchased along with the quantity of the order is not critical. The number of engines will be decided based upon the number of airplanes the defendant decides to buy in the future. The proper indication of the goods is not affected by the condition that according to the proposal the buyer could choose from among the enumerated engines. Therefore, plaintiff's proposal of December 14, 1990, was a legal offer under the CISG.

The next issue was whether defendant's response of December 21, 1990, was an acceptance under Article 18 of the CISG. It is noted that the offer contained the language that the defendant's "acceptance of this proposal is conditional upon the approvals of the governments of Hungary and the United States." This condition does not prevent the formation of a contract. Article 23 of the CISG states that a contract becomes valid when the offeror receives a notification of acceptance. We believe that defendant's response of December 21, 1990, established a valid agreement. The court finds the defendant in breach of contract under the CISG.

Case Highlights

- Although ships, vessels, and aircraft are excluded from the CISG, a sale of parts for such items is covered by the CISG.
- An offer is sufficient even if it allows the offeree to fix the quantity term at some later date.
- A conditional acceptance does not prevent the formation of a contract.

Paragraph 10 passes the costs of any litigation brought by the Seller, including attorneys fees, to the purchaser. The onesided nature of these terms will become important only if the parties are involved in a contract law dispute, but by the time of a dispute, it is too late for the purchaser to object to the onerous terms. Exchanging forms with conflicting or varying terms is referred to as the **battle of the forms.**

A U.S. businessperson familiar only with the UCC will be exposed to unexpected consequences under the CISG in a battle of the forms scenario. Article 19 of the CISG resolves a conflict in the exchange of forms differently than does Arti-

EXHIBIT 8.1 *Purchase Order*

PURCHASE ORDER
(ORDEN DE COMPRA)
January 15, 1999

No. 7777895

To: Latin America Exporting Co.
P.O. Box 54321
Miami, Florida 33152
USA

Date Required: March 15, 1999
Deliver to: Compania Mundial
Mexico City, Mexico
Payment: Irrevocable LOC

Terms of Payment

CASH AGAINST DOCUMENTS

Payment Against the Following Documents:

Commercial Invoice ( ) Packing List ( )
Insurance Certificate ( ) Bill of Lading ( )
Quality Certificate ( ) Airway Bill ( )
Forwarders Receipt ( )

Shipped By: ____________

Final Destination: ____________

Forwarders Insurance Taken By: ____________

Trade terms governed by INCOTERMS 1990 CIF Mexico City

Identifying Marks	Quantity	Description	Unit Price	Amount
C&M "Made in USA"	350	Model #345 HTS # 8059101345	US $45.99	$
C&M "Made in USA"	150	Model #198 HTS # 8059101152	US $74.50	$
			Total	$

Packing: Each in Cardboard Box,144 per double export carton, weighing 14 & 16 kilograms and measuring 25x25x10 cm.

Shipment: via M/V Hathaway from Port of Miami

Payment: Irrevocable Letter of Credit for 110% of CIF value at sight, through Banco de Mexico to Nations Bank, Miami, Florida

Notify Party: Towers of Mexico Customs Broker

Confirmed By: ____________

cle 2-207 of the UCC. For example, a seller responds to a purchase order ("the offer") with a confirming invoice ("the acceptance"). The confirming invoice, however, includes an **additional term** that limits purchaser's ability to make a claim for breach of warranty by providing a short notice period. What is the legal effect of the additional notice requirement? If construed as a nonmaterial modification, the CISG and the UCC would acknowledge the contract formation, incorporating the additional term. Article 19(3) of the CISG, however, broadly defines *material* to include "among other things, price, payment, quality and quantity of the goods, place and time of delivery, *extent of one party's liability to the other,* or relating to the settlement of disputes." In essence, the CISG adopts the old common law **mirror image rule** in which the acceptance must be a mirror image of the offer. Thus,

http://
Guide to the CISG: **http://www.jura.uni-freiburg.de/ipri/cisg.**

EXHIBIT 8.2 *Pro Forma Invoice—Terms and Conditions*

Pro Forma Invoice
Terms and Conditions
(Please read carefully.)

1. Services by Third Parties: Unless the Company carries, stores, or otherwise physically handles the shipment, and the loss, damage, or delay occurs during such activity, the Company assumes no liability as a carrier, but undertakes only to use reasonable care in the selection of carriers, truckmen, lightermen, forwarders, customhouse brokers, warehousemen, and others to whom it may entrust the goods for delivery unless a separate bill of lading or other contract of carriage is issued by the Company, in which event the terms thereof shall govern.
2. Liability Limitations of Third Parties: The Company is authorized to select all necessary third parties as required to transport the goods, all of whom shall be considered as the agents of the Purchaser and subject to all conditions as to limitation of liability and to all rules and regulations and conditions appearing in bills of lading or receipts issued by such third parties. The Company shall not be liable for any loss, damage, expense, or delay to the goods for any reason whatsoever when the goods are in the possession of third parties.
3. Choosing Routes or Agents: Unless specified by the Customer in writing, the Company has complete freedom in choosing the means, route, and procedure to be followed in the handling, transportation, and delivery of the goods.
4. Quotations Not Binding: Quotations as to fees, rates of duty, freight charges, insurance premiums, or other charges are for informational purposes only and are subject to change without notice unless the Company in writing specifically undertakes the transportation of the shipment at the specified rate.
5. Limitation of $50 per Shipment: The Customer agrees that the Company shall in no event be liable for any loss, expense, or delay to the goods resulting from the negligence or fault of the Company for any amount in excess of $50 per shipment.
6. Presenting Claims: In no event shall the Company be liable for any act or omission or default unless the claim is presented to it at its office within 60 days from the date of exportation of the goods in a written statement to which sworn proof of claim shall be attached.
7. General Lien on Any Property: The Company shall have a general lien on any and all property and documents relating thereto of the Purchaser in its possession or en route, for all claims for charges, expenses or advance incurred by the Company in connection with any shipments to the Purchaser, and if such claims remain unsatisfied for a period of thirty days, the Company may sell at public auction or private sale, and apply the net proceeds of the sale to the payment of the amount due Company. The Purchaser remains liable for any deficiency in the sale.
8. No Responsibility for Governmental Requirements: It is the responsibility of the Purchaser to know and inform the Company of the marking requirements of the country of importation, and all other safety and health regulations, and all other requirements of law or official regulations. The Company shall not be responsible for action taken or fines or penalties assessed by any governmental agency against the shipment.
9. Construction of Terms and Venue: The foregoing terms and conditions shall be construed according to the laws of the State of Florida. Unless otherwise consented to in writing by the Company, no legal proceeding against the Company may be instituted by either the Purchaser, its assigns or subrogee, except in the City of Miami, Florida.
10. Costs of Collection: Purchaser shall pay all costs, charges, and expenses including attorney's fees, reasonably incurred or paid by the Company (including attorney's fees for any appeals taken) because of the failure of the Purchaser to perform and comply with the terms and conditions of this agreement including payment of monies due and every such payment shall bear interest from the date at the highest rate permitted by law.

under the CISG the additional term converts the attempted acceptance into a counteroffer, resulting in a finding of no contract.

The impact of the CISG's adoption of the mirror image rule may be profound. The use of standard forms in the formation of modern contracts is a universal practice. Invariably, any time seller's and buyer's forms are exchanged there will be conflicting terms in the fine print that neither party is likely to read unless a dispute arises. Under the CISG's broad materiality standard, the contracts thus formed are technically unenforceable.

A German Court seemed to recognize the reality of standard form contracting and ignored the broad materiality definition in Article 19(3). It held that a restrictive notice provision pertaining to claims of defects was not a material term. The notification of nonconformity term would seem to come within the purview of Article 19(3) as a term relating to the "extent of one party's liability to the other party." The German court's decision demonstrates that until there are enough cases interpreting the CISG, contracting parties are likely to be surprised by some of the decisions produced by national courts applying the CISG. One way to avoid a battle of the forms is to use a single or model contract that both parties sign.

The battle of the forms scenario is illustrated in *Filanto, S.P.A. v. Chilewich International Corp.* In that case one of the parties attempted in its offer to incorporate another document by reference. A belated acceptance attempted to delete the reference in order to avoid an arbitration clause. The issues for the court were whether a contract had been formed and, if so, under whose terms.

Filanto, S.P.A. v. Chilewich International Corp.

789 F. Supp. 1229 (S.D.N.Y. 1992)

Italian footwear manufacturer brought action against New York export-import firm, alleging breach of contract. This case is a striking example of how a lawsuit involving a relatively straightforward international commercial transaction can raise an array of complex questions. Defendant Chilewich signed a contract with a Russian importer for a long-term supply of footwear. This "Russian Contract" contained an arbitration clause: "All disputes are to be settled by the Arbitration tribunal of the Chamber of Commerce in Moscow, Russia."

Chilewich then entered into negotiations with Filanto, an Italian manufacturer, to supply the shoes needed for the Russian contract. After a negotiation meeting, Chilewich sent Filanto a letter, dated July 27, 1989, that stated: "Attached please find our contract to cover the purchases from you. Same is governed by the conditions which are enumerated in the standard contract in effect with the Russian buyers, copy of which is also enclosed." Subsequently, Chilewich procured a letter of credit to the benefit of Filanto as required under the contract. Soon thereafter, Filanto began to perform on the contract.

On September 2, 1989, Chilewich received a letter from Filanto that included the following statement: "Returning back the enclosed contracts signed for acceptance, if we do not misunderstand, regarding the Russian contract, we have to respect only the following points: Packing and marking, way of shipment, delivery." After its Russian buyer rejected an earlier shipment of shoes, Chilewich never purchased a subsequent order of 90,000 pairs of boots. It is Chilewich's failure to do so that forms the basis of this lawsuit. Chilewich commenced an arbitration action in Moscow. Filanto moved to enjoin the arbitration, or alternatively, for an order directing that arbitration be held in New York rather than Moscow because of unsettled political conditions in Russia.

Brieant, Chief Judge. The facts indicate that when Filanto thought it was desirable to do so, it recognized that it was bound by the incorporation by reference of portions of the Russian contract. Also, Chapter 2 of the Federal Arbitration Act comprises the Convention on the Recognition and Enforcement of Foreign Arbitral

Awards. The Arbitration Convention requires courts to recognize "any agreement in writing under which the parties undertake to submit to arbitration." The term "agreement in writing" is defined as "an arbitral clause in a contract or an arbitration agreement, signed by the parties or contained in an exchange of letters or telegrams." The threshold question is whether these parties actually agreed to arbitrate their disputes. The Federal Arbitration Act controls this determination.

The "federal law of contracts" to be applied in this case is found in the United Nations Convention on Contracts for the International Sale of Goods (CISG). The parties offer varying interpretations of the numerous letters and documents exchanged between them. There simply is no satisfactory explanation as to why Filanto failed to object to the incorporation by reference of the Russian contract in a timely fashion. Chilewich had in the meantime commenced its performance under the Agreement by furnishing a letter of credit to Filanto. An offeree who, knowing that the offeror has commenced performance, fails to notify the offeror of its objection to the terms of the contract within a reasonable time will be deemed to have assented to those terms. The August 7, 1990, acceptance, noting its objection to the arbitration clause, to Chilewich's March 13, 1990, Memorandum Agreement was untimely due to Filanto's awareness of Chilewich's commencement of performance. Furthermore, Filanto's June 21, 1991, letter makes reference to the "Master Purchase Contract" (the Russian contract). This letter comes within CISG Article 8(3) directive that "in determining the intent of a party due consideration is to be given to any *subsequent conduct* of the parties."

Heeding the presumption in favor of arbitration, which is even stronger in the context of international commercial transactions, the Court holds that Filanto is bound by the terms of the March 13 Memorandum Agreement and so must arbitrate its dispute in Moscow. SO ORDERED.

Case Highlights

- The Federal Arbitration Act requires courts to enforce reasonable arbitration clauses. Any state law that restricts the federal policy in favor of arbitration is preempted.
- The ability of one party to add or delete contract terms in the battle of the forms scenario is lost if the party delays its response beyond a reasonable time or after the other party begins performance.
- A court will take into consideration the conduct of the parties following the formation of the contract (course of performance) when interpreting a contract.

Contract Interpretation

A famous case of contract interpretation involved the judicial attempt to define the word "chicken." The *Frigaliment Importing v. B.N.S. International Sales* case illustrates how a court attempts to define terms in a contract through its reading of the contract itself and its use of evidence of prior dealings, course of performance, and trade usage. It also introduces a number of important legal concepts including the **four-corner analysis,** the **totality of the circumstances,** and the **reasonable person standard.**

The *Frigaliment* case illustrates a hierarchy of tools that courts use in interpreting contracts. The first level is studying the language of the contract to determine its meaning. This is sometimes referred to a four-corners analysis or the plain meaning rule. If the language is unclear, the court proceeds to the next level of analysis. It will analyze the relationship and actions of the contracting parties. First, it will look at evidence of "course of performance" of the parties for the contract in dispute. In short, the postformation conduct of the parties will be reviewed to determine what the parties believed that the contract meant. If the meaning is still unclear, the court

Frigaliment Importing v. B.N.S. International Sales Corp.

190 F. Supp. 116 (S.D. N. Y. 1960)

Action by buyer of fresh frozen chicken against seller for breach of warranty. Two contracts are in suit. In the first, a New York sales corporation confirmed the sale to plaintiff, a Swiss corporation, of: "US fresh Frozen Chicken, Grade A, Government Inspected, 2½ to 3 lbs. each, all chickens individually wrapped, packed in secured fiber cartons suitable for export." The second contract was identical save that only 50,000 lbs. of the heavier "chicken" were called for. When the initial shipment arrived in Switzerland, plaintiff found that the birds were not young chickens suitable for broiling and frying but stewing chickens or "fowl." Protest ensued. Nevertheless, shipment under the second contract was made again being stewing chickens. The issue is: What is a chicken?

Friendly, Circuit Judge. Plaintiff says "chicken" means a young chicken, suitable for broiling and frying. Defendant says "chicken" means any bird of the genus that meets contract specifications on weight and quality, including what it calls "stewing chicken" and plaintiff pejoratively terms "fowl." To support its claim, plaintiff sends a number of volleys over the net; defendant essays to return them and adds a few serves of its own. Assuming that both parties were acting in good faith, the case nicely illustrates Oliver Wendel Holmes's remark "that the making of a contract depends not on the agreement of two minds in one intention, but on the agreement of two sets of external signs—not on the parties' having *meant* the same thing but on having *said* the same thing." Since the word "chicken" standing alone is ambiguous, I turn first to see whether the contract itself offers any aid to its interpretation.

Plaintiff's first contention hinges on an exchange of cablegrams which preceded the formal contracts. After testing the market price, plaintiff accepted, and sent defendant a confirmation. These and subsequent cables between plaintiff and defendant, which laid the basis for the additional quantities under the first and for all of the second contract, were predominantly in German, although they used the English word "chicken." Defendant's agent testified that when asked plaintiff's agent what kind of chicken were wanted, received the answer "any kind of chickens." Defendant relies on conduct by the plaintiff after the first shipment had been received. Defendant argues that if plaintiff was sincere in thinking it was entitled to young chickens, plaintiff would not have allowed the shipment under the second contract to go forward.

Plaintiff's next contention is that there was a definite trade usage that "chicken" meant "young chicken." Here there was no proof of actual knowledge of the alleged usage; indeed it is quite plain that defendant's belief was to the contrary. Plaintiff endeavored to establish such a usage by the testimony of witnesses. However, one witness stated that a careful businessman protected himself by using "broiler" when that was what he wanted and "fowl" when he wished older birds. An employee of a company that publishes a daily market report on the poultry trade gave his view that the trade meaning of "chicken" was "broilers and fryers." Defendant provided a witness that said that in the trade, "chicken" would encompass all the various classifications of chicken. Defendant also provided a regulation of the Department of Agriculture that defined "chickens" as various classes including "*Broiler or fryer,* Roaster, Capon, Stag, Hen or *stewing* chicken or *fowl.*"

When all the evidence is reviewed, it is clear defendant believed it could comply with the contracts by delivering stewing chickens. Plaintiff asserts that it is equally plain that plaintiff's own subjective intent was to obtain broilers and fryers. Because plaintiff has the burden of showing that "chicken" was used in the narrower rather than in the broader sense, and this it has not sustained, judgment shall be entered dismissing the complaint.

Case Highlights

- A four-corners analysis requires a court or arbitral panel to find the answer to the issue in dispute within the contract.
- In a totality of the circumstances analysis the court or arbitrator looks outside of the contract to interpret its meaning.
- In performing a totality of the circumstances analysis, a court will apply the reasonable person standard.
- Under the reasonable person standard, the contract is interpreted from the perspective of a reasonable person in that particular trade or business.

http://
"Contract Interpretation and the Parol Evidence Rule":
http://www.wisbar.org/cle/samples/Contract00_05.pdf.

will study any prior contracts or dealings between the parties to infer a previously established meaning. The final level of analysis is to infer a meaning from outside such as trade usage or custom. In *Frigaliment* none of these levels of analysis provided a clear meaning for the word *chicken*. The result was the plaintiff lost because of its failure to meet its burden of proof regarding the meaning of the word.

The second and third levels of analysis are referred to as a totality of the circumstances analysis. The courts often look to surrounding circumstances surrounding the execution of a written contract to find the parties' intent. Lord Wilberforce in *Reardon Smith Line, Ltd.*[9] defined the totality of the circumstances analysis as the need in "commercial contracts for the court to know the commercial purpose of the contract. This presupposes knowledge of the genesis of the transaction, background, context, and the market in which the parties were operating." The background and context include oral negotiations, prior dealings, trade usage, and custom.

The common law has long used the reasonable person standard as an aid in interpreting and enforcing contracts. The reasonable person reflects the totality of the circumstances analysis because it is often constructed using the trade usage, customs, and practices of businesspersons in a particular trade or business. The role of the reasonable person standard has become more important because of the modern innovation of standard forms, since most terms of standard forms are not the product of negotiations and conscious agreement. The reasonable person standard is used to interpret the so-called fine print or boilerplate terms to see if the terms meet the measure of commercial reasonableness.

The traditional focus held that the act of signing a standard form was evidence that the signer intended to accept all of its terms. This approach became increasingly untenable as it became apparent that in reality there was no such actual consent; usually at least one of the parties does not read or understand the fine print of the preprinted form. The role of the reasonable person was thus expanded to determine what reasonable terms would be included and what unreasonable terms would be excluded.

Karl Llewellyn[10] devised two roles for the reasonable person standard in the area of standard form contracts: (1) to interpret the meaning of the terms expressly negotiated by the parties, and (2) to determine what non-negotiated terms are to be reconstructed or expelled due to unreasonableness. The reasonable person standard is also used to determine what reasonable terms are to be inferred to fill in gaps in the contract. For purposes of determining reasonableness, the reasonable person standard looks to the terms generally found in such contracts. The reasonable person standard is used to conform the boilerplate terms to the spirit of the contract as represented by the negotiated terms and the type of transaction being undertaken.[11]

Duty to Inspect and Proper Notice

A purchaser of goods may reject delivered goods if it gives timely and effective notice of a nonconformity. What is proper notice under the CISG? The buyer has

9. Reardon Smith Line, Ltd. v. Yngvar Hansen-Tangen [1976] 1 W.L.R. 989, 996 (Eng. H.L.).

10. Karl Llewellyn was the reporter and chief architect of the Uniform Commercial Code.

11. See generally Larry A. DiMatteo, "The Counterpoise of Contracts: The Reasonable Person Standard and the Subjectivity of Judgment," 48 South Carolina Law Review 293, 338–41 (1997).

three duties: First, Article 38 (1) requires the buyer to inspect the goods "within as short a period as is practicable." Second, the buyer must inform the seller of the nonconformity "within a reasonable time after he has discovered it or ought to have discovered it." Any claim for nonconformity is time barred if not reported within two years of delivery to the buyer. Third, the notice to the seller must specify the nature of the nonconformity.

A German court dealt with the notion of due diligence in the inspection of goods. Following customer complaints about measurements, sewing quality, and color fading, a German retailer attempted to cancel a second order with an Italian manufacturer. The goods were shipped nonetheless. The retailer inspected only a selected sample of the shoes and failed to detect any nonconformities. Following additional customer complaints, the retailer attempted to reject the order due to nonconformity. The court found in favor of the seller, holding that the expiration of sixteen days rendered the buyer's notice as untimely.[12] The court's rationale smacks of due diligence: Because the buyer was aware of nonconformities stemming from the first order, it should have performed a more detailed inspection of the shoes in the second order. The court presumed that such an inspection would have uncovered the nonconformity at an earlier date.

http://

United Nations Commission on International Trade Law (UNCITRAL)—abstracts of foreign case law on CISG (CLOUT): **http://www.uncitral.org/en-index.htm**.

In another case, pursuant to an installment contract a German clothing retailer gave notice to an Italian seller of fashion goods eight and twelve days after delivery of two shipments. The notice stated that the goods failed to conform because of "poor workmanship and improper fit." The German court bypassed the issue of timeliness and held the notice ineffective due to its lack of specificity.[13] The specificity required under the UCC, however, seems to be less demanding than that required under the CISG. Initially, the rejecting party needs only to state in general terms the reason for the rejection. Comment 1 states that it is the policy of this Section to permit the "buyer to give a quick and informal notice of defects in a tender without penalizing him for omissions in his statement."[14] There is one exception to the general character of the UCC notice requirement. Where the defect in a tender is one which could have been cured by the seller, a buyer who merely rejects without stating his objections is probably acting in commercial bad faith. Except for the situation where the seller has the ability and right to cure, this clarification indicates that a general notice and not a particularized one is sufficient to meet the dictates of the UCC.

Nachfrist *Notice*

Another concept foreign to Anglo-American contract law is the civil law notion of ***nachfrist* notice.** The underlying premise behind this concept is that a delay in performance does not in itself constitute a material breach of the contract. The notion allows a buyer or seller to fix an additional time for performance beyond that which is specified in the contract. The additional time must be of a reasonable duration. The reasonableness of the time extension will depend on the nature, extent, and consequences of the delay, along with the importance to the buyer of prompt delivery.

http://

"*Nachfrist* Notice and Avoidance Under the CISG": **http://www.cisg.law.pace.edu/cisg/biblio/kimbel.html**.

12. General Court of Stuttgart, 3 KFh 97/89, CLOUT Case No. 4 (Case Law on UNCITRAL Text.). CLOUT is a reporting service accessible through the United Nations document services.
13. General Court of München, 17 HKO 3726/89, CLOUT Case No. 3, UNCITRAL Abstract, A/CN.9/SER.C/Abstracts/1(May 19, 1993).
14. UCC § 2-605, Comment 1 (1990).

The civil law's ability to affix additional time was adopted in Articles 47 through 49 and 63 of the CISG. The buyer may give notice to the seller that she will accept delivery beyond the time prescribed. The buyer is then enjoined from taking legal action during the *nachfrist* period and must accept any proper tender of performance during that period. If the seller makes a request for a *nachfrist* extension, then the buyer is obligated to respond to the request. Failure to do so results in the automatic granting of the additional time. The failure of the breaching party to perform during the extension allows the other party to declare an immediate voiding of the contract. (See Comparative Law: A *Nachfrist* Case Study.)

A U.S. businessperson unaware of the practice of *nachfrist* notice will be subject to unintended liabilities. She may mistake a *nachfrist* notice as a meaningless,

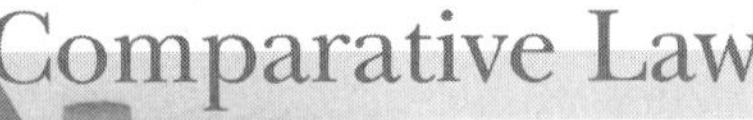

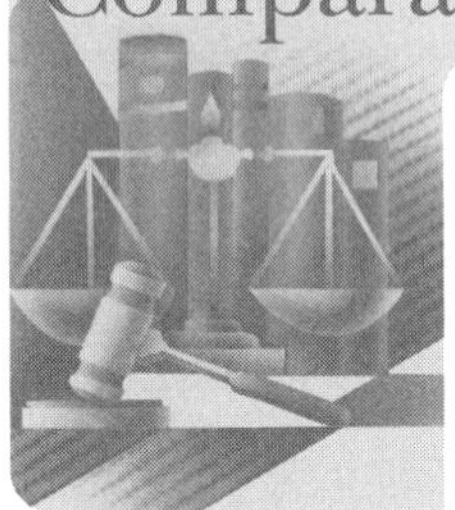

A *Nachfrist* Case Study

A contract between an Italian clothing manufacturer and a German retailer provided for a schedule of delivery dates stating that the clothes were "autumn goods, to be delivered July, August, September, plus or minus." *Municipal Court of Holstein, 5 C 73/89, CLOUT Case No. 7.* The first delivery of the goods was made on September 26. The retailer rejected the delivery of the goods as untimely. The court rejected the buyer's argument that the term "autumn goods" envisioned delivery of three equal shipments for the months of July, August, and September. Such misunderstandings are common given the problems of linguistic and cultural differences, along with the tendency of businesspersons toward brevity in business communiqués. *What could the German importer have done differently to avoid such a misunderstanding?* First, it should have defined the term "autumn goods" more carefully in order to ensure timely and qualitatively effective delivery of the goods. Second, as suggested by the German court, they could have made use of the *nachfrist* notice provision in the CISG. The purchaser should have sent notice pursuant to Article 47 of the CISG. Article 47 states that the "buyer may fix an additional period of time of reasonable length for performance by the seller." Article 48 allows a seller to "request" additional time for performance. Such notice of the granting of an additional time to perform is normally given in conjunction with a fixed and known delivery date. The German court held that "the buyer did not effectively void the contract by refusing acceptance of the goods *without fixing an additional period* in the previous cases of nondelivery."

The implications of this decision could support a number of interpretations. First, the use of *nachfrist* notice in this situation would have been evidence that the parties had indeed intended multiple delivery dates throughout July, August, and September. Second, the decision holds the possibility that *nachfrist* notice may be used to fix an unspecified delivery date. At the minimum, it would have placed a burden upon the exporter to respond to the request for delivery. The failure of the exporter to respond would have allowed the German importer to declare the contract as voided and to seek substituted goods elsewhere. Article 49 provides that the "buyer may declare the contract voided in the case of nondelivery, if the seller does not deliver goods within the additional period of time fixed by the buyer."

nonlegal request for more time. Failure to respond in a proper way will result in an unintended granting of additional time and a freezing of her legal options. This likely will be compounded by her rejecting delivery of goods during the *nachfrist* period as untimely resulting in liability for the purchase price, along with possible additional freight and storage costs. The existence of an express "time of the essence" clause is unlikely to provide a party any further protection from the use of *nachfrist* notice. It is important for a businessperson to realize that the receipt of seemingly meaningless communications should be fully investigated for legal consequences.

Seller's Right to Cure

The seller's **right to cure** defective goods under the CISG is similar to that offered in the UCC. Section 2-508 of the UCC allows a seller to cure the delivery of defective goods if the time for performance has not expired. Article 48 of the CISG allows the seller to cure after the contract date for delivery unless such late delivery would cause the buyer "unreasonable inconvenience or uncertainty." The buyer retains the right to sue for damages and expenses caused by the delay or by the initial delivery of nonconforming goods.[15]

Anticipatory Breach and Adequate Assurance

Anticipatory breach is a concept of Anglo-American legal derivation. The civil law does not recognize the right of a party to avoid or suspend their contract obligation in anticipation of a breach by the other party. Contract avoidance is permitted only at the time of breach or by way of a court order. Article 71 of the CISG allows a party to suspend its performance if it becomes clear that the other party will not perform. It gives two broad grounds for anticipatory breach. First, the other party has become seriously deficient in its ability to perform or in its creditworthiness. Second, the other party's preparation or lack of preparation or insufficiency of its performance to date has called into question its ability or willingness to perform under the contract. When one party anticipates a breach of the other party and suspends performance, it must give immediate notice of the suspension.

The suspending party must lift its suspension in the event that the other party provides **adequate assurance** that it will perform as contracted. Section 2-609 of the UCC provides a similar device for suspending performance. It states that when reasonable grounds for insecurity arise with respect to performance, the concerned party "may in writing demand adequate assurance of due performance" and may suspend performance until such time as such assurance is given. Failure to give such adequate assurance within a reasonable time, not exceeding thirty days, results in a repudiation of the contract.

Damages

The damage provisions in the CISG are found in Articles 74 to 77. Article 74 provides the general measure of damages. It adopts the common law rule that damages should be limited to those that were foreseeable at the time of contract

15. However, an ICC Tribunal held that if the seller is guilty of a fundamental breach, then he has no right to cure beyond the due date in the contract without the buyer's consent (ICC Case No. 7531 of 1994).

formation—what are popularly known as the rules of *Hadley v. Baxendale*.[16] The damages that can be collected are restricted in three ways. First, only foreseeable **consequential damages** related to the breach may be sued upon. Article 74 states that "damages may not exceed the loss which the party in breach foresaw or ought to have foreseen at the time of the conclusion of the contract." Second, damages will be limited to those that are provable with some degree of certainty. Therefore, purely speculative damages may not be collected.

Third, Article 77 provides that even if the loss was foreseeable and its amount is certain, the nonbreaching party will be limited in his recovery in the event he failed to **mitigate** his damages. Article 77 provides that if he "fails to take such measures to mitigate the loss, the party in breach may claim a reduction in damages in the amount by which the loss should have been mitigated." For example, if a buyer has a source for substituted goods, he must make efforts to obtain those substituted goods. If he does not he will be precluded from collecting full loss of profits damages. This is similar to the rule adopted in Section 2-715 of the UCC that holds the breaching party liable for all damages that *could not reasonably be prevented.* In the case of a fundamental breach, Article 75 allows the nonbreaching party to void the contract. It also authorizes the nonbreaching party to obtain substituted goods. The nonbreaching party may then sue the breaching party for the difference between the contract price (of the voided contract) and the price, if higher, of the substituted goods. If the nonbreaching party elects not to procure substituted goods, it may in the alternative sue for lost opportunity damages. Article 76 of the CISG allows him to recover for the difference between the contract price and the market price at the time of avoidance.

The *Delchi Carrier v. Rotorex* case that follows examines the different types of damage available in a typical breach of contract case. The case involves the delivery of defective goods. The goods involved in the transaction were component parts used by the buyer in the production of air conditioning units. The court assesses the damages that the buyer may collect when the delivery of defective goods results in a production slowdown at its plant. The court also decides on the types of out-of-pocket expenses the buyer can collect against the seller.

Unlike the UCC, the CISG does not allow for recovery for breach of warranty that results in injury to persons or property. Article 5 of the CISG states that it does not cover claims resulting from the "liability of the seller for death or personal injury caused by the goods to any person." Therefore, **products liability** remains to be determined under national laws. In contrast, Section 2-715 of the UCC allows for the recovery of consequential damages stemming from the seller's breach due to "injury to person or property proximately resulting from any breach of warranty."

Warranty Provisions

The CISG's warranty provision mimics the warranty provisions found in the UCC. The warranties that are of concern to most seller-exporters are any implied warranties that a court may use to hold the seller liable for nonconforming goods. Section 2-314 of the UCC recognizes the two common law implied warranties of merchantability and particular purpose (see Comparative Law: UCC Section 2-314(2)). A sale of fungible commodities is normally governed by the **implied warranty of**

16. 156 Eng. Rep. 145 (1854).

Delchi Carrier, S.P.A. v. Rotorex Corp.

71 F.3d 1024 (2d Cir. 1995)

The case involved a warranty dispute between a U.S. seller of compressors ("Rotorex") and an Italian purchaser ("Delchi"). The trial court determined that the compressors failed to conform to the specifications provided in the contract or the sample provided by Rotorex to Delchi. After Rotorex failed to cure the defects, Delchi brought suit for breach of contract and recovery of damages, including consequential damages for lost profits. The lost profits were allegedly due to lost volume caused by a closing of the assembly line for four days until the compressors were repaired. They also sued for incidental damages such as the cost to repair the compressors, the cost of storage, and the costs of expediting substitute goods.

Winter, Circuit Judge. The governing law of this case is the CISG. Article 74 allows for Delchi to collect monetary damages that are equal to its loss, including lost profits. Those damages are limited, however, to damages foreseeable at the time at the formation of the contract. Its first claim of damages is the cost of repairing the nonconforming compressors. These damages are recoverable because they were a foreseeable result of Rotorex's breach. Hence, Delchi is entitled to expenses for repairing the units including labor cost, costs of extraordinary inspections, and testing of the units. Pursuant to Article 77 of the CISG Delchi attempted to mitigate its losses by expediting a shipment of previously ordered Sanyo compressors. The expedited shipment cannot be considered as cover under Article 75, because they were previously ordered. Nonetheless, Delchi's actions in expediting the shipment were both commercially reasonable and reasonably foreseeable. Therefore, Delchi is entitled to recover the additional cost of air shipment over the cost of ocean shipment. Delchi is also entitled to the incidental costs of handling and storage of the rejected compressors.

The CISG permits recovery of lost profits resulting from a diminished volume of sales. In conformity to the common law, to recover for lost profit under CISG, a party must provide sufficient evidence to estimate the amount of damages with reasonable certainty. Delchi proved with sufficient certainty a total lost profit of 546,377,62 lire. Delchi did not prove with sufficient certainty lost sales from "anticipated profits." Delchi's claim of 4,000 additional lost sales in Italy is supported only by speculative testimony of Italian sales agents who stated they would have ordered if more were available. Delchi provides no documentation of additional lost sales in Italy and that Delchi's inability to fill those orders was directly attributable to Rotorex's breach.

Delchi is entitled to compensatory damages for those expenses incurred in repairing nonconforming goods, obtaining substituted goods, storage of rejected goods, and reasonably certain lost profits. Lost profits do not include profits that arise from anticipated sales that cannot be determined by reasonable certainty.

Case Highlights

- Article 74 of the CISG allows a party to collect any foreseeable damages incurred due to a breach of contract.
- Article 77 of the CISG requires the plaintiff to mitigate its damages. Expenses incurred, such as expediting shipment of substitute goods, are recoverable against the breaching party.
- The plaintiff may also collect incidental damages, such as cost incurred in repairing, storing, and protecting the defective goods.
- A plaintiff may collect lost profits caused by delivery of defective goods, but only those profits that can be proven with reasonable certainty.
- In sum, under the CISG and the UCC, damages are restricted by three principles: (1) they must have been foreseeable at the time that contract was signed, (2) they were not caused by the plaintiff's failure to mitigate, and (3) they must be proven with reasonable certainty and are not merely speculative.

merchantability. Section 2-314 states it is implied that for the goods to be merchantable they must be "fit for the ordinary purposes for which such goods are used." For example, a toaster should brown toast within a reasonable amount of time and a 20,000 BTU air-conditioning unit should produce 20,000 BTU of air conditioning.

Comparative Law

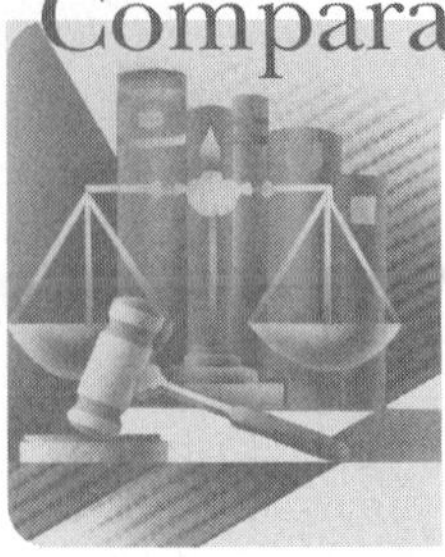

UCC Section 2-314(2)

Goods to be *merchantable* must be at least such as:

(a) pass without objection in the trade under the contract description; and
(b) in the case of fungible goods, are of fair average quality within the description; and
(c) are fit for the ordinary purposes for which such goods are used; and
(d) run, within the variations permitted by the agreement, of even kind, quality, and quantity within each unit and among all units involved; and
(e) are adequately contained, packaged, and labeled as the agreement may require; and
(f) conform to the promises or affirmations of fact made on the container or label if any.

Comment 2: The question when the warranty is imposed turns on the meaning of the terms of the agreement as recognized in the trade. Goods delivered under an agreement made by a merchant in a given line of trade must be of a quality comparable to that generally acceptable in that line of trade under the description of the goods used in the agreement.

Comment 8: Fitness for the ordinary purposes for which goods of the type are used is a fundamental concept of the present section and is covered in paragraph (c). As stated above, merchantability is also a part of the obligation owing to the purchaser for use. Correspondingly, protection, under this aspect of the warranty, of the person buying for resale to the ultimate consumer is equally necessary, and merchantable goods must therefore be *honestly* resalable in the normal course of business because they are what they purport to be.

The **implied warranty for a particular purpose** entails conveying specific requirements from the buyer to the seller. This communication is generally done to take advantage of the seller's superior knowledge or expertise in selecting or producing the product. Article 35 of the CISG states that the goods are to conform to "any purpose expressly or impliedly made known to the seller" at the time of the formation of the contract. Thus, if you visit a licensed air-conditioning company and discuss your needs for air-conditioning, the seller is implied to warrant that the unit being provided is sufficient for your needs. If the air-conditioning company sells you a 20,000 BTU unit that performs as advertised by producing 20,000 BTU, it will be considered defective when in fact your needs dictated a unit with a 50,000 BTU capacity.[17]

The *T.J. Stevenson* case that follows discusses the warranty of merchantability and the importance of giving notice when receiving defective or nonconforming goods. Failure to give timely notice will result in the buyer losing her right to remedies, including the right to reject the defective goods and the right to sue for damages.

Often a seller will attempt to disclaim all warranties, express or implied, or will want to limit its liability through a **limited express warranty.** The UCC allows for such **disclaimer** only by the use of clear and conspicuous language. Language such as the

17. The CISG also specifically makes it a breach of warranty if the seller fails to adequately package the goods for shipment.

T.J. Stevenson & Co. v. Bags of Flour

629 F.2d 338 (5th Cir. 1980)

An *in rem* action, stemming from insect infestation of wheat flour, was brought by an ocean carrier which claimed a lien on the cargo for freight, detention, and expenses, and also sought recovery of damages from milling company (seller) and shipper consignee (buyer), the Republic of Bolivia. The miller filed counterclaims against Bolivia and the carrier and Bolivia counterclaimed for breach of warranty. The Republic of Bolivia had entered into a contract for the purchase of 26,618 metric tons of flour from ADM Milling Co. The contract contained the following delivery term: "Delivery of goods by SELLER to the carrier at point of shipment shall constitute delivery to BUYER." Upon satisfactory delivery, the price was payable by irrevocable letter of credit. The contract also contained an express warranty of merchantability: "Seller warrants that the product sold shall be of merchantable quality." The warranty clause contained the following notice requirements: "BUYER hereby waives any claim based on the quality of the goods unless, within twenty days of the arrival of goods at destination, BUYER sends SELLER a letter by registered mail specifying the nature of the complaint."

Brown, Circuit Judge. With this decision we hopefully end, in all but a minor respect, an amphibious imbroglio and commercial law practitioner's nightmare involving a shipload of flour. Without pause to reflect on the complications that simple insects—confused flour beetles or otherwise—can create in the lives of men and Courts, we proceed to explain our decision. One issue permeates this case: What was the source of the flour infestation? The District Judge rightly concluded that infestation began either on the rail cars or at the mill supplying the flour. Neither the warehouses nor the ships were the source of any significant infestation.

The Warranty

The District Judge rightly held that the flour failed to meet the express warranty provision of the contract. The issue being, infestation and all, whether the flour was of merchantable quality. The Uniform Commercial Code Section 2-314(2) defines merchantable as goods that "are fit for the ordinary purposes for which such goods are used." Official Comments 2 and 8 provide helpful clues to divining the parties' intent. Comment 2: "Goods delivered under an agreement made by a merchant in a given trade *must be of a quality comparable to that generally acceptable in that line of trade.* Comment 8: "Merchantable goods must be *honestly resalable in the normal course of business because they are what they purport to be.*" We have often recognized that no food is completely pure. The FDA has long permitted very small amounts of insect fragments and other *dead* infestation in food products.

Here the question is: How much live infestation renders consumer-destined flour unfit for the ordinary purposes for which it is used? The evidence indicates that consumer-intended flour containing substantial amounts of live infestation is not merchantable under prevailing standards. Trade usage and course of dealing point to but one conclusion: Although flour may be "fit for human consumption" in the sense that it can be eaten without causing sickness, it is nonetheless not of merchantable quality.

Risk of Loss

Since it has been established that consumer-intended flour containing substantial amounts of live infestation is unmerchantable and the infestation in this case began before the flour reached the State Docks warehouses, we are confronted with the issue of which party is to be responsible for the further infestation of the flour as it stood in the warehouses or lay in Stevenson's ships. The delivery term in the contract read as follows: "F.A.S. MOBILE, ALABAMA for export." Section 2-509(1) of the Uniform Commercial Code reads that where there is no breach and where the contract requires the seller to ship the goods by carrier then: "if it does not require him to deliver at a particular destination, the risk of loss passes to the buyer when the goods are duly delivered to the carrier." However, Section 2-510(1) provides that in case of breach "where a tender or delivery of goods so fails to conform to the contract as to give a right of rejection the risk of their loss remains on the seller until cure or acceptance." Since it was materially nonconforming at the time it arrived in Mobile, Bolivia could have rejected the flour at that time. We therefore conclude that under Section 2-510(1)'s plain language, the risk of loss of the infested flour remained on the seller.

Breach of Warranty Claim

In order for Bolivia to win on its warranty claim it must satisfy the relevant notice requirements. Section 2-607(3)(a) of the UCC states that "the buyer must within a reasonable time after he discovers or should have discovered any breach notify the seller of breach or be barred from any remedy." Furthermore, the contract added the contractual requirement that notice must be in writing "within twenty days after arrival of the goods." ADM contends that under Section 2-607(3)(a) and the contract provision, it never received adequate notice of the defects. The facts show that there were informal communications throughout the time there were problems with the flour. The parties were in "continuous communication" with one another from the time the infestation problems were found. Also, Bolivia telexed ADM that no further payments would be permitted under the "irrevocable" letter of credit. From this view of the parties' course of conduct, one may infer that ADM was aware of Bolivia's dissatisfaction with the flour. Its awareness operated as a waiver of the specific notice provisions of the contract. ADM's reply to the telex as well as its informal communications dealt with the substance of Bolivia's complaint and did not fault Bolivia for failing to comply with the contract's notice requirements. ADM's responses to Bolivia's initial complaints established a course of performance in which the registered mail requirement of the contractual notice provision could be disregarded.

Defendant (seller) was liable for breach of warranty and its argument that it did not receive adequate notice is rejected.

Case Highlights

- Under the UCC any defect is ground for rejection. The CISG gives a right of rejection only if there is a fundamental breach.
- The court disregarded the specific notice requirements of the contract by imputing actual notice from the actions and correspondence between the parties after the goods were delivered.
- FAS stands for Free Alongside Ship. Under this term the risk of loss to the goods is transferred to the buyer when the goods are delivered to the port of shipment and ready for loading on to the ship. However, the court found that since the goods were defective upon delivery to the ship the risk of loss never passed to the buyer. FAS is a trade term that will be discussed in detail in Chapter 9.
- If nonconforming goods can be resold for another purpose, then a court is likely to find that the breach did not constitute a fundamental breach. In such a case the buyer has no right to reject the goods. Instead, the buyer may make use of the price reduction remedy provided for in the CISG. Under this remedy the buyer can unilaterally reduce the price of the goods by the difference in value between the goods in their defective condition and the value of conforming goods.

http://
American Bar Association:
http://www.abanet.org/home.html.

"Purchaser Takes As Is" is considered clear disclaimer language. Also, the disclaimer must be conspicuous; it must be easily noticeable when reviewing the contract. It cannot be placed in fine print on a page filled with fine print terms. In contrast, the CISG provides no formal requirements for disclaimers. Any form of disclaimer is enforceable under the CISG. Focus On Transactions: Limited Liability and Disclaimer in Software Contracts was taken from the American Bar Association's collection of software contract forms.[18] It illustrates the disclaimer language often used by merchants.

In the Focus on Transactions: Limited Liability and Disclaimer in Software Contracts, some of the language is printed in capital letters. This capitalization is meant to satisfy U.S. law that requires disclaimers of implied warranties to be conspicuously stated so as to alert a buyer of the existence of the disclaimer. There is no conspicuousness requirement in the CISG. Therefore, a disclaimer may be placed within the fine print terms. The final sentence of the disclaimer is an example of a merger clause. It is meant to bar the buyer from claiming that a different warranty was given by the seller through oral representations or other documents. However,

18. See American Bar Association, "Software Contract Forms," 1-3 (1992).

Focus on Transactions

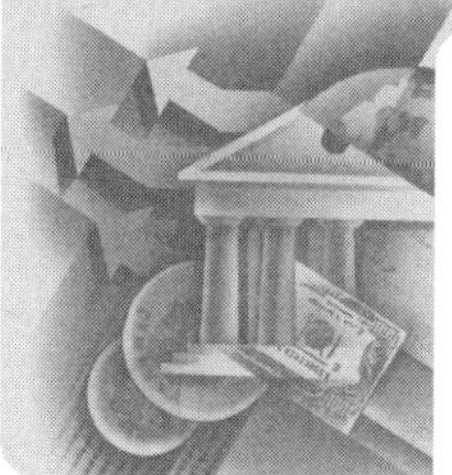

Limited Liability and Disclaimer in Software Contracts

LICENSE: The User shall have a nontransferable license to modify and use the product for functions performed in User's business. This product is sold to the purchaser under this Agreement to be an end user to be modified for certain functions as specified in the documentation for the product. The product includes both hardware and firmware that is proprietary to the seller who retains said rights. RESALE OR OTHER TRANSFER OF THE PRODUCT BY THE FIRST PURCHASER IS A VIOLATION OF THE TERMS OF THIS AGREEMENT. ANY AND ALL WARRANTIES ARE TERMINATED UPON SUCH A TRANSFER.

The User may NOT duplicate, disassemble, modify, translate, or use the Firmware other than as expressly authorized in this Agreement. Upon termination of the license, the User shall destroy all copies of and modifications to the Firmware.

LIMITED WARRANTY & DISCLAIMER: EXCEPT AS EXPRESSLY SET FORTH, THE PRODUCT IS PROVIDED TO THE ORIGINAL USER "AS IS," WITHOUT WARRANTY OF ANY KIND, EITHER EXPRESSED OR IMPLIED, INCLUDING, BUT NOT LIMITED TO, ANY IMPLIED WARRANTIES OF MERCHANTABILITY OR FITNESS FOR A PARTICULAR PURPOSE

LIMITATION OF REMEDIES: Seller's entire liability and User's exclusive remedy shall be: Repair and replacement including materials and labor for a period of one year unless the product has been abused, misused, or modified. IN NO EVENT WILL SELLER BE LIABLE TO THE USER FOR ANY DAMAGES, INCLUDING ANY LOST PROFITS, INCIDENTAL OR CONSEQUENTIAL DAMAGES ARISING OUT OF THE USE OR INABILITY TO USE THE PRODUCT. THE USER FURTHER AGREES THAT THIS DOCUMENT IS THE COMPLETE AND EXCLUSIVE STATEMENT OF THE AGREEMENT BETWEEN THE USER AND THE SELLER WHICH SUPERSEDES ANY PROPOSAL OR PRIOR AGREEMENT, ORAL OR WRITTEN.

under the CISG this other evidence may still be admitted since the CISG states that a contract "may be proved by any means, including witnesses."

Contractual Excuses

All legal systems provide relief for someone who despite good faith intentions is unable to perform. Although in technical breach of the contract, the court will excuse the breaching party from claims of damages. The common law fabricated the **doctrine of impossibility** and the **doctrine of frustration.** The former requires the contracting party to be objectively prevented from performing and generally entails the destruction of the subject matter of the contract. Under the doctrine of frustration the performance may still be objectively possible but the reason for the performance has ceased. For example, a hotel charges five times its normal rate for the weekend of the Super Bowl. Because of the threat of a hurricane, the Super Bowl is postponed. The purpose for renting a room at the exorbitant rate has been frustrated. The booking agent or renter will be relieved of its obligations to pay for the room.

The availability of contractual excuses in the civil law countries vary. In Belgium and France, *pacta sunt servanda* or sanctity of contract generally prevails over any request for an excuse. If the contract does not provide an excuse through a *force majeure* clause, then the contract will be enforced without any modification to its terms.

In England, the doctrine of frustration remains the premier excuse doctrine. The parties are relieved of their contractual obligations as of the date of frustration; the courts do not have the authority to modify or reform the contract. In Germany, if the "basis of the transaction" has evaporated, then the court is free to excuse a party or to reform the contract in accordance with the changed circumstances.

The UCC and the CISG possess their own excuse provisions. The UCC provision found in Section 2-615 is popularly referred to as the **doctrine of impracticability.** It excuses a party from performing if the performance has been "made impracticable by the occurrence of a contingency the nonoccurrence of which was a *basic assumption*" of the contract. Article 79 of the CISG allows for an excuse if nonperformance is due to an **impediment** that is beyond the control of the breaching party and was not foreseeable at the time of contract formation. However, the excuse is not permanent; performance is suspended for the duration of the impediment. The person attempting to exercise an Article 79 impediment must give prompt notice of the impediment to the other party. Failure to do so exposes the party to damages resulting from not giving notice.

All the excuse doctrines revolve around all or some of the following parameters: unforeseeability, undue hardship, and beyond the party's control. Most excuse doctrines require that the changed circumstances were **objectively unforeseeable** at the time of contract formation. If they were foreseeable, then the losses resulting from the breach will be considered as allocated risk. The breaching party will be susceptible to full contract damages. **Undue hardship** generally means more than a mere loss. The fact that the contract becomes unprofitable for one of the parties is insufficient; the loss must be near catastrophic. Beyond control means the event is a type of *force majeure* or superior force. There are no feasible alternatives for the party to perform on the contract. The UNIDROIT Principles summarize these factors[19]:

http://
UNIDROIT (The International Institute for the Unification of Private Law): **http://www.unidroit.org**.

- occurrence of an event or hardship that *fundamentally alters* the contractual equilibrium due to a change in costs or values
- occurrence was not known and the events could not *reasonably* have been taken into account at the time of the conclusion of the contract
- occurrence was *beyond the control* of the breaching party

FRUSTRATION

In some countries, such as the United Kingdom, the excuse of commercial frustration remains the primary excuse doctrine. Commercial frustration does not require that the subject matter of the contract has become objectively impossible to perform. Instead, due to changed circumstances, the purpose or the value of the subject matter of the contract has been severely diminished. The following International Chamber of Commerce arbitration Case No.6281 involves a seller's attempt to claim frustration for an increase in the market price of steel.

The Force Majeure *Clause*

http://
Examples of *force majeure* clauses—licensing digital information: **http://www.library.yale.edu/~llicense/forcecls.shtml**.

The *force majeure* clause lists the type of events that allow the parties an excuse out of the contract. *Force majeure* events may include wars, blockades, strikes, governmental interference or approval, fire, transportation problems, and others. The parties are free to recognize any event as one to be given *force majeure* effect. A *force*

19. See UNIDROIT Principles at Article 6.2.2.

International Chamber of Commerce

Case No. 6281 of 26 August 1989

On August 20, 1987, the parties entered into a contract for the sale of 80,000 metric tons of steel bars at a price of $190 per ton with delivery to a port in Yugoslavia. The contract provided the buyer with an option to purchase an additional 80,000 metric tons. On November 27, 1987, the buyer informed seller that it would exercise the option. The seller requested $215 per ton for the additional delivery. On January 26, 1988, the buyer purchased 80,000 tons from another supplier at a price of $216 and brought suit against seller for the difference between the original contract price and the price spent for the substituted goods.

Paris, France. The arbitrator decided that Yugoslav law was applicable. The arbitrator noted that Article 133 of the Yugoslav Law on Obligations allowed for a rescission of a contract due to "changed circumstances." The seller argues that it should be released from the contract due to changed circumstances, namely the increase in the market price of steel. Article 133 does list "economic events, such as extremely sudden and high increases or decreases of prices" as one of the reasons resulting in a frustration of a contract. However, a party cannot make such a claim if he should have taken such circumstances into account at the time of contracting. The world market prices of products, such as steel, fluctuate, as is known from experience. Also, the amount of damage must exceed a reasonable entrepreneurial risk. An increase in market prices from $190 to $215 amounts to slightly less than 13.16%. This increase is well within the customary margin. Furthermore, the development was also predictable. A reasonable seller had to expect that steel prices might go up further.

The buyer's purchase from another supplier, however, cannot be interpreted as a substitute purchase because he had failed to inform the seller of his intention to do so. Thus buyer's damage is limited to the difference between the $190 and $215 and not the $216 replacement price. It should be remarked in passing that the outcome would have been the same under Articles 74 to 77 of the CISG.

AWARD: Seller shall reimburse the buyer in the amount of $1,920,000 (80,000 × $24).

Case Highlights

- Most price or cost increases will not be considered the type of unforeseeable event that provides a party an excuse for breaching a contract.
- Losses due to cost increases, market price changes, or currency fluctuations are considered allocated risks and are to be borne by the party that is allocated the risk in the contract.
- The nonbreaching party may have to agree to a price increase under the duty to mitigate damages. It would then be able to recoup the price increase by suing for damages.

majeure clause should be custom drafted to take into account the type of industry, the countries, and type of carriage involved. The discussion of the *Harriscom v. Svenska* case and other materials in Chapter 4's coverage of *force majeure* clauses illustrated the importance of a properly drafted clause for avoiding liability.

LIMITATION PERIOD

Another important contract law issue is the statute of limitations or warranty period that will be applied to any future claims of the parties. It is always advisable for the parties to agree upon a reasonable limitation period. But what is a reasonable limitation period? When does the limitation period commence? Should there be any instances when the limitation period should be stopped or "tolled"? The United Nation's sponsored **Convention on the Limitation Period in the**

International Sale of Goods[20] provides uniform rules governing the period of time within which a party may bring a claim in conjunction with a contract for the international sale of goods.

The Convention prescribes a four-year limitation period for most claims. Article 2 of the Convention defines an international sale as one in which "the buyer and seller have their places of business in different states." Article 22 states that the limitation period cannot be modified through contract; however, it does make an exception for arbitral proceedings. "The provisions of this Article shall not affect the validity of a clause in the contract of sale which stipulates that arbitral proceedings shall be commenced within a shorter period of limitation." However, the four-year limitation period, even if applicable, can be truncated through the adoption of restrictive notice provisions. Article 1 states that "this Convention shall not affect a particular time-limit within which one party is required, as a condition for the acquisition or exercise of his claim, to give notice to the other party or perform any act other than the institution of legal proceedings." Also, the Convention does not apply to certain types of claims. For example, claims for personal injury caused by defective products and claims on bills of exchange or drafts are not governed by the Convention (Article 5).

The Convention outlines rules for the determination of the commencement of the limitation period and when the period is to be tolled. Article 9 provides the general rule that the limitation period commences on the date that the "claim accrues." This date is further defined in Article 10 as the date when a breach of contract occurs. Other commencement dates are provided for acts of fraud and claims of defects. "A claim arising from a defect or other lack of conformity" accrues on the date on which the "goods are handed over to or their tender is refused by the buyer." The period for a claim of fraud commences on the date which the fraud was discovered or "reasonably could have been discovered."

A tolling of the limitation period is granted when there is a submission to arbitrate the claim. Article 14 states that when the parties submit a claim to arbitration, "the limitation period shall cease to run when either party commences arbitral proceedings" in accordance with an arbitration clause. In the absence of an arbitration agreement, "arbitral proceedings shall be deemed to commence on the date on which a request that the claim in dispute be referred to arbitration is delivered at the habitual residence or place of business of the other party."

Other tolling provisions for specific types of claims and events are provided elsewhere in the Convention. For example, Article 15 provides for a tolling of the limitation period when a creditor asserts a claim in conjunction with a dissolution or bankruptcy proceeding. Article 18 provides for a further tolling when there are multiple debtors. It states that "where legal proceedings have been commenced against one debtor, the limitation period prescribed in this Convention shall cease to run against any other party jointly and severally liable." This tolling of the limitation period is granted *"provided that the creditor informs such party in writing within that period that the proceedings have been commenced."* Note the importance of notifying any potential debtors.

The Convention does place an outer limit for the tolling of the limitation period through the above provisions. Article 23 states that "notwithstanding the pro-

20. The Convention on the Limitation Period in the International Sale of Goods was concluded in New York on June 14, 1974. An amendment to the Convention, known as the 1980 Protocol, was concluded in Vienna on April 11, 1980. Both instruments entered into force on August 1, 1988.

visions of this Convention, a limitation period shall in any event expire no later than ten years from the date on which it commenced."

Associated limitation periods vary greatly from country to country and from cause of action to cause of action. Two common statutes of limitation periods are generally provided for breach of warranty and products liability claims. European Union law provides for an extended ten-year statute of limitation for products liability claims. In comparison, the limitation period for warranty claims is two years starting from the date of delivery.

Key Terms

acceptance, 220
additional term, 223
adequate assurance, 231
anticipatory breach, 231
battle of the forms, 222
boilerplate, 221
choice of law clause, 212
computer software sale, 215
conflict of law rules, 213
consequential damages, 232
contract formation, 219
Convention on the Limitation Period in the International Sale of Goods, 239
course of performance, 216
disclaimer, 234
doctrine of frustration, 237
doctrine of impossibility, 237
doctrine of impracticability, 238
four-corner analysis, 226
impediment, 238
implied warranty for a particular purpose, 234
implied warranty of merchantability, 232
jurisdiction, 213
lex mercatoria, 213
limited express warranty, 234
mailbox rule, 221
mirror image rule, 223
mitigate, 232
mixed sale, 214
nachfrist notice, 229
objectively unforseeable, 238
offer, 219
offeree, 220
offeror, 220
parol evidence rule, 215
place of business, 213
prior dealings, 216
products liablity, 232
ratification, 219
reasonable person standard, 226
rejection, 220
revocation, 220
right to cure, 231
rights and obligations, 219
specially manufactured goods, 215
statute of frauds, 215
totality of the circumstances, 226
trade usage, 216
undue hardship, 238
Uniform Commercial Code (UCC), 212
United Nations Convention on Contracts for the International Sale of Goods (CISG), 211
virtual goods, 215
written confirmation rule, 215

Chapter Problems

1. Compare the Uniform Commercial Code's treatment of anticipatory repudiation and adequate assurance in 2-609 and 2-610 with the CISG's treatment in Articles 71-73. Can you find any significant differences?

2. In many transactions involving technology transfer, the contract provides for the sale of both goods and services. Does the CISG apply to such contracts?

3. How do courts determine which national laws apply in a given case?

4. Section 2-205 of the Uniform Commercial Code provides an exception to the rule that an offeror is the "master of the offer" or that he has a right to revoke his offer at any time. It provides that "an offer given by a *merchant* in a *signed writing* which gives *assurance* that it will be held open is not revocable, but in no event may such period of irrevocability exceed three months." The CISG's firm offer rule is found in Article 16. It provides that an offer cannot be revoked "if it indicates that it is irrevocable or if it was reasonable for the offeree to rely on the offer being irrevocable and the offeree has acted in reliance on the offer." Do you see any significant differences between these two versions of the firm offer rule? Which version is broader? Why?

5. (A) As a seller and exporter of goods you are negotiating a long-term (three-year) installment contract. Because of the length of the contract, an open price term needs to be negotiated. Write a clause that anticipates the risks involved in entering a long-term supply contract. What cost factors should be described in detail? Also, how would one interrelate the open price term with a *force majeure* clause?

(B) You are negotiating a contract for the shipment of goods from Miami to the Middle East. The risks and costs of the shipment will be yours to the point of destination. Draft a *force majeure* clause. What events would you want to be considered as *force majeure?* Should some occurrences provide for an excuse (termination) and others for suspension?

(C) In a "battle of forms" situation the additional terms in the acceptance often become a part of the contract. Assuming that you are the offeror, draft language for your offer that would preclude those additional terms from entering the contract. Assuming that you are the offeree, draft a clause for your acceptance that would make it clear that there is no contract unless it is on the terms of the acceptance (counteroffer).

6. A business manager corresponds with numerous contacts in the international business world. She sends letters and faxes to agents, customers, suppliers, distributors, lenders, and many others. Most U.S. businesspersons have been educated to believe that they would expose their companies to liability if and only if they enter into a formal written contract. The formal written contract is a product of the company's lawyers. They are also aware that under the UCC's statute of frauds they are not liable for oral promises. They further (incorrectly) rationalize that the statute of frauds requires a fully negotiated, written agreement signed by both parties. Therefore, they often say or write things aimed at encouraging another party to take some action. They say things and write letters under the assumption that they would not be held liable until they enter a formal agreement. How have these assumptions changed with the enactment of the CISG? Can businesspersons be held liable for promises or assurances made in simple business letters? How can a manager avoid such unintended liability?

7. The European Union has a directive pertaining to warranties in consumer transactions. Compare the selected provisions of Directive 99/44/EC with the warranty provisions found in the UCC and CISG. Note that the European word for "warranty" is "guarantee."

8. Review the "Purchase Order" in Exhibit 8.1 and answer the following questions:

(a) Why is payment by "Irrevocable LOC"? What does LOC signify?

(b) What is the importance of the term "Cash Against Documents"? Is this considered to be advance payment or payment through a documentary transaction?

(c) Of the documents listed for possible delivery which one is absolutely needed for purposes of a documentary transaction?

(d) Why is the letter of credit amount based upon "CIF plus 10%"?

(e) What does CIF signify? What does "INCOTERMS" refer to?

(f) What is wrong with the designation "CIF Mexico City"?

(g) What does the acronym "HTS" represent?

(h) What does "M/V Hathaway" represent?

(i) Who is the "notify party"? Can the common carrier deliver the goods to the notify party?

(j) What is the importance of the notation "at sight?"

(k) What roles do the Banco de Mexico and Nations Bank of Miami play? What are these banks called?

Internet Exercises

1. Review the latest revision to Article 2 of the Uniform Commercial Code to see if any changes make it more similar or dissimilar to the CISG. You can use Comparative Law: Selective Comparison of CISG and UCC, page 220, to look up relevant sections. The recent revised drafts of Article 2 can be accessed at **http://www.law.upenn.edu/bll/ulc/ucc2/ucc20600.pdf**.

2. Review how Islamic Law deals with sale of goods and commercial law. See Centre of Islamic and Middle Eastern Studies at **http://www.soas.ac.uk/Centres/IslamicLaw/Materials.html**.

3. Select a country and research its sales law using the Cornell Law School Legal Information Institute at **http://www.law.cornell.edu**. Select "Law by Source or Jurisdiction" and then "Law from Around the World."

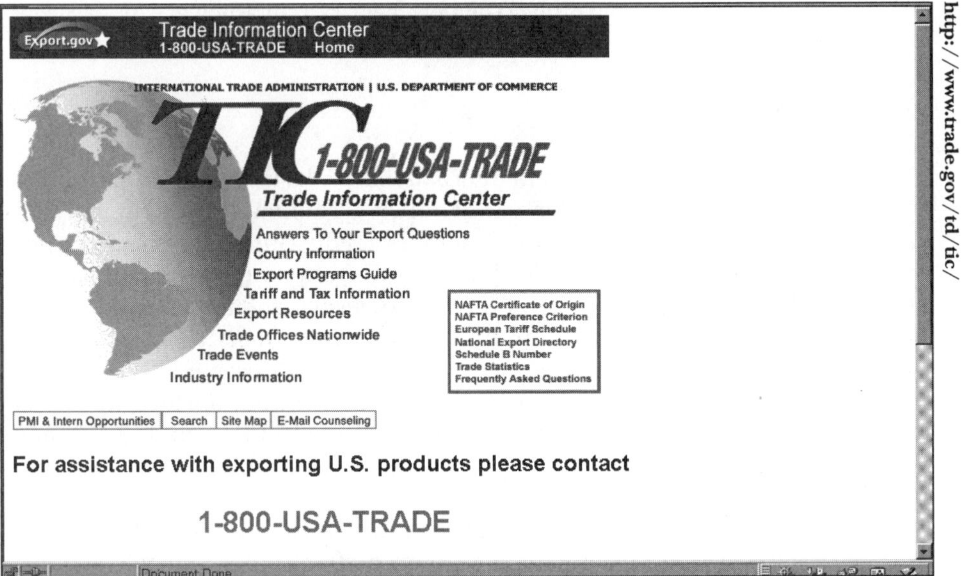

http://www.trade.gov/td/tic/

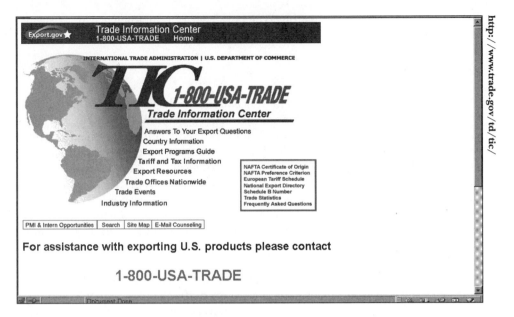

Chapter 9 The Documentary Transaction

The two fundamental risks of international exporting are the seller's payment risk and the buyer's delivery risk. The seller fears relinquishing control over its goods before receiving payment, while the buyer fears making payment before obtaining possession of the goods. The method of payment agreed to by the two parties determines who will bear the burden of these two risks. For sales within the United States, if the buyer has good credit, sales are usually made on open account; if not, cash in advance is required. There are several basic methods of payment for products sold abroad. As with domestic sales, a major factor that determines the method of payment is the seller's level of trust in the buyer's ability and willingness to pay. This chapter begins with a review of the different methods of payment utilized in the sale of goods. It will then focus on the most common method of payment in international transactions—the documentary collections transaction.

METHODS OF PAYMENT

The common methods of payment in international trade, ranked in order from the least secure for the exporter-seller are: (1) open account and consignment sales, (2) documentary collection, (3) documentary credit, and (4) cash in advance. Exhibit 9.1: Methods of Payment Risk Scale lists the different methods of payments on a risk scale from the perspective of the exporter-seller and importer-buyer.

Since getting paid in full and on time is of utmost concern to exporters, exporters should carefully weigh these different methods of payment. For example, the buyer would much prefer an open account transaction in which he will not have to make payment until sometime after the delivery of the goods. In an **open account** transaction, the exporter simply bills the customer, who is expected to pay under agreed terms at a future date. Open account sales do pose risks. The exporter may have to pursue collection abroad, which can be difficult and costly. Also, receivables may be harder to finance, since drafts or other evidence of indebtedness are unavailable. In a foreign transaction, an open account is a satisfactory method of payment if the buyer is well established, has demonstrated a long and favorable payment record, or has been thoroughly checked for creditworthiness. In contrast, **cash in advance** before shipment is the most desirable method from the perspective of the seller. The seller is relieved of all collection problems and has immediate use of the money, especially if a wire transfer is used.

The other methods of payment lie between the two extremes of open account and cash in advance. The two most common come under the label of documentary transactions. **Documentary collections** and **documentary credit transactions** are the

EXHIBIT 9.1 *Methods of Payment Risk Scale*

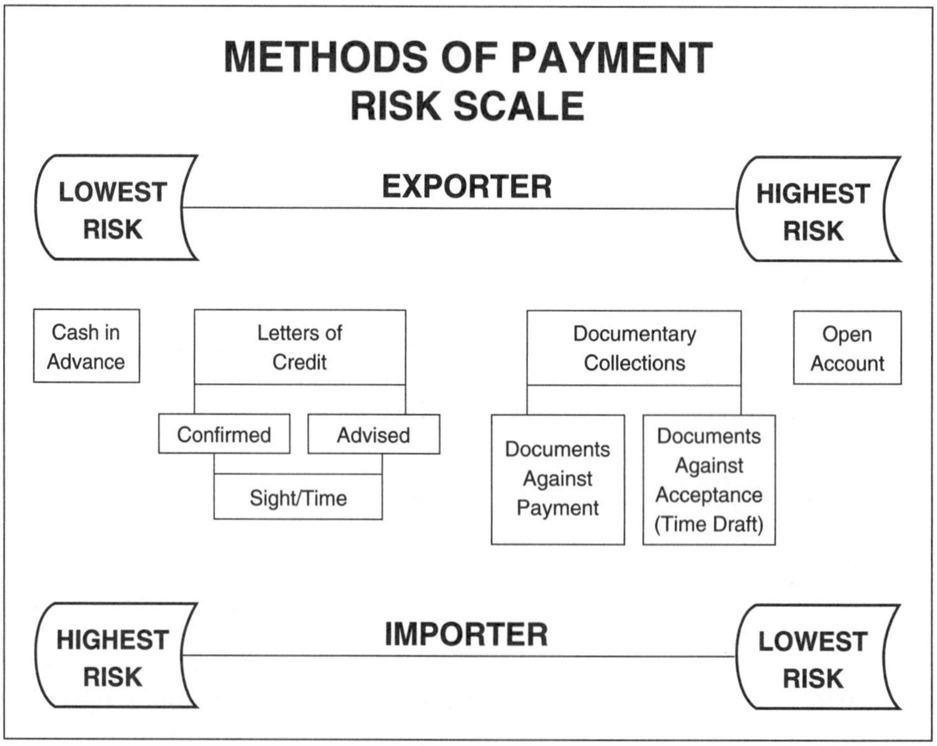

two forms of documentary transactions. The documentary collections transaction is the focus of this chapter. The documentary credit transaction, the use of letters of credit to guarantee payment to the seller, will be the subject of Chapter 11. Both methods involve the use of documents to ensure the passage of title to the goods to the buyer and payment to the seller while the goods are in transit.

http://
International Trade Data System—"International Trade Terms": **http://www.itds.treas.gov/glossaryfrm.html**. This site provides a comprehensive glossary of legal and business terms, many of which appear in the next three chapters.

A documentary collections transaction is one in which the buyer is obligated to pay upon delivery of documents (not delivery of goods). The documentary credit transaction also requires payment upon delivery of documents, but that payment is further guaranteed by a commercial bank through the issuance of a letter of credit. The buyer receives payment through the letter of credit upon presentation of documents to the bank.

Another intermediate method of payment is the **consignment sale.** In international consignment sales, the buyer receives use of the goods, but title remains with the seller until the goods are sold to a third party. This method is most common when goods are shipped to a foreign distributor to be sold on behalf of the exporter. The exporter retains title to the goods until the distributor sells them. Once the goods are sold, payment is sent to the exporter. With this method, the exporter accepts a great deal of risk and loss of control over the goods and may have to wait quite a while to get paid. When this type of sale is contemplated, it may be wise to consider some form of risk insurance.

The Sales Contract and Documentary Transaction

Before exporting to or entering a foreign market an analysis of the factors that relate to the profitability of such an entry should be undertaken. Many new exporters calculate their export price by the **cost-plus method** alone. In the cost-plus method of calculation, the exporter starts with the domestic manufacturing cost and adds administration, research and development, overhead, freight forwarding, distributor margins, customs charges, and profit. The net effect of this pricing approach may be that the export price escalates into an uncompetitive range.

A more competitive method of pricing for market entry is what is termed **marginal cost pricing.** This method considers the direct, out-of-pocket expenses of producing and selling products for export as a floor beneath which prices cannot be set without incurring a loss. For example, export products may have to be modified for the export market to accommodate different sizes, electrical systems, or labeling requirements. Changes of this nature may increase costs. On the other hand, the export product may be a stripped-down version of the domestic product and therefore cost less. Or, if additional products can be produced without increasing fixed costs, the incremental cost of producing additional products for export should be lower than the average production costs for the domestic market only.

In addition to production costs, overhead, and research and development, other costs should be allocated to domestic and export products in proportion to the benefit derived from those expenditures. Additional costs often associated with export sales include: (1) market research and credit checks; (2) business travel; (3) international postage, cable, and telephone rates; (4) translation costs; (5) commissions, training charges, and other costs involving foreign representatives; (6) consultant and freight forwarding costs; and (7) product modification and special packaging.

http://
International Trade Administration—sample export quotation worksheet: **http://www.unzco.com/basicguide/figure10.html**.

As in the domestic market, demand in the foreign market is a key to setting prices. What will the market bear for a specific product or service? For most consumer goods, per capita income is a good gauge of a market's ability to pay. Per capita income for most of the industrialized nations is comparable to that of the United States. For the rest of the world, it is much lower. In lower per capita income markets, simplifying the product to reduce selling price may be the answer. The exporter must also keep in mind that currency valuations alter the affordability of the goods. Thus, pricing should accommodate fluctuations in currency and the relative strength of the dollar. Few companies are free to set prices without carefully evaluating their competitors' pricing policies. Where many competitors are servicing a particular foreign market, the exporter may have little choice but to match the going price in order to establish a market share. If the exporter's product or service is new to a particular foreign market, it may actually be possible to set a higher price than is normally charged domestically. Only after it has estimated the cost, demand, and competition for its goods is the exporter-seller ready to prepare a ***pro forma* invoice** and enter into an export contract.

Pro Forma *Invoice*

The prudent exporter realizes the importance of entering into a well-defined agreement. When the parties are from different countries setting up the transaction clearly in advance is vital. First, the imposition of larger geographical distances, along with customs regulations and special documentary requirements, make the international sale of goods transaction more complicated. Second, the exporting and importing transaction requires the use of various third parties, such as commercial banks, international common carriers, custom brokers, and freight forwarders. Thus, before entering into an international sales contract, the seller should consider the costs associated with these two factors. The form that describes the allocation of these costs between the seller and the buyer is the seller's *pro forma* invoice.

Many export transactions, particularly first-time export transactions, begin with the receipt of an inquiry from abroad, followed by a request for a quotation or a *pro forma* invoice. The *pro forma* invoice is an invoice provided by a seller prior to the shipment of goods, informing the buyer of the kinds and quantities of goods and their costs. It is generally the basis for the formation of the sales contract, along with the buyer's purchase order. A *pro forma* invoice describes the product, states a price for it, sets the time of shipment, and specifies the sale and payment terms. Before preparing the *pro forma* invoice the prudent exporter or importer should develop a checklist of the important terms and documentary requirements that need to be incorporated. An example is provided in Focus on Transactions: "International Shipping Checklist." Most of the documents in the feature will be explained in detail later in the chapter.

http://

International Trade Administration—example of *pro forma* invoice: **http://www.unzco.com/basicguide/figure11.html**.

Since the foreign buyer may not be familiar with the product, the description of it in the *pro forma* invoice must be more detailed than it would be in a domestic quotation. The description should include: (1) buyer's name and address, (2) buyer's reference number and date of inquiry, (3) list of requested products and brief description, (4) price of each item (it is advisable to indicate whether items are new or used and to quote in U.S. dollars to reduce foreign-exchange risk), (5) gross and net shipping weight (in metric units where appropriate), (6) total cubic volume and dimensions (in metric units where appropriate) packed for export, (7) trade discount, if applicable, (8) delivery point, (9) terms of sale, (10) terms of payment, (11) insurance and shipping costs, (12) validity period for quotation, (13) total charges to be paid by customer, (14) estimated shipping date from factory or U.S. port, and (15) estimated date of shipment arrival.

Focus on Transactions

International Shipping Checklist

Commercial Invoice
- Will a commercial invoice suffice or is a customs or consular invoice required?
- Are all charges in accord with the original quotation?
- Are terms of delivery clear? Were INCOTERMS 2000 used?
- Are terms of payment and currency of payment clearly stated?
- Are unit descriptions, measures, and prices recorded the same way as on all other documents? Are they exactly as required by the letter of credit?
- Is a destination control statement required?

Packing List
- Are shipper and consignee clearly identified?
- Are all item descriptions and units of measure per the commercial invoice and the letter of credit?
- Are carton marks and numbers accurate?
- Does the packing list conform to the importing country's requirements?

Shipper's Export Declaration (SED)
- Is an SED required?
- Has the correct export license designation been used? Is a validated export license required?
- Have the commodity, consignee, and destination country been reviewed for export controls?

Bills of Lading
- Are the consignee, shipper, and notify party clearly identified?
- Do descriptions, marks, and numbers match the commercial invoice and packing list?
- Are ocean bills of lading marked "On Board," if required by L/C?
- If freight charges are included on the commercial invoice, is the bill of lading marked "Prepaid"?
- Are any of the items classifiable as hazardous materials?

Certificate of Origin
- Is an origin certificate required by the letter of credit or by the destination country?

Miscellaneous Documents
- Preshipment inspection certificate?
- Insurance certificate?
- Manufacturer's certificate?
- Phytosanitary inspection certificate?
- Weight certificate?

The *pro forma* invoice should not be confused with the commercial invoice. *Pro forma* invoices (see Exhibit 9.2) are not for payment purposes but are essentially quotations in an invoice format. The invoice should be conspicuously marked *"pro forma* invoice." It is important that price quotations state explicitly that they are subject to change without notice. If a specific price is agreed upon or guaranteed by the exporter, the precise period during which the offer remains valid should be specified.

THE DOCUMENTARY TRANSACTION

In order to alleviate the seller's risk of not being paid or the buyer's risk of not receiving the goods after making payment, most export contracts require a documentary transaction. The sale of goods contract is converted into a sale of

EXHIBIT 9.2 *Sample* Pro Forma *Invoice*

Tech International
1000 J Street, N.W.
New York, New York 20005
Telephone: 202-555-1212
Fax: 202-555-1111

Date: Jan. 12, 2002

To: Gomez Y. Cartagena
Bogota, Colombia

Our Reference: Col. 91-14
We hereby quote as follows:

Terms of Payment: Letter of Credit

Terms of Sale: CIF Buenaventura, Colombia

QUANTITY	MODEL	DESCRIPTION	UNIT	EXTENSION
3	2-50	Separators in accordance with attached specifications	$14,750.00	$44,250.00
3	14-40	First-stage Filter Assemblies Per attached specifications	$1,200.00	$3,600.00
3	custom	Drive Units—30 hp each (for operation on 3-phase 440 v., 50 cy. current) complete with remote controls	$4,235.00	$12,705.00

Total FOB New York, New York, domestic packed..$60,555.00

Export processing, packaging, prepaid inland freight to JFK International Airport & forwarder's handling charges FOB Dulles Airport, Virginia..$63,670.00

Estimated air freight and insurance...$2,960.00

Estimated CIF Buenaventura, Colombia...$66,630.00

Estimated gross weight 9,360 lbs.; Estimated cube 520 cu. ft.

Export packed 4,212 kg.; Export packed 15.6 cu. meters

1. All prices quoted herein are U.S. dollars.
2. Prices quoted herein for merchandise only are valid for 60 days from this date.
3. Any changes in shipping costs or insurance rates are for account of the buyer.
4. We estimate ex-factory shipment approximately 60 days from receipt here of purchase order and letter of credit.

Source: National Trade Data Bank, a product of STAT-USA, U.S. Department of Commerce.

documents contract. The buyer contracts to buy documents and the seller promises to provide conforming documents to the buyer while the goods are in transit. In the documentary transaction, the seller is paid and the buyer receives title to the goods while the goods are in transit to the port of destination. In this way, the buyer's delivery and seller's payment risks are diminished. Upon receiving the documents, the buyer is in a position to resell the goods to downstream buyers or to use the documents as collateral to obtain financing. In the event that the buyer refuses to pay for the documents, the seller still retains title and control of the goods. He can mitigate his losses by selling the goods to someone else through negotiation of the documents.

The documentary collections transaction requires drafts to be paid either when presented for payment or at a date after the buyer receives the goods. A draft or **bill of exchange**[1] is analogous to a foreign buyer's check. Drafts that are paid when presented for payment are called **sight drafts.** Drafts that are payable at some time after presentation of the documents are called **time drafts.** Like checks used in domestic commerce, drafts sometimes carry the risk that they will be dishonored. A sight draft is used when the seller wishes to retain title to the shipment until it is paid for.

http://
United States Department of Commerce—guide to international trade: **http://www.unzco.com/basicguide**. Provides information on all aspects of documentary transactions.

Banks use these instruments to effectuate payment to the seller upon the presentation of the documents. A draft is a written, unconditional order for payment from the **drawer** (seller) to the **drawee** (buyer). It directs the drawee to pay a specified sum of money, in a given currency, at a specific date to the payee (seller). The documentary transaction allows the buyer to take possession either by making payment upon the presentation of the draft or by acceptance of the draft. The first type documentary collections transaction is called **"Cash Against Document."** This type is the ordinary means of processing a documentary collections transaction.

The second type is referred to as the **"Documents Against Acceptance"** type of documentary collections. The Cash Against Document transaction requires the buyer to sign a sight draft before receiving the necessary documents. The sight draft is then processed through the banking system for immediate payment to the seller. In the Documents Against Acceptance transaction, instructions are given by the seller to a bank indicating that the documents transferring title to the goods should be delivered to the buyer-drawee upon the buyer's acceptance of the attached time draft. The buyer's signature indicates its guarantee to pay the draft at some future time. The function of drafts as means of payment and as used for purposes of financing are discussed in detail in Chapter 11.

In order for an exporter or importer to understand its responsibilities in a documentary transaction it is advisable to develop an export-import checklist. The Focus on Transactions: Checklist for Export-Import Transactions provides an example of such a checklist. The numbers to the right of the checklist items refer to the description that follows.

Enlisting the services of commercial banks to provide letters of credit (2 and 3) and to transfer documentation (10) is a common requirement of the standard sales contract (1). Following the receipt of the letter of credit, the seller will prepare the goods for shipment (7) and obtain an insurance policy to cover the risk of loss to the goods while they are being transported to the buyer (5). In order to diminish the risk of fraudulent documentation, a prudent buyer will negotiate for inspection rights (6). The inspection of the goods will take place before the goods are loaded at the port of shipment. The inspection company issues an inspection certificate that the seller sends to the buyer, along with the other required documents. The buyer will be able to review the inspection report before paying for the documents and taking possession of the goods at the port of destination.

The international sales contract almost always provides for transit of the goods by ocean carriage. Under the standard **CIF** (Cost, Insurance, Freight) contract, for example, the seller must ship the goods by obtaining the services of a freight forwarding company and a common carrier to transport the goods to the buyer (4). The contract will require that the seller obtain a bill of lading from the common

1. The term *draft* is used commonly in the United States, while *bill of exchange* is the term used in the United Kingdom and some other Commonwealth countries.

Focus on Transactions

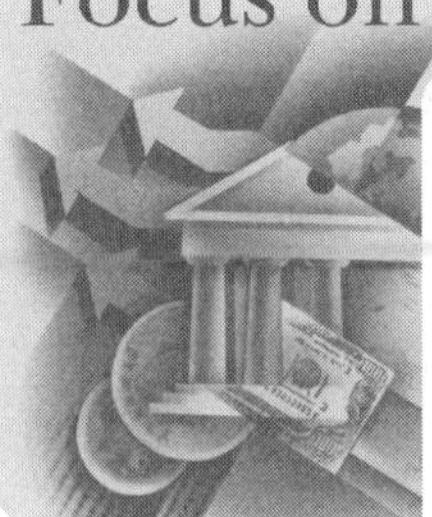

Checklist for Export-Import Transactions

- Enter into a sale contract (1)
- Obtain letter of credit (if required) (2)
- Obtain confirmation of letter of credit (3)
- Hire carrier for transport of goods (4)
- Obtain necessary insurance policies (5)
- Arrange inspection of goods prior to shipment (6)
- Prepare goods for shipment: packing, marking (7)
- Deliver to carrier (8)
- Obtain shipping documents (9)
- Transmit shipping documents (10)
- Obtain payment under letter of credit (11)
- Entry and customs clearance in the country of delivery (12)
- Final liquidation of customs duties and delivery to importer (13)

carrier to prove that the goods have been sent as dictated by the contract (8 and 9). The seller will not be able to receive payment unless it delivers to the bank for transmission to buyer a conforming bill of lading, along with the other documents stated in the sales contract (10). After the bank reviews the documents the seller receives payment (11). Upon receipt of the bill of lading and other documents the buyer is then able to take delivery of the goods for import into the country (12 and 13).

THE DOCUMENTARY COLLECTIONS TRANSACTION

As discussed in the previous section, the seller in a documentary collections transaction is required to present a number of conforming documents as required in the sales contract in order to receive payment. The required documents are generally attached to a draft or bill of exchange. The seller draws the draft on the account of the buyer and makes it payable to the seller. Unlike with a standard check or bank draft, the seller is both the drawer and payee of the documentary draft. To better reduce the payment risk, the seller (exporter) will want to negotiate a sight draft so that it will receive payment immediately upon the presentation of the documents. Some exporters, however, will agree to wait for payment, especially when doing business with an established customer. In such cases, a time draft is utilized that provides for payment within so many days of presentment or from shipment. In that case, the buyer should be required to sign and note "accepted" on the time draft before obtaining possession of the documents.

The typical documentary collections transaction proceeds along a chronological timeline as shown in Exhibit 9.3: Documentary Collections Flowchart. It begins with the negotiation and execution of a sales contract (1). The sales contract is usually formed by the exchange of a *pro forma* invoice or price quotation from the seller and a purchase order from the buyer. The seller often contacts a freight forwarder to obtain freight quotes and insurance information before drafting the *pro forma* invoice. After the contract is formed, the seller contacts the freight forwarder to book shipment on a common carrier (2A and 2B). The freight for-

EXHIBIT 9.3 *Documentary Collections Flowchart*

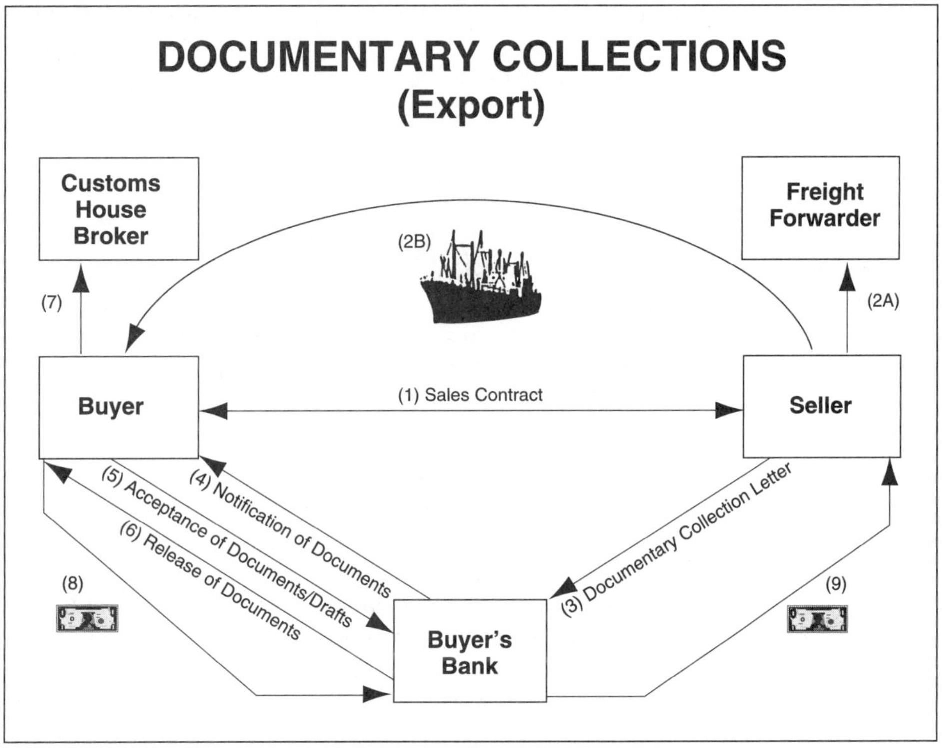

warder coordinates the movement of the goods, submits the export documentation to the Customs Service, obtains the bill of lading from the carrier, and compiles other required documents.

The **bill of lading** is a title document that allows the goods to be transferred while they are in transit to the port of destination. Without the bill of lading, or similar title document, the documentary transaction would not be possible. The bill of lading allows a sale of goods transaction to be converted to a sale of documents. Upon receiving the bill of lading the buyer becomes the owner of the goods. Any dispute over the ownership of goods will be resolved in favor of the party in possession of the bill of lading and not the party in the actual possession of the goods. The functions and characteristics of the bill of lading will be reviewed in detail later in this chapter.

In order to obtain the bill of lading, the goods are delivered to the common carrier. The bill of lading is endorsed by the shipper and sent via the shipper's bank to the buyer's bank or to another intermediary along with a sight draft, invoices, and other supporting documents specified by the buyer, such as packing lists, consular invoices, and insurance certificates. The seller usually does not submit the documents and draft directly to the buyer's bank. Instead, it uses a local bank to transmit the documents through its corresponding relations to the buyer's bank. These documents are presented to the buyer's bank along with a documentary collections letter or order (3). The collection letter or order includes a draft drawn on the buyer's account either payable at sight or at a future time.

The buyer's bank acts as the collecting bank for purposes of transmitting payment to the seller. It notifies the buyer of the receipt of the documents and collects payment on the draft (sight draft) or notifies the seller of the buyer's acceptance of the draft (time draft) (4 and 5). Following the payment or acceptance, the bill of lading and other documents are released to the buyer (6). Before the cargo can be released, the original ocean bill of lading must be properly endorsed by the buyer and surrendered to the carrier, since it is a document that evidences title. Air waybills of lading, on the other hand, do not need to be presented in order for the buyer to claim the goods. The buyer transmits the shipping documents to its customs broker (7). The customs broker clears the goods through customs at the port of importation and arranges inland transport to the buyer's warehouse. Finally, funds are wired through the banking system to the seller's account (8 and 9). If the sales contract requires the purchaser to guarantee payment through a letter of credit, then the first step in the process is the procurement by the buyer of a letter of credit. The role of letters of credit in international business transactions will be examined in Chapter 11.

DOCUMENTATION

The following documents are commonly used in exporting; which of them are actually used in each case depends on the requirements of the exporting and importing countries. First, as in a domestic transaction, the **commercial invoice** is a bill for the goods prepared by the seller (see Exhibit 9.4). A commercial invoice contains basic information about the transaction, including a description of the goods, the address of the buyer and seller, and the delivery and payment terms. The buyer needs the invoice to prove ownership and to arrange payment. Some governments use the commercial invoice to place a value on the goods in assessing customs duties.

http://
International Trade Administration—sample of a straight bill of lading: **http://www.unzco.com/basicguide/figure3.html**.

Second, **bills of lading** are contracts between the owner of the goods and a common carrier. A negotiable or shipper's order bill of lading can be bought, sold, or traded while goods are in transit and is used for letter-of-credit transactions. A straight bill of lading is nonnegotiable. The customer usually needs the original bill of lading to take possession of the goods.

Third, certain countries require a **consular invoice,** which is used to control and identify goods. The consular invoice is purchased from the consulate of the country to which the goods are being shipped and usually must be prepared in the language of that country. Fourth, some countries require a signed statement as to the origin of the export item. Such **certificates of origin** are usually obtained through a semiofficial organization such as a local chamber of commerce.

Fifth, some purchasers and countries may require a **certificate of inspection** attesting to the specifications of the goods shipped. Inspection certificates are often obtained from independent testing organizations. Sixth, if the seller provides insurance, then he must provide an **insurance certificate** or binder stating the type and amount of coverage. This insurance certificate is negotiable so that it can be transferred along with the bill of lading.

http://
International Trade Administration—sample packing list: **http://www.unzco.com/basicguide/figure7. html**.

Seventh, the United States requires a **Shipper's Export Declaration (SED).** The SED is used to control exports and compile trade statistics. It must be prepared and submitted to U.S. Customs for exports valued at more than $2,500.[2] Eighth, U.S. export shipments are required by the U.S. government to have either a general or a validated **export license.**[3] Ninth, an export **packing slip** or list itemizes the mate-

2. See Chapter 6.
3. See Chapter 6.

EXHIBIT 9.4 *Commercial Invoice*

Invoice

Date: __________

Bill of Lading / Air Waybill No.:__________

Invoice Number: __________

Purchase Order No.:__________

Terms of Sale (Incoterm): __________

Reason for Export: __________

Shipper Information:

Tax ID/VAT No.: __________
Contact Name: __________
Company Name: __________
Company Address: __________
City: __________
State/Province: __________
Postal Code: __________
Country: __________
Telephone No.: __________
E-Mail ID: __________

Ship To:

Tax ID/VAT No.: __________
Contact Name: __________
Company Name: __________
Company Address: __________
City: __________
State/Province: __________
Postal Code: __________
Country: __________
Telephone No.: __________
E-Mail ID: __________

Sold To:

Tax ID/VAT No.: __________
Contact Name: __________
Company Name: __________
Company Address: __________
City: __________
State/Province: __________
Postal Code: __________
Country: __________
Telephone No.: __________
E-Mail ID: __________

No. Units	Unit of Measure	Description of Goods (include Harmonized Tariff Number If known)	Country of Origin	Unit Value	Total Value

Additional Comments:

Declaration Statement:

Invoice Line Total:	
Discount/Rebate:	
Invoice Sub-Total:	
Freight Charges:	
Insurance:	
Other (Specify Type)__________:	
Invoice Total Amount:	
Currency Code:	

Shipper Signature / Title __________ **Date:**

Total Number of Packages:__________

Total Weight (indicate LBS or KGS):__________

These commodities, technology, or software were exported from the United States in accordance with the Export Administration Regulations. Diversion contrary to U.S. law prohibited.

rial in each individual package being shipped. It gives the individual and gross weights and measurements for each package, along with the package markings. The packing list is attached to the outside of a package in a waterproof envelope marked "packing list enclosed." It allows the shipper or forwarding agent to determine the total shipment weight, volume, and whether the correct cargo is being shipped. In addition, customs officials use the list to check the cargo. The more common documents used in the documentary transaction are further defined in Doing Business Internationally: "List of Export Documents."

The number of documents the exporter must deal with varies depending on the destination of the shipment. Because each country has different import

Doing Business Internationally

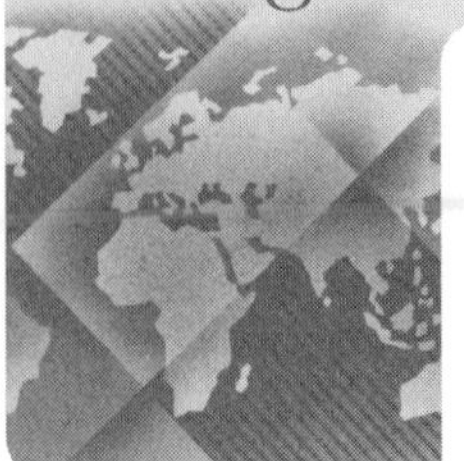

List of Export Documents

Bill of Lading
A title document issued by a shipping company. It also serves as a formal receipt of the goods and a carriage contract. The holder of the bill of lading has a right to claim delivery of the goods from the shipping company at the port of destination. The most common bill of lading in international transport is the ocean bill of lading. A multimodal transport bill of lading may be used when more than one form of transport is being used.

Letter of Credit
A document issued by the importer-purchaser's bank to guarantee the payment of the draft to the exporter for the purchase of the goods or upon the presentation of documents by the exporter. A transferable letter of credit allows the exporter (beneficiary) to make the credit payable to others (suppliers).

Letter of Indemnity
This document allows a carrier to release goods to the consignee not yet in possession of the bill of lading. It is a guarantee to indemnify the carrier from all liability related to the release. It is also called a "steamer guarantee."

Export License
A government-issued document granting permission to export the specific commodity to a specific country.

Dock Receipt
This document certifies the receipt of the goods by a carrier at the port of shipment.

Warehouse Receipt
Acknowledges receipt of the goods by a warehouse operator. A "dock warrant" not only acknowledges receipt, but is also a document of title.

Commercial Invoice
This document is prepared by the exporter and lists and describes the goods. It generally also gives the prices, discounts, quantities, and delivery and payment terms. It is used by governments to place a valuation of the goods for the assessment of customs duties.

Consular Invoice
An invoice certified by the consul of the country of import. It is used by customs officials to verify the value, quantity, and quality of the goods. Also, the consular may compare the export price with the market price in the exporting country to determine if dumping is evident.

Certificate of Inspection
An inspection certificate is issued by an independent inspection company to assure the purchaser of the quantity and quality of the goods being shipped. Preshipment inspection is a requirement for importation of goods into many developing countries.

Certificate of Origin: This document may be required by the country of import. It is provided by a third party such as an official of the local chamber of commerce or an official of the consular office.

Bill of Exchange or Draft
An order addressed to the importer or the importer's bank for the payment of a fixed sum at sight or in the future (time draft).

ATA Carnet
An international customs document for the temporary duty-free import of goods into a country for display, demonstration, or other purposes. A carnet is usually good for one year from the date of issuance. Generally, a bond or cash deposit of 40 percent of the value of the goods is required. Carnets are sold in the United States by the U.S. Council for International Business, 1212 Avenue of the Americas, New York, New York 10036, (212) 354-4480.

ISO 9000 Certificate
International quality standards which certify that the exporter meets certain minimum requirements of quality.

Marine Insurance Certificate or Binder
Generic form of insurance available even in multimodal transport.

regulations, the exporter must be careful to provide proper documentation. Exporters should seriously consider having the freight forwarder handle the documentation. Much of the documentation is routine for freight forwarders or customs brokers acting on the firm's behalf, but the exporter is ultimately responsible for the accuracy of the documentation.

Bill of Lading

The bill of lading is the traditional transport document and serves three functions: (1) carriage contract between the ship owner and the shipper, (2) evidence of receipt that the goods were delivered to the ship, and (3) document of title (see Exhibit 9.5: Bill of Lading).[4] Its function as a title document allows for the sale, transfer, and "collateralization" of the goods while in transit. Lord Mustill in discussing the third function of the bill of lading states that "it is a symbol of constructive possession of the goods which can transfer possession by endorsement and transfer; it is a transferable *key to the warehouse.*"[5]

Although the bill of lading generally serves as a document of title, receipt, and carriage contract, other agreements may preempt its role in one of these areas. For example, a prior agreement, such as a freight or **booking contract,** may control the contractual relationship between the shipper and the common carrier. In *M & Z Trading Corp. v. Cargolift Ltd,*[6] the shipper argued that a prior freight agreement governed, while the common carrier contended that its bill of lading constituted the contract. The court reasoned that the resolution of such disputes turns on factual and legal issues relating to, for example, the parties' negotiations, the documents generated during those negotiations, and the status and legal effect of the bill of lading. By the express terms of the prior agreement, the carrier's general obligations began upon the initial pickup of the goods in Canada and continued until final delivery in Russia. The court held that the bill of lading could have only, at most, supplemented the parties' prior agreement, unless the parties clearly agreed otherwise. Therefore, the bill of lading did not nullify the lengthy course of negotiations that culminated in the prior freight agreement.

A future development that will transform documentary practice is the electronic bill of lading. **Electronic bills of lading** will enable a more efficient sale or transfer of goods while they are in transit. The first electronic bill of lading was developed in conjunction with rail transport (CMI Rules for Electronic Bills of Lading). A more expansive project, known as the Bolero Project, to transmit electronically all standard documents is underway.

CHARACTERISTICS OF BILLS OF LADING

The standard documentary sales contract requires an **on-board bill of lading.** The on-board bill of lading warrants that the cargo has been placed aboard a named vessel and is signed by the master of the vessel. This type of bill ensures the buyer that the goods are indeed on the ship in transit to the port of destination. A

4. See generally Georgios Zekos, "The Contractual Role of Bills of Lading under United States Law"; "The Contractual Role of Bills of Lading under English Law"; and "The Contractual Role of Bills of Lading under Greek Law," all in 39 *Managerial Law* (1997).
5. *The Delfini,*1 Lloyd's Rep. 252, 268 (1990).
6. 2000 U.S. App. LEXIS 11573 (9th Cir. 2000).

EXHIBIT 9.5 *Bill of Lading*

Any Container Line BILL OF LADING

SHIPPER/EXPORTER

BOOKING NUMBER

BILL OF LADING NUMBER

EXPORT REFERENCES

CONSIGNEE

FORWARDING AGENT

FMC NO.
CHB NO.

NOTIFY PARTY

ALSO NOTIFY - ROUTING & INSTRUCTIONS

VESSEL VOYAGE FLAG

PLC OF RECEIPT BY PRECARRIER

RELAY POINT

POINT AND COUNTRY OF ORIGIN OF GOODS

PORT OF LOADING

LOADING PIER

TYPE OF MOVE

PORT OF DISCHARGE

PLACE OF DELIVERY BY ON CARRIER

ORIGINALS TO BE RELEASED AT

PARTICULARS FURNISHED BY SHIPPER

MARKS & NO'S/CONTAINER NO'S	NO.OF PKGS.	DESCRIPTION OF GOODS	WEIGHT	MEASUREMENTS

FREIGHT CHARGES	RATED AS	PER	RATE	TO BE PREPAID IN U.S. DOLLARS	TO BE COLLECTED IN U.S. DOLLARS	FOREIGN CURRENCY
SUBJECT TO SECTION 7 OF CONDITIONS, IF SHIPMENT IS TO BE DELIVERED TO THE CONSIGNEE WITHOUT RECOURSE ON THE CONSIGNOR, THE CONSIGNOR SHALL SIGN THE FOLLOWING STATEMENT; 'THE CARRIER SHALL NOT MAKE DELILVERY OF THIS SHIPMENT WITHOUT PAYMENT OF FREIGHT AND OTHERLAWFUL CHARGES.'			TOTALS			

IN WITNESS WHEREOF THE CARRIER BY ITS AGENT HAS SIGNED

SIGNATURE OF CONSIGNOR ______

RECEIVED THE GOODS OR PACKAGES SHIPPER'S LOAD AND COUNT GOODS HEREINAFTER MENTIONED IN APPARENT GOOD ORDER AND CONDITION UNLESS OTHERWISE INDICATED TO BE RELAYED AS HEREIN PROVIDED, THE RECEIPT, CUSTODY, CARRIAGE, DELIVERY, AND TRANSSHIPPING OF THE GOODS ARE SUBJECT TO THE TERMS APPEARING ON THE FACE AND BACK HEREOF, AND CARRIER'S TARIFFS ON FILE WITH THE INTERSTATE COMMERCE COMMISSION AND/OR THE FEDERAL MARITIME COMMISSION, WASHINGTON, D.C

LIABILITY LIMITED TO AMOUNT SPCIFIED IN SEC 16 UNLESS INCREASED VALUE DECLARED BY SHIPPER AS SPECIFIED BELOW:

ORIGINAL BILLS OF LADING ALL OF THE SAME TENOR AND DATE ONE OF WHICH BEING ACCOMPLISHED THE OTHERS TO STAND VOID.

DECLARED VALUE ______

*APPLICABLE ONLY WHEN USED AS A THROUGH BILL OF LADING AFTER MENTIONED IN APPARENT GOOD ORDER AND CONDITION UNLESS

**INDICATE WHETHER ANY OF THE CARGO IS HAZARDOUS MATERIAL UNDER DOT, INCO,OR OTHER REGULATIONS AND INDICATE THE CORRECT COMMODITY NUMBER IN DESCRIPTION OF PACKAGES AND GOODS ABOVE.

BY ______ CARRIER

BY ______ FOR SHIPPER

DATE ______

received-for-shipment bill of lading recognizes only the delivery of the goods to the common carrier; it does not warrant that the goods have been placed upon the ship.

If the sale contract is silent regarding the type of bill of lading, must the buyer accept a received-for-shipment bill of lading when presented with the documents? The answer for the U.S. exporter is different depending on whether the UCP 500[7] or Article 5 of the Uniform Commercial Code (UCC) is applied. Section 1-201(15) of the UCC defines a document title simply as a "bill of lading." It does not differentiate between "on-board" and "received-for-shipment." Section 1-201(6) further defines bill of lading as "a document evidencing the receipt of goods for shipment issued by a person engaged in the business of transporting or forwarding goods." Section 2-323 specifically authorizes the use of a "received-for-

7. Uniform Customs and Practices for Documentary Credits as published by the International Chamber of Commerce. See Chapter 11.

shipment" bill of lading in CIF or C & F contracts.[8] In contrast, Article 23 of the UCP states that "banks will, unless otherwise stipulated in the Credit, accept a document which: (ii) indicates that the goods have been loaded on board, or shipped on a named vessel."

Bills of lading are contracts between the owner or shipper of goods and the carrier. They do not affect the contractual relationship between the seller and the buyer. The person or firm named in a bill of lading to which goods are to be turned over is the **consignee.** A **straight bill of lading** is nonnegotiable. Such a bill allows only for delivery to the named consignee in the bill. A negotiable or **order bill of lading** can be bought, sold, or traded while the goods are in transit. The order bill is also used for many types of financing transactions.[9] The owner needs the original bill of lading in order to take possession of the goods. A **clean bill of lading** is a receipt for goods issued by a carrier with an indication that the goods were received in "apparent good order and condition." In letter of credit transactions, a "Clean, On-Board, Order Bill of Lading" is necessary for the shipper to obtain payment from the bank.

AIR WAYBILL

Most transport of goods is performed through ocean carriage. In the event of transit by air, however, the operative transport document is the **air waybill** (Exhibit 9.6). The air waybill is a bill of lading that covers both domestic and international flights transporting goods to a specified destination. It is a nonnegotiable instrument that serves as a receipt for the shipper. Unlike the ocean bill of lading, the air waybill does not act as a document of title. Therefore, it merely serves as a contract of carriage and a receipt for goods.

The front of the air waybill makes a number of important representations. First, unless noted otherwise, the "goods are accepted in apparent good order and condition." Second, the shipper is directed to the reverse of the form for an explanation of the carrier's "limitation of liability." Third, the shipper is provided with notice of his right to increase carrier's liability. "Shipper may increase such limitation of liability by declaring a higher value for carriage and paying a supplemental charge." Also provided is a space for the "Amount of Insurance" requested by the shipper. Above the signature line, the shipper is notified that he is certifying that the goods are not dangerous unless described as such. If dangerous by nature, then the shipper certifies that the goods are in "proper condition for carriage by air according to the applicable Dangerous Goods Regulation."

Trade Terms

The insertion of a **trade term** into the sales contract allows the parties to designate the point at which the costs and risks of transport are divided between the seller and buyer. The **risk of loss** allocation determines who has the responsibility for any loss or damage to the goods while they are in transit. The generic costs allocated by the trade term are the costs of freight and insurance. As a practical matter the trade term will also allocate a number of other responsibilities including

8. "Where the contract contemplates overseas shipment and contains a term CIF or C & F or FOB vessel, the seller unless otherwise agreed must obtain a negotiable bill of lading stating that the goods have been loaded on board or, in the case of a term CIF or C & F, received for shipment." UCC § 2-323(1).
9. See Chapter 11.

EXHIBIT 9.6 *Air Waybill*

Shipper's Name and Address
Shipper's Account Number
Not negotiable
Air Waybill *
Issued by
Copies 1, 2 and 3 of this Air Waybill are originals and have the same validity.
Consignee's Name and Address
Consignee's Account Number
It is agreed that the goods described herein are accepted in apparent good order and condition (except as noted) for carriage SUBJECT TO THE CONDITIONS OF CONTRACT ON THE REVERSE HEREOF. ALL GOODS MAY BE CARRIED BY ANY OTHER MEANS INCLUDING ROAD OR ANY OTHER CARRIER UNLESS SPECIFIC CONTRARY INSTRUCTIONS ARE GIVEN HEREON BY THE SHIPPER, AND SHIPPER AGREES THAT THE SHIPMENT MAY BE CARRIED VIA INTERMEDIATE STOPPING PLACES WHICH THE CARRIER DEEMS APPROPRIATE. THE SHIPPER'S ATTENTION DRAWN TO THE NOTICE CONCERNING CARRIER'S LIMITATION OF LIABILITY. Shipper may increase such limitation of liability by declaring a higher value for carriage and paying a supplemental charge if required.
Issuing Carrier's Agent Name and City
Accounting information
Agent's IATA Code
Account No.
Airport of Departure (Addr. of first Carrier) and requested Routing
to | By first Carrier | Routing and Destination | to | by | to | by | Currency | Chgs Code | WT/VAL PPD COLL | Other PPD COLL | Declared Value for Carriage | Declared Value for Customs
Airport of Destination | Flight/Date | For Carrier Use only | Flight/Date | Amount of Insurance | INSURANCE – If carrier offers insurance, and such insurance is requested in accordance with the conditions thereof, indicate amount to be insured in figures in box marked "Amount of Insurance".
Handling Information
These commodities licensed by the U.S. for ultimate destination
Diversion contrary to U.S. law prohibited.

No. of Pieces RCP	Gross Weight	kg lb	Rate Class / Commodity Item No.	Chargeable Weight	Rate / Charge	Total	Nature and Quantity of Goods (incl. Dimensions or Volume)

Prepaid | Weight Charge | Collect
Other Charges
Valuation Charge
Tax
Total other Charges Due Agent
Shipper certifies that the particulars on the face hereof are correct and that **insofar as any part of the consignment contains dangerous goods, such part is properly described by name and is in proper condition for carriage by air according to the applicable Dangerous Goods Regulations.**
Total other Charges Due Carrier
Signature of Shipper or his Agent
Total prepaid | Total collect
Currency Conversion Rates | cc charges in Dest. Currency
Executed on (Date) at (Place) Signature of Issuing Carrier or its Agent
For Carriers Use only at Destination | Charges at Destination | Total collect Charges

Source: A Basic Guide to Exporting, U.S. Department of Commerce in cooperation with Unz & Co., Inc. (1999).

customs clearance, payment of duties, and the loading-unloading of the goods from the common carrier. The trade term is an element in the contract of sale and can normally be found in the *pro forma* invoice. The importance of the trade term and other **risk-shifting clauses**[10] in the international sales contract is explained in the following excerpt:

Harold J. Berman*, The Law of International Commercial Transactions (Lex Mercatoria),** *2* Journal of International Dispute Resolution ***245-248, 276 (1988)

10. Examples of risk-shifting clauses include arbitration, forum selection, choice of law, *force majeure,* and liquidated damages clauses.

The Export-Import Contract

Many of the risks inherent in an international transaction can be allocated by the importer and exporter through their contract of sale, under familiar principles of contract law. . . . Out of the price-delivery term, and especially out of the term "CIF" which is probably the most widely used term in international trade contracts, has come a great deal of law. The price-delivery term defines the title to the goods, time and place of delivery, time and place of payment, importer's right of inspection, the risk of loss or damage to the goods in transit, and the cost of transportation.

***

An international sales contract typically contains other risk-shifting clauses. Force majeure *and other contingency clauses are added to escape liability where unforeseen circumstances prevent performance of an assumed obligation. Choice of law, choice of forum, and arbitration clauses seek to avoid the vagaries, uncertainties, and delays of foreign litigation. The tendency to spell out in detail such matters as inspection rights and remedies for breach may also be an attempt to substitute the law of the contract for that of any national legal system.*

***

Destination and Shipment Contracts

An importer may ask his foreign supplier to place the goods on board a vessel bound for the country of destination and to bear the risks of the voyage. Such a contract is called a "destination contract." . . . "Shipment contracts" cast the risk of loss upon the purchaser from the moment of loading or shipment. The seller typically agrees to place the goods on board or alongside the vessel, but the risks of transit are shifted to the buyer. Typical shipment contracts include FAS, FOB, CIF, and CFR.

http://
International Chamber of Commerce: **http://www.iccwbo.org**.

The trade term controls the parties' respective obligations regarding contracting for shipping and insurance services. The trade term is also important in determining the conformity of documents in the documentary transaction. A trade term, whether taken from the international trade terms manual (INCOTERMS) as published by the International Chamber of Commerce or the UCC, is a three-letter acronym that allocates the cost, risk of loss, and responsibilities of transporting the goods between the seller and buyer.

In addition, the trade term affects documentary requirements. For example, the **FOB** (free on board) trade term generally dictates that the bill of lading need not show that the freight has been paid since freight costs and shipping arrangements are delegated to the buyer in a FOB contract. There are some variations recognized by most parties. For instance, the buyer can negotiate an additional services clause into a FOB contract. This clause often requires the seller to secure liner space and an insurance certificate as agent for the buyer. This type of clause acts as a compromise for the seller who wants to avoid the risk of paying for any escalation in insurance or freight costs. Additionally, such a clause benefits the buyer who is willing to incur such costs but finds it difficult to book a ship or insurance at the port of shipment.

In selecting trade terms, the parties should also be concerned with any conflicts between the chosen trade term and other terms in the contract. For example, a CIF contract shifts the risk of loss to the buyer at the port of shipment. If the contract provides that the seller guarantees a certain weight or quality at arrival, then the risks of loss below that weight would seem to shift back to the seller. What term will dictate liability for loss during transit? "The tendency of courts (in the United States) has been to subordinate conflicting terms to the CIF term."[11] Under the UCC a guarantee of quality clause is likely to be construed only as a guarantee of "ordinary deterioration, shrinkage, and the like in transportation."[12] All other causes of loss or damage remain with the buyer. Furthermore, an occurrence within the "quality clause" does not provide the buyer with a right of rejection but only a right of adjustment. Professor Berman notes that comments to UCC Section 2-321(3) make such a presumption.

> *[T]he express language used in an agreement is frequently a precautionary, fuller statement of the normal CIF terms and hence not intended as a departure or variation from them. Moreover, the dominant outlines of the CIF term are so well understood commercially that any variation should, whenever reasonably possible, be read as falling within those dominant outlines rather than as destroying the whole meaning of a term which essentially indicates a contract for proper shipment rather than one for delivery at destination.*[13]

Nonetheless, it is important for contracting parties not to vary recognized trade terms.

In international contracting, the trade terms as defined in **INCOTERMS 2000** should be used.[14] The dangers of varying the standard trade terms are illustrated by *Kumar Corp. v. Nopal Lines, Ltd.*[15] Kumar entered into a contract to sell goods to Nava in Venezuela on a consignment basis. Consignment is the delivery of goods from an exporter (consignor) to an agent (consignee) under agreement that the agent sells the goods on the account of the exporter. The consignor retains title to the goods until sold. The consignee sells the goods for commission and remits the net proceeds to the consignor. The contract trade term was CIF. Unfortunately, the goods were stolen while in possession of the common carrier at the port of shipment. Since payment was not due until a resale of the goods in Venezuela, Nava was under no obligation to pay against documents. In bringing suit against the common carrier, Kumar would have to overcome the defense that under the CIF term, risk of loss had passed to the buyer and therefore, Kumar had no standing to sue. Failure to overcome that defense would result in Kumar not having any recourse except for a claim under an applicable insurance policy.[16]

International sale of goods contracts are defined as either **shipment** or **destination contracts.** Whether a contract is described as a shipment or destination contract depends on when the risk of loss passes from the seller to the buyer. In a shipment contract the risk of loss passes to the buyer at the point of shipment. In contrast, in a destination contract the risk of loss passes to the buyer at the point of destination. The risk of loss refers to which party will suffer the loss of damaged or lost goods. For example, if the risk of loss has passed to the buyer and the goods are subsequently lost at sea, then the buyer will have to pay for goods it will never receive. The party that has the risk of loss is liable for any damages to the goods that occurred while it retained the risk. The trade term, among other things, allocates the risk of loss. If the contract

11. Berman at 250. Professor Berman notes a more drastic example of inconsistency when a CIF term is coupled with a "no arrival, no sale" clause. "With full risk of loss on the seller, it makes no sense for the buyer to have the right to the insurance proceeds." Ibid. at 251.
12. Ibid. at 253, citing UCC § 2-321(2).
13. UCC § 2-320, Comment 14.
14. Reference to INCOTERMS will generally be to INCOTERMS 1990. However, the International Chamber of Commerce recently published the ICC GUIDE TO INCOTERMS 2000, ICC Pub. No. 620 (1999).
15. 462 So.2d 1178 (Fl. Ct. Appeals 1985).
16. Ironically, Kumar's negligence in not procuring insurance coverage enabled it to sue the common carrier. The court held that since Kumar had failed to obtain insurance as required by the CIF term the risk of loss remained with Kumar. Thus, Kumar had the requisite standing to sue the common carrier.

fails to use a trade term, then generally the risk of loss passes at the time the seller delivers the goods to the carrier.[17] Thus, the presumption is in favor of a shipment contract. In order to avoid risk of loss and performance disputes, the contract should use accepted trade terms to clearly state whether it is a shipment or destination contract.

It is important, as discussed in *Phillips Puerto Rico v. Tradax Petroleum* in Chapter 3, to examine the interrelationship between the trade term and other terms in the contract. This is especially necessary if other language in the contract can be construed as modifying the trade term. This was the issue in *Warner Bros. & Co. v. Israel.*[18] That case involved the purchase of Philippine sugar for shipment to New York City. The trade term in the contract stated "Philippines—C.I.F. Terms." Another provision in the contract provided that the seller was to deliver sugar of a "net delivered weight." The sugar was delayed entry into the United States due to the imposition of a government sugar quota. The buyer attempted to avoid payment by arguing that the "net delivered weight" language converted the contract to a delivery or destination contract. It argued that the net delivered weight could only be determined at the port of destination.

The court rejected the argument holding that it was a CIF contract where the purchaser must pay upon the presentation of documents. It held that the "net delivered weight" language referred to the adjustment of the price based upon the weight of the sugar actually delivered, but was not enough to convert the express trade term into a destination contract. It further noted the general proposition that a delivery term (to be delivered to New York City) does not change an express trade term. "Under the ordinary CIF contract, delivery of the goods would not be a condition precedent to be performed at the risk of the seller. Nor is it made so merely because the obligation to contract for the carriage is expressed in the form of the delivery of the goods at a designated place."[19] The result may be different, however, if the destination term is included in the same provision as the trade term. It is important, therefore, to use the trade term without further explanation and to make sure that other terms in the contract do not expressly conflict with the term chosen.

The contract of carriage (bill of lading) should be consistent with the allocation of responsibilities provided by the trade term in the sales contract. A misunderstanding regarding the trade or delivery term is likely to prevent exporters from meeting contractual obligations or to make them responsible for shipping costs they sought to avoid. It is important to understand and use trade terms correctly; the trade terms in international business transactions often sound similar to those used in domestic business, but they frequently have very different meanings.[20] For this reason, the exporter must know the terms before preparing a quotation or a *pro forma* invoice. A few of the more common terms used in international trade include:

- CIF (cost, insurance, freight) to a named overseas port of import. Under this term, the seller quotes a price for the goods including insurance and all transportation charges to the point of debarkation from the vessel.

17. See CISG Article 67 ("handing the goods over to the first carrier") when the contract envisions carriage of goods and Article 69 (when contract requires buyer to pick up goods at seller's place of business); UCC §2-503 (risk passes at seller's place of business upon notification to buyer if the contract does not require sending the goods) and § 2-504 (when contract envisions "shipment by seller" risk passes when placed in possession of carrier). See generally Berman & Ladd, "Risk of Loss or Damage in Documentary Transactions Under the Convention on the International Sale of Goods," 21 *Cornell International Law Journal* 423 (1988).
18. 101 F.2d 59 (2d Cir. 1939).
19. Ibid. at 61.
20. For example, compare INCOTERMS with Sections 2-319 ("F.O.B. and F.A.S."), 2-320 and 2-321 ("C.I.F. and C. & F."), and 2-322 ("Delivery Ex Ship") of the Uniform Commercial Code.

- CFR (cost and freight) to a named overseas port of import. Under this term, the seller quotes a price for the goods that includes the cost of transportation to the named point of debarkation. The buyer pays the cost of insurance.
- CPT (carriage paid to) and CIP (carriage and insurance paid to) a named place of destination. Used in place of CFR and CIF, respectively, for shipment by modes other than water.
- EXW (ex works) at a named point of origin, such as the seller's factory, mill, or warehouse. Under this term, the price quoted applies only at the point of origin and the seller agrees to place the goods at the disposal of the buyer at the specified place on the specified date. The buyer pays all charges for transport and insurance.
- FAS (free alongside ship) at a named port of export. Under this term, the seller quotes a price for the goods that includes charges for delivery of the goods alongside a vessel at the port. The buyer handles the cost of loading, ocean transportation, and insurance.
- FCA (free carrier) to a named place. This term replaces the former "FOB named inland port" to designate the seller's responsibility for the cost of loading goods at the named shipping point. It may be used for any mode of transport including multimodal.
- FOB (free on board) at a named port of export. The seller quotes the buyer a price that covers all costs up to and including delivery of goods aboard an overseas vessel.
- DES (delivered ex ship) to a named place of destination. The DES term requires the seller to pay the cost of transport and insurance to the port of destination. The buyer is responsible for unloading the ship and for clearing the goods through customs.

The exporter should quote CIF whenever possible, because it has meaning abroad. It shows the foreign buyer that the cost of shipping the product to the port in the country of importation will be borne by the seller. If assistance is needed in figuring the CIF price, an international freight forwarder can help. If at all possible, the exporter should quote the price in U.S. dollars. Doing so eliminates the risk of possible exchange rate fluctuations and the problems of currency conversion. INCOTERMS 2000, a booklet issued by the International Chamber of Commerce (ICC), and the most accepted source of international trade terms is the subject of the next section.

INCOTERMS 2000

http://

Company Guide to Shipping includes materials on INCOTERMS, bills of lading, shipping documents, and a glossary.
http://www.yellowglobal.com/resources/index.jsp.

The rules for interpreting a trade term are of primary importance in international sale of goods transactions. Trade terms are used to allocate the costs of freight and insurance, along with stating the time that the risk of loss passes to the purchaser. The rules of interpretation for trade terms also determine who is responsible for dealing with customs agents and the payment of tariffs. Traditionally, national laws provide the rules of interpretation.[21] In international trade, trade terms as defined in the *INCOTERMS 2000 Manual,* published by the International Chamber of Commerce, has obtained almost universal acceptance. (See Focus on Transactions: INCOTERMS.) INCOTERMS provides 13 terms categorized into four groups: E Group (EXW), F Group (FCA, FAS, FOB), C Group (CFR, CIF, CPT, CIP), and D Group (DAF, DES, DEQ, DDU, DDP). A key advantage in using INCOTERMS is

21. See, e.g., Uniform Commercial Code Sections 2-319 to 2-322.

that they have been consistently updated to reflect contemporary commercial practice.[22] Along with selecting an INCOTERM, the parties should detail any rights and obligations associated with the shipment of the goods, including any special marking, packaging, inspection, and testing requirements.

When using an INCOTERM always cite to the INCOTERMS Manual. Thus, in selecting an INCOTERM, state the three-letter trade term, such as CIF, FOB, or DES, "as defined in INCOTERMS 2000."[23] The 13 INCOTERMS provide a broad range of options regarding the relative responsibilities of the exporter and importer. It is important not to attempt any variation of the terms. Also, some of the terms are to be used only for certain modes of transportation, while others can be used for all modes of transportation. The FAS, FOB, CFR, CIF, DES, and DEQ terms are used for carriage of goods by sea. The EXW, FCA, CIP, CPT, DAF, DDU, and DDP terms can be used generally, including for multimodal means of shipment.

INCOTERMS 2000 made a number of changes to INCOTERMS 1990. The most important differences in substance concern:

- placing the export clearance obligation under FAS on the seller (previously on the buyer)
- the specification of the seller's obligation to load the goods on the buyer's collecting vehicle and the buyer's obligation to receive the seller's arriving vehicle unloaded under FCA
- the placing of the import clearance obligation under DEQ on the buyer (previously on the seller)
- the suggestion that instead of relying on the "crossing the ship's rail" standard found in the FOB, CFR, and CIF terms, the parties are invited to choose such terms as FCA, CPT, and CIP where delivery of the goods is connected to the handing over of the goods to the carrier.

The "crossing the ship's rail" standard shifts the risk of loss to the buyer when the cargo passes an imaginary line above the ship's rail. This murky standard is likely to produce dispute in the event that the goods are damaged while in possession of the carrier prior to loading or while the goods are being loaded on the ship. INCOTERMS list obligations that the terms allocate. These obligations include:

- obtaining necessary export licenses and government authorizations
- satisfying import requirements and formalities
- giving notice regarding a vessel hired for transport
- giving notice of delivery to the common carrier
- checking, packaging, and marking goods
- obtaining transport and other documents

The notice of the hiring of a vessel is normally the responsibility of the buyer under the FOB, FAS, and FCA terms. Notice of delivery to the common carrier is the responsibility of the seller. The next few sections will examine the more important INCOTERMS in greater detail.

FOB AND FAS TERMS

Under FOB (Free on Board), the seller must deliver conforming goods on board the vessel named by the buyer at the stipulated time and must give notice to the

22. As a result, the CISG elected not to provide any competing terms and the current Revision of Article 2 of the Uniform Commercial Code eliminates its provisions dealing with trade terms.

23. The material in this paragraph was taken from ICC, "The ICC Model International Sale Contract," Pub. No. 556(E) (1997) at 30-31.

buyer of the delivery. The seller bears all costs up to the passing of the ship's rail at the port of shipment including exportation fees, the packing and checking of the goods, and the costs of obtaining a document evidencing the loading of the goods. He is also obligated to obtain a certificate of origin at the buyer's request and expense.

In turn, the buyer must book the carriage and give notice to seller of the name, loading berth, and dates for delivery to vessel. The buyer, along with bearing the costs of freight and insurance, pays the costs of obtaining most documents including the certificate of origin, consular invoice, and in some incidences the bill of lading.[24] It should be noted that it is a common practice in the United States to use the FOB term in conjunction with the place of destination, such as "FOB Buffalo (place of destination)." This would, in essence convert the contract into a destination contract whereby the risk of loss would not pass until arrival in Buffalo.

FAS or Free Alongside Ship is essentially the same as FOB except that the seller's responsibilities end when the goods are brought alongside the ship. This is performed when the goods are delivered on the dock or placed in lighters at the port of shipment. The buyer has to bear all costs and risks of loss, including the loading of the goods onto the ship, at the moment the goods are placed alongside the ship. The responsibility of obtaining export clearance is also placed upon the buyer. Therefore, this term is not for use by an unsophisticated buyer who is not familiar with the formalities of exporting. INCOTERMS 2000 requires the seller to "Obtain at his own risk and expense any export license or other official authorization and carry out, where applicable, all customs formalities necessary for the export of the goods."

CIF AND CFR TERMS

Under the CIF term the seller's responsibilities include obtaining a marine insurance policy and a carriage contract. He must also at his expense obtain any export license and arrange for the loading of the goods. The marine insurance policy shall be in the amount of CIF value plus 10 percent. The seller must also obtain war risk coverage at the request and expense of the buyer. He must obtain a "clean, on-board bill of lading." It should be noted that some clauses commonly inserted into the bill of lading that refer to the condition of the packaging do not render the bill of lading "unclean." For example, clauses that note that the packages are "used" or "secondhand" are considered descriptive and not a notation of perceived damage or nonconformity. Such statements as "condition unknown" in the above clauses do not remove the presumption that the carrier guarantees that the goods were "in apparent good order and condition."

The costs of packing and checking the goods are those of the seller. In turn, the buyer is required to pay the cost of unloading, along with lighterage and wharfage charges. The buyer can transfer the costs of unloading by negotiating a "CIF landed" term. The buyer also pays for the costs of obtaining the certificate of origin and any necessary import licenses or permits, along with all customs duties.

Other related responsibilities should be expressly allocated in the contract. For example, the CIF term requires the seller to obtain only a basic ("free of particular average") marine insurance policy in the currency of the contract. The parties should agree to any special risk endorsements that may be appropriate including theft, pilferage, leakage, breakage, and other risks of concern for the particular goods and the particular point of destination. The contract should specify how delivery is to take place, who is responsible for loading and unloading, how much insurance coverage is

24. The need for the buyer to obtain a bill of lading may occur when he charters a vessel and the seller is issued a mate's receipt instead of a bill of lading.

required, as well as the contract's duration and geographical scope, and details regarding the type of carriage (e.g., above deck or below, refrigerated container, etc.). Also, the party responsible for customs clearance or delivery should negotiate a *force majeure* or **time-extension clause** in case of delay in clearing customs or making delivery.

The **CFR** term is also referred to in the United States as the C & F term. It is essentially the same as the CIF term except that the responsibility to obtain and pay for the marine insurance is shifted to the buyer. It remains the responsibility of the seller to clear the goods through customs at the place of shipment or exportation. It is important to understand that the "C terms" are "shipment contracts" and not "arrival or destination contracts." The risk of loss is transferred, like in the "F terms," at the port of shipment.

CPT, CIP, AND FCA TERMS

The traditional prevalence of the FOB, CFR, and CIF terms is likely to give way to increased use of the **CPT, CIP,** and **FCA** terms. The traditional supremacy of FOB, CFR, and CIF contracts was due to the central importance of marine carriage. The advent of modern containerization and multimodal transport is likely to result in these terms yielding to the FCA, CPT, and CIP terms, simply because the traditional function of the ship's rail as the dividing point between sellers' and buyers' functions has been replaced by other points, such as cargo terminals or other reception facilities. This has also influenced documentation and reduced significantly the use of on-board bills of lading. Thus, even in the carriage of goods by sea, non-negotiable sea waybills have replaced bills of lading.[25] Under INCOTERMS 2000, the FCA term now provides that delivery by seller is completed only when the goods have been loaded on the transport provided by the carrier.

EX WORKS TERM

The **ex works** term is the most pro-seller trade term. It means that the seller fulfills his obligation to deliver when he notifies the buyer that the goods are available at his factory, warehouse, or office. The seller is not responsible for loading the goods on the vehicles provided by the buyer or for clearing the goods for export. The buyer bears all the costs and risks of transport from seller's place of business to the point of destination. Only an expert importer willing to undertake satisfying export formalities in a foreign country should use this term.

D TERMS

The D group terms (DAF, DES, DEQ, DDU, DDP) are the only terms that are considered to be destination contracts. The **DES** term is the most longstanding of the D terms. DES obligates the seller to bear the costs and risks of shipment to the port of destination. Seller's responsibilities end when the goods have been made available to the buyer on board the ship at the port of destination. It is the buyer's responsibility to unload the goods from the ship and to clear the goods through customs in the country of delivery. This term, along with the **DEQ** term, are to be used only for water transport.

The DEQ term gives the seller the added responsibility of unloading the goods and makes the goods available to the buyer at the wharf (quay). This also means that it is the seller's responsibility to clear the goods through customs. The seller then bears

25. Jan Ramberg, "Novel Features of the ICC Incoterms 1990" in UNITED NATIONS UNIFORM COMMERCIAL LAW IN THE TWENTY-FIRST CENTURY 80 (1992).

Focus on Transactions

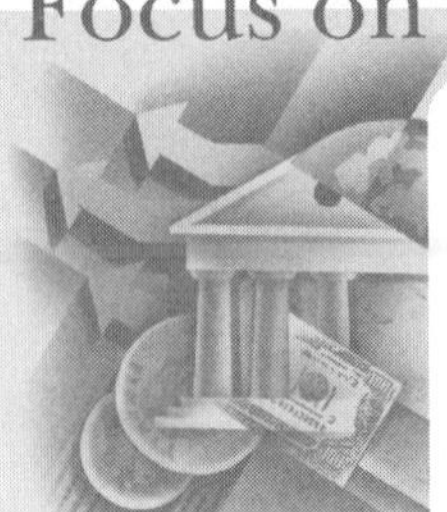

INCOTERMS[26]

EX WORKS (. . . named place)

Ex works means that the seller fulfils his obligation to deliver when he has made the goods available at his premises (works, factory, warehouse, etc.) to the buyer. In particular, he is not responsible for loading the goods on the vehicle provided by the buyer or for clearing the goods for export, unless otherwise agreed. The buyer bears all costs and risks involved in taking the goods from the seller's premises to the desired destination. This term thus represents the minimum obligation for the seller. This should not be used when the buyer cannot carry out directly or indirectly the export formalities. In such circumstances, the FCA term should be used.

FCA Free Carrier (. . . named place)

Free carrier means that the seller fulfils his obligation to deliver when he has handed over the goods, cleared for export, into the charge of the carrier named by the buyer at the named place or point. If no precise point is indicated by the buyer, the seller may choose within the place or range stipulated where the carrier shall take the goods into his charge. When, according to commercial practice, the seller's assistance is required in making the contract with the carrier (such as in rail or air transport) the seller may act at the buyer's risk and expense. This term may be used for any mode of transport, including multimodal transport. Carrier means any person who, in a contract of carriage, undertakes to perform or to procure the performance of carriage by rail, road, sea, air, or inland waterway or by a combination of such modes. If the buyer instructs the seller to deliver the cargo to a person, for example, a freight forwarder who is not a carrier, the seller is deemed to have fulfilled his obligation to deliver the goods when they are in the custody of that person. Transport terminal means a railway terminal, a freight station, a container terminal or yard, a multipurpose cargo terminal, or any similar receiving point. Container includes any equipment used to unload cargo, for example, all types of containers and/or flats whether ISO accepted or not, trailers, swap bodies, ro-ro equipment, or igloos, and applies to all modes of transport.

FAS Free Alongside Ship (. . . named port of shipment)

Free alongside ship means that the seller fulfils his obligation to deliver when the goods have been placed alongside the vessel on the quay or in lighters at the named port of shipment. This means that the buyer has to bear all costs and risks of loss of or damage to the goods from that moment. The FAS term requires the buyer to clear the goods for export. It should not be used when the buyer cannot carry out directly or indirectly the export formalities. This term can only be used for sea or inland waterway transport.

FOB Free on Board (. . . named port of shipment)

Free on board means that the seller fulfils his obligation to deliver when the goods have passed over the ship's rail at the named port of shipment. This means that the buyer has to bear all costs and risks of loss of or damage to the goods from that point. The FOB term requires the seller to clear the goods for export. This term can be used only for sea or inland waterway transport. When the ship's rail serves no practical purpose, such as in the case of roll-on/roll-off or container traffic, the FCA term is more appropriate to use.

CFR Cost and Freight (. . . named port of destination)

Cost and freight means that the seller must pay the costs and freight necessary to bring the goods to the named port of destination but the risk of loss of or damage to the goods, as well as any additional costs due to events occurring after the time the goods have been delivered on board the vessel, is transferred from the seller to the buyer when the goods pass the ship's rail in the port of shipment. The CFR term requires the seller to clear the goods for export. This

26. For a complete explanation of INCOTERMS, see Jan Ramberg, *ICC Guide to Incoterms* 2000 (Pub. No. 620) (1999).

term can be used only for sea and inland waterway transport. When the ship's rail serves no practical purpose, such as in the case of roll-on/roll-off or container traffic, the CPT term is appropriate to use.

CIF Cost, Insurance, and Freight (. . . named port of destination)
Cost, insurance, and freight means that the seller has the same obligations as under CFR but with the addition that he has to procure marine insurance against the buyer's risk of loss of or damage to the goods during the carriage. The seller contracts for insurance and pays the insurance premium. The buyer should note that under the CIF term the seller is required to obtain insurance only on minimum coverage. The CIF term requires the seller to clear the goods for export. This term can be used only for sea and inland waterway transport. When the ship's rail serves no practical purposes such as in the case of roll-on/roll-off or container traffic, the CIP term is more appropriate to use.

CPT Carriage Paid To (. . . named place of destination)
Carriage paid to means that the seller pays the freight for the carriage of the goods to the named destination. The risk of loss of or damage to the goods, as well as any additional costs due to events occurring after the time the goods have been delivered to the carrier, is transferred from the seller to the buyer when the goods have been delivered into the custody of the carrier. Carrier means any person who, in a contract of carriage, undertakes to perform or to procure the performance of carriage, by rail, road, sea, air, or inland waterway or by a combination of such modes. If subsequent carriers are used for the carriage to the agreed destination, the risk passes when the goods have been delivered to the first carrier. The CPT term requires the seller to clear the goods for export. This term may be used for any mode of transport including multimodal transport.

CIP Carriage and Insurance Paid To (. . . named place of destination)
Carriage and insurance paid to (. . .) means that the seller has the same obligations as under CPT but with the addition that the seller has to procure cargo insurance against the buyer's risk of loss of or damage to the goods during the carriage. The seller contracts for insurance and pays the insurance premium. The buyer should note that under the CIP term the seller is required to obtain insurance only on minimum coverage. The CIP term requires the seller to clear the goods for export. This term may be used for any mode of transport including multimodal transport.

DAF Delivered at Frontier (. . . named place)
Delivered at frontier means that the seller fulfils his obligation to deliver when the goods have been made available, cleared for export, at the named point and place at the frontier, but before the customs border of the adjoining country. The term frontier may be used for any frontier including that of the country of export. Therefore, it is of vital importance that the frontier in question be defined precisely by always naming the point and place in the term. The term is intended to be used primarily when goods are to be carried by rail or road, but it may be used for any mode of transport.

DES Delivered Ex Ship (. . . named port of destination)
Delivered ex ship means that the seller fulfils his obligation to deliver when the goods have been made available to the buyer on board the ship uncleared for import at the named port of destination. The seller has to bear all the costs and risks involved in bringing the goods to the named port of destination. This term can be used only for sea or inland waterway transport.

DEQ Delivered Ex Quay (Duty Paid) (. . . named port of destination)
Delivered ex quay (duty paid) means that the seller fulfils his obligation to deliver when he has made the goods available to the buyer on the quay (wharf) at the named port of destination, cleared for importation. The seller has to bear all risks and costs including duties, taxes, and other charges of delivering the goods thereto. This term should not be used if the seller is unable directly or indirectly to obtain the import license. If the

Focus on Transactions *(continued)*

parties wish the buyer to clear the goods for importation and pay the duty the words duty unpaid should be used instead of duty paid. If the parties wish to exclude from the seller's obligations some of the costs payable upon importation of the goods (such as value-added tax [VAT]), this should be made clear by adding words to this effect: Delivered ex quay. VAT unpaid (. . . named port of destination). This term can be used only for sea or inland waterway transport.

DDU Delivered Duty Unpaid (. . . named place of destination)
Delivered duty unpaid means that the seller fulfils his obligation to deliver when the goods have been made available at the named place in the country of importation. The seller has to bear the costs and risks involved in bringing the goods thereto (excluding duties, taxes, and other official charges payable upon importation as well as the costs and risks of carrying out customs formalities). The buyer has to pay any additional costs and to bear any risks caused by his failure to clear the goods for import in time. If the parties wish the seller to carry out customs formalities and bear the costs and risks resulting therefrom, this has to be made clear by adding words to this effect. If the parties wish to include in the seller's obligations some of the costs payable upon importation of the goods (such as value-added tax [VAT]), this should be made clear by adding words to this effect: Delivered duty unpaid. VAT paid, (. . . named place of destination). This term may be used irrespective of the mode of transport.

DDP Delivered Duty Paid (. . . named place of destination)
Delivered duty paid means that the seller fulfils his obligation to deliver when the goods have been made available at the named place in the country of importation. The seller has to bear the risks and costs, including duties, taxes, and other charges of delivering the goods thereto, cleared for importation. Whilst the Ex Works term represents the minimum obligation for the seller, DDP represents the maximum obligation. This term should not be used if the seller is unable directly or indirectly to obtain the import license. If the parties wish the buyer to clear the goods for importation and to pay the duty, the term DDU should be used. If the parties wish to exclude from the seller's obligations some of the costs payable upon importation of the goods (such as value-added tax [VAT]), this should be made clear by adding words to this effect: Delivered duty paid, VAT unpaid (. . . named place of destination). This term may be used irrespective of the mode of transport.

the costs of any duties, taxes, or other charges associated with the importation of the goods. A relatively unsophisticated exporter who is unprepared to obtain the necessary import license in a foreign country should not use this term.

The remaining D terms, DAF, DDU, and DDP, can be used in association with any mode of transport, including ocean, rail, and truck. The **DAF** or delivered at frontier requires the seller to clear the goods for export and deliver the goods to the border of an adjoining country. This term is used primarily in conjunction with rail or road transport, but may also be used for ocean carriage. The frontier needs to be expressly defined because it can mean either the border of the country of import or export. The **DDU** term stands for delivered duty unpaid, while the **DDP** term stands for delivered duty paid.

While Ex Works signifies the seller's minimum obligation, DDP, when followed by words naming the buyer's place of business, denotes the seller's maximum obligation. The seller must clear the goods for import into the buyer's country. A DDU contract is a destination contract in which the buyer is responsible for clearing the goods through customs. This entails paying any duties, taxes, and charges. Any additional costs and risks caused by the failure to clear the goods for import is borne by the buyer. This is essentially another version of the DES term that can be used for all modes of transport. The DDP term places the costs and risks of importation clearance on the seller. It is the same as the DEQ term, but may be used for all modes of transport.

Both the DDP and DDU terms may be modified in the event the buyer and seller want to allocate specific costs associated with the importation. If the parties agree that the buyer will pay all the import costs and fees except for any value-added tax, then they could modify the DDU term to read *Delivered Duty Unpaid, VAT Paid.* The parties may instead want the seller to pay for all import costs except for any value-added taxes. In this regard, they could modify the DDP term to read *Delivered Duty Paid, VAT Unpaid.*

MODERN TREND IN INCOTERMS

Under the FOB and FCA terms, practice often overtakes the legal obligation that the seller needs only turn over the goods to the carrier hired by the buyer. In practice, the seller generally books the shipment for carriage. This practice is noted in the INCOTERMS FCA trade term: "If requested by the buyer or if it is commercial practice and the buyer does not give an instruction to the contrary in due time, the seller may contract for carriage on usual terms at the buyer's risk and expense. The seller may decline to make the contract and, if he does, shall promptly notify the buyer accordingly."[27]

In practice, there are a variety of FOB contracts. Under the strict definition of the FOB term, the buyer nominates the ship, and the seller delivers the goods to that ship in exchange for the bill of lading. However, the FOB term in conjunction with "additional services" requires the seller to arrange the shipping and insurance on behalf of the buyer. The only distinction between the CIF contract and "FOB additional services" is that the arrangements are made at the expense of the buyer in the FOB additional services contract.[28] It is also important to note that the allocation of costs for loading and unloading under FOB, CIF, and C & F may be impacted by the customs of a given port. The FCA term is the trade term most likely to become more important because it applies to all modes of transport.

Key Terms

air waybill, 257
bill of exchange, 249
bill of lading, 251
booking contract, 255
cash against document, 249
cash in advance, 244
certificate of inspection, 242
certificate of origin, 252
CFR, 265
CIF, 249
CIP, 265
clean bill of lading, 257
commercial invoice, 252
consignee, 257
consignment sale, 245
consular invoice, 252
cost-plus method, 245
CPT, 265
DAF, 268
DDP, 268
DDU, 268

27. Jan Ramberg, *ICC Guide to Incoterms 2000* (1999).
28. Ralph H. Folsom, Michael W. Gordon, & John A. Spanogle, Jr., INTERNATIONAL BUSINESS TRANSACTIONS 90 (3d ed. 1995).

DEQ, 265
DES, 265
destination contract, 260
documentary collections transaction, 244
documentary credit transaction, 244
documents against acceptance, 249
drawee, 249
drawer, 249
electronic bill of lading, 255
ex works, 265
export license, 252
FAS, 264
FCA, 265
FOB, 259
INCOTERMS 2000, 260
insurance certificate, 252
marginal cost pricing, 245
on-board bill of lading, 255
open account, 244
order bill of lading, 257
packing slip, 252
pro forma invoice, 245
received-for-shipment bill of lading, 256
risk of loss, 257
risk-shifting clause, 258
shipment contract, 260
Shipper's Export Declaration (SED), 252
sight draft, 249
straight bill of lading, 257
time draft, 249
time-extension clause, 265
trade term, 257

Chapter Problems

1. A buyer and seller entered into a contract for the sale of widgets "CIF Omaha." A further provision stated that delivery was to be at a "factory in Omaha, Tulsa, or Kansas City, to be designated by the buyer." The widgets were lost in transit. The buyer refused to pay on the presentation of the documents arguing that the additional provision had converted the shipment contract to a destination contract. What type of contract was this and why? What advice would you give someone regarding the use of trade terms?

2. You are the purchasing agent for a U.S. luggage manufacturer. You are asked to outsource some of the components, including steel strips used in the fabrication of the structural frames of the larger pieces of luggage. Your company's manufacturing plant is located in Peoria, Illinois. Your research finds that the companies best able to supply the strips are located in Windsor, Canada; São Paulo, Brazil; and Padang, Indonesia. In asking for price quotations what types of documents should you require? From your perspective, which trade term should be used in the price quotations?

3. You are a manufacturer of precision industrial tools and parts based in Ithaca, New York. You have been contacted by a manufacturer in Budapest, Hungary, to begin supplying it with an assortment of your products. Using INCOTERMS, prepare a *pro forma* invoice with three different shipping options. For each option (INCOTERM) itemize the costs and relative responsibilities of the two parties. Consider how you will get the goods from Ithaca to Budapest. What modes of transport will need to be utilized? Who can you contact for information needed to prepare the invoice?

4. An export contract required that the seller provide: "A full set of 3 original clean on board bills of lading." Instead, the seller presented a full set of 3 clean on board bills of lading but only one was marked "Original." The other two bills of lading were marked "Duplicate" and "Triplicate." Can the buyer reject the bills of lading as not conforming to the documentary requirements of the contract?

5. A foreign buyer negotiates with a foreign exporter for goods to be shipped out of a foreign port. To protect itself from fraud in the transaction the buyer requires that the exporter provide an inspection certificate as one of the documents to be presented for payment. When the documents were presented for payment, the buyer noticed that the date on the inspection certificate was later than the shipment date on the bill of lading. The certificate failed to state when the inspection occurred. Can the buyer refuse payment due to this discrepancy?

Internet Exercises

1. You are unsure of what trade term to use in negotiating an export contract. You are willing to be responsible for the loading and shipping costs to the port of destination, along with the cost of unloading, but do not want to be responsible for import and customs clearance. What INCOTERM would best serve your needs? See **http://www.itds.treas.gov/incoterms.html**.

2. Select a country and research the documentary requirements for the importation of goods into that country. Such information can be obtained from the following sources: (1) U.S. Department of Commerce, (2) foreign government web sites, especially consulate sites, (3) Bureau of National Affairs Export Shipping Manual, and (4) National Council on International Trade Documentation (NCITD).

CARRIAGE OF GOODS BY SEA ACT 1 OF 1986

Incorporating the Hague Visby Rules

[As amended by the Shipping General Amendment Act, 1997 with effect from 1 September 1997]

[ASSENTED TO 4 MARCH 1986] [DATE OF COMMENCEMENT: 4 JULY 1986]

(Afrikaans text signed by the State President)

ACT

To amend the law with respect to the carriage of goods by sea, and to provide for matters connected therewith.

1 Application of Hague Rules

(1) Those Rules contained in the International Convention for the Unification of Certain Rules of Law Relating to Bills of Lading signed at Brussels on 25 August 1924, as amended by the Protocol signed at Brussels on 23 February 1968, which are set out in the Schedule (hereinafter referred to as the Rules) shall, subject to the provisions of this Act, have the force of law and apply in respect of the Republic in relation to and in connection with-

(a) the carriage of goods by sea in ships where the port of shipment is a port in the Republic, whether or not the carriage is between ports in two different States within the meaning of Article X of the Rules;

(b) any bill of lading if the contract contained in or evidenced by it expressly provides that the Rules shall govern the contract;

(c) any receipt which is a non-negotiable document marked as such if the contract contained in it or evidenced by it or pursuant to which it is issued is a contract for the carriage of goods by sea which expressly provides that the Rules are to govern the contract as if the receipt were a bill of lading, but subject to any necessary modifications and in particular with the omission in Article III of the Rules of the second sentence of paragraph 4 and paragraph 7; and

(d) deck cargo or live animals, if and in so far as the contract contained in or evidenced by a bill of lading or receipt referred to in paragraph (b) or (c) applies to deck cargo or live animals, as if Article I (c) of the Rules did not exclude deck cargo and live animals, and in this paragraph 'deck cargo' means cargo which by the contract of carriage is stated as being carried on deck and is so carried.

(2) The State President may by proclamation in the Gazette amend the Schedule and subsection (1) of this section to give effect to any amendment of or addition to the Rules which may be made from time to time and adopted by the Government of the Republic.

http://www.uctshiplaw.com/cogsa.htm

Chapter 10
Transport of Goods

In transporting goods throughout the world, a number of different types of **common carriers** are utilized. A common carrier is a company that contracts with the public for transportation of goods or persons; commercial airlines, overnight courier services, and international shipping lines are all examples of common carriers. Each type of common carrier or carriage contract is governed by its own **unimodal transport convention.** The most important international transport conventions are listed in Doing Business Internationally: International Transport Conventions.

The application of different carriage liability regimes in an international transport of goods transaction is potentially overwhelming. The leg of transport (land, rail, ocean) in which the loss-inducing event occurs determines the convention to be applied. Determining liability is further complicated by the existence of different legal regimes for a given mode of transport. For example, in ocean carriage

http://
Transportation Law Navigator—air and ocean transport: **http://www.cargolaw.com.** Comprehensive web site on issues pertaining to the transport of goods.

there are three alternative legal regimes—**Hague, Hague-Visby,** and the **Hamburg Rules.** If a loss is sustained during an ocean voyage, then it must be determined which ocean carriage convention is applicable.

The most established and important of the international carriage conventions is the Hague Rules.[1] The Hague Rules have been enacted into law in the United States as the **Carriage of Goods by Sea Act (COGSA).**[2] Most international transport of goods necessarily includes ocean carriage, and despite the increased use of multimodal transport documents, the **ocean bill of lading** remains the paramount title document. This chapter will focus on the legal regime instituted by the Hague Rules. The chapter concludes with a review of the related topic of marine insurance. We will first discuss briefly the premier air carriage convention—the **Warsaw Convention.**

AIR WAYBILL AND THE WARSAW CONVENTION

http://
Text of the Warsaw Convention: **http://www.forwarderlaw.com/archive/warsaw.htm.**

As a contract of carriage, the **air waybill** incorporates by reference the pertinent international carriage convention, namely the Warsaw Convention. Like the Hague Rules, the Warsaw Convention limits liability for the common carrier. The standard terms and conditions of the air waybill generally state that the liability limitation is "250 French Gold Francs per kilogram or approximately $20 per kilogram." The Warsaw Convention shares numerous similarities with the Hague

Doing Business Internationally

International Transport Conventions

Carriage by Air
Convention for the Unification of Certain Rules Relating to International Carriage by Air (Warsaw Convention)

Additional Protocols Nos. 1–4 to Amend the Warsaw Convention (Montreal Accord)

Carriage by Rail
International Convention Concerning the Carriage of Goods by Rail (CIM Convention)

Convention Concerning International Carriage by Rail (COTIF) (1990)

Carriage by Road
Convention on the Contract for the International Carriage of Goods by Road (CMR)

Carriage by Sea
Brussels Convention on Bills of Lading or International Convention for the Unification of Certain Rules of Law Relating to Bills of Lading (Hague Rules)

Protocol to Amend the Hague Rules (Hague-Visby Rules)

Hamburg Rules of 1978

Multimodal Transport
UNCTAD/ICC Rules for Multimodal Transport Documents (1991)

1. The formal name of the Hague Rules is the Brussels Convention for the Unification of Certain Rules Relating to Bills of Lading. See 51 Stat. 233 (1924).
2. Unless stated otherwise the Hague Rules and COGSA will be used interchangeably.

Rules. For example, it allows for the extension of coverage to other parties involved in the carriage through a Himalaya clause. It states that "any exclusion or limitation of liability applicable to the carrier shall apply to the benefit of the carrier's agents, servants, and representatives and any person whose aircraft is used by carrier for carriage."

The carrier is also protected from most claims of material deviation. The Convention states that "carriers may substitute alternative carriers or may without notice and with due regard to the interests of the shipper substitute other means of transportation. Carrier is authorized to select the routing or to change or deviate from the routing shown on the face of the air waybill." In the area of notice of damage, the consignee or person entitled to take delivery must promptly inspect the goods. He then must make a written complaint "of visible damage to the goods, immediately after discovery of the damage and at the latest within 14 days from receipt of the goods." The Convention provides for a two-year statute of limitation for the filing of claims.

INTERNATIONAL OCEAN CARRIAGE CONVENTIONS

Liability of common carriers is fixed by a combination of international conventions and national laws. National laws define issues of title and negotiability, while the international conventions impose the minimum duties of the carriers and provide limits to carrier liability. This was not always the case. Carriers, at one time, were able to shield themselves from liability by incorporating broad limitation of liability or **exculpatory clauses.** After many disputes with shippers, a compromise on issues of liability, know as the Hague Rules, was adopted in 1924. The Hague Rules established a number of carrier responsibilities such as the requirement to undertake due diligence in providing a seaworthy ship, to not deviate materially from the carriage contract, and to provide shippers with the opportunity to declare a higher value for their goods. In return, the shipping companies are provided a limitation of liability to cap their potential liabilities, along with a number of exemptions from liability.

> http://
> Megalaw.com—Admiralty/Maritime law: **http://www.megalaw.com/top/admiralty.php3**. Provides links to all of the major maritime laws in the United States, including the Harter Act.

There are three international conventions that regulate the liability of common carriers in the international transport of goods by sea: the Hague Rules, the Hague-Visby Rules, and the Hamburg Rules. There was, however, a predecessor to these international conventions—the U.S. **Harter Act** of 1893.[3] The primary objective of the Harter Act was to prohibit clauses whereby carriers attempted to eliminate their liability for acts of negligence. The Harter Act prohibited the enforcement of broad exculpatory clauses incorporated into the standard bills of lading by the shipping industry. It did not, however, attempt to regulate the relationships between carriers and shippers comprehensively. The Harter Act remains in force for goods shipped from one U.S. port to another U.S. port.

The Hague-Visby rules updated the Hague rules, but some countries, including the United States, have failed to ratify the update. The liability of the carrier and associated companies is directly affected depending on which version is applied. Under the Hague-Visby rules, the limit of liability is significantly increased. The Hamburg Rules are more pro-shipper than the Hague and Hague-Visby Rules.

3. 46 U.S.C. App. §§ 190-196 (1988).

Comparative Law

International Ocean Carriage of Goods Conventions

	Hague-Visby Rules	Hamburg Rules	Multimodal Convention (United Nations)[4]
Transport Document	Bill of lading	Any transport document including sea waybill	Multimodal document
Negotiable Transport Document	Yes	Optional	Optional
Application	Loaded in contracting state or stated in bill of lading	Between two contracting countries	Place of charge or delivery in contracting country; two different modes
Basis of Carrier's Liability	Due diligence in providing seaworthy ship; not liable for exceptions	Liable unless it proves it took all reasonable measures	Multimodal transport operator liable unless it proves it took all reasonable measures
Limitation of Carrier's Liability	10,000 gold francs per package or 30 gold francs per Kg[5]	835 SDR[6] per package or 2.5 SDR per Kg of gross weight	920 SDR per package or 2.75 per Kg or the higher amount provided under national law for a particular mode or leg of the transit
Limitation Period for Legal Action	1 year	2 years	2 years but notice must be given within 6 months of delivery

However, carrier liability protections are automatically extended to the servants or third-party contractors of the carriers under the Hamburg Rules.

The *Prima U.S. v. M/V Addiriyah* case on the next page illustrates a number of points. First, it provides an introduction to the different third parties involved in the international shipment of goods, including the common carrier, stevedores, freight forwarder, non-vessel operating common carrier, and the custom broker. Second, it analyzes the importance of being designated a common carrier under the above carriage conventions, along with the potential liabilities of the freight forwarder.

4. This convention has not come into force due to a lack of support. It is placed here to illustrate what a future multimodal convention may look like.
5. Under the U.S. Carriage of Goods by Sea Act (Hague Rules) the per package limitation is fixed at $500. The Hague-Visby Rules' per-package limitation translates to $1,000.
6. SDR is the acronym for "Special Drawing Rights," which is a standard of value based upon the rates of a basket of different national currencies.

COGSA

The Carriage of Goods by Sea Act or COGSA is the U.S. domestic version of the Hague or Hague-Visby Rules.[7] Most of the major maritime nations of the world have adopted one of these two conventions into their national laws. The U.S. Carriage of Goods by Sea Act is modeled after the Hague Rules; the United Kingdom's is modeled on the Hague-Visby Rules.

Prima U.S. Inc. v. M/V *Addiriyah*

223 F.3d 126 (2d Cir. 2000)

McLaughlin, Circuit Judge. The Westinghouse Electric Corporation ("Westinghouse") contracted in writing with Panalpina, Inc. ("Panalpina"), a "freight forwarder," for the transportation and shipment of an electric transformer from the manufacturer in Italy to the ultimate consignee, the 3M Corporation in Iowa. Panalpina, as freight forwarder, was to oversee all of the transportation for the transformer, both on land and over sea. Panalpina's obligations under the contract included ensuring that the transformer was properly secured and lashed onto a flat-rack for ocean shipment. As is the industry custom, Panalpina did not issue a bill of lading for the shipment.

Pursuant to the standard terms and conditions listed on the reverse side of its contract, Panalpina undertook to exercise "reasonable care" in the selection of those who would actually carry, store, or otherwise handle the goods. The standard terms also limited Panalpina's liability for losses to $50 per shipment, and they disclaimed liability for all consequential or special damages in excess of this amount. These were the same terms utilized in the prior ten-year course of dealing involving more than 1,000 transactions between Westinghouse and Panalpina. When the time came to ship the transformer, Panalpina arranged for it to be picked up at a factory in Melegano, Italy, and brought to the Port of Genoa for an ocean trip.

In Genoa, Panalpina hired Ligure Toscano, a customs broker, to coordinate the movement of the transformer through the Genoa Port. Because the transformer was oversized, it had to be secured to a forty-foot "flat-rack" container for ocean shipment. Through Toscano, Panalpina hired CSM, a local stevedore, to load the transformer onto the appropriate container, and to lash it securely for the trip. The transformer, on its flat-rack, was loaded aboard the M/V *Addiriyah* for the voyage to the United States.

During the ocean voyage, the M/V *Addiriyah* encountered heavy seas and the transformer, which CSM had negligently lashed to its flat-rack, broke loose, crushing a laser cutting machine owned by Prima (U.S.A), Inc. ("Prima"). Prima, via its subrogated insurer, filed a complaint against Westinghouse and Panalpina. Prima sought damages for the loss of its laser. A third-party action was then filed by Westinghouse against Panalpina for indemnification. The district court went on to find Panalpina liable to Westinghouse, in indemnity. Panalpina now appeals, challenging the district court's decision that it must indemnify Westinghouse for CSM's negligent actions. Panalpina asserts that it is only a freight forwarder, and hence, should not be made to indemnify Westinghouse.

Panalpina was a freight forwarder, not a carrier

The job of a "non-vessel operating common carrier" (NVOCC) is to consolidate cargo from numerous shippers into larger groups for shipment by an ocean carrier. An NVOCC issues a bill of lading to each shipper. If anything happens to the goods during the voyage the NVOCC is liable to the shipper because of the bill of lading that it issued. A freight forwarder like Panalpina, on the other hand, simply facilitates the movement of cargo to the ocean vessel. The freight forwarder secures cargo space with a steamship company, gives advice on governmental licensing requirements, proper port of exit and letter of credit intricacies, and arranges to have the cargo reach the seaboard in time to meet the designated vessel.

Unlike a carrier, a freight forwarder does not issue a bill of lading, and is therefore not liable to a shipper for anything that occurs to the goods being shipped. As long as the freight forwarder limits its role to arranging for

7. 46 U.S.C.A. § 1304.

transportation, it will not be held liable to the shipper. By analogy, Panalpina was hired to act as a "travel agent" for the transformer: it set things up and made reservations, but did not engage in any hands-on heavy lifting. Of course, a party that calls itself a freight forwarder might in fact be performing the functions of a carrier in which case function would govern over form. But the burden of demonstrating any deviation from what freight forwarders normally do in the maritime context must rest, and heavily so, on the party who would show such deviation. Moreover, when a freight forwarder selects someone to perform transportation services, that selection fulfills the forwarder's obligations in the absence of proof that the selection itself was negligent. We REVERSE the district court's order that Panalpina indemnify Westinghouse.

Case Highlights

- The "non-vessel operating common carrier" (NVOCC) consolidates cargo from numerous shippers into larger groups for shipment by an ocean carrier.
- Unlike a carrier, a freight forwarder does not issue a bill of lading and is not liable for damage to the goods while in the possession of a carrier.
- The freight forwarder is liable if it negligently selects a third party, such as a common carrier or customs broker, who proves to be incompetent.

http://

English Carriage of Goods Act of 1971: **http://www.jus.uio.no/lm/england.carriage.of.goods.by.sea.act.1971/doc.html**. For a complete version of Hague-Visby Rules select "Schedule of The Hague-Visby Rules."

http://

Recent Developments—the need to change COGSA: **http://www.hhgfaa.org/Portal/feb_00/feb55.asp** or **http://www.forwarderlaw.com/archive/arch2.htm**. For a bibliography of articles by Professor Sturley of the University of Texas Law School analyzing the proposed changes to COGSA: **http://www.utexas.edu/law/faculty/msturley/publist.html**.

The application of COGSA in the United Kingdom differs from its counterpart in the United States in two fundamental ways. First, Hague-Visby Rules apply to any shipments *from* a port in the United Kingdom. This differs in application from the Hague Rules as adopted in the United States. COGSA in the United States applies to all shipments *from* and *to* U.S. ports. In the United Kingdom COGSA does not automatically apply to shipments from a foreign port to the United Kingdom. Second, COGSA does apply to shipments *from* one port in the United Kingdom to another such port. In contrast, the Harter Act covers shipments from one U.S. port to another U.S. port, unless the parties expressly agree that COGSA is to be the governing law. All future references in this chapter will be to COGSA as the codified version of the Hague Rules.

COGSA applies only to shipments evidenced by a bill of lading. COGSA states that it applies only to carriage of goods by sea where the carriage contract "expressly or by implication provides for the issue of a bill of lading or any similar document." The carriage contract is the bill of lading that is issued by either a common carrier or a charter party. A **charter party** is one who leases the entire ship from the ship's owner. COGSA would apply if the charter party then enters into carriage contracts with third parties and issues bills of lading in conjunction with these contracts.

The period of coverage under COGSA is limited to "the time when the goods are loaded on to the time they are discharged from the ship." Therefore, unless the bill of lading extends the period of coverage COGSA does not cover the period of time when the goods are in the possession of the common carrier before loading and after discharge. Bills of lading generally incorporate a marine extension or **warehouse-to-warehouse clause** to extend the period of coverage.

In addition, specialized companies, such as stevedore companies, are used by the common carrier to move the goods to and from the ship and to load and off load the goods. COGSA protection is extended to these third-party companies through the use of a **Himalaya clause.** The third party need not be specifically named in the Himalaya clause in order for the protection of a carriage convention to be extended. General language, for example, is sufficient to extend defenses under the bill of lading to stevedores.[8] The following provision is an example of a typical Himalaya clause:

8. See Secrest Machine Corp. v. S.S. *Tiber*, 450 F.2d 285 (5th Cir. 1971).

> *No servant or agent of the Carrier (including every independent contractor from time to time employed by the Carrier) shall in any circumstances whatsoever be under any liability whatsoever to the Merchant (shipper). Every right, exemption, defense and immunity of whatsoever nature applicable to the Carrier shall also be available and shall extend to protect every such servant or agent of the Carrier.*[9]

The above clause was held to be sufficient to extend coverage to a stevedore company and a consultant hired to supervise the stowage of the cargo. Almost any company working in conjunction with the common carrier is extended the same COGSA protections. For example, marine terminal operators have been extended protection under a general Himalaya clause.[10]

The primary objective of COGSA is to limit the liability of the common carrier while at the same time ensuring a claim for damages by shippers. COGSA limits the liability of the common carrier to $500 (Hague Rules) or $1,000 (Hague-Visby Rules) per package. It also provides 17 exemptions that fully exempt the common carrier from all liability for damage or loss to the goods. If the losses relate to a number of enumerated duties, however, the **per package limitation** and 17 exemptions are removed, and the common carrier becomes liable for all damages. First, losses attributed to the carrier's failure to perform **due diligence** in providing a seaworthy ship. Second, the carrier commits a **material deviation.** Third, the carrier fails to provide a **fair opportunity** for the shipper to declare a value above the per package limitation.

Carrier Liability

The primary grounds for common carrier liability are outlined in a single paragraph, Section 1304 (5), of COGSA. The numbers within the paragraph signify important liability issues and are explained below.

> *§1304 (5):*
>
> *Neither the carrier nor the ship shall in any event be or become liable for any loss or damage to or in connection with the transportation of goods in an amount exceeding $500 per package (1) lawful money of the United States, or in case of goods not shipped in packages, per customary freight unit (2), or the equivalent of that sum in other currency, unless the nature and value of such goods have been declared by the shipper before shipment and inserted in the bill of lading (3). This declaration, if embodied in the bill of lading, shall be* prima facie *evidence, but shall not be conclusive on the carrier. In no event shall the carrier be liable for more than the amount of damage actually sustained (4).*[11]

The carrier's liability under COGSA is determined in one of two ways. First, an amount (not to exceed $500) per package multiplied by the number of packages listed or described in the bill of lading (1). Second, an amount declared by the shipper on the bill of lading (3). The per package limitation is the default provision meaning that if the shipper fails to declare a higher amount then the carrier's liability is automatically capped at $500 per package.

9. General Elec. Co. v. Inter-Ocean Shipping, 862 F.Supp. 166, 169 (S.D. Tex. 1994).
10. See Wemhoener Pressen v. Ceres Marine Terminals, 5 F.3d 734 (4th Cir. 1993).
11. 46 U.S.C.App. §1304 (5).

Some types of goods, however, are not packaged for shipment. There are, therefore, no packages for purposes of calculating the carrier's liability. COGSA provides an alternative in such cases known as the **customary freight unit** or **CFU** (2) to determine the number of packages. For example, in *Caterpillar Overseas v. Marine Transport, Inc.,* the court determined that each tractor in a shipment of tractors was a CFU.[12] Other examples are measurements used for bulk goods, such as tons (coal), cubic yards (wheat), or barrels (oil). It is important to note that the $500 per package amount is an upper limit (4). If the goods have a value of less than $500 per package, then the carrier is liable only for the lesser amount.[13] COGSA provides that the actual loss figure is to be determined based upon the value of the goods "at the time and place of discharge." It then offers three sources for the determination of value: commodity exchange price, current market price, or "the normal value of goods of the same kind and quality."

http://
Download the text of the United States Carriage of Goods by Sea Act: **http://uscode.house.gov/title_46.html**.

As discussed above, the cap of $500 per package or CFU is overridden by any higher value declared by the shipper on the bill of lading. Implied in this right of the shipper to declare a higher value is a correlative duty of the carrier to provide an opportunity for such a declaration. The carrier is liable for an undeclared higher value if it failed to give the shipper "a *fair opportunity* to choose a higher liability by paying a corresponding greater charge."[14] Common carriers generally honor their duty to provide fair opportunity to declare a higher value by providing notice and a space to declare a higher value on the face of the bill of lading. Although good practice, some courts have held placing a space on face of the bill of lading is not required. Language found in the fine print on the back of the bill of lading form may be sufficient.[15]

Carrier Duties

COGSA not only restricts the common carrier's ability to limit its liabilities, but also sets out a number of mandatory responsibilities. COGSA lists a number of duties of the carrier that pertain to its issuance of bills of lading. First, there is a general duty on the carrier to issue a bill of lading when receiving goods from the shipper. Second, the bill must include basic information including "leading marks" provided by the shipper for the identification of the goods; the number of packages or pieces, or the quantity, or weight as furnished by the shipper; and the apparent order or condition of the goods. Any such statements regarding the above requirements shall be *prima facie evidence* that the goods were so delivered to the carrier. Thus, the carrier becomes a guarantor of the information provided by the shipper and placed on the bill of lading.

If the goods delivered are not in the condition as stated on the bill of lading or there is a **shortage** as to quantity, then the shipper or the party receiving goods meets its burden of proof by providing the bill of lading as evidence. However, a party's right to make claim against the carrier is limited by two procedural requirements. First, the receiving party must give notice of loss either at the port of discharge or at the time of receiving the goods from the carrier. If the loss is not apparent at the time of receiving the goods, then notice must be given in writing

12. 900 F.2d 714 (4th Cir. 1990).
13. The same is true in the case where the shipper declares a higher value. If the value of the goods are less than the amount declared, then the carrier is liable only for the true value.
14. Cincinnati Milacron Ltd. v. M/V *American Legend,* 784 F.2d1161 (4th Cir. 1986).
15. See e.g., Mori Seiki USA, Inc. v. M/V *Alligator Triumph,* 990 F.2d 440 (9th Cir. 1993).

within three days. Failure to give notice is *prima facie* evidence that the goods received were as indicated on the bill of lading. Upon the giving of the required notice of loss, COGSA provides a one-year **statute of limitations.** The party suffering a loss must commence suit within one year of the delivery of the goods.

COGSA prohibits any attempts by the carrier to insert into its bill of lading more restrictive procedural requirements or attempts to limit its duties and liabilities. COGSA states that "any clause in a contract of carriage relieving the carrier from liability shall be null and void." The question has arisen whether an arbitration clause in the bill of lading is subject to challenge under this limitation. The Supreme Court in *Vimar Seguros y Reaseguros v. M/V Sky Reefer*[16] found that an arbitration clause in the bill of lading was not subject to attack under COGSA. The Court referred to the **Federal Arbitration Act**[17] for the general premise that arbitration is a favored means of dispute resolution in the United States. Regarding COGSA, it held that an arbitration clause is not to be considered as a type disclaimer or limitation of liability that is generally prohibited under COGSA.

The arbitration clause was held not to lessen the liability of the common carrier by increasing the costs of obtaining relief. The added cost argument pertained not so much to the fact that arbitration was mandated but that the arbitration was to be held in Tokyo, Japan. The lessening of liability argument was not strengthened by the fact that both Japanese and American laws were based upon the Hague Rules. The Court did outline one exception to the enforcement of arbitration clauses in bills of lading. This would be where a forum selection clause and a choice of law clause are used in tandem to prevent a shipper from pursuing its statutory remedies under COGSA.

A clause that limits carrier liability that is generally recognized by the courts is the ***force majeure* clause.** The *force majeure* clause is a standard clause in a marine contract exempting the parties from liability for nonperformance resulting from a condition beyond their control, such as government interference, wars, and "Acts of God." The next part of the chapter will analyze more fully the carrier's duty to shippers and its liabilities for failing to perform those duties.

SEAWORTHINESS

The common carrier must satisfy two general duties in order to gain the protections of COGSA. It must undertake due diligence in the preparation and inspection of the ship in order to ensure its **seaworthiness.** The due diligence undertaking is to be performed before the ship departs from the port of shipment. The seaworthiness determination is done at the time of departure. In the event that the ship becomes unseaworthy after it leaves the port of shipment the common carrier remains protected under COGSA.

Four parameters must be met in order for a ship to be considered seaworthy under COGSA. First, the ship used must be appropriate for the type of carriage. Factors in making this determination include the type of goods being transported and the anticipated route of transit: a ship that may be seaworthy for lake or river travel may be unseaworthy for ocean carriage; a ship that may be seaworthy for the carriage of containers may be unseaworthy for the shipment of bulk goods. Second, the ship must be properly equipped for the "reception, carriage, and preservation" of the goods. Thus, all mechanical devices such as fire suppression equipment and refrigeration units must be properly maintained and functioning.

16. 515 U.S. 526 (1995).
17. 9 U.S.C.A. §§ 1, 2, 201 *et seq.*, 202.

Third, the common carrier must man the vessel with a competent crew, properly trained to operate the ship and its equipment. Fourth, the carrier must "properly and carefully load, handle, stow, keep, and discharge the goods carried." Proper **stowage** varies according to the types of goods being transported. Goods that are susceptible to motion must be properly lashed or secured in the hull of the ship. The *Manifest Shipping* case that follows focuses upon the "equipment" and "competency" of the crew elements of seaworthiness.

Per Package Limitation

Section 1304(5) of COGSA, as discussed earlier, provides a liability limitation to the common carrier of $500 per package. An issue often litigated is what is a "package" for purposes of calculating damages? Congress did not define the term "package"

Manifest Shipping v. Uni-Polaris Insurance Co.

1 Lloyd's L. R. 651 (Q.B. 1995)

Justice Tuckey. *Star Sea* had an engine room and cargo holds that were protected from fire by a full flood carbon dioxide extinguishing system. It also had an electrically powered fire pump in the engine room and an emergency fire pump in the forepeak. While in transit from Brazil with a load of bananas she was inspected by the Belgian port authority and found to have a nonworking emergency fire pump. The chief engineer in repairing the pump cut the suction pipe. The emergency fire pump was repaired but the cut pipe was never repaired. On the return trip to South America a fire started in the engine room. The shipowner filed a claim under its marine insurance policy for a constructive total loss. The insurance company denied liability contending that the ship had been sent to sea in an unseaworthy state. The lower court held that the cut pipe made the vessel unseaworthy; however, as the fire involved electrical cables, the fact that the emergency pipe was not working would not have materially affected the spread of the fire.

The present court holds that the ship was unseaworthy on another matter. The ship was unseaworthy pertaining to this claim because of the incompetence of the ship's master. The master's conduct demonstrated a massive ignorance of the working of the carbon dioxide fire suppression system. Furthermore, this incompetence is attributable to the ship's owner because it looked to the maintenance of the fire equipment and the training of the master with a blind eye.

The essence of this allegation is that the master was unaware of the need to use the carbon dioxide system as soon as he realized that the fire could not be fought in any other way. Instead the system was not discharged until at least two and one-half hours after the fire had started. I have no doubt that this was negligent, but does it indicate that the master was incompetent so as to render the ship unseaworthy? I accept that just because the master made a mistake or mistakes, it does not follow that he was incompetent. In fact, given the master's years of experience, I do not doubt his general competence. However, since he did not undergo fire training when he was first certified his competence regarding the particular fire suppression system is in doubt. The master's conduct demonstrates a massive ignorance of its essentials which can only be characterized as incompetence. Due to this incompetence I find that the vessel was unseaworthy. Judgment is REVERSED.

Case Highlights

- Under COGSA, for a ship to be seaworthy its equipment must be in good working order and the crew must be competent in operating the equipment.
- A nonoperational fire suppression system will generally render a ship unseaworthy.
- A ship's captain or master may possess general competence but still be judged incompetent regarding the operation of the ship's equipment.

in COGSA. Clearly, cargo fully boxed or crated is a "package," particularly "where the mode of packaging conceals the identity of the goods being shipped." Similarly, freestanding cargo not enclosed in a box or crate clearly constitutes "goods not shipped in a package." But, what about cargos where some preparation for transportation has been made, but the mode of packaging does not completely conceal or enclose the goods? The answer is not always obvious.

In *London Underwriters v. Sea-Land Service, Inc.,*[18] the court held that a yacht shipped in an on-deck cradle constituted a package. In comparison, another court held that a transformer to which a wooden skid was attached did not constitute a package. A package is likely to be presumed if the cargo fits a plain, ordinary definition of "package." In short, if the cargo could not have been simply dumped in a hold, then it is likely to have been carried with some sort of packaging. Also, most courts will give great weight to the designation of the cargo as packages in the bill of lading.

A common problem is the existence of a number of different "packages" for a court to choose in assessing COGSA damages. The different means of quantifying a shipment of goods may stem from how the goods are packaged or how they are described in the bill of lading. In *Sony Magnetic Products Inc. v. Merivienti,*[19] Sony packed a standard cargo container with video cassette tapes. Sony first placed the tapes into 1,320 cardboard cartons and then strapped the cartons onto 52 wooden pallets. The carrier issued Sony a bill of lading with the following description: "Description of Packages and Goods, 1 x 40 foot container STC [said to contain]: 1,320 Ctns." The bill of lading did not reserve space for designating the value of the cargo, but the attached export certificate showed a value of $424,765.44. The court found that each of the 1,320 cartons was a "package" for purposes of COGSA, capping liability at $660,000, and then awarded $424,765.44, the actual damages sustained by Sony as evidenced by the invoice value of the tapes.

Previously, the court in *Vegas v. Compania Anonima Venzolana*[20] decided that an ambiguity on a bill of lading regarding the number of COGSA packages should be resolved in favor of the shipper. Like the shipper in the *Sony* case, Vegas had consolidated cartons of goods onto pallets and informed the carrier on the bill of lading of the number of individual cartons. Unlike the shipper in *Sony,* however, Vegas not only disclosed the number of cartons but also disclosed that they had been consolidated onto pallets. The *Vegas* court resolved the ambiguity, a stated number of cartons and a lesser number of pallets, on the bill of lading in favor of the shipper. It is important to note that the *Sony* court used only the value listed in the export certificate as evidence of value. It did not hold that the value of the goods listed on the attached export certificate was a declaration of a higher value for purposes of COGSA. Section 1304(5) expressly requires that any declared value be "inserted in the bill of lading."

Once it is determined that goods have been lost or damaged, a number of procedural issues must be faced by any prospective plaintiff. First, who has the burden of proof in proving damages and how can such proof be rebutted? Second, what parties have standing to sue the carrier? The *Polo Ralph Lauren v. Tropical Shipping* case that follows reviews these different procedural issues relevant to all claims under COGSA.

18. 881 F.2d at 761, 768 (9th Cir. 1989).

19. An excerpt of this case is used in this chapter because it pertains to the enumerated exemption of "latent defect."

20. 720 F.2d 629 (11th Cir. 1983).

Polo Ralph Lauren, L.P. v. Tropical Shipping & Construction Co.

215 F.3d 1217 (11th Cir. 2000)

Kravitch, Circuit Judge. This appeal centers on what recourse, if any, an owner of goods lost at sea has against the carrier when the owner of the goods is not a named party to the bill of lading. Plaintiff Polo Ralph Lauren, L.P. ("Polo"), seeks damages for cargo lost overboard while in transport with Tropical Shipping & Construction Company ("Tropical"). Polo apparently entered into a bailment contract with Drusco, Inc. ("Drusco") for the manufacture and delivery of 4,643 pairs of pants. Under the terms of this agreement, Polo sent fabric to Drusco in Florida, which Drusco cut and preassembled before shipping the fabric pieces to the Dominican Republic to be sewed into finished pants. Drusco entered into similar arrangements with several other clothing manufacturers and combined the pants from all of the manufacturers into two large sealed containers that it delivered to Tropical. Drusco also arranged for the return shipment of the finished trousers to Florida where it would add designer accoutrements before returning them to the manufacturers for sale to retailers.

While en route from the Dominican Republic to Florida, the container containing Polo's cargo was lost overboard in rough seas. Polo asserted claims for breach of contract, bailment, and negligence. The district court granted the motion as to the contract claim on the ground that Polo did not have standing because it was not named in the bills of lading. The court also granted summary judgment to Tropical on the bailment and negligence claims as preempted by COGSA.

COGSA—An Exclusive Remedy

COGSA, enacted in 1936, governs "all contracts for carriage of goods by sea to or from ports of the United States in foreign trade." The purpose of COGSA was to achieve international uniformity and to redress the edge in bargaining power enjoyed by carriers over shipper and cargo interests by setting out certain duties and responsibilities of carriers that cannot be avoided even by express contractual provision. Plaintiff states a *prima facie* claim under COGSA by demonstrating delivery of goods in sound condition to a carrier and their subsequent receipt in damaged condition. The burden then shifts to the carrier to establish that the damage was not caused by its negligence.

We conclude that because COGSA applies in this case, it provides Polo's exclusive remedy and preempts Polo's tort claims. We have found no cases in which a court has allowed a tort claim to proceed when COGSA applies. Polo's complaint therefore should have stated a single COGSA claim instead of three separate causes of action. Many courts have recognized that a COGSA claim against a negligent carrier for lost or damaged goods comprises elements of both contract, arising from the breach of the contract of carriage, and tort, issuing from the breach of the carrier's duty of care.

Although recognizing the COGSA claim's hybrid nature, these cases do not stand for the proposition that COGSA provides various causes of action, both contract and tort, from which a plaintiff may choose in seeking redress from a negligent carrier. Nothing in the language of COGSA or the cases interpreting it leads us to believe otherwise. We therefore conclude that COGSA affords one cause of action for lost or damaged goods. The district court properly granted summary judgment on Polo's actions in bailment and negligence.

Polo's Standing to Bring a COGSA Claim

The district court rejected Polo's argument that it was a third-party beneficiary to the bills of lading and granted summary judgment. Polo is not named in the bills of lading. Contracts bind only named parties unless both parties to the contract clearly express a mutual intent to benefit a third party. This rule of strict construction applies with equal force in contracts of carriage. The third party need not be mentioned by name as long as the contract refers to a "well-defined class of readily identifiable persons" that it intends to benefit.

Polo argues that the inclusion of the "owner of the goods" in the bills of lading evinces a clear intent to benefit that class of persons. The back of the bills of lading uses the phrase "shipper, consignee, or owner of the goods" repeatedly in defining the conditions of the contract of carriage. The final clause of the bills iterates that the "Shippers, Consignees, and Owners of the goods and the Holder of the Bill of Lading" expressly agree to all its terms. Polo argues that these recurring references to the "owner of the goods" intend to benefit Polo.

In *All Pacific Trading, Inc. v. Vessel M/V Hanjin Yosu*, 7 F.3d 1427 (9th Cir.1993), the court considered a consolidated action brought by nine owners of damaged goods and their insurers. Eight of the nine plaintiffs delivered their goods to different non-vessel-operating common carriers ("NVOCCs") who issued bills of lading to the shippers and then delivered the goods to the carrier, who in turn executed separate bills of lading with the NVOCCs. The cargo owners were not named in the bills of lading with the carrier. The court rejected the carrier's argument that the plaintiff cargo owners lacked standing to sue because it found that the cargo owners were actual parties to the bills of lading. As with the bills of lading before us, those bills of lading contained a clause obligating the "owner of the goods" to their terms.

The bills of lading between Tropical and Drusco recurrently refer to the "owner of the goods" and specifically bind the "owner of the goods" to its terms and obligations, creating the possibility that Polo would have standing to sue as owner of the goods or as a third-party beneficiary to the bills of lading. There was sufficient evidence before the district court of Polo's ownership to render improvident its grant of summary judgment on Polo's COGSA claim.

AFFIRMED in part; REVERSED in part.

Case Highlights

- COGSA governs all contracts for carriage of goods by sea to or from ports of the United States in foreign trade.
- The initial burden of proof is on the shipper to prove that the goods delivered to the carrier were in sound condition. This burden is met by providing a "clean" bill of lading. The burden then shifts to the carrier to prove that the damage was not caused by its negligence.
- A party does not have to be named in the bill of lading to have standing to sue the carrier if it is a member of a class of persons that were intended to benefit from the carriage contract.

COGSA Coverage

COGSA[21] is more comprehensive than the Harter Act in regulating the carrier-shipper relationship. The Hamburg Rules are even more so. All three provide a relatively fair allocation of liability between the carrier and the shipper. There are some important differences, however, between the different carriage conventions. For example, COGSA limits the liability of the carrier to the time frame represented from "tackle to tackle" or from time of loading to time of discharge. This does not take into account the time when the goods are in the control of the carrier before the loading and after the unloading of the cargo.

http://

Text of Hamburg Rules: **http://www.jus.uio.no/lm/un.sea.carriage.hamburg.rules.1978/doc.html**.

The Hamburg Rules extend the period of responsibility to include when the goods are in the control of the carrier but not on the ship. Article 7 of the Hague Rules (COGSA) allow the parties to agree to extend the period of application to the period "prior to the loading, and subsequent to the discharge." This is generally done through the insertion of a warehouse-to-warehouse clause into the bill of lading. The *Mori Seiki USA v. M/V Alligator Triumph* case on the next page reviews the "tackle to tackle" coverage of COGSA, the duty of the carrier to provide an opportunity to declare a higher value, and the use of the Himalaya clause to extend COGSA to third parties.

Carrier is defined more broadly by the Hamburg Rules. They define carrier as "any person by whom a contract of carriage of goods by sea has been concluded with a shipper." By not referring to "carrier," as COGSA does, the Hamburg Rules apply to parties such as freight forwarders and terminal or non-vessel common carriers. COGSA applies only to shipments covered by a bill of lading. In contrast, Hamburg Rules apply to any contracts of carriage by sea such as straight or non-negotiable bills of lading and electronic documents.

In addition, the Hamburg Rules provide specific rules for carriage above deck, while the Hague Rules exclude deck carriage from its application. COGSA does

21. In the United States see Article 7 of the Uniform Commercial Code for domestic transactions. For international transactions involving bills of lading refer to the Federal Bills of Lading Act, 49 U.S.C.A. §§ 80101-16.

Mori Seiki USA, Inc. v. M/V *Alligator Triumph*, Mitsui O.S.K. Lines, Ltd., and Marine Terminals Corp.

990 F.2d 444 (9th Cir. 1993)

Hug, Circuit Judge. Appellant, Mori Seiki USA, Inc. ("Mori Seiki"), was the consignee of a precision lathe that was damaged while being transported from Nagoya, Japan to Houston, Texas. The lathe was damaged after it was unloaded from an ocean vessel at the Port of Los Angeles, but before it was released from the seaport. Mori Seiki filed suit in district court seeking damages from the ocean carrier (Mitsui), the ship (M.V. *Alligator Triumph*), the seaport operator (Trans Pacific Container), and the stevedore services firm which unloaded and handled its lathe (Marine Terminals Corporation).

Applicability of COGSA after Discharge

COGSA applies to all cargo shipments carried by sea, to or from the United States. By its own terms, COGSA limits its liability for cargo damage to $500, if the damage occurs between the time the cargo is loaded on to the ship and the time it is discharged from the ship ("tackle to tackle"). Parties to a shipping agreement, however, may contractually extend the limitation period.

The bill of lading at issue in this case stated that "with respect to loss or damage occurring during the period from the time when the Goods arrived at the sea terminal at the port of loading to the time when they left the sea terminal at the port of discharge the carrier shall be responsible for such loss or damage to the extent prescribed by the Hague Rules (COGSA)." The plain meaning of this language is that COGSA's liability limitation would extend to the period after the lathe was discharged from the ship, but before it was released from the sea terminal. Although it is true that a bill of lading is a contract of adhesion, which is "strictly construed against the carrier," and that "any ambiguity in the bill of lading must be construed in favor of the shipper and against the carrier," we are not persuaded that such an ambiguity exists here. The bill of lading extended COGSA's $500 liability limitation to the period during which the lathe was damaged.

Extension of Liability Limitation under the Himalaya Clause

Mitsui's bill of lading included a so-called "Himalaya clause," which is commonly used to extend a carrier's defenses and liability limitations to certain third parties performing services on its behalf. The district court concluded that the seaport operator and the stevedore services company were covered by the Himalaya clause in Mitsui's bill of lading. We conclude, therefore, that the Himalaya clause extended Mitsui's COGSA defenses, including the $500 package liability limitation, to Marine Terminal Corporation. AFFIRMED.

Case Highlights

- COGSA covers only the "tackle to tackle" portion of the carriage unless contractually extended in the bill of lading.
- The Himalaya clause is commonly inserted in the freight contract to extend a carrier's defenses and liability limitations (COGSA) to third parties performing services on its behalf, such as a stevedore company.

permit the parties to agree to above-deck carriage. This is done through the incorporation of a **clause paramount** into the bill of lading. The burden of proof is on the shipper under COGSA to prove that any loss was due to the fault of the carrier. The burden is satisfied generally by the presentment of a *clean* bill of lading. In contrast, carrier fault is presumed under the Hamburg Rules. Article 5 of the Hamburg Rules states that "the carrier is liable for loss, damage, or delay that occurred while the goods were in its charge." It then expressly states "that, as a rule, the burden of proof rests on the carrier."

A still unresolved issue is how best to deal with combined or **multimodal transport** contracts. The Hague Rules and COGSA were enacted prior to the advent of **containerization.** Containerization allows a single container to be used in different modes of transit.[22] A container can be attached to a truck, placed on the bed of a railroad car, and loaded on to a ship. The current approach is the recognition that the different unimodal conventions form a network of liability. Each segment of the transport is governed by the convention applicable to that type of transportation.

http://

The ICC also works to uncover and prevent maritime crimes (and fraud) through its International Maritime Bureau: **http://www.iccwbo.org/ccs/menu_imb_bureau.asp**

Under the International Chamber of Commerce's **Rules for Multimodal Transport Documents,** "the carrier must prove during which stage of the multimodal transport the damage occurred." It also places a presumption in favor of the shipper in the event that the carrier does not meet its burden. "If the stage cannot be established, the system of liability most favorable to the claimant of the relevant modes of transport is deemed to apply."[23]

Containerization poses a number of concerns as it relates to the application of COGSA. First, multimodal transport raises questions about the continued relevancy and importance of the traditional ocean bill of lading; newer multimodal transport documents have increasingly become popular. Second, can a container filled with packages of goods be itself considered a single package for purposes of calculating per package liability? COGSA provides guidance in defining the word "package." It states that "where a container, pallet, or similar article of transport is used to consolidate goods, the number of packages or units enumerated in the bill of lading as packed in such article of transport shall be deemed the number of packages or units." Courts, in order to protect shippers, have generally held that a container cannot be considered a package. This is especially true when the bill of lading lists a more specific number of units or packages. The more specific description prevails over any general statement referring to the number of "containers."

The court in *Marcraft Clothes, Inc. v. M/V Kurobe Maru*[24] held that multimodal containers are generally not to be considered as packages for the calculation of COGSA liability of the common carrier. The enumeration on the bill of lading that the container was filled with 4,400 men's suits made each suit a "package" for purposes of COGSA liability. The issue remains, however, whether the common carrier can expressly designate the container as the package for purposes of COGSA's per package limitation? Generally courts have rejected the notion that a container can be designated as a package to limit the carrier's liability to $500 for the entire shipment.

In *All Pacific Trading v. Vessel M/V Hanjin Yosu,* the carrier inserted the following clause into the bill of lading: "Where the cargo has been packed into containers it is expressly agreed that the number of such containers shown on the face hereof shall be considered the number of packages for the purpose of the application of the limitation of liability provided for herein." The carrier further argued that the container was the proper package because the rate agreement was determined based upon the number of containers and not by the number of packages within

22. A *container* is a uniform, reusable metal box in which goods are shipped by vessel, truck, or rail. Standard lengths include 10, 20, 30, and 40 feet (40-foot containers generally hold about 40,000 pounds of cargo). See generally, Simon, "The Law of Shipping Containers," *Journal of Maritime Law & Commerce* 507 (1974); Bissel, "The Operational Realities of Containerization and Their Effects on the 'Package' Limitation and the 'On-Deck' Prohibition: Review and Suggestions," 45 *Tulane Law Rev.* 902 (1971); L. Alexander, "Containerization, the Per Package Limitation, and the Concept of 'Fair Opportunity,'" 11 *The Maritime Lawyer* 123 (1986).

23. Frank G.M. Smeele, "The Contract of Carriage" in *International Contracts: Aspects of Jurisdiction, Arbitration and Private International Law* (Marieele Koppenol-Laforce, ed. 257 1996).

24. 575 F. Supp. 239 (S.D.N.Y. 1983).

the containers. The court rejected the carrier's arguments that the containers were indeed the "packages." It focused upon the fact that elsewhere on the bill of lading there was a listing of the number of packages in each container.[25]

The law on this topic remains unsettled as indicated by the court in *St. Paul Ins. v. Sea Land Service*:

> *The court notes with some trepidation that it is its view that the determination that the $500 per package or per customary freight unit limitation should not apply to a container said to contain packages should be re-examined. Cases seeking to apply the limitation to containers pursuant to bills of lading are all too common particularly because carriers have drafted bills of lading with all sorts of terms relating to its applicability to container shipments. Furthermore, because of reasons of reductions of cost and prevention of theft or damage, containers have become a* customary freight unit, *if not the customary freight unit recognized by COGSA.*[26]

In order to avoid the classification of a container as a COGSA package, the shipper should request a detailed description in the bill of lading expressly stating the number of packages within each container.

Material Deviation

The next three sections will explore areas of carrier fault that result in the removal of a carrier's liability limitation under the per package rule. The three areas where the common carrier is held to be fully liable for all damages are material deviation, failure to give fair opportunity to declare a higher value, and **misdelivery.** The first of these three areas of full carrier liability will be reviewed in this section. Material deviation claims can generally be divided into two groups—those involving the above-deck carriage of goods and a change in the expected route of the ship.

Above-deck carriage has historically been considered a material deviation, but this claim has severely diminished in modern times. The advent of containerization and more powerful ships has made above-deck carriage commonplace, since containers help protect the cargo from the adverse conditions of sea travel. Furthermore, modern ships allow for larger cargo capacity by the stacking of containers below and above the deck. For this reason, ocean carriage has become more efficient and reasonable. COGSA permits the parties to agree to above-deck shipment. It states that *"deck cargo* means cargo which by the contract of carriage is stated as being carried on deck." Most bills of lading now reflect the practice of above-deck carriage by the incorporation of a clause paramount.

The second ground for a claim of material deviation is an unreasonable route change. If the common carrier fails to follow a customary or reasonable shipping route, then it will be liable for damages resulting from late delivery. A defense to a material deviation in the route would be a change resulting from an emergency such as mechanical failure or governmental intervention. For example, it would be reasonable for the common carrier to follow instructions to dock at a port for required government inspection or to change route in order to avoid hostilities. The *St. Johns Shipping Corp.* case that follows reviews the material deviation of above-deck stowage.

25. See also Universal Leaf Tobacco Co. v. Companhia De Navegacao Maritima Netumar, 993 F.2d 414 (4th Cir. 1993) (courts will not consider a container as a package if the bill of lading discloses the number of packages within the container); Cia Panamena de Seguros, S.A. v. Prudential Lines, Inc., 416 F. Supp. 641 (D.C. 1976) (court rejected bill of lading definition of container as package).

26. 745 F. Supp. 186, 189.

St. Johns N. F. Shipping Corp. v. S. A. Companhia Geral Commercial de Rio de Janeiro

263 U.S. 119 (1923)

Where rosin shipped under a clean bill of lading was stowed on deck, and was jettisoned during the voyage to relieve the ship in a storm, held, that the ship was liable as for a deviation, could not escape by reason of relieving clauses in the bill, and must pay damages measured by the value of the goods at destination. There are three leading classes of cases: (1) where shipment under deck is customary and there is no controlling contract; (2) where shipment on or under deck, at ship's option, is customary and there is no controlling contract; (3) where custom is controlled by contract.

Generally, courts construe the bill of lading, which thus constituted the entire contract between the parties, to give a promise to carry under deck. In the absence of a proved contract modifying the custom, the custom speaks when the bill of lading is silent. However, deck shipment can be controlled by a separate freight contract. There is nothing inconsistent between a bill of lading with no loading endorsement on it, and a written contract allowing shipment on deck. In such a case, there is no duty on the carrier to notify the shipper as to stowage; if the shipper required notice as to how the option was to be exercised, it should have so provided in the contract of affreightment. It was error to hold that the bill of lading and all its terms were wiped out by the absence of a notation on the bill of lading that the shipment was on deck. The consent to deck stowage was sufficiently evidenced in the bill of lading as issued when that document is read in conjunction with the freight contract that preceded it.

Justice McReynolds. The rosin was loaded on board June 11 and clean receipts—without endorsement concerning stowage—were given. Before reaching Rio de Janeiro the vessel encountered a storm and for sufficient cause the master jettisoned the rosin in order to relieve her. The loss resulted directly from the on-deck stowage. We are not dealing with a case arising under a general port custom permitting above-deck stowage notwithstanding a clean bill, with notice of which all shippers are charged.

When there is no such custom and no express contract in a form available as evidence, a clean bill of lading imports under deck stowage. Upon this implication respondent had the right to rely. To say that the shipper assented to stowage on deck is not correct. It gave the vessel an option, and the clean bill of lading amounted to a positive representation by her that this had been exercised and that the goods would go under deck. By stowing the goods on deck the vessel broke her contract, exposed them to greater risk than had been agreed and thereby directly caused the loss. She accordingly became liable as for a deviation, cannot escape by reason of the relieving clauses inserted in the bill of lading for her benefit, and must account for the value at destination. The decree below is AFFIRMED

Case Highlights

- Consent to deck stowage can be determined by reviewing the bill of lading in conjunction with other evidence of the freight contract.
- When the bill of lading does not expressly allow for on-deck stowage and there is no port custom permitting on-deck stowage, then above-deck stowage would be considered a material deviation.
- A material deviation precludes the common carrier from utilizing the limitation of liability (per package) protection under COGSA.

The court in *DuPont de Nemours International v. Mormacvega*[27] recognized an implied exception to the COGSA principle that carriage on the deck of the ship is a material deviation. It held that it is not an unreasonable deviation from the carriage contract to carry the goods above deck if the ship is one designed for above-deck containerized carriage. This can be seen as judicial recognition of the technological developments since the writing of the Hague Rules.

27. 493 F.2d 97 (2d Cir. 1974). See also Electro-Tec Corp. v. S.S. Dart Atlantica, 598 F. Supp. 929 (D. Md. 1984).

The common carrier generally prevents a material deviation claim for above-deck carriage by inserting a clause paramount in the bill of lading. In essence, the shipper agrees to allow the common carrier to decide whether the goods are to be carried below or above deck. The clause asserts that the Hague Rules (COGSA) or other pertinent convention will apply to goods stowed above deck. The clause below is an example of a clause paramount. The numbers in parentheses refer to the statements immediately before them and are explained in the paragraph that follows.

> *The bill of lading shall have effect subject to all the provisions of the Carriage of Goods by Sea Act of the United States, as approved on April 16, 1936. The defenses and limitations of said Act shall apply to goods whether carried on or under the deck (1), to carriage of goods between U.S. ports, or between non-U.S. ports (4), before the goods are loaded on and after they are discharged from the vessel, and throughout the entire time the goods are in the actual custody of Carrier (2), whether acting as carrier, bailee, or stevedore (3). Carrier shall be entitled to the full benefit of all rights and immunity under and all limitations and exemptions from liability contained in any law of the United States or any other place whose law shall be compulsorily applicable. If any term of this bill of lading be repugnant to the Carriage of Goods by Sea Act or any other law compulsorily applicable, such term only shall be void. This bill of lading shall be construed and the rights of the parties determined according to the laws of the United States (5).*[28]

http://

For an example of a more expansive clause paramount: **http://www.oocl.com/BL/Terms_p3.htm**.

The above clause does more than simply extend COGSA to above-deck carriage (1). It also extends COGSA's coverage beyond tackle-to-tackle to the entire period that the goods are in the possession of the carrier (2). Some courts have recognized this extension of COGSA even when the bill of lading fails to incorporate such a clause.[29] Second, it extends COGSA protection to all third parties involved with the transport of the goods by sea including stevedores (3) (Himalaya Clause). Third, it preempts the application of the Harter Act extending coverage to shipments between U.S. ports (4). Finally, it selects U.S. law as the law to be used to interpret the carriers' obligations and liabilities under the bill of lading (5) (choice of law).

Fair Opportunity

There are a limited number of exceptions to the per package limitation afforded to carriers. One exception is when the shipper is not given a fair opportunity to declare a higher per package value for the goods. Courts will carefully examine the bill of lading itself in deciding whether the common carrier has fulfilled its fair opportunity responsibilities. The court in *Komatsu, Ltd. v. States S.S. Co.*[30] held that common carriers' fair opportunity obligations are satisfied when they incorporate the language of Section 1304(5) on the *face* of the bill of lading. The *Travelers Indemnity Company v. Waterman Steamship* case on the next page further explores the nuances of the carrier's duty to provide an opportunity to declare a higher value.

Misdelivery of Goods

Under COGSA, the carrier is obligated to deliver the goods to the holder, and only the holder, of the bill of lading. A cause of action accrues to the shipper in the

28. This clause was taken from St. Paul Fire & Marine Ins. v. Sea-Land Service, 745 F.Supp. 186, 188 (S.D.N.Y. 1990).
29. See, e.g., Binladen BSB Landscaping v. M.V. Nedlloyd Totterdam, 759 F.2d 1006 (2d Cir. 1985).
30. 674 F.2d 806 (9th Cir. 1982).

Travelers Indemnity Company v. Waterman Steamship Corp. ("The Vessel *Sam Houston*")

26 F.3d 895 (Court of Appeals Ninth Circuit 1994)

Wiggins, Circuit Judge. This action arose when a barge owned and operated by Waterman sank in the inner harbor of Alexandria, Egypt. The barge was carrying machinery and materials for appellant's assured. The shipment consisted of steel, valves, pumps, and other materials to be used in the erection of sewage treatment plants and elevated water tanks. Travelers sustained a loss of $1,174,876 when a portion of the cargo was lost or damaged. Travelers brought suit against Waterman in federal district court. The district court found that the $500 per package or per customary freight unit limitation on liability, set forth in the Carriage of Goods by Sea Act (COGSA), controlled. In addition, the district court found that 77 "packages" were damaged or lost. Thus, the district court entered final judgment for $38,500.

COGSA regulates the liability of international carriers for loss or damage to cargo. Specifically, Section 4(5) of COGSA provides that a carrier is liable for $500 per package or per customary freight unit. 46 U.S.C. § 1304(5). The shipper may increase the carrier's liability, however, by declaring on the bill of lading the nature and value of the goods shipped and paying a higher freight rate. A carrier may take advantage of COGSA's $500 per package or per customary freight unit limitation on liability "only if the shipper is given a 'fair opportunity' to opt for a higher liability by paying a correspondingly greater charge."

The fair opportunity requirement is meant to give the shipper notice of the legal consequences of failing to opt for a higher carrier liability. Thus, the carrier must "bear an initial burden of producing *prima facie* evidence that demonstrates that it provided notice of a choice of liabilities and rates to the shipper." Normally, the carrier can meet this initial burden by showing that the language of COGSA Section 4(5) is contained in the bill of lading. Travelers offered two pieces of evidence. First, L.A. Water submitted to Waterman prior to shipment the export declaration it prepared for customs. This export declaration reported the value of the total cargo to be $6,000,000. Second, Waterman's bill of lading did not contain a designated space in which to declare a higher value. Travelers noted that the *Nemeth* court considered "the fact that the bill of lading contains no designated place for an excess value declaration" to be evidence that the shipper did not have a fair opportunity to opt out of COGSA's liability limitation.

The export declaration does not, in fact, constitute evidence that the shipper "would have opted for a higher liability had it been given a fair opportunity to do so." The party in this case was a sophisticated shipper of goods. And it had shipped its goods with Waterman on several previous occasions. Thus, the shipper was familiar with Waterman's shipping procedures and its bill of lading. Second, a designated place for an excess value declaration is not mandatory. AFFIRMED.

Case Highlights

- A common carrier can take advantage of the $500 per package limitation only if it gives the shipper a "fair opportunity" to declare a higher value.
- A common carrier will generally meet its burden to provide a fair opportunity to declare a higher value by incorporating the language of §4(5) of COGSA into the bill of lading.
- Designating a space on the front of the bill of lading to declare a higher value is not required by COGSA.
- A statement of higher value in a document other than the bill of lading, even if provided to the common carrier, is of no consequence.

event that delivery is made to someone not holding the bill of lading. The common carrier is liable for misdelivery, even after the goods are discharged from its ship, because the carrier remains a **bailee** of the goods until they are delivered to the holder of the bill of lading. The *law of bailment* places special duties of care on a party (bailee) who is entrusted with the goods of another party.

The special status of the common carrier under the law of bailment is explored in the *Allied Chemical International Corp. v. Compania de Navegacao Lloyd Brasileiro* case.

Allied Chemical International v. Companhia de Navegacao Lloyd Brasileiro

775 F.2d 476 (2d Cir. 1985)

Meskill, Circuit Judge. Compania de Navegacao Lloyd Brasileiro (Lloyd), an ocean carrier, appeals from a judgment of the United States District Court for the Southern District of New York finding Lloyd liable to Allied Chemical International Corporation (Allied), a shipper, for the misdelivery of goods to the consignee, Banylsa Tecelagem do Brasil S.A. (Banylsa). The carrier caused the goods to be delivered without requiring Banylsa to produce the original order bill of lading.

Allied, an exporter of chemical products, received from Banylsa an order for a quantity of caprolactam, a crystalline cyclic amide used in the manufacture of nylon. The sale was to be in two lots of 6,000 bags on terms of sight drafts against documents through Banco Bamerindus do Brasil S.A. of Sao Paulo, Brazil (Brazilian bank). Lloyd's vessel arrived at the Port of Salvador and in accordance with local custom and usage, the carrier unloaded the caprolactam at a warehouse under the control of the Administration of the Port of Salvador, an agency of the Brazilian government.

Banylsa requested and received from Lloyd in accordance with Brazilian import regulations a "carta declaratoria," a letter declaring that the freight had been paid at the port of origin and that the Merchant Marine Renewal Tax had been paid in Salvador. By virtue of the *carta declaratoria,* Banylsa was able to obtain possession although it had not paid for the goods and it was not in possession of the bill of lading. Soon thereafter, Banylsa filed a voluntary receivership proceeding in the Civil Court of the District of Salvador, Brazil. Allied made a demand on Lloyd for losses incurred as a result of the carrier's failure to request proper documentation before authorizing the release of the caprolactam.

The liability question in this case inextricably involves the critical importance of the documentary transaction in overseas trade. The documentary sale enables the distant seller to protect himself from an insolvent or fraudulent foreign buyer by ensuring that the buyer ordinarily cannot take possession of the goods until he has paid for them. It accomplishes this rather simply. The seller tenders shipping documents, including a negotiable bill of lading, rather than goods to the buyer. By paying for the documents, the buyer gets possession of the original bill of lading.

Possession of the bill of lading entitles the holder to possession of the goods; it represents the goods and conveys title to them. Most likely, the bill will be an order bill of lading, made to the order of or endorsed to the buyer. The carrier, the issuer of the bill of lading, is responsible for releasing the cargo only to the party who presents the original bill of lading. Delivery to the consignee named in the bill of lading does not suffice to discharge the carrier where the consignee does not hold the bill of lading. If the carrier delivers the goods to one other than the authorized holder of the bill of lading, the carrier is liable for misdelivery.

Lloyd contends that clauses 1 and 12 of the bill of lading absolve it from liability. Clause 1 provides that "the Carrier shall not be liable in any capacity whatsoever for any delay, nondelivery or misdelivery, or loss of or damage to the goods occurring while the goods are not in the actual custody of the Carrier." Clause 12 provides that "the responsibility of the Carrier, in any capacity, shall altogether cease and the goods shall be considered to be delivered and at their own risk and expense in every respect when taken into the custody of customs or other authorities." However, when Lloyd discharged the cargo, it assumed the status of a bailee. A bailee is absolutely liable for misdelivering cargo. Therefore, under COGSA, the Harter Act (which still governs the periods prior to loading and after the goods are discharged until proper delivery is made), and the law of bailment, Lloyd is liable for misdelivery. The judgment of the district court is AFFIRMED.

Case Highlights

- The issuer of the bill of lading is responsible for releasing the cargo only to the party who presents the original bill of lading.
- A common carrier is considered as a *bailee* of the goods put in its charge. Therefore, it may be liable in the law of bailment even after it discharges its obligations under COGSA
- Despite the protections provided for under COGSA and other carriage conventions, it is important to know the local customs and practices of the country of importation.

In addition, the case illustrates that even though the bill of lading is the universally accepted document of title, national maritime customs and shipping practices need to be understood in order to protect against misdelivery. Misdelivery can occur when a country's import documentation allows for such a release or when the receiving party and the common carrier make alternative arrangements.

Alternative arrangements are sometimes made for delivery to someone not holding a bill of lading. One common practice is where the common carrier agrees to release the goods to a consignee, not in possession of the bill of lading, upon the presentment of a bank guarantee. The bank guarantee absolves the carrier from any liability for misdelivery. It is important to note that the carrier remains liable for misdelivery under COGSA, but is able to seek indemnification through the guarantee.

In *C-Art, Ltd. v. Hong Kong Islands Line America, S.A.,*[31] the parties' prior course of dealing allowed the importer to present a bank guarantee, rather than wait to receive the bill of lading. However, instead of presenting its normal bank guarantee, the buyer presented a corporate guarantee and received a release of the goods. The court held the carrier liable for misdelivery by reasoning that "the carrier, the issuer of the bill of lading, is responsible for releasing the cargo only to the party who presents the original bill of lading."[32] It would seem that even if the importer had presented a bank guarantee or indemnity, the carrier still remains liable to the shipper for misdelivery unless the shipper-seller expressly agreed to such a delivery arrangement.

COGSA Exemptions

If the carrier fulfills its obligations as outlined previously, then its liability is limited to not more than $500 per package. In addition, it obtains the protection of **17 COGSA exemptions** (see Comparative Law: The 17 COGSA Exemptions). There are 16 enumerated exemptions and one "catch-all" known as the **Q-clause exception.** The 16 enumerated exemptions include losses due to errors in navigation and management of the ship, fire, perils of the sea, acts of God, war, acts of public enemies, government seizure, quarantine restrictions, act or omission of the shipper, strikes, wastage due to inherent vice, insufficiency of packing, and latent defects. Perils of the sea would include violent or catastrophic storms, but not normal storms at sea. Latent defects are those defects not discoverable by due diligence.

The courts have narrowly interpreted most of the exemptions in order to allow shippers to collect on their claims. For example, the latent defect exception has not provided carriers much protection even when they perform due diligent inspections and testing. The "catch-all" exception or Q-clause exception grants the carrier a general exemption for any damages that arise from a cause that was not the "actual fault of the carrier or those of the agents or servants of the carrier." However, COGSA states that the burden of proof is on the carrier to prove that its fault or negligence had not contributed to the loss or damage. Courts have rarely granted an exemption from liability under the Q-clause. If there is any possibility that the loss or damage occurred while the goods were in the possession of the carrier, no matter how remote, then the court will likely rule against the carrier's claim of a Q-clause exemption.

31. 940 F.2d 530 (9th Cir. 1991).
32. Ibid. at 532. See also The Caledonia, 157 U.S. 124 (1895).

Damage to goods attributable to one of these 17 causes, nonetheless, relieves the carrier of *all* liability. In contrast, the Hamburg Rules eliminate these exceptions and provide a presumption of carrier liability for loss except when occasioned by a fire. In addition, COGSA requires the consignee to make a notice of loss "before or after the time of the removal of the cargo, if apparent." It further provides a limitation period of one year for any claims of loss. The Hamburg Rules allow a claim of loss within one working day after delivery to the consignee. Also, the limitation period is extended to two years. COGSA provides for liability when goods are lost or damaged but make no mention of liability for a delay in delivery. The Hamburg Rules designate "delay" as an equal ground for recovery.

The *Sony Magnetic Products v. Merivienti* case on the next page explains the shifting of the burden of proof between the carrier and the shipper. It also serves to highlight the enumerated exemption of latent defect. The *Lamb Head Shipping v. Jennings* case on page 294 reviews the perils of the sea exemption and how it interrelates with the carrier's duty of due diligence.

FREIGHT FORWARDERS AND MULTIMODAL TRANSPORT OPERATORS

The final two parts of this chapter will focus on the role and duties of other essential third parties in the transport of goods. These include the **freight forwarder, multimodal transport operator,** and **marine insurance company.** The freight forwarder serves three vital functions for importers and exporters: (1) arrange for the

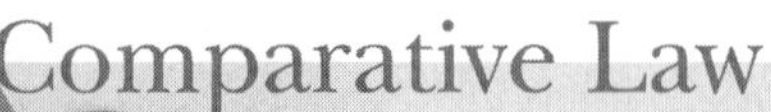

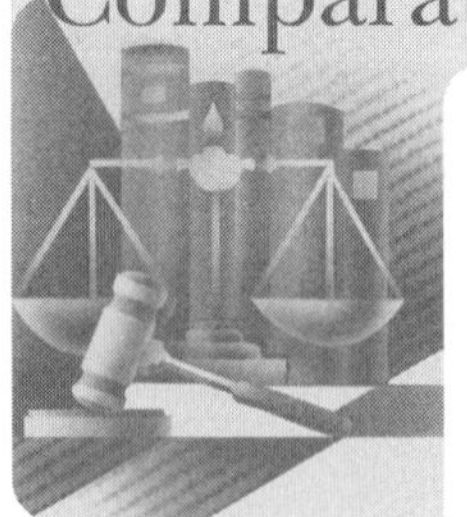

The 17 COGSA Exemptions

Neither the carrier nor the ship shall be responsible for loss or damage arising or resulting from:

(a) Act, neglect, or default of master or employees in the navigation or in the management of the ship.
(b) Fire.
(c) Perils of the sea.
(d) Act of God.
(e) Act of war.
(f) Act of public enemies.
(g) Arrest or restraint or seizure under legal process.
(h) Quarantine restrictions.
(i) Act or omission of the shipper or owner of the goods.
(j) Strikes, lockouts, or stoppage of labor.
(k) Riots and civil commotions.
(l) Saving or attempting to save life or property at sea.
(m) Wastage in bulk or weight or any other loss arising from inherent vice of the goods.
(n) Insufficiency of packing.
(o) Insufficiency of marks.
(p) Latent defects not discoverable by due diligence.
(q) Any other cause arising without actual fault or privity of the carrier, but the burden of proof shall be on the person claiming the benefit of this exception.

Sony Magnetic Products Inc. v. Merivienti

863 F.2d 1537 (11th Cir. 1989)

Kravitch, Circuit Judge. Sony Magnetic Products, Inc., of America contacted Page & Jones, a freight forwarder with offices in Mobile, Alabama, to arrange for the transportation of a container of video cassette tapes to England. Page & Jones reserved space for Sony's cargo with Atlantic Cargo Services on board the *Finnhawk.* Sony packed its cargo of video cassette tapes into a standard shipping container, measuring 40 feet long by 8 feet wide by 8 feet high. As the *Finnhawk's* deck crane was lifting the container of Sony's tapes up to the vessel's cargo deck, the hydraulic motor of the crane exploded causing the container to drop approximately 60 feet to the concrete loading deck below.

The first issue on appeal is whether the district court properly imposed liability on the defendants under COGSA for the damage to Sony's video cassette tapes. A shipper establishes a *prima facie* case under COGSA by proving that the carrier received the cargo in good condition but unloaded it in a damaged condition. A carrier can rebut a shipper's *prima facie* case by establishing either that it exercised due diligence to prevent the damage to the cargo by properly handling, stowing, and caring for it in a seaworthy ship or that the harm resulted from one of the excepted causes listed in section 1304(2). If the carrier is able to rebut the shipper's *prima facie* case, the burden then shifts back to the shipper to show that the carrier's negligence was, at the least, a concurrent cause of the loss.

The defendants attempted to establish that the accident that caused the damage to Sony's cargo was the result of a latent defect in the motor of the *Finnhawk's* crane, one of the enumerated exceptions. In addition, crew members of the *Finnhawk* maintained that there had been no complaints about or problems with the crane and that it had always been properly maintained and inspected. In pertinent part, § 1304 of COGSA provides as follows:

(2) Neither the carrier nor the ship shall be responsible for loss or damage arising or resulting from—(p) Latent defects not discoverable by due diligence. A latent defect is one that could not be discovered upon reasonable inspection or by any known and customary test.

The district court concluded, as a matter of law, that the defendants had not sustained their burden of proving that Sony's loss was caused by a latent defect. For the foregoing reasons, the judgment of the district court is AFFIRMED.

Case Highlights

- Often times the bill of lading is prepared by the freight forwarder, on behalf of the shipper, and submitted to the carrier for signature.
- Presenting a clean bill of lading satisfies the shipper's initial burden of proving that it had delivered cargo in good condition to the carrier.
- A carrier can rebut a shipper's *prima facie* case by establishing either that it exercised due diligence to prevent the damage to the cargo by properly handling, stowing, and caring for it in a seaworthy ship or that the harm resulted from one of the enumerated exemptions or causes.
- The carrier has a heavy burden in proving that the loss was due to a "latent defect."

shipment of goods with carriers,[33] (2) act as a freight consolidator, and (3) process required documentation.

In arranging for the shipment the forwarder negotiates a freight rate with the carrier as an agent for the shipper. The negative repercussion of the role of the freight forwarder as agent is that it may bind the shipper to modifications made by the carrier to the standard carriage contract. The *Constructores Tecnicos v. Sea-Land Service* case on page 295, for example, examines the ability of a freight forwarder to bind the shipper to a material deviation. It addresses the question of whether the forwarder acts as an agent for the shipper for purposes of imputing the forwarder's knowledge to the shipper.

33. The freight forwarder reserves space on the carrier well before actual shipment date by entering into a *booking contract.*

Lamb Head Shipping v. Jennings

1 Lloyd's L. R. 624 (C.A. 1994)

The *Marel* sailed from Greece to Ghent with a load of Greek corn. While in route it encountered adverse weather conditions with the wind reaching NE force 7 with a swell of about two or three metres. According to the evidence, witnesses felt a "bump" sufficient to cause the crew to be thrown off balance. Less than one hour later the ship sank. The plaintiffs claimed under their marine hull insurance contending that the vessel was lost due to *perils of the sea* which was covered under the policy. The sole issue was whether the loss was caused by perils of the sea.

Justice Dillon. The burden of proving on the balance of probabilities that a vessel was lost by perils of the sea was on the owners. It is not sufficient for the owners merely to prove the incursion of seawater into the insured vessel. In fact, *Marel* was not overwhelmed by exceptionally bad weather. It is very nearly impossible that the only form of unidentified object that was suggested as a possibility, a derelict container, caused the casualty. The crucial question is how the flooding of the engine room came about. The plaintiffs assert that it came about by perils of the sea. "Perils of the sea" does not include the ordinary action of wind and waves.

The primary submission for the plaintiff was that *Marel* had hit a floating container that had fallen from some other ship. However, there was no evidence that there had been any report of any container having been lost in the vicinity. The lower court accordingly found that it was wholly improbable that entry of seawater was due to a collision. Though the general condition of the vessel was good for her age, there had been various botched repairs and the owners were not enthusiastic about spending money unnecessarily. We therefore AFFIRM the lower court's dismissal.

Case Highlights

- The ship owner has the burden to prove a loss due to a "peril of sea" in making a claim under its marine insurance.
- Perils of the sea does not include the ordinary action of wind and waves.
- Failure to properly repair a ship opens the ship owner to a charge of a lack of due diligence in maintaining the seaworthiness of the vessel.

http://

The role of the freight forwarder and the law of freight forwarding: **http://www.itds.treas.gov/freight.html**; **http://www.unzco.com/basicguide/c10.html**; and **http://www.forwarderlaw.com**.

It has become a common practice for the forwarder to issue carrier-type documents such as the **forwarder's bill of lading** or receipt. In such cases, the forwarder assumes the liability of a carrier or possibly of a multimodal transport operator. Carrier liability, therefore, may extend not only to the actual carriers, but also to *contractual* carriers. The freight forwarder also serves the important function of consolidating the shipments of a number of shippers to fill all available space being offered by the carrier in order to reduce the freight costs to the individual shippers. Finally, the freight forwarder provides assistance in preparing the necessary documentation needed for customs clearance. **Customs brokers** are also utilized to deal with customs authorities and to comply with customs regulations.[34]

Multimodal transport operators (MTOs), also known as combined transport operators, arrange for the shipment of goods using different modes of transport such as sea, rail, road, and air. They enter into separate contracts with the individual carriers. The major benefit to the shipper is that the MTO issues a single transport document for the entire transport. The shipper may make a claim for loss against the MTO no matter where the loss occurs during the transport.

Because of the increased use of MTOs and freight forwarders as common carriers, the **through bill of lading** has become a more commonly used document of

34. See Chapter 6, National Export and Import Regulation.

Constructores Tecnicos v. Sea-Land Service, Inc.

945 F.2d 841 (5th Cir. 1991)

King, Circuit Judge. The Honduran government awarded Constructores Tecnicos (Contec), a Honduran company, a contract for the construction of 20 testing wells and 13 water wells in Honduras. In order to perform the work, Contec purchased a Ford LT 9000 Tandem Chassis diesel truck and various drilling accessories, including a portable drilling rig unit from JWS Equipment, Inc., of Moore, Oklahoma. Contec partner Julio Pineda contacted Charles Pagan of Golden Eagle International Forwarding Co. (Golden Eagle), a freight forwarder, and requested that Golden Eagle arrange for transportation of the truck from Oklahoma to Puerto Cortes, Honduras.

Pagan made the transportation arrangements through Sea-Land Service, Inc. (Sea-Land). He filled out a Sea-Land bill of lading, listing the cargo to be shipped but leaving the space for the freight rate blank. The bill of lading did not indicate whether the cargo was to be stowed on deck or below deck. Pagan then delivered the draft bill of lading to Sea-Land's office. The truck and equipment were loaded on the M/V *Vermillion Bay,* a vessel chartered by Sea-Land. The truck and some of the equipment were secured to a flatrack, a form of open container, by chain lashings and stowed on deck.

The M/V *Vermillion Bay* encountered severe weather in the Gulf of Mexico on the fringes of Hurricane Gilbert. During the storm, nearby containers broke free of their lashings causing severe damage to the truck. The ship changed course and docked at Port Everglades, Florida, where the truck was unloaded and deemed a constructive total loss. Contec brought suit against Golden Eagle, Sea-Land, and International Cargo and Surety Insurance Co. (International Cargo).

COGSA limits an ocean carrier's liability for lost or damaged cargo to $500 per package. A carrier loses this protection, however, if a deviation from the specifications contained in its contract of carriage with the shipper amounts to more than a reasonable deviation. The district court held that a clean bill of lading entitles the shipper to presume below-deck stowage. The lower court, citing a line of authority dating back to the late 19th century, described the legal effect of a clean bill of lading: "A clean bill of lading imports that the goods are to be safely and properly stowed under deck. Absent an express agreement to the contrary or a port custom permitting on-deck stowage, a shipper may presume that a clean bill of lading will result in carriage of the cargo below deck."

The appellants argue that Contec had not dealt directly with the carrier, but rather through an intermediary freight forwarder who had the power to bind the shipper to on-deck shipment. We disagree with appellants' suggestion that there is a hard and fast rule deeming freight forwarders to be agents of shippers. In regard to the shipper's selection of the forwarder, obviously this is an indication that the forwarder's actions can be attributed to the shipper. Control of the manner in which the forwarder performs his duties, however, rather than selection, has been the more important factor in deciding the agency question. It is undisputed that the shipper did not control the forwarder's actions in booking cargo. The forwarder was free to select the carrier or line on which to ship the goods and the shipper had little knowledge of the manner in which the forwarder performed its duties, much less controlled the forwarder's performance.

Appellants correctly argue from these facts that Golden Eagle "entered into the contract of carriage on behalf of the shipper," but the conclusion it believes follows—that Golden Eagle's knowledge concerning Sea-Land's practices may be imputed to Contec as a result of an agency relationship—is incorrect without the missing link of control by the shipper over the forwarder's actions. The legal relationship of agency is the threshold question. Only then could the agent's knowledge of the carrier's usual custom of storing oversized containers on deck be deemed sufficient to bind the shipper to a contract in which the shipper consented to on-deck stowage. If the shipper has in no way consented to on-deck stowage, and cannot be deemed to have done so through a freight forwarder acting as its agent, the law's concern is with the shipper's expectations. WE AFFIRM the judgment awarding damages in excess of the COGSA limitation of liability.

Case Highlights

- The freight forwarder acts as agent for the shipper in selecting a common carrier and booking cargo space.
- The freight forwarder's knowledge of a common carrier's practices that would be deemed to be material deviations is not imputed to the shipper.
- An express provision in the bill of lading or port custom may overcome the presumption in favor of below-deck stowage.

title. The through bill of lading and the liabilities that emanate from it are explained in the *Mannesman Demag Corp.* case that follows. The case also explains how containerization has transformed the shipping industry and its legal regimes, along with the continued use of the Harter Act to fill in gaps in coverage before and after the goods are loaded or discharged from a ship.

Mannesman Demag Corp. v. M/V *Concert Express*

225 F.3d 587 (5th Cir. 2000)

Smith, Circuit Judge. This case arises from damage sustained to an oxygen compressor owned by Mannesman while in transport from Bremerhaven, Germany, to Terre Haute, Indiana. Atlantic carried the goods from Bremerhaven to the Port of Baltimore, Maryland, aboard the M/V *Concert Express.* Trism carried the goods from Baltimore to Terre Haute. While in route from Baltimore to Terre Haute, the goods were damaged when Trism's trailer overturned.

There was only one bill of lading for the entire transportation, issued by Atlantic, reflecting an agreement to transport the goods from Bremerhaven, Germany, to the midwestern United States. The bill is what is called a "through bill of lading." A through bill of lading is one by which an ocean carrier agrees to transport goods to their final destination. Someone else (e.g., railroad, trucker, or air carrier) performs a portion of the contracted carriage. The bill obligates the common carrier to transport the cargo "through" the port to its ultimate destination.

This case presents an issue of first impression regarding the applicability of federal maritime statutes to inland transport under a through bill of lading. Until the advent of the containerization of cargo, the cargo owner typically would enter into a new shipment contract with a new carrier each time the mode of transport changed. An inland carrier—a railroad, trucker, or, in some cases, an inland barge operator—would carry the goods to a seaport under one contract of carriage. There someone, usually a "freight forwarder" acting on behalf of the cargo owner, would arrange to place the goods in the hands of a steamship line. Different legal regimes arose to govern the parties' rights and liabilities, depending upon the mode of shipment. If the railroad did the damage, then the rules of liability governing railroads would apply. Maritime law would govern the liability of the steamship or ocean leg of the transport.

Along came multimodal or intermodal shipping containers and everything changed. Now, the same steel cargo container can move freely between different modes of transport. Ocean carriers began to offer "door to door" service. Rail carriers, truckers, or other transporters now contract, not with the owner of the goods, but as a subcontractor to the steamship line who has offered a complete transport package. The U.S. Carriage of Goods by Sea Act (COGSA) governs the liability of an ocean carrier on an international through bill of lading. COGSA contains important benefits to the carrier. Inland carriers frequently attempt to take advantage of the benefits afforded by COGSA.

One of COGSA's most important provisions limits a carrier's liability to five hundred dollars ($500) per package unless a higher value is declared by the shipper. COGSA also contains a one-year limitation for cargo claims. By its terms, COGSA applies "tackle-to-tackle" only; it does not extend to losses that occur prior to loading or subsequent to discharge from a vessel. A Period of Responsibility Clause can be used to extend COGSA's application to the entire time the goods are within the carrier's custody.

Atlantic's bill references two statutes, the Carriage of Goods by Sea Act (COGSA) and the Harter Act. Under COGSA, a carrier of goods in international commerce must "properly and carefully load, handle, stow, carry, keep, care for, and discharge the goods carried." The Harter Act imposes a duty of "proper loading, stowage, custody, care, and proper delivery." Although the Harter Act's applicability to international commerce was partially superseded by COGSA, COGSA is applicable only from the time goods are loaded onto the ship until the time the cargo is released from the ship's tackle at port. Therefore, the Harter Act applies to the period between the discharge of the cargo from the vessel and "proper delivery."

Atlantic's bill of lading provides that, to the extent the Harter Act is compulsorily applicable, the Carrier's "responsibility shall be subject to COGSA." It further states that "where COGSA applies, the Carrier shall not be or become liable for any loss or damage in an amount per package or unit in excess of $500." Therefore, if the Harter Act is compulsorily applicable to Trism's inland transport, the court correctly limited Atlantic's liability to $500 per package. The Harter Act is at its core a maritime law; the Court is unwilling to rule that simply because private parties enter an intermodal agreement federal maritime legislation is thus extended far beyond its congressionally intended bounds. The Harter Act is designed solely to regulate the liability of seagoing carriers.

That said, the Court finds that the Harter Act does reach to the point at which goods are loaded onto the vehicles of an inland trucker, whether hired by the shipper or the carrier.

In this age of "containerized" cargoes subject to "multimodal" bills of lading, it is often difficult to locate precisely the points of legal delivery. Increasing efficiency and integration in cargo transport continues to blur the lines separating sea carrier responsibilities from those of others. The Court finds it advisable to keep sea carriers to the standards imposed by the Harter Act until goods are in the hands of land carriers and actually leaving the maritime arena. With COGSA covering carriers' legal responsibilities through discharge, Harter fills a potential gap between discharge and inland transit in those situations where goods, though on the dock, are still within the control and responsibility of the sea carrier.

Case Highlights

- A through bill of lading is one by which an ocean carrier or MTO agrees to transport goods to their final destination.
- The Harter Act fills a potential gap between discharge and inland transit in those situations where goods, though on the dock, are still within the control and responsibility of the sea carrier.
- The Harter Act does reach the point at which goods are loaded onto the vehicles of an inland trucker, whether hired by the shipper or the carrier.

MARINE INSURANCE

Under international conventions, such as the Hague Rules and Warsaw Convention, a common carrier's liability is frequently limited. Buyers or sellers of goods protect themselves from carrier liability limitations by making arrangements for cargo insurance against losses due to damage or delay in transit. If the buyer neglects to obtain coverage or obtains too little, damage to the cargo may cause a major financial loss to the exporter. Therefore, even if the terms of sale make the foreign buyer responsible, the exporter should still contemplate obtaining insurance on its own behalf.

Due to the advent of containerization, an insurance policy or policies will need to cover multiple modes of transportation. Shipping goods across national boundaries—from one inland destination to a port of shipment, then to a port of destination and the inland point of destination—involves different types of insurance, including marine, war risk, comprehensive general liability, protection and indemnity, and excess insurance. This is further complicated by the fact that insurance providers will often distribute the risk through reinsurance.[35]

In order to deal with these different issues of coverage, the transit insurance industry has produced a host of standard forms and clauses. The existence of such standardization, however, should not cloud the fact that the transit insurance policy is often a very specific custom contract. "Even with the extensive use of form policies there are inevitable variations negotiated by the parties. There is simply no substitute for a thorough review of the particular insurance contract in the manner of its negotiation and placement."[36]

35. Marine insurance is a contractual relationship between an underwriter and the insured (shipper), while reinsurance is a contract between different underwriters. As a general rule the insurer may not reinsure on broader terms than are found in the underlying policy.

36. Raymond P. Hayden & Sanford E, Balick, "Marine Insurance: Varieties, Combinations, and Coverages," 66 *Tulane Law Review* 311, 313 (1991). Most of the information in this section was gleaned from this article. See generally Arthur E. Brunck, et al., OCEAN MARINE INSURANCE (1988).

Highly specialized, the marine insurance industry provides a variety of insurance policies, including hull, cargo, and liability policies. These policies protect ship and cargo owners from an assortment of exposures including damage to goods, damage to the ship, damage to other's property, and liability for injury and death. The most common property coverage is provided by **hull insurance.** The owner or charter party of a vessel generally obtains hull insurance. This protects the owner or charter party from losses due to damage to the vessel or its equipment. War risk coverage is ordinarily excluded from the standard hull and cargo policies. The hull policy is a perils-only type of policy in that one may collect only for losses resulting from expressly listed causes. Therefore, clauses that extend coverage should be carefully considered.

http://

Definitions of Inchmaree clause and other cargo insurance terms: **http://www.tsbic.com/cargo/glossary.htm**.

The two most popular extensions are through the **Inchmaree clause** and the **running down clause.** The Inchmaree or additional perils clause extends the list of covered perils usually to include losses due to negligence of the crew and damage arising from a latent defect. This clause is also commonly inserted in cargo insurance polices. The running down clause provides protection from liability for damages to another vessel caused by a collision with the insured ship. The best sources for hull insurance forms and clauses are Lloyd's of London and the American Institute's Hull Clauses.

Liability coverage is provided through protection and indemnity insurance, offered through associations of shipping companies popularly known as P & I clubs. The **Protection and Indemnity (P & I) Policy** provides two broad categories of protection: third-party liability and contractual liability protection. Third-party liability coverage protects against damages caused to others due to marine collision. Contractual liability coverage includes protection against passenger liability, liability for loss and damaged cargo, pollution, and general average. Thus, when a cargo owner or its insurance company sues the common carrier for cargo damage the carrier's insurance company will be required to defend or pay the claim.

With the advent of container transport, the **through-transport policy** form of P & I insurance has become popular. A through-transport policy provides indemnification for third-party damage caused during inland transit. Indemnity policies become operative only upon payment by the insured. Another popular policy is the **comprehensive general liability (CGL) coverage.** The **Insurance Services Office (ISO),** a private trade association, drafts this policy.[37] Two points will be made regarding CGL policies. Their most salient feature is their comprehensiveness. Second, they provide a rather broad duty on the part of the insurer to defend. Thus, the insured is provided with the luxury of having legal services paid for by the insurance company even on claims where insurance coverage is suspect.

http://

Insurance Services Office, Inc.: **http://www.iso.com/**.

Shippers also commonly obtain umbrella or **excess insurance.** Insurance is often multilayered due to the fact that the underlying insurance provider may be unwilling to provide the amount of coverage requested by the insured. The insured may further limit its exposure by obtaining excess coverage for claims that exceed the amount of the underlying policies. The excess insurance policy incorporates one of a number of popular clauses that control when that coverage becomes operational. These clauses relate the excess coverage to the coverage provided by underlying policies. For example, an escape clause precludes any recovery if the type of claim is covered under an existing policy even if that claim exceeds the amount of coverage provided by the underlying policy. An **excess clause** covers all claims

37. Ibid. at 339.

outside the coverage of the underlying policy. The ***pro rata* clause** proportions the amount paid under the policy based upon the limits provided by all relevant policies.[38]

Marine Cargo Insurance

The most relevant policy for exporter and importers of goods is the **cargo policy** (see Exhibit 10.1: Sample Insurance Certificate). The restrictions on coverage in cargo insurance revolve around three factors: (1) the causes of loss that it protects against, (2) amount of coverage, and (3) duration of the coverage. The first factor determines whether to obtain perils or an all-risk policy. The second factor affects

EXHIBIT 10.1 *Sample Insurance Certificate*

SAMPLE INSURANCE CERTIFICATE

FIREMAN'S FUND INSURANCE COMPANY
SAN FRANCISCO, CALIFORNIA
ATLANTIC DIVISION, 110 WILLIAMS STREET
NEW YORK, NEW YORK 10038

SHIPPER/EXPORTER	DOCUMENT NO.	CERTIFICATE NO.
CALIFORNIA CITRUS EXPORT CO. 100 ORANGE GROVE DRIVE SANTA PAULA, CALIFORNIA 93060 U.S.A.		999999999
	EXPORT REFERENCES 61102 SHIPPER'S REF # 681038	
CONSIGNEE (Not negotiable unless consigned to order) NAGOYA IMPORT COMPANY HAMAMATSUCHO OFFICE CENTER 2-4-1, SHIBAKOUEN, MINATO-KU NAGOYA, JAPAN	FORWARDING AGENT-REFERENCES FAR EAST FORWARDERS, Inc. FMC 690 25 OCEAN DRIVE TORRANCE, CALIFORNIA 90501	
	POINT AND COUNTRY OR ORIGIN OF GOODS CALIFORNIA, U.S.A.	
NOTIFY PARTY SAME AS CONSIGNEE	DOMESTIC ROUTING/EXPORT INSTRUCTIONS CALIFORNIA FREIGHT COMPANY 21 RIVER ROAD SANTA PAULA, CALIFORNIA 90501	
PIER OR AIRPORT PIER 24 OAKLAND MARINE TERMINAL		

OCEAN VESSEL/VOY. NO.	PORT OF LOADING	INSURED DESTINATION
PACIFIC PACER V-71	OAKLAND, CA	NAGOYA, JAPAN
PORT OF DISCHARGE NAGOYA, JAPAN	FOR TRANSHIPMENT TO NONE	

PARTICULARS FURNISHED BY SHIPPER

Container No.; Seal No.; Marks & Nos.	No. of Containers or Packages	TYPE OR KIND OF CONTAINERS OR PACKAGES - DESCRIPTION OF GOODS	GROSS WEIGHT	MEASUREMENT
TRIU855204-0	1 x 40'	SHIPPER'S LOAD AND COUNT CY/CY. FREIGHT PREPAID. MAINTAIN TEMPERATURE AT 37 DEG. F. HC REEFER CONTAINER STC: 1001 CARTONS FRESH VALENCIA ORANGES AGREED WEIGHT IS 17.9 KGS/CTN	17935 KGS 39450 LBS	35.431 CM 1251 CFT

DATE OF POLICY	SUM INSURED	AMOUNT IN WORDS
Aug. 11, 1998	$15,837	Fifteen thousand eight hundred and thirty seven dollars

Insured against all risks of physical loss or damage from any external cause irrespective of percentage, but excluding the risks excluded by the F.C. & S and or S.R. &C.C. warranties on the reverse side of this policy except to the extent that such risks may be specifically covered by endorsement: also warranted free from any claim arising out of the inherent vice of the goods insured or consequent upon loss of time or market.

This insurance attaches from the time the goods leave the warehouse at the place named in the policy for the commencement at the transit and continues during the oridinary course of transit until the goods are delivered to the final warehouse at the destination named in the policy.

It is a condition of this insurance that there shall be no interruption or suspension of transit unless due to circumstances beyond the control of the Assured.

The risks covered by this policy include loss, damage or expense resulting from explosion howsoever or wheresoever occurring irrespective of percentage, but it is especcially understood and agreed that this wording is not intended to cover any of the risks excluded by the F. C. & S. and/or S.R. & C.C. Warranties set forth elsewhere in this policy.

This insurance is subject to the American Institute Marine Extension Clauses (1943) and the following American Institute Clauses as if the current form of each were endorsed hereon:
South America 60-Day Clause S.R. & C.C. Endorsement War Risk Insurance

It is hereby understood and agreed that in the cases of loss or damage to the property insured under this policy, same shall be immediately reported as soon as the goods are landed, or the loss known as expected, to the nearest agent of this Company as designated on the reverse side hereof.

(See reverse side for further terms and conditions which are hereby made a part of the Policy.)

Note: – It is necessary for the assured to give prompt notice to underwriters when he becomes aware of an event for which he is "held covered" under this policy and the right to such cover is dependent on compliance with this obligation.

In witness whereof the company named above has caused this policy to be signed by its duly authorized officers, but this policy shall not be valid unless countersigned by an authorized representative of this Company of the Assured.

Secretary President

ENDORSEMENT Countersigned at ____________________

____________________ By ____________________

38. Ibid. at 357.

the decision to insure against only a total loss, known as free of particular average, or to insure against partial losses or *with* average. The third factor involves the incorporation of clauses in the marine insurance that would extend the duration of coverage to periods when the goods are on the shore or in a warehouse. These **extension clauses** include warehouse-to-warehouse, shore, and marine extension clauses

There are two general types of marine insurance policies: (1) **perils only policy** and (2) **all risks policy.** The most common form of cargo insurance is the perils only policy that pays only for losses due to expressly enumerated perils or causes (see Exhibit 10.2: The Standard Perils Only Policy, ULA's Cargo B Clause).

The burden is on the cargo owner to prove that the loss was due to one of the listed perils.[39] Thus, under the perils only policy a loss caused by an unforeseen event or occurrence would be borne by the owner of the goods. In contrast, broader coverage is available through the all risk policy. The all risk policy covers any losses except for those expressly excepted in the policy. The burden to prove that the loss was due to an excluded clause is placed upon the insurance company. Standard cargo policies, both of the perils only and all risk varieties, will not cover risks associated with war, revolution, riot, or strikes. These areas of loss are exempted by the **F.C. & S. clause** (free of capture and seizure) and the **S.R. & C.C. clause** (strikes and riots). The F.C. & S. clause has been interpreted to exclude any losses due to war or civil strife, including rebellion and revolution. Coverage may be requested through an endorsement on the underlying policy or through a separate war risk policy. This decision is likely to be based upon the particular places of shipment and destination, along with the expected route of transport and the types of goods being transported.

Marine insurance polices also generally specify whether they cover less than total losses, known as **with average,** or whether they cover only total losses, **free of particular average (FPA).**[40] The more comprehensive policy is one *with average.*

EXHIBIT 10.2 *The Standard Perils Only Policy (ULA's Cargo B Clause)*

Risks Covered

This insurance covers:

(1) loss or damage to the goods insured reasonably attributable to:
   - (a) fire or explosion
   - (b) vessel or craft being stranded, grounded, sunk, or capsized
   - (c) overturning or derailment of land conveyance
   - (d) collision or contact of vessel or craft with any external object other than water
   - (e) discharge of cargo at a port of distress
   - (f) earthquake, volcanic eruption, or lightning

(2) loss or damage caused by:
   - (a) general average sacrifice
   - (b) entry of sea, lake, or river water into vessel or place of storage
   - (c) jettison or washing overboard

(3) total loss of any package lost overboard or dropped while being loaded on to or unloaded from vessel or craft.

39. Additional coverage can be added through a war and riot risk clause and an Inchmaree clause.

40. The marine term for loss is the word *average.*

This policy protects for partial as well as total losses. However, most with average polices restrict the coverage for partial losses to those losses that exceed 3 percent of the value of the goods. The free of particular average clause states that the insurance company does not have to pay the insured (assured) if he suffers less than a total loss. This type of limited coverage is not favored. More recently, the Institute of London Underwriters opted to eliminate free of particular average from its standard clauses. Instead, it provides an alternative clause that allows the insurance company to narrow the list of specified risks that would be covered under the standard perils only policy.

Marine cargo insurance traditionally covers only the period that the goods are upon the ship. Due primarily to the importance of the bill of lading and the use of multimodal containers, the cargo policy is often made to cover risk of loss for periods of time before the loading and after the unloading of the goods. This is generally done by incorporating a warehouse-to-warehouse or **marine extension** clause in the insurance policy that protects the shipper from the start in the exporter's country until received in the importer's country. (See Exhibit 10.3: Warehouse-to-Warehouse Clause.) The marine extension or warehouse-to-warehouse clause extends the standard marine coverage to the period before the loading of the goods and the period between offloading and delivery to the consignee. It is important to make sure that the clause does not limit the extended coverage through a time limit provision. The best way to ensure this is to provide that the policy remains in operation until the goods are delivered to the consignee.

The *Shaver Transportation Co.* case is an excellent review of some of the standard clauses found in most marine insurance policies. Marine insurance policies are directed at one of two intended beneficiaries—the shipper and the common carrier. The clauses reviewed in *Shaver Transportation Co.* apply equally to both perils only and all risk insurance policies. The clauses in the marine insurance policy that are referred to in the case have been excerpted and placed in Focus on Transactions: Standard Marine Insurance Clauses. It is important to refer to these clauses when reading the case.

Cargo insurance can be obtained for a single voyage or a fixed period of time. The most common form in exporting is the open or **general cover** form of

EXHIBIT 10.3 *Warehouse-to-Warehouse Clause (Institute of London Underwriters, Clause A)*

Duration

This insurance attaches from the time the goods leave the warehouse or place of storage at the place named herein for the commencement of the transit and terminates either

(1) on delivery to the Consignee's or other final warehouse or place of storage at the destination named herein,

(2) on delivery to any warehouse, whether prior to or at the destination named herein, which the assured elects to use either

  (i) for storage in the ordinary course of transit, or

  (ii) for allocation or distribution, or

(3) on the expiration of 60 days after the completion of discharge overside of the goods from the oversea vessel at the final port of discharge, whichever shall occur first.

This insurance shall remain in force during delay beyond the control of the assured, any deviation, forced discharge, reshipment or transhipment arising from the exercise of a liberty granted to shipowners under the contract of affreightment (carriage).

Shaver Transportation Co. v. The Travelers Indemnity Co.

481 F. Supp. 892 (D.C. Oregon 1979)

Skopil, District Judge. Shaver Transportation Company (Shaver), a barge company, contracted with Weyerhaeuser Company (Weyerhaeuser) to transport caustic soda from Weyerhaeuser plants to a buyer of the soda, GATX. Following the terms of the agreement, Shaver arranged for marine cargo insurance with Travelers. Shaver decided on "Free from Particular Average" and "standard perils" provisions supplemented with "specially to cover" clauses. Upon delivery to GATX, it was determined that the soda had been contaminated with tallow.

The parties agree that contamination occurred as Shaver was loading the caustic soda aboard the barge. The barge had previously carried a load of tallow, and Shaver had not thoroughly cleaned the barge input lines. Shortly thereafter Travelers notified Shaver that the contamination did not represent a recoverable loss under the defendant's marine open cargo policy. There is only one major issue in the case: Are the losses incurred by the plaintiffs the consequences of an insured event under the marine cargo insurance policy? Plaintiffs have meticulously examined the policy and argue for recovery under several theories.

I. *Recovery under Perils of the Sea clause and Free from Particular Average clause*

The Perils clause, almost identical to ancient perils provisions dating back several hundred years, defines the risks protected by the policy. In addition to a long list of "perils of the sea," the clause includes "all other perils, losses, and misfortunes, that have or shall, come to the hurt, detriment, or damage to the said goods and merchandise." Plaintiff argues that the "forced" disposition of the caustic soda was like jettison (an enumerated peril) and is covered by the concluding language of the clause.

The contamination of the cargo occurred at the time of loading. Therefore, the plaintiffs cannot recover under the Perils clause of the policy. The term "jettison" also appears in the Free from Particular Average clause. If jettison did occur, this clause affords coverage regardless of the amount of cargo damage. However, I find that a jettison did not occur in this instance.

II. *Recovery under Warehouse-to-Warehouse clause; Marine Extension clause; Shore Coverage clause*

These clauses do not define the nature of the risks covered by the policy but merely define where physically the coverage extends. To recover under either the Warehouse-to-Warehouse or the Marine Extension clause the plaintiffs must show that an insured peril existed and the damage was proximately caused by that peril. The shore coverage clause provides coverage for enumerated risks occurring on shore. Plaintiffs argue that contamination while loading is a shore accident. However, since the contamination occurred within the barge's intake lines, the incident arose "on board." Therefore shore coverage does not apply. Even if it were to apply, contamination of cargo is not within the enumerated risks covered by the shore coverage clause.

III. *Recovery of Extraordinary Expenses under Landing and Warehousing clause; Extra Expenses clause; Sue and Labor clause*

Under these provisions the insured is entitled to recover expenses associated with losses incurred as a result of an insured peril. I find that the losses suffered by plaintiffs were not caused by a peril covered by the policy. Recovery under these provisions is therefore precluded.

IV. *Recovery under Inchmaree clause*

The purpose of the Inchmaree clause is to expand the coverage of the policy beyond the perils provision. It allows a vessel owner to become exempt from liability for fault or error in navigation or management of the ship. In contrast, the shipowner must retain liability for negligence in the care and custody of the cargo. The Ninth Circuit, noting that no precise definitions exist, advocates a case-by-case determination using the following test: "If the act in question has the primary purpose of affecting the ship, it is 'in navigation or in management'; but if the primary purpose is to affect the cargo, it is not 'in navigation or in management.'" Using this test, I find that the contamination of the cargo in this case was caused by fault in the care, custody, and control of the cargo.

V. *Recovery under Negligence clause*

The Negligence clause provides coverage against losses due to enumerated perils caused by the unseaworthiness of the vessel. To recover under this clause plaintiffs must show that the barge was unseaworthy. This unseaworthiness must then cause a loss through one of the enumerated perils: "sinking, stranding, fire, explosion, contact with seawater, or by any other cause of the nature of any of the risks assumed in the policy." "Seaworthiness" depends on such factors as the type of vessel, character of the voyage, reasonable weather, navigational conditions, and type of cargo.

A vessel is unseaworthy if she is not reasonably fit to carry cargo she has undertaken to transport. I find Shaver's barge unseaworthy as a result of improper loading of cargo. Plaintiffs must demonstrate that the unseaworthiness of the barge caused a loss to cargo by one or more of the enumerated perils. Since contamination is not an enumerated peril, no recovery is possible under the Negligence clause of this policy.

Even assuming that a peril existed, defendant claims that contribution cannot be requested when the vessel owner was at fault in creating the situation. Vessel owners have long placed in bills of lading a provision incorporating the protections of the Harter Act and Carriage of Goods by Sea Act. This provision, known as the Jason clause entitles shipowners to contribution notwithstanding negligence in creating the general average situation. However, the shipowner must comply with 46 U.S.C. § 1303(1) (a) requiring due diligence to make the vessel seaworthy. The burden of proving "due diligence" in making the vessel seaworthy falls on the vessel owner. I find that Shaver did not meet this burden. Shaver failed to properly clean or inspect the barge's input lines. Shaver failed to use due diligence to make the barge seaworthy. Judgment shall be entered for the defendant.

Case Highlights

- Warehouse-to-warehouse and shore clauses do not define the nature of the risks covered by the policy but merely define where physically the coverage extends.
- The Inchmaree clause allows a vessel owner to become exempt from liability for fault or error in navigation or management of the ship. In contrast, the shipowner must retain liability for negligence in the care and custody of the cargo (stowage).
- A vessel is unseaworthy if she is not reasonably fit to carry cargo she has undertaken to transport.
- Since contamination is not an enumerated peril, no recovery is possible under the Negligence clause.
- The Jason clause allows shipowners to collect general average damages notwithstanding their negligence in creating the general average situation (see next section on general average).

insurance policy, which is not limited to a specific shipment, but covers numerous shipments for a fixed period of time or until terminated by notice given by the shipper (insured) or the insurance company. The premium is calculated on the basis of the values declared by the shipper on the certificates issued for each shipment. A variant of the open cover policy is the **blanket policy** in which the shipper is not required to declare the individual values of each shipment. Each shipment is covered up to the maximum amount of the policy.

Marine insurance policies have been standardized through the use of common clauses published by one of a number of associations. An example is the **Institute of London Underwriters (ILU).** Founded in 1884, the ILU is an association of marine insurance companies that publishes a manual of standard clauses. The sophisticated international exporter or importer should familiarize herself with the standard forms and clauses published by the ILU, the **American Institute of Marine Underwriters (AIMU),** and Lloyd's of London. An example of such publications is the manual on Cargo Clauses published by the AIMU. Familiarization with the standard forms is important because underwriters will often create their own policies by using clauses found in the standard forms. "Frequently, the standard clauses will be removed from the standard form and used as building blocks in custom policies. In addition the ILU and AIMU have drafted standard terms for particular trades."[41]

http://

American Institute of Marine Underwriters: **http://www.aimu.org** and Institute of London Underwriters: **http://www.iua.co.uk**

41. Hayden & Balick, *supra* note 37 at 325.

Focus on Transactions

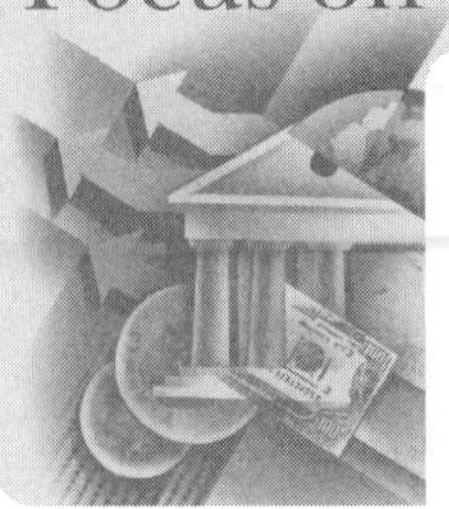

Standard Marine Insurance Clauses (from *Shaver*)

PERILS CLAUSE. Touching the adventures and perils which the said Assurers[42] are contented to bear, and take upon themselves, they are of the seas and inland waters, man of war, fires, enemies, pirates, rovers, assailing thieves, jettisons,[43] letters of mart,[44] reprisals, taking at sea, arrests, restraints and detainments of all kings, princes of people of what nation, condition or quality whatsoever, barratry of the master and mariners,[45] and all other perils, losses and misfortunes, that have or shall come to the hurt, detriment or damage to the said goods and merchandise, or any part thereof.

FREE OF PARTICULAR AVERAGE CLAUSE. Other shipments covered hereunder are insured: Free of Particular Average unless caused by the vessel and/or interest insured being stranded, sunk, burst, on fire or in collision with another ship or vessel or with ice or with any substance other than water, but liable for jettison and/or washing overboard, irrespective of percentage.

WAREHOUSE-TO-WAREHOUSE CLAUSE. This insurance attaches from the time the goods leave the Warehouse and/or Store at the place named in the policy for the commencement of the transit and continues during the ordinary course of transit, including customary transhipment if any, until the goods are discharged overside from the overseas vessel at the final port. Thereafter the insurance continues whilst the goods are in transit and/or awaiting transit until delivered to final warehouse at the destination named in the policy or until the expiry of 15 days (or 30 days if the destination to which the goods are insured is outside the limits of the port) whichever shall first occur. The time limits referred to above to be reckoned from midnight of the day on which the discharge overside of the goods hereby insured from the overseas vessel is completed. Held covered at a premium to be arranged in the event of transhipment, if any, other than as above and/or in the event of delay in excess of the above time limits arising from circumstances beyond the control of the Assured.

MARINE EXTENSION CLAUSE. This policy is extended to cover all shipments which become at risk hereunder in accordance with the following clauses:

I. This insurance attaches from the time the goods leave the warehouse at the place named in this policy . . . and continues until the goods are delivered to the final warehouse.

II. This insurance specially to cover the goods during deviation, delay, forced discharge, reshipment, and transhipment.

III. This insurance shall in no case be deemed to extend to cover loss, damage, or expense proximately caused by delay or inherent vice or nature of the subject-matter insured.

SHORE COVERAGE CLAUSE. Including while on docks, wharves or elsewhere on shore and/or during land transportation, risks of collision, derailment, fire, lightning, sprinkler leakage, cyclones, hurricanes, earthquakes, floods, the rising of navigable waters, or any accident to the conveyance

GENERAL AVERAGE

General average is a venerable doctrine of maritime law that dates back 2,800 years. The doctrine provides that when a portion of a ship's cargo is sacrificed to save the rest from a real and substantial peril, each owner of property saved contributes ratably to make up the loss of the sacrificed property's owners. The United States

42. Assured refers to the party insured by the policy. Assurer refers to the insurance company.
43. Cargo may be voluntarily sacrificed by jettison in the common good, giving rise to a general average loss.
44. Letters of mart or marque are government authorizations to commit piracy against a designated state or person.
45. Barratry is fraud or criminal conduct performed by the captain or the crew.

and/or collapse and/or subsidence of docks and/or structures, and to pay loss or damage caused thereby, even though the insurance be otherwise F.P.A.

LANDING AND WAREHOUSING CLAUSE. Notwithstanding any average warranty contained herein, these Assurers agree to pay landing, warehousing, forwarding or other expenses and/or particular charges should same be incurred, as well as any partial loss arising from transhipment. Also to pay the insured value of any package, piece, or unit totally lost in loading, transhipment, and/or discharge.

EXTRA EXPENSES CLAUSE. Where, by reason of a peril insured against under this policy, extra expenses are incurred to destroy, dump, or otherwise dispose of the damaged goods, or where extra expenses are incurred in discharging from the vessel and/or craft and/or conveyance, such expenses will be recoverable in full in addition to the damage to the insured interest.

SUE AND LABOR CLAUSE. In case of any loss or misfortune, it shall be lawful and necessary to and for the Assured, his or their factors, servants and assigns, to sue, labor, and travel for, in, and about the defense, safeguard, and recovery of the said goods and merchandise, or any part thereof without prejudice to this insurance; nor shall the acts of the insured or insurers, in recovering, saving, and preserving the property insured, in case of disaster, be considered a waiver or an acceptance of abandonment; to the charges whereof the said Assurers will contribute according to the rate and quantity of the sum herein insured.

INCHMAREE CLAUSE. This insurance is also specially to cover any loss of or damage to the interest insured hereunder, through the bursting of boilers, breakage of shafts or through any latent defect in the machinery, hull, or appurtenances, or from faults or errors in the navigation and/or management of the vessel by the Master, Mariners, Mates, Engineers, or Pilots; provided, however, that this clause shall not be construed as covering loss arising out of delay, deterioration or loss of market, unless otherwise provided elsewhere herein.

NEGLIGENCE CLAUSE. The Assured are not to be prejudiced by the presence of the negligence clause and/or latent defect clause in the bills of lading and/or charter party and/or contract of affreightment. The seaworthiness of the vessel and/or craft as between the Assured and Assurers is hereby admitted, and the Assurers agree that in the event unseaworthiness or a wrongful act or misconduct of shipowner, charterer, their agents or servants, shall, directly or indirectly, cause loss or damage to the cargo insured by sinking, stranding, fire, explosion, contact with seawater, or by any other cause of the nature of any of the risks assumed in the policy, the Assurers will (subject to the terms of average and other conditions of the policy) pay to an innocent Assured the resulting loss. With leave to sail with or without pilots, and to tow and assist vessels or craft in all situations and to be towed.

Supreme Court in *Barnard v. Adams*[47] described three events that create a general average situation: (1) a common danger to which ship, cargo, and crew are all exposed and which is imminent; (2) a voluntary sacrifice of a part for the benefit of the whole; and (3) successful avoidance of the peril.

Modern law has eased the imminent requirement by requiring only that a peril be real and substantial. Two classes of general average claim exist: those which arise

http://

Text of the York-Antwerp Rules—1994 Edition: **http://www.jus.uio.no/lm/cmi.york.antwerp.rules.1994/doc.html**.

47. 51 U.S. 270 (1850).

http://
The Association of Average Adjusters of the United States: **http://www.usaverageadjusters.org/Yorkantwerp.htm**.

from sacrifices of part of a ship or cargo made to save the whole venture, and those which arise out of **extraordinary expenses** incurred by the shipowner for the joint benefit of ship and cargo. Thus, general average claims are available to both shipowners and cargo owners. The international convention that governs the calculation of general average losses is the **York-Antwerp Rules.** The *Folger Coffee Company v. Olivebank* case involves a claim for general average by a common carrier against cargo owners.

Folger Coffee Company v. *Olivebank*

201 F.3d 632 (5th Cir. 2000)

Farris, Circuit Judge. In this admiralty and maritime appeal, Folger Coffee Co. and its insurer, Gulf Insurance Company, seek to reverse the district court's judgment that (1) the vessel M/V *Olivebank* is entitled to use general average on a salvage lien and (2) that Folger Coffee and Gulf Insurance owe their proportional share to the general average fund. The M/V *Olivebank* left the Port of Durban, South Africa, with cargo that included granite blocks, steel wire, and earth-moving equipment.

During the voyage the vessel encountered severe weather and extremely rough seas that caused seawater to come over the deck. The vessel's emergency electrical system, required by the Safety of Life at Sea Convention of 1974, should have provided emergency lighting from batteries, followed by the automatic startup of the emergency generator to provide electrical services for steering. The batteries failed and the emergency generator was ultimately started manually. The parties dispute the exact means by which the seawater reached the alternator room. It is, however, undisputed that a skylight, or raised hatch, nine feet above deck and two levels above the alternators was open at some point during the relevant period. It is also undisputed that outside deck-level vent covers to the exhaust vents were open and that these vents lead to the alternator room.

The captain of the vessel put out a Mayday. He entered into a salvage agreement with Pentow Marine, Ltd., a salvage tug, pursuant to a Lloyd's Open Form. The salvors arrived in the late afternoon. The main engines were ultimately started prior to the arrival of the salvors, and, after waiting out the storm, the M/V *Olivebank* sailed to a port of refuge on its own power. The salvors exercised their salvage lien by threatening arrest of the cargo and/or the ship.

The owners of the M/V *Olivebank* declared general average, forcing the cargo interests to provide general average bonds and guarantees. Folger Coffee and Gulf Insurance filed actions in district court seeking a declaration that the vessel was not entitled to general average and recovery for damage to cargo. The district court found that the loss of power was caused by a fortuitous combination of events and that the vessel was seaworthy when it left port.

Folger Coffee and Gulf Insurance maintain that the M/V *Olivebank* was not entitled to general average because the vessel was unseaworthy under the Carriage of Goods at Sea Act, 46 U.S.C. §§ 1300-1315. The parties do not dispute that the bill of lading covering the cargo aboard the M/V *Olivebank* required general average contribution. Under COGSA, once the vessel establishes that a general average act occurred, the cargo owner might avoid liability only by establishing that the vessel was unseaworthy at the start of the voyage and that the unseaworthiness was the proximate cause of the general average event. If the cargo owner proves unseaworthiness, the vessel may still prevail by proving that it exercised due diligence to make the vessel seaworthy prior to the voyage.

The district court held that the evidence did not support the proposed finding that the vessel was unseaworthy due to a defective emergency electrical system. The district court found that the failure of the batteries and emergency system was due to the same intervening event that caused the primary alternators to fail (entry of seawater) and that the collapse of both systems at the same time was fortuitous. The district court held that the M/V *Olivebank* was seaworthy when it left port and that the open skylight and the vent covers were not an issue of seaworthiness but a management decision. The district court did not commit clear error by finding the vessel seaworthy despite the entry of seawater. It found that the water came onto the ship over the stern in a storm with force 11 winds. This finding has support in the record.

Folger Coffee and Gulf Insurance also contend that the conditions of the skylight, or hatch, and vent covers and the fact that these items were not closed made the vessel unseaworthy. The district court found that the most likely explanation for the entry of water into the alternator room was through the hatch and the exhaust vents and that the vessel was relieved of liability because the decision not to close the skylight or the vent covers was a management decision.

COGSA "excepts the carrier for liability from damage caused by 'act, neglect, or default of the master, mariner, pilot, or the servants of the carrier in the navigation or in the management of the ship.'" Failure to detect a flaw prior to sailing constitutes a failure to exercise due diligence and not an error of management. There is a fine line between actions that constitute errors in management and inaction that constitutes a lack of due diligence. Folger Coffee and Gulf Insurance have misconstrued the district court's use of the phrase "management decision." Neglect by management also relieves liability under COGSA. AFFIRMED.

Case Highlights

- Under COGSA, once the vessel establishes that a general average act occurred, the cargo owner might avoid liability only by establishing that the vessel was unseaworthy at the start of the voyage and that the unseaworthiness was the proximate cause of the general average event.
- There is a fine line between actions that constitute errors in management for which the carrier is exempted and inaction that constitutes a lack of due diligence.

Key Terms

17 COGSA exemptions, 291
air waybill, 272
all risk policy, 300
American Institute of Marine Underwriters (AIMU), 303
bailee, 289
blanket policy, 303
cargo policy, 299
charter party, 276
clause paramount, 284
COGSA, 272
comprehensive general liability (CGL) coverage, 298
common carrier, 271
containerization, 285
customs brokers, 294
customary freight unit (CFU), 278
due diligence, 277
excess clause, 298
excess insurance, 298
exculpatory clause, 273
extension clause, 300
extraordinary expenses, 306
F.C. & S. clause, 300
fair opportunity, 277
Federal Arbitration Act, 279
force majeure clause, 279
forwarder's bill of lading, 294
free of particular average (FPA), 300
freight forwarder, 292
general average, 304
general cover, 300
Hague Rules, 272
Hague-Visby Rules, 272
Hamburg Rules, 272
Harter Act of 1893, 273
Himalaya Clause, 276
hull insurance, 298
Inchmaree clause, 298
Institute of London Underwriters (ILU), 303
Insurance Services Office, 298
marine extension clause, 300
marine insurance company, 292
material deviation, 277
misdelivery, 286
multimodal transport, 285
multimodal transport operator, 292
ocean bill of lading, 272
per package limitation, 277
perils only policy, 300
pro rata clause, 299
Protection and Indemnity (P & I) Policy, 298
Q-clause exception, 291
Rules for Multimodal Transport Documents, 285
running down clause, 298
S.R. & C.C. clause, 300
seaworthiness, 279
shortage, 278
statute of limitations, 279
stowage, 280
through bill of lading, 294
through-transport policy, 298
unimodal transport convention, 271
warehouse-to-warehouse clause, 276
Warsaw Convention, 272
with average, 300
York-Antwerp Rules, 306

Chapter Problems

1. A shipper obtains a marine (cargo) insurance policy for $25,000 on goods that had a real or market value of $8,000. If the goods are lost at sea is the insurance company liable for $25,000, $8,000, or nothing?

2. An insured takes out a marine insurance policy on $50,000 worth of goods but fails to disclose his previous claims history. In fact, the insured had filed claims for loss on eight previous policies covering transport of goods. Can the insurance company avoid making payment for loss to the insured goods?

3. A shipper obtains a cargo insurance policy on 400 sealed crates of "Grade A" industrial grinding wheels. In fact, the grinding wheels were contained in 400 burlap sacks and were of secondhand stock. Does such a variation in the description of the insured goods jeopardize the shipper's coverage?

4. Goods are jettisoned from a ship as a general average act. You file a claim against your marine insurance policy and receive full payment. Does the marine insurance company have a claim for general average against the shipowner and the other cargo owners?

5. During a time of hostilities, a shipowner hires a tug to tow the ship to lessen the danger from enemy submarines. Can the shipowner make a general average claim by arguing that the towing costs are extraordinary expenses incurred for the benefit of the ship and its cargo?

6. Plaintiff Tseng boarded an international flight from New York to Tel Aviv. Before being allowed to board, she was subjected to an intrusive security search. Tseng sued the airline in state court in New York for the torts of assault and false imprisonment. The Warsaw Convention does not address such an injury. Will Tseng be allowed to continue her action under New York law? *El Al Israel Airlines, Ltd. v. Tseng,* 119 Sup. Ct. 662 (1999).

7. The plaintiffs are Dutch importers of commodities that included industrial leather gloves. Four shipments of gloves were made in 1982 and 1983. The insurance contract contained the following clause: "This insurance shall in no case be deemed to extend to cover loss damage or expense proximately caused by *inherent vice* or nature of the subject matter insured." The plaintiff claimed that the dropping of water from a source external to the goods damaged the gloves. The defendant asserted that the goods deteriorated as a result of their natural behavior. In short, the goods were damaged because the leather was not properly dried by the plaintiff. Is this a case of inherent vice? *Noten v. Harding,* 2 Lloyd's Law Report 283 (English Court of Appeal 1990).

Internet Exercises

1. Review the web site of the International Maritime Bureau **http://www.iccwbo.org/ccs/menu_imb_bureau.asp**. What types of services does this organization provide to international shippers?

2. Research the status of the BOLERO Project in the development of electronic documentation relating to the shipment of goods at **http://www.bolero.net**.

3. Your company has just entered into an export contract with a company in Chile. It is your job to arrange transport from the Port of Miami to Santiago, Chile. Review shipping schedules in order to determine the best and fastest transit route. See "Shipping Schedules" at Maritime Global Net at **http://www.mglobal.com**.

http://www.exim.gov/index.html

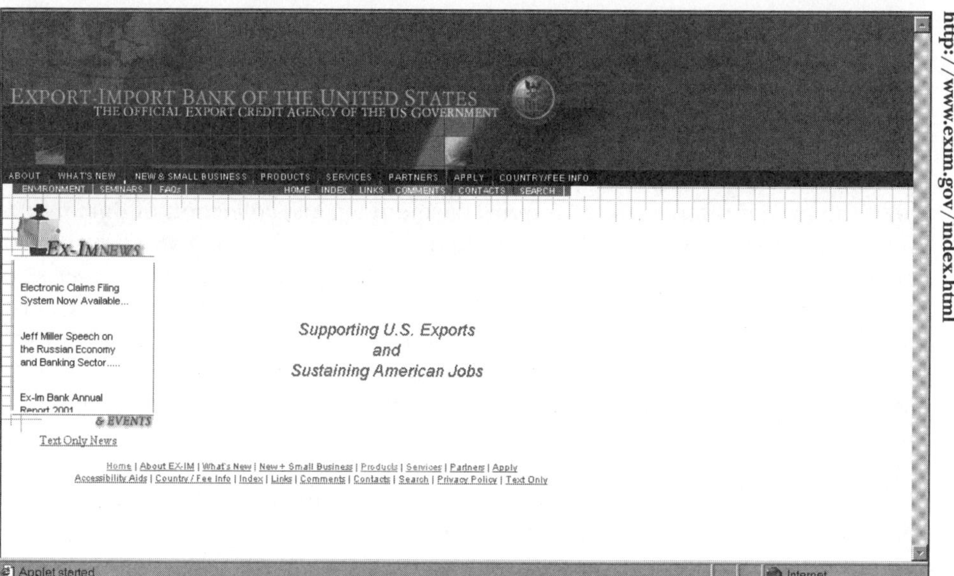

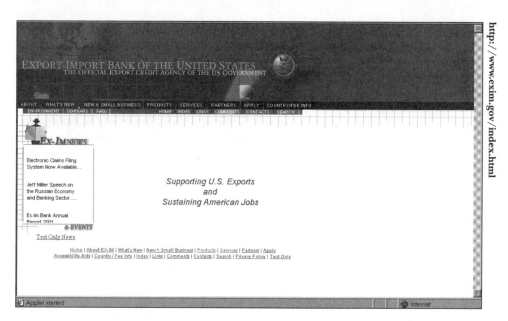

Chapter 11 International Trade Finance

Financing export transactions is a crucial part of most export and import businesses. Financing can be obtained in one of two ways: The first, external to the transaction, is when one of the parties obtains a general loan from a commercial bank or a government agency. The second method, internal to the transaction, is facilitated by two documents found in most export transactions—the bill of lading and the **letter of credit.** The importance of the bill of lading as a document of title was discussed in Chapter 9. A negotiable bill of lading allows for the transfer of the goods while they are in transit. Because it is negotiable it can be used as collateral to secure a loan.

The letter of credit is the main topic of this chapter. The letter of credit is a commercial bank guarantee of either payment by the buyer or performance by the seller. The letter of credit's primary purpose is to guarantee payment to the buyer (letter of credit) or to guarantee performance of one of the parties (standby letter of credit). Its secondary purpose is to allow the seller to finance the production and export of the goods.

As discussed in Chapter 9, in order to lower the risk of nondelivery or nonpayment the parties often agree to require payment against collection of documents. In the **documentary collections transaction** the seller does not give up control of the goods until the buyer purchases the documents minimizing the seller's risk of nonpayment. At the same time, the buyer's nondelivery risk is minimized because, with the documents, it obtains legal control over the goods in transit. The buyer's only remaining risk is fraud, where the documents do not reflect the true shipment. Requiring preshipment inspection minimizes this risk. One risk for the seller remains—the risk that the buyer will dishonor its obligation to purchase the documents. In that case, the seller retains control over the goods, but the goods are in transit to a distant port. The cost of returning or transshipping the goods or finding an alternative buyer is likely to be substantial.

The risk of nonpayment is removed through the use of a **documentary *credit* transaction.** In such a transaction the buyer obtains from a bank a letter of credit that guarantees payment to the seller. Substituting the credit or guarantee of a bank for that of the buyer eliminates the risk of nonpayment. This chapter will examine three uses of letters of credit in international transactions. First, the letter of credit is used as a device to guarantee a payment obligation in a documentary transaction. Second, the letter of credit is used as a *standby* to guarantee a performance obligation. Three, the letter of credit is used to help finance the exporting or importing of goods.

LETTERS OF CREDIT

http://
Dictionary of banking terms: **http://www.ubs.com/e/index/about/bterms/**.

Letters of credit have been called the lifeblood of commerce. The origins of the letter of credit in international transactions may be traced deeply into history. There is evidence letters of credit were used by bankers in Renaissance Europe, Imperial Rome, ancient Greece, Phoenicia, and even early Egypt. These simple instruments have survived because of their inherent reliability, convenience, economy, and flexibility. Letters of credit serve three important functions in international business transactions: payment instrument (transfer of documents and collection of funds), guarantee instrument (performance guarantee), and finance instrument (negotiation and collateral).

Between trusted parties when a letter of credit is not cost-effective, alternatives may be sought to secure payment. The documentary transaction without a letter of credit, where payment is through a **sight** or **time draft,** is utilized. A draft is simply a check drawn on the account of the purchaser. A sight draft allows the seller to "cash" the draft immediately on presenting the documents to the bank or purchaser. A time draft, like a postdated check, can be cashed only some time after the presentation of the documents, most commonly 30, 60, or 90 days. The draft may be sued upon independent of the underlying export contract. The following is a sample acceptance and payment clause relating to a time draft:

> *Buyer shall pay for the goods ordered by means of a documentary collection whereby Seller shall draw a time draft which shall be accepted by buyer against buyer's receipt of documents (specify documents) not less than sixty days after shipment, and payable sixty days after such acceptance. Payment of the draft shall be made by*

buyer's bank upon presentation at bank located (near seller) as shall be designated by buyer's bank and acceptable to seller.[1]

In initial transactions with a new or unknown business party, however, securing payment is a crucial concern. A letter of credit adds a bank's promise to that of the foreign buyer of paying the exporter when the exporter has complied with all the terms and conditions of the letter of credit. The buyer applies for issuance of a letter of credit to the exporter and therefore is called the applicant or **account party**; the exporter is called the **beneficiary party** (see Focus on Transactions: Definitions of Key Letter of Credit and Finance Terms). Payment under a documentary letter of credit is based on documents, not on the terms of sale or the condition of the goods sold. Before payment, the bank responsible for making payment verifies that all documents are exactly as required by the letter of credit. When they are not as required, a discrepancy exists, which must be cured before payment can be made.

Focus on Transactions

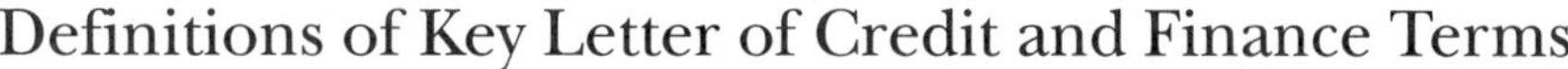

Definitions of Key Letter of Credit and Finance Terms

Account Party
The party requesting or applying for the letter of credit from a bank.

Advising Bank
A bank in the beneficiary's country through which the issuing bank communicates the credit to the beneficiary—sometimes referred to as the correspondent bank.

Back-to-Back Letter of Credit
This term is used when a third bank agrees to issue a second letter of credit at the request of the beneficiary using the first credit as collateral. The second credit is often used to pay or secure the beneficiary's suppliers.

Beneficiary Party
The party for which favor the letter of credit is issued such as the exporter (seller) in an international sale of goods transaction.

Confirming Bank
The bank in the beneficiary's country that further guarantees the issuing bank's commitment to pay the letter of credit.

Documentary Collection
The use of the banking system for an exporter to transfer documents to purchaser and to receive payment. The bank is required to not transfer the documents to the purchaser unless the purchaser makes payment or accepts a bill of exchange (draft). The bank does not act as a guarantor of payment as in the documentary credit transaction.

Documentary Credit (letter of credit)
An instrument requiring a bank to pay a sum of money to the beneficiary against the presentation of documents stipulated in the letter of credit. Used most commonly as a payment mechanism for export sales.

Factoring
The exporter sells its rights to receive payment to a factoring company. The factoring company discounts the amount of the payment owed to the exporter in order to produce the desired rate of return. Used in short-term financing.

Forfaiting
The use of a draft or promissory note given by the purchaser (guaranteed by purchaser's bank) to the exporter to obtain non-recourse financing. The terms are negotiated in advance so that the exporter is assured of payment before shipping the goods. The

1. Dennis J. Murphy, "How to Document International Commercial Transactions," *International Law Quarterly* 70, 85 (1985).

Focus on Transactions *(continued)*

importer assumes the costs of discounting the note or draft. Used in long-term financing.

Nominating Bank
A bank designated by the issuing bank to which the beneficiary party can present documents and obtain payment (may or may not be the advising or confirming bank).

Open Account Transaction
This is the situation where the seller does not require payment until some time after the purchaser receives the goods or documents. This is usually an unsecured type of financing offered by an exporter to a trusted customer.

Red Clause Financing
This is where the seller-exporter is allowed to receive an advance on the letter of credit prior to presenting the required documents. The red clause represents a form of unsecured financing offered by the purchaser to a trusted exporter.

Standby Letter of Credit
A type of credit issued as a guarantee against default by one of the parties to the contract. Generally used to guarantee the performance (not payment) of one of the parties and paid only upon default (nonperformance), it acts as a "standby." Alternative devices that serve the same purpose are the Bank Guarantee and the Performance Bond.

Transferable Credit
A transferable credit can be transferred by the beneficiary party in whole or part to secondary beneficiaries. An exporter may transfer the credit in order to finance the manufacture or purchase of the goods to be exported. The UCP requires that the original credit expressly provide for transferability. If it does not, the credit will be presumed to be nontransferable.

Uniform Commercial Code—Article 5
Provides the basic rules for letter of credit transactions within the United States.

Uniform Customs and Practices for Documentary Credits (UCP)
The international rules for letters of credit published by the International Chamber of Commerce in Paris. The current version is known as the UCP 500.

http://

First Union Commercial Bank—Trade Resource Room: **http://www.firstunion.com/international**. View self-guided tour of a letter of credit transaction.

A letter of credit may be irrevocable or revocable. The **irrevocable letter of credit** is the one used most commonly in export transactions. A revocable letter of credit does not provide the seller with much security given the fact that the bank can revoke it at any time. A change to a letter of credit is best performed by a formal **amendment** issued by the bank and signed by all parties. Since changes can be time-consuming and expensive, every effort should be made to get the letter of credit right the first time.

The letter of credit (bank guarantee) requirement in an export contract produces a number of contractual relationships. The purchaser enlists the services of its commercial bank by way of a letter of credit application (see Exhibit 11.1: Letter of Credit Application). If the bank accepts the application, it issues the letter of credit. The application forms the basis of the contract between the applicant or account party (buyer) and the **issuing bank.** The bank, upon issuing the letter of credit, forms a contract with the beneficiary party (seller) to pay the contract price upon the presentation of the required documents. The letter of credit itself fixes the issuing bank's obligations to the beneficiary party.

EXHIBIT 11.1 *Letter of Credit Application*

APPLICATION FOR
IRREVOCABLE COMMERCIAL LETTER OF CREDIT

PREFERRED BANK

L/C NO. (FOR BANK USE ONLY)

DATE: ______

Please issue for our account an irrevocable Letter of Credit as set forth below by:

☐ AIRMAIL ☐ AIRMAIL, WITH SHORT PRELIMINARY CABLE ADVICE ☐ FULL CABLE

ADVISING BANK (If bank, use your correspondent bank)	APPLICANT
BENEFICIARY	AMOUNT
	EXPIRATION DATE

AVAILABLE BY DRAFTS AT ______ DRAWN, AT YOUR OPTION, ON YOU OR YOUR CORRESPONDENT
PLEASE INDICATE SIGHT OR TENOR

FOR ______ % OF THE INVOICE VALUE.

WHEN ACCOMPANIED BY THE FOLLOWING DOCUMENTS, AS CHECKED: *(CHECK REQUIRED DOCUMENTS)*

☐ COMMERCIAL INVOICE
☐ CUSTOMS INVOICE
☐ INSURANCE POLICY AND OR CERTIFICATE COVERING THE FOLLOWING RISKS: (MARINE, WAR RISK, ETC.) ______
IF OTHER INSURANCE IS REQUIRED, PLEASE STATE RISKS
☐ PACKING LIST
☐ OTHER DOCUMENTS ______

☐ AIR WAYBILL CONSIGNED TO ______
☐ ON BOARD OCEAN BILL OF LADING (IF MORE THAN ONE ORIGINAL HAS BEEN ISSUED ALL ARE REQUIRED)
ISSUED TO ORDER OF **PREFERRED BANK**
MARKED: NOTIFY: ______
FREIGHT: COLLECT/PAID

COVERING: Merchandise described in the invoice as: (Mention commodity only in generic terms omitting details as to grade, quality, etc.)

CHECK ONE: ☐ FAS ☐ FOB ☐ C&F ☐ CIF ☐ C&I ☐ OTHER

SHIPMENT FROM:	PARTIAL SHIPMENTS	TRANSSHIPMENTS
TO:	☐ PERMITTED	☐ PERMITTED
LATEST:	☐ NOT PERMITTED	☐ NOT PERMITTED

(PLEASE CHECK APPLICABLE BOXES)

☐ Documents must be presented to negotiating by paying bank within ______ days after the date of issuance of documents evidencing shipment or dispatch or taken in charge (shipping) (documents) but within validity of letter of credit.
☐ Insurance effected by ourselves. We agree to keep insurance coverage in force until this transaction is completed.
☐ Special Instructions: ______

DISPOSITION OF DOCUMENTS ☐ TO US ☐ OTHER

PLEASE DATE AND OFFICIALLY SIGN THE AGREEMENT ON THE REVERSE OF THE THIS APPLICATION
(SEE REVERSE)
(THE FOLLOWING IS TO BE EXECUTED IF THE APPLICANT IS NOT ALSO THE ACCOUNT PARTY)

The International Chamber of Commerce has developed a number of standard documentary credit forms, along with "Guidance Notes" for their proper use.[2] The ICC forms incorporate the requirements of the UCP. A review of the ICC forms and Guidance Notes will help the purchaser to draft instructions to the issuing bank and help the beneficiary (seller) to prepare the stipulated documents. For example, the letter of credit applicant should understand the repercussions of using broad terminology to describe items of value or amounts of something. The use of

http://
International Chamber of Commerce:
http://www.iccwbo.org.

2. See generally ICC, THE NEW STANDARD DOCUMENTARY CREDIT FORMS FOR THE UCP 500, No. 516 (ed. Charles del Busto 1993). See also, James E. Byrne "Fundamental Issues in the Unification and Harmonization of Letter of Credit Law," 37 *Loyola Law Review* 1 (1991).

words like "approximate" in association with the amount of the credit or the quantity or unit price of the goods will be automatically fixed under Article 39(b) of the UCP. The buyer, for example, will have to accept documents that vary the amount of goods in the range of 5 percent more or less. In order to avoid such a variance, the applicant should state a specific number of packing units, or words to the effect that "the quantity of the goods specified must not be exceeded or reduced."

A balance should be struck between filling out the letter of credit application completely and avoiding excessive detail. In drafting the instructions to the bank it is important to be simple, clear, and precise. Excessive detail in the letter of credit application may lead to unnecessary confusion given the different cultures represented in many international transactions. An overly detailed letter of credit is apt to result in an increased likelihood of documents being rejected that would have ultimately been acceptable to the account party (purchaser). The ICC manual makes these simple suggestions when filling out a letter of credit application:

- Do not call for documents that the Beneficiary cannot obtain. Article 13 (c) deals harshly with such instructions. "If a Credit contains conditions without stating the documents to be presented in compliance therewith, banks will deem such conditions not stated and will disregard them."
- Do not state conditions whose observance cannot be ascertained from the face of a document.

Most often an intermediary bank located near the seller or the port of shipment is used to process the documents. If that bank confirms the letter of credit then two additional contractual relationships are formed: between the **confirming bank** and the beneficiary, and between the confirming bank and the issuing bank. If the intermediary bank elects not to confirm or guarantee the letter, then it is referred to as an **advising bank.** It acts merely as a conduit for transmitting documents and payments. It has no independent legal obligation to the beneficiary party. A corresponding bank that confirms the letter of credit is independently liable for its payment. See Exhibit 11.2 for an example of a bank letter "confirming" a letter of credit. It lists the required documents, which are more fully detailed in the actual letter of credit. The important legal language is the statement that the bank "confirms and undertakes to honor each draft." In contrast, an advising bank is not liable for the dishonoring of the credit by the issuing bank.

The Letter of Credit Transaction

The typical letter of credit transaction follows the chronology below. Each step in the chronology is discussed in the remainder of this section.

- After the U.S. exporter (seller) and buyer agree on the terms of a sale, the buyer arranges for its bank to open a letter of credit.
- The buyer's bank prepares an irrevocable letter of credit, including all instructions to the seller concerning the shipment.
- The buyer's bank sends the irrevocable letter of credit to a U.S. bank, requesting confirmation.
- The U.S. bank prepares a letter of confirmation to forward to the exporter along with the irrevocable letter of credit.
- The exporter arranges with the freight forwarder to deliver the goods to the appropriate port or airport.

EXHIBIT 11.2 *Confirmation Letter*

Confirmed Irrevocable Straight Credit

Original Invoices in Duplicate Covering 1000 Cartons of Fashion Clothes (Ladies and Mens) per Pro-Forma Invoice 63421.

Full Set, Clean On-Board, Original Ocean Bills of Lading, Marked Freight Prepaid and Evidencing Shipment from New York Port to Fortuga.

Full Set Insurance Policy for 110% CIF Value Including War Risk and All Risk Clauses.

Expiring This Office July 4, 19–

We Confirm and Hereby Undertake to Honor Each Draft and Presented as Above Specified.

Signed

W. W. Smith

- When the goods are loaded, the forwarder completes the necessary documents.
- The exporter presents to the U.S. bank documents indicating full compliance.
- The bank reviews the documents. If they are in order, the documents are airmailed to the buyer's bank for review and transmitted to the buyer.
- The buyer gets the documents that may be needed to claim the goods.
- A draft, which accompanies the letter of credit, is paid by the exporter's bank at the time specified or may be discounted at an earlier date.

The typical scenario in an export transaction is that the seller and buyer negotiate a contract in which the buyer agrees to provide the seller with a letter of credit. Prior to signing a contract, the importer may seek advice from a **customs broker** regarding import regulations and the documents that it should require from the seller for import purposes. After the execution of the contract, the buyer places an application for the letter of credit with the prospective issuing bank. Following credit approval, the bank issues the original letter of credit using the details supplied in the letter of credit application.

The original letter of credit is forwarded (mail, telex, or SWIFT[3]) to the exporter's bank. The exporting bank then advises the exporter (beneficiary party) that the letter of credit has been issued. If required, the exporter's bank may also confirm the letter of credit. In order to ensure that the letter of credit is to be confirmed by a local bank, the exporter should negotiate clear language in the contract. The following clause provides for an irrevocable, confirmed letter of credit:

> *The Letter of Credit is to be drawn in IRREVOCABLE form and be subject to the Uniform Customs and Practices for Documentary Credits (UCP) as published and*

3. The SWIFT network was set up to provide banks with a means of handling interbank transactions including bank transfers and foreign exchange confirmations. It is cooperatively owned by more than 1,000 banks in dozens of countries.

updated from time to time by the International Chamber of Commerce. The Letter of Credit must be advised through and CONFIRMED by a bank located at the port of shipment acceptable to the seller. It must be PAYABLE AT THE COUNTERS OF THE CONFIRMING BANK.

The above clause expressly makes the UCP the choice of law and requires payment upon presentation of the documents to the confirming bank. This is especially important to the exporter wanting to receive payment as soon as practicable. The UCP is incorporated by reference into most banks' application and letter of credit forms. Letters of credit in the United States are generally regulated under Article 5 of the Uniform Commercial Code.

Upon receiving a letter of credit, the exporter should carefully compare the letter's terms with the terms of the exporter's *pro forma* invoice or price quotation. The exporter must provide documentation showing that the goods were shipped by the date specified in the letter of credit or it risks not being paid. Exporters should check with their freight forwarders to make sure that no unusual conditions may arise that would delay shipment. In addition, documents must be presented by the date specified in the letter of credit.

Following approval by the beneficiary, the bank is instructed to send the letter of credit to the freight forwarder with instructions to book shipment. The **freight forwarder** coordinates the movement of the goods, secures the bill of lading, and completes other documentation as required in the letter of credit. Generally, to initiate a relationship with a freight forwarder, the exporter completes a **Power of Attorney** form. The Power of Attorney allows the freight forwarder to complete documents in the name of the exporter. The form must be signed by an authorized signatory of the exporter and witnessed by two people.

The original letter of credit and the shipping documents are presented to the advising or confirming bank. If the bank has confirmed the letter of credit, then it will review the documents and pay the exporter. The documents are then sent to the issuing bank with a claim for reimbursement. Upon its approval of the documents, the issuing bank will debit the importer's account for the amount of the letter of credit and any charges due. Following payment, the importer may instruct the bank to forward the documents to a customs broker. The customs broker secures the release of the goods by clearing them through customs. The customs broker will require, among other items, a commercial invoice and a properly endorsed bill of lading for import clearance purposes.

http://

Example of "Draft Transmittal Letter": **http://www.unzco.com/basicguide/figure12.html**. Click on "Figure 12."

An exporter is often not paid until the advising or confirming bank receives the funds from the issuing bank. To expedite the receipt of funds, wire transfers may be used. Bank practices vary, however, and the exporter may be able to receive funds by discounting the letter of credit at the bank, which involves paying a fee to the bank. Exporters should consult with their international bankers about bank policy.

The *Voest-Alpine Int'l v. Chase Manhattan Bank* case that follows describes a typical letter of credit transaction and introduces the **rule of strict compliance.** The rule of strict compliance is the standard by which banks review documents being presented for payment under a letter of credit. The UCP allows a bank to reject any nonconformity or discrepancy between the document being reviewed and the letter of credit requirements. The rule of strict compliance should not be confused with the independence principle or **facial compliance rule.** The facial compliance rule refers to the principle that a bank's only obligation in a letter of credit transaction is to review documents. Under the facial compliance rule, a bank is free to disregard any information, even about a fraud in the transaction, that comes from a source outside of the documents. The rule of strict compliance is simply the standard by which the banks review documents.

Voest-Alpine International v. Chase Manhattan Bank

707 F.2d 680 (2d Cir. 1983)

Cardamone, Circuit Judge. Originally devised to function in international trade, a letter of credit reduced the risk of nonpayment in cases where credit was extended to strangers in distant places. Interposing a known and solvent institution's (usually a bank's) credit for that of a foreign buyer in a sale of goods transaction accomplished this objective. A typical letter of credit transaction, as the case before us illustrates, involves three separate and independent relationships—an underlying sale of goods contract between buyer and seller, an agreement between a bank and its customer (buyer or account party) in which the bank undertakes to issue a letter of credit, and the bank's resulting engagement to pay the beneficiary (seller) providing that certain documents presented to the bank conform ["strict compliance rule"] with the terms and conditions of the credit issued on its customer's behalf.

Significantly, the bank's payment obligation to the beneficiary is primary, direct, and completely independent of any claims that may arise in the underlying sale of goods transaction [independence principle or "facial compliance rule"]. Further, employing concepts which underlie letters of credit in non–sale of goods transactions, enables these devices to serve a financing function. And it is this flexibility that makes letters of credit adaptable to a broad range of commercial uses.

Since the great utility of letters of credit arises from the independent obligation of the issuing bank, attempts to avoid payment premised on extrinsic considerations—contrary to the instruments' formal documentary nature—tend to compromise their chief virtue of predictable reliability as a payment mechanism. Viewed in this light it becomes clear that the doctrine of strict compliance with the terms of the letter of credit functions to protect the bank that carries the absolute obligation to pay the beneficiary. Adherence to this rule ensures that banks, dealing only in documents, will be able to act quickly, enhancing the letter of credit's fluidity. Literal compliance with the credit therefore is also essential so as not to impose an obligation upon the bank that it did not undertake and so as not to jeopardize the bank's right to indemnity from its customer. Documents nearly the same as those required are not good enough.

Metal Scrap Trading Corporation (MSTC) is an agency of the Indian government that had contracted to buy 7,000 tons of scrap steel from Voest-Alpine International Corporation (Voest), a trading subsidiary of an Austrian company. In late 1980 MSTC asked the Bank of Baroda to issue two letters of credit in the total amount of $1,415,550—one for $810,600 and the other $604,950—to Voest to assure payment for the sale. The credits were expressly made subject to the Uniform Customs and Practice for Documentary Credits. The parties originally contemplated that Chase Manhattan Bank, N.A. (Chase or Bank), would serve as an advising bank in the transaction. As such, Chase was to review documents submitted by Voest in connection with its drafts for payment. Amendments to the letters of credit increased Chase's responsibilities and changed its status to that of a confirming bank, independently obligated on the credit to the extent of its confirmation.

The terms and conditions of the credits required proof of shipment, evidenced by clean-on-board bills of lading; certificates of inspection indicating date of shipment; and weight certificates issued by an independent inspector. Sometime between February 2 and February 6 (beyond the January 31 deadline), the cargo was partially loaded aboard the M/V *Atra* at New Haven. Unfortunately, the *Atra* never set sail for India. A mutiny by the ship's crew disabled the ship and rendered it unseaworthy. The scrap steel was later sold to another buyer for slightly over a half million dollars, nearly a million dollars less than the original contract price.

On February 13, two days before the expiration date of the credits, Voest presented three drafts with the required documentation to Chase. The bills of lading indicating receipt on board of the scrap metal were signed and dated January 31 by the captain of the *Atra*. The weight and inspection certificates accompanying the drafts revealed, however, that the cargo was loaded aboard the *Atra* sometime between February 2 and February 6. Despite this glaring discrepancy Chase advised the Bank of Baroda on February 25 that the drafts and documents presented to it by Voest conformed to the terms and conditions set forth in the letters of credit.

The Bank of Baroda apparently looked at the documents with more care than Chase. It promptly advised Chase that the documents did not comply with the requirements of the letters of credit, that it would therefore not honor the drafts, and that it would hold the documents at Chase's disposal. When Voest presented the drafts for payment on July 30 Chase refused to honor them. Voest thereupon instituted the present suit. It asserted that Chase waived the right to demand strict compliance with the terms of the credits and therefore wrongfully dishonored the drafts. Voest further alleged that regardless of whether the documents conformed to the letters of credit Chase was liable on the drafts because it accepted them.

A. *Acceptance*

Claims by a beneficiary of a letter of credit that a bank has waived strict compliance with the terms of the credit should generally be viewed with a somewhat wary eye. Acceptance is the drawee's signed engagement to honor the draft as presented and that it "must be written on the draft." By requiring written acceptance on the draft Section 3-410 of the Uniform Commercial Code impliedly eliminated oral acceptances as well. The present record is silent as to whether Chase actually accepted the drafts by proper notation on them.

B. *Fraud*

Presentation of fraudulent documents to a bank by a beneficiary subverts not only the purposes which letters of credit are designed to serve in general, but also the entire transaction at hand in particular. Falsified documents are the same as no documents at all.

We AFFIRM the judgment in favor of the Bank of Baroda. All parties have acknowledged that the documents tendered Chase did not conform to the established terms and conditions of the letters of credit. The Bank of Baroda, as the issuing bank, was entitled to strict compliance and there is no claim that it waived that right.

Case Highlights

- A typical letter of credit transaction comprises a number of contractual relationships including between the buyer (account party) and its bank (issuing bank), between the issuing bank and the seller (beneficiary), and between the issuing bank and a corresponding bank (confirming bank).
- A confirming bank owes an independent obligation to the beneficiary party.
- The rule of strict compliance protects banks by allowing them to reject documents because of discrepancies.
- A bank is liable for payment if it "accepts" a draft. However, legal acceptance of a draft may be done only by a written endorsement on the draft (Uniform Commercial Code § 3-410).

The *Voest-Alpine v. Chase Manhattan* case illustrates a number of other important items. First, a number of expiration dates exist in most international export transactions. The documents were presented before the expiration of the letters of credit. The documents were untimely, however, because the letter of credit requirements stated that an on-board bill of lading had to be acquired on or before January 31. The UCP also provides another type of expiration date. The **21-day rule** states that the bill of lading, and accompanying documents, must be presented to the bank within 21 days from their procurement. If the exporter obtains the bill of lading and delays presentation past the 21 days, then the letter of credit expires even though the expiration date on the letter has not passed.

The second item highlighted in the above case is the **bill of exchange** or **draft.**[4] The draft was previously discussed in Chapter 9 but will be briefly reviewed again here. The draft is a collections instrument that acts very much like a check. It is the mechanism for payment through the banking system. When a seller presents documents for payment on a letter of credit it presents the bank with a draft drawn on the letter of credit. The draft is an order to the drawee (bank or account party) to pay. The difference between a draft and an ordinary check is that in the documen-

4. The terms *draft* and *bill of exchange* can be used interchangeably. The term used in the United Kingdom is "bill of exchange." The term used in the United States is "draft."

tary draft the seller acts as both the drawer and the payee. The **Uniform Law on Bills of Exchange** states that "a bill of exchange or draft contains an unconditional order to pay a determinate sum of money; the name of the person who is to pay *(drawee);* the time of payment; the place of payment; the name of the person to whom or to whose order payment is to be made *(payee);* and the signature of the person who issues the bill *(drawer)*."

http://
United Nations Convention on International Bills of Exchange and International Promissory Notes: **http://www.UNCITRAL.org** (follow links from "Adopted Texts" to "International Payments").

The two general types of drafts used in export transactions are the sight draft and the time draft. A sight draft requires payment immediately upon the presentation of the documents. A draft in which the time of payment is not specified is deemed payable at sight. Exhibit 11.3 provides an example of a sight draft. Note that if a period of time was entered in the blank following "Sight Days After," then the draft would be converted into a time draft.

If the exporter wants to extend credit to the buyer, a time draft can be used to state that payment is due within a certain time after the buyer accepts the draft and receives the documents. By signing and writing "accepted" on the draft, the buyer is formally obligated to pay within the stated time. When this is done the draft is called a **trade acceptance** and can be either kept by the exporter until maturity or sold to a bank at a discount for immediate payment. **Acceptance** creates an independent obligation on the acceptor (drawee). The independence of the acceptance obligation means that the obligation "can be enforced by subsequent holders of the instrument without regard to the buyer's rights under the sales contract."[5] In short, the acceptance converts the draft into a negotiable instrument.[6] When a bank accepts a draft, the draft becomes an obligation of the bank and a negotiable instrument known as a **banker's acceptance.** A banker's acceptance can be sold to a bank at a discount for immediate payment. The following excerpt from the *Interpane Coatings v. Australia & New Zealand Banking Group* case describes the use of time drafts and the importance of acceptance.

EXHIBIT 11.3 *Sight Draft*

November 26 19____
SIGHT DAYS AFTER ______

PAY TO THE ORDER OF Ourselves $ 22,000.00

Twenty Two Thousand DOLLARS

FOR VALUE RECEIVED AND CHARGE TO ACCOUNT OF CITIBANK LETTER OF CREDIT NO. 10076312

Citibank, N.A.
111 WALL STREET
NEW YORK, NY 10043

Arthur's Clothes for Export Inc.

5. JOHN O. HONNOLD & CURTIS R. REITZ, SALES TRANSACTIONS: DOMESTIC AND INTERNATIONAL LAW (2001). This casebook provides a good summary of sales law including the documentary transaction and letters of credit.

6. In the United States, Article 3 of the UCC governs the liabilities of the acceptor (drawee-buyer) and the drawer (seller).

Interpane Coatings, Inc. v. Australia & New Zealand Banking Group

732 F. Supp. 909 (N.D. Ill. 1990)

Kocoras, District Judge. Underlying this litigation is an international sale of goods run amuck. Interpane, a Wisconsin corporation and the seller in this transaction, delivered the goods to an Australian buyer who then did not pay despite having accepted the goods as well as having endorsed three bills of exchange. In this action, Interpane seeks to hold ANZ, the designated collecting bank in the transaction, liable for its failure to obtain the money from the buyer.

The relevant facts are as follows: Interpane and an Australian entity named McDowell Pacific Pty., Ltd., entered into a contract for the sale of goods whereby Interpane was to ship goods to Australia and McDowell was to pay for them. As is usual in such cases where delivery and payment are to occur at a distant point, the seller used bills of exchange and bills of lading rather than simply shipping the goods to the buyer in Australia with an invoice (open account).

By using this procedure, Interpane reduced the critical transactional points of tender and acceptance to a mere documentary transfer that made acceptance of the bills of exchange a condition precedent to tender. But to do so required the aid of middlemen in the form of banks. The banks involved in the transaction were ANZ and the Chicago branch of Swiss Bank Corporation. ANZ, McDowell's bank, was to act as the presenting and the collecting bank. Swiss Bank was designated Interpane's local representative, forwarding and receiving the relevant documents on behalf of Interpane. It was also the named payee on the bills of exchange. Under the documentary procedure used in this case, Interpane sent ANZ three bills of exchange accompanied by three bills of lading. The bills of exchange were all time drafts with payment to be due 60 days from McDowell's "seeing" them; such bills are called time drafts in order to distinguish them from sight drafts which are actually payable on sight.

There are two principal types of collection orders, those that require mere acceptance by the drawee/buyer and those which require actual payment. If acceptance is required, the collecting bank need only obtain the endorsement of the drawee/buyer before releasing the title documents. By accepting the bills of exchange, the drawee acknowledges the debt and commits to making payment as required by the bill of exchange (in this case 60 days from sight). As the designated collecting bank, ANZ had a contractual duty to follow Interpane's collection orders. Interpane alleges that ANZ breached this contractual duty by not obeying its special instructions, which it alleges required ANZ to endorse the bills of exchange as a guarantor, thus converting them into a banker's acceptances, before releasing the title documents to McDowell.

[Case dismissed on procedural grounds *(forum non conveniens)* not related to the bank's obligations under the letter of credit.]

Case Highlights

- Banks play an intermediary role in effecting the transfer of documents and payments relating to an export transaction.
- Documentary collection transactions condition the release of documents on acceptance or payment of the documentary draft by the buyer.
- Bills of exchange or drafts are the means by which an exporter obtains payment in an international sale of goods transaction.
- Bills of exchange or drafts are orders by the drawer (exporter) to the buyer or buyer's bank (drawee) to pay the exporter (payee). It differs from a check only in that the drawer. and the payee are the same party (exporter).
- A time draft is a bill of exchange that requires payment sometime after the buyer accepts the documents.

UNIFORM CUSTOMS AND PRACTICES FOR DOCUMENTARY CREDITS

The UCP is a set of rules published by the International Chamber of Commerce, the most recent compilation of which is the **UCP 500.** The UCP applies to letters of credit used to guarantee payment to an exporter in a documentary transaction. They may also be used in conjunction with standby letters of credit used to guarantee a performance. As mentioned earlier, the UCP is incorporated in most international letter of credit transactions by references in the application forms supplied by commercial banks (see Exhibit 11.1: Letter of Credit Application). Letters of credit used to guarantee payment to an exporter are called documentary credits. This name refers to the fact that payment under the letter of credit is contingent upon the presentation of documents by the exporter.

As discussed earlier, banks have the duty to use reasonable care in examining documents for conformity to the requirements of the letter of credit. If the documents are in facial compliance then the bank pays the beneficiary party (exporter) through the letter of credit. The issuing bank must examine the documents within a reasonable time and notify the parties promptly of any nonconformity. The documents must comply strictly with the requirements of the letter of credit. Banks are not liable for accepting forged or false documents. The letter of credit instructions of the account party (buyer) should give precise details of the documents required. For example, a bill of lading must indicate that the goods have been loaded on board the named vessel. Insurance documents must be dated prior to the loading of the goods on board the ship. The description of the goods in the commercial invoice must be the same as the one contained in the letter of credit.

The sophisticated importer-purchaser should become familiar with the requirements and rules of the UCP 500. They have a direct bearing on how the applicant completes a letter of credit application. If the applicant places a noncustomary term or instruction in the application, the banks will often disregard that instruction in favor of a default rule found in the UCP 500. The following list is a sampling of some of the more important UCP 500 rules:

- Care should be used in selecting an expiration date to avoid the bother of obtaining extensions. An unnecessarily prolonged expiration date should be avoided in order to avoid incurring additional bank charges.
- For a letter of credit to be transferable, the applicant must request such designation. Article 48 of the UCP should be carefully reviewed before making such a request.
- Under Article 9 of the UCP, the applicant must request that the letter be confirmed. The applicant may designate the confirming bank or leave it to the discretion of the issuing bank. It is best for the applicant and the beneficiary to agree on the identity of the confirming bank before the credit application is submitted.
- The currency of the letter of credit should be designated using the ISO currency codes: USD (United States Dollar), GBP (Pounds Sterling), etc.
- The applicant should designate the bank or banks (nominated banks) at which the credit will be available. An alternative is to insert "freely negotiable by any bank" or "freely negotiable credit." This designation allows the beneficiary to negotiate the documents at any bank willing to negotiate. However, it is desirable for the applicant to limit the free negotiability to a specific country or city.
- The applicant should clearly instruct whether the credit will be made available for partial shipments ("partial shipments allowed" or "partial shipments not allowed"). Shipments by pre-agreed installments should also be clearly stipulated on the credit application.
- The applicant should provide transport details, including where the shipment

is to be "taken in charge, dispatched, or loaded on board" and to where the shipment must be made whether "at the place of unloading, delivery, or final destination." The applicant should also state the latest date for shipment, dispatch, or taking in charge under the space next to the phrase "not later than" on the credit application. Otherwise, the time limit will be the date of expiration as provided in Article 44 of the UCP. If the applicant uses the phrase "on or about," Article 46(c) of the UCP defines an acceptable period as five days before or after the specified date. Also, abbreviations for geographical designation should be avoided. Full names should be used for all cities, states, provinces, and countries.

Under the rule of strict compliance, banks are authorized to reject documents even if they are technically in conformity. The use of abbreviations or acronyms in the description of goods may make strict compliance problematic. People in the industry may use such devices in corresponding among themselves, but banks are not required to know or to investigate trade custom or usage. This was the situation in the English case of *J.H. Rayner & Co. v. Hambros Bank, Ltd.,*[7] in which the bank rejected a bill of lading that used the notation "C.R.S." in describing the goods. In the nut industry C.R.S. is the abbreviation for "Coromandel ground nuts." The letter of credit required that the bill of lading state "Coromandel ground nuts." The accompanying commercial invoice did use the full name. Nonetheless, the court upheld the bank's right to reject the documents. Two rationales were given. First, "that even though the description of the goods in the bill of lading was correct in accordance with the custom of trade, the bank could not be held to be affected with a knowledge of the customs of the various trades in which its customers might be concerned." Second, even if the bank possessed knowledge of the trade custom or usage, it must do exactly what its customer requires it to do. There may be some unknown reason why the account party (importer) wants the documents to be detailed in a certain way. It is not for the bank to impose common sense to abrogate a specific instruction in the letter of credit. The application of the rule of strict compliance is the key issue in *Courtaulds North America v. North Carolina National Bank.*

For the reasons described in the proceeding paragraph, the description of the goods should generally be as brief as possible. In the above case, the result would have been different under the UCP if the letter of credit had not specifically stated that the bill of lading should have that particular description. The UCP requires only that the commercial invoice reflect the description found on the letter of credit. Article 37 states that "the description of the goods in the commercial invoice must correspond with the description in the Credit. In all other documents, the goods may be described in general terms not inconsistent with the description of the goods in the Credit." Therefore, it is advisable to keep the description simple and clear.

In listing documents other than transport documents, insurance documents, and commercial invoices, the applicant should specifically state the issuing entity and what the content of the documents should entail. This is required under Article 21 of the UCP.

Articles 23–30 of the UCP should be reviewed when determining the transport documents that will be required. The rules pertaining to two of the more common transport documents, the ocean bill of lading and a bill of lading issued by a freight

7. 112 K.B. 27 (1943).

forwarder, are found in Articles 23 and 30. If the shipment entails the use of more than one mode of transportation, then the applicant should require a Multimodal Transport Document as described in Article 26.

The content of insurance documents is addressed in Articles 34 through 36 of

Courtaulds North America v. North Carolina National Bank

528 F.2d 802 (4th Cir. 1975)

Bryan, Circuit Judge. A letter of credit with the date of March 21, 1973, was issued by the North Carolina National Bank at the request of and for the account of its customer, Adastra Knitting Mills, Inc. It made available upon the drafts of Courtaulds North America, Inc., "up to" $135,000 at "60 days date" to cover Adastra's purchases of acrylic yarn from Courtaulds. The life of the credit was extended in June to allow the drafts to be "drawn and negotiated on or before August 15, 1973." The Bank refused to honor a draft for $67,346.77 dated August 13, 1973, for yarn sold and delivered to Adastra. Courtaulds brought this action to recover this sum from Bank.

The Bank denied liability chiefly on the assertion that the draft did not agree with the letter's conditions that the draft be accompanied by a commercial invoice stating that it covers "100% acrylic yarn"; instead, the accompanying invoices stated that the goods were "Imported Acrylic Yarn." The District Court held defendant Bank liable to Courtaulds for the amount of the draft, interest, and costs. It concluded that the draft complied with the letter of credit when each invoice is read together with the packing lists stapled to it, for the lists stated on their faces: "Cartons marked: - 100% Acrylic." After considering the insistent rigidity of the law and usage of bank credits and acceptances, we must differ with the District Judge and uphold the Bank's position.

On Monday, August 20, Bank called Adastra and asked if it would waive the discrepancies and thus allow Bank to honor the draft. Courtaulds on August 27 sent amended invoices to Bank which were received by Bank on August 27. They referred to the consignment as "100% Acrylic Yarn", and thus would have conformed to the letter of credit had it not expired. On August 29 Bank wired Courtaulds that the draft remained unaccepted because of the expiration of the letter of credit on August 15. "The only issue presented by the facts of this case is whether the documents tendered by the beneficiary to the issuer were in conformity with the terms of the letter of credit." The letter of credit provided: "Except as otherwise expressly stated herein, this credit is subject to the Uniform Customs and Practice for Documentary Credits (UCP)." Of particular pertinence are these provisions of the UCP:

Article 7. *Banks must examine all documents with reasonable care to ascertain that they* appear on their face *to be in accordance with the terms and conditions of the credit.*
Article 8. *In documentary credit operations all parties concerned deal in documents and not in goods. If, upon receipt of the documents, the issuing bank considers that they* appear on their face *not to be in accordance with the terms and conditions of the credit, that bank must determine, on the basis of the documents alone, whether to claim that payment, acceptance, or negotiation was not effected in accordance with the terms and conditions of the credit.*
Article 9. *"Banks . . . do [not] assume any liability or responsibility* for the description, . . . *quality, . . . of the goods represented thereby. The description of the goods in the commercial* invoice *must correspond with the description in the credit.* In the remaining documents the goods may be described in general terms.

In utilizing the rules of construction embodied in the letter of credit, the UCP states that one must constantly recall that the drawee bank is not to be embroiled in disputes between the buyer and the seller, the beneficiary of the credit. The drawee is involved only with documents, not with merchandise. Its involvement is altogether separate and apart from the transaction between the buyer and seller; its duties and liability are governed exclusively by the terms of the letter, not the terms of the parties' contract with each other. Moreover, as the predominant authorities unequivocally declare, the beneficiary must meet the terms of the credit—and precisely—if it is to exact performance of the issuer. Failing such compliance there can be no recovery from the drawee. That is the specific failure of Courtaulds here. "There is no room for documents which are almost the same, or which will do just as well."

At trial Courtaulds prevailed on the contention that the invoices in actuality met the specifications of the letter of credit in that the packing lists attached to the invoices disclosed on their faces that the packages contained "cartons marked: - 100% acrylic." In this connection it is well to revert to the distinction made in the UCP between the "invoice" and the "remaining documents," emphasizing that in the latter the description may be in general terms while in the invoice the goods must be described in conformity with the credit letter. Bank was not expected to scrutinize the collateral papers, such as the packing lists. Nor was it permitted to read into the instrument the contemplation or intention of the seller and buyer. Had the Bank deviated from the stipulation of the letter and honored the draft, then at once it might have been confronted with the not improbable risk of the bankruptcy trustee's charge of liability for unwarrantably paying the draft to the seller. REVERSED AND REMANDED.

Case Highlights

- Article 7 of the UCP requires that banks review required documents for facial compliance. Banks are not required to know or to research trade custom or usage.
- Article 8 (strict compliance rule) allows for banks to reject documents that do not comply on their face.
- Article 9 requires that the description of the goods in the commercial invoice must strictly correspond to the description in the letter of credit. Descriptions in other documents may be made with more general terms.
- Even if a bank wants to accept an inexact description in the commercial invoice it is precluded from doing so if the letter of credit expressly states otherwise.

the UCP. If the applicant fails to state the amount of the insurance to be procured, then Article 34 (f)(ii) of the UCP requires an amount equal to CIF value plus 10%.

The applicant should specify the time by which the documents need to be presented following shipment of the goods. If a period is not stipulated, then Article 43 (a) of the UCP sets the period as 21 days from the date of shipment. If the applicant wants to allow for presentation irrespective of the date of shipment, he must so state in the space provided for "Additional Instructions."

In amending an irrevocable letter of credit it is advisable to use the standard form titled Irrevocable Documentary Credit Amendment Form. Focus on Transactions: Ten Rules Pertaining to International Letters of Credit further summarizes the rules governing letters of credit.

Rule 6 in the Focus on Transactions feature notes that banks have a reasonable time to review documents not to exceed three days under the Uniform Commercial Code[8] and seven days under UCP 500. If the bank accepts nonconforming documents, then it may sue the beneficiary party if it proceeds in a timely fashion. This was the issue in *Habib Bank Ltd. v. Convermat Corp.*[9] In that case, the bank paid on documents that included a bill of lading with a discrepancy in the shipping date. The account party subsequently rejected the documents. The bank waited a month before making a claim against the beneficiary party. The court held that the claim was not made in a timely fashion and dismissed the action. This duty of the bank to act quickly is implied from Article 14 of the UCP. Article 14(d) requires the bank to give notice "by expeditious means" and such notice "must state *all* discrepancies in respect of which the bank refuses the documents."

8. UCC § Section 5-112.
9. 554 N.Y.S.2d 757 (1990).

Focus on Transactions

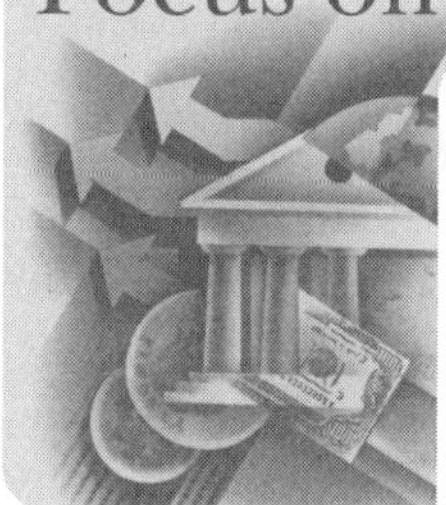

Ten Rules Pertaining to International Letters of Credit

Rule 1
Rule of Facial Compliance: Banks are only required to review documents and compare them to the letter of credit's requirements for conformity (not liable for "fraud in the transaction").

Rule 2
Banks are not required to know or to investigate trade or business usage, custom, or practices.

Rule 3
Rule of Strict Compliance: Banks may reject documents for *any* discrepancy.

Rule 4
A letter of credit must have an expiration date in order to be enforceable.

Rule 5
UCP 500 21-day rule: The beneficiary party must deliver documents within 21 days of receipt (21 days from receipt of bill of lading).

Rule 6
Bank's Period of Review: Banks have a *reasonable period* to review documents, not to exceed three days (UCC Art. 5) or seven days (UCP 500).

Rule 7
Presumption of Irrevocability: UCP 500 and UCC Article 5 presume that a letter of credit is irrevocable unless it clearly states on its face that it is revocable.

Rule 8
Insurance Certificate: Must not be dated later than date of loading and should be in the amount of CIF plus 10%.

Rule 9
Commercial Invoice: Must include the exact description found in the letter of credit. (Other documents may use general descriptions not inconsistent with one found in the letter of credit.)

Rule 10
A letter of credit is not transferable unless it specifically states that it is a transferable credit.

STANDBY LETTERS OF CREDIT

The Federal Reserve of the United States defines **standby letter of credit** as a letter of credit that "represents an obligation to the beneficiary on the part of the issuer: (1) to repay money borrowed by or advanced to or for the account of the customer (account party); (2) to make payment on account of any evidence of indebtedness undertaken by the account party; or (3) to make payment on account of any default by the account party in the performance of an obligation."[10] The UCP has traditionally been applied to both documentary credits and standby letters of credit. However, on January 1, 1999, new **International Standby Practices (ISP98)** governing standby letters of credit took effect.[11]

Standby letters of credit can be used to help secure a variety of contractual obligations associated with the export transaction. In addition to performance

10. Regulation H, 12 C.F.R. §208.8(*d*)(1) (1979).
11. The ISP98 can be obtained through the International Chamber of Commerce as Publication 590 or through the web site of the Institute of International Banking Law and Practice at http://www.isp98.com.

guarantees often associated with construction projects, standby letters have been used to guarantee warranties, to support borrowers under international loans, to ensure availability of suppliers, to secure countertrade commitments, along with acting as deposits in the sale of goods and as prepayment of fees for services.[12] *Itek Corp. v. First National Bank of Boston* illustrates the use of standby letters of credit to guarantee performance of a construction project and for the return of monies paid by the foreign buyer.

Itek Corp. v. First National Bank of Boston

730 F.2d 19 (1st Cir. 1984)

Breyer, Circuit Judge. The First National Bank of Boston ("FNBB"), at the request of Itek Corp., issued several letters of credit running in favor of Bank Melli Iran ("Melli"). Melli demanded payment from FNBB of the money that the letters promised. Itek obtained a federal district court injunction prohibiting FNBB from paying Melli. The basic question that Melli's appeal presents is whether its effort to obtain the money by calling the letters is "fraudulent."

The letters of credit arise out of promises made in a 1977 contract between Itek and Iran's Imperial Ministry of War. The contract provided that Itek would make and sell high-technology optical equipment to the War Ministry at a price of $22.5 million. Iran was to make a 20 percent down payment. It would pay Itek 60 percent of the total price ($13.5 million) as work progressed; it would pay the remaining 20 percent upon satisfactory completion. The contract required Itek to provide two types of bank guarantees. The first, the *down payment guarantee,* was to give the Ministry the right to obtain return of the down payment until Itek produced work of sufficient value. The second, the *good performance guarantee* was for $2.25 million, 10 percent of the contract price. Its object was to protect the Ministry against a breach of contract. The Ministry could call for payment under the guarantees simply by submitting a written request for payment to the bank.

Bank Melli, an instrumentality of the Iranian government, issued the guarantees. Melli required Itek to provide it with similar "standby" letters of credit, issued by an American bank in Melli's favor. The underlying contract provided that if the contract "is cancelled due to *Force Majeure,* all Bank Guarantees of good performance of work will be immediately released." The contract defines *Force Majeure* to include cancellation by the United States of necessary export licenses. Itek's work proceeded uneventfully until Iran's government collapsed in early 1979. In April 1979 the United States suspended Itek's export license. Itek then proceeded to cancel the contract in accordance with the *force majeure* provisions. At that point, Melli demanded payment on the letters of credit.

Section 5-114(2)(b) of the Uniform Commercial Code authorizes a court to enjoin payment on a letter of credit when it finds "fraud in the transaction." It states that:

> *(2) Unless otherwise agreed when documents appear on their face to comply with the terms of a credit but a required document is forged or fraudulent or there is fraud in the transaction:*
>
> *(a) the issuer must honor the draft . . . if honor is demanded by . . . a holder in due course and*
>
> *(b) in all other cases as against its customer, an issuer acting in good faith may honor the draft or demand for payment despite notification from the customer of fraud, forgery or other defect not apparent on the face of the documents but a court of appropriate jurisdiction may enjoin such honor.*

The basic legal question in this case is whether the circumstances surrounding Melli's calls on FNBB's letters of credit establish "fraud in the transaction." We answer this question fully aware of the need to interpret the "fraud" provision narrowly. The very object of a letter of credit is to provide a near foolproof method of placing money in its beneficiary's hands when he complies with the terms contained in the letter itself—when he presents, for example, a shipping document that the letter calls for or (as here) a simple written demand for payment. Despite these reasons for hesitating to enjoin payment of a letter of credit, the need for an exception is apparent. Thus, in a leading case, a seller, contractually committed to ship bristles to a buyer, shipped rubbish instead. The court refused to allow the seller to call the letter, put the money in his pocket, and let the buyer sue

12. See Graham & Geva, "Standby Credits in Canada," 9 *Canadian Business Law Journal* 180 (1982).

him, for in the court's view, the seller did not even have a colorable claim that he had done what the contract called for as a precondition to obtaining the money, namely, ship the bristles. *Sztejn v. J. Henry Schroder Banking Corp.*, 31 N.Y.S.2d 631 (Sup. Ct. 1941). If Melli has no plausible or colorable basis under the contract to call for payment of the letters, its effort to obtain the money is fraudulent and payment can be enjoined.

For these reasons, we find adequate support for the district court's conclusions that Melli was without a plausible legal basis for calling the letters of credit and that its call upon them, in the circumstances revealed in this record, constituted "fraud." The injunction therefore was properly issued. And the district court's order is AFFIRMED.

Case Highlights

- A letter of credit that is used to guarantee a performance or return of a deposit is called a standby letter of credit.
- A bank *may* honor a letter of credit when documents comply on their face even if notified that the documents are forgeries or that there is fraud in the transaction
- The account party can enjoin the bank from honoring a letter of credit by obtaining a court order (injunction).
- A *force majeure* clause describes events that allow a party to be excused from performing a contractual obligation.

The *Itek Corp. v. First National Bank of Boston* case notes that under the Uniform Commercial Code § 5-114(a)(2), a court may enjoin a bank from honoring the demand for payment when the bank has been notified of fraud in the transaction. The "fraud" exception to the traditional reluctance of courts to interfere with commercial letters of credit and guarantees has been liberally construed in the decisional law both before and after the adoption of the Code. However, in most export transactions obtaining an injunction may not be a practical alternative because of the time it takes to obtain such an order.

Alternative Methods of Guaranteeing Performance

Besides the standby letter of credit, there are other methods of guaranteeing a performance or ensuring the return of monies. A **performance bond** minimizes the buyer's risk of nonperformance by the seller in the export transaction or nonperformance by a contractor in a construction project. The performance bond is a guarantee from an insurance company to pay the insured in case of default (nonperformance). It serves the same function as a standby letter of credit. **Bid bonds** insure against the risk that a bidder may not honor its bid. These are usually required to bid on government procurement contracts.

A **credit surety** guarantees repayment to a bank or lender who finances an export transaction or development project. These sureties generally take the form of a payment guarantee from a state agency, such as **Eximbank,** or from a development bank, such as the **World Bank.** A surety may also be in the form of a corporate guarantee from the parent company. A **retention fund** is not a third-party guarantee, but an arrangement between the principal parties. In large projects or government procurement contracts, a percentage of the monies is deducted from each payment due the supplier or contractor and is retained in a fund pending the completion of the contract or the expiration of a warranty period.

http://
World Bank—links to Multilateral Investment Guarantee Agency (MIGA), International Development Association (IDA), and International Finance Corporation (IFC): **http://www.worldbank.org**.

The bank guarantee or **demand guarantee** is a popular means of guaranteeing performance. Like the standby credit, the demand guarantee secures performance of a nonmonetary obligation. It serves as a default device when performance is not satisfactory. Whereas a bank pays a documentary letter of credit only if things go right, a bank will be called upon to pay a demand guarantee or standby letter only if things go wrong.[13] A special concern of demand guarantees is that the lack of rigid documentation requirements allows for the possibility of unfair calls.[14] Often all the beneficiary is required to do is make a written demand for payment. Both the ICC and UNCITRAL have developed rules to govern these types of instruments. The ICC has published the **Uniform Rules for Demand Guarantees** (Uniform Rules)[15] and UNCITRAL has released its **Convention on Independent Letters of Guarantee and Standby Credits.** In order to discourage unfair calls on demand guarantees, Article 20 of the Uniform Rules requires the beneficiary to provide a statement describing the way in which the principal is in breach.

SOURCES OF TRADE FINANCE

Exporters naturally want to get paid quickly, and importers usually prefer to delay payment at least until they have received and resold the goods.[16] Because of the intense competition for export markets, being able to offer good payment terms is often necessary to make a sale. Exporters should be aware of the many financing options open to them. In some cases, the exporter may need financing to produce goods that have been ordered or to finance other aspects of a sale, such as promotion and selling expenses, engineering modifications, and shipping costs.

Various financing sources are available to exporters, depending on the specifics of the transaction and the exporter's overall financing needs. A number of variables need to be assessed before making a decision on export or import financing: (1) cost of financing, (2) length of the financing, and (3) risks of financing. The impact on price and profit of different methods of financing should be well understood before a ***pro forma* invoice** is submitted to the buyer.

The greater the risks associated with the transaction the greater the costs of financing and the more difficult financing will be to obtain. The creditworthiness of the buyer directly affects the probability of payment to the exporter, but it is not the only factor of concern to a potential lender. The political and economic stability of the buyer's country also can be a factor. To provide financing for either accounts receivable or the production or purchase of the product for sale, the lender may require more secure methods of payment, such as a letter of credit or export credit insurance. If a lender is uncertain about the exporter's ability to perform, or if additional credit capacity is needed, a government guarantee program may enable the lender to provide additional financing. The best place to begin, however, is by researching the services provided by commercial banks. Because of their international banking connections and expertise in international business transactions commercial banks are great sources for information.

13. Roy Goode, "Abstract Payment Undertakings in International Transactions," 22 *Brooklyn Journal of International Law* 1, 15 (1996).
14. "[T]he documentation required for a claim on a demand guarantee is skeletal in the extreme, entailing in most cases presentation of no more than the written demand itself." Ibid.
15. ICC, PUBLICATION NO. 458 (1992).
16. A good deal of the material in the following sections was gleaned from the National Trade Data Bank, a product of STAT-USA, U.S. Department of Commerce.

Commercial Banks

More than 300 U.S. banks have international banking departments and specialists familiar with specific foreign countries and various types of commodities and transactions. These large banks, located in major U.S. cities, maintain correspondent relationships with smaller banks throughout the country. Larger banks also maintain correspondent relationships with banks in most foreign countries or operate their own overseas branches, providing a direct channel to foreign customers. International banking specialists are generally well informed about export matters. If they are unable to provide direct guidance or assistance, they may be able to refer inquirers to other specialists who can. Banks frequently provide consultation and guidance free of charge to their clients, since they derive income primarily from loans to the exporter and from fees for special services.

Finally, large banks frequently conduct seminars and workshops on letters of credit, documentary collections, and other banking subjects of concern to exporters. Among the many services a commercial bank may perform for its clients are the following: (1) exchange of currencies, (2) assistance in financing exports, (3) collection of foreign invoices, drafts, and letters of credit, (4) transfer of funds to other countries, and (5) credit information on potential representatives or buyers overseas.

EXPORT FINANCING

A logical first step in obtaining financing is for an exporter to approach its local commercial bank. If the exporter already has a loan for domestic needs, then the lender already has experience with the exporter's ability to perform. Many lenders, therefore, would be willing to provide financing for export transactions if there were a reasonable certainty of repayment. By using letters of credit or export credit insurance, an exporter can reduce the lender's risk. A government guarantee program may offer a lender greater assurance than is afforded by the transaction, enabling the lender to extend credit to the exporter. When selecting a bank, the exporter should ask the following questions: (1) What are the charges for confirming a letter of credit, processing drafts, and collecting payment? (2) Does the bank have foreign branches or correspondent banks? Where are they located? (3) Does the bank have experience with U.S. and state government financing programs that support small business export transactions?

A time draft under an irrevocable letter of credit, confirmed by a U.S. bank, presents relatively little risk of default. To convert these instruments to cash immediately, an exporter must obtain a loan using the draft as collateral or sell the draft to an investor or a bank for a fee. When the draft is sold to an investor or bank, it is sold at a discount. Banks or other lenders may be willing to buy time drafts that a creditworthy foreign buyer has accepted or agreed to pay at a specified future date. These endorsed drafts or bills of exchange are what we earlier described as trade acceptances.

In some cases, banks pre-agree to accept the obligations of paying a draft, usually of a customer, for a fee. As discussed previously, the banker's acceptance is a draft drawn on and accepted by a bank (see Exhibit 11.4: Banker's Acceptance). Depending on the bank's creditworthiness, the acceptance becomes a financial instrument that can be discounted and sold before maturity. The exporter receives an amount less than the face value of the draft so that when the draft is paid at its face value at the specified future date, the investor or bank receives more than it paid to the exporter. The difference between the amount paid to the exporter and

EXHIBIT 11.4 *Banker's Acceptance*

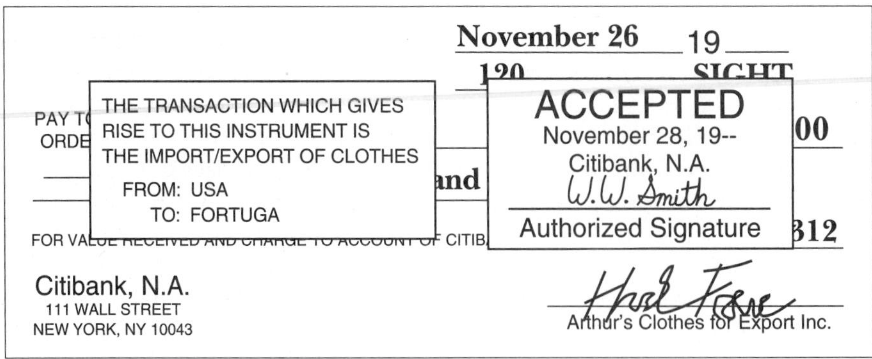

November 26 19___

120 SIGHT

PAY T
ORDE

THE TRANSACTION WHICH GIVES
RISE TO THIS INSTRUMENT IS
THE IMPORT/EXPORT OF CLOTHES
FROM: USA
TO: FORTUGA

ACCEPTED
November 28, 19--
Citibank, N.A.
W.W. Smith
Authorized Signature

00

nd

312

FOR VA F CITIB

Citibank, N.A.
111 WALL STREET
NEW YORK, NY 10043

Arthur's Clothes for Export Inc.

the face amount paid at maturity is called a discount and represents the fees or interest the investor or bank receives for holding the draft until maturity. The bank often discounts drafts **without recourse** to the exporter in case of default by the drawee. Other drafts may be discounted with recourse to the exporter, in which case the exporter must reimburse the investor or bank if the party obligated to pay the draft defaults.

Factoring and Forfaiting

Factoring is the discounting of foreign account receivables without a draft. The exporter transfers title to its account receivables to a factoring company at a discount. These houses specialize in the financing of account receivables by giving cash at a discount from the face value. Although factoring is often done without recourse to the exporter, the exporter should verify the specific arrangement. The factoring company assumes the financial risk of nonpayment and handles the collections on the receivables. Export factoring allows an exporter to sell on **open account,** by which goods are shipped without a guarantee of payment such as a letter of credit.

Forfaiting is the selling at a discount of longer-term account receivables or promissory notes of the foreign buyer. This is a form of supplier credit in which the exporter turns over export receivables, usually guaranteed by a bank in the importer's country, by selling them at a discount to a forfaiter. This arrangement is generally agreed to in advance before the conclusion of the sales contract. The exporter is thus able to incorporate the discount (costs) into the selling price. Forfaiters usually deal in bills of exchange or promissory notes that can be sold on the secondary market. Both U.S. and European forfaiting houses are active in the U.S. market.

Buyer and Supplier Financing

In order to produce the goods under an export contract the seller will often need to obtain financing. This financing will at times come from the buyer or from the seller's suppliers. One form of buyer financing is when a letter of credit allows for progress payments. Under a progress payment, the bank is authorized by the buyer to pay seller on inspection by the buyer's agent or receipt of a statement by the seller that a certain percentage of the product has been completed. This type of partial payment under a letter of credit is known as a **red clause** advance. Under the red clause, the seller may demand a partial payment under the letter of credit before the presentation of documents. It is called a red clause because of the danger associated with it. The buyer is at risk for any red clause payments. If the seller subsequently fails to produce the goods or provide conforming documents, then the buyer must reimburse the bank for any red clause advances. Red clause payments are simply unsecured loans from the buyer to the seller.

Supplier financing is generally obtained through the supplier's selling materials to the exporter on account. Generally the seller produces the goods needed to fulfill the export contract and pays its suppliers before the due date out of the proceeds from the export contract. Suppliers will want some sort of collateral or security for selling materials on account, however. Two methods of providing such security are the **transferable credit** and the **back-to-back letter of credit** (see Exhibit 11.5).

Under the transferable credit arrangement, suppliers accept assignment of a part of the letter of credit that the seller receives from the buyer in the export transaction. If agreeable to the bank a documentary letter of credit can be made expressly transferable. It can then be divided and transferred to numerous suppliers of the exporter in order to guarantee payment to them upon the payment of the underlying letter of credit. Otherwise, some banks allow only a single transfer or assignment of a letter of credit.

The seller arranges the back-to-back letter of credit without the assistance of the buyer or issuing bank. The seller makes arrangements with a third-party bank to take the letter of credit from the export transaction as collateral for a new letter of credit. The third-party bank in partial amounts issues a new letter of credit to the suppliers of the seller. Thus, unlike the transferable credit arrangement, the back-to-back letter or credit scenario involves two separate letters of credit. The documentary letter of credit simply acts as collateral for the second letter of credit. The back-to-back letter of credit highlights the importance of the documentary letter of credit in both guaranteeing payments and in financing international trade.

EXHIBIT 11.5 *Back-to-Back Letter of Credit*

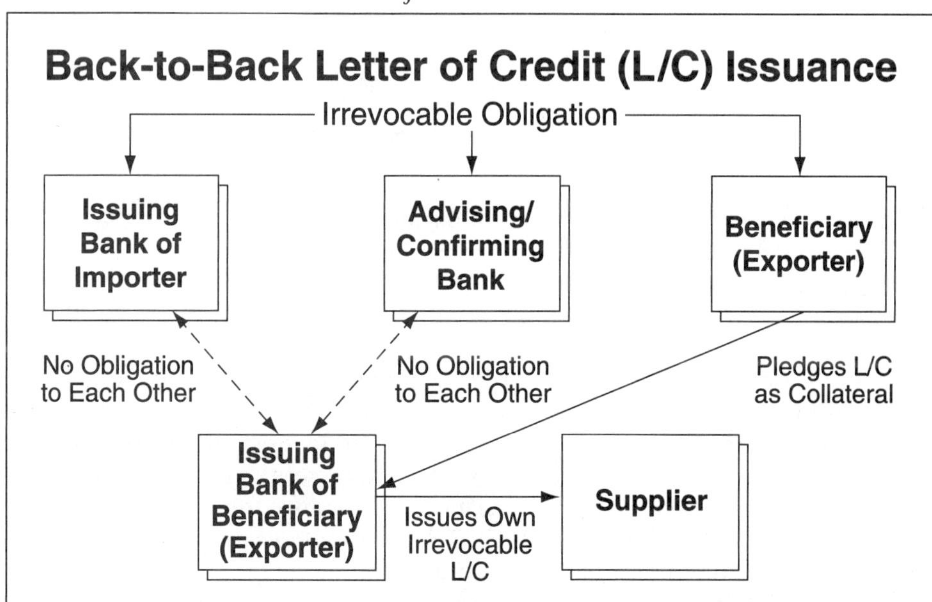

EXHIBIT 11.6 *Letter of Credit—Payment and Risks*

Type	Time of Payment	Goods Available to Importer	Risk to Exporter (seller)	Risk to Importer (buyer)
Irrevocable (confirmed letter of credit)	At sight of presentation of documents to bank or within specified number of days after acceptance	After payment	Provides most security	Fraud in the transaction
Revocable	Same as confirmed	After payment	Provides least security	Easier for issuing bank to cancel if evidence of fraud
Sight Draft	When shipment is made	After payment	Risk lies with confirming bank	Assured shipment is made but relies on exporter to ship goods as described in documents
Time Draft	At maturity of draft	Usually before payment	Loses control over goods	Assured shipment is made but relies on exporter to ship goods as described in documents
Red Clause	A percentage of total amount of letter of credit before shipment	After payment	Risk to confirming and issuing banks	The percentage of payment in advance is at total risk
Standby Letter of Credit	At time shipment is received	Usually before payment	Delay in payment	None
Back-to-Back Letter of Credit	Same as irrevocable	After payment	None	None
Transferable Letter of Credit	Same as irrevocable	After payment	Same as irrevocable	None

Exhibit 11.6 summarizes the times of payment and risks pertaining to the different types and uses of letters of credit reviewed in this chapter.

Government Assistance Programs

Several U.S. government agencies, as well as a number of state and local ones, offer programs to assist exporters with their financing needs. Some are guarantee programs that require the participation of an approved lender; others provide loans or grants to the exporter or a foreign government. Government guarantee and insurance programs are used by commercial banks to reduce the risk associated with loans to exporters. The Eximbank is the U.S. government's general trade finance agency, offering numerous programs to address a broad range of export needs.

Eximbank offers four major export finance programs, including loans, guarantees, working capital guarantees, and insurance. It provides these services to

U.S. exporters and foreign buyers. Eximbank's insurance and guarantee programs are structured to encourage private financial institutions to fund U.S. exports by reducing the commercial risks of nonpayment and political risks, such as war and currency inconvertibility. Credit insurance provided through its affiliate, the **Foreign Corporation Insurance Agency (FCIA),** protects against default on exports sold under open account, drafts, and letters of credit. FCIA's policies cover up to 100 percent of loss due to specified political risks, such as war and expropriation, and up to 95 percent of loss due to other commercial risks, such as buyer default and insolvency.

The **Overseas Private Insurance Corporation (OPIC)** provides specialized assistance to U.S. firms through its performance bond and contractor insurance programs. OPIC facilitates U.S. foreign direct investment in developing nations and Eastern Europe. An independent, financially self-supporting corporation fully owned by the U.S. government, OPIC encourages U.S. investment projects overseas by offering political risk insurance, guarantees, and direct loans. OPIC political risk insurance protects U.S. investment ventures abroad against the risks of civil strife and other violence, expropriation, and inconvertibility of currency. In addition, OPIC can cover business income loss due to political violence or expropriation.

http://

Small Business Administration: **http://www.sba.gov/oit/txt/info/links.html**. Links to SBA exporting guide and trade finance program.

The **Small Business Administration** provides an export **revolving line of credit.** This line of credit guarantees loans to U.S. exporters to help bridge the capital gap between the time inventory and production costs are incurred and the time payment is received from a foreign buyer. The credit line is granted based upon the likelihood of a company completing its export transactions, and the SBA guarantees 85 percent of the credit line. The guarantee covers against default by the exporter; failure on the buyer's side is expected to be covered by letters of credit or export credit insurance.

Key Terms

21-day rule, 318
acceptance, 319
account party, 311
advising bank, 314
amendment, 312
back-to-back letter of credit, 331
banker's acceptance, 319
beneficiary party, 311
bid bond, 327
bill of exchange, 318
confirming bank, 314
Convention on Independent Letters of Guarantee and Standby Credits, 328
credit surety, 327
customs broker, 315
demand guarantee, 327
documentary collections transaction, 310
documentary credit transaction, 310
draft, 318
Eximbank, 327
facial compliance rule, 316
factoring, 330
Foreign Corporation Insurance Agency (FCIA), 333
forfaiting, 330
freight forwarder, 316
International Standby Practices (ISP98), 325
irrevocable letter of credit, 312
issuing bank, 312
letter of credit, 309
open account, 330
Overseas Private Insurance Corporation (OPIC), 333
performance bond, 327
Power of Attorney, 316
pro forma invoice, 328
red clause, 330
retention fund, 327
revolving line of credit, 333
rule of strict compliance, 316
sight draft, 310
Small Business Administration, 333
standby letter of credit, 325
time draft, 310
trade acceptance, 319
transferable credit, 331
UCP 500, 320
Uniform Law on Bills of Exchange, 319
Uniform Rules for Demand Guarantees, 328
without recourse, 330
World Bank, 327

Chapter Problems

1. One topic of great interest at a recent global banking conference was dealing with letters of credit in China. As those who use Chinese letters of credit know, the Chinese will reject a letter of credit on the minutest of discrepancies. Several participants now report that in certain instances the scrutiny has gotten even worse. One member related an instance where a letter of credit was rejected because it was signed in blue ink instead of black. Several members theorized that the reason for the increased inspection is the cash flow problems in certain provinces. What can be done to overcome this problem of overly strict review and enforcement of documentary requirements?

2. Should the parties to a documentary credit include a dispute resolution clause in their letters of credit or allow disputes to be resolved through litigation? Are there any alternatives to arbitration that could be used to minimize the time and cost of litigation or arbitration?

3. A company engaging in the manufacture and sale of telecommunications equipment entered into an agreement with the "Imperial Government of Carpathia" to install and maintain certain telecommunications equipment. As a condition of the contract and to secure the advance payment, the company was required to guarantee its performance by obtaining two irrevocable letters of credit in the amounts equal to the advance payments made by Carpathia. Subsequently, a revolution occurred in Carpathia and the company was at least temporarily prevented from finishing the contract. The company was concerned that a new government would "arbitrarily" demand payment on the letters of credit. In light of the foregoing, the company sought a preliminary injunction preventing the bank from making payment on the letters of credit without first giving the company an opportunity to prove lack of authenticity or the fraudulent nature of the demand. Should the court grant a preliminary injunction? *Stromberg-Carlson Corp. v. Bank Melli Iran*, 467 F. Supp. 530 (S.D.N.Y. 1979).

4. The terms and conditions of a letter of credit state that the beneficiary party (seller) is to provide a certificate of origin listing the goods as originating from "NAFTA Countries." The certificate of origin did state "NAFTA Countries" but the commercial invoice stated only "NAFTA." The issuing bank rejected the documents because the declaration of origin in the commercial invoice was inconsistent with the declaration in the certificate of origin. The beneficiary party bank sues the issuing bank for wrongfully dishonoring the letter of credit. Under the UCP, who wins? Why?

5. A letter of credit is issued with the following terms and conditions: "(1) The beneficiary party must present a full set of clean-on-board bills of lading evidencing shipment from Port A to Port B and (2) documents must arrive at the offices of the issuing bank before arrival of the ship at Port B." The issuing bank rejected the documents for the following reasons: "(1) The bill of lading does not indicate that the goods were placed on board, but instead states that they were taken in charge at Container Freight Yard and (2) the documents were untimely because they were presented to the bank one day after the arrival of the ship." Were the two discrepancies given appropriate for rejecting the documents?

6. Test your knowledge of trade finance terminology. Match the term with its definition.

(A) Irrevocable	(1) A letter of credit that does not require the presentation of specified documents. It is extremely risky for the purchaser in an export transaction.
(B) Negotiable	(2) The letter of credit used in an export transaction that requires the seller to present specified documents in order to receive payment under the letter.
(C) Transferable	(3) A draft or bill of exchange that requires the bank to pay under the letter of credit at the time the documents are presented.
(D) Confirmed	(4) A letter of credit in which the buyer is named as beneficiary. It is used to guarantee performance on a contract and the return of a deposit or installment payments.
(E) Clean	(5) Cannot be revoked without beneficiary's consent. Most common form used in international transactions because it provides greatest security against nonpayment.
(F) Revolving	(6) The provision in a letter of credit allows for the advancement of monies prior to the seller presenting the required documents. This is a means by which a buyer can provide financing to the seller. It is very risky because it is unsecured and the buyer is responsible to reimburse the bank whether the seller performs or not.
(G) Documentary Credit	(7) Permits the accompanying drafts or bills of exchange to be transferred. This allows for the negotiation of a draft at other banks. The issuing bank is required to reimburse any bank that negotiates the letter of credit.

(H) Standby (8) A second bank endorses the letter of credit indicating that it will also guarantee payment upon the presentation of the required documents. In an export transaction the exporter's bank will generally be that bank.

(I) Sight Bill (9) Permits the beneficiary to negotiate the letter of credit to secondary beneficiaries. The original letter of credit must expressly state that it is transferable.

(J) Time Bill (10) The buyer provides the seller with a letter of credit. That credit is used as collateral to obtain a second letter of credit by the seller. The second provides a guarantee to the seller's suppliers. The second letter finances the acquisition of the materials needed by the seller to produce the goods.

(K) Red Clause (11) Generally granted by commercial banks to large importers. The buyer is allowed to reuse the credit after the bank is reimbursed.

(L) Back-to-Back (12) A draft or bill of exchange that orders the bank to pay on the letter of credit only after passage of a certain amount of time after the presentation of the documents. This allows the buyer to resell the goods or to obtain financing before being required to pay the seller.

Internet Exercises

1. Research the availability and requirements of the Small Business Administration's Trade Finance Program at **http://www.sba.gov/oit/txt/info/links.html**.

2. Take a self-guided tour from a Canadian perspective of an international trade transaction at **http://www.royalbank.com/trade**.

3. The U.S. Eximbank is the largest U.S. export financing agency. Explore **http://www.exim.gov** to see how its programs benefit U.S. exporters.

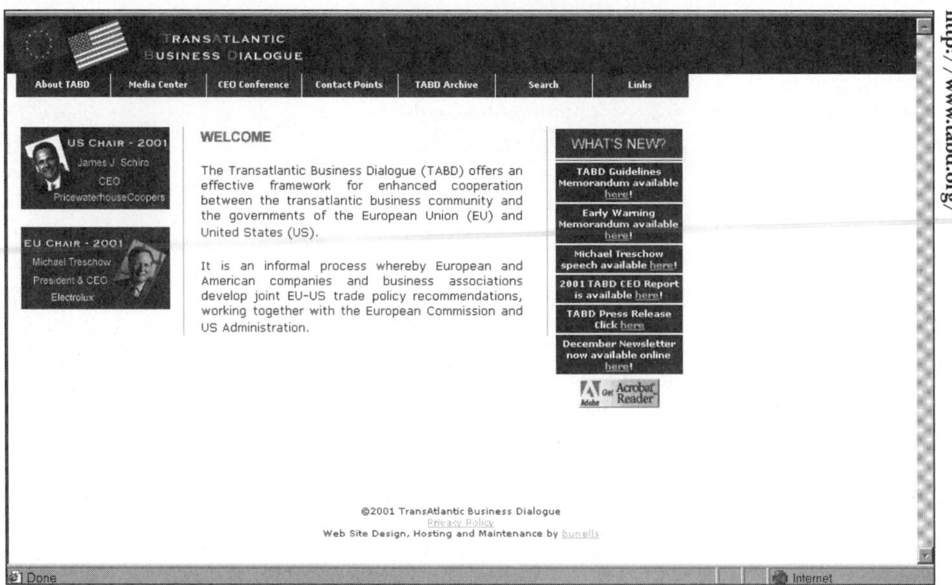

http://www.tabd.org/

Chapter 12
Sale of Services

Traditionally, international business law courses have focused on the sale of goods rather than the sale of services. This chapter is intended to alert the student to the importance of sales of services in international trade. A growing portion of U.S. exports falls in the areas of sale of services and the licensing of technology. This chapter will highlight the former; Chapters 13 and 14 will review the latter. Due to the breadth of the topic, this chapter is formatted somewhat differently than the other chapters in the book. Instead of providing cases for illustrative and pedagogical purposes, the coverage is more descriptive. The focus is on the practical issues that an individual or company faces in hiring foreign personnel. It includes an extensive review of the legalities associated with employment and agency contracts.

Sales of services are generally effectuated through employment and consulting contracts, which would seem to indicate that such transactions are purely private in nature. This is generally true in a domestic sale of services contract in the United States, but a host of restrictions and regulations are imposed on the international sale of services. Unlike the United States, some countries have developed an entire regulatory scheme that covers such transactions. This chapter provides examples of foreign regulations that the international employer, principal, agent, consultant, and employee will need to become accustomed with.

This chapter will review the generic ways people sell services—namely, the employment, foreign sales representation, and commercial agency contracts. The distinction between employment and independent contracting is examined in conjunction with these three ways of selling services. This material can be applied to sales of services in any type of industry and business. As was apparent through the earlier chapters of this book, a number of service industries make the sale of goods transaction possible. This chapter concludes with a review of some specific service areas including logistics, advertising, security offerings, and accounting.

Service contracts exist in almost all industries and businesses. An exact definition of sale of services is difficult to fashion because services comprise a broad range of activities. One way of defining a sale of services is by comparing it to the other two modes of international trade—sale of goods and licensing. A good is something tangible and movable. Sale of goods transactions include the sale of raw materials, component parts, equipment, and consumer products. Licensing involves a less than total transfer of ownership found in the sale transaction. Licenses generally pertain to intangible items such as technology, know-how, trade secrets, and intellectual property rights (trademarks, patents, copyrights). As discussed in Chapter 8, many transactions are **mixed sales** that include two or all three of the above modes of doing business (sale of goods, license, sale of services). A technology transfer, for example, may include a sale of goods (software or computer equipment), a license (right to use the software), and a sale of services (technical assistance and training).

INTERNATIONAL SALE OF SERVICES

The **Organization for Economic Cooperation and Development (OECD)** has estimated that between 60 percent and 70 percent of the business sector in OECD countries[1] relates to the sale of services. The principal markets for U.S. services, Canada, Japan, and the European Union, have been growing at a 10 to 15 percent annual rate. Export growth for services exists in Latin America, Asia, and Central and Eastern Europe. For example, U.S. service exports to Mexico are expected to grow at an astonishing 19 percent annual rate.[2] The means for selling services internationally include international consulting, services related to the export of goods, electronic transfers of knowledge and data, licensing agreements, franchising services, and tourism services. There has been rapid growth in many service sectors, including transport, communications, finance, and business services, along with knowledge-intensive services, such as computing and consultant services.

http://
Organization for Economic Cooperation and Development (OECD): **http://www.oecd.org**.

1. OECD member countries include Australia, Austria, Belgium, Canada, Czech Republic, Denmark, Finland, France, Germany, Greece, Hungary, Iceland, Italy, Japan, Korea, Luxembourg, Mexico, Netherlands, New Zealand, Norway, Poland, Portugal, Spain, Sweden, Switzerland, Turkey, United Kingdom, and United States. The forerunner of the OECD was the Organization for European Economic Cooperation which was formed to administer U.S. and Canadian aid under the Marshall Plan for reconstruction of Europe after WWII.
2. JOE REIF, JANET WHITTLE, ALEXANDRA WOZNICK, MOLLY THURMOND & JANE KELLY, SERVICES: THE EXPORT OF THE 21ST CENTURY (1997).

Advances in innovation, information, knowledge, and communications technologies have driven increased productivity in all segments of business. The United States has become a major international exporter of these types of knowledge and information-based services.

The rules-based multilateral trading system so successful in reducing barriers to trade in goods is now being expanded in the area of trade in services. A number of WTO Agreements, starting with the **General Agreement on Trade in Services (GATS),** concluded during the Uruguay Round of GATT, are targeted to reducing obstacles to trade in services. At the bilateral level, the United States and the European Union reached a number of **Mutual Recognition Agreements (MRA).**[3] These agreements are aimed at reducing trade barriers in specific industries. Trade barrier reduction is to be achieved through the mutual recognition of each other's product testing and certification procedures. At the non-governmental level, the **Trans-Atlantic Business Dialogue (TABD)** "endorsed bilateral and multilateral co-operation in the area of electronic commerce and identified five priority issues: protection of personal data and privacy; digital signatures and harmonized legal framework; encryption; tax, tariff, and customs; and intellectual property, protection, and associated liabilities."[4]

Service industries span a wide variety of enterprises from hamburgers to high technology. The service sector accounts for about 70 percent of the U.S. Gross National Product (GNP) and 75 percent of employment. In 1988, the service sector also accounted for slightly more than two-thirds of all self-employed persons. Internationally, a similar change has taken place. World trade in services grew in the past decade at an average rate of 5 percent a year to constitute approximately 20 percent of overall world trade. The leading exporter of services is the United States. Eighteen percent of all its exports are for services.

In view of the shift toward services both domestically and internationally and the substantial competitive advantage of the United States in the services field, liberalization in the trade for services has become an important U.S. policy objective. This is evidenced by the fact that the United States was a major promoter of GATS. Most business services can be exported, especially the highly innovative, specialized, or technologically advanced services that are efficiently performed in the United States. The following sectors have particularly high export potential for U.S. service providers: (1) construction, design, and engineering, (2) banking and financial services, (3) insurance services, (4) legal and accounting services, (5) computer and data services, (6) teaching services, and (7) management consulting services.

Important features differentiate exporting services from exporting products:

- Services are less tangible than products, providing little in terms of samples that can be seen by the potential foreign buyer. Consequently, communicating a service offer is much more difficult than communicating a product offer. Much more attention must be paid to translating the intangibility of a service into a tangible and saleable offer.
- The intangibility of services makes financing more difficult. Frequently, even financial institutions with international experience are less willing to provide financial support for service exports than for product exports, because the value of services is more difficult to monitor.

3. Charles O. Verrill, Jr., Peter S. Jordan & Timothy C. Brightbill, "International Trade," 32 *International Lawyer* 319, 326 (1998).
4. Ibid.

- Selling services is more personal than selling products, because it quite often requires direct involvement with the customer. This involvement demands greater cultural sensitivity when services are being provided across national borders.
- Services are much more difficult to standardize than products. Service activities must frequently be tailored to the specific needs of the buyer. This need for adaptation often necessitates the service client's direct participation and cooperation in the service delivery.

Demand for certain services is often related to product exports. Many merchandise exports from the United States would not take place if they were not supported by service activities such as banking, insurance, and transportation. For example, the "Big Five" accounting firms have expanded into the customs compliance area. Spurred by globalization and stricter compliance by U.S. Customs, the accounting firms now offer specialized services to help companies comply with Customs regulations. Since enactment of the **Customs Modernization Act of 1993,** importers and exporters are required to submit to periodic customs audits and to comply with strict record-keeping requirements. The accounting firms have expanded their services to include advising exporters and importers on how to minimize payment of duties and value-added tax, as well as on handling transfer-pricing and international tax issues. They also offer consulting in valuation, sourcing, trade strategies, logistics, trade process management, and information technology.

In recognition of the increasing importance of service exports, the U.S. Department of Commerce has made the **Office of Service Industries** responsible for analyzing and promoting services trade. The Office of Service Industries provides information on opportunities and operations of services abroad. A number of its divisions focus on specific industry sectors including information, transportation, tourism, marketing, finance, and management.[5]

General Agreement on Trade in Services

The World Trade Organization's General Agreement on Trade in Services (GATS) is a **Framework Agreement** containing basic obligations that apply to all member countries. It is built of national schedules of commitments and specific goals for continuing liberalization. In addition, it contains a number of annexes addressing individual services sectors.

Part I of the basic Framework Agreement defines the types of services that are covered:

- services supplied from the territory of one party to the territory of another
- services supplied in the territory of one party to the consumers of any other (for example, tourism)
- services provided through the presence of service-providing entities of one party in the territory of any other (for example, banking)
- services provided by nationals of one party in the territory of any other (for example, construction projects or consultancies)

5. Much of the information in this section was taken from the National Trade Data Bank, a product of STAT-USA, U.S. Department of Commerce.

Part II sets out general obligations and disciplines. A **most-favored-nation** obligation states that each party "shall accord immediately and unconditionally to services and service providers of any other member country, treatment no less favorable than that it accords to like services and service providers of any other country." **Transparency** requirements include publication of all relevant laws and regulations pertaining to the providing of services by foreign individuals or companies. Since domestic regulations and not cross-border rules provide the most significant influence on services trade, provisions spell out that all such measures of general application should be administered in a reasonable, objective, and impartial manner. The agreement contains obligations with respect to **recognition requirements** for the purpose of securing authorizations, licenses, or certification to provide a service. These types of requirements pertain mostly to professional trades including legal, engineering, medical, insurance, and accounting.

Part III contains provisions on market access and **national treatment** as listed in national schedules. For example, national restrictions on the kind of legal entity or joint venture through which a service is provided or any foreign capital limitations must be eliminated. The national-treatment provision contains the obligation to treat foreign services suppliers and domestic service suppliers in the same manner. Part IV of the agreement establishes the basis for progressive liberalization in the services area through successive rounds of negotiations and the development of national schedules. Part V of the agreement contains institutional provisions, including consultation and dispute settlement and the establishment of a **Council on Services.**

http://

Text and Guide to GATS: **http://gats-info.eu.int**.

The first annex to the GATS concerns the movement of labor. It permits parties to negotiate specific commitments applying to the movement of people providing services under the GATS. The annex would not apply to measures affecting employment, citizenship, residence, or employment on a permanent basis. It also relates to membership or participation in self-regulatory bodies and securities or futures exchanges. The annex on telecommunications relates to measures that affect access to and use of public telecommunications services and networks. In particular, it requires that such access be accorded to foreign parties on reasonable and nondiscriminatory terms. The annex also encourages technical cooperation to help developing countries to strengthen their own domestic telecommunications sectors. Doing Business Internationally: The New Round of Trade in Services discusses some of the issues relating to the current round of talks involving trade in services.

Services and the Internet

An evolving issue is the role of e-commerce and how the GATS commitments can be responsive to the new opportunities for providing services over the Internet. In nearly all sectors, there will be increasing pressure to allow services to be provided across borders. For example, in the case of financial services, regulators will be challenged to justify the requirement to provide these services through a local subsidiary, when the service can be provided more efficiently from abroad. However, there is also the possibility that nations and free trade areas will respond with specialized laws aimed at controlling cross-border transactions over the Internet. Consumer protection laws are likely to be tailored to protect nationals engaged in Internet transactions with foreign sellers. An example of such a law is the **EU Directive on Distance Contracts,** which is described in the Comparative Law feature on page 342.

Doing Business Internationally

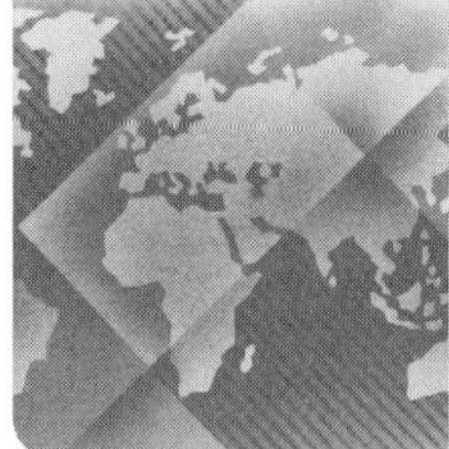

The New Round of Trade in Services[6]

The World Trade Organization's well-publicized failure to launch a comprehensive trade negotiation in Seattle has delayed indefinitely the plans of many of its members to begin negotiations in a number of key trade areas. This is not the case, however, for services. Services rules are relatively new, having become part of the GATT/WTO in 1995 through the General Agreement on Trade in Services (GATS). The WTO rules and disciplines that govern services are different from those of goods, since services do not formally enter a country's customs territory subject to tariffs. They typically reach foreign markets through investment, over the telephone, and by individuals crossing the border. In recent years, services companies have greatly expanded the ability to export their products by way of the Internet. However, many services still must be provided in person.

The GATS, therefore, is structured to address the different "modes of supply," which represent how countries permit or restrict foreign participation in the different services sectors. The GATS establishes its rules in two ways. First, general obligations are negotiated that bind all member countries. Examples include obligations to provide transparency, regulation of the behavior of monopolies and exclusive services providers, and the granting of most-favored-nation treatment. Second, specific commitments to provide market access and national treatment, as well as special regulatory obligations, are assumed by individual countries as a result of negotiations reached bilaterally or among a group of countries. The objectives of the current round of services negotiations fall into three basic categories:

1. Efforts to remove restrictions and limitations on market access and national treatment in sectors generally covered in country commitments. Some of the more important sectors that fall into this category are financial, telecommunications, professional, rental and leasing, computer and software implementation, audiovisual, construction, travel and tourism, and transportation services.
2. The greater inclusion of sectors largely ignored in the Uruguay Round. These include environmental, energy, express delivery, distribution, and health and education services.
3. Initiatives to expand regulatory disciplines. The concern over differences in domestic regulatory systems has generated interest in expanding the GATS to encompass targeted sector areas of interest to individual countries. A model for this sort of agreement is the set of regulatory principles that were developed among 70 participant countries in the negotiations on basic telecommunications.

As in most consumer protection statutes, the EU Directive on Distance Contracts requires the (foreign) seller to disclose certain types of information. The required disclosure information includes location of seller, price and additional costs, and the minimum length of time that the consumer will be bound to the contract. The directive allows the seller to solicit over the telephone, but is required to follow-up with a written confirmation. An e-mail confirmation does satisfy the writing requirement. The statute mandates a consumer right of withdrawal. The consumer has up to seven days to cancel the contract and receive a full refund

6. Richard B. Self, "Trade in Services: The Round Is Underway," *The Metropolitan Corporate Counsel* (2000).

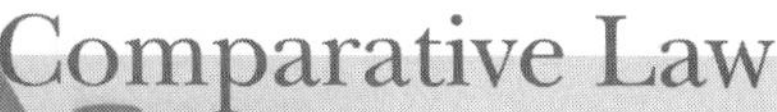

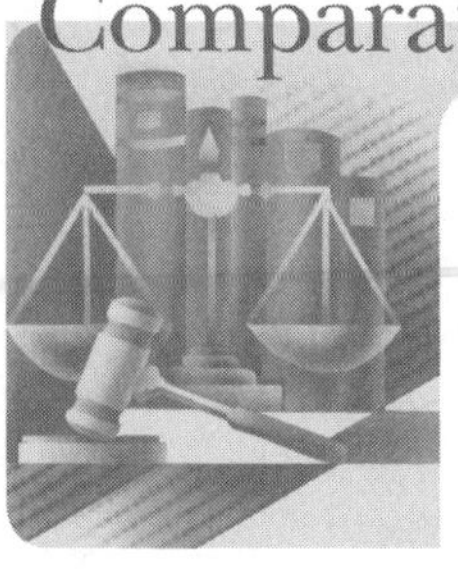

EU Directive 97/7/EC of February 17, 1997, on Protection of Consumers in Distance Contracts[7]

Prior to the conclusion of any distance contract, the consumer must be provided with clear and comprehensible information concerning:

- the identity and possibly the address of the supplier;
- the characteristics of the goods *or services* and their price;
- delivery costs;
- the arrangements for payment, delivery, or performance;
- the existence of a right of withdrawal;
- the period for which the offer or the price remains valid and the minimum duration of the contract, where applicable;
- the cost of using the means of distance communication.

This information must comply with the principles of good faith in commercial transactions and the principles governing the protection of minors. In the case of telephone calls, the caller's identity and commercial purpose must be made clear at the beginning.

The consumer must receive written confirmation or confirmation in another durable medium (electronic mail) at the time of performance of the contract. The following information must also be given in writing:

- arrangements for exercising the right of withdrawal;
- place to which the consumer may address complaints;
- information relating to after-sales service;
- conditions under which the contract may be rescinded.

The consumer has a right of withdrawal. Where the supplier has met his obligations relating to the provision of information, the consumer has at least seven working days to cancel the contract without penalty.

Where the supplier has failed to meet his obligations as regards information, this period is extended to three months. The supplier is obliged to repay the amounts paid by the consumer within thirty days.

Where the supplier fails to perform his side of the contract, the consumer must be informed and any sums paid refunded. In some cases it is possible to supply an equivalent good or service.

Where unsolicited goods are supplied, the consumer's failure to reply does not constitute consent.

The use by the supplier of automatic calling devices or faxes requires the prior consent of the consumer.

The Member States must ensure that consumers are allowed judicial or administrative redress so that they are not deprived of protection under the law of a non-Member country.

The Member States may adopt more stringent provisions, provided that these are compatible with the Treaty, such as a ban on the marketing of certain goods and services through distance contracts.

of any monies paid. The right of withdrawal is extended to three months in the event that the seller has failed to provide the information required by the Directive. This consumer right is akin to the right of rescission found in some federal and state consumer protection statutes in the United States.

7. This directive applies to sales of both goods and services through distance contracts such as mail order, telephone communications, or other means of telecommunications.

It is important to note the second to last paragraph of the Directive. This prevents the seller from avoiding the dictates of the statute by inserting a choice of law clause selecting a country outside of the EU. Therefore, a choice of law clause selecting the State of California as the law of the contract would be ignored in case over a dispute pertaining to issues covered by the Directive. California law would still apply, however, to contract disputes not covered under the Directive. Finally, the statute does not prevent member countries of the EU from enacting more stringent consumer protection legislation. The U.S. exporter, unfortunately, will not only have to satisfy the dictates of the Directive, but will also have to research the consumer protection requirements of each EU country it chooses to export to.

HIRING FOREIGN PERSONNEL

Any company seeking to sell its products internationally will face the need for foreign representation. It will be forced to enter the market for services. For example, exporters contemplating an initial penetration into a foreign market have three alternatives for entry. First, it may elect to use employees, whether those already in place or new foreign hires. Second, it may elect to hire independent contractors to provide the needed services. The most common form of service provided by independent contractors is sales representation. Third, it may elect to enter into a distribution relationship with a foreign distributor. It is estimated that over half of world trade is handled through sales representatives and distributors.[8]

A **foreign sales representative** is an agent who distributes, represents, services, or sells goods on behalf of foreign sellers. The following sections will focus upon the differences between the employment and independent contractor relationships, why those differences are important, and on the law pertaining to the use of foreign sales representatives and distributors. Although the employment or **independent contractor** relationships are largely matters of private contracting, foreign laws heavily impact the classification of a given relationship. Also, once a relationship is designated as an employment or independent contractor relationship, a number of host country laws regulate areas such as notice, termination, and remuneration.

The terminology of agency, employment, and independent contractor as used in the United States may differ from the way it is used in other countries. For example, the general meaning of ***agent*** may differ from country to country.[9] Generally, an agent denotes the person being hired while the party doing the hiring is referred to as the **principal.** The term *agent* encompasses both dependent and independent agents. An employee is a **dependent agent.** A mixture of employment and agency law governs the employer-employee relationship. In contrast, an independent contractor, such as a consultant, is an **independent agent.** Agency law governs the principal-agent relationship between the hiring company and the consultant. It will be seen, however, that in some foreign legal systems this relationship is subject to a good amount of statutory control. The next two sections will examine the general nature of the employment and independent contractor relationships.

8. See generally King, "Legal Aspects of Appointment and Termination of Foreign Distributors and Representatives," 17 *Case Western International Law Journal* 91 (1985).
9. RALPH H. FOLSOM & MICHAEL W. GORDON, INTERNATIONAL BUSINESS TRANSACTIONS 4, n.1 (1995).

The Employment Relationship

The philosophical foundation of the U.S. employment relationship, the **employment at will doctrine,** provides that except for express employment contracts the employment relationship may be terminated at the will of either party. In order to prevent employee-generated lawsuits of unfair dismissal, companies should avoid the use of employment contracts and make clear at the time of hiring that the employment is "at will." A U.S.–based international company's employment manual should make this clear. First, the manual should state that the general employment policy applies to all subsidiaries. Of course, one should bear in mind that the "at will" concept may be defined differently in other legal systems.

Second the employment manual should clearly state that "all employees are hired as *at will* employees." The employer's code of conduct (ethics code) should also delineate prohibited areas of conduct such as:

- rude or discourteous behavior
- theft or personal dishonesty
- use or possession of alcohol or controlled substances on company premises
- maintenance of inappropriate files on the company's internal network
- transmission of confidential information over the e-mail system
- disclosing nonpublic information, including trade secrets
- duplicating software products
- engaging in any act of harassment or discrimination

The U.S. employer should pay special attention to the last item on the above list. Laws and cultural attitudes vary widely among countries. Therefore, a clear policy on sexual harassment should be developed with the international employee in mind. Doing Business Internationally: Standard Sexual Harassment Policy provides a common format for developing a company's **sexual harassment policy.** At the minimum, a policy should state the company's general policy, provide workable definitions of inappropriate conduct, and provide a user-friendly complaint procedure. The problems of cultural or ethical relativism were discussed in Chapter 2. Based upon that discussion, should a U.S. company tailor a policy or modify its existing policy to take into account more relaxed cultural and legal standards of sexual harassment? How can such modifications be justified?

The employment relationship is viewed differently culturally and legally throughout the world. The perspective of legal status of the employee varies from the employment at will doctrine in the United States to **employment as a property right** in Germany and **lifetime employment** in Japan. Understanding these differences is vital to the U.S. manufacturer contemplating the hiring of foreign nationals. In Germany, for example, hiring a single employee can result in the company being designated as having "permanent status," leading to the taxation of the exporter's German-generated revenues. Thus, designating a German national as an independent contractor in a clearly written contract is prudent.

The decision to hire foreign employees, especially in most EU countries, should be made with full knowledge of the obstacles the employer has to overcome under European law in order to terminate the employment relationship. In Germany, the notice required to discharge an employee may vary from four weeks to seven months depending on the longevity of the employment. Dismissals are permitted only following consultation with statutorily mandated **Works Councils.** Also, workers can sue for reinstatement and damages if the dismissal is determined to be

Doing Business Internationally

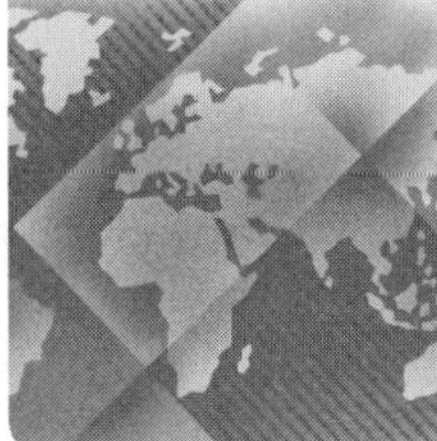

Standard Sexual Harassment Policy

Three typical sections of a sexual harassment policy include:

General Policy
Management personnel are responsible for maintaining a harassment-free environment and are strictly prohibited from stating or in any way implying that submitting or refusing to submit to sexual advances will have any affect upon an individual's hiring, placement, compensation, training, promotion, or any other term or condition of employment.

Definition
All employees are prohibited from making offensive remarks or engaging in unwelcome overtures, either verbal or physical. Such prohibited conduct includes, but is not limited to, offensive and unwelcome flirtations, advances, or propositions; verbal abuse of a racial, ethnic, religious, or sexual nature; graphic or degrading comments about an individual or his or her appearance; the display of sexually suggestive objects or pictures; or any offensive or abusive physical contact. Acts of harassment by any employee are strictly prohibited and will result in disciplinary action that may include termination of employment.

Complaint Procedure
When a complaint is received the company's ethics officer or human resources department will conduct an immediate impartial and confidential investigation. At the conclusion of the investigation, the officer or representative of Human Resources will advise the employee of the results.

"unjustified."[10] A number of protected classes, such as pregnant women and members of the Works Council, are not subject to dismissal. Furthermore, severance payments can reach as high as a full year of salary or more for long-term employees. Thus, the decision to employ should be cautiously entered into.

Under the **French Labor Code,** a meeting with the employee being discharged and notice are required, making immediate termination impossible. A suit for unfair dismissal, like in Germany, is recognized. "In order to avoid civil sanctions for breach of contract, the employer must be able to prove that there were real and serious grounds for the dismissal."[11] The employee also has a right to a severance payment based upon seniority. He may waive this right in favor of a statutorily mandated **conversion contract.** Under the conversion contract, the employee receives, at the cost of the employer, enhanced government unemployment benefits and retraining or educational opportunities. If the ground for dismissal is economic, then the discharged employee has: (1) a right to a transfer if another position is available within the company and (2) a right to re-employment for a period of one year in the event that the economic factors change.

In France, dismissals for reasons of **redundancy** are allowed under certain conditions. Redundancy is the term for "laying off" workers no longer needed because of a restructuring or downsizing. The employer may make such collective dismissals only following consultation with labor unions. Also, the selection of workers to be

10. PRICE WATERHOUSE, DOING BUSINESS IN GERMANY 84 (1996).
11. PRICE WATERHOUSE, DOING BUSINESS IN FRANCE 102 (1995).

dismissed must be based upon the criteria established by law that factors in the number of family dependents, seniority, and organizational needs.

The employment relationship in the former countries of the Soviet Union remains heavily regulated. For example, the **Russian Labor Code** makes it very difficult for the employer to terminate employment. Another policy grants maternity leave for up to *three years* per child. Furthermore, the written contract is the basic form for commencing an employment relationship that must satisfy detailed requirements before an employee can be dismissed. Therefore, before dismissing an employee, it is important to seek legal consultation.

In Italy, trade unions are given standing to sue employers under the law for any violations of rules pertaining to union membership or activities. The law provides for the issuance of injunctions against the employer. The trial is required to begin within two days of the filing of a *recorso* or complaint by the trade union.

A fundamental difference in Italian law is that an employer's freedom to hire is limited. The placement of workers is considered to be a matter of public concern to be implemented by the government. A number of agencies are given the responsibility to place workers. These include the Ministry of Labor, Central Employment Commission, along with regional and provincial employment offices. The employer is required to file an application with the Placement Office indicating the category and qualifications sought. The Placement Office then selects workers among those registered on its **hiring list.** Unemployed workers are given priority over those wanting to change jobs. This procedure is known as *annunzione numerica* or **hiring by number.**

Recently, the Italian hiring by number practice has been liberalized to enable employers to engage in more direct hiring. Employers are now allowed to hire directly: (1) managers and other workers performing managerial duties, (2) 50 percent of all other workers that they were previously required to hire through the Placement Office, and (3) workers paid wholly on a profit-sharing basis. Italian law also includes a provision for **compulsory hiring.** The law provides that companies employing more than 35 employees must hire 15 percent of its workforce from the following categories of people: war disabled, work disabled, blind, deaf, or mute people and orphans and widows by reasons of military service or work.

In the area of termination, the employer must follow a statutory **consultation procedure** that includes the giving of notice provided for either in the collective bargaining agreement or by custom and practice (see Comparative Law: Italian Consultation Procedure). Failure to give notice obligates the employer to pay an **indemnity in lieu of notice.** The indemnity payment is an amount equal to the pay the worker would have received for the period of the required notice. In reviewing the Italian consultation procedure a U.S. employer is likely to be astonished by the complexity of dismissing an employee, the broad rights accorded the employee, and the size of the mandated employee benefits. On average, it can take about three months to dismiss an employee. The employee is given a right to re-employment for up to one year following her dismissal. In addition, the employee is entitled to up to three years of indemnity (unemployment) paid through contributions by the employer to the National Social Security Institute!

The employer in Italy may terminate an employee without notice where the dismissal is for cause. **Dismissal for cause** is defined as something grounded on such grave misconduct, whether intentional or negligent, that the employment relationship is no longer capable of being reasonably continued. Reasons short of theft are unlikely to justify a dismissal for cause. In short, employers are subject to strict conditions when terminating their employees. The dismissal must be based upon *justi-*

Comparative Law

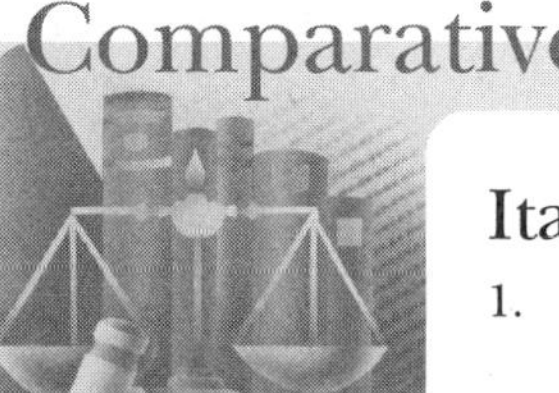

Italian Consultation Procedure

1. The employer must give written notice to the union of intention to dismiss workers.
2. A meeting with the union must be held within seven days of the receipt of the notice to discuss how to avoid the dismissals (such as the possible relocation of workers).
3. If after 45 days a settlement has not been concluded, then they shall continue before the Regional Labor Office or, where the dismissals involve different locations, then before the Ministry of Labor.
4. Negotiations before the Ministry or Labor Office shall not exceed 30 days.
5. If an agreement is not reached before the expiration of the above time limits, then the employer has the right to terminate the redundant workers.
6. The discharged workers are placed on a *mobility list* and shall be given priority for re-employment by the original employer for a period of one year.
7. The dismissed workers are entitled to a notice period or an indemnity in lieu of notice.
8. Dismissed workers are also entitled to a *mobility indemnity* paid by the *Instituto Nazionale della Previdenza Sociale* (National Social Security Institute or INPS). The indemnity is paid for a period of 12 months for workers under the age of 40, 24 months for workers over 40, and 36 months for workers over the age of 50. The employer contributes to this indemnity by paying to INPS an amount equal to nine times the monthly "conventional salary."
9. Workers are also entitled to *termination dues* normally equivalent to one month of salary for each year of service.

fied reasons such as closing a product line, notice must be in writing, and it must give the reasons for the dismissal. Failure to comply with this procedure results in a continuation of the employment.

Any discharged worker may contest her dismissal within 60 days and seek a settlement before a Conciliation Committee. If no settlement is reached the worker may bring suit for wrongful dismissal. The burden of proof in such a lawsuit is placed upon the employer. If a court rules that the dismissal was unlawful, then the employee is entitled to damages ranging from five months to fourteen months of salary and the employer may be required to rehire the discharged employee.

INTERNATIONAL LABOR STANDARDS

Labor regulation has become a controversial issue in both the regional and global contexts. In the global arena, national and international labor groups have criticized the creation of the World Trade Organization (WTO) with its narrow mandate of fostering free trade. These groups believe that free trade agreements should be made conditional on respect for labor standards. Thus far the WTO has rejected demands to adopt standards for the regulation of labor.

Historically, the **International Labor Organization (ILO)** has been associated primarily with the development of international norms applicable to labor issues. The Treaty of Versailles established the ILO in 1919 with the stated principle that "labor should not be regarded merely as a commodity or article of commerce." A common device used to advance labor standards is the inclusion of **labor clauses** in

http://
International Labor Organization: **http://www.ilo.org.**

trade agreements (see Focus on Transactions: ILO Labor Clauses in Public Contracts). This was expressly done in regional free trade agreements such as the North American Free Trade Agreement (NAFTA) and more specifically in EU legislation, but was rejected in the enactment of the WTO Agreements.

The **ILO Declaration on Fundamental Principles and Rights at Work** has enumerated a number of "core labor standards" including:

- freedom of association and the right to collective bargaining
- elimination of all forms of forced or compulsory labor
- abolition of child labor
- elimination of discrimination in respect of employment and occupation

http://
The Apparel Industry and Codes of Conduct: A Solution to the International Child Labor Problem?: **http://www.dol.gov/dol/ilab/public/media/reports/iclp/apparel/main.htm.** U.S. Department of Labor, "By the Sweat and Toil of Children: Efforts to Eliminate Child Labor": **http://www.dol.gov/dol/ilab/public/media/reports/iclp/sweat5/.**

Note the close relationship between these core labor rights or standards and the basic human rights discussed in Chapter 2. Currently, U.S. law reflects this commitment to core labor rights. For example, a developing country may lose preferential tariff rates for violating labor rights. The General System of Preferences (GSP) law states that reduced tariff rates are to be removed if a "country has not taken steps to afford internationally recognized worker rights to workers in the country." The U.S. Tariff Act of 1930, Section 1307, prohibits the importation of goods produced with prison or indentured labor. In 1997, Section 1307 was amended to include goods produced using forced or indentured child labor. The sporadic implementation of these provisions has been an issue for debate.

The EU has addressed labor standards on a piecemeal basis by incorporating them into agreements on specific activities. For example, EU directives require the insertion of labor clauses in public procurement contracts. Another pro-labor device recognized in Europe is the works council discussed above. These employee councils require a company to provide information and seek consultation with its workers on plant and workforce relocations. In 1993, Hoover Europe announced the closing of a plant in France resulting in the loss of 600 of 700 existing jobs. Partially in response to the public outcry, the EU approved a **European Works Council Directive.**[12] The Directive requires large companies, mostly multinational corporations, to establish European Works Councils (EWC). It is estimated that the Directive covers about 1,500 multinational companies operating in Europe.[13]

Focus on Transactions

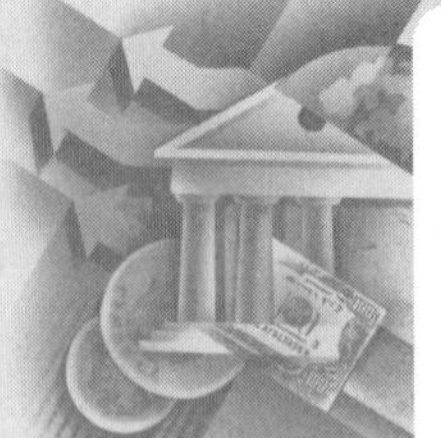

ILO Labor Clauses in Public Contracts

Contractor agrees to ensure working conditions not less favorable than those established for work of the same character in the trade or industry where the work is carried on by collective agreement or other recognized machinery of negotiations between employers and workers. Where such agreements are not in existence, then those working conditions that are at "the general level observed in the trade or industry in which the contractor is engaged by employers whose general circumstances are similar."

12. Directive 94/45/EC of 22 September 1994.
13. Brian Bercusson, "Labor Regulation in a Transnational Economy," 6 *Maastricht Journal of European and Comparative Law* 244 (1999).

The Independent Contractor Contract

The designation of a foreign agent as an employee, partner (joint venture), or independent contractor is crucial. If the foreign agent is hired as an independent contractor, then the host of employment regulations discussed above do not apply to the relationship. Furthermore, the principal, the U.S. company doing the hiring, would not be liable for the acts of the independent contractor, as it would be for acts of an employee or partner.

It is important that independent contractor status be preserved both in any written contract and in the actual carrying out of the contractual relationship. The independent contractor agreement should also include a **nonpartnership clause** to prevent the principal from being vicariously liable under agency principles. A typical nonpartnership clause states that "the party being hired is to perform as an independent contractor and nothing contained herein should be construed as creating a partnership between the parties to this agreement."

In addition, a **work for hire clause** should be inserted into any employment or independent contractor agreement in which the employee or independent contractor is being paid to develop new technology or to perform research and development. This clause makes it clear that all rights to the research and intellectual property rights are to revert to the employer. A typical work for hire clause reads that "all inventions, creations, and research of the employee (or independent contractor) during the term of his employment shall be work for hire and shall be the property of the employer, and that all rights to the intellectual property shall be assigned by the employee to the employer."

The Foreign Sales Representative

The most common use of the independent contractor vehicle for transacting business is to hire a foreign sales representative. This relationship has been defined as the hiring of an agent "to prospect for and visit customers with a view to negotiating and, when appropriate, concluding sales agreements in the name and for account of the exporter of goods, services, technology."[14] This relationship is also referred to as a **commercial agency** arrangement.

The following excerpt from the U.S. State Department's Country Commercial Guide for Indonesia illustrates some of the nuances in hiring foreign sales representatives and agents:

> *The main difference between a representative office and an agent is that the former cannot sell or sign contracts but only market and do research, while the latter can perform all trade activities. Only Indonesians can function as agents. Foreign principals often work out a management agreement that allows the foreign company in Indonesia to play a more active role in the marketing efforts of its Indonesian agent or distributor. Whatever basis is used for remuneration, it must be formulated clearly in the agreement, and it must be applicable under the present Indonesian laws. To protect the foreign company's interests properly, a comprehensive agreement should be drawn between the parties concerned.*

A subsequent determination or conversion, by a foreign government, of an independent sales agent to employment status subjects the exporter to a wide array of

14. ICC, GUIDE FOR THE DRAWING UP OF CONTRACTS—COMMERCIAL AGENCY 5 (1993).

foreign laws including tax and labor laws. An employment designation may also "establish" the company for purposes of personal jurisdiction in the courts of that country. Thus, the structuring and wording of the services contract as one of independent agency, and not dependent agency, is crucial for avoiding such host country laws. The profound differences in the area of agency law between civil law and common law countries require the advice of foreign legal counsel when entering such a relationship.

Before hiring a foreign sales agent or representative, a company should develop a checklist of factors for selection. Each company's checklist should be tailored to reflect the types of products or services to be sold and the differences between targeted countries. The Focus on Transactions feature on the next page provides an example of the type of questions and factors to be considered when hiring a foreign agent.

After developing a hiring checklist, a company's next step is to negotiate the foreign representation or agency agreement. The next section reviews some of the issues relevant to the negotiation of a commercial agency contract.

The Commercial Agency Contract

Provisions related to the termination of the agreement are the most important part of an international agency contract.[15] This is because of the existence of host country laws that restrict a foreign company's right to terminate an agency agreement. These laws, popularly referred to as **evergreen statutes,** will be dealt with in the next section. Because of the existence of these statutes the agency contract should include an escape or **termination clause** in the agreement allowing the exporter or principal to end the relationship. The contract should spell out exactly what constitutes *just cause* for ending the agreement. The following list illustrates the legal questions that should be considered when negotiating a termination clause in an agency contract.

- How far in advance must the representative be notified of the exporter's intention to terminate the agreement? (Three months satisfies the requirements of most countries.)
- What is just cause for terminating a representative? (Specifying causes for termination in the written contract usually strengthens the exporter's position.)
- Which country's laws will govern a contract dispute? (Laws in the representative's country may forbid the representative from waiving its nation's legal jurisdiction.)
- What compensation is due the representative on dismissal? (Depending on the length of the relationship, the added value of the market the representative has created for the exporter, and whether termination is for just cause as defined by the foreign country, the U.S. exporter may be required to pay damages or an indemnity.)
- What must the representative give up if dismissed? (The contract should specify the return of patents, trademarks, name registrations, customer records, and promotional materials.)
- Should the representative be referred to as an agent? (The contract may need to specify that the representative is not a legal agent with power of attorney.)

15. The label "agency contract" is broad enough to include a wide variety of contracts including sales representation, distribution, consulting, advertising, and transportation agreements.

Focus on Transactions

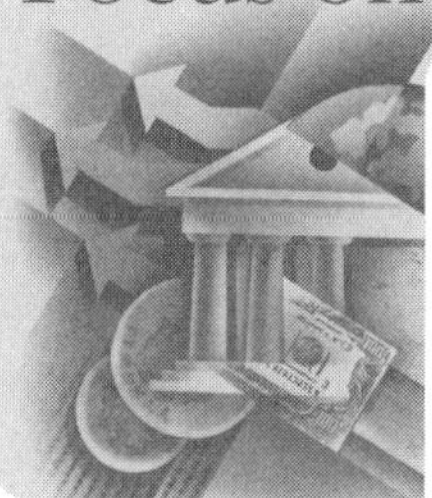

Factors to Consider when Choosing a Foreign Representative or Distributor[16]

Size of sales force

- How many field sales personnel does the representative or distributor have?
- What are the company's short- and long-range expansion plans?
- Would it need to expand to accommodate your account properly? If so, would it be willing to do so?

Sales record

- Has its sales growth been consistent? Try to determine sales volume for the past five years.
- What are its sales objectives for next year?

Territorial analysis

- What territory does it now cover?
- Is its coverage consistent with the coverage you desire? If not, is it able and willing to expand?
- Does it have any branch offices in the territory to be covered?
- Does it have any plans to open additional offices?

Product mix

- How many product lines does it represent?
- Are these product lines compatible with yours?
- Would there be any conflict of interest?
- Does it represent any other U.S. firms? If so, which ones?

Facilities and equipment

- Does it have adequate warehouse facilities?
- What is its method of stock control?
- Does it use computers? Are they compatible with yours?
- If your product requires servicing, is it equipped and qualified to do so? To what extent will you have to share training cost?
- If necessary and customary, is it willing to inventory repair parts and replacement items?

Marketing policies

- How is its sales staff compensated?
- Does it have special incentive or motivation programs?
- How does it monitor sales performance?
- How does it train its sales staff?
- Would it share expenses for sales personnel to attend factory-sponsored seminars?

Customer profile

- Who are its key accounts?
- What kinds of customers is it currently contacting?

Principals represented

- How many principals is it currently representing?
- Would you be its primary supplier?
- If not, how does your percentage compare with other suppliers?

Promotional thrust

- Can it help you compile market research information to be used in making forecasts?
- What media does it use, if any, to promote sales?
- How much of its budget is allocated to advertising? How is advertising distributed among principals?
- Will you be expected to contribute funds for promotional purposes? How will the amount be determined?

16. Source: National Trade Data Bank, a product of STAT-USA, U.S. Department of Commerce.

- In what language should the contract be drafted? (English should be the official language of the contract in most cases.)

The International Chamber of Commerce's **Commercial Agency—Guide for the Drawing up of Contracts** can be used as a checklist for writing an agency contract. Focus on Transactions: ICC Commercial Agency Guide provides a summary. These selected provisions highlight the issues that an international agency contract should address.

Focus on Transactions

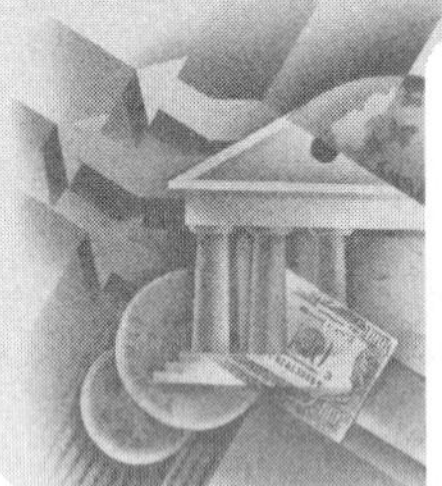

ICC Commercial Agency Guide

- **Independent Contractor Status:** The heading of the agreement should clearly state that it is a commercial agency contract.
- **Identity and Capacity of Parties:** The nationality and legal form of each party should be stated, along with the foreign entity's capacity to act as a commercial agent.[17]
- **Assignments:** If the parties intend to allow assignment, the contract should state the conditions and procedure for assignments.
- **Language of the Contract:** If the contract is written in two languages, it should state which language is to control in the enforcement of the contract.
- **Products:** The contract should be clear regarding the products that are to be sold on behalf of the principal. If the principal produces different classes of products, then the contract should state which classes are subject to the agency contract.[18]
- **Agency Territory:** The contract should precisely delineate the sales territory that is being given to the agent. A further restriction may be placed upon the sales to third parties who are likely to export the goods to another territory. Such restrictions are needed to prevent the gray market problem discussed in Chapters 13 and 14.[19]
- **Solicitation of Customers:** The parties should agree to the groups to be targeted by the agent as potential customers.
- **Acceptance of Orders:** The agreement should clearly state whether the agent has the authority to bind the principal.[20]
- **Intellectual Property Rights Infringement:** The relative responsibilities of the parties as to infringement of intellectual property rights should be defined. For example, the agent's responsibility to notify the principal of any such infringements should be detailed.[21]
- **Advertising and Marketing Materials:** The contract should stipulate whether the principal is to provide any samples or advertising materials, and which party is to pay the costs of such materials. The contract should make clear whether the principal has the right of prior consent for any materials or advertising produced by the agent.

17. For example, in some countries only nationals may act as agents and in others commercial agents must be registered with the government.
18. The contract should also address the issue of the development of new products or subsequent improvements of the products listed in the contract.
19. Host country laws should be reviewed to see if territorial restrictions will violate competition (antitrust) laws.
20. Under some foreign laws, agency authority to bind its principal may result in the loss of independent contractor status.
21. In order to protect its rights, the principal should register its intellectual property rights in the host country prior to entering any agency relationship.

EVERGREEN STATUTES

The most difficult laws to avoid are national agency termination laws, popularly referred to as evergreen statutes. These laws often impose minimum notice requirements for terminating an agent or require the payment of an indemnity upon termination unless the termination is based upon a just cause. These laws are different than the employment regulations discussed earlier in the chapter. Unlike employment regulations, evergreen statutes do apply to agents acting as independent contractors.

- **Best Efforts Provision:** The principal will want to negotiate a clause that requires the agent to use "best efforts" in marketing and selling the principal's products. The agreement should attempt to define the meaning of "best efforts" such as tying them to generally accepted business practices.
- **Noncompetition Clause:** This provision prohibits the agent from selling the products of a competitor.[22]
- **Parts and Service:** The obligations of the agent should be detailed with regard to providing after-sales service and spare parts.
- **Legal Information:** A clause may be inserted that the agent must inform the principal of any changes in national laws or regulations relating to technical requirements, labeling, and customs regulations. This should include information regarding any national requirement to register the agency contract.
- **Confidentiality:** The agreement should require the agent to maintain the secrecy of the principal's trade secrets even after the termination of the relationship.
- **Minimum Sales:** The principal may want to negotiate that the agent is required to meet certain minimum sales levels. It should specify the consequences for the failure to meet sales quotas such as termination, reduction of territory, or loss of exclusivity.
- **Commissions:** The basis of calculation and the rate of commissions should be clearly stated. If the net amount is used as a basis, then the deductions (e.g., freight, insurance, discounts, taxes, packing) should be stated.
- **Termination:** The contract may be for a fixed period or an indefinite time period subject to reasonable notice. Some national laws require that the notice be of a certain length of time. It may be stipulated that certain events, such as bankruptcy, merger, assignment, resignation of a key employee, give a party the right to terminate.
- **Choice of Law and Forum Selection Clauses:** The parties should agree on the law that will apply to any disputes. It should also select the court or arbitration panel in which such disputes are to be brought.

22. This clause should be narrowly constructed so as to not violate national laws that view such restrictions harshly.

Many European countries grant the agent a right upon the termination of the agency relationship to either an indemnity payment, based upon the length of the relationship and the level of past or anticipated payments, or to a claim for *damages* attributed to the termination. In countries like France, a decision not to renew an agency contract is construed as a termination requiring remuneration. **European Union Directive 86/653** provides that agency contracts should provide for a minimum notice of termination. A reasonable notice period is one month per year of service. A commercial agent will be owed an indemnity upon termination to the extent that he has brought new customers to the principal or significantly increased the principal's volume of business.[23]

The EC Directive also allows national laws to provide for a damage claim to the agent, especially if at the time of termination the agent had not completely amortized his costs and expenses relative to the representation.[24] The best approach is to enter into a fixed term contract with no renewal options. As stated earlier, the contract should provide a detailed list of performance standards upon which termination for *just cause* may be based. Also, some country laws, as in Belgium and France, presume that the agent is an employee even if the contract designates the agent as an independent contractor. Therefore, the easiest way to avoid this presumption is to deal with agents who are artificial entities (corporations).[25]

National labor and employment laws will need to be checked for obligations of the principal pertaining to social security and other "employment-related" statutory requirements. Under Italian law, the principal and the agent must pay 5 percent each on all commissions paid to the national agency (ENASARCO) as social security contributions. The principal is legally obligated to withhold the agent's contribution and remit it to the agency, along with an amount to be used toward the **severance indemnity.** A certain percentage is paid on a sliding scale based on the amount of the commissions paid, ranging from 4 percent to 1 percent.

A **foreign consultant** is a variation of the foreign sales representative. The same issues of host country labor laws and agency termination laws apply to the consulting relationship. The **consulting contract** should be specific as to the scope of the engagement, and should emphasize the independent status of the consultant. A separate "independent contractor status clause" should be incorporated into the agreement. The factors often utilized in making the distinction between employee and independent contractor should be incorporated into this clause, including:

- the consultant is not an employee and is not entitled to any employee-type benefits
- the consultant is to perform its tasks based on its own discretion and skills and will be responsible for any acts or omissions
- the consultant is responsible for hiring any subagents or assistants
- the consultant provides its tools, equipment, and materials, and pays its own overhead expenses

The agreement should state that the services are being provided on a nonexclusive basis and that the principal takes no responsibility for the manner in which the consultant performs on the contract.

23. EC Directive 86/653, Article 17(2).
24. Ibid. at Article 17(3). The agent must notify its principal of a claim for indemnity or damages within one year from the date of termination. Ibid. at Article 17(5).
25. For example, in Belgium if the contract subordinates the agent to the authority of the principal, then there is a legal presumption that an employment relationship has been formed. However, this presumption can be overcome if the agent is a corporate entity.

THE DISTRIBUTION AGREEMENT

The distribution agreement is a type of commercial agency relationship. It is also an example of a common form of service contract. Engaging the services of a foreign distributor is the most important decision that an exporter of goods will make. Foreign exporting often rises or falls based upon the strength of the exporter-distributor relationship.[26] Importing goods to a foreign country is of little benefit unless the goods can be sold and delivered to consumers in an efficient manner. It is the job of the foreign distributor to get the goods to market.

Because of the differences in language, culture, and the legal treatment of foreign distributor relationships, it is important to negotiate a foreign distribution agreement that is detailed regarding the respective duties and responsibilities of the parties. Unlike the standard agency relationship where the sales contract is between the principal and the purchaser (consumer), the distributor generally sells the goods on its own account. The sales contract is between the distributor and the purchaser. Because of this, the foreign distributor is by necessity an independent contractor in relationship to the exporter or manufacturer.

The selection of a competent and trustworthy foreign distributor or agent is crucial. The U.S. Department of Commerce provides information on foreign distributors and agents through **Agent-Distributor Searches (ADS).** The U.S. International Trade Administration offers a fee-based service that locates foreign import agents and distributors on behalf of U.S. exporters. It also provides Customized Market Analysis (CMA) reports that identify potential representatives.

The International Chamber of Commerce's **Guide to Drafting International Distribution Agreements**[27] outlines the underlying risks of the distribution relationship and the ways to deal with such risks in the distribution contract. A brief review of this guide is a good starting point for analyzing this pivotal contractual relationship. *Distributor* is defined in the guide as "not a middleman, but a dealer who buys goods in order to resell them in his own name, even if he is often called an agent." Thus, calling a distributor an agent is a misnomer. In contrast, an agent is generally an independent contractor owing certain fiduciary obligations to the principal. It should be noted, however, that a distributor might act as both an agent and as a distributor.

The distributor's relationship with the manufacturer-exporter is purely contractual and is very much akin to a sale of goods transaction. However, it is a special kind of sales relationship because (1) the distributor often deals with the promotion and organization of distribution within its contractual territory, (2) generally the contractual territory is exclusive to the distributor, (3) the transaction is not one-shot but lasts for a certain duration, (4) there exists a certain level of loyalty, namely an obligation to refrain from competition, and (5) the relationship almost always relates to the distribution of brand-name products.

Before entering into an international distribution agreement it is imperative to research the law of the distributor's country in order to comply with mandatory legal provisions. Some countries like Saudi Arabia require distributors to be nationals and register as distributors with the government. Some countries, by statute or case law, require that the distribution agreement provide the distributor some

26. See generally Herold & Knoll, "Negotiating and Drafting International Distribution Agency and Representative Agreements: The United States Exporter's Perspective," 21 *International Lawyer* 939 (1987); King, "Legal Aspects of Appointment and Termination of Foreign Distributors and Representatives," 17 *Case Western Reserve Journal of International Law* 91 (1985); Saltoun & Spudis, "International Distribution and Sales Agency Agreements: Practical Guidelines for U.S. Exporters," 38 *Business Lawyer* 883 (1983).
27. ICC, GUIDE TO DRAFTING INTERNATIONAL DISTRIBUTION AGREEMENTS, ICC Pub. No. 441 (E) (1988).

minimal level of protection regarding issues of termination and compensation. In France, the case law is rich with instances where judges have ordered additional compensation to be paid by the principal when severing a distribution relationship. Germany recognizes a **goodwill indemnity** that is owed to the distributor upon the termination of the distribution agreement.

The exporter should include a clause requiring the distributor to use its best efforts to achieve maximum sales. The best efforts provision may also provide minimum sales quotas in order to meet the best efforts obligation. The "minimum sales quota" might trigger an exporter option to terminate the contract or to preclude a renewal of the contract. The exporter may want to place a clause in the agreement assigning the risk of products liability claims to the distributor, but foreign national law may impose that liability on both the manufacturer-exporter and the distributor. The parties may instead, agree to obtain a prescribed level of products liability insurance to protect them both against products liability risks.

Often the manufacturer will want to ensure that each of its distributors offers the same conditions of sale to their customers, especially regarding guarantees and after-sales service, but the validity of clauses that appear to entail restrictions regarding the types of customers to be solicited, resale pricing, and territorial restrictions is questionable under some national laws. For example, the laws of France, Germany, United Kingdom, and the Scandinavian countries should be closely checked especially with regards to the area of retail price maintenance.

The guide stresses how important it is for the distribution agreement to deal with the issue of changes in **key personnel.** If certain employees are considered essential, they should be recognized in the contract. The contract can then provide for termination in the event that essential persons cease to be associated with the distributor. In addition, in order to avoid the reach of evergreen statutes, the contract should specify specific commencement and expiration dates. Setting a fixed term for the agreement will help minimize the chances of large indemnity payments being owed under certain national laws. Also, renewals should be kept to a minimum. In order to minimize the size of indemnity payments, it is better to enter into an entirely new contract at the expiration of the first contract.

Foreign Competition Law

Most distribution agreements provide exclusive territories to the distributor; the exporter may be prohibited from selling products to customers who are likely to import them into the distributor's territory and the distributor will be prohibited from selling the products outside of its exclusive territory. The developing countries look with skepticism on any such restrictions and generally will not enforce restrictive contract provisions in their courts. Most developed countries allow the contracting parties full freedom to contract and will enforce most restrictive clauses. Under antitrust or competition laws, some forms of exclusivity may be deemed to be anticompetitive, and certain restrictions will be scrutinized.

EU Regulation 1983/83 deals with the legality of exclusive distribution agreements. For example, it generally disfavors clauses that prohibit a distributor from selling within the territory of another distributor. However, certain **block exemptions**[28] can be utilized to defend against such challenges. In addition, foreign com-

28. A block exemption is simply a statutory recognition that certain types of business practices are to be permitted even though they technically violate EU competition (antitrust) law. An example would be exclusive territories pertaining to automobile dealerships.

petition laws need to be researched to see if exclusivity in a distribution agreement will be enforceable.[29] Because of the complexity of foreign competition law, it is advisable to have a specialist review the distribution agreement.[30]

The manufacturer will often insert a clause that obligates the distributor to transmit orders from customers outside its territory to the manufacturer or a distributor within that territory. Such a provision is also likely to be held invalid under EU Regulation 1983/83. A clause prohibiting a distributor from openly soliciting outside its territory is likely to be upheld, however.

Price-fixing and **tying clauses** are those most likely to be held as illegal. For example, many national laws prohibit the principal or licensor from setting pricing guidelines, especially at the retail level. Tying clauses that require the distributor to purchase other items along with the licensed product are generally unenforceable. One exception is when tying products or services is needed to ensure the quality of the licensed or distributed product. In such cases, a requirement that the licensee purchase materials from certified suppliers is likely to be enforced.

Noncompetition clauses are also susceptible to nonenforcement. Generally, a distribution contract cannot prohibit the agent or representative from also selling the products of another company. The one major exception is that U.S. courts will allow such clauses in cases involving patented property rights where the distributor is given an exclusive license. Thus, one strategy to increase the chances of enforceability is to tie exclusivity to noncompetition. For example, the distributor can be given the right to sell the goods of a competitor but in doing so converts the distribution agreement from exclusive to nonexclusive.

LOGISTICAL SERVICES

An exporter must comply with foreign packing, labeling, and documentation requirements. Because of the complexity of these requirements, most exporters will enlist the services of freight forwarders and customs brokers. **Freight forwarders**[31] act as agents of the exporter and importer in transporting cargo worldwide and for importing the goods into a given country. Freight forwarders are familiar with import and export regulations, methods of shipping, and documentation requirements. They are also a good source for freight and insurance cost information. In a documentary transaction, the freight forwarder can be enlisted to review the letter of credit, bill of lading, and other documents. The freight forwarder can also help in the packaging and marking the goods for transport. The freight forwarder will be aware of the internationally recognized symbols for handling and shipping products of all kinds.

29. See, e.g., Jesse A. Finkelstein, "Legislative and Judicial Regulation of Exclusive Distribution Agreements in France," *International Lawyer* 539 (1981); S. Sharma & W. Morrison, "The Use of Local Representatives in Saudi Arabia," *International Lawyer* 453 (1977). It should be noted that these articles are somewhat dated and should be used only as general background reading.

30. Another source for nation-specific regulation of the distribution agreement is a series of articles found in *International Lawyer.* See, e.g., H.T. King, Jr., "Legal Aspects of Appointment and Termination of Foreign Distributors and Representatives," *International Lawyer* 91 (1985); T.W. Simon, "Termination of Sales Agents and Distributors in Belgium," *International Lawyer* 752 (1983); G. Vorbrugg & D.H. Mahler, "Agency and Distribution Agreements Under German Law," *International Lawyer* 607 (1985); David M. Dobson & Rita Gaudenzi, "Agency and Distribution Laws in Italy: Guidelines for the Foreign Principal," *International Lawyer* 997 (1986).

31. Most of the information that follows also applies to customs brokers. However, the services of the freight forwarder are broader in that a freight forwarder provides services pertaining to export requirements, transportation, and importation. The customs brokers expertise generally revolves around the government requirements for the importation of goods.

Law of Freight Forwarding

The freight forwarder plays a crucial role in the transportation of products under an international sales contract. The services provided by the freight forwarder and, to some extent, the customs broker have expanded in modern times. Traditionally they are engaged to assist merchants in preparing and booking the cargo for carriage. In some cases, freight forwarders act as agents for carriers, particularly liner shipping companies for carriage of goods by sea. Freight forwarding services normally include the clearance of goods for export and import. Also, freight forwarders have cooperating partners in other countries to whom instructions are given for the receipt of the cargo and for customs clearance.[32]

The freight forwarder also plays the important role of **cargo consolidator.** Most exporter shipments require booking only a portion of a ship's cargo space. The freight forwarder can obtain more reasonable shipment rates by consolidating the cargo of a number of its clients. In addition, the demands of international **multimodal transport**[33] have transformed the freight forwarder from a mere agent of the shipper to that of an operator with carrier liability. The role of the freight forwarder as a common carrier is recognized in Article 30 of the UCP. It allows freight forwarders to issue bills of lading if they are acting as a carrier or multimodal transport operator.

The multiple roles played by the freight forwarder lead to some ethical concerns. As the agent of the shipper, the freight forwarder is supposed to work on the shipper's behalf as an unbiased advisor,[34] but its multiple roles may generate temptations to give preferential treatment to certain customers or to work more in favor of the transport companies than the shipper. Thus, the shipper is best advised to perform independent checks on the services being provided.

ADVERTISING SERVICES AND LAW

National laws dealing with deceptive advertising vary in scope and enforcement. Because of cultural differences, an advertising campaign that is legal in one country may be illegal in another. Almost all developed countries possess laws that make illegal the use of misleading advertising.[35] Advertising laws are policed by administrative agencies, through private litigation, and via industry self-regulation. These three means of enforcement vary dramatically throughout the world. All three are utilized in the United States.

The **Federal Trade Commission (FTC)** regulates virtually all forms of advertising in the United States. It is empowered to prevent "unfair and deceptive practices."[36] Section 43(a) of the **Lanham Act**[37] created a private cause of action for anyone injured by false advertising.[38] There are also many examples of industry and

32. Jan Ramberg, *Unification of the Law of Freight Forwarding.*
33. For a discussion of "multimodal transport" see Chapter 10.
34. P.R. Murphy, J.M. Daley & P.K. Hall, "Transportation Ethics: A Comparison of Shipper and Carrier Perspectives," 63 *Journal of Transportation Law, Logistics & Policy* 370 (1996); Paul R. Murphy & James M. Daley, "Ethics and the International Freight Forwarder: User Perspectives," 65 *Journal of Transportation Law, Logistics & Policy* 95 (1998).
35. See, e.g., BARBARA S. BAUDOT, INTERNATIONAL ADVERTISING HANDBOOK (1989); Peter L. Tracey, "International Advertising: Regulatory Pitfalls for the Unwary Marketer," 7 *Dickinson Journal of International Law* 229 (1989); NORBERT REICH & HANS W. MICKLITZ, CONSUMER LEGISLATION IN THE EC COUNTRIES: A COMPARATIVE ANALYSIS, (1980).
36. 15 U.S.C. § 45(a)(1)(1982).
37. 15 U.S.C. 1125(a) (1988).
38. See generally Ross D. Petty, "Supplanting Government Regulation with Competitor Lawsuits: The Case of Controlling False Advertising," 25 *Indiana Law Review* 351 (1991).

media self-regulation. One example is the National Advertising Division of the Council of Better Business Bureaus. In contrast, there is no national self-regulation in Saudi Arabia. Instead, a number of agencies, including the Organization for the Prevention of Sins and Order of Good Deeds, seek the enforcement of Islamic laws.[39] In Italy, "industry self-regulation deals with most of the country's advertising disputes."[40]

http://

American Association of Advertising Agencies: **http://www.aaaa.org**; American Advertising Federation: **http://www.aaf.org**.

Civil law countries, including Germany, "rely on advertising law that authorizes private litigation to control misleading advertising."[41] The Scandinavian countries make use of the consumer ombudsman to enact advertising guidelines and to resolve disputes.[42] Because of the vast differences in advertising law enforcement, it is important for the international entrepreneur to seek local counsel before embarking on a marketing campaign. The local counsel can provide information on the substantive law of advertising. However, most exporters will use private advertisement agencies to handle their marketing campaigns. At a minimum, the prospective agency should be a member of that country's professional advertisement association. For example, in Chile most advertising agencies are members of the *Asociacion Chilena de Agencias de Publicidad* (Chilean Association of Advertising Agencies, ACHAP).

Businesses may attempt to minimize the risks of false or improper advertising through insurance. Although insurance is unlikely to protect from government prosecution, it will minimize their exposure to private litigation. The *Heritage Mutual Insurance* case that follows illustrates some of the issues created by the intersection of advertising and insurance law. This case explains the important concepts of **advertising injury** and the **duty to defend.**

Heritage Mutual Insurance v. Advanced Polymer Tech.

97 F. Supp. 2d 913 (S.D. Ind. 2000)

Barker, Chief Judge. This case represents another installment in the ongoing debate about the meaning of "advertising injury," a popular phrase used to describe a type of insurance coverage provided in standard versions of commercial general liability insurance policies issued since the 1970s. Plaintiff, Heritage Mutual Insurance Company ("Heritage"), filed a complaint seeking a declaratory judgment that it has no duty to defend or to indemnify its insured, Advanced Polymer Technology (APT). The policy at issue here, known as the Commercial General Liability ("CGL") form, represents a 1986 version written by the Insurance Services Organization ("ISO"), a for-profit private trade organization that generates standard insurance forms for use by its clients, mainly insurance companies.

While some insurers may alter the forms they receive from ISO and tailor the standard language based upon the unique coverage requested by their insured, insurers often adopt the ISO forms verbatim. ISO periodically revises and clarifies the coverage offered by its standard insurance forms and alters, deletes or adds language accordingly. For instance, the 1998 ISO CGL policy form modified the 1986 version. Coverage "B" of the CGL policy, entitled "Personal and Advertising Injury Liability,"

39. Mushtaq Luqmani, "Advertising in Saudi Arabia: Content and Regulation," 6 *International Marketing Review* 59 (1989).
40. Ross D. Petty, "Advertising Law and Social Issues: The Global Perspective," 17 *Suffolk Transnational Law Review* 309, 319 (1994).
41. Ibid. at 318. See also Warren S. Grimes, "Control of Advertising in the United States and Germany: Volkswagen Has a Better Idea," 84 *Harvard Law Review* 1769 (1971).
42. J.J. Boddewyn, "The Swedish Consumer Ombudsman System of Advertising Self-Regulation," 19 *Journal of Consumer Affairs* 140 (1985).

provided in its "Insuring" clause that Heritage would insure APT for any "advertising injury caused by an offense committed in the course of advertising APT's goods, products or services." The policy defined "advertising injury" as injury arising out of one or more of the following offenses: (a) oral or written publication of material that slanders or libels a person or organization or disparages a person's or organization's goods, products or services; (b) oral or written publication of material that violates a person's right of privacy; (c) misappropriation of advertising ideas or style of doing business; or (d) infringement of copyright, title, or slogan.

One of the policy's coverage exclusions, the "first publication" exclusion, provides that insurance coverage does not apply to "advertising injury . . . arising out of material whose first publication took place before the beginning of the policy period." Additionally, the policy established Heritage's "duty to defend any suit seeking those damages." Under Indiana law, a contract for insurance is subject to the same rules of interpretation as are other contracts. The insured is required to prove that her claims fall within the coverage provisions of her policy, but the insurer bears the burden of proving specific exclusions or limitations to policy coverage.

The insurer's duty to defend, which is broader than its duty to indemnify, is determined by the nature of the claim in the underlying complaint, not its merits. An insurer must defend an action even if only a small portion of the conduct alleged in the complaint falls within the scope of the insurance policy. The intentions of the parties to a contract are to be determined by the "four-corners" of the document. When an insurance contract contains an ambiguity, it should be strictly construed against the insurance company. Yet, when the underlying factual basis of the complaint, even if proved true, would not result in liability under the insurance policy, the insurance company can properly refuse to defend.

Environ, a patent owner, claims that APT willfully infringed on its patents. It also accuses APT of "federal unfair competition" under the Lanham Act by contending that APT made "false and misleading statements as to the creation or ownership" of the piping product "in its application for a patent." The parties have not contended that the patent application constituted an advertisement or an item "in the course of advertising" as required by the Heritage-APT policy. Environ alleges that Defendant APT's marketing of its POLY-TECH piping system as 'patent pending' creates a cloud on its ownership of the Invention, thereby discouraging investment in or purchase of its products.

We find it implausible that the parties would have intended that direct and induced patent infringement would be covered under the policy without expressly listing those offenses in the phrase "infringement of copyright, title, or slogan." Also, the insurer had no duty to defend the insured since the plaintiff's unfair competition and Lanham Act claims did not qualify as allegations of misappropriation of advertising ideas or style of doing business. The allegation that the insured engaged in unfair competition by misappropriating trade secrets does not allege misappropriation of advertising ideas or styles of doing business as such.

APT claims in abbreviated fashion that Environ's allegations fall within the "disparagement category" of advertising injury offenses. Importantly, Environ never contends that APT's advertisements mention Environ, compare the products of the respective companies, or discredit or denigrate Environ's piping products. While we believe that some direct reference to the competitor's product is necessary to fall within the plain meaning of "disparage," we also do not view Environ's allegations as resulting in a reasonable claim of implied disparagement either. The phrase "patent pending" signifies nothing about the quality or state of Environ's product, as the phrase means exactly what it says—a patent is pending.

Heritage's conduct strikes us as sufficiently reasonable under the circumstances of this case, and, as it turns out, correct as a matter of legal contract interpretation. Heritage retained coverage counsel, who clearly examined the insurance policy provisions at issue and the allegations in the underlying complaint. The reasons supplied for denial of coverage were rational and understandable. We hold that Heritage has no duty to defend its insured because the allegations in Environ's complaint do not constitute advertising injury offenses.

Case Highlights

- Insurance Services Organization ("ISO") is a trade association that develops standard insurance forms and clauses.
- "Advertising injury" is a type of insurance coverage provided in standard versions of commercial general liability insurance policies (CGL).
- Under insurance law, the insured is required to prove that her claims fall within the coverage provision of her policy, but the insurer bears the burden of proving specific exclusions or limitations to policy coverage.
- The insurer's duty to defend is broader than its duty to indemnify.
- When an insurance contract contains an ambiguity, it is strictly construed against the insurance company.

CROSS-BORDER SECURITY OFFERINGS

Companies raise capital in a number of ways including borrowing from banks and accepting investments by venture capitalists. The most common way of raising capital is to sell either debt instruments (bonds) or equity instruments (stock shares). The advantage of selling shares in the company is that it raises capital without incurring a debt obligation. From the investor's perspective an equity investment, especially in a new company, is made in the hope that the company will be profitable. The internationalization of the capital markets has been one of the major trends in the business world.[43] It is not uncommon for even small or medium investors to allocate a portion of their portfolios to foreign securities. From a legal perspective, this poses questions as to the enforcement and regulation of international securities transactions.

The key issue with the international sale and purchase of securities is how such offerings are to be regulated. Since there is no international policing institution, regulation comes through the enforcement of national regulatory laws. In the United States, the **Securities and Exchange Commission (SEC)** administers federal securities laws. Can the SEC regulate security offerings originating in a foreign country? Can U.S. security laws be applied extraterritorially? It has been deemed fair by U.S. courts "to demand compliance with U.S. laws and regulations of any person or entity who has purposely made a connection with the United States for the sale or purchase of a security, and its conduct has the *effect* of undermining the stability and fair operation of the securities markets within the United States."[44]

The extraterritorial application of U.S. securities laws follows a standard two-prong test. First, the foreign parties must have had the intent or purpose of selling their securities in the U.S. marketplace. Second, the alleged foreign illegal activities are likely to have an *effect* within the United States. The second prong is commonly referred to as the **effects test.** The effects test has been used to determine the extraterritorial applicability of many U.S. laws such as discrimination, antitrust, and tort law. The effects test stands for the principle that the exercise of jurisdiction is appropriate where the illegal activity abroad injures someone within the United States. However, the effects test does not justify the exertion of SEC jurisdiction where no fraud is committed within the United States and the securities are purchased outside the United States.

Offshore security offerings are those in which the offer to sell is not made to a person in the United States or when a security is sold on a foreign stock exchange. In order to avoid U.S. securities laws a company can take steps to prevent the solicitation of persons within the United States. However, the development of securities transactions over the Internet challenges a company's ability to avoid SEC jurisdiction.

An offering on the Internet not intended for U.S. investors may still be subject to SEC enforcement actions. The global nature of the Internet can lead to the conclusion that such offers are being made "in the United States" and therefore must be registered with the SEC. The SEC has recently provided guidance, in its "Statement of the Commission Regarding the Use of Internet Web Sites to Offer Securities, Solicit Transactions, or Advertise Investment Services Offshore," for those wanting to avoid U.S. securities laws in offshore offerings. It suggests that

43. See generally FERRERA, LICHTENSTEIN, REDER, AUGUST & SCHIANO, CYBERLAW at Chapter 7 (2001).

44. Sharon Drew, "Extraterritoriality of the United States Securities and Exchange Commission, 20 *The Comparative Law Yearbook of International Business* 231, 232 (1998).

the offering party take reasonable precautions to guard against making sales to U.S. persons and to place a disclaimer on the offer stating that it is not intended for persons in the United States.

The **International Organization of Securities Commissions (IOSCO)** has made it a goal to achieve the comparability of information required under national securities laws in order to facilitate cross-border offerings and listings by multinational securities issuers. In order to achieve this goal, IOSCO has proposed the development of a generally accepted body of disclosure standards that could be used in a uniform disclosure statement for cross-border offerings and listings. In 1998, IOSCO published its "International Disclosure Standards for Cross-Border Offerings and Initial Listings by Foreign Issuers." A company planning to sell shares internationally should review these standards when preparing required prospectuses and registration statements.

A problem with international standards is that they fail to provide a definition of **materiality,** which is crucial in determining the accuracy of documents and statements. All countries require that a company or issuer disclose all material information. However, the definition of materiality varies from country to country. In the United States, the Supreme Court in *TSC Industries, Inc. v. Northway, Inc.*[45] defined materiality as follows: "An omitted fact is material if there is a substantial likelihood that a reasonable shareholder or investor would have considered it important." In Quebec, Canada, materiality is considered as something likely to have significant influence on the value or market price of the securities of a reporting issuer.

The Stock Exchange of Hong Kong's Listing Rules defines *materiality* as the disclosing of information "necessary to enable an investor to make an informed assessment of the activities, assets and liabilities, financial position, management, and prospects of the issuer." In contrast, the European Union does not use the concept of "material" and therefore does not provide any definition of materiality. Japanese disclosure rules provide numerical guidelines for determining materiality.

INTERNATIONALIZATION OF ACCOUNTING AND TAXATION

The internationalization of business has placed pressure upon the accounting profession to provide necessary support services.[46] Accounting services, as with most professional services, can be internationalized on a number of fronts. First, domestic regulations can be modified to take into account the special issues of cross-border transactions. Second, international standards can be enumerated for professional services. Third, countries can recognize each others' professional qualifications and national standards.[47] The adoption of harmonized international standards provides the greatest possibility for increased trade in international

45. 426 U.S. 438 (1976).
46. The importance of liberalizing trade in accounting services has been recognized under the WTO Agreements. The WTO's Working Party on Professional Services (WPPS) has focused its attention on the internationalization in accounting services.
47. The problem of recognition is especially acute in former nonmarket countries. It was not until 1996 that Russian accountants first received national qualifications of professional accountants. In the substantive area, Russia has adopted international accounting practices, but some idiosyncrasies remain. For example, the fundamental accounting assumption that financial statements are reviewed so that they are a "true and fair view of financial position, performance, and changes in the financial position of a company" is replaced with a lower threshold that the financial statements are "satisfactorily trustworthy" or *dostovernost. Trustworthiness* is defined as compliance with law and regulations. PRICE WATERHOUSE, DOING BUSINESS IN RUSSIA 104 (1997).

accounting services. The areas where international accounting services are needed include transfer pricing, currency translation,[48] and joint venture accounting.[49]

Transfer pricing refers to a method of tax avoidance. In structuring contracts between itself and its foreign subsidiaries, a corporation will often attempt to recognize or transfer any profits to subsidiaries located in low-tax countries. The U.S. Internal Revenue Service requires that such intra-company transactions be conducted at *arms length.* Contract prices between affiliated companies are to be set at market or reasonable prices. Therefore, multinational corporations need to develop a transfer pricing policy that will be generally accepted in the countries that they do business in. This is needed in order to avoid complicated tax disputes and the potential for double taxation. Tax planning should be done on a country-by-country basis. For example, the social security rates in EU countries range from 20 percent to as high as 40 percent. Some guidance can be obtained through the use of recently developed guidelines for transfer pricing and documentary requirements produced by the OECD.

http://
Association of International Accountants: **http://www.aia.org.uk**.

One approach for taxing multinational corporations or cross-border business transactions is through **unitary taxation.** It is an approach in which corporate profits are apportioned to the different taxing authorities using a formula based on sales, payroll, and property within each jurisdiction. Transfer pricing issues become more confusing in the growing area of international Internet or electronic commerce. The U.S. policy on Internet commerce, as stated in a 1997 release titled "A Framework for Electronic Commerce,"[50] adopts the following principles regarding the issue of taxation of Internet commerce:

- No tax system should discriminate among types of commerce.
- The system should be transparent.
- The system should accommodate tax systems of other countries.

Currently, the two most influential bodies in the movement to harmonize accounting standards and financial statements are the International Accounting Standards Committee (IASC) and the International Organization of Securities Commissions. The diversity of accounting practices throughout the world is an encumbrance to the development of truly global capital markets. Companies currently wishing to raise capital in foreign markets have to contend with costly and complicated national disclosure and reporting requirements. The ability to provide comparable financial statements to be used in cross-border security offerings would significantly decrease the number and types of required filings.

The EU Commission has sought to harmonize reporting requirements at the regional level. At the international level, IASC has developed a number of **International Accounting Standards (IAS).** IOSCO has deferred to IASC by accepting IAS and has focused its attention on developing a common international prospectus that could be used for listing and filing in all exchanges. These efforts will continue and are essential to further enhance the free flow of capital and related services.

48. Currency translation is the process of expressing amounts denominated in one currency in terms of another currency by use of an exchange rate. Translation adjustments result from the process of translating financial statements from the entity's functional currency (primary currency or currency in which its books are maintained) into the reporting currency. See Statement of Financial Accounting Standards, No. 52 (1981). The translation risk of currency devaluation needs to be addressed on both the management and accounting sides. Translation exposure may result in lower reported earnings. See, e.g., C. O. Houston, "Translation Exposure Hedging Post SFAS No. 52," 2 *Journal of International Management & Accounting* 145 (1990).
49. See also International Federation of Accountants (IFAC): **http://ifac.org**.
50. William J. Clinton & Albert Gore, *A Framework for Electronic Commerce* (1997).

Key Terms

advertising injury, 359
agent, 343
Agent-Distributor Searches, 355
block exemption, 356
cargo consolidator, 358
commercial agency, 349
Commercial Agency—Guide for the Drawing Up of Contracts, 352
compulsory hiring, 346
consultation procedure, 346
consulting contract, 354
conversion contract, 345
Council on Services, 340
Customs Modernization Act of 1993, 339
dependent agent, 343
dismissal for cause, 346
duty to defend, 359
effects test, 361
employment as a property right, 344
employment at will doctrine, 344
EU Directive on Distance Contracts, 340
EU Regulation 1983/83, 356
European Union Directive 86/653, 354
European Works Council Directive, 348
evergreen statutes, 350
Federal Trade Commission (FTC), 358
foreign consultant, 354
foreign sales representative, 343
Framework Agreement, 339
freight forwarder, 357
French Labor Code, 345
General Agreement on Trade in Services (GATS), 338
goodwill indemnity, 356
Guide to Drafting International Distribution Agreements, 355
hiring by number, 346
hiring list, 346
ILO Declaration on Fundamental Principles and Rights at Work, 348
indemnity in lieu of notice, 346
independent agent, 343
independent contractor, 343
International Accounting Standards (IAS), 363
International Labor Organization (ILO), 347
International Organization of Securities Commissions (IOSCO), 362
key personnel, 356
labor clause, 347
Lanham Act, 358
lifetime employment, 344
materiality, 362
mixed sales, 337
most-favored-nation, 340
multimodal transport, 358
Mutual Recognition Agreements, 338
national treatment, 340
noncompetition clause, 357
nonpartnership clause, 349
Office of Service Industries, 339
Organization for Economic Cooperation and Development (OECD), 337
price-fixing clause, 357
principal, 343
recognition requirements, 340
redundancy, 345
Russian Labor Code, 346
Securities and Exchange Commission (SEC), 361
severance indemnity, 354
sexual harassment policy, 344
termination clause, 350
Trans-Atlantic Business Dialogue, 338
transfer pricing, 363
transparency, 340
tying clause, 357
unitary taxation, 363
work for hire clause, 349
Works Council, 344

Chapter Problems

1. The chapter introduced the Japanese tradition of lifetime employment. Research the effects of the prolonged economic recession of the 1990s in Japan and see how it has impacted this tradition. Is the notion of lifetime employment still an apt description of the Japanese employment relationship? If not, how is it different? How does it still differ from the employment-at-will system found in the United States?

2. Review the following consulting agreement. What are the purposes of the different clauses? Would these clauses be enforceable in the United States and in the European Union? How would you improve this agreement? How would you make this agreement more pro-principal or more pro-agent?

CONSULTING AGREEMENT

This Agreement dated April 11, 2001, is made by and between Joe "Hot Shot" Muldune of Menton, France ("Consultant"), and Gator Exporting of Gainesville, Florida ("Company"). The above parties agree as follows:

1. Services. The company employs the Consultant to perform certain consulting services. The Consultant will consult with the officers and employees of the Company concerning matters relating to the selling, marketing, and advertising of Company's products in the country of France.

2. Term. The agreement shall begin on June 1, 2001, and terminate on May 30, 2004. Either party may cancel this agreement on thirty (30) days' notice to the other party in writing, by certified mail or personal delivery.

3. Time Devoted by Consultant. It is anticipated that the Consultant will spend approximately 35 hours per week in fulfilling his obligations under this agreement. The amount of time may vary from week to week. However, the Consultant will devote a minimum of 100 hours per month to its duties in accordance with this agreement.

4. Place of Services. The Consultant will perform services at a location of Consultant's discretion.

5. Compensation. The Consultant will be paid at the rate of $125 per hour of work performed. However, the Consultant will be paid a minimum of $15,000 per month regardless of the time actually spent. The Consultant will send an itemized statement, on a monthly basis, setting forth the services and time rendered. The Company shall remit payment within 15 days of the receipt of each itemized statement.

6. Independent Contractor. The Company and Consultant agree that the Consultant is being hired as an independent contractor. Accordingly, the Consultant shall be responsible for payment of all taxes arising out of the Consultant's activities, including but not limited to income tax, social security tax, and unemployment insurance taxes.

7. Confidential Information. The Consultant agrees that any information received from the Company which concerns the personal, financial, or other affairs of the Company will be treated in full confidence and will not be disclosed to any other persons or companies.

8. Subcontractors. The Company may from time to time request that the Consultant arrange for the services of third parties. The Company will pay all costs to the Consultant but in no event shall the Consultant employ others without the prior authorization of the Company.

IT IS HEREBY AGREED THIS 5th day of May, 2001

____

____

Joe Muldane Gator Exporting

Internet Exercises

1. It is estimated that the European Union countries are responsible for 26 percent of the total global trade in services (43 percent if trade between EU members is included). The EU Commission has established a business-driven European services network. Review the EU web site at **http://gats-info.eu.int** for information on this network.

2. The most recognized authority on international labor standards is the International Labor Organization (ILO). Review the ILO web site at **http://www.ilo.org** and become familiar with its standards and its current activities.

3. Review the following web sites promoting good working conditions and encouraging consumers to boycott companies who allegedly do not respect workers' rights: Corpwatch at **http://www.corpwatch.org**; The Maquila Solidarity Network at **http://www.maquilasolidarity.org**; Global Exchange at **http://www.globalexchange.org/economy/corporations/**; and Solidarmonde at **http://www.solidarmonde.fr**.

4. Research some of the following industry organization web sites for information on exporting services in those specific sectors.

- *Management and Public Relations:* Public Relations Society of America at **http://www.prsa.org**; Society for Human Resources Management at **http://www.shrm.org**.
- *Insurance Services:* American Insurance Association at **http://www.aiadc.org**.
- *Information Technology:* International Federation for Information Processing at **http://www.ifip.or.at**; Society for Information Management at **http://www.simnet.org**.
- *Healthcare:* Healthcare Information and Management Systems Society at **http://www.himss.org**.
- *Franchising:* International Franchise Association at **http://www.franchise.org**.
- *Export Services:* Assist International at **http://www.assist-intl.com**.
- *Environmental Technologies:* National Association of Environmental Professionals at **http://www.naep.org**.
- *Banking and Financial Services:* Financial Management Association International at **http://www.fma.org**; International Society of Financiers at **http://www.insofin.com**.

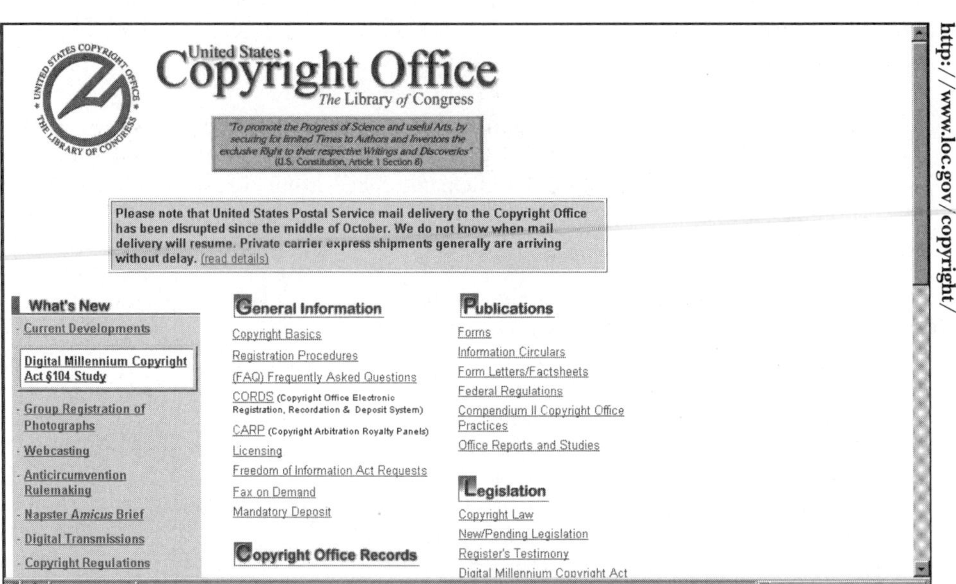

http://www.loc.gov/copyright/

Chapter 13
Law of Intellectual Property Rights

A company may find that building international recognition for a brand is expensive. Protection for brand names varies from one country to another and, in some developing countries, barriers to the use of foreign brands or trademarks may exist. In other countries, piracy of a company's brand names and counterfeiting of its products are widespread. To protect its products and brand names, a company must comply with local laws on patents, copyrights, and trademarks. The rights protected under these statutes are generically referred to as intellectual property rights.[1]

Intellectual property refers to a broad collection of rights relating to such matters as:

1. Other countries of the world often refer to such property under the term *industrial property rights.*

- Works of authorship protected under copyright law
- Product marks, symbols, and trade names protected under trademark law
- Inventions protected under patent law
- Confidential information and methods of doing business protected as trade secrets or by unfair competition laws
- Specialized creations, such as semiconductor chips and mask works, protected by newer statutory rights[2]

No international treaty completely defines these types of intellectual property, so the intellectual property owner needs to refer to national laws to confirm its rights and the means of protecting those rights.

To best understand the problems of protecting intellectual property internationally it is important to understand the basic intellectual property principles common to most legal systems. In this text, a brief review of the intellectual property law of the United States will be the starting point. The intellectual property law of the United States is the most protective in the world. U.S. law provides four general types of intellectual property protection: (1) trademark, (2) copyright, (3) patent, and (4) trade secrets.

Federal statutory law protects primarily the first three, while trade secrets are protected under state laws. **Trademark law** protects words, names, and other symbols used to identify a company's goods and distinguish them from those manufactured by others. Unlike patent and copyright protection, trademark protection can be derived from both federal and state law. For the maximum amount of protection, however, the trademark must be registered in the U.S. Patent and Trademark Office. As long as the trademark does not become generic, the trademark may be renewed perpetually.

http://

General information web sites on intellectual property law: Emory IP Law at **http://www.law.emory.edu/LAW/refdesk/subject/intellectual.html**, LII Intellectual Property Materials at **http://www.law.cornell.edu/topics/topic2.html#intellectual property**, and Hieros Gamos IP Law at **http://www.hg.org/intell.html**.

Federal **copyright law** protects works of original authorship from unauthorized duplication, modification, or distribution. Mere creation of the work results in copyright protection. However, placing a copyright notice on the work and registering it with the Copyright Office provides more complete protection.

Patent law protects inventions that are "novel, useful, and non-obvious." Federal law lists a number of statutory categories of *patentable* subject matter including machines, manufactured articles, processes, and compositions of materials.

A **trade secret** is any device or information that is used in a business and gives its owner an advantage over its competitors. Trade secrets law provides for perpetual protection, unless the protected information becomes publicly known. The next section will review the major tenets of these areas of U.S. law for three purposes: First, to alert the reader to the major issues and concepts found in intellectual property protection. Second, as a basis to compare similar international and foreign laws. Third, the shortcoming of intellectual property laws, especially in the international arena, underscores the importance of transfer and licensing agreements presented in Chapter 14.

INTELLECTUAL PROPERTY RIGHTS IN THE UNITED STATES

The United States provides a wide range of protection for intellectual property, including patents, trademarks, service marks, copyrights, trade secrets, and

2. Semiconductor mask works or integrated circuit layout designs registrations protect the mask works embodied in semiconductor chip products. The Semiconductor Chip Protection Act of 1984 provides the owner of a mask work with the exclusive right to reproduce, import, and distribute such works for a period of 10 years.

semiconductor mask works. Many businesses, particularly high-technology firms, publishers, chemical and pharmaceutical firms, recording companies, and computer software companies depend heavily on the protection afforded their creative products and processes. This section will review the four major areas of protection—trademark, copyright, patent, and trade secrets—found in U.S. law.

Trademark Protection

A trademark is any word, name, symbol, or device or any combination that identifies goods and distinguishes them from those manufactured or sold by others.[3] Trademarks are derived from their *commercial use* in order to identify goods and are protected by registration and filing at state and federal levels, as well as through international treaties and conventions. The federal law that deals with trademark issues is the **Lanham Act** or **Trademark Act.**[4]

A trademark or service mark registered with the U.S. Patent and Trademark Office remains in force for 10 years from the date of registration and may be renewed for successive periods of 10 years, provided the mark continues to be used and has not been previously canceled or surrendered. A **service mark** is a name, phrase, or other device used to identify and distinguish the services of the provider.

http://

The Publishing Law Center—"The Nuts and Bolts of Federal Trademark Registration": **http://www.publaw.com/bolts.html**. The Publishing Law Center maintains a database of legal articles giving brief explanations of important intellectual property terms. These articles will be cited often throughout the chapter.

To prove trademark infringement under U.S. law a party must prove that another's use of the registered mark is likely to cause consumer confusion regarding the source of the product or service. A number of factors are used to determine the likelihood of confusion, including:

- degree of similarity between the marks
- the intent of the alleged infringer
- the similarity of use of the two products or services
- similarity in the marketing of the goods or services
- the degree of care likely to be exercised by the consumer or purchaser
- evidence of actual confusion
- the strength of the registered mark[5]

The *Best Cellars v. Grape Finds* case explores the above factors used in making the determination of likelihood of confusion. The case involves the application of trademark protection to **trade dress.** Trade dress refers to the general way a product, service, or business is packaged or presented to the public. The case also serves to highlight the distinction between legally protected trademarks and unprotected **generic marks.**

3. The material in this and the next two sections was taken from the Trade Data Bank, U.S. Dept of Commerce.

4 The Lanham Act prohibits three forms of unfair competition related to trademark infringement: (1) false advertising, (2) passing off, and (3) false designation of place of origin. The Lanham Act defines *false advertising* as the use of a "false or misleading description of fact, or false or misleading representation of fact in commercial advertising or promotion which misrepresents the nature, characteristics, qualities, or geographic origin of his or another person's goods, services, or commercial activities." The statement must be literally false or likely to confuse or deceive a purchaser.

It is not required that a mark be registered in order to be able to bring a *passing off* or *false designation of origin* claim. In order to prove "passing off" the plaintiff need prove two things. First, she must show an association of origin by the consumer between the mark and the first user of the product. Second, she must prove that there is a likelihood of consumer confusion between the trademarked good or service and the infringer's good or service.

5. See, e.g., First Savings Bank v. First Bank System, Inc., 101 F.3d 645 (10th Cir. 1996).

Best Cellars Inc. v. Grape Finds at Dupont, Inc.

90 F. Supp. 2d 431 (S.D.N.Y. 2000)

Sweet, District Judge. Plaintiff Best Cellars, Inc. ("Best Cellars") has moved for a preliminary injunction to enjoin defendants Grape Finds at Dupont from infringing on various intellectual property rights claimed by Best Cellars under the Lanham Act. This action presents difficult issues, particularly with respect to the law of trade dress protection, itself a complex and shifting field of judicial interpretation. The action involves a unique concept, the retail sale of wine by taste, captured and exemplified in the particular trade dress of the Best Cellars stores. It presents the tension between the protection of certain intellectual property and free and open competition.

Best Cellars operates retail wine stores in New York, Brookline, and Seattle. Joshua Wesson, an internationally recognized wine expert, founded the store. In the early 1990s, he began to think about developing a new kind of retail wine store where people who knew little or nothing about wine could feel as comfortable when shopping as wine connoisseurs, and in which the "wine by style" concept could be implemented. The name "Best Cellars" came to him in 1993. Wesson spent considerable time before and during the design phase of the first Best Cellars store refining the "wine by style" concept.

Wesson eventually reduced the "world of wine" to eight taste categories: sparkling wines, light-, medium-, and full-bodied white wines, light-, medium-, and full-bodied red wines, and dessert wines. A principal reason Wesson reduced the world of wine to eight taste categories was in order to demystify wine for casual, non-connoisseur purchasers who might be intimidated purchasing wine in a traditional wine store, where wines are customarily organized by grape type and place of origin.

The design for the first Best Cellars retail store—on the Upper East Side in Manhattan—evolved to contain the following elements: (1) For each of the eight taste categories in the Best Cellars system, a corresponding color and a graphic image (an "icon-identifier") both to evoke and to reinforce the sensory associations of each category. (2) A display bottle for each wine stands upright on a stainless-steel wire pedestal so that the label is viewable by the customer. (3) Under each display bottle, at eye-level, is a "shelf-talker": a 4" × 4" information card providing the name of the wine, its vintage, a five- or six-line description of its taste, the type of grape from which it is made, its place of origin, the foods which the wine would complement, and its price. (4) The racking system, which is patented by Wesson, is lit from behind, which causes the bottles to glow.

The Grape Finds story begins with Mazur, who while at Columbia Business School discovered the Best Cellars New York store, which he has visited at least ten times. The Grape Finds store opened in Washington, D.C., on December 3, 1999. The store possessed many similarities to the Best Cellars store. The display is organized according to eight taste categories. As with Best Cellars, Grape Finds assigned to each taste category a corresponding color and icon-identifier. Moreover, lights above the racks are directed down causing them to glow. As in Best Cellars, beneath the racks are storage cabinets, creating the same visual look.

Section 43(a) of the Lanham Act provides in pertinent part that:

Any person who in connection with any goods or services, uses any word, term, name, symbol, or device, or any combination *thereof, which is likely to cause confusion, or to deceive as to the affiliation or connection, of such person with another person, shall be liable in a civil action.*

Trade dress has a broad meaning, and includes "all elements making up the total visual image by which a product is presented to customers as defined by its overall composition and design, including size, shape, color, texture, and graphics." For example, the Supreme Court in the *Two Pesos* case upheld a federal district court's finding that a Mexican restaurant was entitled to protection under § 43(a) for a trade dress consisting of a festive eating atmosphere having interior dining and patio areas decorated with artifacts, bright colors, paintings, and murals.

The public policy rationale for trade dress protection is explained by the Supreme Court as follows: "Protection of trade dress, no less than of trademarks, serves the [Lanham] Act's purpose to secure to the owner of the mark the goodwill of his business and to protect the ability of consumers to distinguish among competing producers." To establish a claim of trade dress infringement under § 43(a), a plaintiff must demonstrate (1) "that its trade dress is either inherently distinctive or that it has acquired distinctiveness through a secondary meaning," and (2) "that there is a likelihood of confusion between defendant's trade dress and plaintiff's."

Best Cellars' Trade Dress Is Inherently Distinctive

Trade dress is classified on a spectrum of increasing distinctiveness as generic, descriptive, suggestive, or arbitrary/fanciful. Suggestive and arbitrary or fanciful trade dress is deemed inherently distinctive. A descriptive trade dress may be found inherently distinctive if the plaintiff establishes that its mark has acquired secondary meaning giving it distinctiveness to the consumer. Under this standard, many trade dresses are likely to be found to be inherently distinctive. The Best Cellars stores look like no other wine stores. The essence of the look is the "wall of wine," with color-coded, iconographic wall signs identifying eight taste categories.

Substantial Likelihood of Confusion

Courts generally apply an eight-factor test to determine the likelihood of confusion between the trade dress of two competitors: (1) the strength of the plaintiff's trade dress, (2) the similarity between the two trade dress, (3) the proximity of the products in the marketplace, (4) the likelihood that the prior owner will bridge the gap between the products, (5) evidence of actual confusion, (6) the defendant's bad faith, (7) the quality of defendant's product, and (8) the sophistication of the relevant consumer group. While the factors are meant to be a guide, the inquiry ultimately hinges on whether an ordinarily prudent person would be confused as to the source of the allegedly infringing product.

First, the strength of a trade dress or trademark is measured in terms of its distinctiveness, "or more precisely, by its tendency to identify the goods sold as emanating from a particular source." For instance, generic marks are not entitled to protection under the Lanham Act. "Marks that are descriptive are entitled to protection only if they have acquired a 'secondary meaning' in the marketplace." Under this standard, Best Cellars' trade dress is quite strong.

Second, as described above, the dominant visual element of both the Best Cellars and the Grape Finds stores is the wall of wine. The evidence demonstrates a significant probability that ordinarily prudent customers in the Grape Finds store will be confused as to whether they are, in fact, in a Best Cellars store.

Third, "the 'proximity-of-the-products' inquiry concerns whether and to what extent the two products compete with each other." The products here are indisputably similar: value-priced bottles of wine. The class of customers is nearly identical.

Fourth, this factor applies when the first user sells its products in one field and the second user sells its products in a closely related field, into which the first user might expand, thereby "bridging the gap." Here, there is no gap to bridge: Best Cellars and Grape Finds sell the same products in the same field.

Fifth, Best Cellars has presented some evidence of actual confusion, but no survey or systematic research was conducted. However, it is black letter law that actual confusion need not be shown to prevail under the Lanham Act, since actual confusion is very difficult to prove and the Act requires only a likelihood of confusion as to source.

Sixth, this factor looks to whether the defendant adopted its dress with the intention of capitalizing on plaintiff's reputation and goodwill. Given the overwhelming evidence of copying of so many aspects of the Best Cellars business, it strains credulity to think that the reproduction of the trade dress—in particular, the "wall of wine"—in the Grape Finds store was not meant to capitalize on the reputation, goodwill, and any confusion between Grape Finds and Best Cellars.

Seventh, no evidence has been presented that Grape Finds' products are inferior to those of Best Cellars. This factor therefore favors Grape Finds.

Eighth, this factor also favors Best Cellars. Both stores are specifically targeting non-sophisticated wine purchasers, and the overwhelming majority of wines sold in each store are priced at the lower end of the spectrum.

As set forth above, in this case seven of the eight factors weigh in favor of Best Cellars. This is not a case requiring a careful balancing of the factors. Some factors weigh more strongly than others, but there is no doubt that, taken together, Best Cellars has made a substantial showing of a likelihood of confusion between its trade dress and that of Grape Finds. Because Best Cellars has demonstrated a substantial likelihood that (1) its trade dress is distinctive, and (2) that there is a likelihood of confusion between its trade dress and the trade dress of Grape Finds, it has demonstrated that it is likely to prevail on the merits of its trade dress claim. Therefore, it has met the requirements for a preliminary injunction. SO ORDERED.

Case Highlights

- Trademark law seeks to balance the protection of intellectual property and the need not to deter free and open competition.
- Protection of trade dress is needed to secure to the owner of the mark the goodwill of his business and to protect the ability of consumers to distinguish among competing producers.
- To establish a claim of trade dress infringement, a plaintiff must demonstrate (1) "that its trade dress is either inherently distinctive or that it has acquired distinctiveness through a secondary meaning," and (2) "that there is a likelihood of confusion between defendant's trade dress and plaintiff's."
- Generic marks are not entitled to protection under the Lanham Act

TRADEMARK DILUTION

On January 16, 1996, the Lanham Act was amended to include **trademark dilution.** The **Federal Trademark Dilution Act (FTDA)**[6] defines dilution as "the lessening of the capacity of a *famous mark* to identify and distinguish goods or services, regardless of the presence or absence of competition between the owner of the famous mark and other parties, or likelihood of confusion." A trademark dilution claim entitles the trademark owner to an injunction against another person's commercial use of its mark or trade name.

The two recognized types of dilution are tarnishment and blurring. **Tarnishment** arises when the trademark is linked to products of shoddy quality or is portrayed in an unsavory context likely to evoke unflattering connotations about the product or service. **Blurring** is a diminishing of the selling power and value of the trademark by unauthorized use. The differences between the senior user (trademark owner) and junior user (alleged infringer) marks are blurred to the extent that individuals are prevented from disassociating the two marks.

The court in *Nabisco, Inc. v. PF Brands, Inc.,*[7] recently stated the requirements for a trademark dilution claim under the FDTA. The trademark owner must establish the following elements:

- The senior mark must be famous[8];
- The senior mark must be distinctive;
- The junior user must be a commercial user;
- Use by the junior user must begin after the senior mark has become famous; and
- Use by the junior user must cause dilution of the distinctive quality of the senior mark.

The **junior mark** or user referred to in the above requirements is the party accused of trademark infringement or dilution. The **senior mark** or user refers to the trademark owner bringing the claim of infringement or dilution. A new source of trademark infringement and dilution claims involves the Internet and e-commerce. The application of trademark law to the Internet will be examined in Chapter 15. For now, Focus on Transactions: Trademark Dilution and the Internet provides one example of the intersection between trademark law and the Internet. It discusses the abuse of **meta-tags** to divert Web searchers to Web sites unrelated to a famous name or trademark.

http://

The Publishing Law Center: "Internet Legal Issues—Meta-tags" at **http://www.publaw.com/metatags.html**.

Copyright Protection

Copyright is a form of protection provided to authors of "original works of authorship" fixed in a **tangible form** of expression. Works must be fixed in tangible form in order to receive federal copyright protection; improvisational speeches or performances that have not been recorded or written are not protected. The eight

6. 15 U.S.C. § 1127 (1996).
7. 191 F.3d 208, 215 (2d Cir.1999).
8. The FDTA sets forth eight nonexclusive factors to consider in determining whether a mark or dress is famous: (1) the degree of inherent or acquired distinctiveness of the mark; (2) the duration and extent of use of the mark in connection with the goods; (3) the duration and extent of advertising and publicity of the mark; (4) the geographical extent of the trading area in which the mark is used; (5) the channels of trade for the goods or services with which the mark is used; (6) the degree of recognition of the mark in trading areas and channels of trade used by the mark's owner and the person against whom the injunction is sought; (7) the nature and extent of the use of same or similar marks by third parties; and (8) the mark was registered under the Trademark Act as of March 3, 1981.

Focus on Transactions

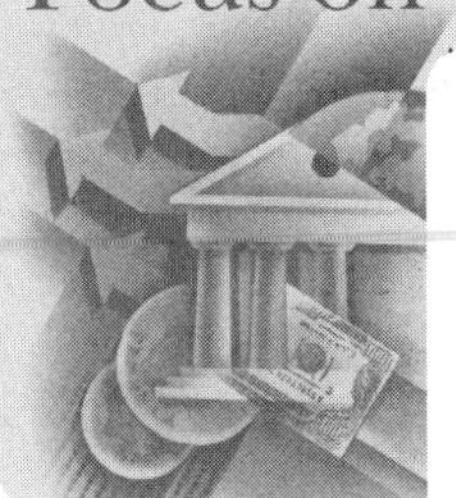

Trademark Dilution and the Internet

The complex questions generated by the intersection of the Internet and copyright or trademark laws are illustrated by *meta-tag* abuse. Internet browsers use search engines to find relevant web sites. For those maintaining web sites, a good listing in a search engine index is crucial for obtaining optimum exposure. The search engines index web sites through the use of HTML (Hypertext Markup Language) source codes. The HTML consists of "mark-up" symbols or codes inserted in a file intended for display on a World Wide Web browser. The markup tells the web browser how to display a web site's words and images for the user. Meta-tags, a portion of this underlying source code, act as signposts that notify the search engines of the content of web sites and facilitate matching search requests to web sites.

Meta-tags are embedded and are not seen by the viewer of the page, but are readable by the search engines. Thus, a party can link itself to a popular web site without overtly using the more popular web site's name in its URL (Uniform Resource Locator) or web address. Instead, it can embed in its source code keywords taken from the more popular web site. As a result, its web site will be found by a search engine in response to a viewer's search request for the more popular site. The legal issue is whether this is a type of trademark of infringement or dilution covered under U.S. trademark law. The global nature of the Internet indicates that amending U.S. trademark laws to deal directly with meta-tag abuse is unlikely to be totally effective.

For further reading see Craig K. Weaver, "Signposts to Oblivion? Meta-Tags Signal the Judiciary to Stop Commercial Internet Regulation and Yield to the Electronic Marketplace," 22 *Seattle University Law Review* 667 (1998).

http://
The Publishing Law Center: "Frequently Asked Questions About Copyright Law" at **http://www.publaw.com/cfaqs.html** and "The Advantages of Copyright Registration" at **http://www.publaw.com/advantage.html**.

http://
U.S. Copyright Office: **http://lcweb.loc.gov/copyright**. For copyright application forms see **http://lcweb.loc.gov/copyright/forms**.

generic categories of copyrightable works include literary, dramatic, musical, choreographic, pictorial (including graphic and sculptural works), motion pictures, sound recordings, and architectural works. These categories are interpreted broadly: for example, computer programs may be registered as "literary works." Copyright protection is available to both published and unpublished works. Copyright protection affixes to the work at the time of its creation. A copyright, as a general rule, has a term that endures for the author's life plus an additional 70 years after the author's death. In the case of works made for hire (owned by a business), the duration of the copyright lasts between 95 and 120 years.

Section 106 of the **Copyright Act of 1976** gives the copyright owner the exclusive *right to reproduce* the work in copies; prepare derivative works; to distribute copies by sale, rental, lease, or lending; and to perform or display the work publicly. It is illegal for anyone to violate any of these rights. However, the rights are not unlimited. Sections 107 through 121 of the Copyright Act provide a number of exemptions from copyright liability. There are three general exceptions to the exclusive rights of copyright ownership: (1) first sale doctrine, (2) fair use doctrine, and (3) materials that are part of the public domain.

The **first sale doctrine** terminates the copyright owner's protections over a copy of the copyrighted work once the work is legally sold. The purchaser gains the right to resell the copy.[9] The Copyright Act states that the owner of a copy is entitled to resell the copy without the consent of the copyright owner.

Section 107 of the Copyright Act allows for certain "fair uses" of copyrighted material without the consent of the copyrighted owner. The **fair use doctrine** allows others to use small portions of a copyrighted work in the creation of another work. The borrower can legally make unauthorized use of copyright materials in limited contexts. The most common contexts include in connection with a criticism of the work, in the course of news reporting, for teaching purposes, and as part of scholarship or research activities. The determination of whether the use was "fair" is done on a case-by-case basis. The factors analyzed include the purpose or character of the use, such as whether it was of a commercial nature, or for non-profit or educational purposes. The courts will also look at the amount of the use in relation to the copyrighted work as a whole and the effect of the use upon the value or market of the copyrighted work.

http://

The Publishing Law Center: "The Fair Use Doctrine" at **http://www.publaw.com/work.html** and **http://www.publaw.com/fairuse.html**.

Finally, material found in the **public domain** is not protected. These materials include government publications and materials whose copyrights have expired. An analogous concept in trademark law is the brand name–generic distinction. A brand name can be protected as a trademark. However, if the name is used widely as a generic name, then it is said to have entered the public domain and is no longer entitled to trademark protection.

http://

The Publishing Law Center: "Public Domain and the Impact of New Legislation" at **http://www.publaw.com/publicdomain.html**.

Authorship of a copyrighted work determines who holds the copyright. A work created by an individual vests copyright ownership in that individual automatically upon its creation. **Work for hire** is the major exception. Section 101 of the Copyright Act of 1976 contains a two-pronged test to determine if a work is for hire. First, a work prepared by an employee within the scope of her employment is a work for hire. The Supreme Court in *Community for Creative Non-Violence (CCNV) v. Reid*[10] listed 13 factors to be used to determine when a third party who is not a regular employee can be considered an "employee" for purposes of copyright ownership (see the Focus on Transactions feature on the next page).

http://

The Publishing Law Center: "Copyright Ownership and the Work for Hire Doctrine" at **http://www.publaw.com/work1.html** and **http://www.publaw.com/work2.html**.

Second, a work is for hire if it was specifically ordered or commissioned for use as a contribution to a collective work or as part of a compilation. The employer or person for whom the work was prepared is considered the author for copyright purposes. In the case of contributions to **collective works,** the contributor of the work retains a copyright for his part, but the creator or producer of the collective work obtains a copyright in the collective work.

Copyright protection is available for all unpublished works, regardless of the nationality of the author. Published works are eligible for copyright protection in the United States if any of the following conditions are met. First, on the date of first publication, one of the authors is a national or is domiciled in the United States. Second, the work is first published in the United States or in a foreign country that is a party to an international treaty to which the United States is also a party. Third, the work is a sound recording that was first *fixed* in a treaty country.

No publication or registration is required to secure a copyright. The mere act of creation and fixing the work in a tangible form automatically creates the copyright. Publication of the work through distribution of copies, although not required, serves a number of purposes. It is a way of informing the public that the work is protected by copyright. It also provides evidence as to the date of copyright in order to determine the duration of the copyright.

9. 17 U.S.C. § 109(a).
10. 490 U.S. 730 (1989).

Focus on Transactions

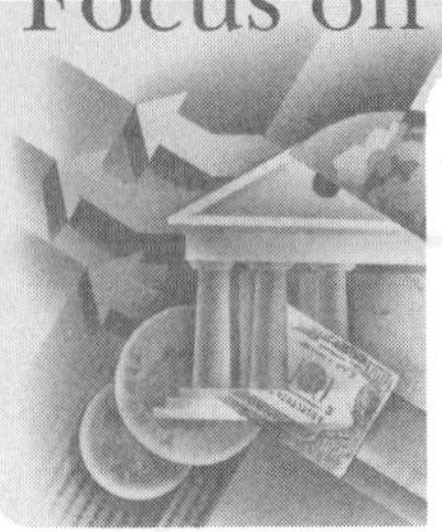

CCNV v. Reid Factors for "Copyright Employee"

- Hiring party's control over the means and manner by which the work is accomplished
- The level of skill required
- The source of the instrumentalities and tools used in creating the work
- The location of the work
- The duration of the relationship between the parties
- Whether the hiring party has the right to assign additional projects to the hired party
- The extent of the hired party's discretion over when and how long to work
- The method of payment
- The hired party's role in hiring and paying assistants
- Whether the work is part of the regular business of the hiring party
- Whether the hiring party is in business
- The provision of employee benefits
- The tax treatment of the hired party

This is not considered to be an exhaustive list and no one factor is considered to be determinative.

Notice of copyright is no longer necessary when publishing a copyrighted work. Before the 1976 Copyright Act, the law did require the use of a copyright notice when publishing or distributing a copyrighted work. The notice needed to use the copyright symbol, give the year of first publication, and name the owner of the copyright. A standard notice looked as follows: © Jane Doe 2001. In 1989, the notice requirement was eliminated when the United States adhered to the **Berne Convention.**[11] Notice is still recommended, however, because it removes the infringer's defense of **innocent infringement.** Under the innocent infringement defense, the infringer is absolved of liability if she can prove that she did not know the work was protected.

Registration of a copyright with the Copyright Office in Washington, D.C., is not a condition for protection, but registration does provide a number of benefits. First, registration of a copyright establishes a public record. A public record will help the owner prove his claim in future infringement or ownership disputes. Registration establishes a *prima facie* case of the validity of the copyright and the facts stated in the registration certificate. Second, registration makes available statutory damages and attorney's fees, while at common law the copyright owner is limited to actual damages. Third, registration allows the copyright owner to record a duplicate registration with the U.S. Customs Service for protection against the importation of infringing copies. A copyright registration is effective on the date that the Copyright Office receives a properly completed application.

Patent Protection

United States patent law confers on the patent owner the exclusive rights to manufacture, use, and sell the patented product or process within the United States for a

11. Notice is still relevant to maintain the copyright status of older works and still should be used to strengthen the owner's case in a copyright infringement lawsuit.

period of 20 years. In order to be fully protected the patent holder or **patentee** should serve notice by affixing the word "patent" or the abbreviation "pat." together with the number of the patent to the patented item or product. The patent law states that failure to mark the package means "no damages shall be recovered by the patentee in any action for infringement." The patentee will be able to obtain an injunction to prevent further infringement, but will not be able to sue for damages for injury caused by the infringement.

The Patent Act defines an infringer as "whoever without authority makes, uses, offers to sell, or sells any patented invention, within the United States or *imports* into the United States any patented invention." Furthermore, anyone who falsely marks goods with the name of the patentee "with the intent of counterfeiting or of deceiving the public" is liable for damages.

http://
U.S. Patent and Trademark Office: **http://www.uspto.gov**.

Under the **doctrine of equivalents** there need not be an exact copying of an invention to prove a case of patent infringement. The patent owner has to show only that there is "equivalence" between the elements of the patented invention and the infringing product. However, if the second invention is an improvement of the first then the patent owner is not likely to benefit from the doctrine of equivalents.[12]

In *Warner-Jenkinson Co. v. Hilton Davis Chemical*[13] the patent owner had developed a process to remove impurities from commercial dyes. Its process operated at pH levels between 6.0 and 9.0. It sought an injunction against the developer of a purification process that worked at a pH of 5.0. The Supreme Court held that the doctrine of the equivalents must be applied to the individual elements of the invention or process and not just the invention as a whole. The fact that both parties had developed a process for the purification of dye did not make them equivalent inventions. Instead, it needed to be determined whether a process that operates at a pH level of 5.0 is equivalent to one that works at 6.0. If the two processes were of equivalent quality, then the owner of the first process was entitled to an injunction under the doctrine of equivalents. If a process that works at a lower pH is qualitatively better, then it is to be considered an improvement and, as such, would be protected as a new invention.

Trade Secrets

Unlike a U.S. patent, a trade secret does not entitle its owner to a government-sanctioned monopoly of her invention for a particular length of time. Nevertheless, a trade secret can be a valuable form of protection. Trade secrets are protected under state law and through private contracts. Trade secret protection is a product of state common law, although many states have adopted the **Uniform Trade Secrets Act.** The Uniform Trade Secrets Act is a model law drafted by the National Conference of Commissioners on Uniform State Laws. It prohibits the misappropriaton of trade secrets by theft, bribery, or misrepresentation. Companies protect their trade secrets through confidentiality agreements between them and their

http://
Text of Uniform Trade Secrets Act: **http://www.nsi.org/Library/Espionage/usta.htm**.

12. The doctrine of equivalents also applies to trademarks. In Enrique Bernat F., S.A. v. Guadalajara, Inc., 210 F.3d 439 (5th Cir. 2000), the seller of "Chupa Chups" sued the seller of "Chupa Gurts" for trademark infringement. Guadalajara, Inc., of Mexico, doing business as Dulces Vero USA, sold frozen yogurt cone–shaped lollipops under the name "Chupa Gurts." Chupa Chups, a Spanish company that sells "Chupa Chups" which are ice cream–flavored lollipops, sued it for trademark infringement. The appeals court held that there was no infringement because the key term, *chupa* is a generic Spanish word. Under the *foreign equivalents doctrine,* courts translate foreign words used as trademarks into what would be their common English meaning in usage to test them for their generic or descriptive meaning. The word *chupa* is a generic Spanish word for lollipop or sucker, so it is due no protection. The court held that there was no likelihood of confusion.
13. 117 S. Ct. 1040 (1997).

employees and by trade secret licensing agreements that prohibit disclosure by licensees.

Recent developments in the area of trade secret law are the passage of the **Economic Espionage Act of 1996 (EEA)**[14] and the designation of customer lists as trade secrets. The EEA makes it a crime to steal not only government secrets but also business trade secrets. One issue recently explored is how to prove a violation of the EAA without first showing that there was a trade secret to be stolen. The court in *U.S. v. Hsu*[15] held that defendants in a criminal case involving conspiracy to steal trade secrets in violation of the Economic Espionage Act, do not have a right to see the trade secrets in question in an effort to prove that there were no trade secrets. In that case, Hsu and others were indicted for violating the EEA by conspiring to steal corporate trade secrets regarding a valuable anti-cancer drug. The defense maintained that constitutional and procedural requirements of criminal prosecutions dictate full access to the documents so they could establish the defense of legal impossibility (they could not steal trade secrets that did not exist). The court ruled that so long as the defendants believed they were going to steal trade secrets, it does not have to be proven that there were actually trade secrets at stake.

http://

Text of Economic Espionage Act of 1996 and other U.S. laws. Scroll down to section titled "U.S. Laws Regarding Electronic Surveillance." **http://www.tscm.com**.

The issue of protecting customer lists as trade secrets was recently examined in *Nowogroski Insurance, Inc. v. Rucker.*[16] The court held that valuable customer lists, which had been reasonably protected by an employer, were protected under the Uniform Trade Secrets Act. An insurance agency sued three former employees for soliciting its clients after they went to work for a competitor, by using confidential information. The fact that written forms of the list had not been taken or copied was held to be immaterial. It is the nature of the employment relationship that imposes a duty on employees and former employees not to use or disclose the employer's trade secrets. A valuable customer list, which has been protected by an employer, is due trade secret protection. The fact that the former employee memorized the information, rather than taking it in written form, made no difference.

EXTRATERRITORIAL APPLICATION OF UNITED STATES LAW

The Lanham Act[17] allows for a claim for false designations of origin.[18] The Court of Appeals in *Scotch Whiskey Assoc. v. Barton Distilling*[19] held that the Lanham Act could be applied extraterritorially where a U.S. producer supplies false labels to a foreign licensee. In that case, the U.S. company supplied labels designating the product as "Scotch Whiskey" to a Panamanian licensee. There was no evidence that the adulterated whiskey was imported into the United States. Nonetheless, the court held that the Lanham Act applied to the U.S. defendant stating that "no prin-

14. 18 U.S.C. § 90 (Economic Espionage Act of 1996).
15. 1998 WL 538221 3d Cir. 1998.
16. 971 P.2d 936 (Sup. Ct., Wash., 1999).
17. 15 U.S.C.A. §§ 1125 (a) and 1127.
18. 15 U.S.C. § 1125(a) states:
    Any person who shall affix, apply, or annex or use in connection with any goods or services, or any container for goods, a false designation of origin, or any false description or representation, including words or other symbols tending falsely to describe or represent the same, and shall cause such goods or services to enter into commerce, and any person who shall with knowledge of the falsity of such designation or origin or description or representation cause or procure the same to be transported or used in commerce or deliver the same to any carrier to be transported or used, shall be liable to a civil action by any person or business in the locality falsely indicated as that of origin or . . .
19. 489 F.2d 809 (7th Cir. 1972).

cipal of international law bars the United States from governing the conduct of its own citizens."

The court in *Scotch Whiskey* relied on the Supreme Court decision in *Steele v. Bulova Watches.*[20] In that case, a U.S. citizen registered the Bulova name in Mexico. He then manufactured watches, using the Bulova name, for sale in Mexico. There was evidence that some of the watches had been imported into the United States. The Supreme Court broadly defined "commerce" in the Lanham Act to include activities of U.S. citizens outside of the country. The court in *Scotch Whiskey* held that "the purpose underlying the Lanham Act, to make actionable the deceptive use of false designations of origin, should not be evaded by the simple device of selecting a foreign license."

The Gray Market

The importation of counterfeited goods is prohibited under the Lanham Act and the Tariff Act.[21] The two pertinent sections of the Lanham Act that apply to the area of counterfeited or pirated goods are Sections 32[22] and 43(a).[23] They make it illegal to falsely affix another's trademark to goods or use an improper place of origin designation. The Customs Service is authorized to seize such goods at the point of entry into the country. In order to assist the Customs Service, trademark and copyright owners should *record* their rights with the Service. Section 133 sets forth the procedures governing recording trademarks with the Customs Service. The Customs Service has established an Intellectual Property Rights Branch to administer the intellectual property components of the U.S. import laws.

http://
Anti-Gray Market Alliance at **http://www.agmatoday.org.**

The so-called **gray market** problem[24] refers to imports bearing a genuine trademark but imported by a party other than the trademark holder or authorized importer. Also referred to as *parallel imports,* they include goods produced outside the United States pursuant to an intellectual transfer agreement and goods licensed in the United States for export that are subsequently reimported into the United States. In these instances, a U.S. licensor will find its own market territory undercut by identical goods produced under a foreign licensing agreement.

The gray market problem as it pertains to the U.S. domestic market involves goods that are:

- legally produced under a license and that are imported or reimported into the United States
- legally produced by a U.S. foreign subsidiary or affiliated firm and then imported into the United States
- imported into the United States by a foreign firm after it licenses or assigns its U.S. trademark rights to another[25]

20. 344 U.S. 280 (1952).
21. 19 U.S.C. Section 1526(e).
22. Section 32 makes it illegal for a person to reproduce or use "any reproduction, counterfeit, copy, or colorable imitation of a registered mark in connection with the sale, offering for sale, distribution, or advertising of any goods or services on or in connection with which such use is likely to cause confusion, or to cause mistake, or to deceive." 15 U.S.C. § 1114(1).
23. Section 43(a) makes it illegal for any person to "affix, apply, or annex, or use in connection with any goods or services, or any container or containers for goods, a false designation of origin, or any false description or representation, including words or other symbols tending falsely to describe or represent the same." 19 C.F.R. Section 133.23a.
24. See Lawrence M. Friedman, "Business and Legal Strategies for Combating Grey-Market Imports," 32 *International Lawyer* 27 (1998).
25. The Supreme Court attempted to deal with the different gray market scenarios in Kmart v. Cartier, Inc., 486 U.S. 281 (1988).

The firm that is hurt by gray market imports will often seek to prevent their importation. Section 526 of the Tariff Act provides relief under the first gray market scenario if the license agreement prohibits such importation. The importance of placing restrictions in international licensing agreements to prevent a gray market problem will be examined closely in the next chapter.

The Customs Service will not prevent importation in the second scenario because the foreign entity is under the *common control* of the domestic company. However, Section 42 of the Lanham Act can be used to prevent the importation of foreign-made goods materially different than the same trademarked goods produced in the United States. This is because of the likelihood that the U.S. consumer will be confused into thinking that the goods are identical.

In general, trademark law generally does not reach the sale of goods legally produced outside the United States and subsequently imported to compete against the same goods produced domestically. This was the situation in *NEC Electronics v. Cal Circuit Abco.*[26] In that case, the defendant had purchased gray market semiconductor chips from a foreign source and imported them to compete against the trademark owner's California subsidiary. The court held that if the trademark owner "chooses to sell abroad at lower prices than those it could obtain for the identical product in the United States, it cannot look to United States trademark law to insulate the American market or to vitiate the effects of international trade."[27] The onus is on the licensor to provide safeguards in its foreign licensing agreements to diminish the chances of parallel importing.

The first sale doctrine, highlighted in the trademark area by the *NEC Electronics* case, protects the importer of copyrighted products from an infringement action if the goods were purchased from or produced by a licensee of the goods. In *Quality King Distributors, Inc. v. L'anza Research International, Inc.*,[28] the Supreme Court held that under the first sale doctrine the owner of copyrighted material is entitled, without permission of the copyright owner, to sell or otherwise dispose of purchased copyrighted materials, imported or not. The domestic owner of the copyright had entered in a distribution agreement with an English distributor. The distributor sold large quantities of the goods to the defendant-importer who resold them at discount prices to unauthorized retailers in the United States. The Supreme Court held that there was no infringement and resale could not be prevented.

The *Columbia Broadcasting v. Scorpio Music Distributors* case on page 380 further examines the first sale defense. In that case, the scope of the first sale doctrine was narrowed in relation to the importation of foreign made phonorecords.

As shown in the *Columbia Broadcasting System* case there is a history of special statutory protection for music and musical performances. Musicians or performers may enjoy copyright or copyright-like protection in three things, which are important to keep distinct. First, a musical composition itself has been protected by statute under copyright law since 1831. Second, in 1971, Congress extended copyright protection to sound recordings under the **Sound Recording Act of 1971.** This means that persons who make unauthorized reproductions of records or tapes can be prosecuted or face civil liability for copyright infringement. Piracy which refers to an unauthorized duplication of a performance already reduced to a sound

26. 810 F.2d 1506 (9th Cir. 1987).
27. Ibid. at 1511. See also A. Bourjois & Co. v. Katzel, 260 U.S. 689 (1923); Olympus Corp. v. United States, 792 F.2d 315 (2d Cir. 1986).
28. 118 S.Ct. 1125 (1998).

NEC Electronics v. Cal Circuit Abco

810 F.2d 1506 (9th Cir. 1987)

Sneed, Circuit Judge. A Japanese manufacturer of computer chips, NEC Corporation (NEC-Japan), assigned its United States trademark rights to its California subsidiary, NEC Electronics (NEC-USA). Defendant, CAL Circuit Abco (Abco), engages in "parallel importation" of NEC-Japan's chips: it buys them abroad at lower prices there prevalent, and then imports and sells them in the United States. NEC-USA sued for trademark infringement under the Lanham Act.

In 1983, NEC-Japan, owner of the trademark "NEC" in this country and elsewhere, assigned all rights to the mark in the United States to NEC-USA, and duly registered this assignment with the U.S. Patent and Trademark Office. NEC-Japan continues to market its computer chips outside the United States, evidently at prices substantially lower than those charged by NEC-USA. Defendant Abco buys these so-called "gray market" chips from a foreign source, imports them, and sells them here in direct competition with NEC-USA. The parties have stipulated that Abco's chips are genuine NEC products. NEC-USA sued Abco for trademark infringement under sections 32 and 43 of Lanham Act. NEC-USA alleges that Abco's use of the "NEC" trademark confuses consumers who believe that Abco's sales are authorized by or connected to NEC-USA.

Section 32 of the Lanham Act provides the registered owner of a trademark with an action against anyone who without his consent uses a "reproduction, counterfeit, copy, or colorable imitation" of the mark in such a way as "is likely to cause confusion, or to cause mistake, or to deceive." Similarly, section 43(a) provides for civil liability if goods are marketed bearing "a false designation of origin." Trademark law generally does not reach the sale of genuine goods bearing a true mark even though such sale is without the mark owner's consent. Once a trademark owner sells his product, the buyer ordinarily may resell the product under the original mark without incurring any trademark law liability.

Because NEC-Japan and NEC-USA are commonly controlled, there is no danger to the latter in being unable to control the quality of the former's products. If, as NEC-USA alleges, Abco sales agents mislead their buyers about the availability of NEC-USA servicing, then Abco may be liable in contract or tort, but not in trademark. If NEC-Japan chooses to sell abroad at lower prices than those it could obtain for the identical product here, that is its business. In doing so, however, it cannot look to United States trademark law to insulate the American market or to vitiate the effects of international trade. This country's trademark law does not offer NEC-Japan a vehicle for establishing a worldwide discriminatory pricing scheme simply through the expedient of setting up an American subsidiary with nominal title to its mark. The grant of partial summary judgment is REVERSED and the preliminary injunction VACATED.

Case Highlights

- Once a trademark owner sells its product, the buyer ordinarily may resell the product under the original mark without incurring any trademark law liability.
- If a company sells a good more cheaply in a foreign market or licenses someone who does so, the company cannot look to trademark law to prevent the importation of such legally produced foreign goods into its domestic market.

recording and commercially released, is conceptually distinct from "bootlegging," which has been defined as the making of "an unauthorized copy of a commercially unreleased performance."

The Sound Recording Act did not expressly cover "bootlegging." Therefore, in 1994, Congress passed a statute, sometimes referred to as the **Anti-Bootlegging Statute,**[29] criminalizing the unauthorized recording, the transmission to the public, and the sale or distribution of or traffic in unauthorized recordings of live musical performances.

29. 18 U.S.C. § 2319A. See United States v. Ali Moghadam, 175 F.3d 1269 (11th Cir. 1999).

Columbia Broadcasting System, Inc. v. Scorpio Music Distributors, Inc.

569 F. Supp. 47 (E.D. Pa. 1983)

Green, Judge. Plaintiff, Columbia Broadcasting System, Inc. ("CBS"), is a New York corporation which owns United States copyrights to six sound recordings, copies of which comprise the subject matter of this copyright infringement case. On or about January 1, 1981, CBS-Sony, Inc., a Japanese corporation, entered into two written agreements with Vicor Music Corporation ("Vicor"), a Philippines corporation, by which Vicor was authorized to manufacture and sell certain phonorecords exclusively in the Philippines.

On November 2, 1981, CBS-Sony severed its manufacturing and licensing agreements with Vicor. CBS-Sony and Vicor agreed that Vicor would have sixty days following termination of the agreements within which to liquidate its stock. International Traders bought the phonorecords from Rainbow Music, Inc., a Philippines corporation, which had purchased them from Vicor before Vicor's sixty-day selloff period expired. CBS filed a complaint on February 1, 1982, alleging that without its consent, Scorpio imported the phonorecords to which CBS owns the copyrights and thereby violated §602 of the Copyright Act which prohibits the importation of phonorecords without consent of the copyright owner.

Scorpio argues that, since the recordings were the subject of a valid first sale from Vicor to Rainbow Music, defendant has not infringed any of CBS' rights. When a work is the subject of a valid first sale, the distribution rights of the copyright owner are extinguished, and title passes to the buyer. Scorpio also argues that it is not an importer within the meaning of §602. Section 602 provides, in pertinent part: "(a) Importation into the United States, without the authority of the owner of the copyright under this title, of copies of phonorecords of a work that have been acquired outside of the United States is an infringement of the exclusive right to distribute copies or phonorecords."

The phonorecords at issue were acquired outside of the United States by International Traders and were imported without authorization from CBS, the copyright owner. Nonetheless, Scorpio argues it is not a proper defendant in this matter because it did not import the records from the Philippines; rather, it transacted its business with International Traders, within the United States. However, the question whether defendant was the importer need not be resolved, in view of the law regarding vicarious and contributory infringement and the undisputed fact that International Traders was an importer. Intent is not a necessary element of infringement, and the copyright holder may proceed against any member in the chain of distribution.

Defendant argues that the exclusive rights of a copyright owner, including the right to distribute, are limited by § 109(a). Section 109(a) provides that "the owner of a particular copy or phonorecord lawfully made under this title, or any person authorized by such owner, is entitled, without the authority of the copyright owner, to sell or otherwise dispose of the possession of that copy or phonorecord." I conclude that the section grants first sale protection to the third-party buyer of copies that have been legally manufactured and sold within the United States and not to purchasers of imports such as are involved here. Moreover, declaring legal the act of purchasing from a United States importer who does not deal directly with a foreign manufacturer, but who buys recordings that have been liquidated overseas, would undermine the purpose of the statute. The copyright owner would be unable to exercise control over copies of the work that entered the American market in competition with copies lawfully manufactured and distributed under this title. This court cannot construe the statute so as to alter the intent of Congress, which has set restrictions on the importation of phonorecords in order that rights of United States copyright owners can be preserved. Accordingly, the defendant's motion to dismiss is DENIED.

Case Highlights

- Generally, when a work is the subject of a valid first sale, the distribution rights of the copyright owner are extinguished.
- Section 602 of the Copyright Act prohibits the importation of phonorecords without consent of the copyright owner.
- Intent is not a necessary element of infringement, and the copyright holder may proceed against any member in the chain of distribution.
- "First sale" protection is available to the third-party buyer of copies of phonorecords that have been legally manufactured and sold within the United States but not to purchasers of imports.

INTERNATIONAL PROPERTY RIGHTS PROTECTION

The rights granted under U.S. patent, trademark, or copyright law can be enforced only in the United States, its territories, and its possessions; they confer no protection in a foreign country. Outside of the United States protection is available through international treaties or foreign intellectual property laws. The relevant international treaties establish minimum standards for protection, but individual country laws and practices can and do differ significantly.

The **World Intellectual Property Organization (WIPO)** is the official depository of most international intellectual property conventions. The WIPO grew out of the 1883 Paris Convention on patents and trademarks and the 1886 Berne Convention on copyrights. Today it serves two main purposes. First, it administers and monitors the enforcement of more than 20 treaties. Second, it promotes the adoption of new intellectual property treaties and conventions.[30] The next Comparative Law feature lists some of the treaties administered by the WIPO, and gives the original date of enactment as well as the date of the most recent amendments. Provisions of the World Trade Organization's **Agreement on Trade-Related Aspects of Intellectual Property (TRIPS)** will be reviewed in depth later in this chapter. This extended coverage is warranted because TRIPS has the potential to provide universal protection for intellectual property rights.

http://
World Intellectual Property Organization: **http://www.wipo.org**. For full text of international treaties see **http://www.wipo.org/treaties/ip/index.html**.

Paris Convention and Patent Cooperation Treaty

To secure patent and trademark rights outside the United States a company must apply for patents or register trademarks on a country-by-country basis. U.S. individuals and corporations are entitled to a **right of priority** and to **national treatment** in the 100 countries that are parties to the **Paris Convention for the Protection of Industrial Property.** The Paris Convention, first adopted in 1883, is the major international agreement providing basic rights for protecting industrial property such as patents, designs, and trademarks.

A person who files for a patent or trademark in one member country is given a right of priority for a fixed period of time to file in other countries. The right of priority gives the holder 12 months for patents, (6 months for trademarks) to file from the date of the first application filed in a Paris Convention country. This right of priority relieves the burden of filing applications in many countries simultaneously. National treatment means that a member country can not discriminate against foreigners in granting patent or trademark protection. Rights conferred may be greater or less than provided under U.S. law, but they must be the same as the country provides its own nationals.

Article 5 of the Convention sanctions member countries to issue **compulsory licenses** to third parties if the patent or trademark owner does not use the patent or trademark. A compulsory license grants patent or trademark rights to third parties without the consent of the patent or trademark owner. Compulsory licenses cannot be issued any sooner than four years from the date of the grant of the patent. A compulsory license is not to be issued if the patentee gives legitimate reasons for its failure to work the patent or trademark. In addition, the parties granted licenses must pay reasonable royalty fees to the patent or trademark owner. U.S. patent law does not authorize the granting of such licenses.

http://
Law firm of Covington & Burling: "Compulsory Licensing" at **http://www.cov.com/publications/253.pdf**.

30. See generally Gerald J. Mossinghoff & Ralph Oman, "The World Intellectual Property Organization: A United Nations Success Story," 79 *Journal of Patent & Trademark Office Society* 691 (1997).

Comparative Law

Treaties Administered by WIPO

- Convention Establishing the World Intellectual Property Organization, July 14, 1967, most recently amended on September 28, 1979
- Paris Convention for the Protection of Industrial Property, signed March 20, 1883, amended October 2, 1979
- Berne Convention for the Protection of Literary and Artistic Works, amended September 28, 1979
- Rome Convention for the Protection of Performers, Producers of Phonograms, and Broadcasting Organizations, October 26, 1961
- Treaty on Intellectual Property in Respect of Integrated Circuits, May 26, 1989
- Madrid Agreement Concerning the International Registration of Marks, April 14, 1891, recently amended January 1, 1998
- The Hague Agreement Concerning the International Deposit of Industrial Designs, November 6, 1925, amended January 1, 1998
- Nice Agreement Concerning the International Classification of Goods and Services for the Purpose of the Registration of Marks, June 15, 1957, amended September 28, 1979
- Lisbon Agreement for the Protection of Appellations of Origin and Their International Registration, October 31, 1958, amended September 28, 1979
- Locarno Agreement Establishing an International Classification for Industrial Designs, October 8, 1968, amended September 28, 1979
- Patent Cooperation Treaty, June 19, 1970, regulations enacted on July 1, 1998
- Strasbourg Agreement Concerning International Patent Classification, March 24, 1971, amended September 28, 1979
- Trademark Law Treaty, October 27, 1994
- Budapest Treaty on the International Recognition of the Deposit of Microorganisms for Purposes of Patent Procedure, September 26, 1980
- Convention Relating to the Distribution of Program-Carrying Signals Transmitted by Satellite, May 21, 1974
- Nairobi Treaty on the Protection of the Olympic Symbol, September 26, 1981

The **Patent Cooperation Treaty (PCT)** addresses procedural requirements, aiming to simplify filing of, searching for, and publication of international patent applications. The PCT entered into force in 1978 and is open to any member of the Paris Convention. The PCT allows companies to file an international application for protection in other member states. Individual national applications, however, must follow within 18 months.

Berne Convention and Universal Copyright Convention

There is no such thing as an international copyright that automatically protects an author's work throughout the world. Protection against unauthorized use depends on the enforcement of national laws on a country-by-country basis. Most country laws, however, do recognize foreign works under certain conditions. This recognition of foreign works has been simplified through the enactment of international copyright treaties. Copyright protection has been seen as a moral right of authors and artists in their works. The moral nature of copyrights is inscribed in the cupola above the lobby at WIPO headquarters. It states that "human genius is the source of all works of art and invention. These works are the guarantee of a life worthy of men. It is the duty of the state to protect the arts and inventions with care."

The level and scope of copyright protection available within a country depends on that country's domestic laws and treaty obligations. In most countries, the place of first publication is an important criterion for determining whether foreign works are eligible for copyright protection. Works first published in the United States are protected in more than 80 countries under the **Berne Convention for the Protection of Literary and Artistic Works.** The United States also maintains copyright relations with a number of countries under a second international agreement called the **Universal Copyright Convention (UCC).**

UCC countries that do not also adhere to the Berne Convention often require compliance with certain formalities to maintain copyright protection. Those formalities require that the copyright be registered and that published copies of a work bear copyright notice, the name of the author, and the date of first publication. The United States also has **bilateral copyright agreements** with a number of countries; the laws of these countries may or may not be consistent with either of the copyright conventions. Before first publication of a work anywhere, it is advisable to investigate the scope of and requirements for maintaining copyright protection for those countries in which copyright protection is desired.

The Berne Convention, originally enacted in 1886, has been amended numerous times. A review of the Convention and its amendments illustrates the types of rights protected under the notion of copyright (see Comparative Law: Ten Rights of Authors and Artists Under the Berne Convention). Although created to protect the author and artists of artistic and literary works directly, the secondary purpose of the Berne Convention has been "to safeguard the large sums of money invested in producing informational goods and services"[31] that are subsequently produced by publishers and others.

The Berne Convention firmly established the rights of authors as a principle of international law, but, left it primarily to national laws to determine the degree of protection required. For example, it is left to national law to determine what types of works shall be given protection. Once a type of work is afforded protection, then a country is required to extend to foreign authors the same protections granted to national authors. A major limitation on this nondiscrimination principle is that if a country's domestic law grants a longer term of protection than the laws of the author's country of origin, then that country need only grant a term of protection equivalent to the law of the author's country of origin and not the longer term that is given under its own laws.

Subsequent amendments to the Convention expanded the scope of its reach, created additional rights, and recognized new technological developments. These amendments included the Berlin Act of 1908, the Rome Act of 1928, the Brussels Act of 1948, the Stockholm Act of 1967, and Paris Act of 1971. The **Berlin Act of 1908** recognized for the first time that photographic works were to be given copyright protection. These rights included the right to authorize the adaptation of an original work and the right over subsequent public performances of recordings of the work. This was a response to the emerging technologies of sound recording, cinematography, and photography. The Berlin Act authorized for the first time the granting of compulsory licenses by individual countries.

31. VINCENT PORTER, BEYOND THE BERNE CONVENTION 1 (1991). The coverage of the Berne Convention borrowed heavily from this source.

The **Rome Act of 1928** recognized the moral rights of authors and the author's broadcast rights in his works. The moral right allows an author to object to any distortion or other modification of the work. The moral rights of authors are now recognized in Article 6*bis* of the Berne Convention. It states that "independently of the author's economic rights, and even after the transfer of those rights, the author shall have the right to object to any distortion, mutilation, or other modification of the work, which would be prejudicial to his honor or reputation." Thus, an author could sell the right to reproduce or publicly display his work, but retain the ability to reject any modification of it in the reproduction or display. The Rome Act through Article 11*bis* established a broadcast right in response to the development of public radio. It states that "the authors of literary and artistic works enjoy the exclusive right to authorize communication of their works to the public by radio diffusion." Thus, for the first time a right was premised not upon a specific act such as reproduction or performing, but on a "process" of communicating the work.

The **Brussels Act of 1948** extended copyright protection to movie films. However, it was left to national law to determine the author or owner of the copyrights to a film. English law places that right with the producer of a film. In contrast, the civil law countries of Europe grant the rights to creative individuals such as the author of the original story or the writer of the screenplay. The Brussels Act also extended the broadcast right recognized in the Rome Act from sound broadcasting (radio) to television. The **Stockholm Act of 1967** and **Paris Act of 1971** allowed less developed countries to impose compulsory licenses for works out of print or for the translation of works not available in the language of the country.

AGREEMENT ON TRADE-RELATED ASPECTS OF INTELLECTUAL PROPERTY

The Agreement on Trade-Related-Aspects of Intellectual Property (TRIPS) is divided into Parts, Sections, and Articles. The first three parts provide the general provisions, scope of intellectual property rights, and enforcement provisions. Part I provides "General Provisions and Basic Principles." This part defines the principles of national treatment, most-favored-nation treatment, and the general objective of the Agreement. Part II is titled "Standards Concerning the Availability, Scope and Use of Intellectual Property Rights." The articles in each of the five sections (see below) in this part make up the operative provisions of intellectual property protections:

Section I: Copyright and Related Rights
Section II: Trademarks
Section III: Geographical Indications (Country of Origin)
Section IV: Industrial Designs
Section V: Patents

Part III provides the type of enforcement mechanisms countries must provide for violations of intellectual property rights. The scope of enforcement mechanisms is shown on the following selected list of articles from Part III:

Article 44: Injunctions
Article 45: Damages
Article 48: Indemnification of the Defendant

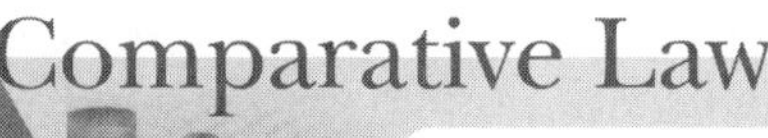

Comparative Law

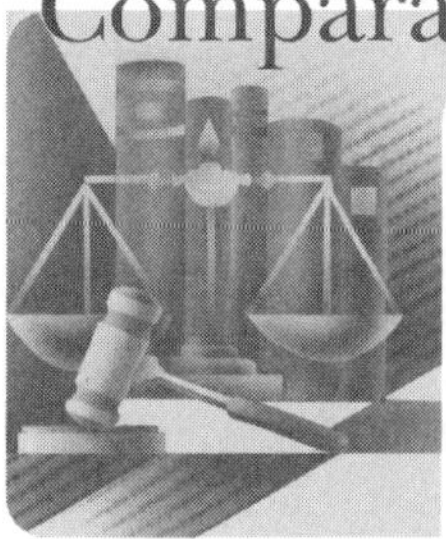

Ten Rights of Authors and Artists Under the Berne Convention

Moral Right
The right to preserve the integrity of the work including the right to publish the work. This is an inalienable right that cannot be assigned to an employer or another.

Reproduction Right
The right over all sound and visual recordings and adaptations of the work.

Translation Right
Right over the authorization of translations into other languages except for the limited right of less developed countries to grant compulsory licenses for translations.

Public Performance Right
Right over the performance of dramatic, musical, and literary works.

Broadcasting Right
Right over performances including radio and television broadcasts.

Adaptation Right
Indicates that a broadcaster needs to obtain permission of both the original author and the adapter or arranger.

Recording Right
This right covers recording of musical or dramatic works.

Author's Film Right
The right of the original author to authorize a film of the work.

Rights of Film Creator
Recognizes the separate rights of the owner or creator of the cinematographic work (film).

Right of Pursuit
Allows national laws to create a right of pursuit to an interest in the secondary and subsequent sales of the work. Thus, if the author or his heirs sell or transfer the rights to the work, they may still claim an interest in the subsequent sale or transfer by the transferee.

Article 51: Suspension by Customs Authorities
Article 57: Rights of Inspection and Information (by rights owner)
Article 61: Criminal Procedures

TRIPS has been described as "the highest expression to date of binding intellectual property law in the international arena." TRIPS became the law of the United States through the enactment of the Uruguay Round Agreements Act of 1994. This framework agreement is to be enforced under the auspices of the World Trade Organization (WTO).[32] With the full force of WTO implementation, TRIPS promises to be the best hope for the recognition of minimum standards for national intellectual property law regimes. TRIPS is a comprehensive agreement that has the potential for widespread implementation. TRIPS covers the four major areas of intellectual property: patent, copyright, trademark, and trade secrets. The following

http://
World Trade Organization: **http://www.wto.org.**

32. The constitutionality of TRIPS was challenged in U.S. v. Moghadam, 175 F.3d 1269 (11th Cir. 1999). The Circuit Court held that the statute enacting TRIPS into the law of the United States was constitutional under the Commerce Clause. The statute was held to be based upon a legally ratified treaty "called for by the World Trade Organization whose purpose was to ensure uniform recognition and treatment of intellectual property in international commerce."

review will not only provide an understanding of TRIPS, but will also reinforce the reader's knowledge of the basic principles of intellectual property protection.

General Principles

The "General Provisions" of TRIPS restate the foundations of the GATT-WTO system including national treatment, most-favored-nation, and transparency. TRIPS requires all signatory countries to apply the national treatment and most-favored-nation principles to the area of intellectual property protection. It states that each signatory "shall accord to the nationals of other Members treatment no less favorable than that it accords to its own nationals with regard to the protection of intellectual property." Article 4 restates the most-favored-nation principle with regard to intellectual property protection as "any advantage, favor, privilege, or immunity granted by a Member to the nationals of any other country shall be accorded immediately and unconditionally to the nationals of all other Members."

The third foundation principal of the WTO, transparency, is mandated in Article 63 of TRIPS. It states that "laws and regulations, and final judicial decisions and administrative rulings of general application, made effective by any Member pertaining to the availability, scope, acquisition, enforcement, and prevention of the abuse of intellectual property rights shall be published." Under the transparency standards of Article 63, countries are required to transmit copies of their laws and regulations to the Council for Trade-Related Aspects of Intellectual Property.

In order to ensure the implementation of the principles, TRIPS established the **Council for Trade-Related Aspects of Intellectual Property.** The Council, along with the WIPO, should be used as a resource for those interested in intellectual property protection. TRIPS instructs the Council to afford members the opportunity to consult on matters relating to the trade-related aspects of intellectual property rights.

The implementation of TRIPS principles is not unlimited. Article 69, for example, implicitly recognizes the problem of "illegal" gray market imports. It requires each country to establish "contact points" in their governments in order to coordinate with other countries in preventing the importation of goods produced in violation of rights recognized under TRIPS. It specifically instructs customs authorities to cooperate in preventing trade in counterfeit trademark goods and pirated copyright goods.

TRIPS recognizes the current roles of the WIPO and existing intellectual property conventions. Article 3 of TRIPS recognizes the continuing roles of existing international conventions, namely the Paris Convention, Berne Convention, Rome Convention, and the Treaty on Intellectual Property in Respect of Integrated Circuits. Article 8 further recognizes countries' rights to limit the grant of intellectual property rights when they violate antitrust laws as unreasonable restraints of trade.

Transitional provisions were incorporated into TRIPS in recognition of the demands TRIPS places on developing countries and former communist countries. These countries are given five years to implement the requirements of TRIPS. The least developed countries are given ten years before TRIPS must be fully implemented. Any developing country member is entitled to delay for a period of five years the date of application. Any other member which is in the process of transformation from a centrally planned into a free-market economy and which is undertaking structural reform of its intellectual property system may also benefit from this transitional period. The least-developed country members are given a period of 10 years to implement TRIPS. It is imperative for the international licensor of intellectual property to check the status of a given country's implementation of TRIPS.

Copyright and Related Rights

TRIPS requires all WTO members to immediately accede to the Berne Convention. In TRIPS as in most national laws, copyright protection shall extend to expressions and not to ideas, procedures, methods of operation, or mathematical concepts as such. As in the Berne Convention, copyright protection is extended to computer programs, whether in source or object code, as literary works.

Copyright protection is also expressly extended to "compilations of data or other material, whether in machine-readable or other form which by reason of the selection or arrangement of their contents constitute intellectual creations." Thus, databases or customer lists are protected under copyright. The minimum **term of protection** for photographic work or a work of applied art is no less than 50 years from the end of the calendar year of authorized publication or, failing such authorized publication, within 50 years from the making of the work.

Trademark Protection

Section 2 of TRIPS outlines the parameters for trademark protection. Article 15 of that section provides a broad definition of trademark akin to recent judicial recognition in the United States. It defines a trademark as "any sign, or any combination of signs, capable of distinguishing the goods or services of one undertaking from those of other undertakings. Such signs, in particular words including personal names, letters, numerals, figurative elements, and combinations of colors, as well as any combination of such signs, are eligible for registration as trademarks."

Once recognized as a trademark, the owner of the trademark has the right to prohibit infringement of the trademark. This right against infringement is defined as "the exclusive right to prevent all third parties not having his consent from using in the course of trade identical or *similar* signs for goods or services that are identical or similar to those in respect of which the trademark is registered." Furthermore, the similarity of the marks and the goods or services must result in a "likelihood of confusion." Article 17 recognizes the fair use concept found in copyright law and applies it as an exception to trademark protection. The period of protection for trademarks and renewals is set at a minimum of seven years. However, TRIPS states that "the registration of a trademark shall be renewable indefinitely."

TRIPS recognizes the principle that trademark rights can be lost through abandonment or nonuse, but rejects the notion of compulsory licensing found in some national laws.[33] Article 19 allows a country to cancel a trademark registration if it is unused for a period of three years. It prohibits such cancellation if the reason for nonuse was due to events outside the control of the registrant, such as import restrictions or government regulation.

The importance of geographical indications or country of origin to the sale of certain products is recognized in Article 22. It recognizes the rights of others to prevent the false use of geographical indications "where a given quality, reputation, or other characteristic of the good is essentially attributable to its geographical

33. TRIPS at Article 21.

origin." Also, an entire section of TRIPS is devoted to the protection of "industrial designs." Section 4 recognizes "independently created industrial designs" as a separate category of protection. It grants a protection period of 10 years for qualifying designs. Article 9 recognizes Article 6*bis* of the Paris Convention, giving the owner of a *well-known* trademark the right to block or cancel an unauthorized registration of its marks in a foreign country.

Patent Protection

Article 27 of TRIPS defines *patentable* as something that is "new, involves an inventive step and is capable of industrial application." For the purposes of this article, the terms "inventive step" and "capable of industrial application" may be deemed by a member to be synonymous with the terms "nonobvious" and "useful" found in U.S. patent law. The immediate impact of the TRIPS patent protections for the United States was the extension of the patent period from 17 to 20 years.

The rights conferred on the patent owner include the right to prevent third parties from the acts of making, using, offering for sale, selling, or *importing* for these purposes the patented product or process. Interestingly, instead of recognizing integrated circuit designs as patentable, TRIPS recognizes such designs separately and provides for a 10-year period of protection from the date of application or from the date of the "first commercial exploitation." It requires members to agree to provide protection for the layout and design of integrated circuits pursuant to the **Treaty on Intellectual Property in Respect of Integrated Circuits.**

Trade Secrets

Trade secrets are recognized under Section 7 of TRIPS. It states that the purpose of recognizing trade secrets is the "protection of undisclosed information." Trade secret is defined as information having commercial value that is not commonly known and for which reasonable steps have been taken to maintain secrecy.[34] The owner of the information may prevent the disclosure of such information if disclosure would be contrary to "commercial practices." **Commercial practice** is further defined in a footnote as, among other things, "breach of contract." Thus, reasonable confidentiality and nondisclosure agreements would be enforceable commercial practices.

Article 40 is of special importance to licensors of intellectual property rights. Countries are allowed to prohibit certain contractual restrictions that have "adverse effects on trade and *may* impede the transfer of technology." Article 40 allows member states to single out for scrutiny contractual restrictions found in exclusive grant-back clauses and clauses that prohibit challenges to the validity of the licensor's rights.[35]

Remedies and Penalties

TRIPS provides a menu of penalties and remedies to parties seeking the enforcement and protection of their intellectual property rights. Countries are required to provide civil and criminal remedies, along with procedures for seizing and destroy-

34. An example of a reasonable step is requiring employees and agents to sign confidentiality agreements.
35. See Chapter 14 (Intellectual Property Licensing).

ing illegal goods. Civil remedies include damages for lost profits and attorney's fees,[36] along with the granting of injunctions to prevent imported goods from entering "the channels of commerce."[37] Regarding counterfeited goods, Article 59 instructs customs authorities not to permit "the re-exportation of the infringing goods in an unaltered state."

Special provisions are included in TRIPS to prevent through the customs authorities the entry of infringing goods. The owner of intellectual property rights may petition the government or customs authority to suspend the importation or exportation of infringing goods.[38] Before granting the suspension, the administrative or judicial authority may require that the petitioner supply security[39] which can be used to indemnify a party whose goods are wrongfully enjoined or suspended.[40] Article 55 provides for an initial suspension period of 10 days. During that period the petitioner must move forward with a proceeding on the merits or request an additional 10-day suspension. Article 57 gives the petitioner the right to inspect the suspended goods in order to substantiate his claim.

Enforcement of Intellectual Property Rights

After intellectual property owners secure rights in foreign markets, enforcement must be pursued diligently through local law. As a general matter, intellectual property rights are private rights to be enforced by the owner. Enforcement varies from country to country and depends on such factors as the attitude of local officials, substantive requirements of the law, and court procedures. The availability of criminal penalties for infringement, either as the exclusive remedy or in addition to private suits, also varies among countries. United States law affords a civil remedy for infringement, including money damages to a successful plaintiff and criminal penalties for more serious offenses.

U.S. exporters with intellectual property concerns should develop a comprehensive strategy for protecting their property. First, they should obtain the available protection provided under U.S. laws covering inventions, trademarks, service marks, copyrights, and semiconductor mask works. Second, before entering into a licensing agreement with a foreign party, licensors should research the intellectual property laws of countries where prospective foreign licensees conduct business. Third, the services of foreign legal counsel should be engaged to file appropriate patent, trademark, or copyright applications within priority periods. Fourth, entering the foreign licensing agreement should be viewed as only the beginning of the process. The use of the licensed rights should be monitored for abuse and infringement. The licensor should be prepared to act promptly to protect its rights in case of a foreign infringement. Finally, trade secrets should be protected through appropriate confidentiality provisions in employment, licensing, marketing, distribution, and joint venture agreements.

The importance of utilizing all the sources of intellectual property protection is illustrated in the *Carell v. Schubert Organization* case that follows. The case involves a claim of copyright infringement. Note that in the opinion reference is made to domestic, foreign, and international copyright laws.

36. TRIPS at Article 45.
37. TRIPS at Article 44.
38. TRIPS at Article 51.
39. TRIPS at Article 53.
40. TRIPS at Article 48 and Article 56.

Carell v. The Shubert Organization, Inc.

2000 U.S. Dist. LEXIS 8807 (S.D.N.Y. 2000)

Schwartz, District Judge. This action arises out of a dispute concerning the copyright in certain makeup designs created for the cast of the Broadway musical *Cats*. Plaintiff Candace Anne Carell filed this action on July 12, 1999, asserting claims for copyright infringement, false designation of origin, antitrust violations, and an accounting for profits, arising out of defendants' use and publication of her Makeup Designs. The show *Cats* is reportedly "the longest running, most financially successful property" in the history of American theater. There have been over 40 productions of the musical in 27 countries. In addition to her claims brought under the U.S. Copyright Act, plaintiff brings infringement claims under several foreign copyright statutes.

In order for a work to be copyrightable, it must be "an original work of authorship"; that is, it must be (i) original and (ii) fixed in a tangible form. 17 U.S.C. § 102(a). Copyright protection for an original work does not extend to "any idea, procedure, process, system, method of operation, concept, principle, or discovery." The Copyright Act provides that ownership "vests initially in the author or authors of the work." There is no disagreement between the parties that the Makeup Designs are copyrightable, or that the creator of such Designs is entitled to protection even if he or she does not apply the makeup to the show's performers' faces. The Designs contain the requisite degree of originality, and are fixed in tangible form on the faces of the actors.

Domestic Infringement Claims

A complaint based on copyright infringement must allege: (1) which original works are the subject of the copyright claim; (2) that the plaintiff owns the copyrights in those works; (3) that the copyrights have been registered in accordance with the statute; and (4) "by what acts during what time" the defendant infringed the copyright. A certificate of registration from the United States Register of Copyrights constitutes *prima facie* evidence of the valid ownership of a copyright, although that presumption of ownership may be rebutted.

Foreign Infringement Claims

Plaintiff asserts her copyright infringement claims not only pursuant to U.S. law but also pursuant to several foreign copyright statutes, specifically those of Australia, Canada, Japan, and the United Kingdom, and pursuant to the Berne Convention for the Protection of Literary and Artistic Works ("Berne Convention"). Several courts and authorities support the exercise of jurisdiction over foreign copyright infringement claims. In *Armstrong v. Virgin Records,* 91 F. Supp. 2d 628 (S.D.N.Y. 2000), recently decided in this district, plaintiff, a jazz musician, claimed that defendants violated his copyright in a song recorded by the music group Massive Attack in the United Kingdom, and which was thereafter distributed worldwide. He filed claims for copyright infringement under the Copyright Act and under unspecified international copyright laws. The court held that it could entertain plaintiff's claims under international copyright laws on the basis of diversity jurisdiction, and, potentially, on the basis of pendent subject matter jurisdiction to plaintiff's domestic infringement claims.

Other authorities, while acknowledging that extraterritorial jurisdiction under the Copyright Act is prohibited, have asserted that there may be a basis for jurisdiction in cases similar to the instant matter. As Professor Nimmer has explained: "Even if the United States Copyright Act is clearly inoperative with respect to acts occurring outside of its jurisdiction, it does not necessarily follow that American courts are without jurisdiction in such a case. If the plaintiff has a valid cause of action under the copyright laws of a foreign country, and if personal jurisdiction of the defendant can be obtained in an American court, it is arguable that an action may be brought in such court for infringement of a foreign copyright law. This would be on a theory that copyright infringement constitutes a transitory cause of action, and hence, may be adjudicated in the courts of a sovereign other than the one in which the cause of action arose."

For the reasons set forth above, defendants' motion to dismiss is denied as to plaintiff's copyright infringement and Lanham Act claims. SO ORDERED.

Case Highlights

- Makeup designs are copyrightable as "original works of authorship."
- U.S. copyright law protects works that are "original" and "fixed in a tangible medium."
- U.S. courts will at time exercise jurisdiction over foreign copyright infringement claims.

FOREIGN INTELLECTUAL PROPERTY LAWS

As stated earlier, industrial property and intellectual property are interchangeable terms. However, it is important to recognize the increasing use of the latter term at the expense of the former term. The term *industrial property* is disappearing from Anglo-American legal terminology. It used to include the protection of inventions, industrial designs, and trademarks. Many countries have entered the postindustrial era, where the line between goods production and information production is increasingly blurred. Copyright, for example, protects purely utilitarian items, such as computer operating systems, while patents may protect quite abstract ideas for ways of doing business.[41] Trademarks have taken on functions quite different from their traditional role of identifying producers of goods. For instance, trademark owners sell their marks as decorations for T-shirts.

The broader and more attractive term *intellectual property* has become the designation for the combination of what used to be industrial property, copyright law, and other related fields.[42] Unification of terminology, however, has not led to a unification of legal institutions. Therefore, it is important to research the different national laws relating to intellectual property. It is important to see how patent, copyright, and trademark laws interrelate in the foreign country of interest.

Foreign Trademark Law

In most countries of the world a trademark is recognized and protected only on the registration of the mark with the appropriate government agency. Article 2 of the **Russian Trademark Law** states that "legal protection of a trademark within the Russian Federation shall be granted upon its registration with the State." The system that allocates rights based upon the "first to register" rule is referred to as an **attributive system.** That is, all rights stem from the registration of the trademark or patent. Most countries, however, as required by international trademark conventions, authorize their trademark offices to reject the registration by third parties of internationally recognized trademarks. Article 7 of the Russian law states that "trademarks of other persons are protected *without* registration by virtue of international treaties to which the Russian Federation is a signatory."

http://

Russian attorney web site with links to patent, trademark, and copyright laws of the Russian Federation: **http://www.palmira.net/~aek/**.

Brazil first recognized the rights of unregistered foreign trademark owners in revising its industrial property law in 1997. The new **Brazilian Industrial Property Law** allows the trademark office to "reject an application for registration of marks that wholly or partially reproduce or imitate a well-known mark." In determining whether a trademark is a well-known mark, the law refers to the Paris Convention. Article 126 of the law states that "trademarks that are well known in the terms of Article 6*bis* of the Paris Convention will enjoy special protection, irrespective of their previous filing or registration in Brazil." However, the window of opportunity to obtain the rights to a trademark is narrow. A contesting party, usually the rightful owner or a licensee, has only 60 days from the time it contests a trademark registration to apply for its own trademark.

41. See generally Larry A. DiMatteo, "The New 'Problem' of Business Method Patents: The Convergence of National Patent Laws and International Internet Transactions," 28 *Rutgers Computer & Technology Law Journal* 1(2002).
42. Peter B. Maggs, "Industrial Property in the Russian Federation," in GEORGE GINSBURGS, DONALD D. BARRY & WILLIAM B. SIMONS (eds.), THE REVIVAL OF PRIVATE LAW IN CENTRAL AND EASTERN EUROPE 377, note 1 (1996).

The Brazilian law also allows the trademark owner to sue for damages. Article 210 provides that the infringer may be sued for lost profits. The lost profit calculation is the one most favorable to the injured party. Thus, the foreign trademark owner can receive the higher of "the benefits it would have received but for the infringement or the value of the benefits received by the violator." Under the old Brazilian law a foreign holder of a trademark not only had to register the trademark, but also had to actively use it within two years of the registration. Because of barriers to investment or non-interest in doing business in Brazil, many international trademarks lost their protection under Brazilian law. Brazil recently changed its law to conform to the Paris Convention and the Stockholm Revision that give protection as long as the trademark is registered in Brazil.

National trademark laws need to be researched for substantive differences. For example, a foreign trademark owner should familiarize itself not only with what is required to register a trademark in a foreign country, but also what is required to preserve the trademark under that national law. Three of the more common areas for concern include:

- the term of the trademark and the requirements for renewal
- preventing infringement of the trademark and having it be transformed from a brand recognition to generic use
- preventing it from being labeled as an abandoned trademark due to nonuse

Under Russian Law, a registration of a trademark is valid for a period of 10 years calculated from the date of receipt of the application. The trademark may be renewed every 10 years by filing a renewal request within the last year of the previous registration period. In the event that a registration or a renewal request is rejected, the applicant has three months to appeal the decision to the Chamber of the Patent Authority. An applicant may appeal the decision of the Patent Authority, within six months, to the Supreme Patent Authority.

Trademark laws are relatively uniform regarding treatment of a trademark that is used generically; it loses its trademark protection. If a trademark or trade name is used to refer to all goods of a certain type and not just to a particular brand name, then all trademark rights are expunged. The *Comite Interprofessional du Vin de Champagne* case explores the generic–brand name distinction. Note that in an international setting a trademark may be considered generic in one country and a protected brand name in another.

Comite Interprofessional du Vin de Champagne v. Wineworths, Ltd.

2 NZLR 432 (1991)

The Comite Interprofessional du Vin de Champagne (CIVC) is a semiofficial body created under French law whose purpose is the protection of the name Champagne. It is disputing with Australian wine interests active in the New Zealand market for sparkling wine that Australian exporters seek to label and sell as champagne. The main dispute is whether the word had in New Zealand crossed the divide from a distinctive word to a generic word. Champagne as we know it is relatively new, having its final development in the 19th century by Dom Perignon of the Benedictine Abbey near Epernay, France. The two features of Champagne of prime importance are the soil and climate in which the grapes are grown, and the method of manufacture by skilled personnel.

The essence of the *methode champenoise* is that the process of second fermentation takes place in the bottle in which it is sold. That requires an operation for shifting the yeast by gradual manipulation down the neck of the inverted bottle for its removal. New Zealanders did not early develop an interest in wines. This was in contrast to Australia where indigenous wine manufacture and drinking became a more integral part of the lifestyle. The plaintiffs recognize that for Australia, like Canada and the United States, there is no legal protection available to them over the use of the appellation *champagne*.

In 1987, Penfolds (Australia) reached an agreement with Wineworths (New Zealand) to export into New Zealand a sparkling wine bearing the label "Australian Champagne." Plaintiffs brought suit claiming that the defendants were guilty of the charge of passing off. It is appropriate to emphasize the plaintiffs' view of what makes the product and name so special. It is avowedly alcoholic and readily capable of producing a pleasurable effect in the stomach. Champagne is appropriate as a wine with which to celebrate; characteristics are that it palpably agitates in the glass, that it is reinforced by exotic origin (France), and its cost.

Is Champagne a Generic Term?

The Court's central task is to determine the overall perception of New Zealanders of the word *champagne*. The following categories of evidence are singled out: (1) dictionaries and linguistic experts, (2) market research, (3) wine expert witnesses, and (4) restaurant wine lists and newspaper advertisements. Based on this evidence, the Court's decision is that the word champagne in New Zealand is not generically used to describe any white sparkling wine.

The Law of Passing Off

The cause of action is not of the classic form whereby one manufacturer seeks to disguise its goods as those of another by imitating name or style of packaging so as to pass off or deceive a buyer as to the true nature of the purchase. This complaint is of a new type of passing off, which is characterized by inconspicuous attachment, and invalid sharing, of a reputation. This new level of passing off makes the identification of the misrepresentation or deceit an indispensable ingredient for liability which is more difficult to prove. The plaintiffs concede that there is no attempt to sell the wine as French wine. They do suggest buyers would think they were buying sparkling wine with all the attractive attributes of Champagne because the product is described by the word.

The essentials of a claim of passing off can be stated within three elements: (1) The case must establish sufficient reputation or goodwill in the name Champagne, (2) The heart of the case is the obligation to show that the challenged actions are likely to cause, or have actually caused, deception, and (3) The plaintiffs suffered or are likely to suffer damage or injury to their business or goodwill. First, there has already been a finding that the word *champagne* retains a distinctive reputation and goodwill and has not become a generic word. Second, the Court's decision is that it is deceptive. Third, the plaintiffs will suffer damage if the word champagne is used on any sparkling wine sold in New Zealand. It follows that the public of New Zealand, by which the Court means the ordinary purchaser without special knowledge of wines and who does not specifically concentrate on differentiation, or is even troubled and carefree about such matters, is likely to be misled. JUDGMENT FOR PLAINTIFFS.

Case Highlights

- "Passing off" is a form of trademark infringement characterized by inconspicuous attachment and invalid sharing of a reputation.
- The crucial factor in passing off is the distinctiveness of the trademark and whether it has become generically used.
- The standard for making the brand name–generic distinction is the perspective of the "ordinary purchaser" or consumer.
- For purposes of conversation at future cocktail parties note the distinction between champagne that is fermented in "the" bottle versus in "this" bottle. The *methode champenoise* requires that the champagne remain in the bottle while impurities are removed during the second fermentation process. Experts turning the bottle over a prolonged period of time "magically" remove the impurities. This is an expensive process and is referred to as in "this" bottle. The cheaper method involves pumping the champagne out of the bottle, removing the impurities by a machine process, and then returning the future champagne by pumping it into another bottle for the second fermentation. This second method is referred to as in "the" bottle. If used adeptly this bit of trivia can help earn you a cosmopolitan reputation.

A large number of countries require the owner of a trademark to use the mark or lose protection under their trademark law. Russian Trademark Law allows the Supreme Patent Chamber to terminate a trademark registration when "any person demonstrates the nonuse of the trademark for a period of five years." The law provides that the registration will not be invalidated in the event that the owner of the trademark shows that its failure to utilize the trademark was for reasons beyond its control. If, for example, the sale of trademarked goods was prevented due to import or export controls, then the owner will retain its trademark rights. Chinese trademark law provides for the canceling of a registered trademark in the event that it has not been used for three consecutive years.

The People's Republic of China views the purpose of intellectual property law in a unique way. Besides the traditional purposes of protecting private property and to encourage technological development, the Chinese see trademark law as a mechanism for quality control and consumer protection. Article 31 of the Chinese Trademark Law authorizes the Trademark Office to revoke a registered trademark if a trademarked good is not of reasonable quality. The law is aimed at providing protection only for trademarks for goods of at least average quality. Thus, a trademark owner that produces goods of inferior quality is seen as deceiving consumers. This deception is based on the assumption that if a good is trademarked, then it is of reasonable quality.

Foreign Patent Law

The fundamental difference between the United States patent system and most foreign patent systems is the time at which patent rights are created. United States law incorporates the **first to invent principle,** where patent rights automatically vest in the inventor at the time of invention. This right is superior to the right of anyone else who may be the first to register the patent with the Patent Office. The inventor has the legal right to have a patent obtained by another party revoked and transferred to him. The United States and the Philippines are the only two countries that award patents on a first to invent basis; all other countries award patents to the first to file or register a patent application. Under the **first to register principle,** the first party to register an invention will receive a legal patent.

http://
State Intellectual Property Law of the People's Republic of China: **http://www.cpo.cn.net/e-page.htm**. Click on link to "Laws and Regulations."

In the area of what types of inventions are protected under patent law there is a great deal of uniformity among the national legal systems. Chinese patent law mimics U.S. law in defining a "patentable" invention as one that possesses *novelty, creativity,* and *utility*. Article 22 of the **Patent Law of the People's Republic of China** describes novelty as an invention that has previously not been published or publicly used. Creativity is defined as a substantial progress over existing technology. Utility requires that the invention be capable of being manufactured or producing a "positive effect."

The **Patent Law of the Russian Federation** defines *patentability* as the invention of something that is "novel, inventive, and can be applied commercially." An invention is novel if it is currently unknown based on the existing level of technology. It is inventive if it does not result from the existing technology in a field. An invention can be applied commercially if it can be employed in industry, agriculture, health, and other spheres of activity. The law further provides that objects of invention include "a device, method, substance, specimen of microorganism, as well as the application of an already known device, method, or substance for a new purpose." Inventions that are not recognized as patentable under Russian law include articles aimed at meeting aesthetic requirements, scientific theories, and programs for computers.

Russian patent law reserves the right to obtain a patent to the employer and not the employee-inventor. Article 8 of the law states that "the right to a patent for an invention created by an employee in the ordinary course of his duties shall belong to the employer, unless otherwise stipulated in a contract between them." The employee-inventor does have a "right to a remuneration proportionate to the profit derived by the employer." The Patent Law invites those applying for a patent to use a patent attorney registered with the Patent Authority. The applicant is required to give the patent attorney a certified power of attorney to act on its behalf. The application must be written in the Russian language, provide an adequate description of the invention, and include a certified receipt of the payment of the required patent duties. Temporary protection is given the applicant beginning on the date of the public notice regarding the nature and content of the application. An approved patent is valid for a period of 20 years unless terminated for cause or due to nonpayment of duties.

Chinese patent law adopts the notion of compulsory licensing found in a large number of developing countries, not often used under U.S. law. Chinese patent law requires the patent holder to *work* the patent in China. To satisfy the work requirement, a foreign patent holder will need to produce the good in China, enter into a joint venture to produce the good in China, or license someone in China to produce the good. In the event that he fails to work the license for a period of three years, the State Patent Bureau is authorized to grant compulsory patent licenses to third parties. Holders of the compulsory licenses are then legally able to produce the patented product. They must, however, pay a reasonable royalty to the original patent holder. Compulsory licenses are also granted to parties who have improved on a previous invention or whose new invention relies upon a previous patent. Often the government will grant a **reciprocal license** to the prior patent holder to be able to use the new invention.

European Union

The European Union has recognized the importance of uniform laws that transcend national laws on intellectual property rights.[43] In EU countries, the intellectual property owner may want to make use of means that provide multinational protections. One example is the availability of a **Single European Patent.** The problem with this patent is that the EU Patent Convention has not been ratified and thus does not provide the intended uniformity and efficiency of application. The single patent is recognized in a number of EU countries, however, along with Switzerland, Sweden, Austria, and Liechtenstein. To acquire the Single European Patent, an application must be submitted to the European Patent Office in Munich.

http://

For a brief description of the European Community Trademark Act: **http://www.lectlaw.com/filesh/il-3.htm.**

In the area of trademarks, the EU Trademark Office in Alicante, Spain, issues a single EU trademark that is valid in all 15 EU countries. It should be noted that national trademarks continue to coexist with the EU trademark. The following Comparative Law feature provides excerpts from Regulation 2868/95 implementing the **EU Trademark Directive.** This regulation is binding in its entirety and directly applicable in all EU countries. Among other things it calls for uniform forms for

43. See generally Andreas Reindl, "Intellectual Property and Intra-Community Trade," 20 *Fordham International Law Journal* 819 (1997).

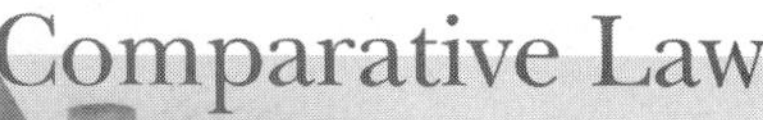

Comparative Law

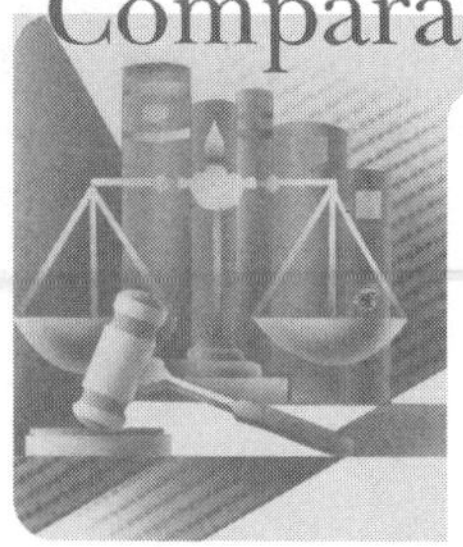

EU Commission Regulation No. 2868/95 on the Community Trademark

This Regulation contains the necessary provisions for a procedure leading to the registration of a Community trademark, as well as for the administration of Community trademarks.

Rule 22: Proof of Use

Where the party has to furnish proof of use or show that there are proper reasons for nonuse, the Office shall invite him to provide the proof required. If the opposing party does not provide such proof before the time limit expires, the Office shall reject the opposition.

Rule 23: Registration of the Trademark and Rule 85: Community Trade Marks Bulletin

The registration shall be published in the Community Trade Marks Bulletin. The Community Trade Marks Bulletin shall also contain publications of applications.

Rule 29: Notification of Expiry

At least six months before expiry of the registration the Office shall inform the proprietor of the Community trademark and any person having a registered right. Failure to give such notification shall not affect the expiry of the registration.

Rule 34: Special Provisions for the Registration of a License

A license in respect of a Community trademark shall be recorded in the Register as an exclusive license if the proprietor of the trademark or the licensee so request.

Rule 42: Application of Provisions

The provisions of these Rules shall apply to Community collective marks.

Rule 44: Application for Conversion

An application may be made for conversion of a Community trademark application or a registered Community trademark into a national trademark application.

Rule 82: Communication by Electronic Means

Where a communication is sent to the Office by electronic means, the indication of the name of the sender shall be deemed to be equivalent to the signature.

Rule 83: Forms

The Office shall make available free of charge forms for the purpose of filing an application, entering opposition to registration, applying for renewal of a registration, and applying for revocation or for a declaration of invalidity of a Community trademark.

applying for, contesting, and renewing trademarks, along with the option of converting a community trademark application into a national application. The regulations also provide for the registering of licenses by licensees.

PROTECTION IN TRANSITIONAL AND EMERGING ECONOMIES

Protection of intellectual property rights in some emerging economies is hampered by inadequate enforcement of relevant laws and regulations. Foreign companies must be vigilant in protecting their products and associated rights from infringement. In some countries novel approaches may be needed because of the lack of government or judicial enforcement. One technique used in countries with weak intellectual property law regimes is to track down counterfeiters and sign them as legal licensees. Ultimately, the courses taken by companies to protect their intellectual property rights will depend on the nature of their products. Some computer software companies, for example, provide free training and sell their software at competitive prices, while warning that copies of their product may contain damaging viruses. Companies with well-known trademarks need to register their marks early and seek the cancellation of any unauthorized registration. In general, a strong local partner or agent can help to defend trademarks and intellectual property.

http://
Office of United States Trade Representative: **http://www.ustr.gov**.

The **U.S. Trade Representative (USTR)** maintains an intellectual property rights "**watch list**" under Section 301 of the United States Trade Act of 1988.[44] This list should be examined prior to making the decision to license in another country.

The new intellectual property law regimes in former Soviet-bloc countries present a special case for scrutiny. The former inventor's certificate system, which gave recognition to an inventor but did not grant a monopoly on profits from the invention, has been mostly abandoned. The newly democratic governments have moved to adopt Western-style intellectual property laws. Unfortunately, the commitment to implement has not been matched with a commitment (or ability) to enforce. Often the new laws begin by fully recognizing international conventions like the Paris Convention, Berne Convention, Patent Cooperation Treaty, and Universal Copyright Convention. Since these conventions dictate minimum standards, domestic legislation is needed to upgrade to the higher standards found in developed countries. Most of the former Soviet-bloc countries have enacted such legislation.

The problem has been in the area of enforcement and remedies. First, the lack of developed remedies under the old inventor's certificate system has carried over to the new systems. When an infringement is recognized, the lack of appropriate remedies or the tendency not to impose harsh remedies results in underenforcement. Second, the court systems are not well equipped to handle claims of intellectual property infringement.

The experience in Russia highlights some of the pitfalls of licensing intellectual property rights in former Soviet-bloc countries. First, Russian patent law[45] adheres to the "first to register" principle in which legal rights are given "solely to those who file applications with a national patent office."[46] Thus, a U.S. patent holder may find it difficult to prevent infringement unless he takes the necessary steps to obtain a Russian patent. The best approach is to secure the services of a **patent agent.**[47]

44. See http://www.ustr.gov/html/special.html for the web site to the 2000 USTR Report containing the watch lists.
45. Patent Law of the Russian Federation, adopted September 23, 1992, available in LEXIS, Intleg Library, Rusleg File. See generally Mark Douma & Rudolph Chistyakov, "The First Patent Law of the Russian Federation," 1 *University of Baltimore Intellectual Property Law Journal* 162 (1993). See also Andrew A. Baev, "Recent Changes in Russian Intellectual Property Law and Their Effect upon the Protection of Intellectual Property Rights in Russia," 19 *Suffolk Transnational Law Review* 361 (1996).
46. It should be noted that Russia is a signatory of the Paris Convention. Therefore, the "true inventor" has 12 months from the filing date in another country to file for a patent in Russia.
47. Russian patent agents are certified under the Statute of Patent Agents enacted in 1993, available in LEXIS, Intleg Library, Rusleg File.

A second issue under Russian patent law is compulsory licensing.[48] If a licensee or a third party makes an improvement on a patent that has not been used for four years, then the law provides that the patent holder must grant the improvement owner a license to use the underlying patent or technology. The "junior" patent holder must argue that it cannot use its patent without infringing on the rights of the other patent. The danger of this provision in the patent law is that "a minor improvement by a second inventor theoretically gives him the right to a license without a reciprocal requirement to grant a license to the first inventor."[49]

Under U.S. law, "if the first inventor refuses to grant a license, the second inventor has no remedy. Russian law provides for compulsory licensing in this situation, thus lessening the value of patent protection."[50] For this reason it is important to periodically use or "work" the patent in order to preclude the creation of second inventor rights. One alternative is to retain the property as a trade secret. If the property is retained as a trade secret, all employment contracts should prohibit the post-employment use of trade secrets. Foreign labor law should always be researched before drafting such clauses, since labor law provisions may protect employees by voiding such clauses.

There have been some hopeful developments aimed at improving the enforceability of Russia's intellectual property law. A recent positive development was the creation of the **Supreme Patent Chamber** by Presidential Edict issued on September 11, 1997. It is hoped that the new judicial body will provide a level of expertise currently lacking in the civil courts. However, its jurisdiction is limited to matters such as the granting of compulsory licenses. The bulk of litigation involving disputes over patent ownership, patent infringement, and licensing contracts remains the jurisdiction of the lower courts.

DEVELOPING AN INTELLECTUAL PROPERTY PROTECTION STRATEGY

Before entering a foreign market, an intellectual property owner or licensor should develop a strategy or checklist to protect its rights. Protection is especially important in countries with weak intellectual property laws or lax enforcement of those laws. A carefully written contract, such as a license, employment, or agency contract or franchise or joint venture agreement, as a mechanism to protect intellectual property will be examined in Chapter 14. The licensor should develop a protection strategy, *before* entering into such an agreement.

Following is an example of such a strategy, using Russia as the target market:

- Explore all protections provided by international conventions. Russia is currently a party to the Patent Cooperation Treaty, Madrid Protocol, Berne Con-

48. See generally Michael Scott, "Compulsory Licensing of Intellectual Property in International Transactions," 10 *European Intellectual Property Review* 319 (1988).
49. Marina Portnova, "Ownership and Enforcement of Patent Rights in Russia: Protecting an Invention in the Existing Environment," 8 *Indiana International Comparative Law Review*, 505, 516 (1998).
50. Maggs, *supra* note 42 at 385.

vention, and Universal Copyright Convention, along with the Paris Convention. These treaty commitments supercede its domestic patent law.

- Enlist expert local guidance. Use a patent agent to obtain a Russian patent, along with any necessary copyrights and trademarks.
- Determine duties or fees payable during the patent term. After obtaining a Russian patent it is important to pay periodic maintenance fees. Failure to pay such fees can result in a termination of the patent.[51]
- Learn where and when notice or registrations are due. In Russia, a licensor is required to record any transfer or assignment of property rights. For example, patent transfers or licenses must be registered with the Patent Office.
- Define ownership rights for employees. In Russia, licensees should be required to enter into employment contracts with their employees that clearly delineate ownership of rights to any improvements made to the licensed technology.
- Explore enforcement options. Because of the poor track record of enforcement by the Russian civil court system, entering license agreements with infringing parties may need to be pursued.
- Protect against compulsory licenses, if necessary. In Russia, a strong best efforts clause should be incorporated into any transfer agreement to prevent claims of abandonment and the issuing of compulsory licenses. Chapter 14 will explain the nature of the best efforts clause.
- The recently enacted **Eurasian Patent Convention** should be utilized when appropriate. This convention allows a Russian patent to be expanded to include a number of other former Soviet republics. The foreign licensor may file an application in the **Eurasian Patent Office** in Moscow.[52]

http://
Eurasian Patent Office: **http://www.eapo.org.**

Finally, the licensor may want to enlist the services of **International Patent Searching Authorities (ISA)** when filing foreign patent applications. A number of national patent offices, including Russia, the United States, and Japan, as well as the European Patent Office, recognize patent search certificates produced by this private company. ISA will forward the search report and the international patent application authorized under the Patent Cooperation Treaty to signatory countries.

http://
International Patent Searching Authorities: **http://www.lib.umich.edu/ummu/pattm/authorities.html.**

Key Terms

Agreement on Trade-Related Aspects of Intellectual Property Rights (TRIPS), 381
Anti-Bootlegging Statute, 379
attributive system, 391
Berlin Act of 1908, 383
Berne Convention for the Protection of Literary and Artistic Works, 383
Berne Convention, 374
bilateral copyright agreements, 383
blurring, 371
Brazilian Industrial Property Law, 391
Brussels Act of 1948, 384
collective works, 373
commercial practice, 388
compulsory license, 381
Copyright Act of 1976, 372
copyright law, 367
Council for Trade-Related Aspects of Intellectual Property, 386
doctrine of equivalents, 375
Economic Espionage Act of 1996 (EFA), 376
EU Trademark Directive, 395
Eurasian Patent Convention, 399

51. See Article 30 of Russian Patent Law.
52. The Eurasian Patent Convention went into effect on January 1, 1996, and provides protection in the countries of Russia, Azerbaijan, Belarus, Kazakhstan, Tajikistan, Turkmenistan, Kyrgystan, Moldova, and Armenia.

Eurasian Patent Office, 399
fair use doctrine, 373
Federal Trademark Dilution Act (FTDA), 371
first sale doctrine, 372
first to invent principle, 394
first to register principle, 394
generic marks, 368
gray market, 377
innocent infringement, 374
International Patent Searching Authorities (ISA), 399
junior mark, 371
Lanham Act, 368
meta-tags, 371
national treatment, 381
Paris Act of 1971, 384
Paris Convention for the Protection of Industrial Property, 381
patent agent, 397
Patent Cooperation Treaty, 382
patent law, 367
Patent Law of People's Republic of China, 394
Patent Law of the Russian Federation, 394
patentee, 375
public domain, 373
reciprocal license, 395
registration, 374
right of priority, 381
Rome Act of 1928, 384
Russian Trademark Law, 391
senior mark, 371
service mark, 368
Single European Patent, 395
Sound Recording Act of 1971, 378
Stockholm Act of 1967, 384
Supreme Patent Chamber, 398
tangible form, 371
tarnishment, 371
term of protection, 387
trade dress, 368
trade secret, 367
Trademark Act, 368
trademark dilution, 371
trademark law, 367
transitional provisions, 386
Treaty on Intellectual Property in Respect of Integrated Circuits, 388
U.S. Trade Representative (USTR), 397
Uniform Trade Secrets Act, 375
Universal Copyright Convention (UCC), 383
watch list, 397
work for hire, 373
World Intellectual Property Organization (WIPO), 381

Chapter Problems

1. What can a U.S. licensor of intellectual property rights do to prevent a gray market problem? See, e.g., Lawrence M. Friedman, "Business and Legal Strategies for Combating Grey-Market Imports," 32 *The International Lawyer* 27 (1998).

2. What are the basic differences between the U.S. patent system and the patent systems found in other countries?

3. *Conflict of law rules* play an important role in the application of national intellectual property laws. Conflict of law rules are applied by courts to determine which national law is to be applied in the case before the court. They are applied when the parties are from different countries or the activities at issue transpired in different countries. The court must decide whether the law of the country of the plaintiff or the defendant, or of some other country should be applied. In a recent case, Itar-Tass Russian News Agency sued *Kurier*, a Russian-language newspaper in New York that copied articles originally published by Itar-Tass, for copyright violation. Itar-Tass claimed *Kurier's* publications of its articles violated the Berne Convention and Universal Copyright Convention. Under what law is the ownership of the articles to be determined? Does the Russian copyright owner have standing to sue for infringement in U.S. courts? *Itar-Tass Russian News Agency v. Russian Kurier, Inc.*, 153 F.3d 82 (2d Cir. 1998).

4. Justice Yates stated more than 200 years ago that: "Ideas are free. But while the author confines them to his study, they are like birds in a cage, which none but he can have a right to let fly: for, till he thinks proper to emancipate them, they are under his dominion." *Millar v. Taylor*, 4 Burr. 2303 (1769). In 1859, Abraham Lincoln commented further that "the patent system added the fuel of interest to the fire of genius." Using these statements explain the purpose of intellectual property laws. Also, how do these laws balance the need to protect the property of "creators" through the granting of "monopolies" over their rights and the goal of free competition?

5. L'Oreal applied for a patent on a sun protection factor (SPF) product in Luxembourg on April 13, 1987. It applied in the U.S. on April 12, 1988. Estee Lauder applied for a patent in the U.S. on the same SPF on December 21, 1987. Assuming that the Paris Convention and Patent Cooperation Treaty applied, who is entitled to the U.S. patent? *Estee Lauder Inc. v. L'Oreal, S.A.*, 129 F.3d 588 (Fed. Cir. 1997)

Internet Exercises

1. Search the United States Copyright Office Web site and report the requirements for filing a copyright registration: **http://www.loc.gov/copyright**.

2. Research the activities of the World International Property Organization by reviewing its Web site at **http://www.wipo.org**.

3. Review the 2000 Special 301 Report of the United States Trade Representative at **http://www.ustr.gov/html/special.html**. What countries are on the Representative's watch lists? Why are these countries on the lists? Be sure to scroll down to the sections titled "Priority Watch List" and "Watch List."

4. Review and compare the texts of the Uniform Trade Secrets Act (**http://www.nsi.org/Library/Espionage/usta.htm**) and the Economic Espionage Act of 1996 (**http://www.tscm.com/**). Scroll down to "U.S. Laws Regarding Electronic Surveillance." What types of activities do they prohibit? What types of information are protected? Are there any defenses to claims under these acts? What remedies or penalties are provided for violations?

5. On May 5, 2000, a Dispute Settlement Panel of the World Trade Organization issued its report in the U.S.-Canada dispute over Canada's term of patent protection. The Panel essentially agreed with the U.S. that Canada's 17-year patent protection fails to comply with the WTO Agreement on Trade-Related Aspects of Intellectual Property Rights. Article 33 of TRIPS requires WTO members to provide a patent protection term of at least 20 years from filing for all patents existing on January 1, 1996. Canada relied on Article 28 of the Vienna Convention, arguing that there is a presumption against retroactivity for treaties. Review the Panel Report available on WTO Web site at **http://www.wto.org**.

6. Review the Web sites of the U.S. Patent and Trademark Office (**http://www.uspto.gov/**), European Patent Office (**http://www.european-patent-office.org/**), and Japanese Patent Office (**http://www.jpo.go.jp/**). Also, through these web sites research the work of the Trilateral Office. The U.S. PTO, EPO, and JPO established the Trilateral offices to facilitate cooperation in the administration of their patent functions (**http://www.uspto.gov/web/tws/gen.htm**).

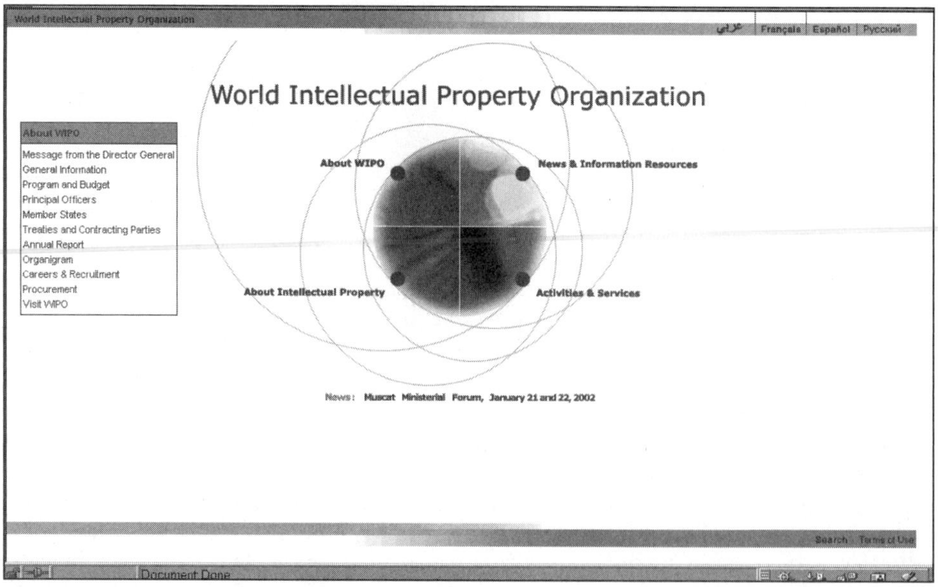

http://www.wipo.org/

Chapter 14 Intellectual Property Licensing

Chapter 13 reviewed some of the shortcomings of foreign and international intellectual property law. These shortcomings mean that the licensor of technology and intellectual property rights must negotiate added protections in international licensing agreements. This chapter will analyze the contractual arrangements used in the field of intellectual property transfer, including a review of common clauses used to protect the rights of the licensor and how best to protect the confidentiality of the licensor's property rights.

An associated issue, introduced in Chapter 13, is the importation of licensed goods into the licensor's market or what is popularly known as the gray market problem. Gray market concerns will be addressed in the discussion of the grant clause and termination of licenses. The post-termination rights and duties of the licensees will also be addressed.

The ability of a licensor to insert contract clauses that will best protect its interests is limited by foreign government regulation of restrictive licensing agreements. The law as applied to international intellectual property transfer is multilayered and complex. Four areas of applicable law need to be studied:

- Whether home country law (law of licensor) applies extraterritorially
- Whether an international convention can be used to protect the property being transferred
- Whether the foreign host country's laws provide sufficient protection
- Whether host country laws exist that regulate the content of the licensing agreement

The first three areas were reviewed in Chapter 13; the fourth will be addressed in this chapter. The fourth area of law becomes especially important when the host country has a propensity for not protecting foreign intellectual property rights. In such countries, the restrictions placed in the transfer agreement may be the only means by which a licensor can protect its intellectual property rights.

LICENSING AND INTELLECTUAL PROPERTY TRANSFER

There are numerous reasons for using licensing or technology transfer agreements to tap into foreign markets. The **licensor** or owner of the technology and intellectual property rights can avoid the costs and time of exporting and importing goods across national borders. She also avoids the panoply of host country laws, such as tax, labor, and environmental laws, that would need to be addressed when directly investing and developing a foreign market.

Licensing, from the licensor perspective, provides an inviting means of generating revenues without committing large amounts of capital. A technology licensing agreement enables a U.S. firm to enter a foreign market quickly, yet poses fewer financial and legal risks than owning and operating a foreign manufacturing facility or participating in an overseas joint venture. Licensing also permits U.S. firms to overcome many of the tariff and nontariff barriers that frequently hamper the export of U.S.–manufactured products. For these reasons, licensing can be a particularly attractive method of exporting for small companies or companies with little international trade experience.

Technology transfer arises from agreements to conduct research and development abroad, to provide technical assistance to a subsidiary or joint venture, or to perform other activities under direct commercial licensing agreements between a manufacturer or intellectual property right owner and a foreign entity. Technology licensing is a contractual arrangement in which the licensor's patents, trademarks, service marks, copyrights, or know-how are sold or otherwise made available to a **licensee** for compensation. Such compensation, known as **royalties,** may consist of a lump sum royalty or a royalty based on volume of production or sales. United States companies frequently license their patents, trademarks, copyrights, and know-how to a foreign company who based on the technology manufactures products for sale in a specific country or group of countries.

http://

National Technology Transfer Center: **http://www.nttc.edu/default.asp**. The mission statement of the Center is to strengthen U.S. industrial competitiveness by promoting the efficient identification and commercialization of marketable research and technologies.

Technology licensing is not limited to the manufacturing sector. Franchising, discussed in Chapter 3, is also an important form of licensing used by many service industries. In franchising, the franchisor (licensor) permits the franchisee (licensee) to employ its trademark or service mark in a contractually specified manner for the marketing of goods or services. The franchisor supports the operation of the franchisee's business by providing advertising, accounting, training, and related services and in many instances also supplies products needed by the franchisee.

Intellectual property licensing in the narrowest sense involves the sale or assignment of statutorily recognized rights of patents, trademarks, and copyrights to a foreign licensee or buyer. Intellectual property is usually expanded to include trade secrets. Trade secrets in the United States are protected under the common law. Technology transfer in its widest sense includes more than the licensing of intellectual property rights. It may include the transfer of technical know-how and skills, along with managerial processes and technical services or assistance. This chapter's coverage applies to both licensing and broader transfer scenarios.

PROTECTING INTELLECTUAL PROPERTY RIGHTS

As a form of exporting, licensing has certain potential drawbacks. The negative aspects of licensing are weakened control over the rights because they have been transferred to an unaffiliated firm and fewer profits than would be generated by exporting goods or services. In certain countries, there are also problems of adequately protecting the licensed property from unauthorized use by third parties.

http://

Text of Section 337 of the Tariff Act of 1930: **http://www.itds.treas.gov/Sec337.htm**.

In considering the licensing of intellectual property rights (IPR), it is important to remember that foreign licensees may attempt to use the licensed IPR to manufacture products to be marketed in the United States or third countries in direct competition with the licensor or its other licensees. In many instances, U.S. licensors will wish to impose territorial restrictions on their foreign licensees if permitted by foreign antitrust and licensing laws. Unauthorized exports to the United States by foreign licensees can sometimes be prevented by filing unfair trade practice complaints with the U.S. International Trade Commission under section 337 of the **Tariff Act of 1930.**

In order to facilitate the denial of entry into the United States of unauthorized foreign imports, the licensor should record its copyrights, trademarks, and patents with the U.S. Customs Service. United States antitrust law, as a general rule, however, prohibits international IPR licensing agreements that unreasonably restrict imports of competing goods or technology into the United States. The U.S. Department of Justice's **Antitrust Enforcement Guidelines for International Operations** contains useful advice about the legality of various types of international transactions, including IPR licensing. In instances when significant federal antitrust issues are presented, U.S. licensors may wish to consider applying for a review from the Department of Commerce or request an **opinion letter** from the Department of Justice.

Before entering a foreign licensing agreement, it is important to investigate not only the prospective licensee but the licensee's country as well. The government of the host country often must approve the licensing agreement before it goes into effect. Some governments, for example, prohibit royalty payments that exceed a certain rate or contractual provisions barring the licensee from exporting products manufactured with or embodying the licensed technology to third countries.

The prospective licensor should review the host country's[1] patent, trademark, and copyright laws; exchange controls; product liability laws; antitrust and tax laws;

1. "Host country" in this context means the country of the foreign licensee.

and attitudes toward repatriation of royalties. The existence of a tax treaty or bilateral investment treaty between the United States and the prospective host country is an important indicator of whether the foreign country is investment and trade friendly.

Prospective U.S. licensors, especially of advanced technology, should also consider the need to obtain an export license from the U.S. Department of Commerce.[2] Because of the potential complexity of international technology licensing agreements, firms should seek qualified legal advice in the United States before entering into such an agreement. In many instances, U.S. licensors should also retain qualified legal counsel in the host country in order to obtain advice on applicable local laws and to receive assistance in securing the foreign government's approval.

Performing **due diligence** is crucial before entering an international licensing agreement. Due diligence should provide answers to the following questions:

- What formalities are needed to register or protect IPR in the host country?
- Will foreign government authorities need to approve the transfer agreement?
- What types of clauses are likely to be disapproved or violate foreign competition (antitrust) laws?
- Are there other mandatory legal rules specific to a particular country?

The next section reviews some of the due diligence issues that should be addressed by the international licensor of intellectual property.

Preventive Due Diligence

In contemplating the exportation of intellectual property rights, the licensor should undertake a due diligence review. For example, foreign national and international IPR laws need to be reviewed in order to take the necessary steps to best protect the licensor's rights. Also, the licensor should review past transfers and infringement actions to determine the types of warranties and protections that it should place in the license agreement. A preventive law checklist should be developed to address these and other concerns (see Focus on Transactions: Checklist for Intellectual Property Transfers). The checklist should be compiled and implemented by an intellectual property review team consisting of both legal and technical personnel.

A licensor's due diligence checklist should include the determination of whether the transfer agreement or license needs to be approved by an agency of the licensee's government. Some countries, unlike the United States, require the **registration** of the license with a government agency. In Russia, for example, all licensing agreements need to be registered. The failure to register the license results in the invalidation of the agreement.[3]

http://

For another example of a due diligence checklist see The Publishing Law Center article titled "Due Diligence: Acquisition of Title and Products" at **http://www.publaw.com/acq.html**.

Licensing the right to use a trademark or trade name is one of the more sensitive issues in negotiating a licensing agreement. As indicated in Chapter 13, the licensor should take all steps to protect its rights to trademarks under the law of the licensee's country. Therefore, before entering any licensing agreement, the licensor should register its trademarks, along with patents and copyrights, under the appropriate foreign national laws. The rights to use the licensor's trademark should be expressly limited to the duration of the agreement. The rights should also be

2. See Chapter 6.
3. Price Waterhouse, DOING BUSINESS IN THE RUSSIAN FEDERATION 53 (1997).

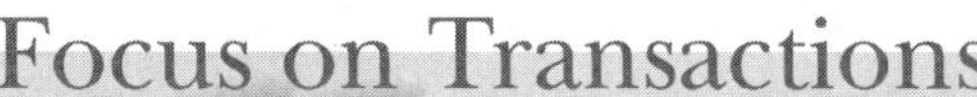

Focus on Transactions

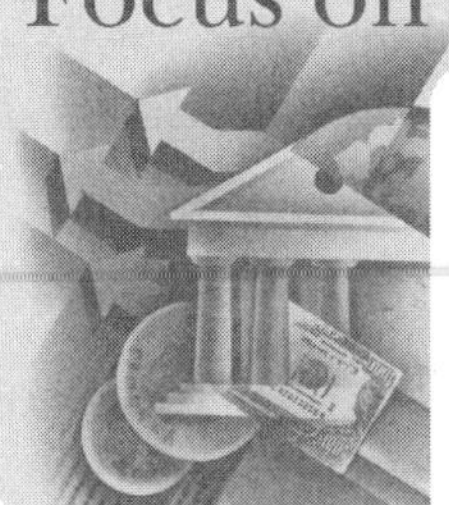

Checklist for Intellectual Property Transfers[4]

Intellectual Property Review Team

Assemble an intellectual property review team. This team should include representatives from management; local and foreign legal counsel; technical personnel, such as representatives from research and development, engineering, and production; sales and marketing; human resources; and financial.

Patents

- What are the times remaining on the patent terms?
- Have patents been used in countries that require *working?*
- Identify all U.S. and foreign patents associated with the transfer.
- Search U.S. and foreign patent office records for title and payment of all necessary fees.
- Identify procedures for protecting inventions, including procedures for determining whether an invention should remain a trade secret, foreign filing requirements, and the timeliness of patent filings.
- Identify all markings to be used in conjunction with the production of the licensed product.
- Identify all existing and pending agreements dealing with the patents.
- Are the patents or licenses transferable? Are improvements included in the transfer? Are there any noncompete provisions? What are the termination dates on the patents and licenses?
- Review all correspondence relating to patent disputes, claims of infringement, and letters threatening lawsuits or other notices received by licensor or licensee.
- What steps have been taken to ensure patent rights in the foreign country of the licensee or the geographic area of the license grant? Has the patent been registered under the appropriate foreign national law?

Trademarks

- Identify all federal, state, and foreign trademark registrations and pending applications.
- Check title and payment of renewal fees.

limited to the territory of the license grant and used only in reference to specific products.

Special attention should be given to the protection of **trade names.** In the United States, a company's trade name is protected by state incorporation statutes. In the process of incorporating, a company reserves a corporate name. Such a reservation prevents anyone else from using a similar name when incorporating. The problem is that trade names are not well protected under some foreign incorporation laws. In a number of countries there is no explicit prohibition against a company using or modifying the name of a pre-existing corporation. Therefore, the license agreement should address the issue of the licensee's use or modification of the licensor's trade names. For example, any registration of the trade name should inure to the benefit of the licensor.

4. See generally Mary Ann Tucker, "Checklist for Due Diligence in Intellectual Property Transactions," 14-1 *Corporate Counsel's Quarterly* 68 (1997).

- Identify all procedures for protecting trademarks, including procedures for deciding whether to seek registrations.
- Provide licensee with samples of the proper use of the trademarks.
- Review copies of all product advertising and promotional materials.
- Check use of the trademark on the Internet.
- Has there been any period of nonuse of the trademarks?
- Have there been any previous assignments of the trademarks? Have these assignments been recorded?
- Are the trademarks and any licenses pertaining to them transferable or assignable?
- Review renewal dates on trademarks.

Copyrights

- Identify all copyrighted materials associated with the transfer or license.
- Check title to copyrights and payment of renewal fees for copyrights by searching the U.S. Copyright Office.
- Review procedures for identifying "copyrightable" material and the protection of those materials, including procedures for deciding whether to mark or register materials.
- Review all previous agreements dealing with the copyrights.
- Does any action need to be taken in the country of the licensee to protect the copyrights?

Miscellaneous

- What procedures, such as site security, employee access, and monitoring of third parties, should the licensee be required to undertake in order to protect the rights being licensed?
- Review employment agreements relating to intellectual property and confidentiality.
- What procedures and responsibilities should the licensee be required to undertake in relationship to third party infringements?
- Does country of licensee require the registration of licenses?

INTELLECTUAL PROPERTY LICENSE REGISTRATION

National laws determine the formalities of preserving and transferring intellectual property rights. In the United States, even though copyrights and patents are automatically protected at the moment of creation, better protection can be achieved by registering them with the appropriate government office. In the area of licensing or intellectual property transfer, compliance with formalities is especially important. In some countries, failure to register a licensing agreement may render it unenforceable.

The **U.S. Copyright Act** allows for the registration of the license or transfer in the Copyright Office. Such registration provides the licensee with important benefits. Section 205 of the Act provides that the recording of copyright transfers constitutes constructive notice of the facts stated in the recording. This becomes important in the event that the copyright owner transfers two conflicting licenses. Section 205(d) states that the license that is recorded first will prevail even against licenses that were granted at an earlier date. Section 204(a) of the Copyright Act states that a transfer of copyright ownership is not valid unless the instrument of transfer is in writing and signed by the owner. "Transfer of copyright ownership" is broadly defined to include the granting of an exclusive license. Thus, both an assignment of all the owner's intellectual property rights and a license of less than total rights need to be in writing.

The formalities of copyright transfers are explored in the *Valente-Kritzer Video v. Callan Productions* case that follows. The case also introduces the concept of how U.S. federal intellectual property statutes preempt other causes of action brought by licensees.

INTELLECTUAL PROPERTY LICENSING AGREEMENT

Once a patent, copyright, or trademark is obtained, the holder is free to assign, transfer, or even mortgage those rights. The licensing agreement is the most com-

Valente-Kritzer Video v. Callan Productions

881 F.2d 772 (9th Cir. 1989)

Sneed, Circuit Judge. VKV produces video programming for sale and distribution. Callan Pinckney is the author of a best-selling book entitled Callenetics. VKV offered to produce a home video based on Pinckney's book. VKV alleges that the parties entered into an oral agreement whereby VKV "was given the exclusive right to shop for a home video deal and to negotiate with major home video cassette manufacturer/distributors for the production and distribution of a home video based upon the book."

Pursuant to the agreement, VKV arranged with MCA Home Video, a nationally recognized producer of home videocassettes, to produce the video. Pinckney, however, refused to perform her part of the agreement. Ultimately, Pinckney and MCA agreed to produce the videocassette that was a commercial success. VKV then filed this action for breach of contract, tortious breach of contract, and fraud. Pinckney moved for summary judgement (dismissal), arguing that the Copyright Act of 1976 preempted all of VKV's claims.

A. *Breach of Contract*

We first address VKV's action for breach of contract. This claim encounters, as VKV concedes, the requirement that a contract transferring an exclusive license in a copyrighted work be in writing. If an oral transfer of a copyright license is later confirmed in writing, the transfer is valid. The right to prepare a derivative work, such as a videocassette based on a copyrighted book, is one of the exclusive rights comprised in a copyright. Section 204(a) not only bars copyright infringement actions but also breach of contract claims based on oral agreements.

B. *Fraud*

VKV's final argument is that the district court improperly held that the Copyright Act preempted the claim for fraud. The district court held that VKV's fraud claim is substantially equivalent to the rights afforded to owners and exclusive licensees of copyrighted works under the Copyright Act, and therefore preempted. We believe that the district court carried preemption too far in this instance. Two district courts have held that common law fraud is not preempted by § 301 because the element of misrepresentation is present. In its complaint, VKV does allege the element of misrepresentation that distinguishes this claim from one based on copyright. AFFIRMED in part and REVERSED in part.

Case Highlights

- A transfer of copyright ownership is not valid unless the instrument of transfer is in writing and signed by the owner.
- "Transfer of copyright ownership" is broadly defined to include the granting of an exclusive license.
- Certain claims, such as common law fraud, are not preempted by the Copyright Act.

mon means of transfer. The intellectual property agreement or license takes on added significance in international transfers as compared to purely domestic transfers in the United States.[5] It is important that the contract provide avenues for lawsuits for breach of contract where an infringement claim is unlikely to be sustained under a foreign intellectual property law regime.

The licensing of technology, intellectual property rights, and know-how involve some of the more complicated and detailed contracts found in international business transactions. National laws that restrict the type of clauses that can be incorporated within a licensing agreement further complicate the license-writing process. Some of these restrictions will be discussed in the last section of this chapter. The next two sections and the section on reviewing a license agreement (page 415) will expose the student to the content of such agreements. The issue of the enforceability of these clauses will be addressed later in the chapter.

Common Licensing Clauses

Because the licensing of IPR is a private contract, the parties are free to formulate their contract as they like. In case of a subsequent dispute, the courts and arbitration panels will look initially to the contract to determine the respective duties and rights of the parties. It is important to note, however, that the licensing agreement is regarded as a *sui generis* contract. Competition (antitrust) laws, for example, will preempt the operation of overly broad territorial restrictions or tying provisions in a licensing agreement.

In most developing countries, certain license clauses are limited by a variety of specific **technology transfer laws.** These laws require approval of the technology transfer agreement by an agency of the government. In essence, the transfer agreement becomes a three-party transaction between the private licensor, the private licensee, and the government.

http://

Yale Library—"Licensing Digital "Information" provides examples of and commentary on a number of important licensing clauses: **http://www.library.yale.edu/~llicense/remcls.shtml**.

Unlike competition law, the aim of technology transfer laws is not to protect competition, but to improve the bargaining strength of the licensee and to promote local technological development. The government approval authorities will examine the contract and rewrite the terms to be more licensee-friendly. The clauses that are most closely examined include the confidentiality, grant-back, choice of law, and export restrictions clauses, and clauses limiting the licensee's use of the technology after the termination of the license. For example, a **duration clause** will often prohibit the use of know-how after the termination of the term of the contract. A technology transfer law may eliminate such a restriction and convert the so-called license into an outright sale.

A **grant-back clause** that requires any improvement of the technology made by the licensee to be assigned back to the licensor is considered invalid under most technology transfer laws. Most countries *will* allow a grant back clause that is reciprocal or nonexclusive. In a reciprocal grant-back clause improvements made by either the licensor or licensee are to be shared with the other party.

A **confidentiality clause** restricts access to the technology to a limited number of **key personnel** of the licensee and prohibits any further disclosure of confidential information to third parties. Many licensors will require licensees to have all their employees sign separate confidentiality agreements. Most developing countries will

5. See generally Byington, "Planning and Drafting of International Licensing Agreements," 6 *North Carolina Journal of International Law & Commercial Regulation* 193 (1984).

insist on a broader dissemination of the technology to its citizens. Therefore, they will often limit the scope of confidentiality clauses and agreements.

A **choice of law clause** or **forum selection clause** that designates the law of the licensor and the licensor's country as the place of dispute resolution is likely to be disregarded by the courts in a developing country. The approval authority in a developing country generally requires that the transfer agreement be subject to the jurisdiction and law of the host country.

In addition, most licensors will desire strict territorial provisions limiting the licensee to selling only in the territory specified in the license. An export restriction clause is generally inserted to prevent the so-called gray market problem where goods are made more cheaply in one country and then exported to compete against the licensor's own goods or those of other licensees. Such restrictions on export may be invalidated under foreign competition law, such as in the European Union, or under technology transfer laws found in many developing countries. Generally, developing countries aggressively promote the export of goods in order to acquire hard currencies and to improve their balance of trade. See Focus on Transactions: Common License Clauses and Explanations for examples and purposes of some other common license clauses.

Foreign competition, technology transfer, and consumer protection laws cannot be avoided through contractual agreement. For example, some foreign contract or consumer laws limit the scope of disclaimers or limitation of liability clauses. Thus, it is imperative that the international licensor determine how such laws, along with differences in customs and trade usage, will impact the operation of their standard licensing agreements. The following sections focus upon some of the standard clauses found in intellectual property agreements.[6]

License Grant and Limitations

The single most important clause in any intellectual property, technology, or software licensing agreement is the **grant clause.** It describes the rights and know-how being transferred, along with any restrictions or limitations on their use. The licensor will want to emphasize that he is granting to the licensee only the right to use the items being transferred. The grant clause should:

- limit or prohibit the licensee's right to copy the licensed material
- prohibit the licensee from reverse engineering
- clearly state that the licensor retains all title, copyright, patents, and other proprietary rights
- call for the licensee to cease using the information upon termination and for the return or destruction of all copies

http://

Licensing Digital Information—The Grant Clause: **http://www.library.yale.edu/~llicense/usecls.shtml** and **http://www.library.yale.edu/~llicense/usegen.shtml**.

The grant clause should itemize the IPR and know-how being transferred. Referencing exhibits that are attached to the agreement is a common technique. The grant should make clear whether the license is exclusive or nonexclusive. The difference is fundamental to issues regarding the degree of competition that may be expected by the licensee and in setting the royalty rate. Also, exclusivity is interconnected to issues dealing with infringement. In an **exclusive license,**[7] the licensee

6. See generally James H. Davis, Kenneth E. Payne & John R. Thomas, "Drafting the Technology License Agreement," *ALI-ABA Course Materials Journal* 13 (Dec. 1996)

7. A hybrid of an exclusive license is the sole license in which the licensor retains the right to produce, sell, or use its rights within the licensed territory.

Focus on Transactions

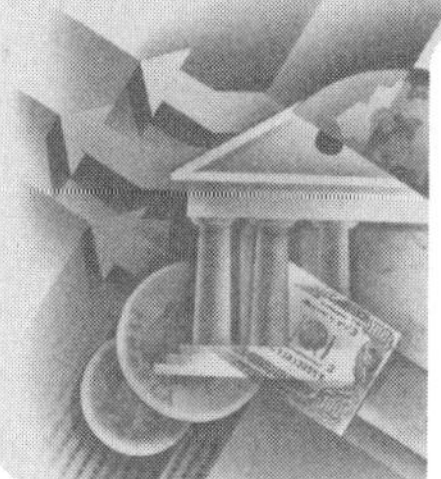

Explanations of Common License Clauses

Compliance with Export Laws

"The licensed products shall not be exported, directly or indirectly, in violation of the export regulations of the United States or be used for any purposes prohibited by the export regulations."

In this clause, the licensee agrees to comply with the export regulations of the licensor's country.

Merger or Integration Clause

"This contract supercedes the terms of any purchase order or ordering document, along with the terms of any unsigned or 'shrinkwrap' license included in any product package."

This clause is especially important where the individual products being transferred come with their own licenses. The licensor would want to supercede such "individual licenses" only if it has provided adequate terms in the master license or transfer agreement.

Limitation of Liability

"The provisions of this Agreement allocate the risks between the licensor and licensee. The licensor's pricing reflects this allocation of risk and the limitation of liability hereto specified."

The parties will generally want to exclude liability for indirect, incidental, special, or consequential damages. The licensor may want to limit the extent of its liability to an amount no greater than the total fees paid by the licensee.

Exclusive Remedy Clause

"The licensee's exclusive remedy and the licensor's total liability shall be the correction of defects in the licensed product or the reperformance of services rendered. Upon failure by the licensor to correct the defects within a reasonable period of time, the licensee may terminate the license and recover any fees paid for the product or for the unsatisfactory services."

An ancillary clause to the limitation of liability clause is one that limits the types of remedies available to the parties.

Infringement Indemnity Clause

"Licensor will defend and indemnify licensee against claims of infringement of patent, copyright, or other intellectual property rights provided that (a) the licensee notifies licensor in writing within 45 days of receiving the claim, (b) the licensor shall have full control over the defense of the claim, and (c) the licensee shall assist the licensor in defending the claim. The licensor shall reimburse the licensee for reasonable expenses incurred in providing such assistance. The licensor shall have the option to (a) modify the licensed products to make them non-infringing or (b) obtain a valid license for the licensee. If the licensor determines that it is not commercially reasonable to perform either (a) or (b), then the licensor may terminate this license and refund the license fees. This shall be licensor's entire liability and the licensee's exclusive remedy for third-party claims of infringement."

The licensee will want assurance that the licensor will defend it against any infringement claims. In turn, the licensor will want to limit its exposure to defending such claims.

Most-Favored-Licensee Clause

"The licensor will notify and offer more favorable terms in the future to ensure that the favored licensee remains on an equal competitive footing with other licensees."[8]

Such a clause requires the licensor to provide the same royalty rate and terms to the licensee that he subsequently gives to another competitive licensee. Such a clause is likely to place the burden in future litigation on the licensor to prove that the most-favored-licensee's competitor was not given a license at a more favorable or lower royalty rate.

8. Carpenter Technology Corp. v. Armco, Inc., 800 F. Supp. 215 (E.D.Pa. 1992).

should negotiate the right to demand that the licensor sue any third-party infringer or the right to sue in the name of the licensor for any infringements in the license territory.

A nonexclusive license grant may include a **most-favored-license** provision in which the licensor is required to amend the license to include more favorable terms negotiated in a subsequent license to another licensee. This ensures that earlier licensees are not placed in an unfair competitive disadvantage.[9] A well written most-favored-license clause would require the licensor to notify the licensee of any new licenses affecting its territory and to provide a copy of any such licenses so that the licensee can determine if the terms of the other license are more favorable. Finally, the most-favored-license clause should provide that if the licensee demands an amendment to its license in order to incorporate any more favorable terms, it must also accept the incorporation of other less favorable terms included in the subsequent license.

The grant clause should also define the grant in terms of its geographic scope, as well as its duration. If the license is for the right to produce, sell, and use the rights in the United States, then the Patent Act implies that the grant is for the entire United States, along with its possessions and territories.[10] If the license is silent as to duration, then a court may imply that it was intended to grant rights for the entire statutory term of the patent, copyright, or trademark.[11]

The grant clause may also restrict the nature of the rights being transferred. For example, for technology with different **fields of use,**[12] the grant clause may restrict the type of use for which the transferred rights are to be utilized. The patent owner (licensor) generally has the right to place any other restrictions that it deems appropriate in protecting its interests.

The *Mallinckrodt, Inc. v. Medipart, Inc.,* case that follows provides an example of a field of use restriction. It also demonstrates that the licensor has the right to sue not only the licensee for violating a grant restriction, but also a third party who assists the licensee in committing the violation. The third party that assists a licensee in the violation of a patent license can be sued for **inducement to infringe.**

A major issue that should be addressed in any IPR license is the right of the licensee to export goods from the licensed territory. Of great concern is the licensee's ability to import goods into the country of the licensor. This gray market issue has become hotly contested throughout the world.[13] If the mobility of the goods being produced under the license is a concern for the licensor, then it should place restrictions in the license in order to prevent gray market imports. The WTO's Agreement on Trade-Related Aspects of Intellectual Property (TRIPS)[14] grants the licensor or intellectual property owner the right to prohibit imports into its home country. Such prohibitions should be clearly delineated in the agreement.

Another method for minimizing gray market risks is for the licensor to negotiate caps on the maximum number of units of the licensed product the licensee can

9. Most-favored-license clauses were held to be enforceable in Carpenter Tech. Corp. v. Armco, Inc., 800 F. Supp. 215 (E.D. Pa. 1992).
10. 35 U.S.C. §§ 100, 271 (a) (1994).
11. See, e.g., United States v. Radio Corp. of America, 117 F. Supp. 449 (D. Del. 1954).
12. For example, the patent owner of laser technology may elect to license the technology separately in the fields of medicine, industry, and government armament or defense.
13. See Chapter 13.
14. Codified in 35 U.S.C. § 271 (a).

Mallinckrodt, Inc. v. Medipart, Inc.

976 F.2d 700 (Fed. Cir. 1992)

Newman, Circuit Judge. This action for patent infringement and inducement to infringe relates to the use of a patented medical device in violation of a "single use only" notice that accompanied the sale of the device. Mallinckrodt sold its patented device to hospitals, which after initial use of the devices sent them to Medipart for servicing that enabled the hospitals to use the device again. Mallinckrodt claimed that Medipart thus induced infringement by the hospitals and itself infringed the patent. The device is marked with the appropriate patent numbers, and bears the trademarks "Mallinckrodt" and "UltraVent" and the inscription "Single Use Only." The package insert provided with each unit states "For Single Patient Use Only" and instructs that the entire contaminated apparatus be disposed of in accordance with procedures for the disposal of biohazardous waste. Instead, the hospitals shipped the used manifold/nebulizer assemblies to Medipart, Inc. The "reconditioned" units, as Medipart calls them, are shipped back to the hospitals from whence they came.

Mallinckrodt filed suit against Medipart, asserting patent infringement and inducement to infringe. The district court granted Medipart's motion on the patent infringement counts, holding that the "Single Use Only" restriction could not be enforced by suit for patent infringement. The court also held that Medipart's activities were permissible repair, not impermissible reconstruction, of the patented apparatus. Mallinckrodt states that the restriction to single patent use is valid and enforceable under the patent law because the use is within the scope of the patent grant, and the restriction does not enlarge the patent grant.

Restrictions on use are judged in terms of their relation to the patentee's right to exclude from all or part of the patent grant, and where an anticompetitive effect is asserted, the rule of reason is the basis of determining the legality of the provision. To sustain a misuse defense involving a licensing arrangement, a factual determination must reveal that the overall effect of the license tends to restrain competition unlawfully in an appropriately defined relevant market.

The district court stated that it intimated no opinion as to whether Mallinckrodt might enforce the restriction on "contract law or property law" or on "equitable grounds." We agree that a patentee may choose among alternate remedies, but to deny a patentee access to statutory remedies is to withhold the protection of the law. Thus whether Mallinckrodt may also have a remedy outside of the patent law is not before us.

It appears that the Court simply applied the rule of contract law that sale may be conditioned. Private parties retain the freedom to contract concerning conditions of sale. The appropriate criterion is whether Mallinckrodt's restriction is reasonably within the patent grant, or whether the patentee has ventured beyond the patent grant and into behavior having an anticompetitive effect not justifiable under the rule of reason. We conclude that the district court erred in holding that the restriction on reuse was, as a matter of law, unenforceable under the patent law. The grant of summary judgment is REVERSED.

Case Highlights

- A license grant may restrict the licensee to a "single patent use."
- A third party that provides a service that allows a licensee to avoid restrictions found in its patent grant (license) is guilty of "induced infringement."
- A patent owner has the right to exclude others from using its invention. Therefore, it has the right to place use restrictions in licensing the patent, unless the restrictions have an unreasonable anticompetitive effect.

produce in a given year. The licensor could also limit the number of units that the licensee may sell to individual purchasers. In addition, the license should state that the licensee is precluded from selling to anyone who is known to import goods into other markets.

In attempting to describe the scope of uses granted by the license, the grant clause may fail to anticipate future unforeseen uses of the intellectual property.

http://

For an analysis of gray market issues: **http://www.managementfirst.com/international_marketing.**

This was the issue addressed by the court in *Cohen v. Paramount Pictures Corp.* In such cases, the court must determine whether the unforeseen use comes within the spirit of the license grant.

Cohen v. Paramount Pictures Corp.

845 F.2d 851 (9th Cir. 1988)

Hug, Circuit Judge. This case involves a novel issue of copyright law of whether a license conferring the right to exhibit a film "by means of television" includes the right to distribute videocassettes of the film. We hold it does not. Herbert Cohen is the owner of the copyright in a musical composition entitled "Merry-Go-Round." Cohen granted H & J Pictures, Inc., a "synchronization" license, which gave H & J the right to use the composition in a film called "Medium Cool" and to exhibit the film in theatres and on television. Subsequently, H & J assigned to Paramount Pictures all of its rights, title, and interest in the movie "Medium Cool," including all of the rights and interests created by the license from Cohen to H & J. Sometime later, Paramount furnished a negative of the film to a videocassette manufacturer, who made copies of the film—including a recording of the composition—and supplied the copies to Paramount. Paramount, in turn, sold approximately 2,725 videocassettes of the film, receiving gross revenue of $69,024.26 from the sales.

On February 20, 1985, Cohen filed suit against Paramount in federal district court alleging copyright infringement. Cohen contended that the license granted to H & J did not confer the right to use the composition in a reproduction of the film in videocassetes distributed for home display.

To resolve this case, we must examine the terms of the license, in order to determine whether the license conveyed the right to use the composition in making and distributing videocassette reproductions of "Medium Cool." The document begins by granting the licensee the "authority to record, in any manner, medium, form or language, the words and music of the musical composition and to make copies of such recordings and to perform said musical composition everywhere, all in accordance with the terms, conditions, and limitations hereinafter set forth." It further states: "The license herein granted to perform said musical composition is granted for: (a) The exhibition of said motion picture to audiences in motion picture theatres and other places of public entertainment where motion pictures are customarily exhibited and (b) The exhibition of said motion picture by means of television, including 'pay television,' 'subscription television,' and 'closed circuit into homes' television." Finally, another provision states that the license reserves to the grantor "all rights and uses in and to said musical composition, except those herein granted to the Licensee."

Although the language of the license permits the recording and copying of the movie with the musical composition in it, in any manner, medium, or form, nothing in the express language of the license authorizes distribution of the copies to the public by sale or rental. One of the separate rights of copyright, as enumerated in section 106 of the Copyright Act, is the right "to distribute copies or phonorecords of the copyrighted work to the public by sale or other transfer of ownership, or by rental, lease, or lending." Thus, the right to distribute copies of the videocassettes by sale or rental remained with the grantor under the *reservation of rights provision.*[15]

It is obvious that the distribution of videocassettes through sale and rental to the general public for viewing in their homes does not fit within the purpose of the license grant that is restricted to showing in theatres and other similar public places. Paramount argues that distribution of videocassettes for showing in private homes is the equivalent of "exhibition by means of television." The words of that paragraph must be tortured to expand the limited right granted by that section to an entirely different means of making that film available to the general public—the distribution of individual videocassettes to the general public for private "performances" in their homes. Television and videocassette display have very little in common besides the fact that a conventional monitor of a television set may be used both to receive television signals and to exhibit a videocassette. Moreover, the license must be construed in accordance with the purpose underlying federal copyright law.

15. See discussion of the reservation of rights clause on pages 416 and 418.

Courts have repeatedly stated that the Copyright Act was "intended definitively to grant valuable, enforceable rights to authors and publishers to afford greater encouragement to the production of literary works of lasting benefit to the world." We would frustrate the purposes of the Act were we to construe this license—with its limiting language—as granting a right in a medium that had not been introduced to the domestic market at the time the parties entered into the agreement.

We hold that the license did not give Paramount the right to use the composition in connection with videocassette production and distribution of the film "Medium Cool." The district court's award of summary judgment in favor of Paramount is REVERSED.

Case Highlights

- In determining the scope of the grant clause, courts will examine any relevant terms of the license for guidance.
- The Copyright Act reserves all rights, whether or not they existed at the time of the creation of the work, to the creator of the work (copyright owner).
- Expanding a license grant to include the application of the licensed property to a medium that had not been developed at the time of the execution of the license would frustrate the purpose of the Copyright Act (protecting the rights of the creator of works).

REVIEW OF TYPICAL LICENSE AGREEMENT

The typical license agreement begins with a preamble that identifies the parties and the nature of the agreement. The generic licensing agreement will have a number of recitals and a definitions section. The recitals are statements of facts pertaining to the parties and the nature of the transaction. The **recitals** will often list the rights being transferred by the licensor. Any untruthful recitals can become the basis for lawsuits asserting breach of warranty or misrepresentation. Because of this, the licensor should verify the status of all its trademarks, copyrights, and patents, along with any patents pending. Definitions will explain the meaning of general and technical terms. Examples include the meaning of "exclusive" license or "net" sales. Because of differences in language and culture definitions take on added significance in an international transfer agreement. Extra care should be taken in defining terms in the definition section of an international transfer agreement.

A number of contract provisions are found in most generic intellectual property licensing agreements.[16] Refer to Doing Business Internationally: License Clause Examples when reading this section. In conjunction with this analysis the student should bear in mind the following questions:

- What issues are being dealt with in the clauses?
- What issues are being neglected?
- How can the clauses be rewritten for added clarity?
- How can the clauses be made more pro-licensor or pro-licensee?

16. Mary Ann Tucker, "Checklist for Due Diligence in Intellectual Property Transactions," 14-1 *Corporate Counsel's Quarterly* 68 (1997). Tucker lists the following clauses as those that should be clearly written: Exclusivity or non-exclusivity of license; assignability or non-assignability of license by licensee; rights or cross-licenses for improvements made by licensee or licensor; rights of licensor to terminate license; licensor's warranty of title; confidentiality provision; post-transaction requirements, e.g., due diligence in returning know-how; details for consulting and support necessary to transfer the technology; and a dispute resolution clause.

In order to address these concerns the reader should draw upon the materials in this chapter and in Chapter 13. The sample clauses provided in Doing Business Internationally: License Clause Examples are brief and need to be customized for a particular transfer. The sample clauses are generally written from the perspective of the licensor.

In a **licensed territory clause,** the licensor defines the appropriate sales areas or distribution channels for the licensed product.[17] If the license grants "exclusive" territory, then the licensor cannot grant other licensees the right to sell in the exclusive territory. The licensor will generally want to restrict the licensee's ability to sell products outside the licensed territory.

Another clause that attempts to limit the licensee's ability to compete against the licensor is the **covenant not to compete.** Much like U.S. courts, foreign courts highly scrutinize and limit these types of clauses. The licensor will often require such a clause in order to prevent the licensee from competing against it after the termination of the license agreement. Article 2596 of the Italian Civil Code typifies the restrictions placed upon covenant not to compete clauses. It requires that such clauses be in writing, be limited to a certain geographical area and activity, and not exceed five years in duration. Italian courts generally favor the licensee in narrowing the restrictions pertaining to area and activity.

In the **reservation of rights clause,** the licensor reserves any intellectual property or contractual rights not expressly transferred by the license. This reservation should always be inserted, even if the license is intended to be exclusive.

The *improvements* or grant-back clause attempts to reserve to the licensor future rights of any subsequent improvements made by the licensee in the licensed property.[18] The licensor will want to stipulate that any modifications or improvements made by the licensee shall revert to the ownership of the licensor. The clause often requires the licensee to assign to the licensor all its rights to any modification.

The grant-back clause should deal with two distinct issues: (1) ownership of the improvement and (2) the right to use the improvement. A one-sided, nonreciprocal grant-back clause, which gives all rights, title, and the right to use any improvements made by the licensee to the licensor, is not enforceable in some countries.[19] Depending upon the country, it may be necessary to provide for reciprocity or sharing within the grant-back clause; any subsequent improvements made by the licensor may also have to be made available to the licensee.

One technique for increasing the likelihood that a grant-back clause will be enforced is to provide for reasonable compensation for the grant back of the licensee's improvements. Also, the grant back can be made nonexclusive. A nonexclusive grant back allows the licensee to continue to use its improvement within the geographical scope of the license.

The licensee generally pays for the licensed property through royalty payments. The **royalty clause** is negotiated along three general parameters: the royalty rate, guaranteed consideration, and momentum royalties. A generic royalty rate is based upon a percentage of sales, determined in one of two ways. The use of gross sales generally favors the licensor, while using net sales favors the licensee.

17. "Licensed product" refers to the products to be produced or sold under the authority granted by the agreement.
18. "Licensed property" refers to the intellectual property rights being transferred under the agreement.
19. In contrast, nonreciprocal grant-back clauses are generally enforced in U.S. courts unless they are held to violate the antitrust laws. See, e.g., Santa Fe Pomeroy. Inc. v. P. & Z. Co., 569 F.2d 1084 (9th Cir. 1978).

The distinction between use of gross sales and net sales is not always significant, however. A net sales definition that allows for very few offsets or deductions will result in a figure very close to a gross sales amount. Conversely, a gross sales definition that allows for a liberal number of setoffs can result in a figure that mimics a net sales figure.

Guaranteed consideration may be a schedule of payments, including a good faith deposit, not connected with sales by the licensee. Guaranteed consideration ensures that the licensee will make reasonable efforts to produce, market, and sell the licensed product. The licensee should negotiate that any advance payments ("Guaranteed Consideration") are to be credited against future royalties.

Momentum royalties are paid when the licensee sells other product lines. These royalties are based upon increases in the licensee's overall sales. This notion is similar to the rental provisions in commercial leases that base the rent on the tenant's sales. Momentum royalties are negotiated in licenses of marquee products that are likely to draw customers to the licensee's other products.

One type of license that creates special problems in drafting the royalty clause is the **hybrid license.** A hybrid license includes patent use rights, along with some other intellectual property right not of the same type or duration as the patent being licensed. One issue that has been disputed is whether the license may provide for payment of royalties past the expiration of the patent.

The U.S. Supreme Court in *Brulotte v. Thys Co.*[20] held that an agreement that extends royalties beyond the life of a patent is *per se* unenforceable. Therefore, royalty clauses must be carefully written to avoid invalidation because of post-expiration royalties. In order to avoid invalidation of royalties in a hybrid license, the license should expressly and realistically allocate royalties between the patent right and the other rights. If the license provides for the use of a number of patents or different intellectual property rights, then it should provide for a reduction in royalties upon the expiration of one of the patents or other rights.

A **best efforts clause** is vital in an exclusive license agreement, since the licensor depends on the licensee to generate sales and royalty payments. Courts have implied such clauses in exclusive licenses,[21] but the licensor would be better served by negotiating a specific best efforts clause with appropriate timetables, benchmarks for production and sales, the amount of monies to be expended by the licensee, and minimum royalty levels. The best efforts clause should provide "penalties" for failure to reach stated goals and for the termination of the license.

Another purpose of the best efforts clause is to prevent a foreign country from issuing a compulsory license on the licensor's technology to a third party. Some countries require a patent owner to use the patent in order to avoid losing the exclusive rights to exploit that patent in the country. Granting a license to a national of that country usually satisfies these so-called "working requirements." The threat remains, however, if the licensee fails to work the license; in that case compulsory licenses may be granted to third parties. A best efforts clause should therefore require that the licensee "work" the license.

Transparency in the licensing relationship should be provided for in the license

20. 379 U.S. 29 (1964).

21. The court in Shearing v. Iolab Corp., 712 F. Supp. 1446 (D. Nev. 1989), extended the implication of best efforts to "improvements." "It is normal and customary in an exclusive licensing arrangement to imply an obligation of the licensee to use its reasonable best efforts with respect to improvements on the invention for which the licensee purchased rights." Ibid. at 1455.

Doing Business Internationally

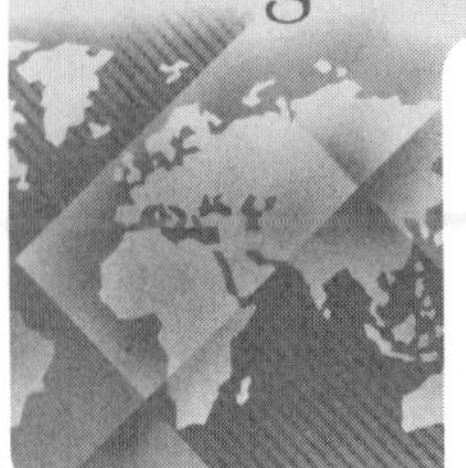

License Clause Examples

License Territory
The licensee may not distribute or sell licensed product to grocery stores or supermarkets. The licensee may sell the licensed product through the following channels of distribution: Gift stores, souvenir stores, and theme parks.

Reservation of Rights
Licensor reserves all rights not expressly conveyed to the licensee. Licensor reserves the right to grant any such reserved rights to other licensees.

Royalties
"Guaranteed Consideration": The sum of $_______ is payable upon the following dates: ____________. These sums as set forth above shall be applied against such royalties as become due to the licensor. No part of such Guaranteed Consideration shall be repayable to the licensee. "Royalty Payments": The Royalty Ratc shall be five percent (5%). The licensee shall pay a sum equal to the Royalty Rate of all "net sales" by the licensee of the Licensed Product. The term "net sales" shall mean gross invoice price billed customers, less actual quantity discounts and actual returns (actual returns not to exceed 5%).

Accounting
Within thirty (30) days of the end of every month, the licensee shall furnish to licensor complete and accurate statements certified by an officer of the licensee with respect to the number of units sold, their gross sale prices, and itemized deductions from the gross sale prices.

Record-keeping
The licensee shall maintain and preserve records pertaining to the license at its principal place of business for at least two years following termination or expiration of the license term or any renewals. These records shall include, without limitation, purchase orders, inventory records, invoices, correspondence, banking and financial records, and any other records pertaining to the Licensed Products. Such records and accounts shall be available for inspection and audit at any time during or after the license term during reasonable business hours and upon at least three (business) days written notice by the licensor.

Indemnification
The licensor shall indemnify the licensee and hold it harmless from any loss or liability arising out of any claims brought against the licensee by reason of the breach by the licensor of the warranties and representations stated within this License Agreement. The licensee shall indemnify the licensor and hold it harmless from any loss or liability arising out of any claims brought against the licensor by reason of the licensee's breach of any provision of this License Agreement including any unauthorized use by the licensee, any improper use of trademarks, copyright, patent, design, or process not specifically granted or approved by the licensor, any noncompliance by the licensee with laws or regulations, and for any defects attributable to the licensee's production of the Licensed Products.

Quality Control
The licensee agrees to strictly comply and maintain compliance with the quality standards, specifications, and rights of approval of the licensor in respect to any and all usage of the Licensed Property. Any modification of the Licensed Product must be submitted in advance for the licensor's written approval as if it were a new product.

Licensor Warranties
The licensor warrants that it possesses the right to license the Licensed Products, including any patents, copyrights, or trademarks, in accordance with the provisions of this License Agreement. The making of this License Agreement does not violate any agreements or rights of any other person, firm, or corporation.

Licensee Warranties
The licensee warrants that it will not harm, misuse, or bring in disrepute the Licensed Property. The licensee will manufacture, sell, and distribute the Licensed Products in accordance with the terms of this License Agreement, and in compliance with applicable government regulations and industry standards. Upon reasonable notice, the licensee shall permit the licensor to inspect

testing records and procedures with respect to the production and sales of the Licensed Products for compliance with applicable quality standards provided in this License Agreement and for compliance with applicable governmental, regulatory, industry, and certification standards.

Confidentiality
The licensee warrants that it will use its best efforts to maintain the confidential nature of all proprietary information and to prevent unauthorized access, reproduction, use, or disclosure of that information. It will restrict access to key employees on a need-to-know basis. In furtherance of this obligation it shall: (a) maintain all copyright notice, trademark notice, and other proprietary markings and (b) not copy or reproduce the proprietary information except as authorized under this agreement.

Copyright and Trademark Protection (Infringement)
The licensee shall cause to be imprinted on each Licensed Product sold under the License Agreement, and on all advertising, promotional, and packaging material, the proper copyright notices and trademarks as instructed by the licensor. The licensee shall promptly notify the licensor in writing of any infringements by others of the Licensed Property. The licensee shall assist the licensor at the licensor's expense in the procurement, protection, and maintenance of the licensor's rights in the Licensed Property. The licensee agrees to cooperate with the licensor in connection with any claims or suits relating to infringements on the licensor's property rights.

Assignment and Sublicensing
This License Agreement is personal to the licensee. The licensee shall not sublicense, franchise, assign, or delegate to third parties any of the rights acquired hereunder. Neither this License Agreement nor any of the rights hereunder shall be sold, transferred, or assigned by the licensee.

Independent Contractor
The licensee is an independent company. Nothing in this agreement is intended to represent that the licensee is to act as an agent or partner of the licensor. The licensee is not granted any rights or authority, express or implied, to bind the licensor in any manner.

Termination
The licensor shall have the right to terminate this Agreement without prejudice to any rights which it may have upon the occurrence of any of the following events: (1) The licensee fails to deliver or maintain the required product liability insurance policy, (2) The licensee becomes delinquent on any payments due under this License Agreement, (3) The licensee fails to provide access to the premises or access to the records required to be maintained under this License Agreement, (4) The licensee fails to comply with applicable laws, regulations, or industry standards, (5) The licensee does not commence in good faith to manufacture, distribute, or sell the Licensed Products throughout the Licensed Territory, and (6) The licensee delivers or sells Licensed Products outside the Licensed Territory or knowingly sells Licensed Products to a third party who the licensee knows intends to or reasonably should suspect intends to sell or deliver[22] such Licensed Products outside the Licensed Territory.[23]

22. The "reason to know" concept would place a requirement of "due diligence" upon the licensee to investigate a third-party purchaser, especially in large volume sales.
23. This provision is clearly aimed at preventing a gray market problem for the licensor. In larger cost products, it would also be prudent to cap the number of units to be produced under the license and the number of units that can be sold to any one purchaser. The overall cap could be determined by calculating an estimate of sales expected for the licensed territory based upon its demographics or based upon sales figures of similar territories.

agreement. This is done through the insertion of accounting and record-keeping requirements. The accounting provision should call for periodic statements of sales and the royalty payments. It should also provide for some form of certification and audit of the sales amount and royalties owing. The licensor should require that an independent accounting firm perform an audit. The licensor should specify payment of interest on delinquent payments and assurances in case of default. The licensee should be required to retain records pertaining to the license and the sales of the licensed products.

Indemnification clauses work both ways between the licensor and the licensee. The licensee generally wants to be indemnified for any liability stemming from the licensor's title or product warranties. The licensor seeks to be indemnified for any misuse of the license by the licensee.

The licensor should also protect itself through a **disclaimer** or limitation of warranty applicable against the ultimate purchaser or consumer. The licensor will want to insert language requiring the licensee to obtain customer signatures agreeing to the disclaimer or limitation.

A good technique used in conjunction with the indemnification clause is to require the licensee to obtain a product liability insurance policy. The best way to prevent liability for product defects is to require the implementation of quality control measures in the production process. The licensor will want to ensure that the licensee complies with quality standards and specifications. It should require that all product modifications require its prior approval. The licensor should also negotiate inspection rights and access to the licensee's testing records and reports.

http://

"Licensing Digital Information"—warranties and indemnification: **http://www.library.yale.edu/~llicense/warrgen.shtml** and **http://www.library.yale.edu/~llicense/warrcls.shtml**.

Warranties and **representations**[24] made in the license are important in liability claims for negligence, misrepresentation, or breach of warranty. The licensor should insert language specifying that only express warranties are enforceable. To further prevent the implication of warranties, the licensor should insert pertinent **negations.** An example of negation includes the statement that the license does not grant the licensee the rights to any subsequent know-how or to additional technical support or information. Another negation may preclude the licensee from using the licensor's trade name. The problem with negation clauses is that a licensor with a U.S. patent cannot be assured that the negation clause will be enforced under foreign law.

The licensee should be required to take all reasonable measures to protect the licensor's copyrights and trademarks. The licensee's duties in this area should be detailed in an **infringement clause.** These duties include affixing the appropriate marks and patent numbers[25] to the products being licensed. The court in *Yarway Corp. v. Eur-Control USA, Inc.,*[26] held that a licensor has a cause of action for damages resulting from the licensee's failure to mark goods as required under the license.

In the area of third-party infringement, the infringement clause places a number of obligations upon the licensee. First, the licensee should be made to act as the "eyes and ears" of the licensor since it is in the best position to uncover in-

24. See Brunsvold, "Negotiating Techniques for Warranty and Enforcement Clauses in International Licensing Agreements," *Vanderbilt Journal of Transnational Law* 281 (1981).

25. Failure to affix the patent numbers may prevent the licensor from collecting damages for past infringements. See 35 U.S.C. § 287.

26. 775 F.2d 268 (Fed. Cir. 1985).

fringement. The licensee should be required to notify the licensor promptly of acts of infringement by third parties. Second, the licensee's cooperation in any infringement proceeding should be required under the transfer agreement.

The license agreement should also detail the rights and duties of the respective parties in the event that a third party sues the licensee for infringement. The most licensee-friendly provision would be an express covenant requiring the licensor to defend and indemnify the licensee against such claims. A licensor-friendly provision, on the other hand, would exclude or limit the licensor's obligations regarding such infringement claims.

One compromise would be to grant the licensee the right to indemnification but limit the indemnity. The licensor can limit its exposure by declaring the option to pay a specified amount to the licensee and terminate the license instead of defending the licensee against an infringement claim. In *Hewlett-Packard Co. v. Bausch & Lomb Inc.*,[27] the court upheld such limited indemnification. Another compromise would be an agreement to share the costs of defending any third-party infringement claims.[28]

From the licensee's perspective, obtaining the right in the license agreement to sue third parties for patent infringement pertaining to the licensed property is not sufficient to actually sue under U.S. patent law. The licensor-patentee must be joined to any such infringement suit.[29] U.S. patent law authorizes infringement actions only by the patentee-licensor[30] or the assignee of a patent.[31] The rationale for this rule is that a license grants to the licensee merely a privilege that protects him from a claim of infringement by the owner. As such, he has no property interest in the patent. "Hence the patent owner may tolerate infringers, and in such a case no right of the patent licensee is violated."[32]

The U.S. Supreme Court has long recognized that the patent owner is an indispensable party to an infringement suit.[33] The courts have also held that granting the licensee the right to sue for third-party infringement does not imply any obligation on the part of the licensor to assist in such actions. "There is no implied agreement by a licensor to protect the licensee by suing. In the absence of a covenant to protect the licensee against infringers there is no obligation on the part of the licensor to do so."[34] Courts have, however, recognized the right of an exclusive licensee to join the licensor as an involuntary plaintiff to an infringement action.[35]

27. 909 F.2d 1464 (Fed. Cir. 1990).
28. See, e.g., Ortho Pharm. Corp. v. Genetics Institute, Inc., 52 F.3d 1026, *cert. denied,* 116 S. Ct. 274 (1995).
29. See, e.g., Yarway Corp. v. Eur-Control USA, Inc., 775 F.2d 258 (Fed. Cir. 1985) (licensee brought claim of infringement against a holder of another patent under the "doctrine of equivalence," where a patent is filed for something that is the design equivalent of another patented device but in which minor changes have been made in order to avoid an infringement claim).
30. 35 U.S.C. § 281.
31. See, e.g., Water Technologies Corp., v. Calco, Ltd., 576 F. Supp. 767 (N.D. Ill. 1983). U.S.C. § 261 authorizes such actions by "assignees, grantees, and successors."
32. Western Electric Co. v. Pacent Reproducer Corp, 42 F.2d 116, 118 (2d Cir. 1930). See also Ortho Pharmaceutical Corp. v. Genetics Institute, Inc., 52 F.3d 1026 (Fed. Cir. 1995).
33. Waterman v. Mackenzie, 138 U.S. 252 (1891).
34. Water Technologies Corp. v. Calco Ltd., 576 F.Supp. 767, 772 (N.D.Ill. 1983). See also Heidelberg Brewing Co. v North American Service Co., 26 F.Supp. 342 (E.D.Ky. 1939); Martin v. New Trinidad Lake Asphalt Co., 255 F. 93 (1919).
35. Independent Wireless Telegraph Co. v. Radio Corporation of America, 269 U.S. 459 (1926). See also Rite-Hite Corp. v. Kelly, 56 F.3d 1538 (Fed. Cir. 1995).

In order to best protect its interests, the licensee should negotiate a clause requiring the licensor to either sue third-party infringers or to join the licensee in any such actions. The clause should state the repercussions for the licensor's failing to fulfill its obligations under the clause. For example, it may authorize the licensee to sue on behalf of the licensor and require the licensor to reimburse the licensee for the costs of the litigation or cease demanding royalty payments. The *Abbott Laboratories v. Diamedix Corp.* case that follows reviews the law regarding whether a licensee has *standing to sue* for the infringement of intellectual property rights included in its license.

Validity or no-challenge clauses prohibit the licensee from challenging the exclusiveness or validity of the licensor's intellectual property rights. Such clauses are generally valid in the United States,[36] but may be invalid in some foreign countries,[37] where they are considered illegal restrictive trade practices. They are also often prohibited in the transfer-of-technology codes found in developing countries.

The license agreement should define the licensee's rights to assign or sublicense its license rights through the insertion of **assignment** and **sublicensing clauses**. The licensor will generally require that the license cannot be sublicensed or assigned.

The **nonpartnership and independent contractor clause** makes clear that the licensee is not acting as an agent or partner of the licensor, hopefully preventing the licensor from being held liable for the actions of the licensee under agency law principles.[38]

http://

"Licensing Digital Information"—duration, renewal, and termination: **http://www.library.yale.edu/~llicense/termgen.shtml** and **http://www.library.yale.edu/~llicense/termcls.shtml**.

Specific termination rights are detailed in a **termination clause.** The termination clause provides the specific grounds upon which the licensor may unilaterally terminate the license agreement. The licensor should make it clear that the termination of the license also requires the termination by the licensee of any sublicenses. Under some foreign laws the unilateral termination of a licensing agreement by the licensor may require the payment of an indemnity. For this reason, the licensor should specify the types of causes that can automatically trigger a termination without indemnity. For example, the failure of the licensee to meet prescribed sales quotas could result in an automatic termination of the license.

The *Paramount Pictures v. Metro Program Network* case on page 424 examines a typical termination clause and the remedies available to the licensor against a licensee that violates the default provisions of the clause. The case also examines post-termination use by the licensee.

All licenses, especially international ones, should provide for dispute resolution. This is done through choice of law and forum selection provisions. Given the unevenness of foreign intellectual property law protections, a U.S. licensor should designate U.S. intellectual property law as the law of any dispute.[39]

The most common forum selection clause in international licensing agreements

36. See, e.g., Shearing v. Iolab Corp., 712 F.Supp. 1446 (D. Nev. 1989); Bausch & Lomb, Inc. v. Barnes-Hind/Hydrocurve, 796 F.2d 443 (Fed. Cir. 1986).
37. See Chapter 13.
38. The expanded liability of a partner or employee under some foreign laws was detailed in Chapter 12.
39. However, a host country court is unlikely to honor a choice of law that avoids its competition, intellectual property transfer, consumer protection, and termination laws.
40. For the specifics of negotiating an adequate arbitration clause refer to Chapter 4.

Abbott Laboratories v. Diamedix Corp.

47 F.3d 1128 (Fed. Cir. 1995)

Bryson, Circuit Judge. Diamedix Corporation appeals from an order denying its motion to intervene in a patent infringement action. The action was brought by Abbott Laboratories, which held a license from Diamedix, against a third party, Ortho Diagnostic Systems, Inc. We conclude that the district court should have permitted Diamedix to join the lawsuit as a party-plaintiff.

In exchange for annual royalty payments, Abbott received a worldwide license to make, use, and sell products incorporating the inventions claimed in the patents. The license was exclusive to Abbott and its affiliates, but was subject to the rights previously granted to Diamedix's other licensees. The agreement was to remain in effect for the life of the patents unless Abbott decided to terminate it earlier. The agreement was not assignable by either party without the consent of the other.

In addition to those general terms, the agreement contained a clause addressing the rights of the parties in suits against third parties for infringement of the patent rights. That clause provided as follows: "If any patent included in PATENT RIGHTS is infringed, Abbott shall have the right, but not the obligation, to bring suit to suppress such infringement against any unlicensed third party."

Abbott filed an action charging appellee Ortho Diagnostic Systems, Inc., with infringing the patents. Ortho denied the allegations of infringement, asserted as an affirmative defense that the patents are invalid, and claimed that Abbott is barred from seeking relief because of its delay in bringing suit. Because Abbott did not join Diamedix as a party to the lawsuit, Diamedix promptly filed a motion to intervene as a plaintiff-intervenor alleging that Ortho had infringed its rights under the two patents. Diamedix argued that Abbott has an incentive not to defend the validity of the patents with great vigor, since a decision invalidating the patents would free Abbott from its royalty obligations.

The Patent Act of 1952 provides that a civil action for infringement may be brought only by "a patentee." The statute defines "patentee" to include the party to whom the patent was issued and the successors in title to the patent, and has been interpreted to require that a suit for infringement ordinarily be brought by a party holding legal title to the patent. Any less complete transfer of rights is a license rather than an assignment. If the patent owner grants only a license, the title remains in the owner of the patent; and suit must be brought in his name, and never in the name of the licensee alone.

The Supreme Court recognized an exception to that rule for cases in which the owner of a patent refuses or is unable to be joined as a co-plaintiff with the exclusive licensee in an infringement action. The Court emphasized, however, that before the exclusive licensee can sue in the patent owner's name, the patent owner must be given an opportunity to join the infringement action. Diamedix retained substantial interests under the patents. Abbott, therefore, does not have an independent right to sue for infringement as a "patentee" under the patent statute. Diamedix retained the right to make and use, for its own benefit, products embodying the inventions claimed in the patents, as well as the right to sell such products to end users, to parties with whom Diamedix had pre-existing contracts, and to pre-existing licensees.

In light of the various rights that Diamedix retains under the agreement, Abbott must be considered a licensee, not an assignee. The district court's decision denying Diamedix's motion to intervene is REVERSED.

Case Highlights

- The invalidity of a patent is an affirmative defense against a claim of patent infringement.
- An assignment of the entire patent, unlike a license of the patent, makes the assignee the owner and gives it standing to sue against third-party infringement.
- An exception to the rule that a licensee does not have independent standing to sue a third-party infringer is made for an exclusive licensee, as long as the patent owner is given an opportunity to join the infringement action.

Paramount Pictures Corp. v. Metro Program Network, Inc.

962 F.2d 775 (8th Cir. 1992)

Magill, Circuit Judge. Metro operates commercial television station KOCR-TV in Cedar Rapids, Iowa. Fitzgerald is the president, general manager, secretary, registered agent, and sole shareholder of Metro. During January 1988, Fitzgerald signed eight interim license agreements with Paramount to broadcast episodes of "Happy Days," "Mork and Mindy," and "Taxi," and packages of motion pictures. Paramount accepted Metro's offers to license these products by letters dated January 28 and March 1.

Under the interim agreements, Metro was to pay Paramount 10 percent of the license fees on January 14, and the remainder in 36 equal monthly installments. Each of the agreements contained the following language: "The license arrangement is subject to those additional provisions as are contained in Paramount's Standard Series Contract and Paramount's Standard Terms and Conditions, copies of which are available on request, and will be fully set forth in a formal written contract." Fitzgerald tendered a check to Paramount dated January 14 in the amount of $26,000. This check was dishonored on March 19 because Metro's account was closed. No other payment was made by Metro under the contracts. Prior to March 19, Paramount had delivered the episodes of "Happy Days," "Mork and Mindy," and "Taxi" to Metro and Metro began to broadcast them.

On May 6, having not received any payments under any of the contracts, Paramount sent Metro a letter terminating the contracts pursuant to the bankruptcy and default provision of the Standard Terms and Conditions and reserving their rights to collect the sums due under the contracts. The provision provides in pertinent part: "If Licensee shall default in the payment of any sums payable in accordance with the terms of this Agreement and such default shall continue for a period of ten (10) days, any and all installments or sums payable under this Agreement remaining unpaid shall immediately become due and payable to Paramount."

"In addition, Paramount shall have the right to (i) terminate each and all of the rights of Licensee under this Agreement and/or (ii) suspend the further delivery of prints until such defaults shall have ceased and shall have been remedied, and/or (iii) seize, wherever found, any print of any licensed picture delivered to Licensee hereunder." On May 20, Paramount sent a second letter, saying that it had been informed that Metro was broadcasting Paramount products "in direct contravention of the Notice of Termination of KOCR's telecast rights dated May 6, 1988," and that the unauthorized broadcast of those products constituted a willful infringement of Paramount's copyrights.

Appellants claim that the district court erred in granting appellees both breach of contract damages and copyright infringement damages because this constitutes an impermissible award of double damages. Under the Copyright Act of 1976, the copyright owner suing an infringer is entitled to either actual damages under § 504(b) or statutory damages under § 504(c).

Section 504 reads, in pertinent part:

(a) In General.—Except as otherwise provided by this title, an infringer of copyright is liable for either —
(1) the copyright owner's actual damages and any additional profits of the infringer, as provided by subsection (b); or
(2) statutory damages, as provided by subsection (c).
(b) Actual Damages and Profits.—The copyright owner is entitled to recover the actual damages suffered by him or her as a result of the infringement, and any profits of the infringer that are attributable to the infringement and are not taken into account in computing the actual damages.
(c) Statutory Damages.—The copyright owner may elect, at any time before final judgment is rendered, to recover, instead of actual damages and profits, an award of statutory damages for all infringements involved in the action, with respect to any one work in a sum of not less than $250 or more than $10,000 as the court considers just.

The district court found that appellants had broadcast 47 episodes of the three sitcoms owned by Paramount after May 20. The court awarded them $500 per infringement, totaling $23,500 in statutory copyright infringement damages. Appellants claim that the breach of contract damages are really an award of actual damages under §504(b) because the claimed infringements occurred during the time the licenses would have been in effect if they had not been terminated and, therefore, appellees are not entitled to both awards.

We find that the breach of contract damages award is not an award of actual damages for copyright infringement under §504(b). The breach of contract claim asserted by Paramount relates solely to events that occurred before May 6. The district court recognized this, and relied strictly on contract law and on the events that took place before May 6 in analyzing this claim. Because appellants did not pay Paramount any of the money owed under the license agreements, they were in default, or breach, of the contracts. Appellants were liable for these damages even if they had not broadcast any Paramount products after the contracts were terminated. In contrast, the copyright infringement claim relates to events that occurred after May 6. Once Paramount exercised its contractual right to terminate the licenses on May 6, appellants no longer had any right to broadcast Paramount products.

Because the damage awards for breach of contract and copyright infringement were for completely separate injuries, the district court correctly awarded both breach of contract damages and copyright infringement damages to appellees. AFFIRMED.

Case Highlights

- A well-worded termination clause allows the licensor to quickly cancel the licensee's rights.
- A licensee who continues to use licensed property following the termination of its license is susceptible to different claims for damages: (1) actual damages for breach of contract and (2) statutory damages for infringement.

is the arbitration clause.[40] To enhance one's ability to obtain and enforce a foreign arbitral award, the place of arbitration should be in a country that has ratified the Convention on the Recognition and Enforcement of Foreign Arbitral Awards ("New York Convention") and where the courts do not have a reputation for interfering with arbitration proceedings.

LAW OF LICENSING

In the event that a licensing agreement fails to resolve a disputed issue, what body of law will be used to interpret and enforce the contract? In the United States, there are two options—the Uniform Commercial Code (UCC) and the Convention for the International Sale of Goods (CISG). For these laws to apply the crucial determination is whether the transaction—the sale of software or license of information—is considered to be a sale of *goods.*

The **mixed sale** articles of the UCC and CISG indicate that software sale contracts are to be considered sales of goods unless a "preponderant part of the obligations consists of labor or services" or the purchaser supplies "a substantial part of the materials."[41] Under the UCC, "off the shelf" software has been determined to be a good. One view of the licensing of information sees the license as a "sale" of the exclusive rights to use that particular copy of the information. In other cases, however, information licensing would seem to fall outside the concept of a "sale of goods" because the licensor retains title to the intellectual property rights and the proprietary information. In such a case, the common law of contracts remains the operative body of law.

Uniform Computer Information Transactions Act

The most recent attempt at creating a series of rules to apply to licensing transactions is the **Uniform Computer Information Transactions Act (UCITA).** A brief review of its provisions is useful for two reasons. First, UCITA highlights some of the issues that confront licensors of IPR, technology, and information. Second, its

41. CISG Article 3.
42. UCITA will be reviewed again in Chapter 15 in conjunction with the "shrinkwrap contract."

http://
Full text of UCITA: **http://www.ucitaonline.com.**

provisions can be used in the negotiation and writing of a license agreement.[42]

The Uniform Computer Information Transactions Act is a model law adopted in July 1999 in Virginia and Maryland to regulate the formation, performance, and enforcement of computer information transactions. Section 104 of UCITA allows parties to opt in or out of UCITA coverage in mixed transactions. It states that "the parties may agree that UCITA governs the transaction in whole or part." **Computer information transactions** are defined as agreements "to create, modify, transfer, or license informational rights."

UCITA expressly states that a license of such rights is not a good for purposes of Article 2 of the UCC. Therefore, in states that enact UCITA it will preempt Article 2 of the UCC in transactions involving the licensing of goods. In UCITA, information is defined as "data, text, images, sounds, or computer programs, including collections and compilations." License means "a contract that authorizes access to, or use, distribution, performance, modification, or reproduction of information including, access contracts,[43] lease of a computer program, and a consignment of a copy." Therefore, the licensing of software or intellectual property rights relating to computer information would be covered under UCITA. UCITA provides rules to deal with legal issues pertaining to contract formation, authentication, duties and rights of performance, breach, remedies, and warranties.

FORMATION OF A LICENSE CONTRACT

The formation or offer-acceptance rules in UCITA mimic those found in Article 2 of the Uniform Commercial Code,[44] with some noticeable variations. The dispatch or **mailbox rule** is modified for electronic acceptance. Under UCITA, an electronic acceptance is effective upon receipt. If the electronic acceptance is by e-mail, is the acceptance received when the message is posted in the offeror's e-mail-box or when the offeror opens its e-mail? Another model law, the **Uniform Electronic Transactions Act (UETA)** states that the acceptance is received when it enters the e-mailbox. Section 15 (b) of UETA states that "an electronic record is received when it enters an information processing system that the recipient has designated for the purpose of receiving electronic records or information." The obtaining and giving of an e-mail address satisfies the designation requirement.

The next issue raised by UCITA is whether a license contract can be formed between computers or between a human and a computer. UCITA answers in the affirmative on both questions. It defines **electronic agent** as "a computer program, or electronic or other automated means, used by a person to initiate an action, or to respond to electronic messages or performances, on the person's behalf without review or action by an individual."[45] Therefore, placing an order through a web page or voice mail creates a contract. Is an offeree able to make a counteroffer when dealing with an electronic agent? No, because electronic agents are unable to evaluate and respond to counteroffers or to acceptances with additional terms. The counteroffer will be construed as an acceptance if it causes the electronic agent to perform, provide benefits, or allow the use or access that is the subject of the counteroffer.

43. Access contract is defined as "a contract to obtain by electronic means access to, or information from, an information processing system." UCITA § 102 (a) (1).
44. See Chapter 8.
45. UCITA § 102 (a) (27). "Electronic message" is defined as "a record or display that is stored, generated, or transmitted by electronic means for the purpose of communication to another person or electronic agent."

UCITA handles the "battle of the forms" scenario differently than does UCC Article 2.[46] In the traditional battle of the forms scenario,[47] a contract is formed between merchants even if the varying or additional terms in the acceptance materially alter the offer. In such a situation, a contract is formed without the additional terms. Under UCITA, additional terms in the acceptance that materially alter the offer prevent the formation of a contract, unless one is formed through the subsequent conduct of the parties.

If the varying terms do not materially alter the offer, then a contract is formed under both UCITA and the UCC. Under UCC Article 2, nonmaterial additional terms in the acceptance become part of the contract. In contrast, UCITA distinguishes between nonmaterial varying terms that conflict with terms in the offer and additional nonmaterial terms that do not conflict with express terms in the offer. In the latter situation, the additional terms do become a part of the contract unless the offeror gives notice of objection within a reasonable period of time.[48] If the nonmaterial additional terms in the acceptance conflict with terms in the offer, then the terms of the offer control.

UCITA also addresses a number of issues pertaining to the writing requirements of the **Statute of Frauds.** First, it expands the Statute of Fraud's notion of a "writing" and "signature" to include **electronic records** and **authentication.** An electronic record is information that is inscribed on a tangible medium or that is stored in an electronic or other medium and is retrievable in perceivable form. To "authenticate" or sign an electronic record is to execute or adopt an electronic symbol, sound message, or process referring to, attached to, included in, or logically associated or linked with that record.[49] One method of proving an authentication is through an attribution procedure. This usually entails the use of algorithms or other codes, identifying words or number, encryption, or callback, or other acknowledgement.[50]

FOREIGN TRANSFER RESTRICTIONS

Some foreign countries attempt to regulate or restrict the transfer of technology and intellectual property to its nationals.[51] Transfer regulations may require government approval. The EU Regulations discussed below, although restrictive, offer the importer of technology or the licensor of intellectual property a degree of harmonization throughout the EU. The People's Republic of China's regulations on the importation of technology will be examined as an example of a restrictive type of transfer regulation. The section concludes with some of the features of registration and approval laws found in developing or emerging-economy countries.

European Union Regulations

In Europe, a foreign licensor must understand the restrictions posed by the competition laws of the European Union and of the individual countries. In

46. See "Battle of Forms" discussion in Chapter 8.
47. See UCC § 2-207.
48. UCITA § 204 (Acceptance with Varying Terms).
49. UCITA § 201 (Formal Requirements).
50. UCITA sets a licensing fee or price amount of $5000 before a writing is required. In contrast, Article 2 of the UCC requires a writing for all sale of goods valued at $500 or more.
51. See, e.g., Ohara, "New Japanese Guidelines for the Commission Regulations of Restrictive Clauses in Patent and Know-How Licensing Agreements," *International Review Industrial Property & Copyright Law* 656 (1991).

some countries, such as Italy, competition law is relatively new[52] and is a close adoption of European Union legislation.

The EU Regulations control the legality and scope of clauses dealing with parallel or gray market imports, infringement, tying clauses, royalties, and term or duration of the license. For example, EU Regulations incorporate the following restrictions:

- A licensing clause cannot prohibit gray market or parallel importing of goods legally produced.
- No-challenge or **validity clauses** are void by law. A licensee cannot be prohibited from challenging the validity of the licensor's right to the intellectual property that is the subject of the license. A license may, however, require the licensee to report acts of third-party infringement to the licensor. It may also require the licensee to take legal action to prevent the infringement.
- A **tying clause** often requires that a licensee purchase its supplies of unlicensed materials from the licensor or a designated supplier. This requirement is allowed only if the licensor justifies the tying to issues of quality control or regularity of supply.
- The license can require the payment of a minimum royalty amount regardless of actual sales, but it cannot require payment of royalties for rights or know-how that subsequently become unprotected or become public information.
- The term of the license may not extend beyond the expiration of the latest patent or intellectual property right.

In general, a licensor may grant exclusive territories, but is prohibited from limiting competition. It may prohibit its licensees from soliciting sales from outside their exclusive territories, but cannot prohibit unsolicited or passive sales. Gray market sales or parallel imports are therefore permitted under EU law. This prohibition against limiting competition prevents a licensor from compartmentalizing territories and artificially setting different prices based on the market conditions in a particular country. EU competition law also prevents the licensor from limiting the licensee to purchasing from a certain supplier. Therefore, nothing prevents one licensee from purchasing licensed products from another licensee.

EU law on gray market sales prevents the licensor from completely prohibiting sales or movement of licensed products outside the licensee's exclusive territory. For example, a licensee or distributor cannot be prohibited under EU competition law from filling unsolicited orders coming from outside its territory. A clause may, however, prohibit the licensee from selling the products of a competitor of the licensor. Despite the fact that exclusivity is a natural characteristic of most licensing, franchising, and distribution agreements, some foreign courts imply that an agreement is nonexclusive if it does not expressly state that it is an exclusive grant of rights.

http://
European Patent Office: **http://www.european-patent-office.org**.

On January 31, 1996, EC **Technology Transfer Regulation 240/96** went into effect.[53] The new regulation is actually two regulations, one pertaining to patents (2349/84) and the other dealing with the transfer of know-how (556/89). The

52. Italy enacted its first Competition Law in 1990 (Law Number 287 of 10 October 1990).
53. See generally, Pierre V. F. Bos & Marco M. Slotboom, "The EC Technology Transfer Regulation—A Practitioner's Perspective," 32 *The International Lawyer* 1 (1998). This regulation provides a *block exemption* for certain license clauses against EU competition (antitrust) law.

purpose of Regulation 240/96 was to simplify patent and know-how licensing. The simplification included clarifying the legality of certain restrictions within transfer agreements in relation to European Union competition law. Exclusive licenses of patents or know-how where the licensor agrees not to work the licensed territory are now expressly exempted from EU competition law. However, the duration of such licenses is limited. An exclusive patent license may extend for a period equivalent to the parallel license of the licensee. A **parallel license** is defined under Regulation 240/96 as the period that such patents would be granted under the national laws of the licensee. Know-how licensing agreements are limited to a period of 10 years from the time that a licensee markets the product.

http://

"Recent Developments in EU Competition Law": **http://www.cov.com/publications/244.pdf.** This article includes checklists for reviewing vertical and horizontal agreements for conformity to EU competition law.[54] It also provides information on popular clauses such as resale price maintenance, territorial, and noncompetition clauses.

Regulation 240/96 also validates certain restrictions placed upon the licensee. Provisions dealing with gray market issues are expressly allowed. Thus, a license clause prohibiting a licensee from using the license outside the licensed territory, or more specifically, in the territory of the licensor, is valid. The Regulation also expands the number of so-called **white-listed clauses** that can be used in know-how and patent transfer agreements. It allows the following contractual restrictions:

- confidentiality provisions prohibiting the licensee from disclosing licensor's know-how
- prohibition of the continued use of the licensor's technology after the expiration or termination of the license
- nonexclusive grant back clauses; however, the licensor may be required to grant an exclusive license to the licensee for subsequent improvements made by the licensor
- best efforts clauses requiring the licensee to fully work the technology in the licensed territory
- clauses giving licensor the right to terminate the license in the event that the licensee challenges the validity of the licensor's patents
- field-of-use restrictions
- production limitations when the licensed product is a component part of another product

In addition, the obligation to pay royalties on sales of nonlicensed products (momentum royalties), a practice which was formerly black-listed, is now permitted.[55]

The Regulation also lists a number of clauses that are prohibited. These **black-listed clauses** include:

- clauses that prohibit all gray market imports by any party
- grant-back clauses that require the licensee to assign the rights to its improvements to the licensor
- general limits on production amounts
- allocation of customers between former competitors

Other types of contracts may be affected by Regulation 240/96. For example, joint ventures between competitors involving technology transfers may benefit from the new regulations. However, to benefit from the block exemption provided

54. The distribution agreement is an example of a vertical agreement. A joint venture agreement for research and development between competitors is an example of a horizontal agreement.
55. See Commission Regulations 556/89, Art. 3(3) and 2349/84, Art. 3(4).

by the Regulation, the parent companies of the joint venture may not have a combined market share of more than 20 percent in a production joint venture or 10 percent in a distribution joint venture.[56]

Another extension of the Regulation is in the area of software licensing. "Software licensing agreements based on copyright are now covered by the Regulation if they are accompanied by patents or know-how within the meaning of the Regulation."[57] Thus, the lists of exempted and prohibited contract clauses are applicable to most types of technology transfer agreements. "Skillful draftsmanship is called for to match the contractual restrictions with the appropriate territories and industrial property. *The Regulation* provides a map with which to steer a legal and effective course through the common market."[58]

Regulations of the People's Republic of China

China's regulations regarding the importation of technology are a serious obstacle to a foreign licensor. The **Regulations Governing Contracts for the Importation of Technology** define imported technology as including the transfer of patents, technical know-how, and technical services. The licensor and licensee must enter into a formal written contract that is to be subsequently submitted to the **Ministry of Foreign Economic Relations and Trade (MOFERT).** The Ministry has 60 days to approve or reject the contract. Other agencies of the government also need to be consulted. For example, approvals often need to be obtained from both the local municipality and the provincial government. Disturbingly, the Regulations impose numerous prohibitions on the substantive content of the transfer contract. For example, Article 8 limits the duration of the agreement to 10 years or "the time period for the recipient to master the imported technology."

The most troublesome provisions are found in Article 9 of the Regulations, which prohibits a number of contractual provisions commonly used by licensors to protect their rights and the rights of other licensees. Some of the prohibited provisions include:

- restrictions on the selection of sources for materials, spare parts, or equipment
- restrictions on acquiring similar technology from a competitor
- unequal conditions for exchanging improvements
- restrictions on the sales channels or exportation of licensed products
- restrictions on post-termination use of the technology

The first two provisions are generally found in exclusive licenses or distribution contracts. The third provision prevents the licensor from negotiating a favorable grant-back clause for improvements to the technology. The fourth provision prohibits clauses aimed at preventing a gray market problem for the licensor or other licensees. The last provision heightens concern for the confidentiality of trade secrets and other sensitive information.

The **Measures for the Examination of Contracts for the Importation of Technology** provides added insight into the restrictive nature of the regulations. Article

56. Pierre V. F. Bops & Marco M. Slotboom, "The EC Technology Transfer Regulation—A Practitioner's Perspective," 32 *International Lawyer* 1, 22 (1998).
57. Ibid. at 24.
58. Ibid. A U.S. exporter contemplating an intellectual property transfer to the European Union should give consideration as to whether Directorate IV (Competition Law) of the European Commission will need to be notified. See generally, Walter Kinn, "New European Union Technology Transfer Block Exemption Regulation," 9 *International Quarterly* 320, 329 (1996).

6 of the Measures mandates that the government review the contract for, among other things, fairness in price and reasonableness of provisions pertaining to property rights, and to ensure that the rights and obligations of the parties are "definite, reciprocal, and reasonable." Thus, the ability of the exporter of technology or licensor of intellectual property rights to protect themselves through a license is heavily circumscribed.

The foreign licensor attempting to negotiate contractual protections should take advantage of the provision for preliminary approval in order to prevent an unexpected disapproval of the final agreement. Article 7 of the Measures provides that the "recipient may prior to or during negotiation seek the opinion of the Approval Authority or submit the contract for preliminary examination with respect to the major contents or certain articles of the contract."

Foreign Registration and Approval

A considerable number of countries, mainly less developed and emerging-economy countries, require some form of government approval of transfer or licensing contracts. These transfer regulations can generally be categorized into two types. First, some require a formal government approval before the agreement becomes valid. Chinese regulations fall into this category.

Second, there are regulations that require the registration of the agreement with a government agency after its execution. This less onerous type of registration regulation should not be discounted in importance. In some countries, such as Russia, failure to register the agreement may result in severe penalties, including the cancellation of the license or contract. Unfortunately, a good many licensors do not bother to register their intellectual property rights in the host country or leave it to a licensee to register. The dangers of such an approach is illustrated in the following excerpt on trademark counterfeiting in Brazil:

> *One of the main causes of trademark counterfeiting in Brazil is a result of association or representation agreements between foreign and local companies. In most cases, when a foreign company enters into an agreement with a local company to represent its products in Brazil and this foreign company is not registered in the country, the first step taken by the local company is to request that the trademark be registered in its name. In this situation, the Brazilian company is justified in acting in this manner to protect the trademark which it represents in Brazil. When this is done in good faith, the Brazilian company subsequently transfers the trademark to the company which it represents and this company then licenses it back to the Brazilian company. In many cases, as the foreign company does not immediately request the transfer, not even as a condition in negotiating the representation, such fact is not usually noticed. If there is a misunderstanding between the two for use by the local company of the trademark registration which it registered in its own name, the local company can use this to its advantage in pressuring the foreign company in negotiations.*[59]

In those countries that require approval, the type of approval varies in scope and application. In some countries such approval is required only for certain types of technology transfers. When approval is required, the parties have to submit documentation that usually includes the draft agreement, financial statements, and proof of ownership of the technology. Provisions of the contract are generally

59. Mauro J. G. Arruda & Pinheiro Neto-Advogados, "Trademark Counterfeiting and Unfair Competition in Brazil," 21 *Comparative Law Yearbook of International Business* 205, 208 (1999).

reviewed with a view to protecting the national licensee. "Governmental bodies charged with reviewing technology transfer agreements often refer to statutory lists of objectionable business practices which must be excised from any agreement as a condition of approval."[60] The most troublesome clauses under approval schemes are those that allow the licensor overly restrictive control, such as one-sided grant-back clauses, and dispute resolution and choice of law clauses that remove all disputes from the host country's courts.

Key Terms

Antitrust Enforcement Guidelines for International Operations, 404
assignment clause, 422
authentication, 427
best efforts clause, 417
black-listed clauses, 429
choice of law clause, 410
computer information transactions, 426
confidentiality clause, 409
covenant not to compete, 416
disclaimer, 420
due diligence, 405
duration clause, 409
electronic agent, 426
electronic records, 427
exclusive license, 410
fields of use, 412
forum selection clause, 410
grant clause, 410
grant-back clause, 409
guaranteed consideration, 417
hybrid license, 417
indemnification clauses, 420
inducement to infringe, 412
infringement clause, 420
key personnel, 409
licensed territory clause, 416
licensee, 403
licensor, 403
mailbox rule, 426
Measures for the Examination of Contracts for the Importation of Technology, 430
Ministry of Foreign Economic Relations and Trade (MOFERT), 430
mixed sale, 425
momentum royalties, 417
most-favored-license, 412
negations, 420
nonpartnership and independent contractor clause, 422
opinion letter, 404
parallel license, 429
recitals, 415
registration, 405
Regulations Governing Contracts for the Importation of Technology, 430
representations, 420
reservation of rights clause, 416
royalties, 403
royalty clause, 416
Statute of Frauds, 427
sublicensing clause, 422
Tariff Act of 1930, 404
technology transfer, 403
technology transfer laws, 409
Technology Transfer Regulations 240/96, 428
termination clause, 422
trade names, 406
tying clause, 428
U.S. Copyright Act, 407
Uniform Computer Information Transactions Act (UCITA), 425
Uniform Electronic Transactions Act (UETA), 426
validity clause, 428
warranties, 420
white-listed clauses, 429

Chapter Problems

1. McCoy hired Mitsuboshi to make and supply shrimp knives covered by McCoy's patent and trademarks. When Mitsuboshi produced the knives, McCoy refused to pay for them. Mitsuboshi resold the knives to Admiral Craft. McCoy sued Mitsuboshi Cutlery, Inc. for patent and trademark infringement in violation of U.S. federal law. Is Mitsuboshi guilty of patent and trademark infringement? *McCoy v. Mitsuboshi Cutlery, Inc.*, 67 F.3d 917 (Fed. Cir. 1995).

2. "Green River" is the trademark under which Sethness-Greenleaf, Inc., sold to bottlers a soft drink, according to a formula that was Sethness-Greenleaf's trade secret. Sethness-Greenleaf sold the Green River business, including the trademark and the trade secret, to Green River Corp. The purchase price was to be paid in installments. When the price was paid in full, the secret formula for the manufacture of Green River beverage and syrup, till then held in escrow, would be released to

60. Alan S. Gutterman, "Regulation of Foreign Inbound Technology Transfers and Direct Investments," 7 *International Quarterly* 599, 600 (1995).

Green River Corp. Green River Corp. fell behind in its payments and Sethness-Greenleaf declared a default, stopped supplying Green River Corp., and demanded the return of the formula from the escrow agent. Unwilling to stop doing business under the "Green River" name, Green River Corp. procured a green soft drink from another producer and sold it under the "Green River" name, precipitating this suit by Sethness-Greenleaf. Green River Corp. counterclaimed that it is not guilty of infringement because Sethness-Greenleaf's failure to continue to supply it with the product was a breach of contract. Assuming that Sethness-Greenleaf is guilty of breach, is Green River Corp. correct? *Green River Bottling Co. v. Green River Corp.*, 997 F.2d 359 (7th Cir. 1993).

3. Your company produces a quality component product that is used in the manufacture of high-scale stereo equipment. The component is manufactured through the use of special software developed by your company. The component and associated software are covered under a number of U.S. patents and copyrights. In addition, your company holds a federally registered trademark that stereo manufacturers are allowed to use in the marketing of their products. Your company has made it a strategic goal to expand the production and sale of the components overseas. It is considering licensing the technology in exchange for royalties; however, it wants to protect the market of its domestic manufacturers. What steps should be taken to maximize protection of the company's intellectual property rights? What license terms should your company insist upon?

4. The premier German manufacturer of compact discs decides to export its discs to markets in Eastern Europe. Because of the economic realities of these emerging-economy countries, the manufacturer is forced to sell the discs at a lower price than it sells them in the German market in order to obtain market share. A wily entrepreneur purchases large quantities of the exported disks and re-imports them into the higher priced German market. What is the likely result under European Union law of the German manufacturer's attempt to prevent the importation of the disks?

5. Your company, a technology company based in the United States, holds a number of patents on Internet-related business applications. It is negotiating a licensing agreement with a major French innovator of Internet technologies. Your company's standard grant-back clause provides a nonreciprocal reversion of all licensee improvements. The French company is refusing to execute the agreement because of the one-sided nature of the clause. Your job is to draft a fair grant-back clause that provides reciprocal rights to the licensor and licensee. How should such a clause deal with the questions of ownership and use? What will be the status of these rights after the termination of the license?

Internet Exercises

1. Review the web site of The Cyberspace Law Institute for information on how the Internet interrelates with intellectual property law: **http://www.cli.org**.

2. Review the web site of the U.S. Copyright Office to determine the requirements for registering a copyright license: **http://www.lcweb.loc.gov**.

3. You own publishing rights to a catalog of popular "do-it-yourself" home and electronic repair manuals. Distributors located in Germany, Italy, and India have approached you. What are your concerns regarding the licensing of the copyrights to these manuals? Develop a due diligence checklist to be used in the negotiation of these licenses. How would your checklist differ for the three countries? Examples of such a checklist can be found at **http://www.publaw.com/acq.html** and **http://www.marklitwak.com/pub_list.htm**. As part of your due diligence research be sure to see USTR's "priority watch" list and "watch list" noted in Internet Exercise 3 at the end of Chapter 13.

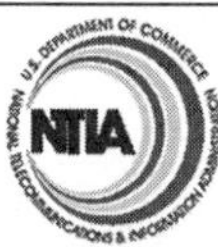

Americans in the Information Age
Falling Through the Net

10-16-2000

Statement by President Clinton

Press Release

Related Department of Commerce Reports

America's New Deficit -- The Digital Work Force: Building Infotech Skills at the Speed of Innovation (PDF file)

U.S. Government Electronic Commerce Policy

Digital Divide Summit
On December 9, 1999, the Secretary of Commerce held a Digital Divide Summit, and announced a new web site, digitaldivide.gov.

October 2000:
The fourth in the ***Falling Through the Net*** series has been released as an HTML file and as a .pdf file. ***Falling Through the Net, Toward Digital Inclusion*** measures the extent of digital inclusion by looking at households and individuals that have a computer and an Internet connection. Executive Summary in html format

The Survey Instrument and Raw Data are posted at http://www.bls.census.gov/cps/computer/computer.htm
This U.S. Census Bureau site contains the survey questionnaire and search tools to access the raw data used in this study.

Previous Reports in the Falling Through the Net Series

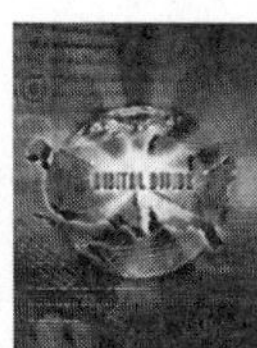

Falling Through the Net: Defining the Digital Divide
Released July 8, 1999, revised November 1999. Third report in the Falling Through the Net series on the Telecommunications and Information Technology Gap in America.

A PDF version of the report is also available (500KB).

http://www.ntia.doc.gov/ntiahome/digitaldivide/

Chapter 15 Electronic Business Transactions

The advance of telecommunications, the advent of the information age, the growth of the Internet, and the exploitation of knowledge as a commodity has accelerated the trend toward purely electronic transactions. Exhibit 15.1 shows that current business trends will result by the end of the present decade in 40 percent of all transactions being conducted by electronic means. Only 13 percent of all transactions were conducted electronically in 1980.

The potential of Internet marketing and sales makes it one of the most important developments to hit the international marketplace.[1] But because the Internet is within the public domain, it and electronic commerce (e-commerce) pose a

1. See generally Jeffrey B. Ritter, "Defining International Electronic Commerce," 13 *Northwestern Journal of International Law and Business* 3 (1992).

EXHIBIT 15.1 *Electronic Transactions (Percentage of all Transactions)*[2]

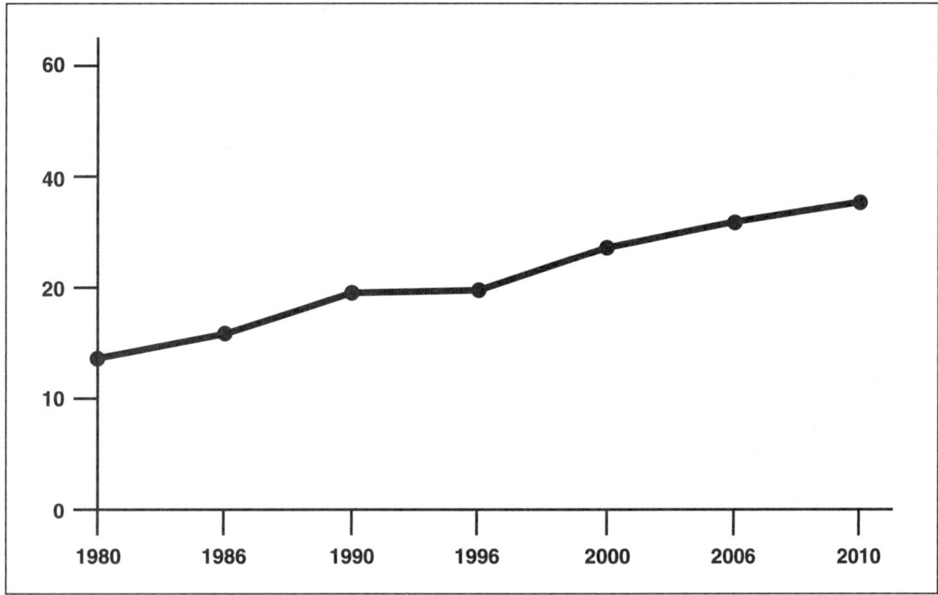

number of risks that have yet to be fully resolved. The scope of e-commerce issues is widespread and touches upon many different areas of business and law. A 1999 EU Council Resolution ("Consumer Dimension of the Information Society") outlined the areas of concern for consumers and the conditions needed for e-commerce to thrive as follows:

- accessibility and affordability
- transparency including in quantity and quality of information
- fair marketing practices, offers, and contract terms
- protection of children against unsuitable content
- security of payment systems, including electronic signatures
- determination of which legal rules are applicable to consumer transactions in the new environment as regards both the choice of law and practicability of existing provisions
- apportionment of responsibility and liability
- privacy and the protection of personal data
- access to efficient systems of redress and dispute resolution

This chapter will survey a number of these issues including personal jurisdiction, protection of personal information, and content regulation.

Despite the technological nature of the Internet, the same issues that are found in more traditional international business transactions apply to Internet transactions.[3] For example, does an Internet transaction bring the seller within the scope

http://

Cyberspace law for nonlawyers (Electronic Frontier Foundation): **http://www.eff.org/Government/Legislation/Legal/CyberLaw_Course/**. An excellent general web site for explanations of many of the issues in this chapter. Topics covered include copyright law, trademark law, privacy law, content regulation, dispute resolution, free speech, and libel law.

2. Source: Adapted from "Technology in Finance," *The Economist* 4 (Oct. 26, 1996).
3. For problems of applying traditional contract and commercial law constructs to electronic commerce and cyberspace see, Joel R. Reidenberg, "Governing Networks and Rule-Making in Cyberspace," 45 *Emory Law Journal* 911 (1996); David R. Johnson & David Post, "Law and Borders—The Rise of Law in Cyberspace," 48 *Stanford Law Review* 1367 (1996); John T. Delacourt, "The International Impact of Internet Regulation," 38 *Harvard International Law Journal* 207 (1997).

of the laws and jurisdiction of the country of the buyer? Will the seller be liable for foreign income, sales, and value-added taxes?[4] Is the transaction subject to foreign consumer protection laws?

This chapter begins with a brief look at how questions of jurisdiction are being applied to electronic transactions. It then focuses directly on issues specific to e-commerce, such as trademark infringement, privacy, and database protection. After a brief introduction to electronic data interchange, an analysis of legal issues related to e-contracting is undertaken. The chapter concludes with the topic of e-commerce ethics.

PERSONAL JURISDICTION

A key issue for the person making an initial foray into e-commerce is whether that person will become amenable to the jurisdiction of a foreign court. Does advertising or processing an order over the Internet provide enough contact with the jurisdiction of the other party to give a foreign court personal jurisdiction? Jurisdiction means the power of a court to hear a case. **Personal jurisdiction** pertains to the power or authority of a judge to require a defendant to defend herself in the judge's court. Under the Due Process Clause of the U.S. Constitution, a court gains personal jurisdiction over a defendant only if the defendant has had **minimum contacts** with the forum state.

A number of recent U.S. court decisions offer some guidance regarding personal jurisdiction in Internet transactions. A Federal Circuit Court in *Bensusan Restaurant Corp. v. King*[5] held that the creation of a Web site did not constitute transacting business in a foreign jurisdiction. A restaurant operated under the same name as a trademarked nightclub in New York City. The trademark owner brought suit for tortious infringement of trademark in federal court in New York. The court held that the mere creation of a web site accessible in New York was not enough to prove sufficient intent to do business in New York. The case was dismissed for lack of personal jurisdiction.

http://

Chicago-Kent Law School Project on Internet Jurisdiction: **http://www.kentlaw.edu/cyberlaw/**.

In the case of *Cybersell, Inc. v. Cybersell, Inc.*,[6] a trademark owner brought suit for tortious infringement of trademark. A Florida company created a web page to advertise its web construction services. An Arizona company had a trademark for the same name. In dismissing the case, the court stated that "no court has ever held that an Internet advertisement alone is sufficient to subject the advertiser to jurisdiction in another state." The court further emphasized that the Florida company had not contracted or sold to anyone in Arizona.

We turn now to two cases that represent opposite ends of the jurisdictional spectrum: *CompuServe, Inc. v. Patterson* and *Bensusan Restaurant Corp. v. King*. The

4. The evolving law and issues relating to Internet taxation are beyond the scope of this chapter. See generally David L. Forst, "Old and New Issues in the Taxation of Electronic Commerce," 14 *Berkeley Technology Law Journal* 711 (1999); Patrick Thibodeau, "Europe Wants U.S. Firms to Pay E-Commerce Taxes," 33 *Computerworld* 41 (Aug. 30, 1999); John K. Sweet, "Formulating International Tax Law in the Age of Electronic Commerce: The Possible Ascendancy of Residence-Based Taxation in an Era of Eroding Traditional Income Tax Principles," 146 *University of Pennsylvania Law Review* 1949 (1998); Anne Murrath, Stan Beelen & Martin Fish, "European Union: The Internet and VAT in the EU," 8 *International Tax Review* 49 (1997).

5. 126 F3d 25 (2d Cir. 1997). Compare, Inset Systems, Inc. v. Instruction Set, Inc., 937 F. Supp. 161 (D. Conn. 1996).

6. 130 F3d 414 (9th Cir. 1997). For a case finding personal jurisdiction, see CompuServe, Inc. v. Patterson, 89 F.3d 1257 (6th Cir. 1996) (a subscriber to a service held to have purposefully availed himself of doing business in the state of the shareware distributor).

CompuServe case introduces the method of licensing software known as **shareware.** In that case, Patterson in effect used CompuServe as a distribution center to market his software. Because Patterson had chosen to transmit his product from Texas to CompuServe's system in Ohio, and because that system provided access to his product to others to whom he advertised and sold his product, the court concluded that Patterson purposefully availed himself of the privilege of doing business in Ohio.

CompuServe, Inc. v. Patterson

89 F.3d 1257 (6th Cir. 1996)

Brown, Circuit Judge. CompuServe is a computer information service headquartered in Columbus, Ohio. CompuServe operates as an electronic conduit to provide its subscribers computer software products, which may originate either from CompuServe itself or from other parties. Computer software generated and distributed in this manner is, according to CompuServe, often referred to as "shareware." Shareware makes money only through the voluntary compliance of an "end user," that is, another CompuServe subscriber who pays the creator's suggested licensing fee if she uses the software beyond a specified trial period. The "end user" pays that fee directly to CompuServe in Ohio, and CompuServe takes a 15 percent fee for its trouble before remitting the balance to the shareware's creator.

Defendant, Richard Patterson, subscribed to CompuServe, and he had placed items of "shareware" on the CompuServe system for others to use and purchase. When he became a shareware "provider," Patterson entered into a "Shareware Registration Agreement" (SRA). This Agreement expressly provides that both parties entered into the contract in Ohio, and that it is to "be governed by and construed in accordance with" Ohio law. From 1991 through 1994, Patterson electronically transmitted 32 master software files to CompuServe. Patterson's software product was, apparently, a program designed to help people navigate their way around the larger Internet network. CompuServe began to market a similar product, however, with markings and names that Patterson took to be too similar to his own.

CompuServe filed this declaratory judgment action in the federal district court for the Southern District of Ohio. CompuServe sought, among other things, a declaration that it had not infringed any common law trademarks of Patterson. Patterson responded with a motion to dismiss for lack of personal jurisdiction.

The "purposeful availment" requirement is satisfied when the defendant's contacts with the forum state "creates a 'substantial connection' with the forum State," and when the defendant's conduct and connection are such that he "should reasonably anticipate being haled into court there." Patterson chose to transmit his software from Texas to CompuServe's system in Ohio, myriad others gained access to Patterson's software via that system, and Patterson advertised and sold his product through that system. Moreover, this was a relationship intended to be ongoing in nature; it was not a "one-shot affair."

Finally, because of the unique nature of this case, we deem it important to note what we do not hold. We need not and do not hold that Patterson would be subject to suit in any state where his software was purchased or used; that is not the case before us. We also do not have before us an attempt by another party from a third state to sue Patterson in Ohio for, say, a "computer virus" caused by his software; thus we need not address whether personal jurisdiction could be found on those facts. Finally, we need not and do not hold that CompuServe may sue any regular subscriber to its service for nonpayment in Ohio.

Because we believe that Patterson had sufficient contacts with Ohio to support the exercise of personal jurisdiction over him, we REVERSE the district court's dismissal.

Case Highlights

- Shareware is a way of selling software where the user is permitted to download and use that software for a trial period, after which the user is asked to pay a fee to the author for continued use.
- Due process considerations for purposes of personal jurisdiction are satisfied if the defendant "purposely avails" itself to the laws of the forum state.

By contrast, the *Bensusan* case involved the use of a **passive web page.**[7] The court observed that whereas the Internet user in *CompuServe* specifically targeted Ohio by entering into an agreement to sell his software over the Internet to out-of-state purchasers, mere advertising on a passive web site does not subject one to the jurisdiction of another state's courts.

Bensusan Restaurant Corp. v. King

126 F.3d 25 (2d Cir. 1997)

Van Graafeiland, Circuit Judge. Plaintiff, Bensusan Restaurant Corp., alleges in its complaint that it is the creator of an enormously successful jazz club in New York City called The Blue Note, which name was registered as a federal trademark for cabaret services on May 14, 1985. Around 1993, a Bensusan representative wrote to King demanding that he cease and desist from calling his club in Missouri The Blue Note. King, at the suggestion of a local Web site design company, permitted that company to create a Web site on the Internet for King's cabaret.

Bensusan then brought the instant action in the Southern District of New York, alleging violations of the Lanham Act and the Federal Trademark Dilution Act of 1995, as well as common law unfair competition. The Web site described King's establishment as "Mid-Missouri's finest live entertainment venue located in beautiful Columbia, Missouri," and it contained the following text: The Blue Note's Web site should not be confused with one of the world's finest jazz clubs, Blue Note, located in the heart of New York's Greenwich Village. Although we realize that attempting to apply established trademark law in the fast-developing world of the Internet is somewhat like trying to board a moving bus, we believe that well-established doctrines of personal jurisdiction law support the result reached by the district court.

New York law states in pertinent part that a New York court may exercise personal jurisdiction over a non-domiciliary who "in person or though an agent" commits a tortious act within the state. Even if Bensusan suffered injury in New York that does not establish a tortious act in the state of New York. Accordingly, in 1966 the New York Legislature enacted an amendment that provides in pertinent part that New York courts may exercise jurisdiction over a non-domiciliary who commits a tortious act without the state, causing injury to person or property within the state. However, the exercise of jurisdiction is limited to persons who expect or should reasonably expect the tortious act to have consequences in the state and in addition derive substantial revenue from interstate commerce.

Because the alleged facts were not sufficient to establish that substantial revenues were derived from interstate commerce, a requirement that is intended to exclude non-domiciliaries whose business operations are of a local character, personal jurisdiction can not be determined. AFFIRMED.

Case Highlights

- The "minimum contacts" standard for establishing personal jurisdiction over a defendant must be applied to Internet activities.
- A long-arm statute grants jurisdiction where a tort (such as trademark infringement) that occurs outside the state causes injury inside the state.
- Mere creation of a Web site containing trademark-infringing material does not satisfy the long-arm statute's requirements for personal jurisdiction.
- Personal jurisdiction does not attach to a tort committed outside of a state unless the defendant purposely directed its activities to the state and derived substantial revenue from those activities.

7. See also E-Data Corp v. Micropatent Corp., 1997 WL805282 (D. Conn. 1997). In this case, the court held that the purchasing of services by downloading material from the Internet was insufficient for purposes of obtaining personal jurisdiction. A key factor in the case was that the accused infringer did not actively advertise its web site. A user had to obtain its web address, access it, browse the information, and then download.

The *Zippo Manufacturing Co. v. Zippo Dot Com, Inc.,*[8] case that follows established a sliding-scale approach to the establishment of personal jurisdiction for Internet activities. In that case, the defendant's web advertisement was followed by the sale of services to more than 3,000 subscribers in the state of Pennsylvania. The number of contacts and sales within a given state is likely to bc considered the major factor in the personal jurisdiction decision. In order to avoid being amenable to suit in a given jurisdiction, it is advisable to place clear **disclaimers** within a web site that your intent is not to engage in transactions with residents in that jurisdiction.

Zippo Manufacturing Co. v. Zippo Dot Com, Inc.

952 F. Supp. 1119 (W.D.Pa. 1997)

McLaughlin, District Judge. This is an Internet domain name dispute. Domain names serve as a primary identifier of an Internet user. Internet companies commonly use their business names as part of the their domain names (e.g., IBM.com). The designation ".com" identifies the user as a commercial entity. We must decide the Constitutionally permissible reach of Pennsylvania's Long-Arm Statute through cyberspace. Zippo Manufacturing Corporation ("Manufacturing") has filed a complaint against Zippo Dot Com, Inc. ("Dot Com"), alleging trademark dilution, infringement, and false designation under the Federal Trademark Act. Dot Com has moved to dismiss for lack of personal jurisdiction.

Manufacturing is a Pennsylvania corporation with its principal place of business in Bradford, Pennsylvania. Manufacturing makes, among other things, the well-known "Zippo" tobacco lighters. Dot Com is a California corporation with its principal place of business in Sunnyvale, California. Dot Com operates an Internet Web site and an Internet news service and has obtained the exclusive right to use the domain names "zippo.com," "zippo.net" and "zipponews.com" on the Internet. A "site" is an Internet address that permits the exchange of information with a host computer. The "Web" or "World Wide Web" refers to the collection of sites available on the Internet. Dot Com has registered these domain names with Network Solutions, Inc., which has contracted with the National Science Foundation to provide registration services for Internet domain names. Once a domain name is registered to one user, it may not be used by another.

Dot Com's contacts with Pennsylvania have occurred almost exclusively over the Internet. Dot Com's offices, employees, and Internet servers are located in California. Dot Com maintains no offices, employees, or agents in Pennsylvania. Dot Com's advertising for its service to Pennsylvania residents involves posting information about its service on its Web page, which is accessible to Pennsylvania residents via the Internet. Defendant has approximately 140,000 paying subscribers worldwide. Approximately 2 percent (3,000) of those subscribers are Pennsylvania residents.

Personal Jurisdiction

Our authority to exercise personal jurisdiction in this case is conferred by state law. The extent to which we may exercise that authority is governed by the Due Process Clause of the Fourteenth Amendment to the Federal Constitution. Pennsylvania's long arm jurisdiction statute permits the exercise of jurisdiction over nonresident defendants upon: "Contracting to supply services or things in this Commonwealth." General jurisdiction permits a court to exercise personal jurisdiction over a nonresident defendant for nonforum related activities when the defendant has engaged in "systematic and continuous" activities in the forum state.

In the absence of general jurisdiction, specific jurisdiction permits a court to exercise personal jurisdiction over a nonresident defendant for forum-related activities, where the "relationship between the defendant and the forum falls within the 'minimum contacts' framework." A three-pronged test has emerged for determining whether the exercise of specific personal jurisdiction over a nonresident defendant is appropriate: (1) the defendant must have sufficient "minimum contacts" with the forum state, (2) the claim asserted against the defendant must arise out of those contacts, and (3) the exercise of jurisdiction must be reasonable.

8. 952 F. Supp. 1119 (W.D.Pa. 1997). See also Maritz, Inc. v. Cybergold, 947 F.Supp. 1328 (E.D.Mo. 1996).

The Internet and Jurisdiction

The Supreme Court noted that "as technological progress has increased the flow of commerce between States, the need for jurisdiction has undergone a similar increase." Enter the Internet, a global "'super-network' of over 15,000 computer networks used by millions of individuals, corporations, organizations, and educational institutions worldwide." With this global revolution looming on the horizon, the development of the law concerning the permissible scope of personal jurisdiction based on Internet use is in its infant stages. The likelihood that personal jurisdiction can be constitutionally exercised is directly proportionate to the nature and quality of commercial activity that an entity conducts over the Internet.

At one end of the spectrum are situations where a defendant clearly does business over the Internet. If the defendant enters into contracts with residents of a foreign jurisdiction that involves the knowing and repeated transmission of computer files over the Internet, personal jurisdiction is proper.

At the opposite end are situations where a defendant has simply posted information on an Internet Web site that is accessible to users in foreign jurisdictions. A passive Web site that does little more than make information available to those who are interested in it, is not grounds for the exercise of personal jurisdiction.

Interactive Web sites where a user can exchange information with a host computer occupy the middle ground. In these cases, the exercise of jurisdiction is determined by examining the level of interactivity and commercial nature of the exchange of information that occurs on the Web site.

Application to this Case

First, we must note that this is not an Internet advertising case. Dot Com has not just posted information on a Web site that is accessible to Pennsylvania residents connected to the Internet. This is not even an interactivity case, since Dot Com has done more than create an interactive Web site through which it exchanges information with Pennsylvania residents in hopes of using that information for commercial gain later. We are not being asked to determine whether Dot Com's Web site alone constitutes the purposeful availment of doing business in Pennsylvania. We are being asked to determine whether Dot Com's conducting of electronic commerce with Pennsylvania residents constitutes the purposeful availment of doing business in Pennsylvania.

We conclude that it does. Dot Com has contracted with approximately 3,000 individuals and seven Internet access providers in Pennsylvania. The intended object of these transactions has been the downloading of the electronic messages that form the basis of this suit in Pennsylvania. We conclude that this Court may appropriately exercise personal jurisdiction over the Defendant and that venue is proper in this judicial district.

Case Highlights

- A sliding scale is used to determine if an Internet activity is sufficient to qualify as "minimum contacts" for purposes of attaching personal jurisdiction to a defendant.
- A company that clearly does business over the Internet is amenable to the personal jurisdiction of a foreign state in which it transacts business.
- A person or company that merely maintains a "passive" Web site is not subject to the jurisdiction of a foreign court.
- Personal jurisdiction based upon an interactive Web site will depend on the level of interactivity and the commercial nature of the site.

The Comparative Law: Proposed Council Regulation on Jurisdiction, Recognition, and Enforcement of Judgments offers excerpts from a proposed EU regulation that would require an Internet retailer to defend itself in the courts of a consumer located in a European Union country. This statutory intervention would make the minimum contacts analysis required in the United States, as used in the *Zippo, CompuServe,* and *Bensusan* cases, irrelevant. The proposed EU regulation would also void the forum selection clause of a license or web page.

The proposed EU regulation brings up a crucial issue of whether a court's exercise of personal jurisdiction over a foreign defendant will be recognized and enforced by a foreign court system. A winning plaintiff in international litigation will often be forced to seek execution of the judgment in a foreign court system. A defendant may not pay on the judgment voluntarily. In such a case, the judgment

Comparative Law

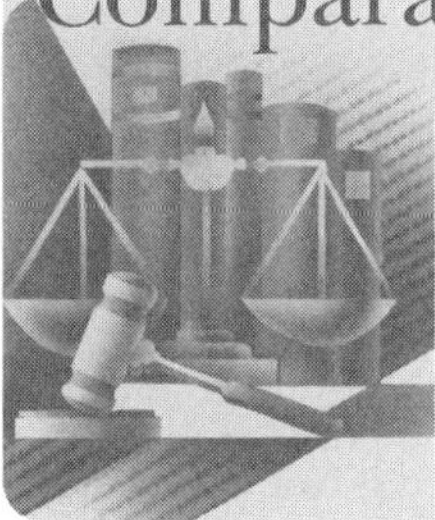

Proposed Council Regulation on Jurisdiction, Recognition, and Enforcement of Judgments

Section 4—Jurisdiction over Consumer Contracts

Article 15

In matters relating to a contract concluded by a person, the consumer, for a purpose which can be regarded as being outside his trade or profession, jurisdiction shall be determined by this Section, if:

(1) it is a contract for the sale of goods on installment credit terms; or
(2) it is a contract for a loan repayable by installments, or for any other form of credit, made to finance the sale of goods; or
(3) in all other cases, the contract has been concluded with a person who pursues commercial or professional activities in the Member State of the consumer's domicile or, by any means, directs such activities to that Member State or to several countries including that Member State, and the contract falls within the scope of such activities.

Article 16

A consumer may bring proceedings against the other party to a contract either in the courts of the Member State in which that party is domiciled or in the courts for the place where the consumer is domiciled. Proceedings may be brought against a consumer by the other party to the contract only in the courts of the Member State in which the consumer is domiciled.

Section 5—Jurisdiction over Individual Contracts of Employment

Article 18

In matters relating to individual contracts of employment, jurisdiction shall be determined by this Section. Where an employee enters into an individual contract of employment with an employer who is not domiciled in a Member State but has a branch, agency, or other establishment in one of the Member States, the employer shall, in disputes arising out of the operations of the branch, agency, or establishment, be deemed to be domiciled in that Member State.

Article 20

An employer may bring proceedings only in the courts of the Member State in which the employee is domiciled. The provisions of this Section shall not affect the right to bring a counterclaim in the court in which, in accordance with this Section, the original claim is pending.

holder will have to obtain satisfaction of the judgment by taking the assets of the defendant. In order to do this he will have to gain the cooperation of a foreign court.

Under the international law principle of **comity,** countries are expected to honor the judicial judgments and orders of a foreign court. However, as discussed in Chapter 4, this recognition is sometimes denied. The *Braintech, Inc. v. Kostiuk* case that follows demonstrates that even closely aligned legal systems, such as those of the United States and Canada, will not enforce the judgment of the other if they determine that the exercise of personal jurisdiction was improper. The case is an issue of first instance involving the posting of defamatory information on an Internet bulletin board.

Braintech, Inc. v. Kostiuk

British Columbia Court of Appeals (1999)

Goldie, Justice. The Plaintiff was a technology company incorporated in Nevada and doing business in various United States jurisdictions. It brought an action in Texas against a resident of British Columbia, alleging the Defendant had published defamatory information about the corporation on an Internet bulletin board. The Texas Civil Code deems a nonresident to do business in the jurisdiction if it commits a tort there.

The Plaintiff obtained a default judgment in Texas and commenced an action on that judgment in British Columbia. British Columbia is obligated to recognize foreign judgments according to principles of [reciprocity and] comity. However, there is a constitutional limitation in the United States on the exercise of personal jurisdiction that requires the Defendant to have sufficient minimum contacts with the jurisdiction. Furthermore, the court must consider whether there was a "real and substantial" connection to Texas. The Defendant's only connection to Texas was passive posting on an Internet bulletin board. To enforce recovery of the default judgment would encourage a multiplicity of actions wherever the Internet is available.

The issue in this case is whether there was a real and substantial connection between Texas and the wrongdoing alleged to have taken place. In my opinion, the trial judge erred in failing to consider whether there were any contacts between the Texas court and the parties which could, with the due process clause of the 14th Amendment to the Constitution of the United States, amount to a real and substantial presence. In the circumstances revealed by the record before this Court, British Columbia is the only natural forum and Texas is not an appropriate forum. That being so, comity does not require that the courts of this province to recognize the default judgment in question. DISMISSED.

Case Highlights

- One country is obligated under international law (principle of comity) to recognize the judicial judgments of a foreign court.
- This recognition is not required unless the exercise of personal jurisdiction satisfies the requirements of due process
- The passive posting of a defamatory statement on an Internet bulletin board does not establish a "real and substantial" connection with a foreign state for purposes of personal jurisdiction.

TRADEMARK INFRINGEMENT, DILUTION, AND CYBERSQUATTING

Trademark protection is "the law's recognition of the psychological function of symbols." Two goals of trademark law are reflected in the federal scheme. On the one hand, the law seeks to protect consumers who have formed particular associations with a mark. On the other hand, trademark law seeks to protect the investment in a mark made by the owner. A recurring problem in Internet commerce has been the misappropriation of names by so-called **cybersquatters**"[9] Cybersquatters are parties that register a famous brand name or trademark as their Internet domain name. The cybersquatter then attempts to extort a payment from the trademark owner for its registered domain name.

The two statutory recourses available in the United States to the trademark owner are the **Lanham Act**[10] and the **Federal Trademark Dilution Act of 1995.**[11]

9. This term and coverage was taken from L. KEITH WHITNEY, DEFEATING THE CYBERSQUATTER: PROTECTING TRADEMARKS AND THE INTERNET (unpublished manuscript) (1999).
10. 15 U.S.C. 1114.
11. 15 U.S.C. 1125 (c).

The Lanham Act requires a likelihood of confusion between the junior user's (infringing party) and the senior user's products. Courts have held that when the goods or services are unrelated to the trademark owner's products, such as when the domain name is registered on behalf of no particular product or service, there is no likelihood of confusion. The Federal Trademark Dilution Act, however, does not require proof of a likelihood of confusion.

Courts have held that the registering of a domain name for the purpose of selling it to a trademark owner is actionable under the Diluton Act.[12] This was confirmed in *Avery Dennison Corp. v. Sumpton,*[13] where the court labeled the defendant a cybersquatter. The court concluded that the defendant's use diluted the well-known trademark of the plaintiffs. In holding against the defendant, the court noted that it had registered more than 12,000 domain names.

http://
The Publishing Law center—"Trademark Protection in Cyberspace": **http://www.publaw.com/cyber.html**.

Unlike infringement and unfair competition laws, in a dilution case competition between the parties and a likelihood of confusion are not required to present a claim for relief. Rather, injunctive relief is available under the Federal Trademark Dilution Act if a plaintiff can establish that (1) its mark is famous; (2) the defendant is making commercial use of the mark in commerce; (3) the defendant's use began after the plaintiff's mark became famous; and (4) the defendant's use presents a likelihood of dilution of the distinctive value of the mark. The Federal Trademark Dilution Act lists eight nonexclusive considerations for the famousness inquiry:

- the degree of inherent or acquired distinctiveness of the mark
- the duration and extent of use of the mark in connection with the goods or services with which the mark is used
- the duration and extent of advertising and publicity of the mark
- the geographical extent of the trading area in which the mark is used
- the channels of trade for the goods or services with which the mark is used
- the degree of recognition of the mark in the trading areas and channels of trade used by the mark's owner and the person against whom the injunction is sought
- the nature and extent of use of the same or similar marks by third parties
- whether the mark was registered on the principal register

In *Panavision Int'l, L.P. v. Toeppen*[14] it was held that the Federal Trademark Dilution Act was implicated when the defendant registered domain-name combinations using famous trademarks and sought to sell the registrations to the trademark owners. Commercial use under the Federal Trademark Dilution Act requires the defendant to be using the trademark as a trademark, capitalizing on its trademark status. In this classic "cybersquatter" case, the court determined that the infringer's intent was to "arbitrage" the registration that included the plaintiff's trademark.

As discussed in Chapter 13, **blurring** is a type of trademark dilution where it is unlikely that consumers will mistake the two companies' products because the products may be dissimilar. Nonetheless, the dilutor's use of the mark still may dilute the uniqueness of the more famous mark. The court in *Toys "R" Us v. Feinberg*[15] held that a gun company's use of the domain name "gunsareus" neither infringed

12. See Intermatic, Inc. v. Toeppen, 947 F. Supp. 1227 (N.D. Ill. 1996); Panavision Int'l L.P. v. Toeppen, 945 F. Supp.1296 (C.D. Cal. 1997).
13. 1998 U.S. Dist. LEXIS 4373 (C.D. Cal. 1998).
14. 141 F.3d 1318.
15. 1998 Dist. LEXIS 17217 (S.D.N.Y. 1998).

nor diluted the senior mark. The court held that any blurring was tenuous because the average consumer would not connect the two names or marks. It confirmed nonetheless that dilution is applicable to Internet cases.

In 1999, Congress enacted the **Anti-Cybersquatting Consumer Protection Act (ACPA).** The *Mattel, Inc. v. Internet Dimensions* case that follows was one of the first cases to apply the ACPA. It is important to note that three types of claims can be made under federal law: trademark infringement, trademark dilution, and violation of ACPA.

Mattel, Inc. v. Internet Dimensions, Inc.

2000 U.S. Dist. LEXIS 9747 (S.D.N.Y. 2000)

Baer, District Judge. Plaintiff Mattel, Inc. ("Mattel"), commenced this action against defendants Internet Dimensions, Inc. ("Internet Dimensions"), and Benjamin Schiff asserting causes of action for (1) trademark infringement under Section 43(a) of the Lanham Act, (2) trademark dilution under Section 43(c) of the Lanham Act, and (3) violation of the Anti-Cybersquatting Consumer Protection Act of 1999 ("ACPA" or "the Act"). Mattel is a publicly held corporation organized and existing under the laws of the State of Delaware. One of its principal products is the trademarked "Barbie" doll.

In 1991, the Second Circuit observed that "the 'Barbie' doll is the best selling toy doll in the world—96 percent of three- to eleven-year-old girls in the United States own at least one. In the past 30 years 600 million Barbie dolls have been sold—one is sold every two seconds—and, in 1990 alone, 26 million of them were sold, earning gross revenues for Mattel of $740 million."

Internet Dimensions is a corporation organized and existing under the laws of the State of Nevada. Internet Dimensions owns Internet domain names for sites that provide, among other things, "adult" entertainment. One of its domain names is "barbiesplaypen.com."

Mattel's primary claim in this action is that defendants violated the Anti-Cybersquatting Consumer Protection Act. The ACPA, signed into law on November 29, 1999, provides that "a court may order the forfeiture or cancellation of the domain name or the transfer of the domain name to the owner of the mark." It also provides that damages can be awarded for violations of the Act.

The ACPA was passed to "protect consumers and American businesses, to promote the growth of online commerce, and to provide clarity in the law for trademark owners, by prohibiting the bad-faith and abusive registration of distinctive marks as Internet domain names with the intent to profit from the goodwill associated with such marks—a practice commonly referred to as 'cybersquatting.'" The Act provides civil liability for cybersquatting as follows:

A person shall be liable in a civil action by the owner of a mark if that person (i) has a bad faith intent to profit from that mark and (ii) registers, traffics in, or uses a domain name that:

(I) in the case of a mark that is distinctive at the time of registration of the domain name, is identical or confusingly similar to that mark;
(II) in the case of a famous mark that is famous at the time of registration of the domain name, is identical or confusingly similar to or dilutive of that mark;
(III) is a trademark, word, or name.[16]

While there is no particular inherent distinctiveness in the name "Barbie," the mark, as it applies to Mattel, has acquired distinctiveness through four decades of exposure in the American consumer market. The Court concludes that the name "Barbie" and the font normally used to advertise BARBIE products is widely recognized throughout the world on the basis of the marketing efforts that have been undertaken by Mattel over the past four decades. The Court finds that the trademark BAR-

16. The terms "distinctive" and "famous" are defined in 15 U.S.C. § 1125(c)(1):
In determining whether a mark is distinctive and famous, a court may consider factors such as, but not limited to:
(A) the degree of inherent or acquired distinctiveness of the mark;
(B) the duration and extent of use of the mark in connection with the goods or services with which the mark is used;
(C) the duration and extent of advertising and publicity of the mark;
(D) the geographical extent of the trading area in which the mark is used;
(E) the channels of trade for the goods or services with which the mark is used;
(F) the degree of recognition of the mark in the trading areas and channels of trade used by the mark's owner and the person against whom the injunction is sought;
(G) the nature and extent of use of the same or similar marks by third parties.

BIE is both "distinctive" and "famous" for purposes of § 1125(d).

The next question is whether the domain name "barbiesplaypen.com" is "identical or confusingly similar to" the BARBIE mark. The similarities between "barbiesplaypen.com" and the BARBIE trademark are as follows: (1) both contain the name "barbie;" (2) the name "Barbie" on the front page of the Web site and the logo BARBIE both have approximately the same font, slant, size, etc.; (3) both BARBIE and "barbiesplaypen.com" are inextricably associated with the verb "play," in the broad sense of the term. All of the above similarities make the Web site 'barbiesplaypen.com," and its domain name, "confusingly similar," though not "identical" to the BARBIE mark.

I next turn to the issue of whether the defendants registered, used, or trafficked in the domain name "barbiesplaypen.com" with a "bad faith intent to profit" from the Barbie mark. We find that the defendants did engage in a "bad faith attempt to profit" from the BARBIE trademark by maintaining the infringing domain name and Web site. It is clear that the defendants expected the same advertising result as Mattel from the use of the domain name "barbiesplaypen.com." The defendants must have expected that consumers searching under the word BARBIE, or perhaps the words "BARBIE and PLAY," in an Internet search engine would be directed to defendants' pornographic "barbiesplaypen.com" site. The diversion of Internet users to a site containing pornographic images may well *tarnish* the image of Mattel's BARBIE products in the minds of those consumers.

Under the ACPA, Mattel is entitled to an order directing defendants to transfer the registration of the domain name "barbiesplaypen.com" to Mattel. This Court finds that a permanent injunction barring defendants from the commercial use and infringement of any of Mattel's BARBIE trademarks is also warranted. Finally, the plaintiff is also entitled to statutory damages and attorneys' fees. SO ORDERED.

Case Highlights

- A party can be liable for trademark infringement even if it sells a product dissimilar to the products sold by the trademark owner. For example, if the infringing use of the trademark "tarnishes" the image of the trademark owner, then the user is guilty of trademark dilution.
- Domain names serve to identify the Internet user. Therefore, businesses prefer to use their trade names as part of their domain names.
- Cybersquatting is the bad faith registration of distinctive trademarks as Internet domain names.
- The Anti-Cybersquatting Consumer Protection Act (ACPA) protects trademark owners from the bad faith use of their trade name by others who register infringing domain names.

INTERNET PRIVACY AND DATABASE PROTECTION

Justice Brandeis once stated that "the right to be left alone is the most comprehensive of rights, and the most valued by civilized persons."[17] The problem of Internet privacy involves the need to balance the individual's right to privacy with the right to develop, transfer, and sell databases compiled with personal data. One issue is the ability of one company to sell its customers list to another company. In this instance, information that an individual believes to be submitted confidentially to one party can end up being used by other parties for different purposes.

In a recent case, the Federal Trade Commission brought suit against Toysmart.com, which had filed for bankruptcy protection, to prevent it from selling its list of 250,000 customer names, addresses, and credit card numbers in order to satisfy its debts. The proposed sale contradicted the e-company's own assurances to its customers that their registered information would "never be shared with a third party." A settlement was reached that allowed Toysmart.com to sell its list under a number of conditions. First, the list could only be sold as part of a package that

17. Olmstead v. United States, 277 U.S. 438, 478 (1928).

included the entire web site. Second, it could only be sold to a qualified buyer in a related market. Third, the buyer must agree to abide by the web site's privacy policy. If a qualified buyer is not found, then Toysmart.com must destroy the customer information.[18]

The United States and the European Union (EU) have elected two different approaches to this problem, not surprising since ingrained cultural attitudes about personal privacy separate the United States from many of the European countries. Europeans are more restrictive in regulating the way companies collect and process personal data. The EU has enacted comprehensive legislation to deal with personal privacy on the Internet. In contrast, the United States has not enacted data protection legislation, instead electing to allow the Internet industry to self-regulate.

Many of today's most popular web sites serve as data collection instruments. Personal information given by a visitor to a web site is collected for future use, sometimes covertly through the use of **cookies** or tags. Cookies are used to identify visitors to a web site. They allow the web site to obtain the visitor's e-mail address, name, the specific pages of the web site that were visited, and what electronic transactions were made. This personal information can then be used for future marketing purposes or sold to others by the web site owners.

Although the United States does not have a comprehensive Internet privacy law, a number of existing statutes offer some protections. The federal statutes focus upon specific industries. For example, the **Fair Credit Reporting Act**[19] governs the use of data by the credit reporting industry. The **Privacy Act of 1994**[20] restricts government agencies from releasing personal information found in its documents and records. The **Telephone Consumer Protection Act**[21] is directed at the abuse of telemarketing activities through telephone solicitations. This Act may be applicable to bulk e-mail solicitations known as **spamming.**[22]

The **Electronic Communications Privacy Act of 1986**[23] extends federal wiretap requirements to new forms of electronic communications such as e-mail and applies to service providers engaged in the transmission and storage of electronic communications. It does not prevent the recipient of the communication from disclosing the contents to others. The **Telecommunications Act of 1996**[24] restricts the disclosure by telecommunications companies of information about subscribers' use of their services.

In contrast, the European Union has enacted comprehensive laws dealing with the protection and use of databases. **Directive 96/9/EC on the Legal Protection of Databases** defines the term *database* as "literary, artistic, musical, or other collections of works or collections of other material such as texts, sound, images, numbers, facts, and data systematically or methodically arranged and that can be individually accessed."

In 1995, the European Union enacted the **Directive on the Protection of Individuals with Regard to the Processing of Personal Data and the Free Movement of Such Data (Directive 95/46).** It states the following standards of data quality:

18. Toysmart.com may still be prevented from selling its customer list since still pending is a suit brought by 39 state attorneys general asserting that such a sale violates their states' consumer protection laws.
19. 15 U.S.C. §§ 1681-1681u (1994).
20. 5 U.S.C. § 552a.
21. 47 U.S.C. § 227.
22. "Spamming" is sending bulk e-mailings of unsolicited advertisements for goods and services.
23. 18 U.S.C. § 2510.
24. 47 U.S.C.A. § 222 (West Supp. 2000).

- personal data must be "processed fairly and lawfully"
- personal data must be "collected for specific, explicit, and legitimate purposes and not further processed in a way incompatible with those purposes"
- personal data must be "accurate and kept up to date"
- every reasonable step must be taken to ensure that data which are inaccurate or incomplete are erased or rectified
- personal data that permits identification of the subject should be kept "no longer than is necessary for the purposes for which the data was collected."

The further processing of collected data is limited to where the data subject (consumer) has given his "consent unambiguously." An exception is made when the processing of personal data is performed "in the public interest or in the exercise of official authority." (See the Comparative Law Feature on the next page.)

Directive 95/46 grants the data subject a number of rights. First, every subject has a **right of access** to obtain "confirmation as to whether data relating to him are processed and as to the purposes of the processing, the categories of data being processed, and the recipients to whom the data are disclosed." Second, a **blocking right** and **right of correction** are granted whereby the subject has the right to "the rectification, erasure, or blocking of data, the processing of which does not comply with this Directive, in particular because of the incomplete or inaccurate nature of the data." Third, there is a limited **right of objection** "on compelling legitimate grounds" to a particular processing of data relating to him.

In addition, Article 25 of the Directive prohibits the transfer of data outside the EU to a third country that does not provide an adequate level of protection. Therefore, the Directive prohibits the transfer of data to the United Sates and other non-EU countries not meeting EU standards for the protection of personal privacy. Such transfers are permissible, however, even if a third country lacks adequate controls if the subject consents to the transfer or if the transfer is necessary for the performance of a contract between the subject and the data possessor. Article 25 offers the possibility of a severe interruption of data flows from Europe to the United States because the United States has not enacted "adequate" data protection laws.

Initially, the EU continued to permit U.S. companies to export personal data from Europe and entered into negotiations in order to avert a trade war. In 2000, the United States and the EU completed negotiations on the **safe harbor agreement.** This accord allows for privacy protection that is deemed adequate, but not equivalent to that under EU law. If U.S. companies comply voluntarily, they will be given *safe harbor* from lawsuits by EU countries. A controversial part of the safe harbor principles is that a company can self-certify by filing a letter annually with the Department of Commerce. The certification can be performed through self-assessment or outside review. Any self-assessment should state the company's privacy policy, along with confirming the existence of procedures for conducting periodic reviews, for training employees, and for disciplining violations. The only specific sanction for misrepresentations in the self-certification letter is by way of an action by the Federal Trade Commission.

http://

Article—"Review of Safe Harbor Agreement after One Year": **http://www.cov.com/publications/254.pdf**.

The EU has also enacted a directive to grant special protection to databases that are a product of "considerable investment of human, technical, and financial resources" (see Comparative Law: Directive 96/9/EC, Legal Protection of Databases). If a database is a product of such investment, then the Directive grants its creator or owner a 15-year term of protection.

U.S. law, in contrast, does not protect databases other than by prohibiting the verbatim copying of databases under copyright law. An alternative means of

Comparative Law

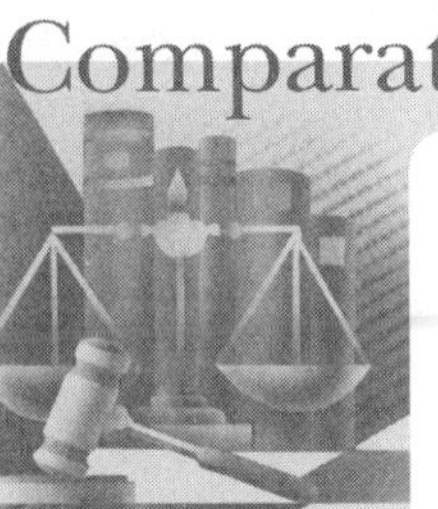

Directive 95/46/EC—European Union Data Privacy Protection (Protection of Individuals with Regard to the Processing of Personal Data)

WHEREAS, cross-border flows of personal data are necessary to the expansion of international trade; the protection of individuals guaranteed in the Community by this Directive does not stand in the way of transfers of personal data to third countries which ensure an adequate level of protection;

WHEREAS, on the other hand, the transfer of personal data to a third country which does not ensure an adequate level of protection must be prohibited;

Principle Relating to Data Quality
Article 6: Member States shall provide that personal data must be:

(a) processed fairly and lawfully;
(b) collected for specified, explicit, and legitimate purposes and not further processed in a way incompatible with those purposes.
(c) adequate, relevant, and not excessive in relation to the purposes for which they are collected and/or further processed;
(d) accurate and, where necessary, kept up to date; every reasonable step must be taken to ensure that data which are inaccurate or incomplete, having regard to the purposes for which they were collected or for which they are further processed, are erased or rectified;

The Data Subject's Right of Access to Data
Article 12: Right of access: Member States shall guarantee every data subject the right to obtain from the controller:

(a) (1) confirmation as to whether or not data relating to him are being processed and information at least as to the purposes of the processing, the categories of data concerned, and the recipients or categories of recipients to whom the data are disclosed,
(2) communication to him in an intelligible form of the data undergoing processing and of any available information as to their source,

The Data Subject's Right to Object
Article 14: Member States shall grant the data subject the right:

(b) to object, on request and free of charge, to the processing of personal data relating to him which the controller anticipates being processed for the purposes of direct marketing, or to be informed before personal data are disclosed for the first time to third parties or used on their behalf for the purposes of direct marketing, and to be expressly offered the right to object free of charge to such disclosures or uses.

Article 23: Liability. Member States shall provide that any person who has suffered damage as a result of an unlawful processing operation or of any act incompatible with the national provisions adopted pursuant to this Directive is entitled to receive compensation from the controller for the damage suffered.

protecting a database in the United States is through trade secrets law. However, it is difficult to maintain a database or customers list as a trade secret if it is accessible by a large pool of employees. It is strategically prudent for U.S. companies to review Directive 96/9/EC in order to obtain the directive's protection for its European operations.

Comparative Law

Directive 96/9/EC, Legal Protection of Databases (March 11, 1996)

(1) The making of databases requires the investment of considerable human, technical, and financial resources while such databases can be copied or accessed at a fraction of the cost needed to design them independently;

(2) This Directive protects collections, sometimes called *compilations,* of works, data, or other materials which are arranged, stored, and accessed by means which include electronic processes;

(3) No criterion other than originality, in the sense of the author's intellectual creation, should be applied to determine the eligibility of the database for copyright protection, and in particular no aesthetic or qualitative criteria should be applied;

(4) Works protected by copyright and subject matter protected by related rights that are incorporated into a database remain, nevertheless, protected by the respective exclusive rights and may not be incorporated into, or extracted from, the database without the permission of the right holder or his successors in title;

Article 3: Object of Protection

1. In accordance with this Directive, databases which, by reason of the selection or arrangement of their contents, constitute the author's own intellectual creation shall be protected as such by copyright.
2. The copyright protection of databases provided for by this Directive shall not extend to their contents and shall be without prejudice to any rights subsisting in those contents themselves.

Article 10: Term of Protection

The right provided for in this Directive shall run from the date of completion of the making of the database and shall expire 15 years from the first of January of the year following the date of completion.

E-COMMERCE AND E-CONTRACTING

The first generation of electronic contracting was performed through the use of **electronic data interchange (EDI).**[25] EDI is the computer-to-computer communication of information.[26] The use of EDI for purposes of forming contracts will continue to grow.[27] For example, in the documentary transaction, contracts will be electronically formed, electronic bills of lading will be sent to a third-party recordkeeping service, letters of credit will be issued based upon pre-existing templates,[28] and other necessary documents like insurance certificates will be requested and

25. See, e.g., Randy V. Sabett, "International Harmonization in Electronic Commerce and Electronic Data Interchange: A Proposed First Step Toward Signing on the Digital Dotted Line," 46 *American University Law Review* 511 (1996).
26. See generally H. PERITT, LAW AND THE INFORMATION SUPERHIGHWAY: PRIVACY, ACCESS, INTELLECTUAL PROPERTY, COMMERCE AND LIABILITY (1996); P. SOKOL, FROM EDI TO ELECTRONIC COMMERCE: A BUSINESS INITIATIVE (1995); B. WRIGHT, THE LAW OF ELECTRONIC COMMERCE: EDI, E-MAIL, AND INTERNET TECHNOLOGY, PROOF AND LIABILITY (2d ed. 1995).
27. See generally BERNARD D. REAMS, JR., ET AL., ELECTRONIC CONRACTING LAW: EDI AND BUSINESS TRANSACTIONS (1993-94 ed.).
28. See, e.g., R. David Whitaker, "Letters of Credit and Electronic Commerce," 31 *Idaho Law Review* 699 (1995).

transmitted by computers. The closed nature of the EDI system allows private parties to create their own law to fill the void created by a lack of legislation.[29]

The rules governing EDI transactions are provided in contracts known as **trading partner agreements** or interchange agreements. This form of contracting makes sense only when one contemplates a long-term contractual relationship with a relatively modest number of contracting parties. (This is in contrast to Internet commerce that often includes many one-time transactions with relatively unknown purchasers and sellers.) The American Bar Association has developed a **Model Electronic Data Interchange Trading Partner Agreement**[30] that can be tailored to particular types of transactions.

The Internet represents the future of electronic commerce: It has become a powerful tool for marketing and selling products internationally. There are three major commercial effects of the increased use of electronic technologies:

1. Commercial parties have begun to restructure their business practices using electronic technologies to communicate internally as well as externally.
2. New industries have emerged to provide needed services to companies engaging in electronic commerce.
3. New types of property with commercial value have become commodities for trade domestically and internationally.

The first effect has been reflected in the increasing use of electronic contracting in place of paper transactions. The development of electronic bills of lading and letters of credit are examples of this trend, along with the use of electronic purchase orders and confirmations. The second effect has resulted in the creation of entirely new businesses. Aggregation, discussed later in the chapter, is an example. The final effect pertains to the changing nature or subject matter of business transactions. The creation of new commodities is reflected by the growing business of selling and transferring information.

Framework for Global Electronic Commerce

In 1999, the Clinton White House published **A Framework for Global Electronic Commerce** in which it sets out U.S. policy regarding electronic commerce. The Framework's general premise is that regulation of the Internet and e-commerce should be primarily by private and not public means. "Governments must adopt a non-regulatory, market-oriented approach to electronic commerce, one that facilitates the emergence of a transparent and predictable legal environment to support global business." The market approach is one in which the parties, through private contract, police their rights and obligations. There will nonetheless be a need for international agreement and governmental regulation in a number of areas.

The paper notes that three areas require international agreement: financial, legal, and market access. In the legal area, the paper calls for a "Uniform Commercial Code for Electronic Commerce," enhanced intellectual property protection, privacy protection, and security initiatives. In the area of developing domestic and international rules and norms, the paper acknowledges the work of the United Nations Commission on International Trade Law (UNCITRAL) in developing its

29. See ABA Model Agreement as reported in "Model Electronic Data Interchange Trading Partner Agreement and Commentary," 45 *Business Lawyer* 1717 (1990).

30. See "ABA's Model Electronic Data Interchange Trading Partner Agreement," 45 *Business Lawyer* 1645 (1990).

Model Law on Electronic Commerce. Two fundamental principles are given to guide the development of such rules. First, contract and other rules should be technology-neutral. Second, existing rules should be applied or modified before the adoption of new rules for electronic contracting. In addition, the Framework advises that these principles are best met internationally through the efforts of organizations like UNCITRAL, UNIDROIT,[31] and the International Chamber of Commerce in developing model provisions and uniform principles.

In the area of intellectual property, the Framework specifically recognizes the problem of trademark infringement and registration of domain names. It poses the preferred solution as the "development of a global market-based system to register Internet domain names." In the area of security, the paper highlights the need to develop "trusted certification services" that permit the secured use of digital signatures.[32]

The enactment, however, of a set of comprehensive and generally accepted international rules for governing electronic commerce is unlikely in the foreseeable future. Instead, the law of contracts is likely to remain the governing institution for electronic commerce. The establishment of a contractual relationship in e-commerce generally begins with customer registration. By requiring customers to register, the international vendor is better able to alleviate the concerns for authentication, security, and payment. In order to place an order, the customer will be required to provide a digital signature. Encryption is used to secure the transmission of the digital signature and credit information. The customer by clicking at appropriate places accepts the terms of the contract.

It should be noted that sales over the Internet that resemble "catalog sales" are likely to come under the purview of consumer protection laws, and so the e-commerce contract will need to comply with legal disclosure requirements. Within the United States, compliance can be achieved through the use of icons and links. The purchaser needs only to click the appropriate icon or link to obtain the required disclosures. Foreign consumer protection laws will need to be reviewed to determine their applicability to e-commerce.

E-Contracting Law Issues

The open nature of the Internet calls for a more proactive government regulation. A legal framework needs to be built to ensure the security and integrity of open network (Internet) transactions. The three major concerns for international electronic contracting are authenticity, enforceability, and confidentiality. Authenticity involves the verification of the identity of the party one is dealing with electronically. Enforceability includes the legal scope of the license granted or the warranty given under a national law. It also includes the provability and verification of the contractual terms of an on-line transaction.

Confidentiality revolves around the protection of sensitive information such as payment information and trade secrets. The fear is that the public nature of e-commerce makes such information susceptible to fraud and misappropriation by third parties. The minimum level of due diligence pertaining to these three concerns demands a workable knowledge of the legal requirements of forming and proving a contract through the Internet.

31. International Institute for the Unification of Private Law.
32. See generally Amelia H. Boss, "The Emerging Law of International Electronic Commerce," 6 *Temple International and Comparative Law Journal* 293, 301-304 (1992).

Electronic contracting poses a number of questions about the application of contract law to this new medium for transacting business.[33] For example, what communications are considered offers and acceptances? When and where does an electronic acceptance reach the offeror? The answers depend on the type of communications and information being provided. A noninteractive web page is more like an advertisement or an invitation to make an offer. Conversely, an interactive web page designed to accept payment information such as credit card numbers could be construed as a standing offer.

The use of e-mail to negotiate contracts opens up the offeror to an acceptance by e-mail. Does the acceptance reach the offeror upon receipt by the service provider and placement in the offeror's mailbox or when the offeror opens his mailbox? The better answer would seem to be the former, because the offeror is inviting acceptance by e-mail and is thus under an implied duty to retrieve his mail in a timely fashion.[34] The next section will review a model law that attempts to provide answers to these and other formation questions

Uniform Computer Information Transactions Act

http://

Text of UCITA: **http://www.law.upenn.edu/bll/ulc/ucita/ucita200.htm** or UCITA online at **http://www.ucitaonline.com**.

Uniform Computer Information Transactions Act (UCITA)[35] is a model law enacted to cover the creation, transfer, and licensing of computer information and software. UCITA provides rules for sales of software and the licensing of information. A **license** is a contract that grants a licensee limited use of the intellectual and informational property rights of the licensor.[36] The licensor retains ownership of the rights being licensed. Generally, the licensee obtains a right to use a particular copy of the licensor's property.

The formation of a contract under UCITA depends on the receipt of the acceptance by the offeror. This is opposite to the common law's acceptance-upon-dispatch or mailbox rule. Receipt of an electronic notice is defined as "coming into existence in an information processing system or at an address in that system in a form capable of being processed by or perceived from a system of that type by a recipient, if the recipient uses, or otherwise has designated or holds out, that place or system for receipt of notices."[37] Thus, a contract is formed even if the receiving party fails to open or read the message of acceptance. Other offer and acceptance issues addressed by UCITA include:

- Can the downloading of information constitute an acceptance? Alternatively stated, can *clicking* approval to terms be considered an acceptance? The answer to both of these questions seems to be yes. Both fulfill the fundamental requirement that an acceptance must merely be a definite expression of acceptance.
- In shrink-wrap licensing, how is the additional terms scenario of § 2-207 likely to be handled? UCITA states that the additional terms found in the

33. See generally Raymond T. Nimmer, "Electronic Contracting: Legal Issues," 14 *John Marshall Journal of Computer and Information Law,* 211 (1996). See also Raymond T. Nimmer, "Breaking Barriers: The Relation Between Contract and Intellectual Property Law," 13 *Berkeley Technology Law Journal* 827 (1998), and Raymond T. Nimmer, "Information Age in Law: New Frontiers in Property and Contract," 68 *New York State Bar Journal* 28 (1996).
34. This information was gleaned from Christoph Glatt, "Comparative Issues in the Formation of Electronic Contracts," 6 *Journal of Law and Information Technology* 34, 50-53 (1996).
35. This is a model law published in 1999 that has been enacted in the states of Virginia and Maryland. Approved by the National Conference of Commissioners on Uniform State Laws in July 1999.
36. UCITA defines a license as "a contract that authorizes access to, or use, distribution, performance, modification, or reproduction of information or information rights."
37. UCITA, Section 102 (52).

shrink-wrapped license do become a part of the contract if the purchaser or licensee is able to review them prior to being obligated to pay. After reviewing the license, the purchaser has a right to return the item for a full refund.[38]

- The use of an **electronic agent,** such as a computer or voice ordering system, to effect a transaction raises a number of legal issues, including: (1) Can contracts be formed through electronic agents? (2) Is a contract formed when a human makes a conditional acceptance to an electronic agent? (3) What if the human attempts to insert additional terms into the contract? Do these additional terms become a part of the contract? UCITA provides rules for such scenarios. Section 206 states that "a contract may be formed by the interaction of electronic agents" and "a contract may be formed by the interaction of an electronic agent and an individual."[39] The contract is formed if the individual takes actions or makes statements that he knows will cause the electronic agent to perform. Additional terms incorporated into the acceptance do not become a part of the contract if the individual "had reason to know that the electronic agent could not react to the terms as provided."

An additional issue that needs to be addressed is whether statutory warranty laws apply to Internet transactions. U.S. warranty law, as discussed in Chapters 7 and 8, does pertain to Internet consumer transactions.[40] Therefore, under U.S. law, all warranties for products sold through the Internet must expressly state:

- the parties protected by the warranty
- any limitations on implied warranties
- any limitation of damages
- availability of alternative dispute resolution
- the coverage of the warranty (parts, characteristics of product)
- the responsibility of the seller in case of defect
- the procedure for making a warranty claim
- the commencement and expiration of the warranty period

Foreign statutory warranty laws would need to be researched for sales in other countries.

THE "SHRINK-WRAP" CONTRACT

Computer software is generally sold encased in plastic wrappers. Inside the wrapper are the terms, including warranty provisions, of the contract intended to govern the sale. Besides a provision triggering the purchaser's acceptance of the **shrink-wrap license** upon opening the package, other provisions commonly found in shrink-wrap contracts include:

- a clause stating that the customer has not purchased the software itself, but has merely obtained a personal, nontransferable license to use the program
- a disclaimer of all warranties, except for a warranty covering physical defects in the diskettes

38. UCITA, Section 112 (Manifesting Assent; Opportunity to Review).
39. An "electronic agent" is defined as a "computer program, or electronic or other automated means, used by a person to initiate an action, or to respond to electronic messages or performances, on the person's behalf without review or action by an individual at the time of action, or response to a message or performance." UCITA, Section 102 (27).
40. See, for example, the Magnuson-Moss Act (federal warranty law), 15 U.S.C. § 2301, *et seq.*

- a clause purporting to limit the purchaser's remedies to repair and replacement of defective disks, and to exclude all consequential or incidental damages caused by the software
- an integration clause providing that the license is the final and complete expression of the agreement
- a provision prohibiting assignment of the program or license without the express prior consent of the licensor

The purchaser does not see the license containing these provisions until after purchasing and taking possession of the software.

Computer equipment and software are also often purchased on-line. The purchaser places an order and pays for an item on-line, but does not see the terms of the sale or license until she opens the box at delivery. At issue is whether the parties have actually agreed to the terms provided in the packaged or shrink-wrapped license. U.S. law has increasingly recognized the shrink-wrap license or contract. The agreement found in the package, or sent by the vendor, typically states something to this effect: "Purchaser's receipt of services [or software] constitutes acceptance of all terms and conditions of this Agreement."

A number of states have passed laws recognizing the shrink-wrap contract. For example, Illinois passed the following law in 1986: "A person who acquires a copy of computer software will be conclusively deemed to have accepted and agreed to those provisions of the license agreement accompanying the copy." However, it places a number of requirements on the seller-licensor before granting the presumption of enforceability. First, there must be a written notation or notice affixed to the package that states clearly that opening the sealed package will constitute acceptance of the terms of the accompanying license agreement. Second, the notice must be clearly and conspicuously visible so as to be readily noticeable to a person viewing the package.

The court in *Arizona Retail Systems v. Software Link*[41] applied Sections 2-207 (additional terms) and 2-209 (modification) of the Uniform Commercial Code to a shrink-wrap license. The issue in the case was whether a disclaimer of implied warranties found in the license had become a part of the contract. The court rejected the argument that the terms of the shrink-wrap license included in each package of software were additional terms under Section 2-207's battle of the forms scenario or a modification of the contract under Section 2-209.

The court concluded that, at best, the license agreement was "a proposal to modify the contract between the parties." Thus, unless expressly agreed to by the purchaser, the warranty disclaimer did not become a part of the contract since the license was delivered after the contract had already been formed. The court suggested that sellers can protect themselves by not shipping until they obtain assent to those terms they consider essential to the formation of a contract.

Shrink-wrap contracts are generally a U.S. phenomenon. If an international seller hopes to use a shrink-wrap contract, it should determine if such a contract will be recognized in the country of importation. In order to protect the seller of software, it may be necessary to require its foreign sales representative or agent to procure a signature on the license agreement from the foreign purchaser.

Another modern form of contracting is the **click-wrap license.** Consumers often purchase software over the Internet. After providing the necessary payment information, the purchaser is allowed to directly download the software; however, the

41. 831 F.Supp. 759 (D.Ariz 1993). See also Step-Saver Data Systems v. Wyse Technology, 939 F.2d 91 (3d Cir. 1991).

purchaser must first agree to the terms of the software license. In order to do so she must click the "accept" icon. The problem is that the actual license is embedded in another file that the purchaser can easily ignore. Thus, web pages can be designed to obtain the purchaser's "acceptance" with very little likelihood that the purchaser will actually view the terms of the offer. (See Focus on Transactions: Key Provisions of UCITA.)

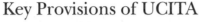

Focus on Transactions

Key Provisions of UCITA

- UCITA provisions deal directly with software licenses that grant the licensee the right to access information of the licensor. This type of license is referred to as an **access contract.** See UCITA § 611.
- A contract is formed only when a person has an opportunity to review the terms of the contract. A party's "opportunity to review" the terms of a contract only after paying or beginning performance (as in a shrink-wrap contract) does not form a contract on those terms unless the party has a right to return. UCITA § 112(e)(3).
- A contract may be formed with an electronic agent such as a Web page order system. A contract is formed when an individual acts in a way that he knows will cause the electronic agent to perform. UCITA § 206.
- Counteroffers or additional terms are ineffectual against electronic agents. Terms added by an individual do not become a part of the contract if the individual had reason to know that the electronic agent could not react to the terms. UCITA § 206.
- A licensor that makes information available by electronic means from its Internet site must give the licensee an opportunity to review the terms of the license (click-wrap contract). The opportunity to review requirement is satisfied if the licensor makes the terms readily available for review before the licensee is obligated to pay, by displaying the terms or a reference to an electronic location prominently and in close proximity to a description of the information or by disclosing the availability of the terms in a prominent place on the site. UCITA § 211.
- UCITA recognizes four warranties: (1) Warranty of Noninterference and Noninfringement (§ 401); (2) Implied Warranty of Merchantability of Computer Program (§ 403); (3) Implied Warranty of Licensee's Purpose (§ 405); and (4) Implied Warranty of Informational Content (§ 404).
- The Implied Warranty of Informational Content warrants to the licensee that there is "no inaccuracy in the informational content caused by the merchant's failure to perform with reasonable care."
- The licensor has a defense for modification made by the licensee to a computer program, other than by using a capability of the program intended for that purpose. Such a modification invalidates any warranties, express or implied, regarding performance of the modified copy. UCITA § 407.
- A licensor is limited in its ability to use self-help remedies such as *disabling bugs* or *time bombs.* A licensor may use self-help means only on the cancellation of a license if the licensee separately manifested assent to the term. Also, the self-help term must require the licensor to give a 15-day notice before exercising the remedy. The notice must give the nature of the licensee's breach and the name, address, and telephone number of a contact person. A wrongful use of electronic self-help makes the licensor liable for the consequential damages of the licensee. UCITA § 816.

STATUTE OF FRAUDS REQUIREMENTS AND AUTHENTICATION

A major obstacle to electronic commerce is the need for a signed writing to form a contract, as is required by the Uniform Commercial Code Article 2 (sale of goods) and Article 5 (letters of credit), and UCITA (licensing). The Uniform Customs and Practices for Documentary Credits (UCP 500) recognized this problem by replacing the requirement for signatures with a requirement for "**authentication.**" In response, the American Bar Association has issued **digital signatures guidelines** whose purpose is to "establish a safe harbor—a secure, computer-based signature equivalent—which will:

- minimize the incidence of electronic forgeries
- enable and foster the reliable authentication of documents in computer form
- facilitate commerce by means of computerized communications
- give legal effect to the general import of the technical standards for authentication of computerized messages."

The ABA guidelines recommend the existing protocol of a public-key and private-key cryptography system with third-party certification authorities. The ABA notes the role of signatures in forming contracts:

> *Evidence: A signature authenticates a writing by identifying the signer with a signed document. When a signer makes a mark in a distinctive manner, the writing becomes attributable to the signer. Ceremony: The act of signing a document calls to the signer's attention the legal significance of his act, and thereby helps prevent 'inconsiderate engagements.' Approval: A signature expresses the signer's approval or authorization of the writing or her intention that it have legal effect. Checks, for example, rely on the formal requirements of a signature to change hands rapidly and with minimal interruption.*

At least 14 states have passed legislation formally recognizing digital signatures; others states are following suit. The 1995 Utah Digital Signature Act[42] is considered a model statute. It is designed to encourage the use of digital signatures and minimize the incidence of forged signatures. The Act provides that a digital signature is "as valid as if it had been written on paper." A signature using a public key from a government-licensed certificate authority "is a legally valid signature" unless the presumption can be rebutted by evidence.

Until the use of digital signatures becomes commonplace, other techniques should be used to authenticate the identity of the other party and to confirm the terms of the contractual undertaking. These techniques include acknowledgement, use of independent agents or value-added networks, and encryption. Acknowledgement can be as simple as an e-mail or a facsimile to confirm the on-line transaction. Private computer networks have become a popular means to broker e-commerce: They provide the vital independent record-keeping function needed to respond to the evidentiary concerns of proving the contract in case of a future breach. Finally, encryption is the strongest vehicle for alleviating concerns about confidentiality.

International E-Commerce Developments

Developments in e-commerce and Internet law are ongoing at both the national and international level. The International Chamber of Commerce published in

42. Utah Code Ann. § 46-3-101.

1997 a guide titled **General Usage for International Digitally Ensured Commerce (GUIDEC)** that addresses some of the definitional and legal aspects relating to methods of overcoming e-commerce authentication and confidentiality problems.[43] GUIDEC gives a general framework for ensuring (authenticating) and certifying digital messages. In order to do this, it had to develop some original nomenclature as well as provide "clear descriptions of the rights and responsibilities of subscribers, certifiers, and relying parties." GUIDEC's operative concept of affixing a signature or verifying the author of the data message is referred to as ensuring. The stated goals of GUIDEC are "to enhance the ability of the international business community, to execute secure digital transactions, to establish legal principles that promote reliable digital ensuring and certification practices, and to define and clarify the duties of participants in the emerging ensuring and certification system."

http://
"GUIDEC, A Living Document": **http://www.iccwbo.org/home/guidec/guidec.asp**.

On June 13, 1997, Germany enacted a broad Internet-multimedia law, titled the Federal Act Establishing the General Conditions for Information and Communications Services or "Information and Services Act." One of the substantive provisions of the Act calls for at least a limited amount of liability for **Internet service providers (ISPs)** for the content of materials accessed through their services. However, this liability extends only if the ISP knew of the content and has the technical means to prevent its use. The law provides a reasonableness standard in determining if the ISP is jointly liable with the creator or provider of the material.[44]

http://
For more information on the German Internet-multimedia law: **http://www.iid.de**, **http://www.iukdg.de**, or **http://www.bmbf.de**.

The European Union has made recent strides to deal with the issues impeding the development of EDI and electronic commerce. In 1997, the European Commission published the "European Initiative on Electronic Commerce" or COM (97) 157. Before that initiative, the EU's first foray into e-commerce was the publication of a **Model EDI Agreement.**[45] The Model Agreement guides contracting parties on a number of important topics including the regulation of the processing and acknowledgment of EDI messages, security precautions, operational requirements, and confidentiality protections.

http://
The European Initiative on Electronic Commerce: **http://www.cordis.lu/esprit/src/ecomcom.htm**.

The United Nations Commission on International Trade Law (UNCITRAL) adopted a **Model Law on Electronic Commerce** (Model Law) on June 12, 1996.[46] The Model Law provides "a *framework* law that does not itself set forth all the rules and regulations that may be necessary to implement those techniques in an enacting country."[47] The law potentially serves three purposes. Individual governments can use it as a model or guide in drafting national legislation. The law can be used as source of language for contract drafting purposes or as a set of default rules incorporated into a contract by reference. Finally, courts and arbitration panels may use it "in interpreting existing international conventions and other instruments as far as they impede electronic commerce."[48]

The Model Law views the place of dispatch as crucial for determining the important issue of the law of the contract and the appropriate court in which to bring a lawsuit. Under Article 15 (4) of the Model Law, the place of dispatch is the place

43. "GUIDEC, A Living Document," accessed at **http://www.iccwbo.org/guidec2.htm**.
44. Similar limitations of liability for ISPs is found in the U.S. Digital Millennium Copyright Act of 1998.
45. The Model Agreement may be accessed through Commission Recommendation 94/820/EC (OJ L 338/98 1994) and Council Decision 87/499/EEC (OJ 1987 L 285/35).
46. UNCITRAL Model Law on Electronic Commerce: **http://www.un.or.at/uncitral**; U.N. Doc. A/51/17 Annex I (1996), reprinted in 36 I.L.M. 200 (1997).
47. UNCITRAL Guide at ¶ 13 (1996).
48. Christopher Glatt, "Comparative Issues in the Formation of Electronic Contracts," 6 *Journal of Law & Information Technology* 34, 57 (1996).

of business of the sender. Therefore, the contract is concluded at the place of the sender. This will be important when there is no express choice of law.

In contrast, Europe's **Brussels Convention** establishes the domicile of the defendant as the fundamental ground for jurisdiction. Article 5 of the Convention provides, however, that the place of performance can be an alternative ground for jurisdiction. For delivery of goods, this would generally be the customer's address. Interestingly, for the online sale and transmission of software, the place of performance will be the place of the service provider, where the data is received. This may not be the same country as where the defendant is located.[49] Regarding choice of law, the **Rome Convention** on law applicable to contractual obligations provides that the contract, in the absence of a choice of law clause, is to be governed "by the law of the country with which it is most closely connected." Article 4(2) provides a presumption in favor of the performing party's principal place of business.

The notion of incorporation by reference is highlighted in Section 46 of GUIDEC. It states that "incorporation by reference is regarded as essential to the widespread use of EDI, electronic mail, digital certificates, [public key certificates], and other forms of electronic commerce. For example, electronic communications are typically structured in such a way that large numbers of messages are exchanged, with each message contracting bits of information, and relying much more frequently than paper documents on reference to information accessible elsewhere."

National consumer protection laws are major obstacles to such contracting by reference, so incorporation by reference in electronic contracting should be done with the mandatory rules of national laws in mind. In an on-line contracting environment where reference is made to the "general terms and conditions" of the seller, the application or form contract should clearly reference the terms and conditions document and make it available for review. For first-time users, the site may automatically display the referenced document before allowing the user to complete a transaction.

ELECTRONIC DOCUMENTATION

In the documentary transaction that is central to the exportation of goods, "paper" is becoming less vital. Cost savings generated by electronic transmission are likely to foster increased use of the electronic communication of documents. "In the transport industry, the cost of raising conventional documents and the attendant delays involved in their issuance and verification constitute 10 percent to 15 percent of total transportation costs."[50] In order to generate cost savings, contracts will be electronically formed, electronic bills of lading will be sent to a third-party record-keeping service, letters of credit will be issued based upon a pre-existing template, and other necessary documents like insurance certificates will be requested and transmitted by computers. The realization that a bill of lading need not be in writing in order to effect a transfer of title led the Comité Maritime International (CMI) to produce the **1990 Rules for Electronic Bills of Lading.**[51] In addi-

49. The information about the Brussels Convention was taken from Christopher Glatt, "Comparative Issues in the Formation of Electronic Contracts," 6 *Journal of Law & Information Technology* 34, 61-63 (1996).

50. Commission of the European Communities, The Legal Position of the Member States with Respect to Electronic Data Interchange: Final Report (Sept. 1989), as cited in Amelia H. Boss, "The International Commercial Use of Electronic Data Interchange and Electronic Communication Technologies," 46 *Business Lawyer* 1787 (1991).

51. See comment, "The CMI Charts a Course on the Sea of Electronic Data Interchange: Rules for Electronic Bills of Lading," 16 *Tulane Maritime Law Journal* 349 (1992).

tion, most of the documents involved in the contract formation process (*pro forma* invoice, purchase order, confirmations) can be transmitted through EDI. Incoterms 2000 also recognizes the trend toward electronic transmissions. Section A8 of Incoterms states that where the seller and buyer have agreed to communicate electronically, documents may be replaced by an "equivalent electronic data interchange (EDI) message."

NEW ELECTRONIC SERVICES INDUSTRY

As electronic commerce grows, so does the need for third-party providers and value-added networks to service the industry. These service companies will perform a number of vital functions including "protocol conversion; storage, transmission, and retrieval services; format translation; message tracing, delivery notification, and integration reports; record retention services; implementation training and consultation; security enhancement; and database development."[52] A first-generation example of the value-added network phenomenon is the Society for Worldwide Interbank Financial Telecommunications (SWIFT) system, which provides a set of rules that govern banks in their telecommunications transactions. The SWIFT system has accelerated the transmission of payments in documentary collections through a private, high-speed communications network between member banks.[53]

The need for Internet security is leading to the development of a growing security service industry. "A vast and increasingly sophisticated computer security industry has developed in response to the critical need to secure electronic information and systems. Its goal is to protect computers, systems, and information from viruses, eavesdropping, hacking, theft, tampering, forgery, and interception."[54] It is estimated that $1.5 trillion will be lost as a result of the activities of computer hackers and computer viruses spread through the Internet.

In 2000, one such virus, the "ILOVEYOU" virus, was spread through e-mail and affected more than 45 million files, costing an estimated $2.6 billion in damages, mostly in lost work time. A new industry of Internet security service providers has blossomed to defend against such crimes. Standard security includes the use of firewalls,[55] antivirus software that must be updated weekly, and systems that deny entry to hackers.[56] Custom insurance policies for computer crimes are also now available through Lloyd's of London.

It is becoming clear that the Internet will continue to spawn the development of completely new industries. One example is the currently developing **aggregation** industry. Aggregators amass on a single web page all information about an individual available on the Internet, including on-line billings, frequent flyer miles,

http://
See site of a leading aggregator: **http://www.yodlee.com.**

52. Amelia Boss, "Electronic Commerce and the Law" in UNITED NATIONS, UNIFORM COMMERCIAL LAW IN THE TWENTY-FIRST CENTURY 163 (1992).

53. It has been estimated that electronic funds transfers have reduced the costs of some transactions by half. G. Mitshell, "Introduction to Electronic Funds Transfer Systems," 2 *Computer Law Journal* 2 (1980). See also Fred M. Greguras & Lynn Kerr, "Transborder Payments: The Legal Issues," 19 *Computer Law Reporter* 628 (1994); Symposium, "The Electronic Future of Cash," 46 *American University Law Review* 967 (1997).

54. GERALD FERRERA, STEPHEN LICHTENSTEIN, MARGO REDER, RAY AUGUST & WILLIAM SCHIANO, CYBERLAW 273 (2001).

55. A firewall is a computer barrier between networked computers and the network (Internet). It allows for the denial of access to certain external users. In essence it allows a company to create its own internal network or intranet, accessible by internal users, but not by external users.

56. One cutting-edge tool is the development of biometrics to authenticate users through the use of human characteristic recognition technologies that include the use of human DNA, palm prints, fingerprint and retina scanning, and voice recognition.

financial, shopping, and e-mail information. The aggregated information is accessible to the individual with the use of a single password.

Aggregation becomes valuable as individuals' on-line activities, accounts, and information become more widespread and complicated. Banks have recently begun to affiliate themselves with aggregators in order to allow customers to review their entire investment and financial portfolio at a single location. Privacy and security concerns need to be resolved for a full flourishing of this new industry.

INTERNET SECURITIES OFFERINGS

There has been a recent trend to offer investment information and securities over the Internet. This has become possible in the United States because the SEC has relaxed a number of regulatory requirements, openly authorizing **direct public offerings (DPOs)** over the Internet. In its 1995 Release 33-7233, the SEC stated that "the use of electronic media should be at least an equal alternative to the use of paper-based media. Accordingly, issuer or third-party information that can be delivered in paper under the federal securities laws may be delivered in electronic format." Thus, companies may make investment information available directly to prospective investors, prospectuses can be posted on-line or delivered on CD-ROM, and sales may be processed over the Internet. The major obstacle to the sale of initial public offerings stock over the Internet is the abscence of a secondary market for the resale of the securities. Already, however, there is evidence of the development of an e-marketplace for stocks not sold on the national securities exchanges.

A problem with electronic securities transactions is fraud. Numerous instances of illegal ponzi and pyramid schemes have been reported, as well as more traditional misrepresentations, such as using the opinion of well-known "investment advisors" who are compensated by the offering party.

In 1998, the SEC created the **Office of Internet Enforcement** to investigate and prosecute cases of Internet securities fraud. Since its establishment the Office of Internet Enforcement has conducted a number of nationwide sweeps of on-line investment scams. The most common is the "pump and dump," where promoters make false claims to artificially drive up the price of a stock in order to sell their own shares at a profit. The Internet enables scam artists to provide false information to a large audience quickly and anonymously.

E-COMMERCE ETHICS

Along with the need for an adequate legal support structure, electronic commerce carries numerous ethical concerns. The e-commerce industry needs to develop its own self-regulatory code of ethics in order to provide guidance to those using the World Wide Web, Internet, and other electronic networks to transact business. The United Nations Educational, Scientific, and Cultural Organization (UNESCO) has raised a number of themes focusing on the ethical, legal, and societal aspects of e-commerce and the information society, including:

- What is the appropriate role to be played by governmental agencies in providing Internet access to the public?
- What special measures are needed to help developing countries and disadvantaged communities benefit from available knowledge and information?

UNESCO has noted that while industry and business provide the infrastructure for access to information resources and content, the challenge is to define the concepts of public domain and **universal access** in a global context to promote common public welfare while encouraging private initiative and protecting rightful economic interests.

Another theme addressed by UNESCO is the special plight of developing countries, especially their inability to benefit fully from the new information age. In light of an emerging **digital divide,** how should governments balance commercial interests with moral obligations to promote equitable access? To answer this question it is important to gain an understanding of the practical obstacles to greater access. For example, what are the most important economic obstacles to information access (telecommunications tariffs, Internet access fees, taxes and duties, for example)?

UNESCO asserts that the principle of free access to and free flow of information as defined in Article 19 of the Universal Declaration on Human Rights must include access to digital media. There is also an important concern that greater access may cause unexpected harm to the culture or society of a developing country. UNESCO asks, How can the cultural, artistic, and scientific heritage of developing countries, including traditional and indigenous information, be suitably protected and made fairly available? UNESCO's plan of action states that the following elements need to be addressed within a global context:

- broader and fairer access to information and communication networks and services
- application of legal exceptions to copyright for developing countries through international conventions
- promotion of freedom of expression while protecting privacy on global networks

Advertising and Marketing Ethics

The International Chamber of Commerce has developed **Guidelines on Advertising and Marketing on the Internet (Guidelines).** The Guidelines' main philosophical mandate is to encourage advertisers and marketers "to create an electronic environment which all the world's consumers can fully trust." Article 1 states that "all advertising and marketing should be legal, decent, honest, and truthful." Although aspirational in character, the Guidelines do provide some concrete rules:

- Advertisers and marketers should identify themselves and the nature of their connection to any commercial messages placed on the Internet (Article 2).
- The addressees of commercial messages should be clearly informed of the cost of accessing the message or service (Article 3).
- Advertisers and marketers should take reasonable precautions to safeguard the security of their files (Article 5).
- Advertisers and marketers should post a **privacy policy statement** on their online sites.

Another issue of Internet ethics is the obtaining and monitoring of user information without the consent of the user. Technology exists that allows retailers and others to monitor the activities of Internet users and to collect personal information such as names, addresses, purchasing patterns, and credit card information. For example, when Company X receives an inquiry or order through the Internet, it can insert small text files known as cookies in the user's computer. Cookies store information about the user's Internet use, including frequency and what files and pages are accessed. When the user revisits Company X's web site, Company X can retrieve the information from the implanted cookie files.

The key fear about cookies is that they give a company the ability to link a user's Internet browsing habits to the user's name and provide that information to other companies. A controversy involving one of the largest Internet advertising companies evolved over this very practice. DoubleClick Inc. has acknowledged its use of cookies to gather information on the habits of Internet users often without their informed consent. The DoubleClick controversy revolved around its ability to link supposedly anonymous online information to specific individuals through the use of its enormous direct marketing database. The Federal Trade Commission and some state attorneys general have commenced an investigation of DoubleClick's marketing practices.[57]

http://

The Publishing Law Center—"Internet Legal Issues (Spam, Framing, and Linking)": **http://www.publaw.com/spam.html**; **http://www.publaw.com/framing.html**; and **http://www.publaw.com/linking.html**.

Unlike traditional mass mailing marketing, the use of uninvited bulk e-mails is considered an unethical business practice and violates most "acceptable use policies." Most Internet service providers state acceptable use policies (AUPs) that prohibit users from engaging in bulk e-mail advertising or "spamming." It is prudent for a prospective user to review the AUP of an Internet access provider before engaging its services.

Key Terms

1990 Rules for Electronic Bills of Lading, 458
A Framework for Global Electronic Commerce, 450
access contract, 455
aggregation, 459
Anti-Cybersquatting Consumer Protection Act (ACPA), 444
authentication, 456
blocking right, 447
blurring, 443
Brussels Convention, 458
click-wrap license, 454
comity, 441
cookies, 446
cybersquatters, 442
digital divide, 461
digital signatures guidelines, 456
direct public offerings, 460
Directive 96/9/EC on the Legal Protection of Databases, 446
Directive on the Protection of Individuals with Regard to the Processing of Personal Data and the Free Movement of Such Data (Directive 95/46), 446
disclaimers, 439
electronic agent, 453
Electronic Communications Privacy Act of 1986, 446
electronic data interchange (EDI), 449
Fair Credit Reporting Act, 446
Federal Trademark Dilution Act of 1995, 442
General Usage for International Digitally Ensured Commerce (GUIDEC), 457
Guidelines on Advertising and Marketing on the Internet (Guidelines), 461
internet service providers (ISPs), 457
Lanham Act, 442
license, 452
minimum contacts, 436
Model EDI Agreement, 457
Model Electronic Data Interchange Trading Partner Agreement, 450
Model Law on Electronic Commerce, 457
Office of Internet Enforcement, 460
passive web page, 438
personal jurisdiction, 436
Privacy Act 1994, 446
privacy policy statement, 461
right of access, 447
right of correction, 447
right of objection, 447
Rome Convention, 458
safe harbor agreements, 447
shareware, 437
shrink-wrap license, 453
spamming, 446
Telecommunications Act of 1996, 446
Telephone Consumer Protection Act, 446
trading partner agreements, 450
Uniform Computer Information Transactions Act (UCITA), 452
universal access, 461

57. A user can prevent the insertion of cookie files into her computer by following the procedures outlined at http://Privacychoices.org or by following the links on the site of the Electronic Privacy Information Center at http://www.epic.org.

Chapter Problems

1. Marobie released copyrighted clip art for use by the fire service industry. The National Association of Fire Equipment Distributors (NAFED) had a web page on which it placed Marobie's clip art so that any web user could download it. Marobie sued NAFED and Northwest, the provider of the host computer for NAFED's web page, for infringement. Is the Internet service provider liable for infringement? *Marobie-FL, Inc. v. Natl. Assn. of Fire Equipment Distributors,* (1997 WL 709747 (N.D. Ill. 1997)

2. The defendant in a recent case had put up a web site as a promotion for its upcoming Internet service. The service consisted of assigning users an electronic mailbox and then forwarding advertisements for products and services that matched the users' interests to those electronic mailboxes. The defendant planned to charge advertisers and provide users with incentives to view the advertisements. The defendant argues that the court did not possess personal jurisdiction because the web site in its current form was passive provider of information pertaining to future services. What do you think? *Maritz, Inc. v. Cybergold, Inc.*, 947 F.Supp. 1328 (E.D. Mo. 1996)

3. E-Data Corporation ("E-Data") is a Utah corporation with a business office in Connecticut. West Stock, a Washington corporation with its principal place of business in Seattle, Washington, licenses stock photography to commercial users. It has no offices in Connecticut, it owns no property and maintains no financial accounts in this forum, and does not have any employees or other agents in Connecticut. Since December 1995, West Stock has operated "Muse," an Internet-based stock photography service through which purchasers may electronically select a photograph, license its use, pay for that use, and download the image—all via the Internet. E-Data claims that West Stock has infringed on its patent. The patented invention is a system for reproducing information embodied in material objects, such as recordings, video games, motion pictures, books, sheet music, greeting cards and the like, at point-of-sale locations with the permission of the owner of the information. Specifically, plaintiff claims that defendant West Stock infringes the patent when it offers consumers the opportunity to purchase photography images via the Internet by paying a licensing fee to unlock and instantly download photography images on the consumer's computer. West Stock moves to dismiss contending that the court lacks personal jurisdiction over it in Connecticut. Does the Connecticut court have personal jurisdiction over West Stock? *E-Data Corp. v. Micropatent Corp.*, 989 F. Supp. 173 (D.Conn 1997)

4. Sportsman's is a mail order company that is well known in the aviation field. It began using the logo "sporty" in the 1960s and registered "sporty's" as a trademark in 1985. It spends about $10 million a year advertising its sporty's logo. A competitor, Pilot's Depot, was set up in early 1995 and registered the domain name sportys.com. The competitor then set up another company, Sporty's Farm, which used the domain name sportys.com to advertise the sale of its Christmas trees on that web site. The question before the court was which company had the right to the domain name. Which company do you think has a right to the domain name? Does Sportsman have to prove that Pilot's Depot acted in bad faith? How does the Anti-cybersquatting Consumer Protection Act apply to this case? *Sporty's Farm L.L.C. v. Sportsman's Market, Inc.*, 202 F.3d 489 (2nd Cir. 2000).

5. Employees may send personal e-mails at work just as they may have personal phone conversations. Do employees have a right of privacy in the e-mails? Do employers have the right to monitor employee e-mail? Does an employer have to notify its employees of its intent to monitor? Can an employer monitor e-mail after stating that it would not monitor? What would be a proper ethical approach to employer monitoring? *Smith v. Pillsbury Co.*, 914 F.Supp. 97 (E.D. Pa., 1996).

Internet Exercises

1. (a) Visit the web site of the CyberSpace Law Center at **http://www.cyberlaw.com**. Prepare a report on recent developments in the area of international piracy and patent infringement. (b) Visit the web site of Internet Legal Services at **http://www.legalethics.com**. This site covers legal issues dealing with advertising on the Internet and the confidentiality of e-mail. Report on employer and employee rights pertaining to e-mail privacy. (c) Review the directory of firewall and computer security information at **http://www.firewall.com**.

2. (a) Review the *International Safe Harbor Privacy Principles* and report on their requirements: **http://www.exports.gov/safeharbor/sh_overview.html**. (b) Review the privacy policy of a major online retailer such as Amazon or L.L. Bean. (c) Review industry-based privacy principles and programs such as **http://www.bbbonline.**

org (Council of Better Business Bureaus, Inc., privacy program) or **http://www.truste.org/** (TRUSTe is an organization of web publishers who have agreed to certain privacy principles).

3. The Digital Millennium Copyright Act (DMCA) provides Internet service providers a measure of immunity from liability for illegal content (pornography, defamation). What are the responsibilities of the provider in order to obtain this immunity from prosecution? What are the similarities and differences between DMCA and the German MultiMedia Law discussed in the chapter? For coverage of the DMCA see Educase at **http://www.educause.edu/issues/dmca.html** and Association of Research Libraries, "DMCA: Status & Analysis" at **http://www.arl.org/info/frn/copy/dmca.html**. For materials on the German MultiMedia Law see **http://www.iid.de**, **http://www.iukdg.de**, or **http://www.bmbf.de**.

Appendix A United Nations Convention on Contracts for the International Sale of Goods

(Not Including Sections 91-101 on Ratification)

PART I
SPHERE OF APPLICATION AND GENERAL PROVISIONS

Chapter I
Sphere of Application

ARTICLE 1

(1) This Convention applies to contracts of sale of goods between parties whose places of business are in different States:

  (a) when the States are Contracting States; or

  (b) when the rules of private international law lead to the application of the law of a Contracting State.

(2) The fact that the parties have their places of business in different States is to be disregarded whenever this fact does not appear either from the contract or from any dealings between, or from information disclosed by, the parties at any time before or at the conclusion of the contract.

(3) Neither the nationality of the parties nor the civil or commercial character of the parties or of the contract is to be taken into consideration in determining the application of this Convention.

ARTICLE 2

This Convention does not apply to sales:

(a) of goods bought for personal, family or household use, unless the seller, at any time before or at the conclusion of the contract, neither knew nor ought to have known that the goods were bought for any such use;

(b) by auction;

(c) on execution or otherwise by authority of law;

(d) of stocks, shares, investment securities, negotiable instruments or money;

(e) of ships, vessels, hovercraft or aircraft;

(f) of electricity.

ARTICLE 3

(1) Contracts for the supply of goods to be manufactured or produced are to be considered sales unless the party who orders the goods undertakes to supply a substantial part of the materials necessary for such manufacture or production.

(2) This Convention does not apply to contracts in which the preponderant part of the obligations of the party who furnishes the goods consists in the supply of labour or other services.

ARTICLE 4

This Convention governs only the formation of the contract of sale and the rights and obligations of the seller and the buyer arising from such a contract. In particular, except as otherwise expressly provided in this Convention, it is not concerned with:

(a) the validity of the contract or of any of its provisions or of any usage;

(b) the effect which the contract may have on the property in the goods sold.

ARTICLE 5

This Convention does not apply to the liability of the seller for death or personal injury caused by the goods to any person.

ARTICLE 6

The parties may exclude the application of this Convention or, subject to article 12, derogate from or vary the effect of any of its provisions.

Chapter II
General Provisions

ARTICLE 7

(1) In the interpretation of this Convention, regard is to be had to its international character and to the need to promote uniformity in its application and the observance of good faith in international trade.

(2) Questions concerning matters governed by this Convention which are not expressly settled in it are to be settled in conformity with the general principles on which it is based or, in the absence of such principles, in conformity with the law applicable by virtue of the rules of private international law.

ARTICLE 8

(1) For the purposes of this Convention statements made by and other conduct of a party are to be interpreted according to his intent where the other party knew or could not have been unaware what that intent was.

(2) If the preceding paragraph is not applicable, statements made by and other conduct of a party are to be interpreted according to the understanding that a reasonable person of the same kind as the other party would have had in the same circumstances.

(3) In determining the intent of a party or the understanding a reasonable person would have had, due consideration is to be given to all relevant circumstances of the case including the negotiations, any practices which the parties have established between themselves, usages and any subsequent conduct of the parties.

ARTICLE 9

(1) The parties are bound by any usage to which they have agreed and by any practices which they have established between themselves.

(2) The parties are considered, unless otherwise agreed, to have impliedly made applicable to their contract or its formation a usage of which the parties knew or ought to have known and which in international trade is widely known to, and regularly observed by, parties to contracts of the type involved in the particular trade concerned.

ARTICLE 10

For the purposes of this Convention:

(a) if a party has more than one place of business, the place of business is that which has the closest relationship to the contract and its performance, having regard to the circumstances known to or contemplated by the parties at any time before or at the conclusion of the contract;

(b) if a party does not have a place of business, reference is to be made to his habitual residence.

ARTICLE 11

A contract of sale need not be concluded in or evidenced by writing and is not subject to any other requirement as to form. It may be proved by any means, including witnesses.

ARTICLE 12

Any provision of article 11, article 29 or Part II of this Convention that allows a contract of sale or its modification or termination by agreement or any offer, acceptance or other indication of intention to be made in any form other than in writing does not apply where any party has his place of business in a Contracting State which has made a declaration under article 96 of this Convention. The parties may not derogate from or vary the effect or this article.

ARTICLE 13

For the purposes of this Convention "writing" includes telegram and telex.

PART II
FORMATION OF THE CONTRACT

ARTICLE 14

(1) A proposal for concluding a contract addressed to one or more specific persons constitutes an offer if it is sufficiently definite and indicates the intention of the offeror to be bound in case of acceptance. A proposal is sufficiently definite if it indicates the goods and expressly or implicitly fixes or makes provision for determining the quantity and the price.

(2) A proposal other than one addressed to one or more specific persons is to be considered merely as an invitation to make offers, unless the contrary is clearly indicated by the person making the proposal.

ARTICLE 15

(1) An offer becomes effective when it reaches the offeree.

(2) An offer, even if it is irrevocable, may be withdrawn if the withdrawal reaches the offeree before or at the same time as the offer.

ARTICLE 16

(1) Until a contract is concluded an offer may be revoked if the revocation reaches the offeree before he has dispatched an acceptance.

(2) However, an offer cannot be revoked:

 (a) if it indicates, whether by stating a fixed time for acceptance or otherwise, that it is irrevocable; or

 (b) if it was reasonable for the offeree to rely on the offer as being irrevocable and the offeree has acted in reliance on the offer.

ARTICLE 17

An offer, even if it is irrevocable, is terminated when a rejection reaches the offeror.

ARTICLE 18

(1) A statement made by or other conduct of the offeree indicating assent to an offer is an acceptance. Silence or inactivity does not in itself amount to acceptance.

(2) An acceptance of an offer becomes effective at the moment the indication of assent reaches the offeror. An acceptance is not effective if the indication of assent does not reach the offeror within the time he has fixed or, if no time is fixed, within a reasonable time, due account being taken of the circumstances of the transaction, including the rapidity of the means of communication employed by the offeror. An oral offer must be accepted immediately unless the circumstances indicate otherwise.

(3) However, if, by virtue of the offer or as a result of practices which the parties have established between themselves or of usage, the offeree may indicate assent by performing an act, such as one relating to the dispatch of the goods or payment of the price, without notice to the offeror, the acceptance is effective at the moment the act is performed, provided that the act is performed within the period of time laid down in the preceding paragraph.

ARTICLE 19

(1) A reply to an offer which purports to be an acceptance but contains additions, limitations or other modifications is a rejection of the offer and constitutes a counter-offer.

(2) However, a reply to an offer which purports to be an acceptance but contains additional or different terms which do not materially alter the terms of the offer constitutes an acceptance, unless the offeror, without undue delay, objects orally to the discrepancy or dispatches a notice to that effect. If he does not so object, the terms of the contract are the terms of the offer with the modifications contained in the acceptance.

(3) Additional or different terms relating, among other things, to the price, payment, quality and quantity of the goods, place and time of delivery, extent of one party's liability to the other or the settlement of disputes are considered to alter the terms of the offer materially.

ARTICLE 20

(1) A period of time for acceptance fixed by the offeror in a telegram or a letter begins to run from the moment the telegram is handed in for dispatch or from the date shown on the letter or, if no such date is shown, from the date shown on the envelope. A period of time for acceptance fixed by the offeror by telephone, telex or other means of instantaneous communication, begins to run from the moment that the offer reaches the offeree.

(2) Official holidays or non-business days occurring during the period for acceptance are included in calculating the period. However, if a notice of acceptance cannot be delivered at the address of the offeror on the last day of the period because that day falls on an official holiday or a non-business day at the place of business of the offeror, the period is extended until the first business day which follows.

ARTICLE 21

(1) A late acceptance is nevertheless effective as an acceptance if without delay the offeror orally so informs the offeree or dispatches a notice to that effect.

(2) If a letter or other writing containing a late acceptance shows that it has been sent in such circumstances that if its transmission had been normal it would have reached the offeror in due time, the late acceptance is effective as an acceptance unless, without delay, the offeror orally informs the offeree that he considers his offer as having lapsed or dispatches a notice to that effect.

ARTICLE 22

An acceptance may be withdrawn if the withdrawal reaches the offeror before or at the same time as the acceptance would have become effective.

ARTICLE 23

A contract is concluded at the moment when an acceptance of an offer becomes effective in accordance with the provisions of this Convention.

ARTICLE 24

For the purposes of this Part of the Convention, an offer, declaration of acceptance or any other indication of intention "reaches" the addressee when it is made orally to him or delivered by any other means to him personally, to his place of business or mailing address or, if he does not have a place of business or mailing address, to his habitual residence.

PART III
SALE OF GOODS

Chapter I
General Provisions

ARTICLE 25

A breach of contract committed by one of the parties is fundamental if it results in such detriment to the other party as substantially to deprive him of what he is entitled to expect under the contract, unless the party in breach did not foresee and a reasonable person of the same kind in the same circumstances would not have foreseen such a result.

ARTICLE 26

A declaration of avoidance of the contract is effective only if made by notice to the other party.

ARTICLE 27

Unless otherwise expressly provided in this Part of the Convention, if any notice, request or other communication is given or made by a party in accordance with this Part and by means appropriate in the circumstances, a delay or error in the transmission of the communication or its failure to arrive does not deprive that party of the right to rely on the communication.

ARTICLE 28

If, in accordance with the provisions of this Convention, one party is entitled to require performance of any obligation by the other party, a court is not bound to enter a judgement for specific performance unless the court would do so under its own law in respect of similar contracts of sale not governed by this Convention.

ARTICLE 29

(1) A contract may be modified or terminated by the mere agreement of the parties.

(2) A contract in writing which contains a provision requiring any modification or termination by agreement to be in writing may not be otherwise modified or terminated by agreement. However, a party may be precluded by his conduct from asserting such a provision to the extent that the other party has relied on that conduct.

Chapter II
Obligations of the Seller

ARTICLE 30

The seller must deliver the goods, hand over any documents relating to them and transfer the property in the goods, as required by the contract and this Convention.

Section I. Delivery of the Goods and Handing Over of Documents

ARTICLE 31

If the seller is not bound to deliver the goods at any other particular place, his obligation to deliver consists:

(a) if the contract of sale involves carriage of the goods—in handing the goods over to the first carrier for transmission to the buyer;
(b) if, in cases not within the preceding subparagraph, the contract relates to specific goods, or unidentified goods to be drawn from a specific stock or to be manufactured or produced, and at the time of the conclusion of the contract the parties knew that the goods were at, or were to be manufactured or produced at, a particular place—in placing the goods at the buyer's disposal at that place;
(c) in other cases—in placing the goods at the buyer's disposal at the place where the seller had his place of business at the time of the conclusion of the contract.

ARTICLE 32
(1) If the seller, in accordance with the contract or this Convention, hands the goods over to a carrier and if the goods are not clearly identified to the contract by markings on the goods, by shipping documents or otherwise, the seller must give the buyer notice of the consignment specifying the goods.
(2) If the seller is bound to arrange for carriage of the goods, he must make such contracts as are necessary for carriage to the place fixed by means of transportation appropriate in the circumstances and according to the usual terms for such transportation.
(3) If the seller is not bound to effect insurance in respect of the carriage of the goods, he must, at the buyer's request, provide him with all available information necessary to enable him to effect such insurance.

ARTICLE 33
The seller must deliver the goods:
(a) if a date is fixed by or determinable from the contract, on that date;
(b) if a period of time is fixed by or determinable from the contract, at any time within that period unless circumstances indicate that the buyer is to choose a date; or
(c) in any other case, within a reasonable time after the conclusion of the contract.

ARTICLE 34
If the seller is bound to hand over documents relating to the goods, he must hand them over at the time and place and in the form required by the contract. If the seller has handed over documents before that time, he may, up to that time, cure any lack of conformity in the documents, if the exercise of this right does not cause the buyer unreasonable inconvenience or unreasonable expense. However, the buyer retains any right to claim damages as provided for in this Convention.

Section II. Conformity of the Goods and Third Party Claims

ARTICLE 35
(1) The seller must deliver goods which are of the quantity, quality and description required by the contract and which are contained or packaged in the manner required by the contract.
(2) Except where the parties have agreed otherwise, the goods do not conform with the contract unless they:
   (a) are fit for the purposes for which goods of the same description would ordinarily be used;

(b) are fit for any particular purpose expressly or impliedly made known to the seller at the time of the conclusion of the contract, except where the circumstances show that the buyer did not rely, or that it was unreasonable for him to rely, on the seller's skill and judgement;

(c) possess the qualities of goods which the seller has held out to the buyer as a sample or model;

(d) are contained or packaged in the manner usual for such goods or, where there is no such manner, in a manner adequate to preserve and protect the goods.

(3) The seller is not liable under subparagraphs (a) to (d) of the preceding paragraph for any lack of conformity of the goods if at the time of the conclusion of the contract the buyer knew or could not have been unaware of such lack of conformity.

ARTICLE 36

(1) The seller is liable in accordance with the contract and this Convention for any lack of conformity which exists at the time when the risk passes to the buyer, even though the lack of conformity becomes apparent only after that time.

(2) The seller is also liable for any lack of conformity which occurs after the time indicated in the preceding paragraph and which is due to a breach of any of his obligations, including a breach of any guarantee that for a period of time the goods will remain fit for their ordinary purpose or for some particular purpose or will retain specified qualities or characteristics.

ARTICLE 37

If the seller has delivered goods before the date for delivery, he may, up to that date, deliver any missing part or make up any deficiency in the quantity of the goods delivered, or deliver goods in replacement of any non-conforming goods delivered or remedy any lack of conformity in the goods delivered, provided that the exercise of this right does not cause the buyer unreasonable inconvenience or unreasonable expense. However, the buyer retains any right to claim damages as provided for in this Convention.

ARTICLE 38

(1) The buyer must examine the goods, or cause them to be examined, within as short a period as is practicable in the circumstances.

(2) If the contract involves carriage of the goods, examination may be deferred until after the goods have arrived at their destination.

(3) If the goods are redirected in transit or redispatched by the buyer without a reasonable opportunity for examination by him and at the time of the conclusion of the contract the seller knew or ought to have known of the possibility of such redirection or redispatch, examination may be deferred until after the goods have arrived at the new destination.

ARTICLE 39

(1) The buyer loses the right to rely on a lack of conformity of the goods if he does not give notice to the seller specifying the nature of the lack of conformity within a reasonable time after he has discovered it or ought to have discovered it.

(2) In any event, the buyer loses the right to rely on a lack of conformity of the goods if he does not give the seller notice thereof at the latest within a period

of two years from the date on which the goods were actually handed over to the buyer, unless this time-limit is inconsistent with a contractual period of guarantee.

ARTICLE 40

The seller is not entitled to rely on the provisions of articles 38 and 39 if the lack of conformity relates to facts of which he knew or could not have been unaware and which he did not disclose to the buyer.

ARTICLE 41

The seller must deliver goods which are free from any right or claim of a third party, unless the buyer agreed to take the goods subject to that right or claim. However, if such right or claim is based on industrial property or other intellectual property, the seller's obligation is governed by article 42.

ARTICLE 42

(1) The seller must deliver goods which are free from any right or claim of a third party based on industrial property or other intellectual property, of which at the time of the conclusion of the contract the seller knew or could not have been unaware, provided that the right or claim is based on industrial property or other intellectual property:

(a) under the law of the State where the goods will be resold or otherwise used, if it was contemplated by the parties at the time of the conclusion of the contract that the goods would be resold or otherwise used in that State; or

(b) in any other case, under the law of the State where the buyer has his place of business.

(2) The obligation of the seller under the preceding paragraph does not extend to cases where:

(a) at the time of the conclusion of the contract the buyer knew or could not have been unaware of the right or claim; or

(b) the right or claim results from the seller's compliance with technical drawings, designs, formulae or other such specifications furnished by the buyer.

ARTICLE 43

(1) The buyer loses the right to rely on the provisions of article 41 or article 42 if he does not give notice to the seller specifying the nature of the right or claim of the third party within a reasonable time after he has become aware or ought to have become aware of the right or claim.

(2) The seller is not entitled to rely on the provisions of the preceding paragraph if he knew of the right or claim of the third party and the nature of it.

ARTICLE 44

Notwithstanding the provisions of paragraph (1) of article 39 and paragraph (1) of article 43, the buyer may reduce the price in accordance with article 50 or claim damages, except for loss of profit, if he has a reasonable excuse for his failure to give the required notice.

Section III. Remedies for Breach of Contract by the Seller

ARTICLE 45

(1) If the seller fails to perform any of his obligations under the contract or this Convention, the buyer may:

   (a) exercise the rights provided in articles 46 to 52;

   (b) claim damages as provided in articles 74 to 77.

(2) The buyer is not deprived of any right he may have to claim damages by exercising his right to other remedies.

(3) No period of grace may be granted to the seller by a court or arbitral tribunal when the buyer resorts to a remedy for breach of contract.

ARTICLE 46

(1) The buyer may require performance by the seller of his obligations unless the buyer has resorted to a remedy which is inconsistent with this requirement.

(2) If the goods do not conform with the contract, the buyer may require delivery of substitute goods only if the lack of conformity constitutes a fundamental breach of contract and a request for substitute goods is made either in conjunction with notice given under article 39 or within a reasonable time thereafter.

(3) If the goods do not conform with the contract, the buyer may require the seller to remedy the lack of conformity by repair, unless this is unreasonable having regard to all the circumstances. A request for repair must be made either in conjunction with notice given under article 39 or within a reasonable time thereafter.

ARTICLE 47

(1) The buyer may fix an additional period of time of reasonable length for performance by the seller of his obligations.

(2) Unless the buyer has received notice from the seller that he will not perform within the period so fixed, the buyer may not, during that period, resort to any remedy for breach of contract. However, the buyer is not deprived thereby of any right he may have to claim damages for delay in performance.

ARTICLE 48

(1) Subject to article 49, the seller may, even after the date for delivery, remedy at his own expense any failure to perform his obligations, if he can do so without unreasonable delay and without causing the buyer unreasonable inconvenience or uncertainty of reimbursement by the seller of expenses advanced by the buyer. However, the buyer retains any right to claim damages as provided for in this Convention.

(2) If the seller requests the buyer to make known whether he will accept performance and the buyer does not comply with the request within a reasonable time, the seller may perform within the time indicated in his request. The buyer may not, during that period of time, resort to any remedy which is inconsistent with performance by the seller.

(3) A notice by the seller that he will perform within a specified period of time is assumed to include a request, under the preceding paragraph, that the buyer make known his decision.

(4) A request or notice by the seller under paragraph (2) or (3) of this article is not effective unless received by the buyer.

ARTICLE 49

(1) The buyer may declare the contract avoided:

  (a) if the failure by the seller to perform any of his obligations under the contract or this Convention amounts to a fundamental breach of contract; or

  (b) in case of non-delivery, if the seller does not deliver the goods within the additional period of time fixed by the buyer in accordance with paragraph (1) of article 47 or declares that he will not deliver within the period so fixed.

(2) However, in cases where the seller has delivered the goods, the buyer loses the right to declare the contract avoided unless he does so:

  (a) in respect of late delivery, within a reasonable time after he has become aware that delivery has been made;

  (b) in respect of any breach other than late delivery, within a reasonable time:

    (i) after he knew or ought to have known of the breach;

    (ii) after the expiration of any additional period of time fixed by the buyer in accordance with paragraph (1) of article 47, or after the seller has declared that he will not perform his obligations within such an additional period; or

    (iii) after the expiration of any additional period of time indicated by the seller in accordance with paragraph (2) of article 48, or after the buyer has declared that he will not accept performance.

ARTICLE 50

If the goods do not conform with the contract and whether or not the price has already been paid, the buyer may reduce the price in the same proportion as the value that the goods actually delivered had at the time of the delivery bears to the value that conforming goods would have had at that time. However, if the seller remedies any failure to perform his obligations in accordance with article 37 or article 48 or if the buyer refuses to accept performance by the seller in accordance with those articles, the buyer may not reduce the price.

ARTICLE 51

(1) If the seller delivers only a part of the goods or if only a part of the goods delivered is in conformity with the contract, articles 46 to 50 apply in respect of the part which is missing or which does not conform.

(2) The buyer may declare the contract avoided in its entirety only if the failure to make delivery completely or in conformity with the contract amounts to a fundamental breach of the contract.

ARTICLE 52

(1) If the seller delivers the goods before the date fixed, the buyer may take delivery or refuse to take delivery.

(2) If the seller delivers a quantity of goods greater than that provided for in the contract, the buyer may take delivery or refuse to take delivery of the excess quantity. If the buyer takes delivery of all or part of the excess quantity, he must pay for it at the contract rate.

Chapter III
Obligations of the Buyer

ARTICLE 53

The buyer must pay the price for the goods and take delivery of them as required by the contract and this Convention.

Section I. Payment of the Price

ARTICLE 54

The buyer's obligation to pay the price includes taking such steps and complying with such formalities as may be required under the contract or any laws and regulations to enable payment to be made.

ARTICLE 55

Where a contract has been validly concluded but does not expressly or implicitly fix or make provision for determining the price, the parties are considered, in the absence of any indication to the contrary, to have impliedly made reference to the price generally charged at the time of the conclusion of the contract for such goods sold under comparable circumstances in the trade concerned.

ARTICLE 56

If the price is fixed according to the weight of the goods, in case of doubt it is to be determined by the net weight.

ARTICLE 57

(1) If the buyer is not bound to pay the price at any other particular place, he must pay it to the seller:
 (a) at the seller's place of business; or
 (b) if the payment is to be made against the handing over of the goods or of documents, at the place where the handing over takes place.

(2) The seller must bear any increases in the expenses incidental to payment which is caused by a change in his place of business subsequent to the conclusion of the contract.

ARTICLE 58

(1) If the buyer is not bound to pay the price at any other specific time, he must pay it when the seller places either the goods or documents controlling their disposition at the buyer's disposal in accordance with the contract and this Convention. The seller may make such payment a condition for handing over the goods or documents.

(2) If the contract involves carriage of the goods, the seller may dispatch the goods on terms whereby the goods, or documents controlling their disposition, will not be handed over to the buyer except against payment of the price.

(3) The buyer is not bound to pay the price until he has had an opportunity to examine the goods, unless the procedures for delivery or payment agreed upon by the parties are inconsistent with his having such an opportunity.

ARTICLE 59

The buyer must pay the price on the date fixed by or determinable from the contract and this Convention without the need for any request or compliance with any formality on the part of the seller.

Section II. Taking Delivery

ARTICLE 60

The buyer's obligation to take delivery consists:

(a) in doing all the acts which could reasonably be expected of him in order to enable the seller to make delivery; and
(b) in taking over the goods.

Section III. Remedies for Breach of Contract by the Buyer

ARTICLE 61
(1) If the buyer fails to perform any of his obligations under the contract or this Convention, the seller may:
   (a) exercise the rights provided in articles 62 to 65;
   (b) claim damages as provided in articles 74 to 77.
(2) The seller is not deprived of any right he may have to claim damages by exercising his right to other remedies.
(3) No period of grace may be granted to the buyer by a court or arbitral tribunal when the seller resorts to a remedy for breach of contract.

ARTICLE 62
The seller may require the buyer to pay the price, take delivery or perform his other obligations, unless the seller has resorted to a remedy which is inconsistent with this requirement.

ARTICLE 63
(1) The seller may fix an additional period of time of reasonable length for performance by the buyer of his obligations.
(2) Unless the seller has received notice from the buyer that he will not perform within the period so fixed, the seller may not, during that period, resort to any remedy for breach of contract. However, the seller is not deprived thereby of any right he may have to claim damages for delay in performance.

ARTICLE 64
(1) The seller may declare the contract avoided:
   (a) if the failure by the buyer to perform any of his obligations under the contract or this Convention amounts to a fundamental breach of contract; or
   (b) if the buyer does not, within the additional period of time fixed by the seller in accordance with paragraph (1) of article 63, perform his obligation to pay the price or take delivery of the goods, or if he declares that he will not do so within the period so fixed.
(2) However, in cases where the buyer has paid the price, the seller loses the right to declare the contract avoided unless he does so:
   (a) in respect of late performance by the buyer, before the seller has become aware that performance has been rendered; or
   (b) in respect of any breach other than late performance by the buyer, within a reasonable time:
      (i) after the seller knew or ought to have known of the breach; or
      (ii) after the expiration of any additional period of time fixed by the seller in accordance with paragraph (1) of article 63, or after the buyer has declared that he will not perform his obligations within such an additional period.

ARTICLE 65

(1) If under the contract the buyer is to specify the form, measurement or other features of the goods and he fails to make such specification either on the date agreed upon or within a reasonable time after receipt of a request from the seller, the seller may, without prejudice to any other rights he may have, make the specification himself in accordance with the requirements of the buyer that may be known to him.

(2) If the seller makes the specification himself, he must inform the buyer of the details thereof and must fix a reasonable time within which the buyer may make a different specification. If, after receipt of such a communication, the buyer fails to do so within the time so fixed, the specification made by the seller is binding.

Chapter IV
Passing of Risk

ARTICLE 66

Loss of or damage to the goods after the risk has passed to the buyer does not discharge him from his obligation to pay the price, unless the loss or damage is due to an act or omission of the seller.

ARTICLE 67

(1) If the contract of sale involves carriage of the goods and the seller is not bound to hand them over at a particular place, the risk passes to the buyer when the goods are handed over to the first carrier for transmission to the buyer in accordance with the contract of sale. If the seller is bound to hand the goods over to a carrier at a particular place, the risk does not pass to the buyer until the goods are handed over to the carrier at that place. The fact that the seller is authorized to retain documents controlling the disposition of the goods does not affect the passage of the risk.

(2) Nevertheless, the risk does not pass to the buyer until the goods are clearly identified to the contract, whether by markings on the goods, by shipping documents, by notice given to the buyer or otherwise.

ARTICLE 68

The risk in respect of goods sold in transit passes to the buyer from the time of the conclusion of the contract. However, if the circumstances so indicate, the risk is assumed by the buyer from the time the goods were handed over to the carrier who issued the documents embodying the contract of carriage. Nevertheless, if at the time of the conclusion of the contract of sale the seller knew or ought to have known that the goods had been lost or damaged and did not disclose this to the buyer, the loss or damage is at the risk of the seller.

ARTICLE 69

(1) In cases not within articles 67 and 68, the risk passes to the buyer when he takes over the goods or, if he does not do so in due time, from the time when the goods are placed at his disposal and he commits a breach of contract by failing to take delivery.

(2) However, if the buyer is bound to take over the goods at a place other than a place of business of the seller, the risk passes when delivery is due and the buyer is aware of the fact that the goods are placed at his disposal at that place.

(3) If the contract relates to goods not then identified, the goods are considered not to be placed at the disposal of the buyer until they are clearly identified to the contract.

ARTICLE 70

If the seller has committed a fundamental breach of contract, articles 67, 68 and 69 do not impair the remedies available to the buyer on account of the breach.

Chapter V
Provisions Common to the Obligations of the Seller and of the Buyer

Section I. Anticipatory Breach and Instalment Contracts

ARTICLE 71

(1) A party may suspend the performance of his obligations if, after the conclusion of the contract, it becomes apparent that the other party will not perform a substantial part of his obligations as a result of:

(a) a serious deficiency in his ability to perform or in his creditworthiness; or

(b) his conduct in preparing to perform or in performing the contract.

(2) If the seller has already dispatched the goods before the grounds described in the preceding paragraph become evident, he may prevent the handing over of the goods to the buyer even though the buyer holds a document which entitles him to obtain them. The present paragraph relates only to the rights in the goods as between the buyer and the seller.

(3) A party suspending performance, whether before or after dispatch of the goods, must immediately give notice of the suspension to the other party and must continue with performance if the other party provides adequate assurance of his performance.

ARTICLE 72

(1) If prior to the date for performance of the contract it is clear that one of the parties will commit a fundamental breach of contract, the other party may declare the contract avoided.

(2) If time allows, the party intending to declare the contract avoided must give reasonable notice to the other party in order to permit him to provide adequate assurance of his performance.

(3) The requirements of the preceding paragraph do not apply if the other party has declared that he will not perform his obligations.

ARTICLE 73

(1) In the case of a contract for delivery of goods by instalments, if the failure of one party to perform any of his obligations in respect of any instalment constitutes a fundamental breach of contract with respect to that instalment, the other party may declare the contract avoided with respect to that instalment.

(2) If one party's failure to perform any of his obligations in respect of any instalment gives the other party good grounds to conclude that a fundamental breach of contract will occur with respect to future instalments, he may declare the contract avoided for the future, provided that he does so within a reasonable time.

(3) A buyer who declares the contract avoided in respect of any delivery may, at the same time, declare it avoided in respect of deliveries already made or of future deliveries if, by reason of their interdependence, those deliveries could not be used for the purpose contemplated by the parties at the time of the conclusion of the contract.

Section II. Damages

ARTICLE 74

Damages for breach of contract by one party consist of a sum equal to the loss, including loss of profit, suffered by the other party as a consequence of the breach. Such damages may not exceed the loss which the party in breach foresaw or ought to have foreseen at the time of the conclusion of the contract, in the light of the facts and matters of which he then knew or ought to have known, as a possible consequence of the breach of contract.

ARTICLE 75

If the contract is avoided and if, in a reasonable manner and within a reasonable time after avoidance, the buyer has bought goods in replacement or the seller has resold the goods, the party claiming damages may recover the difference between the contract price and the price in the substitute transaction as well as any further damages recoverable under article 74.

ARTICLE 76

(1) If the contract is avoided and there is a current price for the goods, the party claiming damages may, if he has not made a purchase or resale under article 75, recover the difference between the price fixed by the contract and the current price at the time of avoidance as well as any further damages recoverable under article 74. If, however, the party claiming damages has avoided the contract after taking over the goods, the current price at the time of such taking over shall be applied instead of the current price at the time of avoidance.

(2) For the purposes of the preceding paragraph, the current price is the price prevailing at the place where delivery of the goods should have been made or, if there is no current price at that place, the price at such other place as serves as a reasonable substitute, making due allowance for differences in the cost of transporting the goods.

ARTICLE 77

A party who relies on a breach of contract must take such measures as are reasonable in the circumstances to mitigate the loss, including loss of profit, resulting from the breach. If he fails to take such measures, the party in breach may claim a reduction in the damages in the amount by which the loss should have been mitigated.

Section III. Interest

ARTICLE 78

If a party fails to pay the price or any other sum that is in arrears, the other party is entitled to interest on it, without prejudice to any claim for damages recoverable under article 74.

Section IV. Exemptions

ARTICLE 79

(1) A party is not liable for a failure to perform any of his obligations if he proves that the failure was due to an impediment beyond his control and that he could not reasonably be expected to have taken the impediment into account at the time of the conclusion of the contract or to have avoided or overcome it or its consequences.

(2) If the party's failure is due to the failure by a third person whom he has engaged to perform the whole or a part of the contract, that party is exempt from liability only if:

(a) he is exempt under the preceding paragraph; and

(b) the person whom he has so engaged would be so exempt if the provisions of that paragraph were applied to him.

(3) The exemption provided by this article has effect for the period during which the impediment exists.

(4) The party who fails to perform must give notice to the other party of the impediment and its effect on his ability to perform. If the notice is not received by the other party within a reasonable time after the party who fails to perform knew or ought to have known of the impediment, he is liable for damages resulting from such non-receipt.

(5) Nothing in this article prevents either party from exercising any right other than to claim damages under this Convention.

ARTICLE 80

A party may not rely on a failure of the other party to perform, to the extent that such failure was caused by the first party's act or omission.

Section V. Effects of Avoidance

ARTICLE 81

(1) Avoidance of the contract releases both parties from their obligations under it, subject to any damages which may be due. Avoidance does not affect any provision of the contract for the settlement of disputes or any other provision of the contract governing the rights and obligations of the parties consequent upon the avoidance of the contract.

(2) A party who has performed the contract either wholly or in part may claim restitution from the other party of whatever the first party has supplied or paid under the contract. If both parties are bound to make restitution, they must do so concurrently.

ARTICLE 82

(1) The buyer loses the right to declare the contract avoided or to require the seller to deliver substitute goods if it is impossible for him to make restitution of the goods substantially in the condition in which he received them.

(2) The preceding paragraph does not apply:

(a) if the impossibility of making restitution of the goods or of making restitution of the goods substantially in the condition in which the buyer received them is not due to his act or omission;

(b) if the goods or part of the goods have perished or deteriorated as a result of the examination provided for in article 38; or

(c) if the goods or part of the goods have been sold in the normal course of business or have been consumed or transformed by the buyer in the course of normal use before he discovered or ought to have discovered the lack of conformity.

ARTICLE 83

A buyer who has lost the right to declare the contract avoided or to require the seller to deliver substitute goods in accordance with article 82 retains all other remedies under the contract and this Convention.

ARTICLE 84

(1) If the seller is bound to refund the price, he must also pay interest on it, from the date on which the price was paid.

(2) The buyer must account to the seller for all benefits which he has derived from the goods or part of them:

(a) if he must make restitution of the goods or part of them; or

(b) if it is impossible for him to make restitution of all or part of the goods or to make restitution of all or part of the goods substantially in the condition in which he received them, but he has nevertheless declared the contract avoided or required the seller to deliver substitute goods.

Section VI. Preservation of the Goods

ARTICLE 85

If the buyer is in delay in taking delivery of the goods or, where payment of the price and delivery of the goods are to be made concurrently, if he fails to pay the price, and the seller is either in possession of the goods or otherwise able to control their disposition, the seller must take such steps as are reasonable in the circumstances to preserve them. He is entitled to retain them until he has been reimbursed his reasonable expenses by the buyer.

ARTICLE 86

(1) If the buyer has received the goods and intends to exercise any right under the contract or this Convention to reject them, he must take such steps to preserve them as are reasonable in the circumstances. He is entitled to retain them until he has been reimbursed his reasonable expenses by the seller.

(2) If goods dispatched to the buyer have been placed at his disposal at their destination and he exercises the right to reject them, he must take possession of them on behalf of the seller, provided that this can be done without payment of the price and without unreasonable inconvenience or unreasonable expense. This provision does not apply if the seller or a person authorized to take charge of the goods on his behalf is present at the destination. If the buyer takes possession of the goods under this paragraph, his rights and obligations are governed by the preceding paragraph.

ARTICLE 87

A party who is bound to take steps to preserve the goods may deposit them in a warehouse of a third person at the expense of the other party provided that the expense incurred is not unreasonable.

ARTICLE 88

(1) A party who is bound to preserve the goods in accordance with article 85 or 86 may sell them by any appropriate means if there has been an unreasonable delay by the other party in taking possession of the goods or in taking them back or in paying the price or the cost of preservation, provided that reasonable notice of the intention to sell has been given to the other party.

(2) If the goods are subject to rapid deterioration or their preservation would involve unreasonable expense, a party who is bound to preserve the goods in accordance with article 85 or 86 must take reasonable measures to sell them. To the extent possible he must give notice to the other party of his intention to sell.

(3) A party selling the goods has the right to retain out of the proceeds of sale an amount equal to the reasonable expenses of preserving the goods and of selling them. He must account to the other party for the balance.

PART IV
FINAL PROVISIONS

ARTICLE 89

The Secretary-General of the United Nations is hereby designated as the depositary for this Convention.

ARTICLE 90

This Convention does not prevail over any international agreement which has already been or may be entered into and which contains provisions concerning the matters governed by this Convention, provided that the parties have their places of business in States parties to such agreement.

Appendix B Uniform Commercial Code

(Selected Provisions)

§ 2-201. Formal Requirements; Statute of Frauds.

(1) Except as otherwise provided in this section a *contract* for the *sale* of *goods* for the price of $500 or more is not enforceable by way of action or defense unless there is some writing sufficient to indicate that a *contract for sale* has been made between the parties and signed by the party against whom enforcement is sought or by his authorized agent or broker. A writing is not insufficient because it omits or incorrectly states a term agreed upon but the contract is not enforceable under this paragraph beyond the quantity of *goods* shown in such writing.

(2) *Between merchants* if within a reasonable time a writing in confirmation of the *contract* and sufficient against the sender is received and the party receiving it has reason to know its contents, it satisfies the requirements of subsection (1)

against such party unless written notice of objection to its contents is given within 10 days after it is received.

§ 2-202. Final Written Expression: Parol or Extrinsic Evidence.

Terms with respect to which the confirmatory memoranda of the parties agree or which are otherwise set forth in a writing intended by the parties as a final expression of their *agreement* with respect to such terms as are included therein may not be contradicted by evidence of any prior agreement or of a contemporaneous oral agreement but may be explained or supplemented

(a) by course of dealing or usage of trade (Section *1-205*) or by course of performance (Section *2-208*); and

(b) by evidence of consistent additional terms unless the court finds the writing to have been intended also as a complete and exclusive statement of the terms of the *agreement.*

§ 2-204. Formation in General.

(1) A *contract for sale* of *goods* may be made in any manner sufficient to show *agreement,* including conduct by both parties which recognizes the existence of such a *contract.*

(2) An *agreement* sufficient to constitute a *contract for sale* may be found even though the moment of its making is undetermined.

(3) Even though one or more terms are left open a *contract for sale* does not fail for indefiniteness if the parties have intended to make a *contract* and there is a reasonably certain basis for giving an appropriate remedy.

§ 2-205. Firm Offers.

An offer by a *merchant* to buy or sell *goods* in a signed writing which by its terms gives assurance that it will be held open is not revocable, for lack of consideration, during the time stated or if no time is stated for a reasonable time, but in no event may such period of irrevocability exceed three months; but any such term of assurance on a form supplied by the offeree must be separately signed by the offeror.

§ 2-206. Offer and Acceptance in Formation of Contract.

(1) Unless otherwise unambiguously indicated by the language or circumstances

  (a) an offer to make a *contract* shall be construed as inviting acceptance in any manner and by any medium reasonable in the circumstances;

  (b) an order or other offer to buy *goods* for prompt or current shipment shall be construed as inviting acceptance either by a prompt promise to ship or by the prompt or current shipment of *conforming* or non-conforming goods, but such a shipment of non-conforming goods does not constitute an acceptance if the *seller* seasonably notifies the *buyer* that the shipment is offered only as an accommodation to the buyer.

(2) Where the beginning of a requested performance is a reasonable mode of acceptance an offeror who is not notified of acceptance within a reasonable time may treat the offer as having lapsed before acceptance.

§ 2-207. Additional Terms in Acceptance or Confirmation.

(1) A definite and seasonable expression of acceptance or a written confirmation which is sent within a reasonable time operates as an acceptance even though it states terms additional to or different from those offered or agreed upon, unless acceptance is expressly made conditional on assent to the additional or different terms.

(2) The additional terms are to be construed as proposals for addition to the *contract. Between merchants* such terms become part of the contract unless:

(a) the offer expressly limits acceptance to the terms of the offer;

(b) they materially alter it; or

(c) notification of objection to them has already been given or is given within a reasonable time after notice of them is received.

(3) Conduct by both parties which recognizes the existence of a *contract* is sufficient to establish a *contract for sale* although the writings of the parties do not otherwise establish a contract. In such case the terms of the particular contract consist of those terms on which the writings of the parties agree, together with any supplementary terms incorporated under any other provisions of this Act.

§ 2-305. Open Price Term.

(1) The parties if they so intend can conclude a *contract for sale* even though the price is not settled. In such a case the price is a reasonable price at the time for delivery if

(a) nothing is said as to price; or

(b) the price is left to be agreed by the parties and they fail to agree; or

(c) the price is to be fixed in terms of some agreed market or other standard as set or recorded by a third person or agency and it is not so set or recorded.

(2) A price to be fixed by the *seller* or by the *buyer* means a price for him to fix in *good faith.*

(3) When a price left to be fixed otherwise than by *agreement* of the parties fails to be fixed through fault of one party the other may at his option treat the *contract* as cancelled or himself fix a reasonable price.

(4) Where, however, the parties intend not to be bound unless the price be fixed or agreed and it is not fixed or agreed there is no *contract.* In such a case the *buyer* must return any *goods* already received or if unable so to do must pay their reasonable value at the time of delivery and the *seller* must return any portion of the price paid on account.

§ 2-308. Absence of Specified Place for Delivery.

Unless otherwise agreed

(a) the place for delivery of *goods* is the *seller's* place of business or if he has none his residence; but

(b) in a *contract for sale* of identified *goods* which to the knowledge of the parties at the time of contracting are in some other place, that place is the place for their delivery; and

(c) documents of title may be delivered through customary banking channels.

§ 2-309. Absence of Specific Time Provisions; Notice of Termination.

(1) The time for shipment or delivery or any other action under a *contract* if not provided in this Article or agreed upon shall be a reasonable time.

(2) Where the *contract* provides for successive performances but is indefinite in duration it is valid for a reasonable time but unless otherwise agreed may be terminated at any time by either party.

(3) *Termination* of a *contract* by one party except on the happening of an agreed event requires that reasonable notification be received by the other party and an *agreement* dispensing with notification is invalid if its operation would be unconscionable.

§ 2-310. Open Time for Payment or Running of Credit; Authority to Ship Under Reservation.

Unless otherwise agreed

(a) payment is due at the time and place at which the *buyer* is to receive the *goods* even though the place of shipment is the place of delivery; and

(b) if the *seller* is authorized to send the *goods* he may ship them under reservation, and may tender the documents of title, but the *buyer* may inspect the *goods* after their arrival before payment is due unless such inspection is inconsistent with the terms of the *contract* (Section *2-513*); and

(c) if delivery is authorized and made by way of documents of title otherwise than by subsection (b) then payment is due at the time and place at which the *buyer* is to receive the documents regardless of where the *goods* are to be received; and

(d) where the *seller* is required or authorized to ship the *goods* on credit the credit period runs from the time of shipment but post-dating the invoice or delaying its dispatch will correspondingly delay the starting of the credit period.

§ 2-313. Express Warranties by Affirmation, Promise, Description, Sample.

(1) Express warranties by the *seller* are created as follows:

  (a) Any affirmation of fact or promise made by the *seller* to the *buyer* which relates to the *goods* and becomes part of the basis of the bargain creates an express warranty that the goods shall conform to the affirmation or promise.

  (b) Any description of the *goods* which is made part of the basis of the bargain creates an express warranty that the goods shall conform to the description.

  (c) Any sample or model which is made part of the basis of the bargain creates an express warranty that the whole of the *goods* shall conform to the sample or model.

(2) It is not necessary to the creation of an express warranty that the *seller* use formal words such as "warrant" or "guarantee" or that he have a specific intention to make a warranty, but an affirmation merely of the value of the *goods* or a statement purporting to be merely the seller's opinion or commendation of the goods does not create a warranty.

§ 2-314. Implied Warranty: Merchantability; Usage of Trade.

(1) Unless excluded or modified (Section *2-316*), a warranty that the *goods* shall be merchantable is implied in a *contract* for their *sale* if the *seller* is a *merchant* with respect to goods of that kind. Under this section the serving for value of food or drink to be consumed either on the premises or elsewhere is a sale.

(2) *Goods* to be merchantable must be at least such as

(a) pass without objection in the trade under the *contract* description; and

(b) in the case of fungible *goods,* are of fair average quality within the description; and

(c) are fit for the ordinary purposes for which such *goods* are used; and

(d) run, within the variations permitted by the *agreement,* of even kind, quality and quantity within each unit and among all units involved; and

(e) are adequately contained, packaged, and labeled as the *agreement* may require; and

(f) conform to the promise or affirmations of fact made on the container or label if any.

(3) Unless excluded or modified (Section *2-316*) other implied warranties may arise from course of dealing or usage of trade.

§ 2-315. Implied Warranty: Fitness for Particular Purpose.

Where the *seller* at the time of contracting has reason to know any particular purpose for which the *goods* are required and that the *buyer* is relying on the seller's skill or judgment to select or furnish suitable goods, there is unless excluded or modified under the next section an implied warranty that the goods shall be fit for such purpose.

§ 2-316. Exclusion or Modification of Warranties.

(1) Words or conduct relevant to the creation of an express warranty and words or conduct tending to negate or limit warranty shall be construed wherever reasonable as consistent with each other; but subject to the provisions of this Article on parol or extrinsic evidence (Section *2-202*) negation or limitation is inoperative to the extent that such construction is unreasonable.

(2) Subject to subsection (3), to exclude or modify the implied warranty of merchantability or any part of it the language must mention merchantability and in case of a writing must be conspicuous, and to exclude or modify any implied warranty of fitness the exclusion must be by a writing and conspicuous. Language to exclude all implied warranties of fitness is sufficient if it states, for example, that "There are no warranties which extend beyond the description on the face hereof."

(3) Notwithstanding subsection (2)

(a) unless the circumstances indicate otherwise, all implied warranties are excluded by expressions like "as is", "with all faults" or other language which in common understanding calls the *buyer's* attention to the exclusion of warranties and makes plain that there is no implied warranty; and

(b) when the *buyer* before entering into the *contract* has examined the *goods* or the sample or model as fully as he desired or has refused to examine the goods there is no implied warranty with regard to defects which an examination ought in the circumstances to have revealed to him; and

(c) an implied warranty can also be excluded or modified by course of dealing or course of performance or usage of trade.

(4) Remedies for breach of warranty can be limited in accordance with the provisions of this Article on liquidation or limitation of damages and on contractual modification of remedy (Sections *2-718* and *2-719*).

§ 2-513. Buyer's Right to Inspection of Goods.

(1) Unless otherwise agreed and subject to subsection (3), where *goods* are tendered or delivered or identified to the *contract for sale,* the *buyer* has a right before payment or acceptance to inspect them at any reasonable place and time and in any reasonable manner. When the *seller* is required or authorized to send the goods to the buyer, the inspection may be after their arrival.

(2) Expenses of inspection must be borne by the *buyer* but may be recovered from the *seller* if the *goods* do not conform and are rejected.

(3) Unless otherwise agreed and subject to the provisions of this Article on C.I.F. *contracts* (subsection (3) of Section *2-321*), the *buyer* is not entitled to inspect the *goods* before payment of the price when the contract provides

(a) for delivery "C.O.D." or on other like terms; or

(b) for payment against documents of title, except where such payment is due only after the *goods* are to become available for inspection.

(4) A place or method of inspection fixed by the parties is presumed to be exclusive but unless otherwise expressly agreed it does not postpone identification or shift the place for delivery or for passing the risk of loss. If compliance becomes impossible, inspection shall be as provided in this section unless the place or method fixed was clearly intended as an indispensable condition failure of which avoids the *contract.*

§ 2-601. Buyer's Rights on Improper Delivery.

Subject to the provisions of this Article on breach in installment contracts (Section *2-612*) and unless otherwise agreed under the sections on contractual limitations of remedy (Sections *2-718* and *2-719*), if the *goods* or the tender of delivery fail in any respect to conform to the *contract,* the *buyer* may

(a) reject the whole; or

(b) accept the whole; or

(c) accept any *commercial unit* or units and reject the rest.

§ 2-602. Manner and Effect of Rightful Rejection.

(1) Rejection of *goods* must be within a reasonable time after their delivery or tender. It is ineffective unless the *buyer* seasonably notifies the *seller.*

(2) Subject to the provisions of the two following sections on rejected *goods* (Sections *2-603* and *2-604*),

(a) after rejection any exercise of ownership by the *buyer* with respect to any *commercial unit* is wrongful as against the *seller;* and

(b) if the *buyer* has before rejection taken physical possession of *goods* in which he does not have a security interest under the provisions of this Article (subsection (3) of Section *2-711*), he is under a duty after rejection to hold them with reasonable care at the *seller's* disposition for a time sufficient to permit the seller to remove them; but

(c) the *buyer* has no further obligations with regard to *goods* rightfully rejected.

(3) The *seller's* rights with respect to *goods* wrongfully rejected are governed by the provisions of this Article on seller's remedies in general (Section *2-703*).

§ 2-605. Waiver of Buyer's Objections by Failure to Particularize.

(1) The *buyer's* failure to state in connection with rejection a particular defect which is ascertainable by reasonable inspection precludes him from relying on the unstated defect to justify rejection or to establish breach

(a) where the *seller* could have cured it if stated seasonably; or

(b) *between merchants* when the *seller* has after rejection made a request in writing for a full and final written statement of all defects on which the *buyer* proposes to rely.

(2) Payment against documents made without reservation of rights precludes recovery of the payment for defects apparent on the face of the documents.

§ 2-606. What Constitutes Acceptance of Goods.

(1) Acceptance of *goods* occurs when the *buyer*

(a) after a reasonable opportunity to inspect the *goods* signifies to the *seller* that the goods are *conforming* or that he will take or retain them in spite of their non-conformity; or

(b) fails to make an effective rejection (subsection (1) of Section *2-602*), but such acceptance does not occur until the *buyer* has had a reasonable opportunity to inspect them; or

(c) does any act inconsistent with the *seller's* ownership; but if such act is wrongful as against the seller it is an acceptance only if ratified by him.

(2) Acceptance of a part of any *commercial unit* is acceptance of that entire unit.

§ 2-607. Effect of Acceptance; Notice of Breach; Burden of Establishing Breach After Acceptance; Notice of Claim or Litigation to Person Answerable Over.

(1) The *buyer* must pay at the *contract* rate for any *goods* accepted.

(2) Acceptance of *goods* by the *buyer* precludes rejection of the goods accepted and if made with knowledge of a non-conformity cannot be revoked because of it unless the acceptance was on the reasonable assumption that the non-conformity would be seasonably cured but acceptance does not of itself impair any other remedy provided by this Article for non-conformity.

(3) Where a tender has been accepted

(a) the *buyer* must within a reasonable time after he discovers or should have discovered any breach notify the *seller* of breach or be barred from any remedy;

§ 2-608. Revocation of Acceptance in Whole or in Part.

(1) The *buyer* may revoke his acceptance of a *lot* or *commercial unit* whose non-conformity substantially impairs its value to him if he has accepted it

(a) on the reasonable assumption that its non-conformity would be cured and it has not been seasonably cured; or

(b) without discovery of such non-conformity if his acceptance was reasonably induced either by the difficulty of discovery before acceptance or by the *seller's* assurances.

(2) Revocation of acceptance must occur within a reasonable time after the *buyer* discovers or should have discovered the ground for it and before any substantial change in condition of the *goods* which is not caused by their own defects. It is not effective until the buyer notifies the *seller* of it.

(3) A *buyer* who so revokes has the same rights and duties with regard to the *goods* involved as if he had rejected them.

§ 2-609. Right to Adequate Assurance of Performance.

(1) A *contract for sale* imposes an obligation on each party that the other's expectation of receiving due performance will not be impaired. When reasonable grounds for insecurity arise with respect to the performance of either party the other may in writing demand adequate assurance of due performance and until he receives such assurance may if commercially reasonable suspend any performance for which he has not already received the agreed return.

(2) *Between merchants* the reasonableness of grounds for insecurity and the adequacy of any assurance offered shall be determined according to commercial standards.

(3) Acceptance of any improper delivery or payment does not prejudice the aggrieved party's right to demand adequate assurance of future performance.

(4) After *receipt* of a justified demand failure to provide within a reasonable time not exceeding thirty days such assurance of due performance as is adequate under the circumstances of the particular case is a repudiation of the *contract.*

§ 2-610. Anticipatory Repudiation.

When either party repudiates the *contract* with respect to a performance not yet due the loss of which will substantially impair the value of the contract to the other, the aggrieved party may

(a) for a commercially reasonable time await performance by the repudiating party; or

(b) resort to any remedy for breach (Section *2-703* or Section *2-711*), even though he has notified the repudiating party that he would await the latter's performance and has urged retraction; and

(c) in either case suspend his own performance or proceed in accordance with the provisions of this Article on the *seller's* right to identify *goods* to the *contract* notwithstanding breach or to salvage unfinished goods (Section *2-704*).

§ 2-615. Excuse by Failure of Presupposed Conditions.

Except so far as a *seller* may have assumed a greater obligation and subject to the preceding section on substituted performance:

(a) Delay in delivery or non-delivery in whole or in part by a *seller* who complies with paragraphs (b) and (c) is not a breach of his duty under a *contract for sale* if performance as agreed has been made impracticable by the occurrence of a contingency the non-occurrence of which was a basic assumption on which the *contract* was made or by compliance in *good faith* with any applicable foreign or domestic governmental regulation or order whether or not it later proves to be invalid.

(b) Where the causes mentioned in paragraph (a) affect only a part of the *seller's* capacity to perform, he must allocate production and deliveries among his customers but may at his option include regular customers not then under *contract* as well as his own requirements for further manufacture. He may so allocate in any manner which is fair and reasonable.

(c) The *seller* must notify the *buyer* seasonably that there will be delay or non-delivery and, when allocation is required under paragraph (b), of the estimated quota thus made available for the buyer.

§ 2-616. Procedure on Notice Claiming Excuse.

(1) Where the *buyer* receives notification of a material or indefinite delay or an allocation justified under the preceding section he may by written notification to the *seller* as to any delivery concerned, and where the prospective deficiency substantially impairs the value of the whole *contract* under the provisions of this Article relating to breach of installment contracts (Section *2-612*), then also as to the whole,

  (a) terminate and thereby discharge any unexecuted portion of the *contract;* or

  (b) modify the *contract* by agreeing to take his available quota in substitution.

(2) If after *receipt* of such notification from the *seller* the *buyer* fails so to modify the *contract* within a reasonable time not exceeding thirty days the contract lapses with respect to any deliveries affected.

(3) The provisions of this section may not be negated by *agreement* except in so far as the *seller* has assumed a greater obligation under the preceding section.

Appendix C
Agreement Establishing the World Trade Organization

(Selected Provisions)

ARTICLE I
ESTABLISHMENT OF THE ORGANIZATION

The World Trade Organization (hereinafter referred to as "the WTO") is hereby established.

ARTICLE II
SCOPE OF THE WTO

1. The WTO shall provide the common institutional framework for the conduct of trade relations among its Members in matters related to the agreements and associated legal instruments included in the Annexes to this Agreement.

2. The agreements and associated legal instruments included in Annexes 1, 2 and 3 (hereinafter referred to as "Multilateral Trade Agreements") are integral parts of this Agreement, binding on all Members.
3. The agreements and associated legal instruments included in Annex 4 (hereinafter referred to as "Plurilateral Trade Agreements") are also part of this Agreement for those Members that have accepted them, and are binding on those Members. The Plurilateral Trade Agreements do not create either obligations or rights for Members that have not accepted them.
4. The General Agreement on Tariffs and Trade 1994 as specified in Annex 1A (hereinafter referred to as "GATT 1994") is legally distinct from the General Agreement on Tariffs and Trade, dated 30 October 1947, annexed to the Final Act Adopted at the Conclusion of the Second Session of the Preparatory Committee of the United Nations Conference on Trade and Employment, as subsequently rectified, amended or modified (hereinafter referred to as "GATT 1947").

ARTICLE III
FUNCTIONS OF THE WTO

1. The WTO shall facilitate the implementation, administration and operation, and further the objectives, of this Agreement and of the Multilateral Trade Agreements, and shall also provide the framework for the implementation, administration and operation of the Plurilateral Trade Agreements.
2. The WTO shall provide the forum for negotiations among its Members concerning their multilateral trade relations in matters dealt with under the agreements in the Annexes to this Agreement. The WTO may also provide a forum for further negotiations among its Members concerning their multilateral trade relations, and a framework for the implementation of the results of such negotiations, as may be decided by the Ministerial Conference.
3. The WTO shall administer the Understanding on Rules and Procedures Governing the Settlement of Disputes (hereinafter referred to as the "Dispute Settlement Understanding" or "DSU") in Annex 2 to this Agreement.
4. The WTO shall administer the Trade Policy Review Mechanism (hereinafter referred to as the "TPRM") provided for in Annex 3 to this Agreement.
5. With a view to achieving greater coherence in global economic policy-making, the WTO shall cooperate, as appropriate, with the International Monetary Fund and with the International Bank for Reconstruction and Development and its affiliated agencies.

ARTICLE IV
STRUCTURE OF THE WTO

1. There shall be a Ministerial Conference composed of representatives of all the Members, which shall meet at least once every two years. The Ministerial Conference shall carry out the functions of the WTO and take actions necessary to this effect. The Ministerial Conference shall have the authority to take decisions on all matters under any of the Multilateral Trade Agreements, if so requested by a Member, in accordance with the specific requirements for

decision-making in this Agreement and in the relevant Multilateral Trade Agreement.

2. There shall be a General Council composed of representatives of all the Members, which shall meet as appropriate. In the intervals between meetings of the Ministerial Conference, its functions shall be conducted by the General Council. The General Council shall also carry out the functions assigned to it by this Agreement. The General Council shall establish its rules of procedure and approve the rules of procedure for the Committees provided for in paragraph 7.

3. The General Council shall convene as appropriate to discharge the responsibilities of the Dispute Settlement Body provided for in the Dispute Settlement Understanding. The Dispute Settlement Body may have its own chairman and shall establish such rules of procedure as it deems necessary for the fulfilment of those responsibilities.

4. The General Council shall convene as appropriate to discharge the responsibilities of the Trade Policy Review Body provided for in the TPRM. The Trade Policy Review Body may have its own chairman and shall establish such rules of procedure as it deems necessary for the fulfilment of those responsibilities.

5. There shall be a Council for Trade in Goods, a Council for Trade in Services and a Council for Trade-Related Aspects of Intellectual Property Rights (hereinafter referred to as the "Council for TRIPS"), which shall operate under the general guidance of the General Council. The Council for Trade in Goods shall oversee the functioning of the Multilateral Trade Agreements in Annex 1A. The Council for Trade in Services shall oversee the functioning of the General Agreement on Trade in Services (hereinafter referred to as "GATS"). The Council for TRIPS shall oversee the functioning of the Agreement on Trade-Related Aspects of Intellectual Property Rights (hereinafter referred to as the "Agreement on TRIPS"). These Councils shall carry out the functions assigned to them by their respective agreements and by the General Council. They shall establish their respective rules of procedure subject to the approval of the General Council. Membership in these Councils shall be open to representatives of all Members. These Councils shall meet as necessary to carry out their functions.

6. The Council for Trade in Goods, the Council for Trade in Services and the Council for TRIPS shall establish subsidiary bodies as required. These subsidiary bodies shall establish their respective rules of procedure subject to the approval of their respective Councils.

7. The Ministerial Conference shall establish a Committee on Trade and Development, a Committee on Balance-of-Payments Restrictions and a Committee on Budget, Finance and Administration, which shall carry out the functions assigned to them by this Agreement and by the Multilateral Trade Agreements, and any additional functions assigned to them by the General Council, and may establish such additional Committees with such functions as it may deem appropriate. As part of its functions, the Committee on Trade and Development shall periodically review the special provisions in the Multilateral Trade Agreements in favour of the least-developed country Members and report to the General Council for appropriate action. Membership in these Committees shall be open to representatives of all Members.

8. The bodies provided for under the Plurilateral Trade Agreements shall carry out the functions assigned to them under those Agreements and shall operate within the institutional framework of the WTO. These bodies shall keep the General Council informed of their activities on a regular basis.

ARTICLE VI
THE SECRETARIAT

1. There shall be a Secretariat of the WTO (hereinafter referred to as "the Secretariat") headed by a Director-General.
2. The Ministerial Conference shall appoint the Director-General and adopt regulations setting out the powers, duties, conditions of service and term of office of the Director-General.
3. The Director-General shall appoint the members of the staff of the Secretariat and determine their duties and conditions of service in accordance with regulations adopted by the Ministerial Conference.
4. The responsibilities of the Director-General and of the staff of the Secretariat shall be exclusively international in character. In the discharge of their duties, the Director-General and the staff of the Secretariat shall not seek or accept instructions from any government or any other authority external to the WTO. They shall refrain from any action which might adversely reflect on their position as international officials. The Members of the WTO shall respect the international character of the responsibilities of the Director-General and of the staff of the Secretariat and shall not seek to influence them in the discharge of their duties.

ARTICLE IX
DECISION-MAKING

1. The WTO shall continue the practice of decision-making by consensus followed under GATT 1947.[1] Except as otherwise provided, where a decision cannot be arrived at by consensus, the matter at issue shall be decided by voting. At meetings of the Ministerial Conference and the General Council, each Member of the WTO shall have one vote. Where the European Communities exercise their right to vote, they shall have a number of votes equal to the number of their member States[2] which are Members of the WTO. Decisions of the Ministerial Conference and the General Council shall be taken by a majority of the votes cast, unless otherwise provided in this Agreement or in the relevant Multilateral Trade Agreement.[3]

ARTICLE X
AMENDMENTS

2. Amendments to the provisions of this Article and to the provisions of the following Articles shall take effect only upon acceptance by all Members:

   Article IX of this Agreement;
   Articles I and II of GATT 1994;

1 The body concerned shall be deemed to have decided by consensus on a matter submitted for its consideration, if no Member, present at the meeting when the decision is taken, formally objects to the proposed decision.

2 The number of votes of the European Communities and their member States shall in no case exceed the number of the member States of the European Communities.

3 Decisions by the General Council when convened as the Dispute Settlement Body shall be taken only in accordance with the provisions of paragraph 4 of Article 2 of the Dispute Settlement Understanding.

Article II:1 of GATS;
Article 4 of the Agreement on TRIPS.

ARTICLE XI
ORIGINAL MEMBERSHIP

1. The contracting parties to GATT 1947 as of the date of entry into force of this Agreement, and the European Communities, which accept this Agreement and the Multilateral Trade Agreements and for which Schedules of Concessions and Commitments are annexed to GATT 1994 and for which Schedules of Specific Commitments are annexed to GATS shall become original Members of the WTO.
2. The least-developed countries recognized as such by the United Nations will only be required to undertake commitments and concessions to the extent consistent with their individual development, financial and trade needs or their administrative and institutional capabilities.

ARTICLE XII
ACCESSION

1. Any State or separate customs territory possessing full autonomy in the conduct of its external commercial relations and of the other matters provided for in this Agreement and the Multilateral Trade Agreements may accede to this Agreement, on terms to be agreed between it and the WTO. Such accession shall apply to this Agreement and the Multilateral Trade Agreements annexed thereto.
2. Decisions on accession shall be taken by the Ministerial Conference. The Ministerial Conference shall approve the agreement on the terms of accession by a two-thirds majority of the Members of the WTO.
3. Accession to a Plurilateral Trade Agreement shall be governed by the provisions of that Agreement.
3. In the event of a conflict between a provision of this Agreement and a provision of any of the Multilateral Trade Agreements, the provision of this Agreement shall prevail to the extent of the conflict.

ARTICLE XVI
MISCELLANEOUS PROVISIONS

4. Each Member shall ensure the conformity of its laws, regulations and administrative procedures with its obligations as provided in the annexed Agreements.
5. No reservations may be made in respect of any provision of this Agreement. Reservations in respect of any of the provisions of the Multilateral Trade Agreements may only be made to the extent provided for in those Agreements.

DONE at Marrakesh this fifteenth day of April one thousand nine hundred and ninety-four, in a single copy, in the English, French and Spanish languages, each text being authentic.

LIST OF ANNEXES

ANNEX 1

ANNEX 1A: MULTILATERAL AGREEMENTS ON TRADE IN GOODS

General Agreement on Tariffs and Trade 1994

Agreement on Agriculture

Agreement on the Application of Sanitary and Phytosanitary Measures

Agreement on Textiles and Clothing

Agreement on Technical Barriers to Trade

Agreement on Trade-Related Investment Measures

Agreement on Implementation of Article VI of the General Agreement on Tariffs and Trade 1994

Agreement on Implementation of Article VII of the General Agreement on Tariffs and Trade 1994

Agreement on Preshipment Inspection

Agreement on Rules of Origin

Agreement on Import Licensing Procedures

Agreement on Subsidies and Countervailing Measures

Agreement on Safeguards

ANNEX 1B: General Agreement on Trade in Services and Annexes

ANNEX 1C: Agreement on Trade-Related Aspects of Intellectual Property Rights

ANNEX 4 PLURILATERAL TRADE AGREEMENTS

Agreement on Trade in Civil Aircraft

Agreement on Government Procurement

International Dairy Agreement

International Bovine Meat Agreement

Appendix D
Agreement on Trade-Related Aspects of Intellectual Property Rights

(Selected Provisions)

PART I: GENERAL PROVISIONS AND BASIC PRINCIPLES

ARTICLE 2—INTELLECTUAL PROPERTY CONVENTIONS

2. Nothing in Parts I to IV of this Agreement shall derogate from existing obligations that Members may have to each other under the Paris Convention, the Berne Convention, the Rome Convention and the Treaty on Intellectual Property in Respect of Integrated Circuits.

ARTICLE 3—NATIONAL TREATMENT

1. Each Member shall accord to the nationals of other Members treatment no less favourable than that it accords to its own nationals with regard to the protection 3 of intellectual property, subject to the exceptions already provided in, respectively, the Paris Convention (1967), the Berne Convention (1971), the

Rome Convention and the Treaty on Intellectual Property in Respect of Integrated Circuits.

ARTICLE 4—MOST-FAVORED-NATION TREATMENT

With regard to the protection of intellectual property, any advantage, favour, privilege or immunity granted by a Member to the nationals of any other country shall be accorded immediately and unconditionally to the nationals of all other Members. Exempted from this obligation are any advantage, favour, privilege or immunity accorded by a Member:

ARTICLE 7—OBJECTIVES

The protection and enforcement of intellectual property rights should contribute to the promotion of technological innovation and to the transfer and dissemination of technology, to the mutual advantage of producers and users of technological knowledge and in a manner conducive to social and economic welfare, and to a balance of rights and obligations.

PART II: STANDARDS CONCERNING THE AVAILABILITY, SCOPE AND USE OF INTELLECTUAL PROPERTY RIGHTS

Section 1: Copyright and Related Rights

ARTICLE 9—RELATION TO BERNE CONVENTION

1. Members shall comply with . . . the Berne Convention (1971).
2. Copyright protection shall extend to expressions and not to ideas, procedures, methods of operation or mathematical concepts as such.

ARTICLE 10—COMPUTER PROGRAMS AND COMPILATIONS OF DATA

1. Computer programs, whether in source or object code, shall be protected as literary works under the Berne Convention (1971).
2. Compilations of data or other material, whether in machine readable or other form, which by reason of the selection or arrangement of their contents constitute intellectual creations shall be protected as such. Such protection, which shall not extend to the data or material itself, shall be without prejudice to any copyright subsisting in the data or material itself.

ARTICLE 12—TERM OF PROTECTION

Whenever the term of protection of a work, other than a photographic work or a work of applied art, is calculated on a basis other than the life of a natural person, such term shall be no less than fifty years from the end of the calendar year of authorized publication, or, failing such authorized publication within fifty years from the making of the work, fifty years from the end of the calendar year of making.

Section 2: Trademarks

ARTICLE 15—PROTECTABLE SUBJECT MATTER

1. Any sign, or any combination of signs, capable of distinguishing the goods or services of one undertaking from those of other undertakings, shall be capable of constituting a trademark. Such signs, in particular words including personal

names, letters, numerals, figurative elements and combinations of colours as well as any combination of such signs, shall be eligible for registration as trademarks. Where signs are not inherently capable of distinguishing the relevant goods or services, Members may make registrability depend on distinctiveness acquired through use. Members may require, as a condition of registration, that signs be visually perceptible.

3. Members may make registrability depend on use. However, actual use of a trademark shall not be a condition for filing an application for registration. An application shall not be refused solely on the ground that intended use has not taken place before the expiry of a period of three years from the date of application.
4. The nature of the goods or services to which a trademark is to be applied shall in no case form an obstacle to registration of the trademark.
5. Members shall publish each trademark either before it is registered or promptly after it is registered and shall afford a reasonable opportunity for petitions to cancel the registration. In addition, Members may afford an opportunity for the registration of a trademark to be opposed.

ARTICLE 16—RIGHTS CONFERRED

1. The owner of a registered trademark shall have the exclusive right to prevent all third parties not having his consent from using in the course of trade identical or similar signs for goods or services which are identical or similar to those in respect of which the trademark is registered where such use would result in a likelihood of confusion. In case of the use of an identical sign for identical goods or services, a likelihood of confusion shall be presumed. The rights described above shall not prejudice any existing prior rights, nor shall they affect the possibility of Members making rights available on the basis of use.
2. Article 6bis of the Paris Convention (1967) shall apply, mutatis mutandis, to services. In determining whether a trademark is well-known, account shall be taken of the knowledge of the trademark in the relevant sector of the public, including knowledge in that Member obtained as a result of the promotion of the trademark.

ARTICLE 18—TERM OF PROTECTION

Initial registration, and each renewal of registration, of a trademark shall be for a term of no less than seven years. The registration of a trademark shall be renewable indefinitely.

ARTICLE 19—REQUIREMENT OF USE

1. If use is required to maintain a registration, the registration may be cancelled only after an uninterrupted period of at least three years of non-use, unless valid reasons based on the existence of obstacles to such use are shown by the trademark owner. Circumstances arising independently of the will of the owner of the trademark which constitute an obstacle to the use of the trademark, such as import restrictions on or other government requirements for goods or services protected by the trademark, shall be recognized as valid reasons for non-use.
2. When subject to the control of its owner, use of a trademark by another person shall be recognized as use of the trademark for the purpose of maintaining the registration.

ARTICLE 20—OTHER REQUIREMENTS

The use of a trademark in the course of trade shall not be unjustifiably encumbered by special requirements, such as use with another trademark, use in a special form or use in a manner detrimental to its capability to distinguish the goods or services of one undertaking from those of other undertakings. This will not preclude a requirement prescribing the use of the trademark identifying the undertaking producing the goods or services along with, but without linking it to, the trademark distinguishing the specific goods or services in question of that undertaking.

ARTICLE 21—LICENSING AND ASSIGNMENT
Members may determine conditions on the licensing and assignment of trademarks, it being understood that the compulsory licensing of trademarks shall not be permitted and that the owner of a registered trademark shall have the right to assign his trademark with or without the transfer of the business to which the trademark belongs.

Section 3: Geographical Indications

ARTICLE 22—PROTECTION OF GEOGRAPHICAL INDICATIONS

1. Geographical indications are, for the purposes of this Agreement, indications which identify a good as originating in the territory of a Member, or a region or locality in that territory, where a given quality, reputation or other characteristic of the good is essentially attributable to its geographical origin.
2. In respect of geographical indications, Members shall provide the legal means for interested parties to prevent:
   (a) the use of any means in the designation or presentation of a good that indicates or suggests that the good in question originates in a geographical area other than the true place of origin in a manner which misleads the public as to the geographical origin of the good;
   (b) any use which constitutes an act of unfair competition within the meaning of Article 10bis of the Paris Convention (1967).
3. A Member shall, ex officio if its legislation so permits or at the request of an interested party, refuse or invalidate the registration of a trademark which contains or consists of a geographical indication with respect to goods not originating in the territory indicated, if use of the indication in the trademark for such goods in that Member is of such a nature as to mislead the public as to the true place of origin.
4. The provisions of the preceding paragraphs of this Article shall apply to a geographical indication which, although literally true as to the territory, region or locality in which the goods originate, falsely represents to the public that the goods originate in another territory.

Section 4: Industrial Designs

ARTICLE 25—REQUIREMENTS FOR PROTECTION

1. Members shall provide for the protection of independently created industrial designs that are new or original. Members may provide that designs are not new or original if they do not significantly differ from known designs or combinations of known design features. Members may provide that such protection shall not extend to designs dictated essentially by technical or functional considerations.

ARTICLE 26—PROTECTION

1. The owner of a protected industrial design shall have the right to prevent third parties not having his consent from making, selling or importing articles bear-

ing or embodying a design which is a copy, or substantially a copy, of the protected design, when such acts are undertaken for commercial purposes.

3. The duration of protection available shall amount to at least ten years.

Section 5: Patents

ARTICLE 27—PATENTABLE SUBJECT MATTER

1. Subject to the provisions of paragraphs 2 and 3 below, patents shall be available for any inventions, whether products or processes, in all fields of technology, provided that they are new, involve an inventive step and are capable of industrial application. 5 Subject to paragraph 4 of Article 65, paragraph 8 of Article 70 and paragraph 3 of this Article, patents shall be available and patent rights enjoyable without discrimination as to the place of invention, the field of technology and whether products are imported or locally produced.
2. Members may exclude from patentability inventions, the prevention within their territory of the commercial exploitation of which is necessary to protect public order or morality, including to protect human, animal or plant life or health or to avoid serious prejudice to the environment, provided that such exclusion is not made merely because the exploitation is prohibited by domestic law.
3. Members may also exclude from patentability:
   (a) diagnostic, therapeutic and surgical methods for the treatment of humans or animals;
   (b) plants and animals other than microorganisms, and essentially biological processes for the production of plants or animals other than non-biological and microbiological processes. However, Members shall provide for the protection of plant varieties either by patents or by an effective sui generis system or by any combination thereof. The provisions of this sub-paragraph shall be reviewed four years after the entry into force of the Agreement Establishing the WTO.

ARTICLE 28—RIGHTS CONFERRED

1. A patent shall confer on its owner the following exclusive rights:
   (a) where the subject matter of a patent is a product, to prevent third parties not having his consent from the acts of: making, using, offering for sale, selling, or importing for these purposes that product;
   (b) where the subject matter of a patent is a process, to prevent third parties not having his consent from the act of using the process, and from the acts of: using, offering for sale, selling, or importing for these purposes at least the product obtained directly by that process.
2. Patent owners shall also have the right to assign, or transfer by succession, the patent and to conclude licensing contracts.

ARTICLE 29—CONDITIONS ON PATENT APPLICANTS

1. Members shall require that an applicant for a patent shall disclose the invention in a manner sufficiently clear and complete for the invention to be carried out by a person skilled in the art and may require the applicant to indicate the best mode for carrying out the invention known to the inventor at the filing date or, where priority is claimed, at the priority date of the application.
2. Members may require an applicant for a patent to provide information concerning his corresponding foreign applications and grants.

ARTICLE 31— OTHER USE WITHOUT AUTHORIZATION OF THE RIGHT HOLDER

Where the law of a Member allows for other use of the subject matter of a patent without the authorization of the right holder, including use by the government or third parties authorized by the government, the following provisions shall be respected:

(a) authorization of such use shall be considered on its individual merits;

(b) such use may only be permitted if, prior to such use, the proposed user has made efforts to obtain authorization from the right holder on reasonable commercial terms and conditions and that such efforts have not been successful within a reasonable period of time. This requirement may be waived by a Member in the case of a national emergency or other circumstances of extreme urgency or in cases of public non-commercial use. In situations of national emergency or other circumstances of extreme urgency, the right holder shall, nevertheless, be notified as soon as reasonably practicable. In the case of public non-commercial use, where the government or contractor, without making a patent search, knows or has demonstrable grounds to know that a valid patent is or will be used by or for the government, the right holder shall be informed promptly;

(c) the scope and duration of such use shall be limited to the purpose for which it was authorized, and in the case of semi-conductor technology shall only be for public non-commercial use or to remedy a practice determined after judicial or administrative process to be anti-competitive.

(d) such use shall be non-exclusive;

(e) such use shall be non-assignable, except with that part of the enterprise or goodwill which enjoys such use;

(f) any such use shall be authorized predominantly for the supply of the domestic market of the Member authorizing such use;

(g) authorization for such use shall be liable, subject to adequate protection of the legitimate interests of the persons so authorized, to be terminated if and when the circumstances which led to it cease to exist and are unlikely to recur. The competent authority shall have the authority to review, upon motivated request, the continued existence of these circumstances;

(h) the right holder shall be paid adequate remuneration in the circumstances of each case, taking into account the economic value of the authorization;

ARTICLE 33—TERM OF PROTECTION

The term of protection available shall not end before the expiration of a period of twenty years counted from the filing date.

Section 6: Layout-Designs (Topographies) of Integrated Circuits

ARTICLE 35—RELATION TO IPIC TREATY

Members agree to provide protection to the layout-designs (topographies) of integrated circuits (hereinafter referred to as "layout-designs") in accordance with Articles 2-7 (other than paragraph 3 of Article 6), Article 12 and paragraph 3 of Article 16 of the Treaty on Intellectual Property in Respect of Integrated Circuits and, in addition, to comply with the following provisions.

ARTICLE 38—TERM OF PROTECTION

1. In Members requiring registration as a condition of protection, the term of protection of layout-designs shall not end before the expiration of a period of ten

years counted from the date of filing an application for registration or from the first commercial exploitation wherever in the world it occurs.

Section 7: Protection of Undisclosed Information

ARTICLE 39

1. In the course of ensuring effective protection against unfair competition as provided in Article 10bis of the Paris Convention (1967), Members shall protect undisclosed information in accordance with paragraph 2 below and data submitted to governments or governmental agencies in accordance with paragraph 3 below.
2. Natural and legal persons shall have the possibility of preventing information lawfully within their control from being disclosed to, acquired by, or used by others without their consent in a manner contrary to honest commercial practices so long as such information:

   is secret in the sense that it is not, as a body or in the precise configuration and assembly of its components, generally known among or readily accessible to persons within the circles that normally deal with the kind of information in question;

   has commercial value because it is secret; and

   has been subject to reasonable steps under the circumstances, by the person lawfully in control of the information, to keep it secret.

PART III: ENFORCEMENT OF INTELLECTUAL PROPERTY RIGHTS

ARTICLE 41

1. Members shall ensure that enforcement procedures as specified in this Part are available under their national laws so as to permit effective action against any act of infringement of intellectual property rights covered by this Agreement, including expeditious remedies to prevent infringements and remedies which constitute a deterrent to further infringements. These procedures shall be applied in such a manner as to avoid the creation of barriers to legitimate trade and to provide for safeguards against their abuse.
2. Procedures concerning the enforcement of intellectual property rights shall be fair and equitable. They shall not be unnecessarily complicated or costly, or entail unreasonable time-limits or unwarranted delays.
3. Decisions on the merits of a case shall preferably be in writing and reasoned. They shall be made available at least to the parties to the proceeding without undue delay. Decisions on the merits of a case shall be based only on evidence in respect of which parties were offered the opportunity to be heard.
4. Parties to a proceeding shall have an opportunity for review by a judicial authority of final administrative decisions and, subject to jurisdictional provisions in national laws concerning the importance of a case, of at least the legal aspects of initial judicial decisions on the merits of a case. However, there shall be no obligation to provide an opportunity for review of acquittals in criminal cases.

ARTICLE 42—FAIR AND EQUITABLE PROCEDURES

Members shall make available to right holders civil judicial procedures concerning the enforcement of any intellectual property right covered by this Agreement. Defendants shall have the right to written notice which is timely and contains sufficient detail, including the basis of the claims. Parties shall be allowed to be represented by independent legal counsel, and procedures shall not impose overly burdensome requirements concerning mandatory personal appearances. All parties to such procedures shall be duly entitled to substantiate their claims and to present all relevant evidence. The procedure shall provide a means to identify and protect confidential information, unless this would be contrary to existing constitutional requirements.

ARTICLE 44—INJUNCTIONS

1. The judicial authorities shall have the authority to order a party to desist from an infringement, inter alia to prevent the entry into the channels of commerce in their jurisdiction of imported goods that involve the infringement of an intellectual property right, immediately after customs clearance of such goods. Members are not obliged to accord such authority in respect of protected subject matter acquired or ordered by a person prior to knowing or having reasonable grounds to know that dealing in such subject matter would entail the infringement of an intellectual property right.

ARTICLE 45—DAMAGES

1. The judicial authorities shall have the authority to order the infringer to pay the right holder damages adequate to compensate for the injury the right holder has suffered because of an infringement of his intellectual property right by an infringer who knew or had reasonable grounds to know that he was engaged in infringing activity.

Section 4: Special Requirements Related to Border Measures

ARTICLE 51—SUSPENSION OF RELEASE BY CUSTOMS AUTHORITIES

Members shall, in conformity with the provisions set out below, adopt procedures to enable a right holder, who has valid grounds for suspecting that the importation of counterfeit trademark or pirated copyright goods may take place, to lodge an application in writing with competent authorities, administrative or judicial, for the suspension by the customs authorities of the release into free circulation of such goods.

ARTICLE 53—SECURITY OR EQUIVALENT ASSURANCE

1. The competent authorities shall have the authority to require an applicant to provide a security or equivalent assurance sufficient to protect the defendant and the competent authorities and to prevent abuse. Such security or equivalent assurance shall not unreasonably deter recourse to these procedures.

ARTICLE 57—RIGHT OF INSPECTION AND INFORMATION

Without prejudice to the protection of confidential information, Members shall provide the competent authorities the authority to give the right holder sufficient opportunity to have any product detained by the customs authorities inspected in order to substantiate his claims. The competent authorities shall also have authority to give the importer an equivalent opportunity to have any such product inspected. Where a positive determination has been made on the merits of a case, Members may provide the competent authorities the authority to inform the right holder of the names and addresses of the consignor, the importer and the consignee and of the quantity of the goods in question.

PART V: DISPUTE PREVENTION AND SETTLEMENT

ARTICLE 63—TRANSPARENCY

1. Laws and regulations, and final judicial decisions and administrative rulings of general application, made effective by any Member pertaining to the subject matter of this Agreement (the availability, scope, acquisition, enforcement and prevention of the abuse of intellectual property rights) shall be published, or where such publication is not practicable made publicly available, in a national language, in such a manner as to enable governments and right holders to become acquainted with them.
2. Members shall notify the laws and regulations referred to in paragraph 1 above to the Council for Trade-Related Aspects of Intellectual Property Rights in order to assist that Council in its review of the operation of this Agreement.

ARTICLE 66—LEAST-DEVELOPED COUNTRY MEMBERS

1. In view of their special needs and requirements, their economic, financial and administrative constraints, and their need for flexibility to create a viable technological base, least-developed country Members shall not be required to apply the provisions of this Agreement, other than Articles 3, 4 and 5, for a period of 10 years from the date of application as defined under paragraph 1 of Article 65 above. The Council shall, upon duly motivated request by a least-developed country Member, accord extensions of this period.

ARTICLE 68—COUNCIL FOR TRADE-RELATED ASPECTS OF INTELLECTUAL PROPERTY RIGHTS

The Council for Trade-Related Aspects of Intellectual Property Rights shall monitor the operation of this Agreement and, in particular, Members' compliance with their obligations hereunder, and shall afford Members the opportunity of consulting on matters relating to the trade-related aspects of intellectual property rights.

Appendix E Excerpts from International Convention for the Unification of Certain Rules of Law Relating to Bills of Lading ("Hague Rules")

ARTICLE 1

In this Convention the following words are employed with the meanings set out below:

(a) "Carrier" includes the owner or the charterer who enters into a contract of carriage with a shipper.

(b) "Contract of carriage" applies only to contracts of carriage covered by a bill of lading or any similar document of title, in so far as such document relates to the carriage of goods by sea, including any bill of lading or any similar document as aforesaid issued under or pursuant to a charter party from the moment at which such bill of lading or similar document of title regulates the relations between a carrier and a holder of the same.

(c) "Goods" includes goods, wares, merchandise and articles of every kind whatsoever except live animals and cargo which by the contract of carriage in stated as being carried on deck and is so carried.
(d) "Ship" means any vessel used for the carriage of goods by sea.
(e) "Carriage of goods" covers the period from the time when the goods are loaded on to the time they are discharged from the ship.

ARTICLE 2

Subject to the provisions of Article 6, under every contract of carriage of goods by sea the carrier, in relation to the loading, handling, stowage, carriage, custody, care and discharge of such goods, shall be subject to the responsibilities and liabilities, and entitled to the rights and immunities hereinafter set forth.

ARTICLE 3

1. The carrier shall be bound before and at the beginning of the voyage to exercise due diligence to:
   (a) Make the ship seaworthy.
   (b) Properly man, equip and supply the ship.
   (c) Make the holds, refrigerating and cool chambers, and all other parts of the ship in which goods are carried, fit and safe for their reception, carriage and preservation.
2. Subject to the provisions of Article 4, the carrier shall properly and carefully load, handle, stow, carry, keep, care for, and discharge the goods carried.
3. After receiving the goods into his charge the carrier or the master or agent of the carrier shall, on demand of the shipper, issue to the shipper a bill of lading showing among other things:
   (a) The leading marks necessary for identification of the goods as the same are furnished in writing by the shipper before the loading of such goods starts, provided such marks are stamped or otherwise shown clearly upon the goods if uncovered, or on the cases or coverings in which such goods are contained, in such a manner as should ordinarily remain legible until the end of the voyage.
   (b) Either the number of packages or pieces, or the quantity, or weight, as the case may be, as furnished in writing by the shipper.
   (c) The apparent order and condition of the goods.

   Provided that no carrier, master or agent of the carrier shall be bound to state or show in the bill of lading any marks, number, quantity, or weight which he has reasonable ground for suspecting not accurately to represent the goods actually received, or which he has had no reasonable means of checking.
4. Such a bill of lading shall be prima facie evidence of the receipt by the carrier of the goods as therein described in accordance with paragraph 3(a), (b) and (c).
5. The shipper shall be deemed to have guaranteed to the carrier the accuracy at the time of shipment of the marks, number, quantity and weight, as furnished by him, and the shipper shall indemnify the carrier against all loss, damages and expenses arising or resulting from inaccuracies in such particulars. The right of the carrier to such indemnity shall in no way limit his responsibility and liability under the contract of carriage to any person other than the shipper.

6. Unless notice of loss or damage and the general nature of such loss or damage be given in writing to the carrier or his agent at the port of discharge before or at the time of the removal of the goods into the custody of the person entitled to delivery thereof under the contract of carriage, or, if the loss or damage be not apparent, within three days, such removal shall be prima facie evidence of the delivery by the carrier of the goods as described in the bill of lading.

   If the loss or damage is not apparent, the notice must be given within three days of the delivery of the goods.

   The notice in writing need not be given if the state of the goods has, at the time of their receipt, been the subject of joint survey or inspection.

   In any event the carrier and the ship shall be discharged from all liability in respect of loss or damage unless suit is brought within one year after delivery of the goods or the date when the goods should have been delivered.

   In the case of any actual or apprehended loss or damage the carrier and the receiver shall give all reasonable facilities to each other for inspecting and tallying the goods.
7. After the goods are loaded the bill of lading to be issued by the carrier, master, or agent of the carrier, to the shipper shall, if the shipper so demands, be a "shipped" bill of lading, provided that if the shipper shall have previously taken up any document of title to such goods, he shall surrender the same as against the issue of the "shipped" bill of lading, but at the option of the carrier such document of title may be noted at the port of shipment by the carrier, master, or agent with the name or names of the ship or ships upon which the goods have been shipped and the date or dates of shipment, and when so noted, if it shows the particulars mentioned in paragraph 3 of Article 3, shall for the purpose of this Article be deemed to constitute a "shipped" bill of lading.
8. Any clause, covenant, or agreement in a contract of carriage relieving the carrier or the ship from liability for loss or damage to, or in connexion with, goods arising from negligence, fault, or failure in the duties and obligations provided in this Article or lessening such liability otherwise than as provided in this Convention, shall be null and void and of no effect. A benefit of insurance in favour of the carrier or similar clause shall be deemed to be a clause relieving the carrier from liability.

ARTICLE 4

1. Neither the carrier nor the ship shall be liable for loss or damage arising or resulting from unseaworthiness unless caused by want of due diligence on the part of the carrier to make the ship seaworthy and to secure that the ship is properly manned, equipped and supplied, and to make the holds, refrigerating and cool chambers and all other parts of the ship in which goods are carried fit and safe for their reception, carriage and preservation in accordance with the provisions of paragraph 1 of Article 3. Whenever loss or damage has resulted from unseaworthiness the burden of proving the exercise of due diligence shall be on the carrier or other person claiming exemption under this Article.
2. Neither the carrier nor the ship shall be responsible for loss or damage arising or resulting from:
   (a) Act, neglect, or default of the master, mariner, pilot, or the servants of the carrier in the navigation or in the management of the ship.
   (b) Fire, unless caused by the actual fault or privity of the carrier.
   (c) Perils, dangers and accidents of the sea or other navigable waters.

(d) Act of God.
(e) Act of war.
(f) Act of public enemies.
(g) Arrest or restraint or princes, rulers or people, or seizure under legal process.
(h) Quarantine restrictions.
(i) Act or omission of the shipper or owner of the goods, his agent or representative.
(j) Strikes or lockouts or stoppage or restraint of labour from whatever cause, whether partial or general.
(k) Riots and civil commotions.
(l) Saving or attempting to save life or property at sea.
(m) Wastage in bulk or weight or any other loss or damage arising from inherent defect, quality or vice of the goods.
(n) Insufficiency of packing.
(o) Insufficiency or inadequacy of marks.
(p) Latent defects not discoverable by due diligence.
(q) Any other cause arising without the actual fault or privity of the carrier, or without the actual fault or neglect of the agents or servants of the carrier, but the burden of proof shall be on the person claiming the benefit of this exception to show that neither the actual fault or privity of the carrier nor the fault or neglect of the agents or servants of the carrier contributed to the loss or damage.

3. The shipper shall not be responsible for loss or damage sustained by the carrier or the ship arising or resulting from any cause without the act, fault or neglect of the shipper, his agents or his servants.
4. Any deviation in saving or attempting to save life or property at sea or any reasonable deviation shall not be deemed to be an infringement or breach of this Convention or of the contract of carriage, and the carrier shall not be liable for any loss or damage resulting therefrom.
5. Neither the carrier nor the ship shall in any event be or become liable for any loss or damage to or in connection with goods in an amount exceeding 100 pounds sterling per package or unit, or the equivalent of that sum in other currency unless the nature and value of such goods have been declared by the shipper before shipment and inserted in the bill of lading.

   This declaration if embodied in the bill of lading shall be prima facie evidence, but shall not be binding or conclusive on the carrier.

   By agreement between the carrier, master or agent of the carrier and the shipper another maximum amount than that mentioned in this paragraph may be fixed, provided that such maximum shall not be less than the figure above named.

   Neither the carrier nor the ship shall be responsible in any event for loss or damage to, or in connection with, goods if the nature or value thereof has been knowingly misstated by the shipper in the bill of lading.
6. Goods of an inflammable, explosive or dangerous nature to the shipment whereof the carrier, master or agent of the carrier has not consented with knowledge of their nature and character, may at any time before discharge be landed at any place, or destroyed or rendered innocuous by the carrier without compensation and the shipper of such goods shall be liable for all damage and expenses directly or indirectly arising out of or resulting from such shipment. If any such goods shipped with such knowledge and consent shall become a

danger to the ship or cargo, they may in like manner be landed at any place, or destroyed or rendered innocuous by the carrier without liability on the part of the carrier except to general average, if any.

ARTICLE 5

A carrier shall be at liberty to surrender in whole or in part all or any of his rights and immunities or to increase any of his responsibilities and obligations under this Convention, provided such surrender or increase shall be embodied in the bill of lading issued to the shipper.

The provisions of this Convention shall not be applicable to charter parties, but if bills of lading are issued in the case of a ship under a charter party they shall comply with the terms of this Convention. Nothing in these rules shall be held to prevent the insertion in a bill of lading of any lawful provision regarding general average.

ARTICLE 6

Notwithstanding the provisions of the preceding Articles, a carrier, master or agent of the carrier and a shipper shall in regard to any particular goods be at liberty to enter into any agreement in any terms as to the responsibility and liability of the carrier for such goods, and as to the rights and immunities of the carrier in respect of such goods, or his obligation as to seaworthiness, so far as this stipulation is not contrary to public policy, or the care or diligence of his servants or agents in regard to the loading, handling, stowage, carriage, custody, care and discharge of the goods carried by sea, provided that in this case no bill of lading has been or shall be issued and that the terms agreed shall be embodied in a receipt which shall be a non-negotiable document and shall be marked as such.

Any agreement so entered into shall have full legal effect.

Provided that this Article shall not apply to ordinary commercial shipments made in the ordinary course of trade, but only to other shipments where the character or condition of the property to be carried or the circumstances, terms and conditions under which the carriage is to be performed are such as reasonably to justify a special agreement.

ARTICLE 7

Nothing herein contained shall prevent a carrier or a shipper from entering into any agreement, stipulation, condition, reservation or exemption as to the responsibility and liability of the carrier or the ship for the loss or damage to, or in connexion with, the custody and care and handling of goods prior to the loading on, and subsequent to, the discharge from the ship on which the goods are carried by sea.

ARTICLE 10

The provisions of this Convention shall apply to all bills of lading issued in any of the contracting States.

Index

A

AAA. *See* American Arbitration Association
Abbott Laboratories v. Diamedix Corp., 422, 423
Above-deck carriage, 283–284, 286, 287, 288
Abus de droit concept, 182
Acceptance, in European contract law, 195–196
Access contract, 455
Accounting
  internationalization of, 362–363
  and IPR licensing agreements, 418
Account party, 311
ACPA. *See* Anti-Cybersquatting Consumer Protection Act
Act of State defenses, 102
Adequate assurance, 231
ADS. *See* Agent-Distributor Searches
Ad valorem duties, 155
Advertising
  comparative, 62
  ethics of, 61–63, 461–462
  FTC regulations, 358
  ICC International Code of Advertising Practice, 63
  insurance, 359
  national laws, 358–359
  use of Made in USA label, 165
Advertising injury, 359, 360
Advising bank, 311, 314
AES. *See* Automated Export System
Affiliate branch office, 69
Affirmative defenses (bribery), 51
Agency relationship, in European contract law, 197
Agent
  dependent and independent, 343
  electronic, 426, 453
Agent-Distributor Searches (ADS), 355
Aggregation, 459–460
Agreement on Customs Valuation, 162
Agreement on Import Licensing Procedures, 130, 132
Agreement on Preshipment Inspection, 130, 132
Agreement on the Application of Sanitary and Phytosanitary Measures (SPS), 130, 131
Agreement on Trade-Related Aspects of Intellectual Property Rights (TRIPS)
  copyright and related rights, 387
  and customary law, 6
  definition of, 27
  enforcement, 389
  establishment of, 127
  general principles of, 386–387
  import prohibition clause, 412
  parts, sections, and articles, 384–386
  patent protection, 388
  remedies and penalties under, 388–389
  trademark protection, 387–388
  trade secrets, 388
AIMU. *See* American Institute of Marine Underwriters
Air waybill, 257, 258, 272–273
Allied Chemical International Corp. v. Companhia de Navegacao Lloyd Brasileiro, 289, 290, 291
All Pacific Trading v. Vessel M/V Hanjin Yosu, 285–286
All risks policy, 300
Alpine View Co., Ltd. v. Atlas Copco AB, 99, 100–101
Alter-ego doctrine, 100–101
American Arbitration Association (AAA), 113–114
American Institute of Marine Underwriters (AIMU), 303
Amoral international businessperson, 46–47
Anheuser-Busch Ass'n v. United States, 162–163
Anti-Bootlegging Statute, 379
Anticipatory breach, 231
Anti-Cybersquatting Consumer Protection Act (ACPA), 444, 445
Antidumping procedures, 135–136
Antitrust Enforcement Guidelines for International Operations, 404
Arbitrage, 22
Arbitration
  advantages of, 111
  and choice of law, 108
  and CISG, 214, 231–232
  custom clauses, 114, 116, 117
  enforceability of, 119
  Federal Arbitration Act, 279

Arbitration (*continued*)
ICC Rules of Optional Conciliation, 116
injunctive relief, 113
international, 109–114
legality of, 116, 118, 119–120
and mediation clauses, 113–114
release of information, 113, 114
Arendt, Hannah, 47
Aristotle, 44
Arizona Retail Systems v. Software Link, 454
Arms Export Control Act, 120
Arrhes doctrine, 124, 187
Assent, genuineness of, 197
Assists, value of, 158–159
ATA Carnet, 254
Attorney General Option, 52
Attributive system, of trademark law, 391
Authentication, 427, 456
Automated Export System (AES), 165
Avery Dennison Corp. v. Sumpton, 443

B

Back-to-back letter of credit, 311
Bailee, 289
"Bananas dispute," 134–135, 138
Banker's acceptance, 319
Banks
advising, 311, 314
confirming, 311, 314
issuing, 312
nominating, 312
Banque Libanaise Pour le Commerce v. Khreich, 107
Barnard v. Adams, 305
Barter transactions, 30, 32
Basel Convention, 173
Basket of risks, 8
Battle of forms, 196, 221–223, 225–226, 427
Belgium
commercial agency in, 354
culpa in contrahendo, 207
sanctity of contract, 237
Bende & Sons, Inc. v. Crown Recreation, Inc., 121
Beneficiary party, of letter of credit, 311
Benefit-cost analysis, 40
Benron-ken wakai, 110
Bensusan Restaurant Corp. v. King, 436–437, 438
Berlin Act of 1908, 383
Berne Convention, 14, 374, 383–384, 385, 387
Bernina Distributors, Inc. v. Bernina Sewing Mach., 22–23
Best Cellars Inc. v. Grade Finds at Dupont, Inc., 368, 369–370
Best efforts clause, 417
BFOQ. *See* Bona fide occupational qualification
Bhopal disaster, 43, 44, 48
Bilateral copyright agreements, 383
Bilateral investment treaties, 15, 28, 29
Bill of exchange, 249, 254, 319–320
Bill of lading, 251, 252, 254, 255–257
clause paramount, 284, 286, 288
and COGSA, 276
electronic, 458–459
exculpatory clauses and Hague Rules, 273–274
and freight forwarder, 293, 294
and higher value, 289
Himalaya clause, 273, 276–277, 284
ocean, 272
Q-clause, 291–292
through, 294, 296
warehouse-to-warehouse clause, 276
Binding assessment, on country of origin, 164
Binding commitments, due to Uruguay Round, 127
Black-listed clauses, 429
Blanket policy, 303
Block exemptions, 85, 356–357
Blocking right, 447
Blurring, 371, 443–444
Boilerplate, 221, 228
Bona fide occupational qualification (BFOQ), 20
Bonded warehouse, 151–152
Booking contract, 255
Bootlegging. *See* Gray market
Bower v. Gateway, 119
Braintech, Inc. v. Kostiuk, 441, 442
Branch office
affiliate, 69
in foreign market, 74
in the United States, 67
Brazil
industrial property (trademark) law, 391–392
intellectual property licensing in, 431–432
Breach of confidentiality, 196–197
Bremen v. Zapata Off-Shore Co., 118
Brennan v. Carvel Corp., 89
Bribery
creeping expropriation, 27
enforcement of laws, 25
FCPA provisions and penalties, 51
gift-giving, 19
in Nigeria, 14
OECD Bribery Convention, 57–58
sharism (Indonesia), 50–51
tax deductibility of, 57
third-party, 52–53, 54, 55
U.S. federal sentencing guidelines, 58–60
See also Foreign Corrupt Practices Act
Broussard v. Meineke Discount Muffler Shops, 87–88
Brussels Act of 1948, 384
Brussels Convention on Jurisdiction and Judgments in Civil and Commercial Matters, 106, 458
Bureau of Export Administration (BXA), 167
Business America, 11
Business protocol, 19
Business review letter, 79
Buy-back transactions, 31–32
Buyer
as drawee, 249
duty to inspect and proper notice, 229
Buying agents, 9
BXA. *See* Bureau of Export Administration

C

Call option, 23
Canada
incorporation in, 75
risks of selling goods in, 14
Canada-United States Free Trade Agreement value-added test, 163
Capital Currency Exchange v. National Westminster Bank and Barclays Bank, 101, 103
Carell v. Schubert Organization, Inc., 389, 390
Cargo consolidator. *See* Freight forwarders
Cargo policy, 299–300
Carriage of Goods by Sea Act (COGSA), 272, 275–277
carrier duties, 278–280
carrier liability, 277–278
coverage, 283–286
exemptions, 291–292
fair opportunity, 277, 278, 288, 289
material deviation, 277, 286–288
misdelivery of goods, 286, 288–289, 291
per package limitation, 277-278, 280–281, 288
seaworthiness, 279–280
statute of limitations, 279
C-Art, Ltd. v. Hong Kong Islands Line America, S.A., 291
Cash against document, 249
Cash in advance, 244
Categorical imperatives, 43
Caterpillar Overseas v. Marine Transport, Inc., 278
Caux Round Table Principles for International Business, 48
CBD. *See* Commerce Business Daily
CE mark, 61, 166
Central Bank of the Philippines v. Ferdinand E. Marcos, 99, 102–103
Certificate of corporation, 68
Certificate of inspection, 252, 254
Certificate of origin, 252
CFR (cost and freight), 262, 265, 266–267
CFU. *See* Customary freight unit
CGL. *See* Comprehensive general liability (CGL) coverage
Change in tariff classification, 163–164
Charter party, 276
Chemco Leasing Spa v. Rediffusion Plc., 208
Chevron U.S.A. Inc. v. Natural Resources Defense Council, Inc., 154
Chile
advertising law, 359
China
approval process for foreign investment, 69
deposits for damages, 124

  foreign economic contracts law, 192–194
  insurance, regulation of, 29
  intellectual property law, 394
  joint ventures in, 68–69, 83–85
  labor contracts in, 84–85
  licensing technology in, 14
  Ministry of Foreign Economic Relations and Trade (MOFERT), 85, 429
  and New York Convention, 112
  patent law, 394, 395
  quanxi (connections), 69
  shareholder power in, 70
  technology transfer regulations, 430–431
Choice of law clause, 107
  and EU Directive on Distance Contracts, 343
  in intellectual property transfer agreement, 410
  judicial abrogation of, 107–108
  used to avoid application of CISG, 212–213
Chotei (conciliation), 179, 181
CIF contract, 249–250, 259–260, 267
CIF (cost, insurance, freight), 261, 264–265
CIP (carriage and insurance paid), 265, 267
CISG. *See* Convention on Contracts for the International Sale of Goods
Clause paramount, 284
Clean bill of lading, 257
Clearing agreements, 32
Click-wrap license, 454–455
CMA. *See* Customized Market Analysis
Code of Federal Regulations, 172–173
Codetermination, 71
COGSA. *See* Carriage of Goods by Sea Act
Cohen v. Paramount Pictures Corp., 414–415
Collection-through-export transactions, 33
Collective works, 373
Columbia Broadcasting v. Scorpio Music Distributors, 378, 380
Comfort instruments, 208
Comite Interprofessional du Vin Champagne v. Wineworths, Ltd., 392–393
Comity, 441
Commerce Business Daily (CBD), 11
Commercial agency contract, 349, 350, 352–356
Commercial invoice, 252, 253, 254
Commission agents, 9
Commission Decision of 17/11/99, 76–77
Committee on Rules of Origin, 164
Commodity control list, 167, 170, 171
Common carrier
  as defined by Hamburg Rules, 283
  definition of, 271
  duties, under COGSA, 278–280
  liability, under COGSA, 277–278
Community for Creative Non-Violence (CCNV) v. Reid, 373, 374
Comparative advertising, 62
Comparison Shopping Service (CSS), 12
Compensation transactions, 31–32
Competition law, 75, 356–357
Comprehensive general liability (CGL) coverage, 298
Compulsory hiring, 346
Compulsory trademark or patent licenses, 381
CompuServe, Inc. v. Patterson, 436–437
Computed value, of imported goods, 159
Computer software sales, 215
  and intellectual property licensing agreements, 425
  limited liability and disclaimer in, 236, 237
  shrink-wrap contracts, 453–455
  Uniform Computer Information Transactions Act, 425–426
Concession agreement, 28
Confidentiality clause, 81, 409–410, 419
Confirmation letter, sample, 315
Confirmed letter of credit, 14
Confirming bank, 311, 314
Conflict of cultural tradition, 42–43
Conflict of law rules, 107, 108–109, 213–214
Conflict of relative development, 42
Consequentalism, 39
Consequential damages, 232
Consignment sale, 245
Constructores Technicos v. Sea-Land Service, 293, 295
Consular invoice, 252, 254
Consulting contract, 354
Containerization, 285–286, 297
Contract of carriage. *See* Bill of lading
Contracts
  access contract, 455
  of adhesion, 189
  ambiguous language in, 24
  booking, 255
  CIF, 249–250
  CISG and UCC interpretation of, 226, 228
  CISG requirements on, 7
  click-wrap license, 454–455
  commercial agency, 349, 350, 352–356
  contractual excuses, 237–239
  electronic, 449–450, 451–452, 453–455
  forward, 22
  futures, 22
  of honor, 208
  ICC Commercial Agency Guide, 352–353
  important clauses, 184
  independent contractor, 343, 349
  international, and cultural differences, 177–178
  interpretation, 184–185
  national contract codes, 188–200
  and national laws, 185–188
  negotiating, 178–181
  noncompetition clauses, 357
  penal clauses, 186
  poorly written, as source of disputes, 6
  precontract instruments, 208
  precontract liability, 196, 200–202, 204–207
  price-fixing clauses, 357
  principles of international contract law, 181–184
  private, as source of international law, 5
  standard form, 182
  tips for, 200
  tying clauses, 357
Contractual joint venture, 68–69
Convention for the International Sale of Goods (CISG)
  anticipatory breach and adequate assurance, 231
  choice of law clause, 212–213
  commercial sale of goods, 214–215
  conflict of law rules, 213–214
  contractual excuses, 237–238
  contracts, interpretation of, 7, 226, 228
  damages, 231–232
  disclaimers, 236
  divisions of, 219
  force majeure as impediment, 122, 238–239
  history of, 212
  and intellectual property licensing agreement, 425
  jurisdiction, 213
  nachfrist notice, 183, 229–231
  parol evidence rule, 215–216
  seller's right to cure, 231
  and Uniform Commercial Code, 219–239
  warranty provisions, 232–237
Convention on the Limitation Period in the International Sale of Goods, 239–241
Conversion contract, 345
Convertibility. *See* Currency, convertibility
Cookies, 446
Cooperative venture contract, 84
Copyright Act of 1976, 372–373, 407–408
Copyright employee, 373, 374
Copyright law, 371–374
  bilateral agreements, 383
  checklist, 407
  collective works, 373
  copyright transfers, 408
  definition of, 367
  fair use doctrine, 373
  first sale doctrine, 372–373
  infringement protection clause, 419
  international, 382
  public domain, 373
  registration, 374, 406–408

Copyright law (*continued*),
tangible form of expression, 371
TRIPS protection, 387
Universal Copyright Convention, 383
and work for hire, 373
See also Intellectual property rights
Corporate codes of conduct, 45
Corporation
creation of, 68
foreign investor in the United States, 68
terms for, 75
See also Foreign corporation law
Corruption Index, 14
Cost-plus formula, 23, 245
Council for Trade-Related Aspects of Intellectual Property Rights, 386
Council of Europe penalty clauses resolution, 124, 185, 186
Council on Services, 340
Counterfeited goods, 377
See also Gray market
Counter-indemnity clause, 81
Counterpurchase, 30–31
Countertrade, 30–34
and currency convertibility and repatriation problems, 14
definition of, 8–9
Countervailing duty, 128, 136
Countervailing subsidy, 138
Country groups list, 167
Country of Origin Rules, 132, 151, 162–164
Course of performance, 216
Courtaulds North America v. North Carolina National Bank, 322, 323–324
Covenant not to compete, 416
CPT (carriage paid), 262, 265, 267
Credit reports, 10
Creeping expropriation, 27
Cross-border security offerings, 361–362
CSS. *See* Comparison Shopping Service
Culpa in contrahendo concept, 182–183, 204–207
Cultural relativism, 39
Culture
conflict of traditions, 42–43
and corporate code of conduct, 45–46
differences, as business risk, 18–20, 178, 180
Currency
arbitrage, 22
convertibility, 14, 20, 21
fluctuation, 21–22
forward contract, 22
futures contract, 22
hard and soft, 21
option contract, 23
regulation of, in Russia, 16
repatriation, 21
Currency option, 23
Customary freight unit (CFU), 278
Customary international business law, 181, 182
Customary law, 6–8
Customized Market Analysis (CMA), 355
Customs brokers, 30, 294, 315
Customs Electronic Bulletin Board, 152
Customs Modernization Act, 165
Customs Modernization Act of 1993, 339
Customs Valuation Code, 130
Cybersell, Inc. v. Cybersell, Inc., 436
Cybersquatters, 442

D

Daedalus Enterprises, Inc., v. Baldridge, 172, 173
DAF (delivered on frontier), 267, 268
Database protection, 445–449
Databases, definition of, 446
DDP (delivered duty paid), 268–269
DDU (delivered duty unpaid), 268–269
Declaration on Trade in Information Technology Products (ITA), 153
Deductive value, of imported goods, 159, 160
Default judgment, and personal jurisdiction, 99
Delchi Carrier, S.P.A. v. Rotorex Corp., 232, 233
Delverde USA, Inc., v. United States, 139–140
Denmark, penalty clauses in, 123
Dependent agent, 343
DEQ (delivered ex quay), 265, 267–268
DES (delivered ex ship), 262, 265, 267
Destination Control Statement, 167–168
Developing countries, risk in, 15–16
Digital divide, 461
Digital signatures guidelines, 456
Diplomatic immunity, 99, 101–103
Direct exporting, 10
Direct foreign investment
in Mexico, 16
risk characteristics, 8
risks of, 15
Directive 95/46, 446–447, 448
Directive 96/9/EC on the Legal Protection of Databases, 446, 449
Direct public offerings (DPOs), 460
Direct representation, in European contract law, 197
Disagio (discount), 34
Disclaimer, 439
CISG, 236
UCC, 234, 236
Discovery, international, 104
Disguised barriers to trade, 129, 130, 132
Dismissal for cause, 346–347
Dispute resolution
arbitration, 109–114, 116
choice of law, 107–109
force majeure, 120–123
forum selection, 116, 118–120
international litigation, 99, 101–102, 106
in Japan, 181
liquidated damages, 123–124
WTO system, 132–135
Distribution agreement
in commercial agency contract, 355–356
in joint ventures, 82
Distributive justice, 40–41
Distributor, definition of, 355
Dock receipt, 254
Doctrine of frustration, 237
Doctrine of impossibility, 237
Doctrine of impracticability, 238
Documentary collections
bill of exchange, 249
bill of lading, 251, 252, 254, 255–257
cash against document, 249
definition of, 244–245, 311
documents against acceptance, 249
process, 250–252
sight drafts, 249
time drafts, 249
Documentary credit transaction, 310, 311
See also Letter of credit
Documentary credit transactions
definition of, 244–245
as means of lowering risk, 310
Documentary transaction
definition of, 247–249
import-export checklist, 249–250
Documents against acceptance, 249
Dominant considerations, 40
DoubleClick Inc., 462
Double parenting, 81–82
DPO. *See* Direct public offerings
Draft. *See* Bill of exchange
Drawback, of customs duties, 161
Drawer and drawee, 249, 319
Dual service of process, 99
Due diligence, and international licensing agreement, 405–407
Dumping goods, 128, 129, 135–136
DuPont de Nemours International v. Mormacvega, 287
Dutch law, three–stage contract negotiations, 205
Duties
ad valorem, 155
on articles assembled abroad, 155–157, 158, 162–163
assessment of, 155–159, 161
drawback of, 161
and foreign trade zones, 77
specific, 155
Duty to defend, 359
Duty to inspect, 229

E

EAR. *See* Export Administration Regulations
EBB. *See* Economic Bulletin Board
Eco-label, 61, 166
e-commerce
developments in, 456–458
and e-contracting, 449–456
EU Council Resolution on, 435

sale of services, 340–343
See also Electronic business transactions
Economic Bulletin Board (EBB), 11
Economic duress, 197
Economic Espionage Act of 1966 (EEA), 376
E-contracting
documentation, 458–459
law issues, 451–452
shrink-wrap contracts, 453–455
statute of frauds requirements and authentication, 456
under UCITA, 452–456
EDI. *See* Electronic data interchange
EEA. *See* Economic Espionage Act of 1996
Effects test, 361
Egoism, 40
Eichman in Jerusalem: A Report on the Banality of Evil, 47–48
Electronic agent, 426, 453
Electronic bill of lading, 255
Electronic business transactions
authentication, 456
cybersquatting, 442–444
electronic contracting, 449–450, 451–452
electronic documentation, 458–459
electronic services industry, 459–460
ethics, 460, 460–462
Framework for Global Electronic Commerce, 450–451
growth of, 435
Internet privacy and database protection, 445–449
Internet securities offerings, 460
personal jurisdiction, 436–442
trademark infringement and dilution, 442–444
See also e-commerce; Uniform Computer Information Transactions Act
Electronic Communications Privacy Act of 1986, 446
Electronic data interchange (EDI), 165–166, 449–450
Electronic records, 427
e-mail
contract negotiation by, 452
sales confirmations by, 341–342
viruses, 459
EMC. *See* Export management companies
Employment, 15
commercial agency contract, 349, 350, 352–356
employment at will doctrine, 344
European law, 344–346
evergreen statutes, 7, 25, 350, 353–354
foreign sales representatives, 343, 349–350, 351
independent contractor contracts, 343, 349
international labor standards, 347–348
lifetime, 344
as property right, 344
service sector, 338
sexual harassment policy, 344, 345
termination, 344–347, 350
Encryption, 451, 456
Enterprise liability, 73–74
Environmental ethics, 48–49
Equity joint venture, 68
Equity ownership, limitations on, 25–26
Equivalents, doctrine of, 375
Essential character, of imported goods, 152
ETC. *See* Export trading companies
Ethics
of advertising, 61–63, 461–462
amoral international businessperson, 46–47
of care, 44–45
compliance program, 14
e-commerce, 460–462
environmental, 48–49
ethics of care, 44–45
Foreign Corrupt Practices Act (FCPA), 50–53, 55–60
host- and home-country standards, 49–50
integrative approach to, 45–46
international standards, 60–61
organizational, 47–48
relativism, 39
rights and duties, 41–43
utilitarianism, 39–41
virtue ethics, 44
EU. *See* European Union
EU Directive on Distance Contracts, 340–343
Eurasian Patent Convention, 399
EU Regulation 1983/83, 356–357
Europcar Italia, S.P.A. v. Maiellano Tours, Inc., 120
Europe Agreement, 146
European contract law, 194–198
European Principles, 194–198
European Union (EU)
"banana dispute", 134–135, 138
block exemption, 85
CE mark, 61, 166
Common Community Customs Code, 140
comparative advertising regulation, 62
competition law in, 75, 76–77, 81
Customs Code, 159, 161
Directive on Distance Contracts, 340–343
Directive on Unfair Terms, 189–190
duty on company capital, 80
eco-label, 61, 166
electronic business jurisdiction proposal, 440–441
expansion of, 146
as factor in growth of international trade, 2
franchising regulations, 91–92, 95–96
and Georgia, partnership and cooperation agreement between, 147
intellectual property rights laws, 395–396
and intellectual property rights regulations, 14
Internet and database privacy legislation, 446–449
Model EDI Agreement, 457
and most-favored-nation principle, 128
Mutual Recognition Agreements (MRA), 338
Section 301 challenge, 140
specified processes test, 163
technology transfer regulations, 427–430
European Works Council Directive, 348
EU Trademark Directive, 395–396
Evergreen provisions
and commercial agency contracts, 350, 353–354
definition of, 7
enforcement of, 25
Exceptions clause, 80
Excess clause, 298–299
Excise taxes, and foreign trade zones, 77
Exculpatory clauses, 273
Eximbank, 14, 28
Export Administration Regulations (EAR), 167, 168–175
Export agent, 9
Export Information System (XIS), 12
Exporting
agent, 9
developing plan for, 34–35
documentary collections transactions, 250–252
documents used in, 252–262
government agencies related to, 175
information systems (XIS), 12
licensing, 167, 171–173
management companies, 9, 34
regulations, 167–175
risks of, 8, 9–10
trade certificate, 79
trading companies, 9, 34
Export license, 252, 254
Export management companies (EMCs), 9, 34
Export trade certificate, 79
Export trading companies (ETCs), 9, 34
Expropriation, risks of, 27–28
Extension clauses, in marine insurance, 300, 301, 304
Extra expenses clause, 305
EXW (ex works), 262, 265, 266

F

Fabrication abroad, 155–157, 158, 162–163
Facial compliance rule, 316–317
Factoring, 311, 330
Fair Credit Reporting Act, 446
Fair opportunity, 277, 278, 288, 289
Fair use doctrine, 373
Falcoal, Inc. v. Kurumu, 16–18
Farrel Corporation v. International Trade Commission, 114, 115

FAS (free alongside ship), 262, 264, 266
F.C. & S.. *See* Free of capture and seizure clause
FCA (free carrier), 262, 265, 266
FCIA. *See* Foreign Credit Insurance Association
FCPA. *See* Foreign Corrupt Practices Act
FDI. *See* Foreign direct investment
Federal Arbitration Act, 279
Federal Rules of Civil Procedure, 25
Federal Trade Commission (FTC) advertising regulation, 358
Federal Trademark Dilution Act (FTDA), 371, 442–444
Fields of use, 412
Filanto, S.P.A. v. Chilewich International Corp., 225–226
Financing export transactions
- back-to-back letter of credit, 331
- buyer and supplier financing, 330–332
- credit surety, 327
- demand guarantee, 327–328
- factoring and forfaiting, 330
- government assistance programs, 332–333
- letter of credit, 310–319, 325
- letter of credit payment and risks, 332
- performance bond, 327
- sources of financing, 328–333
- standby letters of credit, 325–327
- transferable credit, 331
- UPC for documentary credits, 320–324

Finland, penalty clauses in, 123
Finnish Fur Sales Co., Ltd. v. Juliette Shulof Furs, Inc., 72–73
Firm offer rule, in European contract law, 195
First sale doctrine, 372–373
First to invent principle, 394
First to register principle, 394
FOB (free on board), 259, 262, 263–264, 266
Folger Coffee Company v. Olivebank, 306–307
Force majeure
- and common carrier liability, 279
- in dispute resolution, 120–123
- as impediment, CISG, 122, 237, 238–239

Foreign consultant. *See* Foreign sales representative
Foreign corporation law, 69–71, 73–74
Foreign Corrupt Practices Act (FCPA), 14, 49
- accounting provisions, 56–60
- Amendments of 1988, 52, 56
- Attorney General Option, 52
- bribery provisions, 51
- civil and criminal penalties, 51, 58–60
- compliance program, designing, 59
- degrees of ownership, 55
- five elements of offense, 56
- purpose of, 50
- reason to know requirement, 55
- third-party bribery, 52–53, 55

Foreign Credit Insurance Association (FCIA), 28
Foreign direct investment (FDI), as measure of globalization, 3
Foreign distributor, 10
Foreign lawyers, finding and managing, 35–36
Foreign sales representative, 10, 343, 349–350, 351
Foreign subsidiary, 69, 74–75
Foreign Trade Report: Monthly Exports and Imports, 12
Foreign-trade zones, 161–162
Forfaiting, 311–312, 330
Forum non conveniens doctrine, 101, 103
Forum selection clause, 410
Forward contract, 22
Four-corner analysis, 226, 227
FPA. *See* Free of particular average
Framework for Global Electronic Commerce, 450–451
Framework transactions, 32
France
- *arrhes* doctrine, 124, 187
- commercial agency in, 354
- corporate law in, 70
- distributor requirements, 356
- franchising in, 93–94
- incorporation in, 75
- labor code, 345–346
- licensing technology in, 14
- liquidated damages clauses, 123
- Rights of Man, 41
- sanctity of contract, 237

Franchisee review clause, 91
Franchising
- agreement, 89–91
- definition of, 8, 92
- in foreign countries, 85–87
- foreign regulation of, 95–96
- in Germany, 85
- international, 92–93, 94
- law, 87, 89
- master, 91–92
- and technology licensing, 403–404
- UNIDROIT Guide, 92

Frauds, statute of, 189, 203, 204, 217, 427
Free market economics, 40
Free of capture and seizure (F.C. & S.) clause, 300
Free of particular average (FPA), 300–301, 304
Free trade zones, 151–152
Freight forwarders, 30, 275–276, 292–297, 316, 357, 358
Friedman, Milton, 46–47
Frigaliment Importing v. B.N.S. International Sales Corp., 226, 227, 228
Frustration, doctrine of, 237
FTDA. *See* Federal Trademark Dilution Act
Fukayama, Francis, 47
Futures contract, 22

G

GATS. *See* General Agreement on Trade in Services
General Agreement on Tariffs and Trade (GATT)
- Code on Subsidies and Countervailing Duties, 136
- as example of customary law, 6
- as factor in growth of international trade, 2, 3–4
- and foreign trade zones, 77
- Origin Agreement, 164
- original, 26
- principles of, 127, 128–129
- Valuations Code, 157–159
- *See also* Uruguay Round

General Agreement on Trade in Services (GATS), 127, 167, 338
- Framework Agreement, 339–340
- objectives of negotiations, 341

General average doctrine, 304–306
General cover insurance policy, 301, 303
Generalized system of preferences (GSP), 151
General license, for export, 167
General partnership, 67, 80
General Rules of Interpretation of HTS, 152–154
General System of Preferences (GSP), 348
General Usage for International Digitally Ensured Commerce (GUIDEC), 457, 458
Generic marks, 368
Gentlemen's agreement, 208
George E. Warren Corp. v. U.S. Environmental Protection Agency, 128, 129
Germany
- advertising law, 359
- contractual excuses, 238
- corporate governance in, 71
- corporate law in, 79
- employment as property right, 344
- franchising in, 85
- goodwill indemnity, 356
- *nachfrist* notice, 24–25
- precontractual liability in, 201–202
- prohibition on advertising by lawyers, 36
- purchasing a company in, 15
- replacement parts supply law (Article 433), 187
- Works Councils, 344–345

Gift-giving, 19
Globalization
- protests against, 141, 142–143
- responses to, 6
- *See also* International trade

Good faith negotiation, 182–183, 199
- *See also Culpa in contrahendo* concept

Goods
counterfeited, 377
definition of, 337
exporting, differences from services, 338–339
merchantable, 234
mixed, 214
pirated, 377
specially manufactured, 215–216
transport of, 271–307
virtual, 215
Goods, sale of
to Canada, 14
CISG coverage of, 214–216
computer software sale, 215
documentary collections transaction, 244–245, 250–252
documentary transaction, 247–250
documentation, 252–262
INCOTERMS 2000, 262–269
methods of payment for, 244–247
mixed sale, 214, 425
to Nigeria, 14
shipment and destination contracts, 260
virtual goods, 215
Goodwill indemnity, 356
Government approval clause, 123
GPL Treatment Ltd. v. Louisiana-Pacific, 216, 217
Grant-back clause, 409, 416
Grant clause, 410
Gray market, 377–380, 412–413, 428
Gray market goods, 14
Great Britain
doctrine of frustration, 238
and Hague-Visby Rules, 276
incorporation in, 75
Unfair Contract Terms Act, 108
Grifoni v. European Atomic Energy Community (Euratom), 206
GSP. *See* Generalized system of preferences
Guaranteed consideration, 417
GUIDEC. *See* General Usage for International Digitally Ensured Commerce
Guide to Drafting International Distribution Agreements, 355

H

Habib Bank Ltd. v. Convermat Corp., 324
Hadley v. Baxendale, 193, 232
Hague Convention, 99, 104, 106
Hague Rules
and customary law, 6, 182
and liability of common carriers, 272, 273
Hague-Visby Rules
and Hague Rules, differences, 276
and ocean carriage liability, 272, 273–274
Hamburg Rules
and allocation of liability, 283
carrier fault presumption, 284
definition of common carrier, 283
and ocean carriage liability, 272, 273, 274
Q-clause exceptions, elimination of, 292
rules for carriage above deck, 283
Hardship, UNIDROIT Principles, 200
Hardship clause, 122–123
Harmonized Commodity Description and Coding System (HS), 153, 163
Harmonized tariff schedule (HTS), 151, 153
change in tariff classification, 163–164
General Rules of Interpretation, 152–154, 157
Harriscom v. Svenska, 120–121, 239
Harter Act of 1893, 273, 283
Head-of-state immunity, 102
Health and safety standards, WTO, 166–167
Hedging, 14
Heritage Mutual Insurance v. Advance Polymer Tech, 359–360
Hewlett-Packaged Co. v. Bausch & Lomb Inc., 421
Hilton v. Guyot, 104, 105
Himalaya clause, 273, 276–277, 284
Hiring by number, 346
Hiring list, 346
Hoover Europe, 348
Host country laws
and direct foreign investment, 13, 15
employment laws, 15, 344–347, 350, 352–356
evergreen statutes, 7, 25, 350, 353–354
Host-home country standards, 49–50
HS. *See* Harmonized Commodity Description and Coding System
HTS. *See* Harmonized tariff schedule
Hull insurance, 298
Hungary, conflict of law rules, 108
Hybrid license, 417

I

IAS. *See* International Accounting Standards
IASC. *See* International Accounting Standards Committee
ICC. *See* International Chamber of Commerce
ICSID. *See* International Center for Settlement of Investment Disputes
ILO. *See* International Labor Organization
ILU. *See* Institute of London Underwriters
Impediment
in European Principles, 198
force majeure as, 122
Implied warranty of merchantability, 232–234
Importing regulations, 151–167
See also Duties; Tariffs
Impossibility, doctrine of, 237
Impracticability, doctrine of, 238
Inchmaree clause, 298, 305
Incommensurability, 40
INCOTERM (glossary of trade terms), 181, 182, 211, 260, 262–263
CFR, 262, 265, 266–267
CIF, 261, 264–265, 267
CIP, 265
CPT, 262, 265, 267
D terms, 265, 268–269
ex works, 262, 265, 266
FAS, 262, 265, 266
FCA, 262, 265, 266
FOB, 259, 262, 263–264, 266
modern trends in, 269
recent changes to, 263
Indemnification clause, 418, 420
Indemnity in lieu of notice, 346
Independent contractor, 343, 349, 419, 422
Indirect exporting, 9
Indirect representation, in European contract law, 197
Indonesia
branch office in, 74
franchising in, 85–87
hiring foreign sales representatives in, 349
joint ventures and licensing in, 83
sharism, 50–51
tariff reductions, 165
Inducement to infringe, 412
Industrial property, 391
Industry Sector Analyses (ISAs), 12
Infringement clause, 419, 420–421
Innocent infringement, of copyright, 374
Institute of London Underwriters (ILU), 303
Insurance
against false or improper advertising, 359
blanket policy, 303
cargo, 299–301, 303–307
certificate, 252
clause, in franchising agreement, 90–91
for computer crime, 459
excess, 298
general cover policy, 301, 303
managing risk through, 29–30
marine, 297–307
war risk, 298
Insurance Services Office (ISO), 298, 359–360
Integrative approach to business ethics, 45–46
Intellectual property licensing
benefits of, 403–404
drawbacks of, 404
license registration, 407–408
licensing agreement, 408–415
registration of license, 405
typical agreement, 415–417, 420–422, 425
See also Technology transfers

Intellectual property rights
Agreement on Trade–Related Aspects of Intellectual Property (TRIPS), 6, 27, 127, 381, 384–390
Berne Convention, 14, 374, 383–384, 385, 387
definition of, 366–367
enforcement of laws, 25, 27
extraterritorial application of U.S. law, 376–380
foreign laws, 391–396
and franchising, 86, 91
and joint ventures, 82–83
Paris Convention, 381, 382
Patent Cooperation Treaty (PCT), 382
protecting, 404–407
and Section 337 of the Tariff Act, 140–141
strategy, developing, 398–399
trade agreements governing, 27
and trade with China and France, 14
in transitional and emerging economies, 396–398
in the United States, 367–376
Universal Copyright Convention (UCC), 383
WIPO, 381, 382
See also Copyright law; Patent law; Trademark law
Intellectual property transfer
in franchising agreement, 91
in joint ventures, 83
Inter-American Convention on the Extraterritorial Validity of Foreign Judgments, 106
International Accounting Standards (IAS), 363
International Accounting Standards Committee (IASC), 363
International Center for Settlement of Investment Disputes (ICSID), 28
International Chamber of Commerce (ICC)
as arbitration body, 109
Arbitration Case No. 5713, 214
Arbitration Case No. 6281, 239
Commercial Agency-Guide for the Drawing up of Contracts, 352–353
contract checklist, 183, 184
and evolution of *lex mercatoria,* 7
force majeure clause, 122–123
General Usage for International Digitally Ensured Commerce (GUIDEC), 457
Guidelines on Advertising and Marketing on the Internet, 461
Guide to Drafting International Distribution Agreements, 355
INCOTERM, 181, 182, 211, 259–269
international advertising ethical standard codes, 62–63
letters of credit, 181
Rules for Multimodal Transport Documents, 285
rules of optional conciliation, 116
services of, 7
standard credit forms, 313–314
International Court of Justice, 4–5
International Institute for the Unification of Private Law (UNIDROIT), 91–92, 183, 184, 198–200, 238
International Labor Organization (ILO), 38, 167, 347–348
International law
customary international business law, 181, 182
customary law, 6–8
definition of, 4
lex mercatoria, 182
sources of, 4–6
International law societies, 36
International Organization for Standardization (ISO), 60–61
International Organization of Securities Commissions (IOSCO), 362, 363
International Patent Searching Authorities (ISA), 399
International Standby Practices (ISP98), 325
International taxation, 78
International trade
exporting, 9–10
factors in growth of, 2–4
risk management, 28–34
risks, 8–9, 10–28
in services, 4
trends in integration, 3
See also Regulation, international; Regulation, national import and export
International Trade Commission
harmonized tariff schedule (HTS), 151–154
and Section 337 of the Tariff Act of 1930, 140
International trade consultants, 34
Internet
aggregation, 459–460
and cross-border securities offerings, 361–362
fraud, 460
meta-tags and trademark dilution, 371, 372
privacy, 445–446
sale of services on, 340–343
security, 459
U.S. framework for taxation of commerce on, 363
See also Electronic business transactions
Internet service provides (ISPs), 457
Interpane Coatings v. Australia & New Zealand Banking Group, 319, 320
Invoices
commercial, 252, 253, 254
consular, 252, 254
pro forma, 246–247, 248, 258
IOSCO. *See* International Organization of Securities Commissions
IPR. *See* Intellectual property licensing
Iran Aircraft Industries v. Avco Corporation, 112, 113
Irrevocable letter of credit, 312
ISA. *See* Industry Sector Analyses
Islamic law, 187–188, 359
ISO 14000, 61
ISO 9000, 60, 254
ISP. *See* Internet service providers
ISP98. *See* International Standby Practices
Issuing bank, of letter of credit, 312
Italy
commercial agency in, 354
Consultation procedure, 346, 347
culpa in contrahendo, 206
incorporation in, 75
labor laws and trade unions in, 346–347
licensing requirements, 416
Itek Corp. v. First National Bank of Boston, 326–327

J

Jacob v. State, 185
Japan
arbitration vs. litigation in, 109, 110
benron-ken wakai, 110
chotei, 179, 181
contract negotiation in, 178–181
corporate governance in, 71
corporate law in, 69–70
incorporation in, 75
lifetime employment, 344
penalty clauses in, 123
ring-sho, 180
soshjno wakai, 110
wa (harmony of negotiation), 179
J.H. Rayner & Co. v. Hambros Bank, Ltd., 322
Joint stock company, 75
Joint venture
agreement, 79–82
ancillary agreements, 82–83
in China, 68–69, 83–84
contractual, 68–69
definition of, 8, 79
equity, 68
foreign government regulation of, 83–85
in Indonesia, 83
international, 78–79
local partner, 68
in the United States, 67
Junior mark, 371

K

Kant, Immanuel, 43
Kern v. Dynalectron Corp., 20–21
Key personnel, 409–410
Komatsu, Ltd. v. States S.S. Co., 288
Korea, environmental impact of economic growth in, 48–49
Kumar Corp. v. Nopal Lines, Ltd., 260
Kyosei, 48

L

Labor laws
in China, 84–85
and employment relationship, 344
in European nations, 344–347
German, 15
indentured, prison, and child labor, 348
in Japan, 344
sexual harassment, 344, 345
and transaction risks, 15
See also Employment; International Labor Organization
Labor standards, international, 347–348
Lamb Head Shipping v. Jennings, 294
Lamb v. Philip Morris, Inc., 52, 53
Landing and warehousing clause, 305
Language
of business, as source of international law, 5–6
differences, as business risk, 16, 178
See also Lex mercatoria
Lanham Act, 358, 368, 371
and cybersquatting, 442–443
exterritorial application of, 376–377
and gray market, 378
Latin America, ethical standards in politics in, 51
Law of bailment, 289–290
Law of recognition, 105
Lawyers, foreign, 35–36
Legal Guide on International Countertrade Transactions, 32–33
Legal risk, 23–26
Letter of indemnity, 254
Letters of credit
21-day rule, 318
account party, 311
application form, 313
beneficiary party, 311
bill of exchange (draft), 319–320
confirmed, 14
definition of, 309–310
facial compliance rule, 316–317
history of, 310
ICC, 181
irrevocable, 312
key terms, 311–312
as part of documentary credit transaction, 245, 254
rule of strict compliance, 316, 317–318
standby, 312, 325–327
steps in transaction process, 314–319
ten rules pertaining to, 325
transactions without (sight or time draft), 310–311
UCP 500, 320–325
Letters of Request, 104
Lex mercatoria (law of merchants), 5–6
and drafting international contracts, 181–183
and European contract law, 194
evolution of, 7
and history of CISG, 212
as justification for arbitration awards, 214
sources of, 182
Liability
and COGSA, 277–278
of common carriers, 272–274, 277–278
and containerization, 285–286
enterprise, 73–74
exculpatory clauses and Hague Rules, 273–274
and freight forwarder, 294
limited, with additional liability, 75
and Warsaw Convention, 272–273
License, 452
Licensed territory clause, 416, 418
Licensee, 403
Licensee warrantees, 418
Licensing
agreement on, 130, 132
common clauses, 409–410, 411
for export, 167, 171–173
grant and limitations, 410, 412–414
in Indonesia, 83
and intellectual property transfer, 403–404
law of, 425–427
parallel license, 429
risk characteristics, 8
technology, in China, 14
technology, in France, 14
See also Uniform Computer Information Transactions Act; Uniform Electronic Transactions Act
Licensor, 403
Licensor warrantees, 418
Limited express warranty, 234, 236
Limited liability company (LLC), 68
Limited partnership, 67
Liquidated damages clause, 123–124, 186
Litigation
bringing suit, 99, 101–102
discovery, 104
enforceability of judgments, 104, 106
LLC. *See* Limited liability company
Llewellyn, Karl, 228
Locke, John, 41
London Underwriters v. Sea-Land Service, Inc., 281
Long-arm statute, 438
Lugano Convention, 106

M

M & Z Trading Corp. v. Cargolift Ltd., 255
McAlpine v. AAMCO Automatic Transmission, Inc., 92–93
McGann, Brenda, 71
Made in the USA Foundation v. United States of America, 144
Made in USA labels, 164–165
Mailbox rule, 195–196, 221, 426
Mail fraud, 59
Mallinckrodt, Inc. v. Medipart, Inc., 412, 413
Management agreements, 74
Manifest Shipping v. Uni-Polaris Insurance Co., 280
Mannesman Demag Corp. v. M/V Concert Express, 296–297
Maquiladora, 156
Marcraft Clothes, Inc. v. M.V. Kurobe Maru, 285
Marginal cost pricing, 245
Marine insurance, 297–299
cargo insurance, 299–301, 303–307
sample certificate, 299
standard clauses, 304–305
Marine insurance certificate, 254
Market research, 10–13
Marking requirements, on imported goods, 164–165
Massachusetts Burma Law, 156
Master franchise, 91–92
Material deviation, 277, 286–288
Materiality, 362
Mattel, Inc. v. Internet Dimensions, Inc., 444–445
MCC-Marble Ceramic Center v. Ceramica Nuova D'Agostino, S.P.A., 216, 218–219
Med-arb clause, 114, 116
Mediation, 114–115
See also Arbitration
Merck code of ethics, 47
Merger clause, 194–195
Meta-tags, 371, 446
Mexico
foreign investment in, 16
maquiladora (foreign assembly) industry, 156, 158
U.S. service exports to, 337
Micro Data Systems, Inc. v. Dharma Systems, 214–215
MIGA. *See* Multilateral Guarantee Agency
Millennium Round, 141
Minimum contacts standard, 436, 438, 440
Minority interests, in joint ventures, 81
Mirror image rule, 223, 225
Misdelivery of goods, 286, 288–289, 291
Mixed sale, 214, 337, 425
Model EDI Agreement, 457
Model Electronic Data Interchange Trading Partner Agreement, 450
Model Law on Electronic Commerce, 457–458
Modification clause, 194
MOFERT. *See* China, Ministry of Foreign Economic Relations and Trade
Momentum royalties, 417
Moral minimum, 46–47
Moral rights and duties, 41–43
Mori Seiki USA, Inc. v. M/V Alligator Triumph, 283, 284
Most-favored licensee clause, 411, 412
Most-favored-nation principle, 128, 340
Motorola corporate code of conduct, 45, 46
MRA. *See* Mutual Recognition Agreements
MTO. *See* Multimodal transport operator

Mulitmodal transport, 272
Multilateral Guarantee Agency (MIGA), 14, 29
Multimodal transport conventions, 272, 274, 285, 292–297, 358
Multimodal transport operator (MTO), 292–297
Mutual Recognition Agreements (MRA), 338
Myanmar, importing goods from, 154, 156

N

Nabisco, Inc. v. PF Brands, Inc., 371
Nachfrist notice, 24–25, 183, 229–231
NAFTA. *See* North American Free Trade Agreement
Names and titles, and cultural differences, 19
National Foreign Trade Council v. Baker, 154, 156
Nationalization, risks of, 27–28
National Trade Data Bank (NTDB), 11
National treatment principle, 128
NEC Electronics v. Cal Circuit Abco, 378, 379
Negations, 420
Negligence clause, in marine insurance, 305
Nelson Bunker Hunt v. BP Exploration Ltd., 104, 105–106
New York Convention
  articles of, 111
  enforcement of foreign arbitration awards, 86, 106, 110
  vacating of award, 113
Niger, third-party bribery in, 54
Nigeria, risks of selling goods in, 14
Nimrod Marketing v. Texas Energy Corp, 201
Nominating bank, 312
Noncompetition clauses, 81, 357
Nonpartnership clause, 349, 422, 425
Non-tariff barriers, 26
Non-vessel operating common carrier (NVOCC), 275–276
North American Free Trade Agreement (NAFTA)
  aims and provisions of, 145–146
  constitutionality of, 144
  country of origin rules, 162
  as factor in growth of international trade, 2
  labor clause, 348
  marking requirements, 164–165
  and most-favored-nation principle, 128
  value-added test, 163
Northeast Trailer Inc., 70–71, 73
Norway, penalty clauses in, 123
Notice, in European contract law, 195
Novecon Ltd. v. Bulgarian-American Enterprise Fund, 204
Nowogroski Insurance, Inc. v. Rucker, 376
NTDB. *See* National Trade Data Bank
NVOCC. *See* Non-vessel operating common carrier

O

Obligations de faire, 208
Occidental Petroleum, 32
Ocean bill of lading, 272
Ocean carriage conventions, 273–274
OECD. *See* Organization for Economic Cooperation and Development
Offer, in European contract law, 195
Office of Internet Enforcement, 460
Office of Service Industries, 339
Offset agreement, 31
On-board bill of lading, 255
Open account transaction, 244, 312
Open price term, 22
Open terms, 198
Operational standards clause, 89
OPIC. *See* Overseas Private Investment Corporation
Orbisphere Corp. v. United States, 160
Order bill of lading, 257
Oregon Natural Resources Council, v. Animal and Plant Health Inspection Service, 130, 131–132
Organizational ethics, 47–48
Organization for Economic Cooperation and Development (OECD), 337
  Bribery Convention, 57–58
  as example of customary law, 6
Origin Agreement, of GATT, 164
Overseas Private Investment Corporation (OPIC), 12, 14, 28, 29

P

Packing slip, 252–253
Pacta sunt servanda doctrine, 182
Panavision Int'l, L.P. v. Toeppen, 443
Parallel imports. *See* Gray market
Parallel license, 429
Paramount Pictures v. Metro Program Network, Inc., 422, 424–425
Paris Act of 1971, 384
Paris Convention, 381, 382
Parol evidence rule, 215–216, 218–219
Partnership, 67, 68, 80
  general, in the United States, 67, 80
  limited, in the United States, 67
  local, 68
Partnership and Cooperation Agreement, EU, 146, 147
Passive Web page, 438, 440
Patent agent, 397
Patent Cooperation Treaty (PCT), 382
Patent infringement. *See* Intellectual property rights
Patent law
  checklist, 406
  definition of, 367
  Eurasian Patent Convention, 399
  first to invent principle, 394
  first to register principle, 394
  foreign, 394–395, 397–398
  International Patent Search Authorities (ISA), 399
  registering, 405–406
  TRIPS protection, 388
  in U.S., 374
Payment, methods of
  cash in advance, 244
  consignment sale, 245
  documentary collections, 244–245, 250–252
  documentary credit transactions, 244–245
  open account transaction, 244
  risk scale, 244
PCT. *See* Patent Cooperation Treaty
Penalty clauses, 123–124, 185–188
Perfect tender rule, 198
Performance requirements, 33
Perils clause, 304
Perils only policy, 300
Per package limitation, 277–278, 280–281, 288
Personal jurisdiction, 99, 100–101 436–442
Phillips Puerto Rico Core, Inc. v. Tradax Petroleum, 121–122, 261
Piercing the corporate veil doctrine, 70–71, 73–74
Pinto automobile case, 40
Pirated goods. *See* Gray market
Plant relocation, ethics of, 45
Plas v. Valburg, Hoge Road, 205, 206
Political risk, 26–28
Political risk report, 14
Polo Ralph Lauren, L.P. v. Tropical Shipping & Construction Co., 281, 282–283
Positive countertrade, 33
Power of attorney, for freight forwarded, 316
Pratt & Whiney Corp. v. Malev Hungarian Airlines, 222
Precontract liability, 196, 200–202, 204
Precontractual instruments, 208
Price-fixing clauses, 357
Price reduction, 198
Pricing methods
  cost-plus, 23, 245
  and foreign markets, 245–246
  marginal cost pricing, 245
  transfer, 363
Prima U.S. Inc. v. M/V Addiriyah, 274, 275–276
Prior dealings, 216
Privacy, 445–449
Privacy Act of 1994, 446
Privacy policy statement, 461
Privatization, risks of, 27–28
Pro forma invoice, 246–247, 248, 250, 258, 261
Promissory estoppel, 203, 204
Proper notice, 229
Pro rata clause, 299

Protection and Indemnity (P & I) Policy, 298
Protests, antiglobalization, 141, 142–143
Public domain, 373
Punctuality, and cultural differences, 19
Purchase order, CISG and UCC, 221–225
Purpose clause, joint venture, 80
Put option, 23

Q

Q-clause exemption, 291–292
Quality control, and IPR licensing agreements, 418
Quality King Distributors, Inc. v. L'anza Research International, Inc., 378
Quanxi (connections), 69

R

Rational self-interest, 40
Ravens Metal Products v. McGunn, 70–71, 73
Raymond Dayan v. McDonald's Corp., 93–94
Reardon SmithLine, Ltd. v. Yngvar Hansen-Tangen, 228
Reasonable person standard, 226, 227, 228
Reason to know, 184–185
Received-for-shipment bill of lading, 256–257
Red clause financing, 312
Redundancy, 345–346
Regional goods, 145
Regional trading blocks, 141, 145
  See also European Union (EU); North American Free Trade Agreement (NAFTA)
Regulation, export, 167–168, 171–175
Regulation, import
  assessment of duties, 155–161
  classification system, 151
  country of origin, 162–164
  deferred duties, 151–152
  foreign (free) trade zones, 161–162
  foreign national import restrictions, requirements, and standards, 165–166
  General Rules of Interpretation, 152–154
  marking requirements, 164–165
  standards requirements, 166–167
  World Customs Organization (WCO), 152
Regulation, international
  GATT principles, 128–129
  multilateral trade negotiations, 141
  regional expansion of free trade, 141, 145–146
  world trading system, 127
  WTO agreements, 130, 132–136, 138–141
Reliance theory, in U.S. common law, 200–201
Remarketer, 9
Renewal clause, in franchising agreement, 90
Renvoi, doctrine of, 107
Repatriation, and nonconvertible currency, 14
  See also Currency, convertibility
Representative office, 68
Reservation of rights clause, 416, 418
Restatement (Second) of Contracts. *See* Second Restatement of Contracts
Reverse countertrade, 33
R.G. Group, Inc, v. Bojangles' of America, Inc., 202–203, 204
Righteous American perspective, 50
Right of access, 447
Right of correction, 447
Right of objection, 447
Right of priority, 381
Rights of Man, 41
Right to cure, 231
Ring-sho (consensus), 180
Risk
  currency, 20–23
  in developing countries, 15–16
  evaluating through market research, 10–13
  language and cultural, 16, 18–20
  legal, 23–26
  management of, 28–34
  and methods of payment, 244
  political, 26–28
  scope of, 8–10
  transaction, 13, 15
Risk management
  countertrade, 30–34
  through insurance, 29–30
  through intermediaries, 30
Risk of loss allocation, 257
Risk-shifting clauses, 258–259
Rome Act of 1928, 384
Rome Convention, 458
Rose & Frank Co. v. Crompton, 208
Royalties, 403, 417, 418, 428
Royalties clause, in franchising agreement, 90
Royalty clause, 416–417
Rule of reciprocity, 104
Rule of specificity, 152
Rule of strict compliance, 316, 317–318
Running down clause, 298
Russian Federation
  civil code, 188–192
  customs valuation procedures, 166
  franchising in, 92
  incorporation in, 75
  intellectual property protection strategy example, 398–399
  joint stock company in, 75
  labor code, 346
  nationalization protection in, 27–28
  patent law, 394–395, 397–398
  penalty clauses in, 123
  purchasing a company in, 15
  registration of licensing agreements, 405
  Regulation of Hard Currency Control, 16
  trademark law, 391, 394

S

Safe harbor agreement, 447
St. Johns N.F. Shipping Corp. v. S.A. Companhia Geral Commerical de Rio de Janeiro, 286, 287
St. Paul Inc. v. Sea Land Service, 286
Sales representatives, 10, 343, 349–350, 351
Samsonite Corp. v. United States, 157, 158
Sanctity of contract, 182
SA Pasquasy v. Cosmair, Inc., 207
Saudi Arabia
  advertising in, regulation of, 359
  distributor requirements, 355
  glass ceiling for women in, 43
  Shari'a and contract law in, 188
SBA. *See* Small Business Administration
Scotch Whiskey Assoc. v. Barton Distilling, 376–377
Seaworthiness, 279–280
SEC. *See* Securities and Exchange Commission
Secondment agreements, in joint ventures, 82
Second Restatement of Contracts, 184, 186, 201
Securities
  cross-border offerings, 361–362
  Internet offerings, 460
Securities and Exchange Commission (SEC), 361–362
Security, Internet, 459
SEC v. Tesoro Petroleum Corp., 55
SED. *See* Shipper's Export Declaration
Seller
  as drawer, 249
  right to cure, 231
  warranties, 232–237
Selling practices, and cultural differences, 19
Senior mark, 371
Service mark, 368
Service of process, 99
Services, electronic, 459–460
Services, sale of
  accounting and taxation, 362–363
  advertising, 358–360
  commercial agency contract, 349, 350, 352–356
  computer software sale, 215
  cross-border security offerings, 361–362
  definition of, 337
  differences from exporting goods, 338–339
  distribution agreement, 355–356
  foreign competition law, 356–357
  foreign personnel, 343–357
  and the Internet, 340–343
  logistical services, 357–358
  mixed sales, 337, 425
  principal markets, U.S., 337
  risk characteristics, 8
  sectors, U.S., 338
  WTO Agreements, 338
  See also General Agreement on Trade in Services

Severance indemnity, 354
Sexual harassment policy, 344, 345
Share allocation, in joint ventures, 80
Shareware, 437
Shari'a, 187–188
Sharism, 50–51
Shaver Transportation Co. v. The Travelers Indemnity Co., 301, 302–303
Shipper's Export Declaration (SED), 167, 168, 169, 252
Shipping checklist, 247
Shore coverage clause, 304–305
Shrink-wrap license, 453–455
Shulof, George and Juliette, 72–73
Sight draft sample, 319
  See also Time drafts
Sight drafts, 249
Single European Patent, 395
Site selection clause, in franchising agreement, 89
Small Business Administration (SBA), 11
Smith, Adam, 40
Smoot-Hawley Act of 1930, 127, 135–136, 140–141
Snapback provisions, of NAFTA, 145
Social Accountability Standard, 61
Society for Worldwide Interbank Financial Telecommunications (SWIFT), 459
Sony Magnetic Products Inc. v. Merivienti, 281, 293
Soshjno wakai, 110
Sound Recording Act of 1971, 378–379
South Africa, apartheid, MNC defiance of, 43
Sovereign immunity, 99, 101–102
Soviet Union
  ammonia countertrade transaction with Occidental Petroleum, 32
  disintegration of, and growth of international trade, 2
Spain, incorporation in, 75
Spamming, 446, 462
Specific duties, 155
Specific performance, in European Principles, 198
Specified processes test, 163
SPS. *See* Agreement on the Application of Sanitary and Phytosanitary Measures
S.R. & C.C. *See* Strikes and riots clause
Standards. *See* Harmonized tariff schedule (HTS); International Organization for Standardization (ISO); Regulations, import
Standby letter of credit, 312, 325–327
Statement of Ultimate Consignee and Purchaser, 173, 174
Statute of frauds, 189, 203, 204, 217, 427
Steele v. Bulova Watches, 377
Stock Exchange of Hong Kong, definition of materiality, 362
Stockholm Act of 1967, 384
Stowage, 280
Straight bill of lading, 257
Strategies for doing business
  entering a foreign market, 68–74
  establishing a business in a foreign country, 74–78
  franchising, 85–96
  joint ventures, 78–85
  in the United States, 67–68
Stream-of-commerce theory, 100
Strikes and riots (S.R. & C.C.) clause, 300
Subordinate responsibility, 47–48
Subsidiaries, 69, 74–75
Subsidies
  countervailing, 138
  Delverde USA, Inc. v. United States, 139–140
  GATT code, 136
  illegal, and most-favored-nation principle, 128
  illegal, U.S., 134
Substantial transformation, 162
Substantial transformation, test of, 145
Sue and labor clause, 305
Sweden, penalty clauses in, 123
SWIFT. *See* Society for Worldwide Interbank Financial Telecommunications

T

TABD. *See* Trans-Atlantic Business Dialogue
Tangible form of expression, 371
Taric tariff structure, 161
Tariff Act of 1930
  and gray market importing, 378
  illegal subsidies, 135–136
  labor provisions, 348
  rates of duties, 152
  Section 337, 140–141
  Section 402, 157
  unfair trade practice complaints, 404
Tariffs
  harmonized tariff schedule (HTS), 151–154
  Taric structure, 161
  See also Duties; General Agreement on Tariffs and Trade (GATT)
Tarnishment, 371
Taxes
  deductibility of bribes, 57
  and foreign trade zones, 77
  international, 78
  internationalization of, 362–363
  and management agreements, 74
  transfer pricing as means of reducing liability, 69
  value-added (VAT), 27
TC Industries, Inc. v. Northway, Inc., 362
Technical Committee on Rules of Origin, 164
Technical trade barriers, 26
Technology Transfer Regulation 240/96, 428–430
Technology transfers
  to China, 14
  China regulations, 430–431
  EU regulations, 427–430
  foreign registration and approval, 431–432
  to France, 14
  laws, 409
  limitations on, 26
  and technology licensing, 403–404
  WTO declaration on (ITA), 153
  See also Intellectual property licensing
Telecommunications Act of 1996, 446
Teleology, 39
Telephone Consumer Protection Act, 446
Tennessee Imports, Inc. v. Pier Paulo, 118–119
Termination clause
  in commercial agency contract, 350, 352, 354
  in IPR agreement, 419, 422, 425
  in joint ventures, 82
Territorial clauses, in franchising agreement, 90
Texaco v. Pennzoil, 204–205
Theory of Moral Sentiments, A, 40
Third-party bribery, 52–53, 54, 55
Through-transport policy, 298
Time drafts, 249, 310–311, 319–320
T.J. Stevenson & Co. v. Bags of Flour, 234, 235–236
Totality of the circumstances analysis, 185, 226, 227, 228
Touche-Ross & Co. v. Bank I ntercontinental, Ltd., 74
Toymart.com, 445–446
Toys"R"Us v. Feinberg, 443–444
Trade acceptance, 319
Trade and Tariff Act of 1984, 161
Trade barriers
  non–tariff, 26
  technical, 26
  U.S. Department of Commerce definition of, 127
  See also General Agreement on Tariffs and Trade (GATT); Uruguay Round; World Trade Organization (WTO)
Trade dress, 368
Trade Information Center, 11
Trade in goods, growth in, as measure of globalization, 3
Trademark Act. *See* Lanham Act
Trademark law
  checklist, 406–407
  cybersquatting, 442–444, 451
  definition of, 367
  dilution, 371, 372, 443–444
  foreign, 391–392, 394
  generic marks, 368
  junior mark, 371
  meta-tags, 371, 372
  registering, 405–406
  senior mark, 371
  TRIPS protection, 387–388
  in U.S. (Lanham Act), 368–371
  See also Intellectual property rights

Trade names, protection of, in foreign market, 74, 406
Trade secrets
definition of, 367
protecting, in franchising agreement, 95
under TRIPS, 388
in U.S. law, 375–376
Trade terms, 257–262
Trade unions, in Italy, 346
Trade usage, 216
Trade zones, 77
Trading partner agreements, 450
Transaction risks, 13, 15
Transaction value, GATT, 157–159
Trans-Atlantic Business Dialogue (TABD), 338
Transferable credit, 312
Transfer pricing, 28, 69, 363
Transparency International, 50
Corruption Index, 14
Transparency principle, 128–129, 340, 417, 420
Transport conventions, 272
carriage by air, 272
carriage by rail, 272
carriage by road, 272
carriage by sea, 272
multimodal, 272, 274, 285, 292–297, 358
unimodal, 271
Travelers Indemnity Company v. Waterman Steamship, 288, 289
Treaty of Rome, 103
Treaty on Intellectual Property in Respect of Integrated Circuits, 388
TRIPS. *See* Agreement on Trade-Related Aspects of Intellectual Property Rights.
21-day rule, 318
Tying clauses, 357, 428

U

UCC. *See* Uniform Commercial Code; Universal Copyright Convention
UCITA. *See* Uniform Computer Information Transactions Act
UCP. *See* Uniform Customs and Practices for Documentary Credits
UCP 500, 320–325
UETA. *See* Uniform Electronic Transactions Act
UFOC. *See* Uniform Franchise Offering Circular
Ultimate purchaser, of imported goods, 164
UNCITRAL. *See* United Nations, Commission on International Trade Law
Undue hardship, as contractual excuse, 238
Unfair Contract Terms Act, 108, 185
UNIDROIT Principles, 91–92, 183, 184, 198–200, 238
Uniform Commercial Code (UCC), 177, 212
and CISG, 219–239
course of performance, 216
disclaimers, 234, 236
doctrine of impracticability, 238
and intellectual property licensing agreement, 425, 427
and letters of credit, 312, 316
liquidation or limitation of damages, 123–124, 186
merchantable goods, definition of, 234
parol evidence rule, 215
reasonable person approach, 184, 226, 227, 228
statute of frauds, 215
written confirmation rule, 215–216
Uniform Computer Information Transactions Act (UCITA), 425–427, 452–456
Uniform Customs and Practices for Documentary Credits (UCP), 181, 211, 312, 320–325
Uniform Electronic Transactions Act (UETA), 426
Uniform Foreign Money-Judgment Recognition Act, 105, 106
Uniform Franchise Offering Circular (UFOC), 88
Uniform Law on Bills of Exchange, 319
Uniform Trade Secrets Act, 95, 375–376
Unimodal transport convention, 271
Union Carbide (Bhopal disaster), 43, 44, 48
Unitary taxation, 363
United Nations
Commission on International Trade Law (UNCITRAL), 32–33, 450–451, 457
Convention on the limitation period in the International Sale of Goods, 239–241
Declaration of Human Rights, 41, 42
Declaration on the Right to Development, 41
and ethics of e-commerce, 460–461
Global Impact Program, 48
International Labor Organization (ILO), 38, 167
Multimodal ocean carriage of goods convention, 272, 274
Statistical Yearbook, 12
UNIDROIT Principles, 91–92, 183, 184, 198–200, 238
See also Convention on Contracts for the International Sale of Goods (CISG)
United States
"banana dispute", 134–135, 138
corporate governance in, 71
illegal subsidies, 134
intellectual property rights in, 367–376
Internet and database privacy legislation, 446–448
joint venture in, 80
Mutual Recognition Agreements (MRA), 338
United States v. Donald Shetterly, 170–171
United States v. Haggar Apparel Company, 154–155
United States v. Leibo, 52–53, 54, 55
Universal access, 461
Universal Copyright Convention (UCC), 383
Uruguay Round, 26
Agreement on Customs Valuation, 162
binding commitments, 127
summary of, 127
U.S. Bureau of the Census, World Population, 12
U.S. Customs Service
classification and assessment of duties, 153–154
country of origin laws, 164
imported goods review, 152
Intellectual Property Rights Branch, 377, 378
U.S. Department of Commerce
Agent-Distributor Searches (ADS), 355
antidumping duties, 136
countertrade requirements advice, 32
market research publications, 12
Office of Service Industries, 339
U.S. Federal Trade Commission, comparative advertising regulation, 62
U.S. Industrial Outlook, 12
U.S. trade preferences, 157
U.S. Trade Representative (USTR), 136–138, 397
U.S. v. Hsu, 376
Utilitarianism, 39–41

V

Valente-Kritzer Video v. Callan Productions, 408
Validated license, for export, 167
Validity clauses, 428
Value-added tax (VAT), 166
Value-added test, 163
Vegas v. Compania Anonima Venzolana, 281
Vienna Convention on Treaties, 182
Vimar Seguros y Reaseuros v. M/V Sky Reefer, 279
Virtual goods, 215
Virtue ethics, 44
Voest-Alpine Int'l. v. Chase Manhattan Bank, 316, 317–318

W

Wa, Japanese harmony of negotiation, 179
Warehouse receipt, 254
Warehouse-to-warehouse clause
in bill of lading, 276
in marine insurance policy, 301, 304
Warner Bros. & Co. v. Israel, 261
Warner-Jenkinson Co. v. Hilton Davis Chemical, 375
Warranty provisions
of CISG, 232–237
disclaimer, in shrink-wrap contract, 453

Warranty provisions (*continued*)
- implied warranty for a particular purpose, 234
- implied warranty of merchantability, 232–233
- and Internet consumer transactions, 453
- in IPR agreements, 420
- limited express warranty, 234, 236

War risk insurance, 298
Warsaw Convention, 272–273
Warsaw Pact, 2
WCO. *See* World Customs Organization
Wealth of Nations, The, 40
White-listed clauses, 429
WIPO. *See* World Intellectual Property Organization
Work for hire, 349, 373
World Bank, 143
World Customs Organization (WCO), 152
World Intellectual Property Organization (WIPO), 381, 382
World Trade Organization (WTO)
- Agreement on Preshipment Inspection, 130, 132
- Agreement on Technical Barriers to Trade (TBT), 166–167
- Agreement on the Application of Sanitary and Phytosanitary Measures (SPS), 130, 166–167
- Agreement on Trade-Related Aspects of Intellectual Property (TRIPS), 6, 27, 127, 381, 384–390, 412
- antidumping procedures, 135–136
- China's membership in, and enforcement of intellectual property rights, 14
- criticism of, 141, 142–143, 347
- Customs Valuation Code, 130
- Declaration on Trade in Information Technology Products (ITA), 153
- dispute settlement system, 132–135
- establishment of, 127
- as factor in growth of international trade, 2
- General Agreement on Trade in Services (GATS), 338, 339–340, 341
- health and safety standards, 166–167
- Millennium Round, 141
- Section 301, 136–140
- Section 337, 140–141
- and trade barriers, 26

World Traders Data Report, 10
Written confirmation rule, 215–216

X

XIS. *See* Export Information System

Y

Yarway Corp. v. Eur-Control USA, Inc., 420
York-Antwerp Rules, 306
Yugoslavia, jet aircraft counterpurchase agreement with U.S., 31

Z

Zippo Manufacturing Co. v. Zippo Dot Com, Inc., 439–440

Photo Credits

Page 1 Courtesy of International Court of Justice
38 Permission of Dr. Lawrence M. Hinman
66 Courtesy of U.S. International Trade Administration
98 Courtesy of U.S. Business Advisor web site, courtesy of Small Business Administration (SBA)
126 Courtesy of World Trade Organization
150 Courtesy of U.S. Customs Service
177 Courtesy of International Trade/Commercial Law & e-Commerce Monitor
211 Courtesy of Institute of Foreign and International Private Law
243 Courtesy of U.S. International Trade Administration
271 Courtesy of Faculty of Law of the University of Cape Town
309 Courtesy of the Export-Import Bank of the United States
336 Courtesy of Burrells.com, Inc.
366 Courtesy of U.S. Library of Congress
402 Courtesy of World Intellectual Property Organization
434 Courtesy of National Telecommunications and Information Administration